160 87282

P O W E R

&

C U L T U R E

ALSO BY HERBERT G. GUTMAN

The Black Family in Slavery and Freedom, 1750–1925

Work, Culture, and Society in Industrializing America
Essays in American Working-Class and Social History

Slavery and the Numbers Game
A Critique of *Time on the Cross*

P O W E R

&

C U L T U R E

ESSAYS ON
THE AMERICAN WORKING CLASS

Herbert G. Gutman
Edited by Ira Berlin

PANTHEON BOOKS · NEW YORK

Grateful acknowledgment is made to the following for permission to
reprint previously published material:

Alfred A. Knopf, Inc.: "A Brief Postscript" from *Work, Culture, and Society
in Industrializing America* by Herbert G. Gutman. Copyright © 1973 by
Herbert G. Gutman.

Pantheon Books, a Division of Random House, Inc.: "Herbert Gutman" from
Visions of History by MARHO: The Radical Historians Organization, pp.
185–216. Copyright © 1976, 1977, 1979, 1980, 1981, 1983 by MARHO:
The Radical Historians Organization. This interview with Herbert
Gutman originally appeared, in slightly different form, in *Radical History
Review* (published by MARHO: The Radical Historians Organization),
vol. 27 (1983), pp. 202–22.

Syracuse University Press: Excerpt from *The Gilded Age: A Reappraisal*, rev.
ed., edited by H. Wayne Morgan (Syracuse, N.Y., Syracuse University
Press, 1963, 1970).

University of Illinois Press: Excerpt from *Slavery and the Numbers Game: A
Critique of "Time on the Cross"* by Herbert G. Gutman, pp. 14–41. Copyright © 1975 by Herbert G. Gutman.

Library of Congress Cataloging-in-Publication Data
Gutman, Herbert George, 1928–1985
  Power and culture.
  Bibliography: p.
  Includes index.
  1. Labor and laboring classes—United States
—History. 2. Afro-Americans—History. 3. Slavery
—United States—History. I. Berlin, Ira, 1941–
II. Title.
HD8072.G97 1987   305.5'62'0973   87-43018
ISBN 0-394-56026-4

Designed by Marie-Hélène Fredericks
Manufactured in the United States of America
First Edition

CONTENTS

PREFACE

HERBERT GUTMAN loved life. He loved people and enjoyed sharing his own enthusiasm for good food, good fun, and—most important—for a deeper understanding of life itself. Perhaps that was why he was such a good teacher. Certainly that was why students queued up for his classes and why scholars, particularly young ones, crowded around him. They sensed his special combination of deep learning, humane sensibility, and political commitment. They knew instinctively that for Gutman there was no holding back, no half way, no secret agenda. His gift for conveying his knowledge and for infusing others with his spirit made him a historian's historian and one of the most influential scholars of his time.

As Gutman orchestrated them, the combination of high jinks—the red socks and the mismatched plaid suits—and high scholarship was nearly irresistible. Gutman delighted in the strange amalgam as much as any observer. But there was no question which took precedence, for Herbert Gutman was a man of great seriousness of purpose. He took his work seriously and demanded that others do the same. He had powerful, principled commitments, and these manifested themselves in his scholarship. Gutman knew what was good history and what was bad, and he made his opinions known. His outspoken commitments made him a subject of great controversy.

Critics charged that Herbert Gutman was romantic. They meant that he was soft. That he sympathized with the poor and dispossessed. That he failed to acknowledge that mean conditions made mean people. That he allowed his sympathy for those at the bottom of society to blind him to the fact that they were losers—and often nasty losers. That he dwelled upon culture when he should have been concerned with power. That he avoided the tough, political issues that must necessarily inform our understanding of the past.

They also meant that his ideas were soft. That he loved people too much to say the hard things that needed to be said. That his democratic sensibility overwhelmed his critical judgment. That his humanistic concerns shaded toward sentimentality, antiquarianism, and irrelevance. That his desire for a more just society befuddled his view of the past and befogged his vision of the future.

Whatever else Herbert Gutman was, he was not "soft." Although he spoke in the language of culture, he was preoccupied with questions of power. Indeed, as the essays in this volume make evident, the relationship between the two—power and culture—was the central theme of his work. His ideas were hard-edged. He had little patience with fools and could be a merciless critic. Gutman's agenda was political in the broadest sense.

In other ways, however, the critics were right. Gutman was a romantic; he might even be called a paleo-Romantic. Like the original Romantics, he wanted to understand the world as a whole. Also like them, he believed that all manner of things, certainly people and ideas, grow and change. In Gutman's view, there was no mold that could stamp out history of a predetermined sort. Each man and woman had to be considered on his or her own. In this too he was at one with the earlier Romantics, for Gutman had a profound respect for the sovereignty of the human spirit. He was not naive about the price the poor and disfranchised paid for their subordinate status, and, indeed, he documented it in great detail. But his own interest was in understanding what people, particularly working people, did for themselves, not what was done *to* them or *for* them. These concerns made Gutman's work a model of socially informed history, an inspiration to working people, and a testimony to the human spirit. Gutman himself became a guide for countless young scholars inspired by his combination of political engagement and scholarly detachment.

But, like the history he wrote, Gutman was too human to remain a distant idol. He made friends easily and I, like many others, came to know and to respect him—passionate, funny, sometimes dead-eye right, and sometimes overbearing and outrageously out of line. In retrospect, what seems so remarkable about Gutman was that there was no difference between his person and his history. Because he wrote about history and life as one, his legacy of humane letters will continue to inform and inspire those who believe, as he liked to say, that what mattered was "not what 'one' has done to man, but what man does with what 'one' has done to him."

In drawing together this collection of Herbert Gutman's essays I have had several purposes. Some of them were historiographic, some professional, and some frankly personal. First, I wanted to understand how Gutman's ideas evolved. His career spanned one of the most significant periods in American history, a period in which the study of history moved from the periphery of American intellectual life to the center, and then back to the periphery again. I wanted to understand something of that process and Gutman's role in it. Second, I wanted to explore the connection between what I sensed were the two dominant themes in Gutman's thought: power and culture. Gutman believed that he was concerned with power; his critics believed he was concerned with culture. The tension beween the two not only defined his work but also encompassed much of the contested terrain of modern historical study. Third, I wanted to connect Gutman's studies of wage and slave workers. Gutman maintained that they were of one piece. But the structure of American historiography—both the way it was written and the way it was taught—made it difficult for him to gain a hearing. Historians of the North, of urbanization and industrialization, and of wage workers inhabited one world, while historians of the South, of plantation life, and of slavery inhabited another. Gutman understood the institutional and intellectual forces that sustained this arbitrary division, but he never accepted them. If he failed to obliterate the division, he never let it affect his work. As one whose own work spans the subjects of wage and slave labor, I particularly wanted to understand how Gutman had made his peace. Finally, I wanted to connect Gutman's historical, political, and personal concerns. He was a political person, and he believed that history was a political subject. At the same time, he was extraordinarily sensitive to the ways in which history had been abused, and he despised those who flouted the canons of historical scholarship for any purpose. Few historians had greater respect for the rules of evidence than Herbert Gutman. I wanted to understand the ties that connected his history and his politics and the intellectual ligaments that allowed simultaneously for scholarly detachment and political engagement. Gutman also personalized his politics and his history. For better or for worse, his political and historical disagreements became personal disagreements. I wanted to understand how they impinged upon one another, shaped his work, and so affected the course of American historiography.

When I began this study, I thought I had the answers to many of these questions. I quickly became disabused of that idea. Gutman and I had become friends during the academic year 1975–1976 when we were thrown together at Princeton's Shelby Cullom Davis Center for Historical Studies. We shared a house, lunched together, worked collaboratively, and talked endlessly of history and politics. Thereafter, we stayed in touch, met periodically, and tried in vain to complete our collaborative work at long distance. I thought I knew him and his work. But as I began to read Gutman's work systematically, beginning with his master's thesis and concluding with his last essays, I soon realized that there were large parts of the man and his work of which I knew nothing, and that even those parts I "knew," I knew only partially and imperfectly. I have tried to enlarge my knowledge by speaking with others and by reading some of Gutman's voluminous correspondence, but I have not done so systematically. This collection of essays and my own introduction thus do not satisfactorily answer all my questions. I believe, however, that they make a start. They are presented as a contribution toward an intellectual biography of Herbert Gutman.

The essays included in this collection have been selected to provide a full view of Gutman's work and to illustrate the development of his ideas. To that end, whenever possible, I have tried to choose from among his many unpublished essays, knowing full well that they were unpublished because they did not meet his own high standards. With one exception—chapter 7, "Schools for Freedom: The Post-Emancipation Origins of Afro-American Education"—they have not been altered beyond standard editorial practice. "Schools for Freedom" was originally a chapter in an early draft of Gutman's history of the Afro-American family. Like the larger study of which it was a part, it emphasized the activities initiated by former slaves and connected them to the experience of the slave community. Although length prevented its inclusion in *The Black Family in Slavery and Freedom*, Gutman continued to work on it, apparently with an eye toward a separate volume on the establishment of black schools and their ties to the postwar reconstruction of the black family. However, like so many other projects, it was elbowed aside by other commitments. Eric Foner generously found time in his own demanding schedule to edit portions of Gutman's draft for inclusion in this volume. I am greatly in his debt.

Along with these previously unpublished essays, I have selected from among Gutman's published works. Here too I have tried to choose works that illustrate the range of his historical study and suggest its development. Generally, I have picked from among his least accessible essays. This volume, then, is meant to complement his earlier collection of essays, *Work, Culture, and Society in Industrializing America*, and his major book, *The Black Family in Slavery and Freedom*. Together they provide a full view of Gutman's America.

Obviously a collection of this sort cannot be constructed without a good deal of assistance and encouragement. I have had a large measure of both. Judith Mara Gutman gave me full access to her husband's papers, openly shared her very special knowledge of Herb, and answered endless questions, while at the same time giving me free rein to draw my own conclusions. Andrew Gyory, who has undertaken the daunting task of bringing order to Gutman's files, was unstinting in his assistance. He also constructed the bibliography of Gutman's published work that appears at the end of this volume. Michael Merrill and Paul Buhle allowed me to read and quote from the transcripts of interviews they conducted with Gutman. Others have generously answered my queries, and some have taken time from their own work to evaluate these essays and my commentary. I would like especially to thank Martha Berlin, Stephen Brier, Alan Dawley, Leon Fink, Eric Foner, Steven Hahn, Ronald Hoffman, Steven F. Miller, Leslie S. Rowland, André Schiffrin, Dorothy Thompson, E. P. Thompson, and Alfred A. Young. Loraine Lee and Claire Dimsdale typed and retyped the many versions of my introductory essay with unfailing accuracy, checked citations, and generally kept the trains running on time.

Finally, a word should be said about my own role in this venture. Gutman was a partisan, a contentious partisan. As I have tried to make clear, his partisanship—political, historiographic, and personal—gave meaning to his history. It is difficult to write about him without myself being partisan, and I am not so foolish as to believe that I have. But in my selection from his work and in my own introductory essay, I have tried to be fair to those who crossed swords with Gutman. I have also tried to read his work with a critical eye, and I have entered my own judgments. Herb would not have had it any other way. However, these are Herb's essays, and ultimately they speak for themselves. He would not have had that any other way, either.

College Park, Maryland   IRA BERLIN
November 1986

P O W E R

&

C U L T U R E

INTRODUCTION

HERBERT G. GUTMAN
AND THE AMERICAN
WORKING CLASS

HERBERT G. GUTMAN began writing history during the presidency of Dwight D. Eisenhower. It was an era of material prosperity and social peace, when scholars, searching for the sources of America's seeming immunity to the internal discord that racked other nations, emphasized the exceptional nature of the American experience. Whatever the origins of American exceptionalism—be it the absence of a feudal past, the richness of the American domain, or the openness of the political system—most scholars held it as an article of faith that the American social order worked to incorporate outsiders and co-opt dissenters. Disputes were of limited duration and importance. Since all Americans accepted the tenets of the "liberal tradition," differences among them tended to be conflicts of interest rather than of first principles. And, with the possible exception of the Civil War, the sources of those conflicts tended to be transient rather than endemic—for example, the slow incorporation of immigrants into mainstream society or the residual differences rooted in Old World ideologies. Unlike other divided, class-riven nations, the American people stood as one.

Such a vision left precious little room for an American working class whose interests were opposed to those of an entrenched owning class. Workers, like other Americans, belonged to the great middle. They shared the ideas of Main Street and aspired to its material standards. They had no unique values, institutions, or language. They were simply middle class without money. The central theme of the history of American workers was not persistent conflict with their bosses, but the workers' desire to escape the material limitations and social stigma of wage labor, thereby lifting themselves and their children closer to the middle-class ideal. Social mobility was not merely a fact of American life; it was the story of American life.

The unity of American society and the universal desire for *embourgeoisement* were reflected in the peculiar nature of labor organizations. Trade unions, like other American institutions, tended to be nonideological or, more accurately, to espouse the ideology of the society at large. Workers and their leaders had no fundamental quarrel with the

American way. They spoke in the clichés of American patriotism and wanted, not a new system, but the perfection of the existing one. In the words of Samuel Gompers, they wanted "more," a goal which was most understandable within the confines of liberal society and the middle-class ethos.

Since workers only mimicked—or, at best, reflected—the ideals of the larger society, they played a subordinate role in American history. The acts of farseeing presidents and legislators determined the course of American nationality, and the decisions of shrewd entrepreneurs shaped the American economy. Politicians and businessmen—with rare exception, men of Northern European extraction—naturally and rightfully dominated the history books. After all, they had made American history.

Experience, temperament, and politics made Herbert Gutman uncomfortable with this view of the American past. As the child of immigrants in a city of immigrants, Gutman knew what it meant to be an outsider. His sense of the oppositional nature of working-class life was nurtured by the oppositional culture in which he grew up. Socialism was common coin among the Jewish workers and shopkeepers of New York's outer boroughs. Gutman's father, who had migrated from Poland in the 1920s, had been a partisan of the Bolshevik Revolution. After arriving in the United States, he took a degree in pharmacology, married another recent arrival from Poland, and opened a small drugstore in Queens. The Gutmans kept their old politics and much of their culture, maintaining membership in the International Workers' Order and only slowly exchanging Yiddish for English. Yiddish became Herbert's first language, and it remained his "home" language as well as the language of many of the customers at his parents' drugstore. The store placed the Gutmans at the center of neighborhood controversies and allowed a young Herbert to listen in on the debates—in English and in Yiddish. Jewish radicalism deeply influenced him. As an adolescent, he attended the Communist-sponsored Camp Kinderland and later joined the Labor Youth League.[1]

Gutman followed the trail of other bright working-class youths through the New York public schools to Queens College, where he enrolled in 1945. He was "interested in history," but saw little point in its study. Instead, he selected journalism as his major and continued in that program until his senior year, despite the entreaties of a determined history major and special friend, Judith Markowitz. However, it was history that he liked best, especially in the classes of classicist Oscar Shaftel, labor economist Vera Shlakman, and historian Henry David. David, a crusty social democrat, was Gutman's favorite. His classes, each of which opened with a bruising ten-minute inquisition, offered a particularly attractive model of intellectual discourse.

Gutman also liked David's scholarship. Unlike the Popular Front lecturers who had played an important role in Gutman's early education, David told no predetermined tale. Although often "harsh" in his judgments, he dwelled upon the details and tried to show how particular circumstances altered the course of events. His book on the Haymarket Affair was a densely descriptive account of the causes and consequences of the fateful bombing in Chicago.[2] It not only sorted through the myths and half-truths that surrounded Haymarket, but also tried to unravel how circumstances—the struggle between labor and capital, the relations between labor and the law, and the character of various socialist and anarchist movements—shaped its origins and its outcome. The book spoke to Gutman's own interests: the city and its most recent arrivals—immigrants from Europe, like his parents and neighbors, and from the South, like some of his fellow campers at Kinderland. Most important, David's book demonstrated that a deep commitment to social justice need not be compromised by a like commitment to scholarly objectivity. By his senior year, Gutman was ready to transfer to the history department. He seemed pleased with the decision, and upon graduation in 1949, he decided to pursue an advanced degree in history at New York's most prestigious university, Columbia.

Although just a subway ride from his home in Queens, Columbia University was light-years from the world in which Gutman had been raised. The Ivy League college stood at the pinnacle of the New York intellectual community, and its history department enjoyed a national reputation. Allan Nevins and Henry Steele Commager dominated the department. Their many books influenced the way professional historians wrote history, but also addressed the concerns of a broad segment of the American reading public. They enjoyed a large and influential audience. Richard Hofstadter, the department's rising young star, also sought to capture that audience. His recently published book *The American Political Tradition and the Men Who Made It* had received rave reviews. A series of elegant biographical sketches, *The American Political Tradition* was both a critique of an older Progressive history and a blueprint for postwar liberal historiography. Rather than dwell upon conflict in the past, Hofstadter searched for "the common climate of American opinion" and found it in a commitment to entrepreneurial economics and opportunistic politics. Americans were joined together by a desire to seize the main chance. In Hofstadter's view, the United States was "a democracy in cupidity rather than a democracy of fraternity."[3] Political ideology and social philosophy, such as they existed, were little more than flimsy covers for upward-striving businessmen and ambitious politicians. Conflict arose because outsiders wanted in, and, for the most part, they got in. Although not without a critical edge (indeed, self-consciously iconoclastic) and far more subtle than those historians who would subsequently transform his "common climate" into a consensus, Hofstadter celebrated America as an open society in which popular democracy had tamed the exploitative thrust of modern capitalism.

Gutman chose to work with Hofstadter and ended up regretting the decision. His own beliefs, training, and sense of history—however rudimentary—contrasted sharply with those of his mentor. Whatever Gutman understood as "the common climate of American opinion," it was not acceptance of "the economic virtues of capitalist culture as necessary qualities of man."[4] While Hofstadter, in full flight from Progressivism, searched for the assumptions that joined Americans together, Gutman believed conflict to be at the center of the American experience. Gutman also questioned the kind of history Hofstadter wrote. The absence of the sort of detailed primary research that characterized Henry David's study of Haymarket left Gutman uneasy. To make matters worse, Hofstadter had little time for his students. He seemed to believe that they would learn by emulation: he would write and publish; they would do likewise. Gutman had hoped for a more "hands-on" education. At the end of his first semester, he considered shifting to Richard B. Morris, whose close investigation of labor and government in colonial American seemed more in accord with his own interests. But Gutman had already begun a master's thesis on the depression of the 1870s, and the subject was closer to Hofstadter's than to Morris's bailiwick.

Gutman's choice of subject was not arbitrary. The Great Depression of the 1930s loomed large in Gutman's life. He knew its most powerful effects only indirectly, but the trauma of that era resonated through his community. Although the prosperity that accompanied World War II had repaired much of the damage done by the Depression, the great collapse continued to shape people's lives, expectations, and possibilities. It was a never-ending subject of discussion. Quiet talk of an uncle who went bust and never recovered his fortune, of a cousin who had delayed his education and never fulfilled his promise, or of a neighbor who had been idled for lack of work and now seemed incapable of holding a job. And loud talk of politics, elevating Franklin Roosevelt and his Democratic party to the status of saints in the eyes of some and propelling others to more radical political possibilities. Those possibilities—whether Communist or Zionist—were part of the debate that formed Gutman's politics. At Queens College during the late 1940s, he became deeply involved in various Popular Front organizations, joined the Communist party, and campaigned for Henry Wallace. Although Gutman "soon grew wary of and then disgusted with vanguard leftist politics," he remained a socialist and very much a son of the Jewish Old Left.[5]

Although the cataclysm of the thirties and the rubble of its political aftermath were themselves too close for historical analysis, they indicated the importance of such economic climacterics and the attendant social struggles. The first global depression—the panic and subsequent economic collapse of the 1870s—seemed a natural choice to someone who saw history and politics as one. It was distant enough to be historical, yet close enough to have contemporary meaning.

Gutman had hoped to investigate the Tompkins Square Riot, a bitter and violent if little-known confrontation between New York workers and the police during the hard January of 1874. But he soon became caught up in the daily lives of New York's working people. Rather than study "one exciting event," Gutman tried instead to "grasp its total impact as a social and economic catastrophe upon the working men and women of America. The human misery evoked by this depression," he announced with a touch of graduate-student pomposity, "must be tabulated, itemized, and recorded fully."[6]

Although Gutman later dismissed his master's thesis as "conventional," it fulfilled his stated promise to a considerable degree. It recounted "the daily lives of thousands of male and female laborers and mechanics of New York City" as their standard of living slipped under the weight of the depression. Gutman traced the rise of unemployment, the decline of wages, and the spread of destitution among the city's working people. Like much of the history that would later bear his stamp, the thesis was filled with charts and tables assessing the ways in which the depression affected patterns of employment, wage levels, and prices. But in the thicket of statistics, Gutman never lost sight of what he believed to be the larger purpose of his work—indeed, of all labor history: to see workers not as "the products of 'forces' or as statistical data, but rather as living men and women."[7]

Gutman was not content to study the demolition of the workers' standard of living and the dismemberment of their organizations. Seeing men and women as active makers of their own lives, he focused upon the workers' resistance to the many attempts to deprive them of what they believed to be "their rights." Although his narrative never reached the Tompkins Square Riot, Gutman documented the formation of cooperative workshops, the movement of tramping artisans, and the course of a series of strikes, as New York workers drew on their collective experience to protect themselves from the rigors of the depression. In Gutman's view, this common experience—not leadership, organization, or emulation—guided the city's workers. Their activities represented, "not a European importation of 'miserable class warfare,' but an organized expression of the needs of the working people."[8] From his earliest writing, Gutman thus dismissed the notion of an ideal type of class consciousness against which American workers ought to be judged and rejected a history that searched for harbingers of some coming revolution. His emphasis on workers' experiences marked a subtle shift from his original intention to study the "impact" of the depression. The shift became increasingly pronounced as his graduate studies progressed.

Gutman completed his thesis, received a Master of Arts degree from Columbia in 1950, and prepared to continue his formal education. Somehow, Columbia seemed an inappropriate place to study working-class life. Although he had developed an enormous respect for Morris, Gutman had little interest in the field of early American history. Hofstadter, who had directed his thesis, was unconcerned with the questions that mattered most to him. He decided to leave Columbia. Judith concurred. Her opinion now carried additional weight, as she and Herbert were to be married that summer. Anxious to be off on their own, to loosen the bonds of family, and to escape the often suffocating grip of New York provincialism, the couple looked beyond the city for a graduate school. Gutman applied to and was accepted at the University of Wisconsin.

Although in the midst of a fierce bout with Senator Joseph McCarthy, the University of Wisconsin retained its reputation as a stronghold of Progressivism. The history department reflected that political persuasion. Although the scholars who composed the department could scarcely be called a "school"—indeed, they hardly agreed upon anything and some members evinced a cordial dislike for their colleagues—taken together they emphasized what had come to be called the Beardian interpretation of American history. Charles Beard, the colossus of Progressive historiography, had given his name to this mode of historical interpretation, emphasizing the material bases of social conflict in a manner that derived more from James Madison than from Karl Marx. In the hands of many of its practitioners and sometimes of Beard himself, Beardian analysis had often degenerated into crude economic determinism. It would soon be picked apart by critics from both the right and the left. Gutman had already witnessed some of the demolition firsthand in Hofstadter's seminar. But at its best, the Progressive interpretation offered a means of understanding a sharply divided society. When wedded to a rigorous tradition of empirical research, it offered the impetus for close study of those on top and those at the bottom. Perhaps most significantly, the Progressive interpretation provided a model of scholarship that had engaged the central problems of its own time.

It was this perspective that, more than anything else, attracted many left-leaning graduate students to Wisconsin and made the history department a hotbed of dissent in a profession fast becoming famous for its warm appreciation of American life. Many of these graduate students—who included Charles Forcey, William Preston, Warren Susman, and William Appleman Williams—shared Gutman's perspective, along with a passionate belief that the study of history was a proper vehicle for political expression. A determination to unite scholarship and politics became the distinguishing mark of the young historians who came together in Madison in the early 1950s. Although sensitive to the ways history had been abused, they had no desire to study the past for its own sake. As they moved in their own directions—Williams into studies of American foreign policy, Susman into cultural criticism, and Gutman into labor history—each of them carried an understanding that history was and must be a political subject.[9]

For Gutman, his years at the University of Wisconsin were a liberating experience. The Old Left had no presence there, and the endless rounds of self-criticism that had made New York radical politics "a caricature of a serious political movement" seemed self-evidently "banal and ridiculous" in Madison. At the same time, leftist criticism of the Soviet Union was forcing Gutman to reconsider many of his earlier beliefs. Young members of the faculty and his fellow graduate students pushed Gutman in this direction. William Appleman Williams, who had left Madison for the University of Oregon but returned to teach summer school, was working out his own "radical critique of sterile Stalinism." Gutman was also impressed by the ideological liberation of the younger graduate students and undergraduates, some of whom would go on to found *Studies on the Left.* Their free spirit and willingness to question conventional wisdom contrasted sharply with the "Old Left True Believers" with whom Gutman had grown up. Several black graduate students, their presence in Madison a product of the exclusionary policies of their native South, also had an impact on Gutman. They sensitized him to the onrushing civil rights revolution. "Anyone listening to them debate whether and when to return South," he later recalled, "would have known there was going to be a civil rights movement very soon." Taken together, Madison's diverse political and intellectual currents made Gutman realize that he had not understood "America west (and even east) of the Hudson River. Not in the slightest." Gutman described his Madison years as a time when his "dogmatic blinders" were lifted.[10]

Gutman set his political and intellectual course during his years in Madison. His politics would be embedded in his history, and his history would be part of "an effort to redefine socialism, to free up socialism from the totalitarian shroud that it [had] lived in for fifty years." He wanted no part of a history that "filled in the answers." His history would "junk the determinist teleological core of Marxism" and instead draw from Marx "a set of really good questions." Gutman was confident that the unvarnished historical record would "free people for creative and critical thought, or radical thought."[11]

Wisconsin had another tradition that attracted Gutman. The great labor economist John R. Commons had done his work there. The multivolume *Documentary History of American Industrial Society*, edited by Commons and his associates, defined the field of labor history and remained the primary source for and interpretation of the history of American workers.[12] Commons and his followers had built a small empire of economic activists who did much to influence state and federal policy during the first half of the twentieth century. The most important disciple of the Commons school was Selig Perlman, who was nearing retirement after a distinguished career in the economics department.

Perlman saw the trade union as the institutional embodiment of the American worker. His *Theory of the Labor Movement*, which was more historical than theoretical, had located the heroic story of American workers in the struggle to organize and gain the right to bargain collectively. Perlman's argument thus legitimated the changes in the status of labor that had accompanied the New Deal.[13] By the 1950s, however, labor's right to organize did not require an elaborate theoretical justification, and organized labor did not look quite so heroic. Self-satisfied, apathetic, and often corrupt, union leaders no longer appeared to represent the highest ideals of working people. The purge of labor's left wing and the narrow economist definition of labor's interests made union bosses increasingly difficult to distinguish from their corporate counterparts. For many observers, unions had become simply another pressure group, whose interests did not extend beyond its sagging membership.[14] For Gutman, the time had arrived to look elsewhere for the history of working people.

Gutman took a minor field in the economics department, where labor history was taught. He struck up a warm friendship with Perlman, whom he found to be "a very charming and quite dogmatic fellow." Perlman warned Gutman that history was an "Anglo-Saxon profession" and suggested that he would have better opportunities to study working people as an economist.[15] Gutman appreciated the harsh reality that prompted Perlman's advice. Labor history remained outside the "traditional political narrative" that dominated the study of American history. And aside from a handful of municipal colleges, Jews held few positions in the history departments of major American universities. There were none at Wisconsin, despite the university's liberal reputation. Nonetheless, Gutman's approach to the study of workers was quintessentially historical. He rejected Perlman's advice, along with much of his approach to labor history. Rather than add to the history of trade unionism, Gutman became increasingly determined to learn about workers outside the union movement. Indeed, during his years in Madison, Gutman's focus shifted steadily away from the union hall and the shop floor to the neighborhood and the kitchen table. As he had in his father's pharmacy, he wanted to meet workers where they lived as well as where they worked, and he wanted to know them as members of a community as well as employees of a factory. "A good deal has been written about trade unions," Gutman would observe in the introduction to his dissertation, "but less attention has been given to the working population itself and the relationship between labor organizations and the communities of which they were a part."[16]

Gutman took a variety of history courses, working with Merle Curti, Fred Harvey Harrington, and Merrill Jensen. He studied Civil War Reconstruction with John Hope Franklin, who visited Wisconsin for a year. But Gutman remained determined to continue his history of workers during America's first great depression. Howard K. Beale, an expert on post–Civil War America and the author of significant studies of Presidents Andrew Johnson and Theodore Roosevelt, had nominal charge of students working in late-nineteenth-century history. Beale was a neo-Beardian with a strong empirical bent, and his progressive politics, his racial egalitarianism, and his admonitions to stay close to the sources appealed to Gutman. The fit was less than perfect in other ways. Beale was a man of independent wealth and imperious bearing, who made much of gentlemanly deportment, Standard English, and clean fingernails. Gutman was an enthusiast who could neither shake his New York accent nor get the dirt from under his nails. Try as he might, he could not fit Beale's model of a gentleman scholar. Nonetheless, Beale respected Gutman's talent and intense commitment to the study of history, and Gutman recognized Beale's standing in the profession. It would not be an easy relationship for either man, but when Gutman decided to study the 1870s, Beale agreed to supervise his doctoral work.

Beale was a demanding supervisor. He believed his students should be fully committed to their work and only slightly less committed to him. In Gutman's case, Beale had no doubts about the former; however, he worried about the latter. When Gutman informed him that Judith was pregnant, Beale was furious. Relations between teacher and student cooled, so much so that Herbert and Judith agreed that distance might help. In 1953, with required course work completed and a small grant from the Social Science Research Council in hand, the Gutmans— Herbert, Judith, and the newly arrived Marta—returned to New York.

During the next five years, Gutman worked on his dissertation. He loved to research and pore over manuscript collections, published government reports, and newspapers. He found newspapers especially revealing and gained a deep understanding of nineteenth-century society by a close reading of the press, particularly the labor press. Beginning with the assumption "that no one had written anything about . . . American labor in that period, he divided the country into about 6 or 7 regions . . . picked one or two major newspapers in each region and read through them to find out what was going on." Slowly he "began to pick up stories. Little tiny stories in the Cincinnati paper that would say things like: 'Special to the *Cincinnati Commercial*. Hocking Valley miners' strike has entered into its fifth month,' or 'The "long vacation" in Fall River continues.' . . . Or, in the Philadelphia paper: 'To the great surprise of everyone, the Scranton jury freed the miners.' "[17] But the writing was slow, painfully slow, and with the arrival of Nell in 1957, the bills piled up. Gutman taught an occasional course at the New School for Social Research and at Columbia's College of General Studies. He also did some historical research for attorneys in the final stages of the landmark suit challenging school segregation, *Brown* v. *Board of Education of Topeka*.

Although he was more an apprentice historian than a political activist, Gutman's politics were enough to bring him to the attention of the guardians of American patriotism. In 1955, he was called before the Committee on Un-American Activities for allegedly luring a twelve-year-old camper at Kinderland into the Communist party. Gutman refused to answer the committee's questions and ended his testimony with a ringing assertion of the rights of American citizens.[18] But the experience shook Gutman, so much so that he never spoke of it. It also may have affected his career, for despite the growing shortage of university teachers, no regular academic appointment was forthcoming. So Gutman continued to write his dissertation, but the more he wrote the more he wanted to know. It always seemed easier to return to the sources—Beale's empiricism had complemented his own proclivity—than to face the tyranny of the blank page. But slowly, with Judith's encouragement, the dissertation took shape.

Gutman's doctoral dissertation began where his master's thesis had left off. It too traced the impact of the 1873 depression on workers. But, like Gutman himself, the focus of his work left New York and migrated west across Pennsylvania and Ohio into the industrial heartland of the United States. Gutman had chosen his terrain carefully, for he suspected that local and regional studies might be the source of a new labor history. By the time he had completed his dissertation, suspicion had hardened into certitude. Local communities, not the national capital, were the ground upon which the history of the working people after the Civil War could be built, Gutman announced in the introduction to his dissertation. For one thing, "the 'labor history' of that time . . . had little to do with national unions." Moreover, the dramatic events that had caught the eye of the nation and had subsequently preoccupied historians "were not 'typical' incidents." Most important, "a 'national' perspective often misinterpret[ed] those issues that were important to large segments of the post–Civil War working population and to other economic and social groups that had contact with the wage-earners."[19]

With this declaration, Gutman established his scholarly agenda. His focus would be local and would reach beyond the workplace. He would study workers not only where they worked but also where they lived, voted, worshipped, and played. The crucial relationships would not be those between workers and their bosses, but among workers themselves and between workers and their neighbors. Indeed, for Gutman, the "other social classes" would be essential in understanding the nature of working-class life and the conflict between wageworkers and their employers. He spoke less and less of the workers' response and more and more of the workers' initiative.

Gutman divided his dissertation into three parts. The first dealt with workers in small Northeastern and Midwestern communities, the second with urban workers, and the third with the unemployed. Much of parts two and three drew upon his master's thesis, although the last chapter finally reached the Tompkins Square Riot. These portions of his dissertation retained an Old Left preoccupation with material conditions, economic institutions, and industrial organization, and in that context, Gutman dubbed the Tompkins Square Riot the "New York 'Commune.' "[20] Although the themes of parts two and three reflected Gutman's continuing interest in social structure, class composition, and family economy—themes that would later play a large role in his work—these sections belonged more to the older tradition of labor history that he criticized than to the new one that he was attempting to establish. Instead of placing workers, their ideas, and their activities at the center, parts two and three welded descriptive economic history to a traditional labor-history narrative.

The first section of Gutman's dissertation reversed this emphasis and assigned workers an active role in determining the course of events. In the Illinois coal-mining community of Braidwood, Gutman discovered a story that riveted his attention. Industrialists in New York and other great metropolises, aided by state officials, had used the depression to reduce wages, discipline workers, and dismantle unions. Their actions seemed to affirm the power of the new corporate magnates to command the state and to humble labor. In Braidwood, however, workers stood toe-to-toe with the captains of industry and defeated "a wealthy, powerful, and hitherto invincible opponent."[21]

The workers' strength surprised Gutman. According to the history of the Gilded Age that he had been taught, the period following the Civil War was a time when businessmen secured their preeminence within the nation. The reigning historiography debated only whether they should be praised as "industrial statesmen" who had transformed the United States into a leading industrial power, or denounced as "robber barons" who had perverted the democratic process and created untold misery. In either case, they had translated their enormous resources into virtually limitless political power. Gutman's findings questioned this historiography, and with it one of the central tenets of consensus history: that the acceptance of capitalism came early and, by the nineteenth century, was nearly universal. Far from representing the triumph of capital, the industrialists' regular recourse to the authority of the state revealed capital's weakness and the important role labor continued to play in small-town, and perhaps big-city, America.

Central to the workers' success was their place in the community. Although Braidwood miners had early joined together to form the Illinois Benevolent and Protective Association and would become among the first to affiliate with the Miners' National Association, the union alone did not account for the miners' eventual triumph. Instead, Gutman focused on the crucial relationship between miners and nonminers, and the willingness of nonminers—"the mayor, sheriff, police officials, and business people"—to rally to the miners' cause. Braidwood's leading men saw something alien and frightening in the behavior of the Chicago-based mine operators, who could muster state power in the form of injunctions and national guardsmen. When Braidwood's "best men" joined with workers, they were protecting a familiar world. The local elite acted from its knowledge of workers, whom they knew as friends and neighbors, and in opposition to the industrialists, who were distant strangers. Sympathy for the workers ran deep within the confines of small-town life; consequently, workers and local businessmen could join together, defeat the coal operators, elect a mayor, and eventually send a Greenbacker to Congress.[22]

Gutman did not quite know what to make of his discovery. He offered a variety of interpretations, sometimes seeing the alliance between workers and local businessmen as a union of neighbors, sometimes as part of a larger conflict between an older commercialism and a newer industrialism, and sometimes invoking the sociological distinction between community and society. However he looked at it, he clearly was intrigued. What engaged him was the seeming newness of the situation. The actions of these small-town businessmen—mostly shopkeepers but also newspaper editors, judges, and elected officials—suggested a fluidity that permitted the kind of historical analysis with which he felt comfortable. It freed him from the determinism of economic domination, the kind of determinism that was so prevalent in the fraternity of labor historians, in the Beardian school, and in the politics of his youth. Yet this fluidity did not diminish the importance of social and political relations that grew from economic ones. The history of the Gilded Age was not the relentless march of industry, whether led by industrial statesmen or robber barons. Instead, the actions of individual men and women—lowly workers and petty tradesmen as well as great industrialists—shaped the course of events.

As Gutman moved toward the completion of his dissertation, the scenario he had discovered in Braidwood loomed increasingly large. In investigating iron-manufacturing communities in the Ohio River Valley, for example, Gutman found that the social structure of these communities "as well as the ideology of many residents . . . strengthened the hand of the local workers and worked to the disadvantage of the manufacturers. . . . Tradesmen and shopkeepers did not share the values of the industrialists and manufacturers." When manufacturers mobilized outsiders, whether strikebreakers or state militiamen, the local elite objected, often loudly, and hurried to the defense of the beleaguered workers. "We are not living under a monarchy," declared the Portsmouth, Ohio, *Times* in denouncing the mill owners' arbitrary use of power.[23] In each of the communities he studied, Gutman found that industrialists had yet to legitimate their authority in the eyes of workers and others. This discovery became the main theme of his dissertation, and in a more generalized form, the relationship between power and authority would echo through his life's work.

Gutman elaborated the themes of class and community, power and authority in analyses of workers in railheads, mine pits, and factory towns in Pennsylvania, Ohio, Indiana, and Illinois. In each case, he delineated the character of the local economy, the type of ownership, the nature of production, and the composition of the work force to understand how the 1873 depression affected workers. Everywhere he pressed beyond the hard facts of economic history for a fuller understanding of how the social and economic structure shaped evolving patterns of social relations to give citizens an active role in determining their own destiny.

In 1958, Gutman completed a draft of his dissertation. Beale nodded his approval, and before long Gutman received a lectureship at Fairleigh Dickinson College in Rutherford, New Jersey. Gutman taught five classes each semester, including several in the economics department, and still found time to serve as first president of the newly established local of the American Association of University Professors. Between lectures and grievance hearings, he began to polish his doctoral dissertation and prepare it for publication. Although Gutman had considered publishing the entire dissertation in book form, he could not wait to share his discoveries. As he revised each chapter, he sent it to a state historical journal. One by one, the chapters on workers in Braidwood and Portsmouth, and then in Newport, Kentucky, and Blossburg and Susquehanna Depot, Pennsylvania, found their way into print.[24] These early publications brought a glimmer of professional recognition and with it the offer of an assistant professorship at the State University of New York at Buffalo. Eager for a chance to escape the long hours of teaching and the heavy-handed administration at Fairleigh Dickinson, Gutman accepted. In the fall of 1963, he assumed the new position.

The luxury of teaching only three courses, all of them within the history department, permitted Gutman to reconsider his work. For several years, he had been trying to draw together the divergent themes of his dissertation on the depression in small towns and in large cities, and now he had the time. Before long, he had the opportunity. Several young scholars were preparing an anthology of new work on post–Civil War America. They asked Gutman to write on industrial workers.

"The Workers' Search for Power: Labor in the Gilded Age" distilled Gutman's dissertation and the articles derived from it into a single powerful argument. The essay challenged notions that workers in the postwar period were "isolated from the rest of society; that the employer had an easy time and a relatively free hand in imposing the new disciplines; that the spirit of the times, the ethic of the Gilded Age, worked to the advantage of the owner of industrial property; that workers found little if any sympathy from nonworkers; that the quest for wealth obliterated nonpecuniary values; and that industrialists swept aside countless obstacles with great ease."[25] In so doing, Gutman focused attention on the newness of the industrial regime. He emphasized how the relative openness of the arena in which workers and industrialists struggled for power allowed other social groups—"particularly nonworkers"—to play a role in the outcome of that struggle. Nothing was determined, nothing asumed. The as yet unformed nature of American capitalism allowed wage earners, wage payers, and those not yet fully identified with either to affect the course of events.

The struggle between workers and owners could be understood only by close study of local conditions. In reworking his dissertation and his articles, Gutman tried to show how this could be done. But like many pioneers, he failed to heed his own good advice. In comparing the reception of big business in small towns and in large cities, Gutman argued that face-to-face relationships in small towns created more cross-class solidarity than did the relative anonymity of large-city life. Gutman had studied economic and social structure in both towns and cities, relying on the published censuses and government reports, and he had investigated popular opinion, relying mostly on newspapers. But the small-town and big-city newspapers provided unequal access to local opinion. Whereas the small-town press gave voice to the local establishment, which often included workers, the great metropolitan dailies spoke for a more select group. As Gutman soon realized, his comparison of the struggle for power in industrial towns and cities was seriously flawed. He would deeply regret the gaffe and would continually refuse to republish a work he deemed in error.[26]

Despite its limitations, "The Workers' Search for Power" suggested how labor history could be transformed into a history of the working class. As Gutman had hoped, his essay moved the locus of labor history from a national to a local or regional stage and from an institutional to a cultural emphasis. It shifted attention from trade unions, secret societies, and *émigré* intellectuals. Instead, it stressed what Gutman had come to believe was the real business of labor history, "the workers themselves, their communities, and the day-to-day occurrences that shaped their outlook."[27]

But the influence of "The Workers' Search for Power" reached beyond the field of labor history. Gutman's focus on the community as a crucible in which social classes struggled for supremacy at once dismissed the condescending assumptions of the consensus school and put the Old Left's preoccupation with the quality of union leadership in a new context. His emphasis on experience, "day-to-day occurrences," and what he would later call culture broke sharply with the main thrust of contemporary American historiography.

"The Workers' Search for Power" also suggested the close ties between Gutman's history and his politics. Although nothing in the essay touched directly on current events—certainly not on the civil rights movement that occupied his political attention—the very title of the essay and its main theme spoke to the willingness of working people to challenge their social superiors and to make their own world. Boycotts, sit-ins, freedom rides, and marches affirmed Gutman's appreciation of the force of popular activism. History—declared historian Jesse Lemisch—was not "made from the top down but from the bottom up," a phrase that sounded the tocsin for a new history.[28]

"The Workers' Search for Power" made Gutman a spokesman for a history that as yet had no name. Others were also struggling to break from an older tradition of electoral history or a newer one of textual exegesis. Like Gutman, they wanted to avoid the deterministic formulations of the Progressives and the bland pap of the salons of consensus. Like Gutman, many of these young scholars were new to the academy, children of immigrants, anxious to write a history that would include their forebears in America's past. Frontiers and farms played but a small role in their experience; they knew of cities and factories and wanted to give them a part in the national epic. And like Gutman, these young scholars were touched by the unfolding drama of the struggle for racial equality. The democratic upheavals of the 1960s gave the creation of such a history special urgency. How could a nation based upon the principle of "one man, one vote" ignore the majority in its past?

Within the historical profession, the movement to democratize historical scholarship took the form of an assault on the cult of consensus, a reemphasis on conflict, and an expansion of those subjects considered legitimate areas for historical study. Before long, history's boundaries extended across the color line and beyond the divide of gender, greatly enlarging the fields of black and women's history. But the first subjects to be incorporated into this new historiography were workers and immigrants. Labor history was no longer a minor subspeciality within the profession. It now stood at the center, and Herbert Gutman was one of its most prominent practitioners.

Gutman enjoyed the recognition. Having labored in near anonymity at Fairleigh Dickinson, he welcomed the chance to comment at historical conventions, address graduate students, review books, and contribute to texts. His contagious enthusiasm made him an especially effective spokesman for the new history. Connecting the political significance of studying history's disinherited with the revolutionary events of the day, he helped place history on the cutting edge of American intellectual life. In so doing, he invited young men and women to join him in an enterprise that would not only write history but also make history. The vision that he and others had shared in Madison was fast becoming a reality.

The exact form the new history would take was far from certain. The absence of a clear agenda sent historians scurrying in all directions, incorporating insights from other disciplines, adopting new methods, and tinkering with new technologies. Gutman began to read widely in the history of other countries, since it was generally acknowledged that the new history would be comparative. He also studied other disciplines: economics, sociology, and especially anthropology. Two new books published in the United States in 1964 had a particularly profound impact on his thinking.

The most important was E. P. Thompson's *The Making of the English Working Class*.[29] Thompson set out "to rescue the poor stockinger, the Luddite cropper, the 'obsolete' handloom weaver, . . . and even the deluded follower of Joanna Southcott, from the enormous condescension of posterity," much as Gutman had wanted to understand "the workers themselves, their communities, and the day-to-day occurrences that shaped their outlook." But a long line of labor studies and a yeasty

British Marxist tradition broadened Thompson's perspective and gave his work a deeper resonance. In *Making*, Thompson not only presented a monumental history of the English working class but also offered a theory of how that class came into being, indeed, of how to understand the very concept of class. For Thompson, the English working class was not created by the "spontaneous generation of the factory-system" or the inexorable operation of some "external force—the 'industrial revolution'—working upon some nondescript undifferentiated raw material of humanity."[30] Like any class, it was the product of history, and understanding its origins required a close knowledge of historical circumstances at the moment of its creation.

Although the first reviews of Thompson's work were negative—sometimes even dismissive—Gutman immediately recognized the genius of Thompson's book and its connection with his own work. Liberal historians had long offered sympathetic portraits of the dismal conditions of working-class life, and Marxist scholars had linked such portrayals to economic and social structure. But too often liberalism added little more than sympathy, and often condescending sympathy at that. Marxism, particularly the American variety, was dogmatic and deterministic. In explaining the working-class experience neither liberal nor Marxist historiography moved far beyond exploitation and victimization. Thompson vaulted these hurdles and directly addressed the subject of class formation, thereby offering a means of escaping both liberal condescension and Marxist reductionism.

Gutman had not formulated his work in terms of class formation. He used the term "class" gingerly, preferring "workers" and other descriptive synonyms precisely because "class" analysis had been identified with a belief that economic structure determined behavior and belief. Nonetheless, Thompson's twin nemeses—smug liberalism and vulgar Marxism—were also Gutman's, and as a matter of practice, the revisionist formulations central to *The Making of the English Working Class* were already embedded in Gutman's essays. Thompson's understanding of class as the precipitate of common experiences within a system of productive relations, and of class consciousness as the cultural articulation of those experiences, was also Gutman's. Gutman's repeated denial of any necessary connection between economic structure and behavior, his emphasis on experience, and his overarching commitment to empirical research were also Thompson's. Indeed, it was not so much the emphasis on culture that drew Gutman to Thompson as it was Thompson's explicit avowal, indeed his outright celebration, of human agency. Like Gutman, Thompson insisted that human action mattered. Gutman and Thompson had traveled along parallel paths to reach similar conclusions, although differences between American and English intellectual life gave their ideas different forms. Thompson's powerful articulation of this common perspective—his elegant prose, his evocative imagery, his compelling logic, and his commitment to a more humane society—affirmed Gutman's own commitment to this perspective and encouraged him to press it with still greater force.

Still, Gutman had much to learn from Thompson. Thompson introduced a theoretical rigor previously absent in Gutman's work. Although Gutman stepped cautiously onto Marxist terrain and was never fully comfortable there, he nonetheless saw the utility of Marxism, at least as Thompson had presented it. Gutman began to write of capitalism—although he still kept the language of "industrialism"—and increasingly of classes, not workers and owners. He initiated a correspondence with Thompson, and before long the two became fast friends. In 1966, Gutman arranged for Thompson to visit the State University at Buffalo. The visit had a lasting impact on Gutman's work. Previously, Gutman had wanted to write a history of American workers. Now he would write of how American workers had made their own history.

Another book published in 1964, Stephan Thernstrom's *Poverty and Progress: Social Mobility in a Nineteenth Century City*, also had a powerful effect on Gutman's thinking.[31] In its tone and content, it was nothing like *Making*. Indeed, in many ways the differences in the two books suggested the vast distance between history written on the two sides of the Atlantic. If Thompson's opus was the product of an intense theoretical debate (and, indeed, it would unleash an even more ferocious debate between hard-line "structuralists" and Thompsonian "culturalists"), *Poverty and Progress* was nearly innocent of social theory. Instead, it was meant to test the reality of the American dream—the ability of Americans to better themselves, to move up the economic and social ladder, to gain wealth and status. Its great strength derived from its innovative method, particularly the systematic use of the federal manuscript census. Actually, Thernstrom's conclusions—that great jumps in social status were rare and that most mobility was intraclass, not interclass—were rather equivocal. Historians read them differently. Some claimed that Thernstrom's work confirmed the reality of social mobility, while others saw his conclusions as evidence of an empty promise: the glass was both half empty and half full. On both sides of the debate, scholars—indeed, Thernstrom himself—called for more research before the question could be settled. As with similar questions that seem susceptible to empirical validation but actually require conceptual redefinition, more research always appeared necessary. But amid the general enthusiasm for the study of social mobility, few historians were yet willing to look beyond the culture-bound question that Thernstrom asked.[32]

Gutman greeted Thernstrom's work with high praise, declaring it "a spectacular book, exceedingly well-written, free of the painful jargon and secret language that often passes as social science, filled with original insights, and, by any measure, a first-rate work of major importance." Not content to stop there, Gutman asked "Why such enthusiasm?" and went on to heap still more praise on *Poverty and Progress*. Gutman clearly liked Thernstrom's focus on local history, his emphasis on the lives of individual men and women, and his apparent attack on the notion that the ideal of social mobility was the reality of American life. Still, what most attracted Gutman was Thernstrom's method. In utilizing "dry census schedules and dull tax lists," Thernstrom had shown how these mute sources could be made to tell the history of previously anonymous men and women.[33] These were the people Gutman wanted to write about. Thernstrom's sources were weapons Gutman needed in his arsenal.

The influence of *Making* and *Poverty and Progress* would soon manifest itself in Gutman's work. While teaching at Fairleigh Dickinson, Gutman had begun a study of nearby Paterson, New Jersey. A decaying industrial city at the fag end of metropolitan New York, Paterson was once a major industrial center. Alexander Hamilton had singled out the falls of the Passaic River as a prime site for an American manufactory. The early appearance of machine shops promoted the growth of a machine-tool industry and transformed Paterson into a center for the manufacture of railroad locomotives. By the mid-nineteenth century, Paterson produced more than a quarter of the locomotives built in the United States. The town was also a major producer of textiles and became the home of the American silk industry. Workers dominated the population of Paterson, and the city boasted a powerful labor press and a large number of active unions. It became a stronghold for the Industrial Workers of the World, and in 1913 Big Bill Haywood himself led immigrant silk workers in a strike that paralyzed the city and brought American silk production to a halt. Long after the defeat of the IWW, workers in Paterson kept that moment of triumph alive. Gutman had family in Paterson, and had visited the town as a boy and heard tales of the great strike. The town's history and Gutman's personal connection with it made Paterson an especially appealing place to study the transit of American workers from the world of Alexander Hamilton to that of Bill Haywood and thus to understand how an American working class made itself.

But Gutman's first work on Paterson owed more to the influence of Stephan Thernstrom than to that of E. P. Thompson. Indeed, Gutman initially focused not on workers but on the manufacturers. Contemporary scholarship had concluded that America's industrial elite was not the product of a Horatio Alger–like rise from rags to riches; however, Gutman noted that the industrialists who had thus far been studied stood at the pinnacle of the American economic pyramid. Gutman thought social mobility might look different from the local rather than the national perspective. In fact, his investigations in Paterson showed that most successful entrepreneurs had their roots in the ranks of skilled artisans and that many were foreign-born. They "were not 'princes' prepared by training and education to become 'kings' of industry."[34]

Gutman did not conclude his study of "rags to riches" merely by correcting a misperception. What seemed significant about the artisanal origins of Paterson's elite was not so much the validity of the rags-to-riches myth as it was the role that artisans-turned-manufacturers played in the struggle for power. Gutman thus took the question of social mobility out of its narrow confines and placed it in the context of the ongoing struggle between labor and capital. In that context, the success of some artisans cut two ways: it opened to workers the possibility of escaping wage labor, and it awakened manufacturers to the workers' world—a world from which they themselves had come. Again, the meaning of social mobility, however carefully measured, was equivocal. As Gutman was fast coming to understand, his conclusions, like the study of social mobility generally, could have no meaning outside the historical circumstances of his subjects. That realization soured him on Thernstrom's work. While Thernstrom and other like-minded scholars pursued the study of social mobility to greater and greater technical sophistication and smaller and smaller historical significance, Gutman became increasingly critical of history that relied upon technical expertise with little concern for the larger struggle for power.

Instead, Gutman drew his inspiration from Marxist revisionists, of whom Thompson was the most important. Just as he tried his hand at a study of social mobility, Gutman began to look for ways that he could write about working-class culture. Again he turned to Paterson, this time focusing on labor radical Joseph P. McDonnell.

Gutman's essay on McDonnell was his first sustained attempt to draw the insights of Thompsonian culturalism into his own work.[35] Few men could have been a more appropriate subject for this enterprise. Born in Ireland, McDonnell carried membership cards in both the nationalist Fenian Brotherhood and the Marxist International Working men's Association when, at age twenty-five, he migrated to the United States. In Paterson, he became a trade union organizer, labor lobbyist, and newspaper editor. As the personification of transatlantic labor radicalism, McDonnell suggested both how the making of the European working class shaped the making of the American working class and how the dynamics of the historical process of class formation united workers on both sides of the Atlantic.

Gutman's essay, which was probably written in the mid-1960s though not published until later,[36] focused attention on McDonnell's career as a socialist editor and his successful efforts to reform labor law in New Jersey. Under McDonnell's prodding, the New Jersey legislature enacted protective laws, improving working conditions, curbing child labor, and expanding the legal rights of organized workers. Earlier Gutman had explained labor's success in the Gilded Age by emphasizing the limited power of the new industrialist and the willingness of local businessmen to stand with the workers. Now he subordinated this argument to another. Rather than seeing the alliance of workers and other classes as the source of labor's power, Gutman looked to the "vital subcultures among the immigrant and native-born poor as well as among the more substantial craftsmen and artisans." He found that "such subcultures were especially important in the Gilded Age industrial town and city." "Politics in the industrial city," declared Gutman, "was affected by these subcultures and an awareness of a potential (and, at times, active) working-class political presence."[37]

McDonnell's legislative successes derived from workers' power. McDonnell might growl loudly at the evils of child labor and archaic labor laws, but "a 'growl' unaccompanied by a 'bite' was hardly enough, and that potential 'bite,'" Gutman averred, originated in "the electoral power that rested in the industrial cities and their diverse but dense clusters of working-class subculture."[38]

Workers' power, workers' culture: one could not be understood without the other. Power and culture: the subjects had always been embedded in Gutman's work, but Thompsonian Marxism had sharpened them and given them a new edge. That edge could be seen in Gutman's long-running critique of the old labor history. Earlier, he had lamented its institutional preoccupation, its national focus, and its concern with "great events." Now he lashed out at a labor history which depicted workers as "passive, ineffective, and alienated victims, practically helpless before their all-powerful employers."[39]

Gutman's essays on Paterson initiated a study of working-class culture that would occupy him the rest of his life. It was a complicated subject, made more so by the multinational and multiracial composition of the American working class. But Gutman had a sense of the terrain upon which his work would stand: "Gilded Age workers had distinct ways of work and leisure, habits, aspirations, conceptions of America and Christianity, notions of right and wrong, and traditions of protest and acquiescence that were linked together in neighborhoods by extensive voluntary associations and other community institutions."[40] Following Thompson, Gutman saw two elements as central to an understanding of working-class culture: republican politics and popular religion. He turned first to religon.

Despite occasional rhetorical invocations, religion was a subject that had hardly made a ripple in Gutman's earlier work. Like most labor historians, he had seen the sermons and writings of Henry Ward Beecher, Russell Conwell, and Dwight Moody as little more than a front for capital. Now, however, Gutman ignored the gospel of wealth and focused on the workers' religious beliefs. He began with the traditions workers carried from preindustrial society. "A preindustrial social order had nurtured particular religious beliefs that did not disappear with the coming of industrialism," Gutman declared, sounding a theme that would continue to inform his work. It "did not easily or quickly conform to the Protestantism of a Henry Ward Beecher or a Dwight Moody and the secular optimism of an Andrew Carnegie or a Horatio Alger."[41] But what kind of theology, polity, and religious practice did workers bring to the new age? Often they were the same as those of the great industrialists; the difference lay in the meaning that workers invested in them.

In "Protestantism and the American Labor Movement," Gutman explored the mechanics by which American workers mobilized Protestant religious belief and practice for their own purposes, searching for what Thompson called the "legitimising notion of right" that permitted workers to make their own world.[42] Gutman demonstrated how workers transformed preindustrial perfectionism into working-class utopianism and how Christianity provided a standard of justice that workers could measure against the new one offered by the industrial regime. He argued that the historical figure of Jesus—who chided the powerful, defended the despised, and found his following among the common people—became a model and an inspiration to workers, and that Christian imagery and rhetoric suffused the language of the labor movement. If the great industrialists and their clerical allies invoked Protestant Christianity to legitimate their rule, workers employed it on their own behalf. They mouthed the same words, called forth the same images, and worshipped the same icons as their adversaries, but gave them different meanings. Protestantism thus sheltered workers from the harshest aspects of the new order and offered a powerful defense against those who would oppress them. More important, giving Protestantism a special meaning allowed workers to fashion themselves into a class, separate from and opposed to the new industrialists. Workers saw themselves as bearers of Jesus' truth. Christ, as countless labor leaders reminded their people, was a carpenter.

Gutman's study of working-class religion drew directly on *Making* and the work of other Marxist revisionists, particularly that of Eric Hobsbawm. Thompson had portrayed Methodism as the religious manifestation of capitalism in nineteenth-century England and blistered it with his harshest invective. But then, in his own search for the "legitimising notion of right," he went on to show that once Methodism became the religion of the working class, workers wielded it against those who oppressed them.[43] Hobsbawm had also written on Methodism (as well as on millenarian religion) as a vehicle of popular protest. The parallel Gutman drew between the role of religion in the formation of the American and the English working classes proved instructive. It introduced American scholars to a new generation of British Marxists, demonstrated the utility of their work for the study of American history, and—perhaps most important—showed how the history of workers in capitalist societies was all of one piece. "Protestantism and the American Labor Movement" gained for Gutman a reputation as a spokesman for British and particularly Thompsonian Marxism in the United States, a reputation that sometimes detracted from an appreciation of his own original contribution.

Gutman welcomed the more general knowledge of the British Marxists, but from his perspective, the importance of "Protestantism and the American Labor Movement" was that it clarified the special circumstances under which an American working class came into being. While religion might be central to the experience of workers on both sides of the Atlantic, there were still important differences of politics, class composition, and national domain. The American Revolution and subsequent political events gave American workers the vote and an active role in partisan politics long before English Chartists took to the streets. The American working class was a mélange of nationalities whose diverse origins overwhelmed the seemingly minor distinctions between the English, Welsh, Scots, and Irish. Finally, the United States itself was a continental empire ruled, at least after the Civil War, under one flag, while the British Empire was constructed in a different manner. Having tested certain of Thompson's insights—not, as he would insist, Thompson's model—Gutman returned to the task of understanding the creation of the American working class.

A fellowship at the Center for Advanced Study in the Behavioral Sciences at Stanford for the academic year 1966–1967 allowed Gutman the opportunity to consider the general history of industrial workers in the United States. By the time he left the frozen shores of Lake Erie for the balmy edge of the Pacific, he had selected a title for his study: "The Shock of Industrialization."[44] But he was also somewhat awed by the task he had set for himself. Perhaps for that reason, he began his assault on familiar turf: the depression of the 1870s.

Gutman returned to his study of the depression armed with new weapons. Data from the federal manuscript census and insights from Thompsonian Marxism provided a new perspective on the history of American workers. Gutman thus began to rework some of his earliest published essays and unpublished portions of his dissertation, revising his studies of the depression in the industrial and mining communities of the Northeast and Midwest. In so doing, he established a pattern that would characterize his subsequent work. He was always rewriting, taking stories familiar to him and examining them in the light of new ideas. But during his stay at the center, Gutman also pressed into previously unexplored areas of the depression, investigating the world of black coal miners and the lives of those who labored for the great industrial corporations. Finally, he launched a major study of industrial workers in Paterson.

Despite the relaxed atmosphere of the Center for Advanced Study, Gutman worked like a man possessed. His earlier difficulties in writing seemed to fall away, and pages flew from the typewriter. Before he left the center, he completed five extended essays, totaling over 600 pages. The work pointed to a fresh interpretation of how the diverse circumstances of work and the complexity of different national origins shaped the workers' struggle for power at the end of the nineteenth century. Taken together the essays were not a general history of industrial workers in the United States, but they were a substantial beginning.

Two of the essays emerged directly from a reappraisal of previous work. "Labor in the Land of Lincoln: Coal Miners on the Prairie" expanded Gutman's study of the impact of the depression in Braidwood, and "Citizen-Miners and the Erosion of Traditional Rights: A Study of the Coming of Italians to the Western Pennsylvania Coal Mines" enlarged his account of "the Buena Vista Affair."[45] Gutman had already addressed these subjects in his dissertation and in published articles. At the Center for Advanced Study, he stretched the chronological limits of the two studies, reaching back to the 1860s and pressing forward into the twentieth century. He also increased their topical scope, in keeping with his new interest in working-class culture. Evangelical religion, republican ideology, national mythology, and associational and leisure activities all entered into Gutman's expanded view of the struggle for power in Braidwood and Buena Vista. "Labor in the Land of Lincoln" and "Citizen-Miners" demonstrated how Gutman's understanding of the development of the American working class had grown during the previous decade.

Yet each essay had its own particular emphasis. In "Labor in the Land of Lincoln," Gutman focused on the evolution of labor politics from the web of work and community relations in Braidwood. He sketched the origins of the working-class community and showed how work patterns, religious practices, political ideology, and leisure activity knit workers together. In Braidwood, the workers' world combined old elements—"Chartist ideology, post-Chartist 'new model' trade unionism, pride in craft, and an ethic that emphasized benevolence, self-help, and mutuality and drew heavily on perfectionist and post-millennial Protestantism"—and a new element—"the Great Republic of the West."[46] Set against absentee mine owners, this "curious mixture" spawned a rich oppositional culture and a powerful union. In a sense, "Labor in the Land of Lincoln" returned Gutman to the locus of the old labor history—the union hall and the picket line—through the study of community life.

Family ties were especially important to Gutman's understanding of the linkages between work, community, and politics. Braidwood miners, Gutman observed, worked in kin groups, which "were not segregated ethnically in the pits." Work patterns, reinforced by the bonds of kinship, "tightened family ties but weakened ethnic distinctions" among miners. The coincidence of work and family organization thereby reinforced the mutuality of the voluntary associations and the solidarity of the union hall.[47]

In keeping with the general transformation of his work, Gutman also presented a new view of Braidwood's shopkeepers and public officials. In his earlier essays, Gutman had depicted them as "other classes," who joined with workers in a "cross-class alliance." Now he saw these men as part of the working class. His study of their social origins revealed that almost all had working-class roots. Their presence in Braidwood suggested, not a cross-class alliance, but the complexity of the working class itself.

In "Labor in the Land of Lincoln," Gutman confronted workers in defeat. In 1874, Braidwood miners emerged triumphant from their battle with the coal operators. In the years that followed, the miners' union prospered and they solidified their control over the town. But a similar confrontation with the operators in 1877 led to military occupation, the introduction of black strikebreakers, and the defeat and eventual destruction of the union. Mine operators slashed the miners' wages, lowered their standard of living, and took greater control of their daily lives through the imposition of company stores, scrip payment, and onerous work rules. The miners' declining power transformed relations between them and the town's elite and altered relations among the miners themselves. Braidwood's shopkeepers, professionals, and officials no longer allied with the miners with quite the same alacrity, and some miners, even a few committed unionists, defected to the operators' camp. However, the destruction of the union did not mark the end of workers' rule in Braidwood. In many ways, their control of the town government became more entrenched. Frustrated in their struggle for power in one arena, workers turned to another.

"The Great Republic of the West" that played so large a role in

"Labor in the Land of Lincoln" also manifested itself in "Citizen-Miners and the Erosion of Traditional Rights." Gutman interpreted the struggle between western Pennsylvania miners and operators in terms of "the meaning of America." Miners and operators held competing conceptions of American society, and their divergent visions of the Republic informed the struggle over the nature of the industrial regime. Throughout the western Pennsylvania coalfields, the "employer notions of industrial discipline conflicted with deeply felt traditions among the miners about America."[48] Those traditions, Gutman believed, derived at least in part from the workers' belief that America was different from Europe. It was not simply that the United States was the land of opportunity—the warmed-over Algerism served up by the operators—but that workers enjoyed *by right* all the privileges of citizenship, making them equal to all others. "What mattered for the miners," Gutman observed, "were the institutions and values that surrounded their work—the fact that workers shared rights equally with nonworkers; the fact that citizenship in a republic conferred a special status on men in lowly occupations."[49]

Gutman elaborated this notion of republicanism in his narrative of the nativist wars that accompanied the introduction of Italian strike-breakers into the western Pennyslvania coalfields. Both miners and operators mixed their conceptions of republicanism with a potent nativism. The miners, often immigrants themselves, defined their rights as citizens by distinguishing themselves from the Italians who were recruited to break their strike. "An American even though he digs his life away in the bowels of the earth or sweats it away before a hot furnace is yet a freeman, a citizen, feeling the responsibility and duties of citizenship," boasted Pittsburgh's *Labor Tribune*. Operators, for their part, defined the Italians' presence in the same nationalist terms and likened those who opposed the newcomers to treasonous Ku Kluxers and Molly Maguires.[50] Citizens' rights thus became the lingua franca of class struggle in much the same way as evangelical Protestantism.

The preeminence of allegiance arising from the workplace or allegiance arising from national origin—"class" or "ethnicity," in the historiographic argot—was a controversial question among labor historians. In "Citizen-Miners," Gutman entered that debate and defined a position that became even more pronounced in his later work. Although ethnic epithets—"greaser," "monkey grinder," and the like—flew wildly as the struggle between the miners and the operators intensified, what impressed Gutman was how both sides used the arrival of foreign workers to stake a claim to American nationality. The conflict at Buena Vista was lengthy, deep, bloody, and, for several would-be Italian miners, deadly. The miners won the first round in

1874 and 1875, but by 1877 the operators had gained the upper hand. Still, the rights of citizens remained at the center. When the operators introduced company stores, paid in scrip, and changed work rules, miners protested in much the same way as they had objected to the Italian strikebreakers. "What did our forefathers fight and bleed and die for in '76, if checkweighmen are to be allowed to watch," complained an angry coal miner a century after the American Revolution. "The theory of Republicanism does not allow the laboring population to be reduced to poverty and dependence on the will of a few, and the virtual abrogation of our political rights and privileges," another miner pronounced.[51] From Gutman's perspective, what often passed as working-class nativism was in fact an attempt by workers to assert their rights as Americans by distinguishing themselves from workers in other countries. In looking ahead a generation to a time when Italians had come to compose a large part of the established labor force in western Pennsylvania and Eastern Europeans of various nationalities were the newcomers, Gutman found the Italian miners protesting the arrival of the new immigrants in the same language of citizen rights. What was most important, then, was not the diverse nationalities that divided workers but the common ideology that bound them together.

Gutman made the same point about racial differences in the mines. Black strikebreakers loomed large in industrial disputes of the 1870s. They entered the Braidwood strike at a crucial point and played a decisive role in the defeat of union miners. Black miners were a significant part of the labor force in Braidwood during the years that followed. In "Labor in the Land of Lincoln," Gutman tried to penetrate the lives of these black miners as he had other portions of the mining community, but the sources were mute. Gutman's frustration was evident, and the obvious lacuna was one of the reasons "Labor in the Land of Lincoln" remained unpublished. Gutman's discovery of Richard L. Davis, a founder and pioneer organizer of the United Mine Workers, enabled him to learn about the lives of black miners and to see them as other than scabs. It also allowed him to address the question of how racial differences shaped the workers' world. As contemporaries noted, it was "an easy matter for employers and foremen to play race, religion, and faction one against the other." It was an even easier matter for historians to affirm the employers' success and to see racism triumphant. Gutman refused to take the easy route, and as a result, his essay on Davis offered a strikingly original view of the relationship between white and black workers at the end of the nineteenth century.[52]

In many ways, Davis's career exemplified the complex relations among black and white miners. Although often recruited as strikebreakers, most black miners were simply unskilled laborers who found employment in an expanding industry. Davis, "a fullblooded colored man," entered the mines that way, became an active unionist, and was blackballed for his trouble. Still, he continued to preach the union doctrine and to work as an organizer. Despite the racial distrust, friction, and violence that accompanied the use of blacks as strike-breakers, Davis won the respect of both black and white miners. His message that "labor organizations have done more to eliminate the color line than all other organizations, the church not even excepted" gained him many converts among black miners. By 1900, blacks composed 10 to 15 percent of the membership of the United Mine Workers. And, as Davis's election to the union's executive committee suggests, he had also earned the respect of white miners.[53]

Nonetheless, Davis spent most of his career in a three-cornered battle, struggling against the suspicion of both black and white miners as well as the opposition of the mine operators. This, not a prefabricated community of brothers, was precisely the world into which Gutman wanted entry. What Gutman's essay revealed was neither an interracial utopia nor an Oceania of racial warfare, but a world in tension. Davis himself personified that tension by simultaneously inhabiting different portions of that world, "one shaped by his experiences as a coal miner and the other as a Negro."[54]

The dualism of Davis's career was writ large in the history of American coal miners at the end of the nineteenth century. Some black miners served as strikebreakers, but others labored as union officials; some white miners donned the Klansman's robes, but others stood with their black brothers; racism was omnipresent in the mines, but so was evangelical egalitarianism and union-bred solidarity. The allegiances that derived from racial identification were no different than the allegiances that derived from national or religious identification. Their meaning depended upon the circumstances in which they were enmeshed. Gutman thus explored Davis's career using the same methods by which he had studied ethnic conflict in western Pennsylvania. His eye for the "common predicament" of working people allowed him to see possibilities others ignored. While the outcome was not always as Gutman would have liked, neither was it as others had presumed.

Gutman's study of Richard Davis demonstrated a deepening appreciation of working-class culture and a growing respect for its importance in the struggle for power. Like his work on European immigrants, Gutman's essay on Davis denied the conventional division between "black history" and "labor history" and pointed to a general history of working people of diverse national origins. Other aspects of his new work at the Center for Advanced Study contributed to this nascent history. However, it looked not so much to labor's culture as to capital's power.

The role of absentee corporate owners in the small towns that Gutman had studied begged the question of the corporate empires such men were constructing. Perhaps because most workers labored in small shops that rarely employed more than a dozen men, little attention had been given to the factories that employed an increasing share of the American work force. Gutman noted that students of business, enamored of the notion of a perfect wage market, ignored the ability of these large units to shape the economy, and labor historian "fussed in excess over craft workers and laborers in small workshops." To broaden his understanding of the events of the 1870s, Gutman undertook an investigation of the "ways preindustrial Americans and European immigrants confronted the large Gilded Age factory." His questions were wide-ranging and significant: "who worked in these factories, how their owners recruited and disciplined workers, how these workers responded to factory conditions and new work norms, and how the surrounding community felt toward the large factory, its owners, and its workers."[55] The target of his questions was equally big: John D. Rockefeller's mammoth Standard Oil Company.

Again, Gutman had selected his subject with care. The debate over Rockefeller's role in American history was intense and had generated fierce partisanship, as the code words "robber baron" and "industrial statesman" denoted. Gutman left no doubt where he stood. He was angered by the depiction of Rockefeller—whose daily earnings exceeded a worker's annual wage—as an employer who "insisted upon good wages and kindly treatment." But he also thought the debate was framed in such a way as to narrow its significance for the study of American history.[56]

Gutman decided to enter the factory and see exactly how Rockefeller's labor policies worked. He focused on the coopers, old-line craftsmen whose work was being transformed by a new technology. Historians had made much of the importance of technology in the transformation of work and workers, and Gutman did not neglect the subject. He traced how the introduction of machinery into the various phases of barrel making disrupted the preindustrial work routine of coopers, who continued to celebrate "Blue Monday" and enjoy a midafternoon "Goose Egg." He emphasized how these artisans protected their preindustrial traditions and resisted the demands of the new technology. Finally, he noted the uneven effects of mechanization on the craft. While some barrels continued to be hewn by native-born coopers in small shops, others were produced by semiskilled immigrants in large factories. Thus, when Rockefeller needed a barrel—and he needed more than a few—he discovered that they were built by unionized old-line crafsmen in New York; by nonunion Bohemian factory hands in Cleveland, and by journeymen of various national origins employed by boss coopers in Pittsburgh. The trade changed, but not all at once.

It was not the force of technology that humbled the barrel makers, but Rockefeller's raw power. Slapping at technological determinism—another denial of human volition—Gutman observed that "technology altered power relationships inside the factory, but power relationships always affected the introduction of technology and its consequences."[57] Standard Oil's ability to make and purchase barrels at various sites throughout the country permitted Rockefeller's agents to play the coopers against one another. When the coopers showed signs of unity, Rockefeller's minions mobilized the police in their employer's behalf. The coopers did not go down without a struggle. Old-line coopers resurrected their union, and immigrant coopers called upon their community; both drew deep drafts from the cultural wellsprings of a bygone age. None of these defenses had much effect. In the end, Rockefeller triumphed, demolishing the coopers' craft, wrecking their union, and reducing the workers themselves to utter dependence. So far as workers were concerned, Gutman concluded, "market power and technological innovation had joined together, destroyed a traditional craft, and turned the powerful skilled craftsman into a powerless factory laborer."[58] Thereafter, coopers worked on Rockefeller's terms or not at all. Like other workers, they had come to understand that the advent of the corporation shifted the struggle between labor and capital onto new terrain.

Paterson, New Jersey, with its large locomotive factories and textile mills provided the ground upon which Gutman proposed to map this new terrain. An emphasis on both workers' culture (as in the revisions of his community studies) and capital's power (as in his essay on Standard Oil) set the direction for "Social Structure and Social Conflict in the Industrial City," his long-planned study of urban industrial workers.[59] The scope and size of the essay expanded rapidly as Gutman elaborated Paterson's social structure, documented its system of production, and characterized its social and political relations. By the time he had described a series of strikes that racked the city during the 1870s and a variety of other conflicts, including legal suits against Joseph McDonnell, the manuscript totaled over 200 pages and was far from complete. Gutman took the incomplete draft with him when he left the Center for Advanced Study in August 1967. He planned two book-length studies, one of industrial workers in Paterson and another—drawing together the essays on Braidwood, Buena Vista, Davis, and Standard Oil—composed of cases in the development of an industrial working class. The theme of both would be "what happened to republican political institutions given the rapid growth of factory capitalism."[60]

Gutman did not return to Buffalo. Instead, he accepted an appointment at the University of Rochester, where scholars like Norman O. Brown and Loren Baritz had already attracted a coterie of politically active graduate students. Gutman looked forward to the opportunity to direct advanced students at a major university. He had long reflected upon his own graduate training and had definite ideas as to the best way to educate young historians.

As his students have testified, Gutman had a special talent for graduate teaching. Unlike his own graduate instructors, he was accessible and egalitarian. A man of enormous energy and intense commitment, Gutman had a gift for conveying his own enthusiasm. Although he was easily distracted and his seminars were often disorganized, he swept students up in the importance of the task set before them: nothing less than the rewriting of American history. And since he assumed that their work—including the meanest seminar paper—would be an important part of that project, not just an educational exercise, he treated his students as fellow workers in a cooperative enterprise. Even the most deferential soon became aware that Herb —seldom Professor Gutman—wanted active co-conspirators, not passive observers.

Gutman got what he wanted. He quickly attracted a group of well-read, theoretically sophisticated students. Experienced in the civil rights and, before long, the antiwar movement, these students were politically engaged and well versed in labor history. They were actively searching for a way to use the past to remake the future. Gutman's message—that the past was made by people, not abstract forces, and the future would be made the same way—fell upon receptive ears. His political project, to use the study of history to "free people for creative and critical thought or radical thought," found many takers.

The Vietnam War—both the war in Southeast Asia and the war at home—drew Gutman even closer to his students. He was one of the few faculty members to whom antiwar students could regularly turn for support. Whereas many leftist academics bridled at what they considered the excesses of the student movement, particularly what was perceived as an attack on freedom of speech and other essentials of academic freedom, Gutman remained true to the students and their cause. For Gutman, the student-based opposition to the war, like the civil rights movement, affirmed the superior wisdom of the people and their ability to act independently of their political superiors.

Although often critical of student radicalism, Gutman feared that the criminal actions of the Johnson administration would alienate students from their own past. He watched in horror as many uncritically accepted a version of the American past as an "unredeeming saga of a crude mixture of corporate exploitation, all-pervasive racism, and a compliant and corrupted working-class and radical movement." He worried that the strength that could be derived from past struggles of working people would be lost. "It was almost as if Mayor Daley and the Chicago police landed at Plymouth Rock and as if agents for General Motors dumped tea in the Boston Harbor," he despairingly wrote to a friend. But even in his darkest moments, Gutman found reason for optimism. The dedication of his students, as well as events on the streets sustained him.

Still, teacher and students did not always march to the same beat. Gutman had little use for the theoretical debates that so attracted some of his best students. The rigorous empiricism of his years at Madison had placed an emphasis on the raw facts of American economic history. Despite the charges by his critics of "culturalism," few scholars knew their data as well. Much to the discomforture of his students, Gutman loved to display his knowledge of changing wage rates, tariff laws, and population shifts.

Gutman also engaged his students on another level. They wanted to know why there was no American socialism; why no American labor party; why American workers failed at their historically preordained task. Gutman inveighed against such questions. "I don't think that way historically," he roared. "I don't know what it means to talk about 'an historical task that workers faced.' Because what we are letting through the back door in that kind of formulation is a notion that historical development is fixed, in a sense predetermined, and we are measuring the American worker or the French worker or the Polish worker against an ideal type." In his classroom as in his writing, Gutman remained adamantly opposed to determinism of any sort. He urged his students to free themselves from notions of what should have happened and to look instead at what in fact had happened. Gutman's seminar thus emphasized "a set of questions having to do with the way in which one examines class relations, the way in which one examines the institutionalization of power, popular movements, and the integration of subordinate or exploited groups into a social system." The "very, very smart questions" that he drew from Marx, while junking the "determinist, teleological core," became the lodestone of Gutman's pedagogy.[61]

Gutman developed a pedagogical triad, and before long, its litany became familiar to his students. "Little is known about . . ." he would begin, sketching the desolate ignorance of modern scholarship on a question that everyone quickly agreed had transcendent importance.

"Much remains to be learned . . ." he would continue, warming to the task by suggesting the many ways the subject at hand could be addressed. Finally, he would deliver the *coup de grâce*: "But enough is known to . . ." This last would signal a veritable free-for-all in which teacher and students would scrape their imaginations for ways in which the extant literature could be made to speak anew. The "hands-on" history for which Gutman had searched in vain at Columbia and which he had found among the graduate students at Wisconsin was alive and well in his classroom at Rochester.

Gutman's method was designed to demonstrate how the alleged absence of sources was no excuse for not writing the history of working people. His students became immersed in primary sources: labor bureau reports, congressional testimony, and especially newspapers— the labor press, the immigrant press, and the big-city press. "Peeling away" the layers of an account of a strike, even a biased or unsympathetic account, revealed the workers' voice; insights could be "teased" from descriptions of the way workers dressed, spoke, or deported themselves: the very words Gutman used to describe the process of revivifing the sources of working-class life bespoke his method. The sources, including those that derived from the elite, could be made to speak to the history of working people, if read with sensitivity and with the right questions.

Gutman's seminars were practicums in learning to read and think historically. He liked nothing better than to share his own discoveries, often reading long passages from freshly unearthed documents and then quizzing all within earshot on the meaning of what they had heard. But the questioning never became an inquisition. His seminars were always more collaborative than competitive. A shared vision that was as much political as it was historical sustained both teacher and students.

Although he rendered his documents with dramatic flair, Gutman's readings were a source of tension in the seminar. Students often squirmed uncomfortably as he read aloud, waiting respectfully for an opportunity to present their ideas. Nonetheless, Gutman's readings pointed to yet another central tenet of his historical practice: the importance of the word. Indeed, he was convinced that contemporary utterances could be used to write history. His essay on Richard Davis was written in the mode of the nineteenth-century life-and-letters biography, sandwiching long passages from Davis's letters between his own commentary. Gutman submitted documentary notes to *Labor History* with such frequency that they almost became a regular feature of that journal.[62] Later, he served as a member of the National Historical Publications and Records Commission and helped launch a number of innovative documentary editions.

Gutman's new responsibilities at Rochester slowed his own work. He continued research on Paterson, including a pioneering reconstruction of the family structure drawn from the manuscript census. However, his larger work did not approach completion. Except for an article on Richard Davis, the essays drafted at the center remained unpublished.[63] His general history of American workers remained unwritten.

Although a grand synthesis eluded him, Gutman began to collect his ideas on the formation of the American working class and its place in American history. He consolidated his critique of the old labor history, his sense of the new one, his understanding of Thompsonian Marxism, and his own research into a single essay that spoke to the unique history of the American working class. He presented one draft at the first Anglo-American Labor History Conference in 1968 and another at the meeting of the Organization of American Historians the following year.[64] In 1973, he published the final version in the *American Historical Review* as "Work, Culture, and Society in Industrializing America, 1815–1919."[65]

"Work, Culture, and Society" surveyed the terrain of working-class life in the United States from a broad perspective. It began from the idea that the demands of the new industrial regime were foreign to working people. Workers resisted, using every weapon at their command. In Gutman's view, their most potent weapons derived from the standard of justice (again, Thompson's "legitimising notion of right") embodied in the rituals, traditions, and institutions of their preindustrial past. Gutman thus reiterated that class struggle was more than a dispute over wages and hours; it was cultural warfare at the highest level. The arena of class conflict extended beyond the picket line to society at large.

In a rich evocation of the texture of working-class life, Gutman sketched the outlines of his own work, incorporating the studies of the British Marxist historians whom he admired, particularly Thompson, Hobsbawm, Sidney Pollard, and Raymond Williams. But it was not the common elements of class formation that he addressed in "Work, Culture, and Society." Instead, Gutman dwelled upon how the unique character of American workers shaped the process in the United States.

What gave the American working class its special history was the continued reinvigoration of preindustrial culture by wave upon wave of new preindustrial recruits. Beginning with New England mill girls, extending through Irish, German, and British immigrants before the Civil War and Eastern and Southern European immigrants after the war, and concluding with the northward movement of Afro-Americans in the wake of World War I, preindustrial peoples continually revitalized the struggle against the discipline of the factory. Workers spoke in different tongues, practiced different rituals, and carried different traditions, but their common opposition to the new regime and their desire to maintain their old values joined them together. If the struggle was always the same, to paraphrase Thompson, it was never quite the same. The changing nature of the American economy, American politics, and American workers themselves created an American history. From these changes over time, Gutman proposed a new chronology to understand the years between 1815 and 1919. Bypassing the Civil War, Gutman divided that long century into three periods and outlined the distinctive features of the process of class formation in each.

Utilizing a rich array of sources—everything from poetry to census returns—"Work, Culture, and Society" also suggested a way of studying class formation. Gutman, borrowing from the work of Sidney Mintz, characterized culture as "a kind of resource" that workers drew upon in their struggle with their employers and society as "a kind of arena" in which the battle took place.[66] Anthropologists frequently treated such rituals, traditions, and institutions in a reified form as "carryovers" or "survivals" from the Old World, the intellectual or physical remnants of a previous life. Gutman never did so. Although fascinated by the diversity and complexity of working-class culture, Gutman understood the cultural heritage that workers brought to their confrontation with the new industrial regime in terms of the struggle itself. Outside the context of class struggle, such cultural baggage appeared merely as a collection of antiquarian curiosities; within that context, it was a powerful instrument of class warfare. The rituals, traditions, and institutions of a preindustrial past were both a means to transmit culture and a means to sustain it against those who would deny workers their perceived rights.

Several other important subthemes informed "Work, Culture, and Society." They spoke to the ways in which Gutman continually incorporated current controveries into his ongoing work. One of these subthemes had to do with the role of artisans in spearheading the resistance to the new industrial order, a large element in Thompson's work. Another had to do with violence, a subject that preoccupied Gutman following the urban riots of the late sixties and the publication of an ahistorical official government report that purported to explain their origins.[67] But perhaps the most significant of these subthemes concerned the place of immigrants in American history.

By far the most influential postwar student of immigrant life was Oscar Handlin. In his first book, *Boston's Immigrants*, Handlin wrote of the painful transition of newly arrived Irish from denizens to citizens.[68] It was a closely researched, detailed analysis of the suffering of displaced peasants with a heavy emphasis on the role of American nativism.

Starkly revisionist in its frank equation of immigrant history and American history, *Boston's Immigrants* bespoke the views of a second-generation American working on the margin of the American intellectual establishment. Handlin's second major book on immigrants, published nearly a decade later, was written from the perspective of a tenured professorship at Harvard University. Although Handlin did not retreat from his condemnation of the horrific conditions of immigrant life or the narrow bias of American nativists, his emphasis changed. He told a tale of disoriented men and women struggling to maintain their cultural balance, of the abrupt obliteration of the dysfunctional habits of peasant life, and of the inevitable acceptance of modernity. Handlin's immigrants carried a heavy burden to the New World, but in time they—or their children—came to embrace American civilization. Sloughing off the primordial ties of the peasant village, they learned of the impersonal solidarity of the modern city. Like Handlin himself, they would assimilate and come to champion the values of American liberalism. Handlin called his book *The Uprooted.* It won a Pulitzer Prize.[69]

"Work, Culture, and Society" was in large part a critique of *The Uprooted.* Gutman's immigrants were not the hapless flotsam and jetsam of the peasant world swept up by the relentless flow of industrialization, reluctantly but inevitably shedding old ways. Their culture did not disintegrate in the icy glare of nativist bigotry or the warm light of American democracy. Gutman lashed out at the Parsonian functionalism that saw peasant life shatter amid "cost-conscious and ill-equipped factories." Far from being obliterated, the culture of the Old World was transformed in the New. In "Work, Culture, and Society," Gutman announced that it was time to "discard the notion that the large-scale uprooting and exploitative processes that accompanied industrialization caused little more than cultural breakdown and social anomie."[70]

Gutman thus joined anthropologists Clifford Geertz, Eric Wolf, and Sidney Mintz in assaulting what Gutman would later call the "breakdown thesis." Rather than depicting the process by which immigrants became Americans as "assimilation," Gutman—and the other critics of Handlin and the school of sociological functionists who had influenced Handlin—would come to speak of cultural transformation or "acculturation."[71] Such a transformation depicted, not the destruction of the old, but its incorporation into the new. The study of cultural transformation took nothing away from the harsh conditions of immigrant life, but rejected the portrayal of immigrants as an alienated, broken people. For Gutman, " 'suffering' and 'strain' were not synonyms for 'breakdown,' " but evidence of cultural creativity that did more than transform the immigrants. Acculturation was a reciprocal process;

immigrants changed as a result of their New World transit, but so too did the New World and its inhabitants.[72]

The central agency for transmitting working-class culture from the Old World to the New was the family. Sociologists had associated "the factory system with the decline of the family and the onset of anonymity." Gutman found little to support this interpretation. Despite widely varying sex ratios, a higher proportion of immigrant than native families were "intact" in the nineteenth-century industrial cities he had studied. These "tough familial and kin ties made possible the transmission and adaptation of European working-class cultural patterns and beliefs to industrializing America."[73] As with Braidwood's miners, the family was the source of cultural adaptivity and political solidarity.

"Work, Culture, and Society" was a significant achievement. It suggested how the American working class, fragmented by national and racial differences as well as by the vast expanse of the continent, could be understood as a whole. It joined "labor history" and "immigrant history" with "family history." It demonstrated how the American experience was different without being exceptional. It pushed back the frontiers of labor history from the industrial period to the seventeenth and eighteenth centuries by showing how labor shaped the culture and politics before the factory. It connected the study of American history with the live questions of European historiography: moral economy, customary rights, and crowd actions. Above all, it suggested a new chronological framework for the American past.

It was this last that Gutman deemed most important. Later, when questioned about "Work, Culture, and Society," he conceded that some of its emphases were misplaced if not wrong and that some of his definitions were crude if not mistaken. Old World culture, as depicted in "Work, Culture, and Society," was far too homogeneous and "tradition" much too static. The concept of "preindustrial culture" was too imprecise. The essay rested too heavily on what had come to be called modernization theory, a theory Gutman would soon dismiss as deterministic. He also admitted that the essay underestimated the indigenous opposition to the industrial regime and paid too little attention to second-generation Americans, many of whom grew up within the factory system.[74] However, Gutman held fast to his innovative chronology. For him, the new chronology marked a sharp break from the electoral and constitutional mold that shaped the history he had learned. Workers, not presidents and constitutions, stood at the center of his America. The recurrent conflict of workers and their bosses, not the quadrennial election of a president, was the pivot around which nineteenth-century American society turned. The history of the American working class was the history of the United States.

Presumably, "Work, Culture, and Society" provided a theoretical backbone for the larger studies of industrial workers, the pieces of which Gutman had assembled while at the Center for Advanced Study. But even before his essay appeared in the *American Historical Review*, Gutman's work had taken a new direction. His study of American workers had moved from the North to the South, from the factory to the plantation, from the descendants of Europeans to the descendants of Africans.

The shift South had begun slowly, while Gutman was still teaching at Buffalo. Following his arrival, Gutman had initiated a study of the history of his new environs, akin to his ongoing work on Paterson.[75] He assigned a graduate student, Laurence A. Glasco, the task of combing the census returns for Buffalo. They turned out to be extraordinarily rich, for in addition to the federal census, the state had conducted its own more detailed enumeration. Glasco would later draw upon state and federal census returns to write a full-fledged study of the city's working population.[76] Meanwhile, he and Gutman began to apply the accumulating evidence to a variety of historical problems.

One of the more striking was the red-hot controversy over the black family. In the wake of the urban riots of the 1960s, Daniel P. Moynihan, an assistant to President Lyndon Johnson, issued a special report explaining the origins of the contemporary racial crisis. Moynihan tipped his hat to the problems of inner-city employment, housing, and education. But he focused on the "deterioration of the Negro family," declaring it the "fundamental source of the weakness of the Negro community at the present time."[77] Moynihan traced the problem of the contemporary black family to slavery, when blacks—legally property—had no right to marry, to choose a spouse, and to nurture their children. He thus rooted his argument in the historic slave family, borrowing openly from the most recent statement on the subject, Stanley Elkins's *Slavery*.[78]

Althouh pioneerng in many ways, Elkins's book was not based upon original research. In fact, Elkins did little more than repeat the conventional wisdom gleaned from the work of E. Franklin Frazier and other sociologists.[79] Frazier maintained that the reality of the slave family was an accurate reflection of slave law, which had denied slaves the right to a normal domestic life. In his view, slave children rarely knew their fathers; women—mothers, grandmothers, and aunts—dominated slave households; and premarital pregnancy characterized the experience of slave women. For all but a privileged few, the slave family was a formless matriarchy. Standing against the racist scholarship of his day, Frazier sought to demonstrate that the disorganization he saw in contemporary black households was simply another of the nightmarish burdens of slavery. It had nothing to do with the innate character of black people or the traditions of Africa. The cultural connections between Africa and America had been severed by the Atlantic slave trade. Black people, cut off from their Old World roots, were the most American of all New World peoples.

But Moynihan did more than paraphrase Frazier's history. He couched his argument in extraordinarily provocative terms. In Moynihan's view, "deep-seated structural distortions in the life of the Negro American," created by slavery and reinforced by segregation, migration, and urban poverty, had transformed the black family into a self-perpetuating "tangle of pathology." It was proof that "white America broke the will of the Negro people." Unlike other immigrants to the United States, blacks lacked the cultural resources to sustain a separate community.[80]

Moynihan later claimed that his harsh words were chosen to emphasize the depth of white racism and to reinforce the claims black people had on the nation. His report was subtitled *The Case for National Action*. But the racial slander implicit in the Moynihan Report provoked a firestorm of controversy.[81] Gutman was among those aroused.

Gutman thus set out to test the historical basis of Moynihan's hypothesis among Buffalo's small black population. He immediately recognized the source of Moynihan's argument as the breakdown thesis in another guise; Handlin's understanding of the immigrant experience had been applied to Afro-American life. Just as Gutman had challenged Handlin's argument by demonstrating the coherence of immigrant families in nineteenth-century industrial cities, so he began to explore the organization of Afro-American family life. Along with Glasco, he reconstructed the city's black families from the 1855 and 1875 New York State censuses. Many Buffalo blacks were refugees from slavery, and Glasco and Gutman reasoned that "if the slave household developed a fatherless, matrifocal pattern sufficiently strong to become self-sustaining and to be transmitted from generation to generation, such a condition necessarily should have been most common among those free Negroes closest in time and in experience to actual slavery." But instead of finding a "tangle of pathology" among Buffalo's black freedpeople, Glasco and Gutman discovered stable households. Most Buffalo blacks lived in nuclear families with both parents present. Although impoverished, the black family in Buffalo was difficult to distinguish from other working-class households. Glasco and Gutman then compared black family structure in Buffalo in 1855 and in 1875 with that of New York City, Brooklyn, and Mobile, Alabama, in 1860. Again, their evidence revealed that the vast majority of free black people lived in male-headed nuclear households with both parents present. Although cautious in imputing behavior and belief "from the formal structure of individual households," Glasco and Gutman believed they had more than enough evidence to refute "speculation concerning the relationship between slavery and post-emancipation Negro family life, particularly the 'historically' conditioned 'tendency' toward matrifocality and male marginality."[82]

As critics were quick to point out, nineteenth-century Buffalo was hardly a center of black life. Nonetheless, the findings set loose a train of questions about the existing literature on slavery and post-emancipation black life, particularly the historical interpretations upon which Moynihan had relied. That literature was itself in flux, and the combination of live political questions and live historical questions was too much for Gutman to resist. When he moved to Rochester in the fall of 1967, he began to trace the origins of the postbellum black family back into the slave period. The presence at Rochester of Stanley Engerman and Robert W. Fogel, who were engaged in studies of Southern slavery, and the arrival off Eugene D. Genovese two years later, spurred Gutman on.

The quest for an understanding of the black family would slowly insinuate itself into Gutman's scholarly agenda, occupying a larger and larger portion of the whole. It necessitated that he master the literature on slavery. Armed with his newly acquired knowledge, Gutman trailed the black family into the South, focusing on the Civil War and its immediate aftermath. He believed the actions of the newly emancipated freedpeople would provide evidence of slave family life. Gutman thus scrutinized large portion of the postbellum manuscript census, reconstructing the black family in a variety of communities: Beaufort, South Carolina, a densely black center of long-staple cotton production; Washington Township, Mississippi, a portion of a Black Belt county; Natchez, Mississippi, a river port; and Richmond, Virginia, the South's leading industrial city. As a matter of principle, Gutman did not merely sample the black households in the census of each locality but enlisted entire populations. It was not simply that Gutman suspected sampling and the statistical theory that stood behind it (although he did), but that not counting each individual violated his conviction that every man and woman mattered. So he gathered up his yellow legal pads—never a coding sheet—and began to count, score, and count again.

Unlike the people he had studied in Buffalo, Brooklyn, and Mobile, nearly all the black men and women in Beaufort, Washington Township, Natchez, and Richmond had been slaves. Yet in the years immediately following the Civil War, the vast majority also resided in nuclear families with both parents present. The strength of the post-emancipation black family was also affirmed in the marriage registers kept by the Freedmen's Bureau and various state agencies. Once given the opportunity, thousands of newly freed slaves legitimated relationships of long standing. In so doing, they often provided information on the origin and duration of their marriages, thus strengthening the argument Gutman had built from postwar census returns. The postbellum black family was not the product of wartime liberation, but had a long history in slavery.

Gutman pressed his search for the slave family backward in time. In rummaging through plantation records, he uncovered long lists—many of them inventories of property—which enumerated slaves in family groups or indicated familial relations. Other historians had seen these lists, but had done little with them except total the size and value of the masters' holdings. Gutman had taught his students that new questions could make traditional sources speak anew. Now he showed them how. Gutman employed the slave lists to construct elaborate family trees that exposed the thicket of kinship in which slaves resided. He analyzed slave lineages to reconstruct the rules by which slaves built their families. He uncovered naming patterns that revealed the important role played by fathers, grandfathers, and uncles in the slave family. And he suggested how slave family lines governed the transfer of precious knowledge, skills, and material possessions from generation to generation.

In sharp contrast to Moynihan and the historians from whom Moynihan had borrowed, Gutman depicted the slave family as an extraordinarily vital institution that sustained a powerful, complex, and vibrant culture. Throughout the years of bondage, most black people married and lived in family groups, although their unions had no legal standing and often existed against their owners' wishes. Slave women generally had all their children by the same father. Although prenuptial intercourse and childbirth occurred often, most unmarried slave mothers later took husbands and remained with them until death (unless sold away by their owners). The vast majority of slave children grew up knowing a slave father and a slave mother. As evidence of the importance of kinship, slaves commonly named their children after relatives. Slave naming practices served to connect slaves to their families of origins and thereby provided a personal and communal history in which a larger Afro-American culture flourished.

The slave family was not a pale imitation of the master's. According to Gutman, the values that governed slave family life differed from those of their owners and from those of white society generally. For example, whereas slaveowning families encouraged cousin marriages— as a means of consolidating property holdings and assuring social exclusivity—slaves rarely married blood cousins. Gutman also found no evidence that "slaves subordinated sexual intercourse to marriage," something most Americans had done by the early years of the nineteenth century, if not before. Throughout the years of American captivity, slave parents accepted premarital pregnancy as a matter of course and supported unmarried daughters and their children. White Americans—slaveowners and nonslaveowners alike—were generally hostile toward women who had children out of wedlock and viewed premarital pregnancy as a disgrace. As a general rule, parents and siblings appeared to play a more important role in the slave community than in the free one, and blood ties counted more than the bonds of marriage among slaves. The opposite tended to be true among their owners.

Although *The Black Family in Slavery and Freedom* did not appear in print until 1976, Gutman had established its major themes well in advance of publication. He announced them in countless private conversations and public lecture and, in 1972, published them in summary form in the French journal *Annales*,[83] so that when the book finally appeared its conclusions had been so fully incorporated into the historiography of slavery that they seemed common knowledge. Nonetheless, during the early 1970s, as his research began to bear fruit, Gutman's findings had revolutionary implications for understanding Southern society and black life. They also provided important insights into the evolution of American racial ideology (as reflected in the development of the ideas about the black family) and the public policies which were the original source of the inquiry.[84] Gutman addressed all these subjects, including the implications of his findings for federal welfare policy. But his interest continued to center on the slaves themselves. The rediscovery of the black family provided "compelling reasons to reexamine historic Afro-American community life and the very meaning of American black culture."[85]

Having discovered the slave family, Gutman sought its origins. He traced it back from the antebellum years, where most studies of slavery resided, to the seventeenth and eighteenth centuries. In some ways, the pre-Revolutionary years were analogous to the post–Civil War period that Gutman understood as the formative years in the history of a Euro-American working class. The colonial period, particularly the middle decades of the eighteenth century, was a time when forced immigrants from Africa became Afro-American slaves, when the culture of black people on British mainland North America was yet to be determined. The form it would take remained an open question. The decisions of men and women had yet to fix the course of history. This was the intellectual milieu in which Gutman was most at home.

Gutman suggested how eighteenth-century slaves wielded their common experience and the inheritance of Africa to make themselves into a class.[86] He located the beginnings of an Afro-American working class in much the same way that he had found the origins of the Euro-

American one century later, and he studied the process of Afro-American class formation in a like manner. Within the limits of his evidence, Gutman explored how black men and women employed their traditions, rituals, and institutions in the struggle against those who would master them. Slave masters, like the great factory owners, tried to force subordinates to accept their values, but they were no more successful. The cultural resources of the black community permitted slaves to forge a world distinct from and opposed to the owning class. Just as wageworkers gave the evangelical religion and republican politics that they shared with their employers a distinctive meaning, so slaves endowed kinship with meanings different than their owners. The divergent marriage rules, familial roles, and naming practices revealed the independence of slave culture. Culture was as much a weapon for the Afro-American field hand as it was for the Irish seamstress, Slavic coal miner, or Bohemian cooper.

Gutman's study of the black family was more than a history of an important institution of Afro-American life or even the most important institution of Afro-American life. It was an attempt to understand the larger dynamic of Afro-American culture: the origins and transmission of that culture, and the role of culture in black resistance to the system of slavery in mainland North America.

The central question of Gutman's work remained unchanged even as its geographic center migrated from North to South and from factory to plantation. Gutman continued to explore the relation of power and culture in the formation of the American working class. Just as he asked the same questions in studying Richard Davis and Joseph McDonnell, so he applied the same methods in studying slaves and free workers. Slaves were workers who were owned. This distinguished them from wage earners, much as indentured servants and apprentices stood apart from free workers. Similarly, slaves were immigrants, albeit forced ones. This distinguished them from those who traveled across the Atlantic of their own volition. Enslaved immigrant workers, like free ones, opposed those who would oppress them and drew upon their own culture to create a powerful oppositional tradition. Slaves had to be studied, like free workers and like voluntary immigrants, by analyzing their behavior, decoding their language, and reconstructing their institutions. Central among these institutions was the family. It served as a source of cultural continuity and political solidarity for Afro-American workers just as it had for European ones. Only by understanding slave family life could the larger system of chattel bondage—the relationship of slave and master—be understood. Only by connecting the experiences of slave and free workers could the history of an American laboring class be written.

POWER & CULTURE

For Gutman, his study of the Afro-American family was not a detour on the road to a history of the American working class, but the center lane on the main highway.

Gutman was not alone in rethinking the nature of Afro-American culture. Pushed forward by the ongoing revolution in race relations, a small army of scholars representing every discipline from anthropology to theology had begun to reinterpret Afro-American life. The subject grew rapidly, with new interpretations sprouting in a hothouse of racial conflict. Conflict drove the process. Activists and scholars alike—often they were the same persons—believed that uncovering the origins of slavery, the character of Afro-American society, the nature of abolition, and a host of other related matters was essential to an understanding of the contemporary crisis and its resolution. As Gutman had maintained from the beginning, history and politics were one. They were not joined in any direct or simple fashion, but in a complex, often dialectical manner. History provided no easy lessons and instead offered insight and direction. Still, the connection was not easily managed as the American people struggled to reformulate the nation's racial order. Violence had become a part of politics. Frequently, the conflict in the streets spilled over into the classroom, the lecture hall, and the scholarly meeting. Indeed, the ferocity of academic debate often resembled the violence of the street. If blows were rarely exchanged (perhaps owing more to the feeble nature of the participants than to a respect for the spirit of free inquiry), scholars stopped just short of violence in assaulting each other with angry words and racial epithets.

Gutman's understanding of slavery evolved in this highly charged atmosphere. Perhaps it was inevitable that a debate which was at once political and historical would also become intensely personal. Such was the case in Gutman's relationship with the dominant figure in the study of American slavery, Eugene D. Genovese.

Gutman had been in the fore when Rochester's history department recommended Genovese's appointment in 1969. Genovese's Marxist scholarship raised hackles among the university's staid administrators. His well-publicized enthusiasm for a Vietcong victory sent them into a panic. They rejected the history department's recommendation. Gutman and the other members of the department refused to accept the administration's blatantly political decision. Gutman resigned his position as assistant chairman (as did the department chairman, Perez Zagorin). Having disassociated himself from the university's administration, Gutman despaired of the fate of the department, if not of his own career. But much to his surprise, the administrators reconsidered. During the summer, they met with Genovese and not only approved his appointment but also elevated him to the chairmanship of the department.

Having gained power, Genovese was determined to use it. He aimed to make Rochester a center of graduate study in history of the first rank. His vision of a department where scholars of all political persuasions could work without fear of harassment excited great enthusiasm, particularly within the embattled community of leftist scholars. At first, Gutman gave him full support and joined with Genovese and Christopher Lasch, another new appointee, in plans to establish a left historical journal. But Genovese's methods soon alienated his allies, Gutman among them. Perhaps because they shared so much and perhaps because Gutman had risked so much in securing Genovese's appointment, the break became increasingly acrimonious. By 1971, only two years after Genovese's arrival, they had stopped talking to each other and were talking about each other. What they had to say was hardly flattering to either man. For Gutman, Rochester was no longer a comfortable place to work, and in 1972, he left to become chairman of the history department at New York's City College. But the bitter controversy with Genovese did not end. It became a near-vendetta. The personal rivalry and intellectual differences fed upon one another. The feud had a profound effect on Gutman's work.

Gutman came to see himself in a personal contest with Genovese. The contest was magnified by Gutman's own professional standing. He was a full professor in a field in which a published book was almost the *sine qua non* of such status. Although few would challenge his credentials, the absence of a published book grated upon him and increased his determination to write not just a book but a great book, one that would eclipse Genovese's forthcoming volume. Gutman continually raised his own standards to ever more unreachable heights, and when he neared those heights, he raised them still higher, as if to assure that they could never be met. Criticism of his manuscript sent him back to the drawing board. Rather than revise, he completely rewrote, creating several different versions of "The Black Family." By the time he turned the manuscript over to a desperate publisher, it was far larger than could fit between two covers. Gutman was forced to shelve whole sections, many of them original contributions to an understanding of black life in the nineteenth century. Among these was a book-length manuscript exploring the role of former slaves in the establishment of schools. It affirmed the freedpeople's commitment to their families. It also amplified their desire for independence by demonstrating how newly freed slaves took the initiative to improve their own world.[87] Thus much was lost in Gutman's effort to perfect his history.

Still, the continued rethinking and rewriting of "The Black Family" improved the manuscript in many ways. Certainly it enlarged its scope, deepened its theoretical base, and broadened its context. Upon publication, *The Black Family in Slavery and Freedom* was the fullest history of any group of American families and—although few realized it— one of the best studies of class formation in the United States. Its stunning presentation of historical evidence made it a model of historical research, and its compelling logic best exemplified how a historian could make mute sources speak. However, *The Black Family* was also overwritten and poorly organized. As Gutman himself doubtless realized, earlier publication would have made it a better book.

But the contest with Genovese had other, more positive results. It moved Gutman to write a sereis of critiques, first of Genovese's history of slavery and then of the work of Robert Fogel and Stanley Engerman. Written in an angry, polemical style rarely seen in historiographic debates in the United States, Gutman's critiques made manifest many of the unspoken theoretical assumptions that undergirded the writing of American history. They also demonstrated the pitfalls of the fads that had overtaken American scholarship during the 1970s. Most important, they stimulated Gutman to address the fundamental purpose of writing history. When Genovese responded in kind and others joined the debate, the terrain of historical scholarship was immeasurably enlarged. The clash of ideas in the bruising warfare suggested that something important was at issue. It drew the best minds to the subject and placed slavery at the center of the study of American history.

Genovese had begun studying the slave South at the same time Gutman was undertaking his work on the industrial North.[88] The son of Italian immigrants, he had followed a path similar to Gutman's through the New York school system to Columbia University. He missed being Gutman's classmate by only a few years. He too had joined the Communist party, only to be unceremoniously expelled while a sophomore at Brooklyn College. But the youthful encounter with Marx left a stronger impression on Genovese than it had on Gutman. He read deeply in Marxist texts and became fascinated with the process by which a ruling class rules. In flight from the same wooden determinism that so repelled Gutman, Genovese discovered Antonio Gramsci, an Italian revisionist, whose studies suggested how the political and economic power of the ruling class manifested itself in the culture shared by both ruler and ruled. For Gramsci, the hegemony of the ruling class derived, not from the point of a gun, but from the force of cultural domination. Genovese, like Gutman, came to see culture as the terrain of class warfare. But while Gutman viewed the struggle from the bottom, Genovese saw it from the top.

Whereas Gutman went off to Wisconsin, Genovese remained at Columbia and wrote a dissertation on the failure of agricultural reform in the antebellum South. He found the roots of this failure in the precapitalist nature of the Southern planter class, and he located the distinctive nature and ideology of that class in the relationship between slaveowning planters and their slaves. Characterizing these relations variously as precapitalist, prebourgeois, seigneurial, and paternalistic, Genovese depicted the society that derived from owned labor as fundamentally different from one that derived from hired labor. Slavery thus "gave the South a social system and a civilization with a distinct class structure, political community, economy, ideology, and set of psychological patterns" that set it apart from the free North.[89] The social relations that rested upon slavery were in fact so different that they provided the basis for a distinctive Southern nation. In Genovese's view, the War Between the States was no civil war; it was a war for Southern independence.

From the first, Genovese's work centered on the planter class.[90] He exhibited an appreciation of slaveholding planters that bordered on admiration, if not affection. Their open critique of capitalism, their frank recognition of their own class interests, and their willingness to defend them to the death appealed to Genovese. Drawing upon Gramsci, much as Gutman had borrowed from Thompson, he suggested how the planter class extended its power over Southern society. Indeed, for Genovese, the culture of the ruling class was, perforce, the culture of the society. Such a view left precious little room for an independent oppositional working class (or any other class, for that matter). Genovese's enthusiasm for the planters' recognition of their own class interest was not matched by a similar recognition of the slaves' self-awareness. When he did write about slaves, his position was not markedly different from that presented in Stanley Elkins's *Slavery*.[91] But, like other scholars, Genovese was moved by the events of the 1960s. Slowly, he turned from the world the slaveholders made to the one the slaves created.

Published in 1974, *Roll, Jordan, Roll: The World the Slaves Made*, Genovese's majestic study of slavery, penetrated deep into slave life and provided the fullest discussion of the social structure, institutional life, and values of the black people during slavery.[92] In fine detail, Genovese elaborated the culture of the slave quarters and explained how slaves were able to wrest a large measure of control over their own lives and create a work ethic, a set of sexual mores, and a religious ethos of their own. However, slave culture evolved within the powerful embrace of the owning class. In return for a recognition of their humanity and a measure of independence, slaves accepted their owners' authority, at least as long as the owners could maintain it. Slaves thus took the paternalism that underlay the masters' hegemonic ideology and turned it on their owners to create their own world. But that world was compromised at its source. In resting their culture upon their masters', slaves crippled their own oppositional potential. Genovese spoke of the slaves as prepolitical. If he saw Afro-American culture during slavery as the basis of a separate black nation, it was not yet a nation that could stand apart from those who mastered it.

Gutman objected to this view. He objected to it on political grounds, on historical grounds, and on personal grounds. Without question, Gutman's personal animus toward Genovese fueled his political objections to seeing a working class in terms of a ruling class and his historical objections to seeing slave culture rooted in that of the master. But the political was primary. Genovese had maintained that slaves, like other working people, preferred the masters' order to no order at all.[93] In so doing, Gutman believed that Genovese implied that working people, left on their own, would live in chaos. Gutman bristled at that.

Gutman protested the writing of the history of slavery from the veranda of the big house. "Suppose one was writing a book on ironworkers and steelworkers in Pittsburgh called *Roll, Monongahela, Roll: The World the Steelworkers Made*," he asked somewhat mischievously. "How would that book begin? It is not a book about the steel industry. It is not a book about class relations in the steel industry. It is subtitled *The World the Steelworkers Made*. Would it begin with a 150-page essay quoting from and explicating Andrew Carnegie's *Autobiography*?" Gutman was quick to answer his own leading question. Historians do not begin studying the world of the worker in the world of the employer. "We begin in the world of the artisan. We begin in the world of the handicraft weaver. We begin with the world before modern capitalism." In the same way, a proper history of the slave would not originate in the interaction of master and slave. Instead, it would begin in the period before slavery. Just as the historic confrontation of proletarians and capitalists would have to be studied with a knowledge of the preindustrial artisans and peasants, so the Afro-American slaves' struggle against their owners had to be studied with a knowledge of free Africans. Gutman granted that Genovese probed established class relationships "imaginatively and brilliantly." He also appreciated the intellectual adroitness by which the slaves Genovese described took their masters' ideology and turned it to their own benefit, perhaps because such an analysis followed the lines of his own favorite explanations. But, argued Gutman, Genovese's static portrait of slavery handicapped *Roll, Jordan, Roll*. Gutman dismissed the book as "functionalist."[94]

Gutman broadened his attack to a more general condemnation of the history of slaves—and, by implication, all workers—written from the perspective of the owning class. For Stanley Elkins, the masters' unchecked power reduced the slave to a fawning, servile embodiment of the Sambo stereotype. Elkins's formulation carried this logic to the extreme, but in Gutman's view the same reasoning lurked in the work of E. Franklin Frazier, Kenneth M. Stampp, and Genovese. Gutman lumped Genovese with liberal scholars who interpreted slave behavior and belief in terms of the "treatment" slaves received. Genovese's historic compromise, wherein slaves accepted their owners' authority in exchange for a measure of independence, was just another variant of what Gutman labeled the "reactive model." From Gutman's perspective, "slave culture was not the mere consequence of good treatment," or, for that matter, bad treatment. It was not what masters did *for* slaves or what masters did *to* slaves, but what slaves did for themselves that was important. To be sure, "Much in the regular behavior of slaves was affected and even determined by their regular interaction with owners and other whites." However, "these and other choices had their origins within the slave experience" and the slaves' "adoptive and protective responses." In Gutman's view, *Roll, Jordan, Roll* did not allow for the full play of the slaves' experience in the making of "the World the Slaves Made."[95]

Like the great industrialists of the Gilded Age, slaveowners enjoyed great power to command their slaves, but Gutman found no evidence in Genovese's analysis to demonstrate that the owners had transformed power into authority. Indeed, for Gutman, slave naming practices and marriage rules were not the product of a paternal compromise but of the Afro-American experience. Slave fathers and mothers posed an alternative to the masters' world. This was precisely the importance of the slave family. It allowed slaves to articulate values that opposed those of the owners and pass those values to generations unborn. Again, culture was a source of power.

Gutman had integrated his critique of Genovese's work into *The Black Family*. In many ways, *The Black Family* was a running polemic against *Roll, Jordan, Roll* and other studies of slavery. As Gutman put the finishing touches on his own manuscript, a second study of slavery, Robert Fogel and Stanley Engerman's *Time on the Cross*, drew his ire.[96]

Economists by training, Fogel and Engerman believed that neoclassical economic theory and quantitative techniques could be profitably applied to the study of history. Fogel had already done so in a contentious, counterfactual history of railroads in nineteenth-century American economic development. Working in a more conventional mode, Engerman had published several significant studies of the Southern economy.[97] As the controversy over slavery warmed, Fogel and Engerman joined forces to write an economic history of slavery.

Aided by large infusions of money in the form of federal grants, they mustered an army of graduate students, amassed a mountain of historical data, and began to massage it with the most advanced statistical techniques.

Fogel and Engerman saw their highly capitalized, high-tech history as the wave of the future. They wrote as Computer Age cliometricians offering salvation to Stone Age chroniclers mired in soft data and softer assumptions. Like other "quantitative historians," they maintained that methodological expertise, not knowledge of a particular subject, would be the distinguishing feature of the new historiographic millennium.

Appearing in the spring of 1974 amid a rush of publicity generally reserved for the marketing of a new detergent, *Time on the Cross* received high praise. Thernstrom, recognizing one of his own, declared it "absolutely stunning, quite simply the most exciting and provocative book I've read in years." A reviewer in the *New York Times* agreed and stamped it the most significant historical study published in the last decade. "With one stroke," he pronounced, Fogel and Engerman had "turned around a whole field of interpretation and exposed the frailty of history done without science."[98]

Actually, *Time on the Cross* was a peculiar amalgam of original research, pure hokum, and conventional wisdom. The emphasis was on the last. Many of the allegedly revolutionary conclusions were already well ensconced in most general texts. For example, loud declarations of slavery's profitability and viability were greeted with a yawn by knowledgeable scholars. Few Southern historians still maintain that slavery was "moribund on the eve of the Civil War," another of Fogel and Engerman's supposed discoveries. Although the question of the relative efficiency of Southern agriculture remained—indeed, the question had not really been posed in that form—earlier criticism of Genovese's work had demonstrated that many slaveholders were shrewd managers and knowledgeable agriculturalists. What was radically new in Fogel and Engerman's analysis was the implications they drew from slavery's profitability and alleged efficiency.[99]

Whereas most scholars maintained that the planters' profits had been squeezed from the labor of slaves, Fogel and Engerman argued that profitability derived from efficiencies of scale and the ability of slaveholders, as rational men of the market, to stimulate slave productivity with incentives, positive and negative. Their emphasis was on the positive. Slaves responded to marketlike incentives, embraced the " 'Protestant' work ethic," and became upward-striving workers. "Sambo," Gutman would later quip, "really was Horatio Alger with a black skin." The Southern economy boomed and slaveowning capitalists prospered; diligent slaves shared in the benefits. They enjoyed a standard of living as high as or higher than most contemporary free workers. To be sure, slaves were exploited, but "the rate of expropriation was much lower than has generally been presumed." Over the course of his life, "the typical slave field hand received about 90% of the income he produced." To say the least, slavery was not so bad. Black people worked hard, and they received a large portion of the fruit of their labor. Although Fogel and Engerman invoked the horrors of chattel bondage, the slavery they depicted appeared to be a benign institution.[100]

Fogel and Engerman presented their findings in a manner that begged criticism. Taunting traditional historians for their lack of technical expertise and economists for their historical ignorance, they invited the long knives to dinner. Before long, they found themselves minced and skewered. Historians and economists questioned Fogel and Engerman's sources, their methods, and their assumptions.[101] When the critics were finished, little survived. Never in the course of American historiography had a book risen so fast and fallen so quickly. *Time on the Cross*, which appeared with such great fanfare, slunk into oblivion and with it the cliometric revolution.

Time on the Cross offended Gutman. A request for a review from the *Journal of Negro History* allowed him the opportunity to vent his rage. He began to write. Gutman's writing had not been going well as he pressed to get "The Black Family" into print. The difficulties which delayed his doctoral thesis had returned. His syntax became garbled and his style increasingly convoluted. But his anger at Fogel and Engerman removed the blocks. The words flowed easily and power-fully. Simple declarative sentences replaced complex ones. Within weeks, Gutman completed a draft of his review. It occupied the entire issue of the *Journal of Negro History* under the whimsical title of "The World Two Cliometricians Made: F + E = T/C."[102] Later, a revised version was published as *Slavery and the Numbers Game*. In many respects, it ranks among the best pieces of sustained criticism in all of American historiography. Certainly, it is the most entertaining.

The sources of Gutman's anger were many. Some were personal, as Fogel and Engerman had stood with Genovese in the Rochester wars. Some were historiographic, having to do with the interpretation of slave culture from economic statistics. But at bottom, Gutman's anger was political. What offended him most was the antidemocratic use of history. Fogel and Engerman's conclusions emerged mysteriously from a forest of statistics, equations, and formulas, which they had consigned to a separate volume. They claimed immunity from criticism by wrapping themselves in "a more complete body of information on the operation of the slave system than has been available to anyone interested in the subject either during the antebellum era or since."[103]

In short, Fogel and Engerman mystified a democratic art. They used history to buttress a position that flew in the face of common sense: slaves benefitted from slavery. As in his earlier critiques of the Moynihan Report and *Roll, Jordan, Roll*, the personal, the political, and the historical joined to drive Gutman's work forward.

Gutman set out to restore the accessibility of history by demonstrating that an "intelligent reader does not need to know the difference between a chi-square test and a multiple-regression analysis to learn that ordinary enslaved Afro-Americans did not conform to the patterns of beliefs and behavior emphasized in T/C."[104] He wanted to show that Fogel and Engerman were not merely wrong in their facts and wrong in their interpretations, but wrong in the kinds of questions they asked and the ways they set about answering them. He wanted to teach history.

Gutman was at his best in his criticism of Fogel and Engerman's use of Bennet Barrow's whipping list. In a rush to quantify everything, Fogel and Engerman had discovered Barrow, a Louisiana planter, who kept a close record of discipline on his plantation. Over the course of a two-year period, he administered some two hundred whippings to the 120 slaves who composed the heart of his work force. With decimal-point precision, Fogel and Engerman calculated "an average of 0.7 whippings per hand per year." To underline the point, they also presented a bar graph depicting the distribution of whipping among Barrow's slaves between 1840 and 1842. The text that accompanied the analysis of Barrow's whippings emphasized that most slaves did not regularly face the lash and that planters, like other good business-men, preferred to motivate their workers with a system of positive rewards that ranged from a dram of hard liquor to a few dollars in hard cash. As one enthusiastic reviewer noted in summarizing *Time on the Cross*, "good businessmen oil their machines."[105]

Gutman demolished Fogel and Engerman's methods and conclu-sions. For one, they had miscalculated the average number of whippings per slave. But the factual error was just a small part of the problem. The seeming precision of "0.7 whippings per hand per year" was a "pseudostatistic," which like the cool phrase "negative incentive" masked both the nightmarish reality of the lash and its political meaning. Whipping was an instrument of social discipline intended to impress not only the immediate victim but also all who witnessed it. From the perspective, Gutman formulated the relevant question: How often did Barrow's slaves see one of their number beaten? The answer: Once every four-and-a-half days. The whipping post was no stranger to Barrow's slaves. Then Gutman asked who was whipped and why. Most of those subjected to the lash worked in Barrow's cotton fields. Between 1840 and 1842, three-quarters of the field hands felt the lash, including seven of the ten women whom Barrow had assigned to field work. Fogel and Engerman had misconstrued their data by asking the wrong questions. Rather than indicating the internalization of the " 'Protestant' work ethic," Barrow's use of the lash revealed the slaves' stubborn resistance to the masters' authority and—more significantly—the slaves' own work ethic. It was that ethic which informed and gave meaning to the slaves' labor and to their lives. And it was that ethic which stood at the center of any interpretation of the nature of Afro-American culture. Moreover, Gutman emphasized, such an interpretation would not be the product of computers, statistical skills, or any other form of esoteric knowledge. It was accessible to anyone with a sharp pencil, a mastery of long division, and the right questions.[106]

Gutman's critiques of *Roll, Jordan, Roll* and *Time on the Cross* did not go unnoticed. While Fogel and Engerman did not respond directly, Genovese was soon on the offensive. Not one to allow a challenge to go unanswered, he rebuked Gutman in a stinging review of *The Black Family*. Genovese found little of value in the work and suggested that if a good editor had pared the book down to, say, 200 pages, *The Black Family* might have been useful to specialists in the field. Genovese conceded that *The Black Family* conveyed "the human texture," "the moving human resiliency, loyalty, integrity, and tragedy" of black life in slavery. But if Genovese found reason to praise Gutman for his sensitivity to the plight of the oppressed, his praise was short-lived. In his view, the theoretical confusion that marred *The Black Family* transformed sensitivity into misplaced sympathy. Fuming at being thrown together with liberals like Stanley Elkins and Kenneth Stampp, Genovese condemned Gutman for equating "treatment" with the larger issue of social relations. Gutman had erred badly in arguing "that the independence and integrity of the slaves' convictions and aspirations [could] be understood in isolation from an analysis of the contradictory effects of the power of the masters." Yielding to no one in his admiration for the cultural creativity of black people during slavery, Genovese emphasized the limited control slaves had over their own lives. "Whatever the black family did," declared Genovese, "and it would be hard to overestimate its contribution—it did not exercise political power, and it exercised only the narrowest of economic options." By divorcing slaveholders from the process of slave socialization, Gutman separated "blacks and whites alike to wholly discrete entities." And by denying the impact of whites on black culture, he simultaneously denied the impact of blacks on white culture. In Genovese's view, Gutman had not placed family relations within the larger context of social relations and had, in consequence, lost sight of the dynamic interaction in which slaves made their world.[107]

Genovese was not finished. Just as Gutman had elevated his assault on *Roll, Jordan, Roll* to a more general critique of the study of workers, Genovese, joined by Elizabeth Fox-Genovese, broadened criticism of *The Black Family* and "Work, Culture, and Society" to a more general reconsideration of the new history. Published in 1979, "The Political Crisis of Social History" addressed large questions in the development of American historiography and gave close attention to Gutman's work, although it studiously avoided mentioning him by name.[108]

More than personal pique led Genovese and Fox-Genovese to target Gutman. Once Gutman had been a pioneer of a history that had no name. Now he was a spokesman for a history that had many names: labor history, ethnic history, urban history, immigrant history, black history, women's history, family history, and of course social history. Publication of *The Black Family, Slavery and the Numbers Game*, an anthology of readings in American social history entitled *Many Pasts* (edited with Gregory S. Kealey), and his collected essays under the title *Work, Culture, and Society* had propelled Gutman into a leadership role. His work was cited as the conventional wisdom by scholars who desired only to imitate it. He had become a featured speaker at scholarly conventions in the United States and lectured widely in Africa, India, and Japan, as well as Western and Eastern Europe. Wherever he went, young historians crowded around him, eager to learn his opinion of various books and interpretations. Gutman did not accept his new status uncritically. He took the occasion of the publication of *Work, Culture, and Society* to protest the "balkanizing thrust in the new social history." He observed that an "Irish born Catholic female Fall River Massachusetts textile worker and union organizer involved in the disorderly 1875 strike" could be studied under nearly a dozen heads, none of which would capture her experience. Gutman took pride in the way his work joined "labor history" and "immigrant history," and decried the manner in which the new history was fragmented and devoid of a central theme.[109]

In "The Political Crisis of Social History," Genovese and Fox-Genovese issued many of the same laments. But their indictment of the new history, especially the social history that was identified with Gutman, reached beyond these matters to what they saw as its fatal weakness: the lack of a concern with power. Genovese and Fox-Genovese argued that Gutman's attempt to see Afro-American culture in terms of its origins and its internal dynamics abstracted culture from class struggle. Gutman had evoked "the family or, worse, the entire popular culture . . . as an autonomous structure, independent of class confrontation, cultural interpenetration and political domination." Denouncing the removal of the master from the slave experience as a retreat from the public to the private, they implied that Gutman purveyed "a politically anesthetized idealism," "a bizarre and ahistorical

. . . view of a lower class life autonomously divorced from the pervasive influence of, and therefore influence on, the ruling classes." He was leading historians into a "neoantiquarian swamp." His history was little more than "a bourgeois swindle."[110]

Gutman and Genovese had savaged each other, but neither had renderd a faithful account of the other's work. When Gutman equated "treatment" with Genovese's sophisticated rendition of social relations in plantation society, he did great injustice to *Roll, Jordan, Roll.* When Genovese charged that Gutman had denied the role of the master, he did a like injustice to *The Black Family.* Nonetheless, neither man was without a point. Both Gutman and Genovese hit upon important tendencies in the other's work. If the polemical style that characterized their debate exaggerated those tendencies, it also placed them in stark relief. Just as Gutman had identified the weakness of Genovese's static analysis of slave culture and his reification of the concept of paternalism, so Genovese recognized the limitations of the study of working-class culture outside a socially defined arena. In his earlier community-based studies, Gutman had stayed well within the bounds of this arena. His emphasis on working-class agency served as a healthy corrective to the easy dismissal of worker activism. But when Gutman moved his focus from the study of the community to the study of culture generally, working-class agency appeared to take on a life of its own. Its limitations often became lost in the celebration of the complexity and richness of working-class life. Culture was power, but power took the form of solidarity to succor a subordinate class, not a challenge to alter the system of subordination. In short, with some exceptions—McDonnell's "growl," for example—culture had become defensive, whereas power remained offensive. This redefinition, so distant from the concerns manifested in "The Workers' Search for Power" and the other early essays, suggests how Gutman's work had shifted as the study of culture came to occupy his attention.

Gutman responded to Genovese's counterattack. He denied that he had portrayed slave culture as autonomous. The behavior, beliefs, and institutions "that exist among all subordinate groups and classes—and especially among slaves," he insisted, "cannot be autonomous." However, he again emphasized the "regularities" of slave behavior and belief, denounced Genovese's "reactive model," and reasserted the "paramount importance" of "the Afro-American historical experience" in the creation of slave culture.[111]

Gutman did more than restate his established position. Accepting Genovese's challenge, he suggested how the Afro-American experience shaped a "distinctive social class" and defined "the *context* that shaped the choices slave men and women regularly made." For Gutman, the slave family was not merely evidence of the distinctiveness of slave belief, but the medium in which an oppositional culture took shape. The family provided slaves—as it provided other working people—with "passageways" through which slaves elaborated their culture in space and time. Fictive kinship permitted slaves to transfer beliefs from individual households to the larger community, "binding unrelated slave adults to one another and thereby infusing these groups with conceptions of reciprocity and obligation that had initially flowed from kin obligations." At the same time, intergenerational ties allowed slave culture to develop over time. "Afro-Americans were never a self-contained social class," Gutman reiterated, but neither did they take their cues from their owners. The cultural alternatives generated and sustained within the black family "served as very important instrumentalities in furthering group solidarities and in ordering a daily life regularly disordered by the choices slaveowners made."[112] Again, culture was power. Whatever the concerns of Gutman's history, politics remained central.

But it was not concerned only with politics. Genovese and Fox-Genovese's challenge induced Gutman to consider the larger purpose of writing the history of working people. Genovese and Fox-Genovese understood history as "the story of who rides whom and how."[113] Drawing upon the French existentialist Jean-Paul Sartre, Gutman defined it in a different manner. For Gutman as for Sartre, the burden of historical understanding was "not what 'one' has done to man, but what man does with what 'one' has done to him." Gutman saw the emphasis on "achievement" as a trivialization of the human condition.[114] Following Sartre, Gutman redefined the central concern of history. Culture was power, but it was also more.

Gutman's battle with Genovese had been bruising, fueled by personal enmity, professional ambition, and political differences. In good part, their dispute reflected two distinctive approaches to the study of the past. The flow of world-historical events preoccupied Genovese. He took intellectual delight in the contradictions, many of them beyond individual control, that shaped human destiny. Understanding the sources of the relationship that allowed slave masters to obtain hegemony but that ultimately limited their power and cleared the way for their demise greatly attracted him. Likewise, Genovese found something compelling in the fact that the very source of the strength of Afro-American culture handicapped slaves in the struggle for liberation. Gutman had little use for such seeming contradictions or, for that matter, any event beyond human agency. From the first, he was concerned with "the workers themselves, their communities, and the day-to-day occurrences that shaped their outlook." It was those concerns which led to his embrace of Thompsonian revisionism, to his assault on those who defined workers in terms of their bosses, and to his emphasis on "what man does with what 'one' has done to him." To a considerable degree, Gutman and Genovese spoke past each other rather than to each other. In the end, both men regretted that their dispute had gone on so long and had taken the form it did. However, all the heat had not been without value in articulating two different understandings of the human condition.

While the dispute with Genovese continued to boil after Gutman left Rochester, other concerns loomed large. Gutman's move to City College placed him in the center of a different sort of conflict—the great New York school war. It was not a war he welcomed. He had spent his formative years in the city college system and had a deep commitment to public higher education and great affection for his alma mater. But the city colleges had changed enormously since he graduated from Queens. At City College itself, the faculty had become inbred. Hiding behind the skirts of a powerful municipal union, the faculty at City College had become one of the highest paid, least distinguished groups of scholars in America. In 1972, when Gutman became chairman, many department members had not written a book or published an article within the last decade. Except for a handful of recent appointees, most members had retired from an active interest in scholarship. The department was demoralized and deeply divided. Gutman's charge as chairman was to change this. He had been promised five new appointments, and in his first two years he hired several promising historians, including Eric Foner, Leon Fink, Eric Perkins, and Virginia Yans. He also revised the department's outmoded curriculum, introducing courses in social history, women's history, and Afro-American history to address the concerns of a diverse working-class student body. His innovations won him the warm support of the younger faculty, who for the first time saw City College as a center of intellectual discourse. Gutman's reforms also reinvigorated some of the older members of the department. But they earned him the implacable opposition of those who wanted things to remain as they had been.

A larger revolution at City College widened the breach within the history department.[115] In 1969, the city university system had adopted a plan of open admission. Gutman welcomed the democratizing thrust of the new policy; indeed, the changes wrought by open admission were among the attractions that drew Gutman to City College. However, not all his colleagues felt quite so sanguine. Under open admission, City College's student body, once composed of the best and brightest of New York's upward-striving immigrants, was instantly transformed from highly skilled to ill-prepared. Professors who used to teach the well-educated sons and daughters of the middle class now faced the poorly trained children of the working class. Few of these students saw a college degree as a ticket to law school or postgraduate training. For the most part, they wanted the immediate benefits of a college education. Many believed that "history" was a luxury they could ill afford, especially when it seemed alien to their own experience. Moreover, with a change in the social origins of the student body came a change of color. Although most of the students who entered City College under the open-admission policy were white, a large proportion were black. Many were Spanish-speaking. Faculty members, themselves graduates of the "old" City College, could not understand these students, whose paucity of academic skills and indifference toward the great issues of Western civilization seemed to suggest laziness, stupidity, or worse. Since most of the teachers were white descendants of European immigrants (many of them Jews) and many of the students were black and brown children of Southern and Puerto Rican emi-grants, the clash soon took on a hard racial edge. Charges of racism and anti-Semitism became commonplace. The politics of open admis-sion tore at City College.

Still, open admission might have worked if the original political commitment had overcome the pedagogical fears of the doubters. But it soon became apparent that the political commitment was itself weak at best. Funds for remedial courses diminished as the new students poured into the system. Dissension arising from open admission enlarged divisions within the department, particularly after the college eliminated the history requirement. Younger faculty members, those most able to address the special concerns of the new student body, filled their classrooms, while older members found themselves lecturing to empty seats. The value of yellowed notes that had once provided the basis of well-worn lectures on European civilization plummeted. Faculty members fought among themselves to teach courses in their academic specialties. Many blamed Gutman for their problems. City College was hardly a place for scholarly reflection.

For a time, the progress of Gutman's graduate students countered the distressing events at City College. He gained great satisfaction as the young men and women who had worked with him at Buffalo and Rochester began to make their mark with published articles and books. Their work, focusing on both free and slave workers and exhibiting a pronounced Thompsonian bias, often took issue with his own conclu-sions. But Gutman welcomed it nonetheless and gladly celebrated their discoveries as if they were his own.

And Gutman's "students" included more than those who studied directly with him. Young historians from all over the United States and beyond gravitated to him. They had read his work, heard him lecture, and met him at conventions and conferences where he inevitably stood surrounded by a cluster of aspiring scholars. They sensed his seriousness of purpose and the camaraderie that he felt with those who were grappling to understand the past. Gutman's willingness to listen to the ideas of young scholars without condescension, to suggest sources and strategies of research without airs of superiority, and to encourage without patronizing made him a singular figure within the historical profession. A lunchtime meeting with Gutman served as a kind of rite of passage—complete with its ritual laying-on of hands—for many a historian. And Gutman's many courtesies were remembered. A review of the "acknowledgments" in books published during the 1970s and 1980s, particularly the "first books," uncovers dozens of notations thanking Gutman for his suggestions, his assistance, and most of all his encouragement. Gutman had become the unofficial mentor to a generation of young scholars.

Yet events at City College operated against the satisfaction Gutman derived from the progress of young scholars. He sought relief as a fellow at the Shelby Cullom Davis Center for Historical Studies during the academic year 1975–1976, but he could not elude the problems of City College. New York City's deepening fiscal crisis struck hard at the history department. As chairman, Gutman was ordered to fire seven members of the history faculty, including all the young scholars he had appointed and others who had tenure at the institution. Ironically, all were productive scholars who had a deep commitment to open enrollment, just the kind of teachers the college badly needed. Gutman was distraught. That summer he worked feverishly to protect as many as he could. Although the untenured members of the department eventually lost their jobs, Gutman did buy some time and eventually helped them find new positions. But his hopes to rebuild City College's history department had been dashed. He saw no reason to return that fall and instead accepted an appointment as Distinguished Professor at William and Mary College. During the next three years, Gutman became the nation's most distinguished academic gypsy, moving from chair to chair and grant to grant. Not until 1979, when he transferred to the Graduate Center of the newly reconstituted City University, would he again enjoy a regular academic appointment.

Gutman's first refuge was the Davis Center, an intellectual home for the new history, which was presided over with gruff good humor by Lawrence Stone. A man of high intellect, Whiggish sensibility, and an unremitting sense of fair play, Stone ran the Davis Center with the discipline of a drill sergeant. The weekly Davis Center seminar gained a reputation as the Parris Island of academia. Stone annually chose a large topic, assembled a group of bright scholars, and lured others with the promise of lively intellectual combat and a free lunch. He then invited all comers to present their work to the assemblage. Somewhat surprisingly, they came. Every Friday between September and May, Stone introduced the proceedings with a fifteen-minute demolition that left guest scholars scrambling to disassociate themselves from their own work. For the stunned invitee, things generally went downhill from there.

The year 1975 was a particularly good one at the center. The subject was popular culture and the scholars in residence were Robert Buzucha, Lynn Lees, Roger Chartier, and Ira Berlin. William Sewell and William Reddy were at the nearby Center for Advanced Study, along with anthropologists Clifford Geertz and Victor Turner. Gutman enjoyed Stone's seminar as much as any, but he was preoccupied by events at City College. Morever, his own fame had spread. He was on the road as much as he was in Princeton, presiding over a symposium at Smith College, delivering a lecture in Jerusalem, and attending conferences here and there. His own project languished.

During the spring, he and Berlin stumbled upon a common problem. They had begun to muse upon the level of skill of urban slaves. Fogel and Engerman had claimed it to be high. Their evidence was thin, but, as Gutman admitted, his evidence was no better than theirs. No systematic list of slave occupations existed, and the federal census indicated only the age, sex, and color (distinguishing between black and mulatto) of nameless slaves who existed only as an appendage to their owners' enumeration. Gutman and Berlin developed a strategy for estimating the level of slave skill by determining what kind of men and women owned or controlled adult slave men, the slaves most likely to enjoy artisan status: the idea being that if skilled workers owned large numbers of slave men, chances were that the slaves too were artisans. Joined by Rebecca Scott, a young graduate student whose enthusiasm eclipsed Gutman's own, the three coded the entire free and slave census schedules for several Southern cities—as usual, Gutman would hear nothing of sampling—and then linked the two schedules by a magical program devised by the wizards at Princeton's computer-science center. The resulting data allowed them to determine who owned what kind of slaves.

As the printouts poured from Princeton's computers, Gutman and Berlin had the answer to their original question. On the eve of the Civil War, artisans owned few slaves and when they did they usually owned young women. When a skilled worker in a Southern city purchased a slave, it was generally a housekeeper for his home rather than a journeyman for his shop. Slaves were consigned to the most backward sectors of the urban economy as house servants and day laborers and to the most advanced as factory hands. Except in a few older cities, slaves rarely labored as skilled craftsmen. These findings had important implications for the evolution of slavery, the character of nonslaveholding society, and the nature of sectional conflict.

But in answering their original query, Gutman and Berlin raised a new one: Who did the artisanal work in Southern cities? Research showed that European immigrants, most of them newly arrived, composed the bulk of the South's skilled urban labor force. It was a striking discovery, not even suggested by existing studies of the Old South. Their conclusion, and a flurry of speculation that derived from it, became the basis of a year-end presentation at the Davis Center.[116] Unlike most such papers, this one survived the seminar. In fact, the assemblage seemed as surprised by the finding as the authors, and pressed Gutman and Berlin to speculate still further. Stone smiled benignly.

Gutman and Berlin left the Davis Center with piles of printouts. They planned a small book on the composition of the American working class. Berlin took charge of the work on the South, pushing it backward in time. Gutman began exploring the role of immigrants in the North. Again, research came easily enough. Before long, Gutman's seminar buzzed with questions about the number of immigrants in Akron, Virginia City, and St. Paul. But little was put down on paper, as the block that had periodically stymied Gutman's work returned. Finally, in an effort to get something into print, Gutman and Berlin agreed to give a paper at the annual meeting of the Organization of American Historians in 1981. The session would be on the composition of the American working class. Nominally, Berlin would deliver the paper on Southern urban workers; Gutman, on Northern ones. In fact, both papers would be jointly authored.

Building upon the Davis Center paper and subsequent research, Gutman and Berlin turned first to the immigrant origins of the free urban workers in the South and the questions raised about the nature of class struggle in that region.[117] In the Northern states, newly arrived artisans played a central role in the Free Soil movement that evolved into the Republican party. The immigrants' notions of the labor theory of value and small-*r* republicanism joined with indigenous American variants of the same ideas to infuse the political assault on slavery with a powerful moral imperative. Immigrants in the Northern states transferred their enmity toward European landlords to Southern planters. A similar class antagonism had occasionally been noted among Southern yeomanry and Southern urban workers, neither of whom owned many slaves. It manifested itself in struggles over the taxation of slave property, the employment of skilled slaves, and sometimes over slavery itself. But historians had dismissed white nonslaveholding opposition to slavery with the wand of racial unity. Gutman and Berlin found some evidence to affirm this conventional wisdom, but they also found much that called it into question. They suggested how the same cultural traditions immigrant artisans brought to the North and transformed into Republicanism also became a part of the class struggle in Southern society. That cultural heritage, of course, did not cause the enmity between the slaveholding planters and nonslaveholding artisans—that derived from the existing system of social relations—but it helped shape the conflict. Indeed, because social relations differed in the North and the South, the ideas and institutions immigrants brought with them gained different meaning in the slaveholding society. That meaning could only be hinted at in a short paper aimed more at defining the urban working class than at analyzing its actions. However, Gutman and Berlin observed that if historians understated the oppositional potential of the immigrant artisans in Southern cities, slaveholders did not. Gutman and Berlin demonstrated how the presence of immigrant artisans played a significant role in the struggle for power within the South and the nation in the decades before the Civil War.

Gutman and Berlin then turned their attention northward. After leaving the Davis Center, Gutman replicated the studies of the composition of the prewar Southern urban working class for postbellum Northern cities. Here, too, he wanted to know who the workers were. His reading of the federal manuscript census was even more of a revelation than the earlier discovery of immigrant artisans in the urban South. By 1880, in almost every major Northern city, immigrants composed a large plurality of the postbellum work force. In many places, they were a clear majority. Native-born workers descended from native-born parents were just a small fraction of the whole. Some of these native-born workers were black. Except for a few trades—notably the building trades—white workers descended from native-born parents were not a significant part of the American working class at the end of the nineteenth century.

This discovery had a profound impact on Gutman's thinking. Since his appointment to the Graduate Center, he had been reconsidering his work from the perspective of two large projects. The first grew out of a summer seminar he and historian Susan Levine held for middle-level union officials in 1977. The young unionists who volunteered to spend part of their vacation in a classroom impressed Gutman with their intelligence and their commitment to their fellow workers. But they were dismally ignorant of their own history. The New History had not touched these labor activists. Neither—as became increasingly evident—had it informed many others. An address by Gutman at the American Writers Congress in 1981 revealed that leading left intellectuals were no more knowledgeable than his unionist students. Historians knew more than ever about the past, but "two decades of important historical discovery and rediscovery had bypassed most of the people in the audience. It was as if the American history written in the 1960s and 1970s had been penned in a foreign language and had probed the national experiences of Albania, New Zealand and Zambia."[118]

Gutman became increasingly preoccupied by the problems of disseminating the New History. He found his summer seminar enormously rewarding, and he repeated it in 1978 and again in 1979, joined by historians David Bensman and Stephen Brier. But teaching unionists fifteen at a time seemed an inefficient way to inform American workers of their past. Gutman and Brier began to construct a more general curriculum of working-class history. Brier, who had a long-standing interest in motion pictures, urged the use of films, tapes, and other nontraditional historical sources. Gutman pressed for "the word" in the form of a book of documents. But the more they explored, the more necessary a collaborative effort appeared. Grants from the National Endowment for the Humanities and the Ford Foundation enabled Gutman and Brier to put additional hands on the job, and in 1981, they launched the American Working-Class History Project (later the American Social History Project) and began to outline a multimedia curriculum which included films, documents, and a synthetic history of the United States entitled "Who Built America?"[119]

Gutman believed "Who Built America?" could successfully address the problems inherent in the fragmented, localistic New History. But as he began to sketch its main themes, he sensed that the difficulties of the New History went beyond the absence of synthesis and instead were lodged in the political bases of historical understanding. Like the bearer of bad news, some history was unwanted. It was ignored, and when not ignored, repressed and silenced. The case of Camella Teoli, brought to Gutman's attention by Paul Cowan in the *Village Voice*, suggested the root of history's problems.[120]

As a young girl working in a mill in Lowell, Massachusetts, Camella Teoli had been scalped when her hair became entangled in a machine for twisting cotton. The case gained considerable notoriety, and Camella later traveled to Washington, where she testified before a congressional investigating committee. Her emotional testimony captured headlines, and Cowan compared its effect to that of Fannie Lou Hamer's statement before the Democratic party's platform committee. Yet fifty years later, Teoli's daughter, who had daily combed her mother's hair to hide the spot where it had been so violently uprooted, was ignorant of its cause and of her mother's historic role. Teoli, like many of the other participants in the famed Lowell strike, had suppressed knowledge of their political past. Her children remembered their mother as "a sweet silent lady who bought and cooked the traditional eels on Christmas Eve, who rarely missed a Sunday Mass." She had denied them access to her history, to their own history.

If some aspects of the past were denied, others received a warm embrace. Gutman contrasted the silence about Teoli's past—so much at odds with the conventional wisdom of assimilation and mobility—with the ready acceptance of the drama of individual striving and family mobility implicit in Alex Haley's *Roots*. Whatever its problems of historical evidence, *Roots* had "succeeded by redefining the central tension in slave society in ways that made it possible to integrate the Afro-American slave experience (a metaphor here for much 'revisionist' social history) into middleclass American culture."[121] *Roots* integrated historic achievement with contemporary American belief; Teoli's scalping did not. Haley's story was celebrated; Teoli's was hidden.

Gutman made the willingness of Americans to celebrate the individual and the utilitarian over the collective and the mutualist the main theme of his address to the Organization of American Historians in 1982, "Historical Consciousness in Contemporary America."[122] He explored how the post–World War II belief in "class convergence" countered the New History. Ruefully, he admitted that the process whereby history would shape politics was working in reverse; politics was determining the reception of history. But was history only those events that ratified the present? only those events that offered assurances of a "predisposed continuity"—in this case an emphasis on individual over collective achievement? Gutman did not think so. Besides, he was confident that the reality of postwar class divergence would soon make itself felt. His own "Who Built America?" would suggest how both individualist and collectivist themes played a role in the American experience, opening the door not only for new scholarly interpretations but also for new political possibilities.

At the same time that Gutman initiated this synthesis of American working-class history, he also began to rethink his previous work, from his earliest essays on the depression of the 1870s to "Work, Culture, and Society." Gutman was particularly concerned with the second generation of industrial workers, workers whose experience had eluded him in "Work, Culture, and Society." His own recent research on composition of the postbellum working class and his interpretation of contemporary historical consciousness left him dissatisfied with his old formulations. He thought he had been studying class formation, but discovered that what he had been describing was class *re-formation* or *development*, the transformation of an existing class. He had asked how the American working class was made when he should have asked how it was remade—"How does one examine working-class behavior in a developed capitalist society as contrasted with a new capitalist society?"[123] The question of class re-formation took on particular urgency in light of the changes in the nature of the American working class, changes that would soon resonate powerfully when workers abandoned the Democratic party en masse for Ronald Reagan.

In 1981, an invitation from the Hungarian Academy of Science allowed Gutman and Berlin the chance to address the question how an established American working class developed. In "Class Composition and the Development of the American Working Class, 1840–1890," Gutman and Berlin viewed the question of class re-formation from the perspective of the composition of the American working class in 1880.[124] At that moment, few white Americans descended from parents of native birth labored in cities as skilled or unskilled workers. Although an American working class had arisen during the first decades of the nineteenth century and developed its own critique of capitalism, it had not survived into the late nineteenth century. Native-born white workers descended from native-born parents were nearly invisible in the American working class in 1880. The men and women who had shaped the initial working-class critique of capitalist social relations and dependent wage labor had left the stage in the era following the Civil War. Between 1840 and 1880, the American working class had been remade by an influx of foreign-born workers. To be sure, significant regional distinctions existed, but immigrants, blacks, and the children of immigrants composed the overwhelming majority of the working class everywhere in the United States.

The last point was of cardinal significance. How should the children of immigrants be categorized? They were of course native-born, and if they were considered natives like the children of native-born Americans, immigrants would still have a considerable presence in the American working class, extending in some cities to a majority. However, if the children of immigrants were included with their parents as part of a larger transatlantic immigrant generation, then the "immigrant presence" was overwhelming. Gutman's own experience—as a native son who spoke Yiddish before he spoke English—suggested one possible interpretation. But Gutman was reluctant to write his own experience into American history. Instead, he began again to reconsider the process of acculturation and class integration in the United States. Pending that reconsideration, Gutman and Berlin made several preliminary observations. First, they warned against lumping native workers of native parents with native workers of foreign-born parents. For one thing, these two "streams" were unequal: one was a sluggish rivulet and the other a massive torrent; for another, the experiences of the two "streams" were as different as their origins. Second, immigrant workers could no longer be considered outsiders to the history of the American working class, disrupting the development of an established class. Third, and most important, the process of class formation in the United States had to be considered anew. In 1880, an established American working class of immigrant origins began to reproduce itself. But its roots did not travel backward in time to the Puritan fathers. Instead, they traveled laterally in space to the capitalist labor gangs, workshops, and factories of Europe. Little wonder that the language of nationality mediated class struggle in the United States at the end of the nineteenth century. "Ethnicity" became the banner under which workers organized.

Redefining the origins of the American working class required reinterpreting the process by which that class came into being. As throughout his career, Gutman did not simply integrate new facts into an old understanding. For him, writing history was not an additive process. New facts altered his understanding of the whole. Working from the assumption that classes were not formed but were in a continuous process of re-formation, Gutman began to explore the question of class reconstruction in the United States. He planned to do so in a major revision of *Work, Culture, and Society* and in the general history being prepared in cooperation with his colleagues on the American Social History Project. Gutman had thus begun to rethink a lifetime of study of American workers when, in the summer of 1985, he was cut down by a massive heart attack. He died a young man of fifty-six.

Herbert Gutman died during the presidency of Ronald Reagan. In large measure, consensus had been banished from the historiographic landscape. However, abetted by the Reagan revolution, the marketplace as the arbiter of human relations once again manifested itself as an explanatory force in the writing of American history. Some historians saw capitalism, not as an alien social order implanted at great cost, but as the natural system of human relations that was universally accepted. Among these scholars, Hofstadter's America, where "the virtues of capitalist culture [were] the necessary qualities of man," was back in vogue. Working people were as acquisitive as anyone else, and their values not much different from those of the businessmen who employed them or the presidents who governed them. Workers could claim no special place in the American past. Once again, some scholars relegated them to the historical sidelines. The study of history, like much else in American life, was tracking back toward the Age of Eisenhower.

Between the Age of Eisenhower and the Age of Reagan, the history of the American working class flourished, in no small measure due to the work of Herbert Gutman. Gutman sensed that a new era needed a new history. His writing, his teaching, his socially informed criticism, and his example created a history of the American people in which workers played a central role. He inspired a generation of scholars who wrote a history in which working people were not passive recipients of their fate but active makers of their own past. Alive to the revolutionary spirit of the 1960s and 1970s, these young scholars also asked "not what 'one' has done to man, but what man does with what 'one' has done to him." In so doing, they thought differently about the present as well as about the past. The history of working people was seen anew, and with it the history of the United States. Political upheavals might propel some to challenge that history and again attempt to deny working people their rightful place, but Gutman's work assured there would be no disregarding the central role of working people in the American past or denying their vision of a more humane and just society in the American future. For Herbert Gutman, there could be no higher reward.

1

THE WORKERS' SEARCH
FOR POWER
Labor in the Gilded Age

UNTIL VERY recent times, the worker never seemed as glamorous or important as the entrepreneur. This is especially true of the Gilded Age, where attention focuses more readily upon Jim Fisk, Commodore Vanderbilt, or John D. Rockefeller than on the men whose labor built their fortunes. Most studies have devoted too much attention to too little. Excessive interest in the Haymarket riot, the "Molly Maguires," the great strikes of 1877, the Homestead lockout, and the Pullman strike has obscured the more important currents of which these things were only symptoms. Close attention has also focused on the small craft unions, the Knights of Labor, and the early Socialists, excluding the great mass of workers who belonged to none of these groups and creating an uneven picture of labor in the Gilded Age.[1]

Labor history had little to do with those matters scholars traditionally and excessively emphasize. Too few workers belonged to trade unions to make the unions important. There was a fundmental distinction between wage earners as a social class and the small minority of the working population that belonged to labor organizations. The full story of the wage earner is much more than the tale of struggling craft unions and the exhortations of committed trade unionists and assorted reformers and radicals. A national perspective often misrepresented those issues important to large segments of the postbellum working population and to other economic and social groups who had contact with the wage earners.[2] Most of the available literature about labor in the Gilded Age is thin, and there are huge gaps in our knowledge of the entire period.[3] Little was written about the workers themselves, their communities, and the day-to-day occurrences that shaped their outlook. Excessive concern with craft workers has meant the serious neglect of the impact of industrial capitalism—a new way of life— upon large segments of the population.

A rather stereotyped conception of labor and of industrial relations

This essay first appeared in H. Wayne Morgan, ed., *The Gilded Age: A Reappraisal* (Syracuse, N.Y.: Syracuse University Press, 1963), 38–68. It is reprinted here from the revised and enlarged edition of that book, published in 1970.

in the Gilded Age has gained widespread credence, and final and conclusive generalizations about labor abound.

> During the depression from 1873 to 1879, employers sought to eliminate trade unions by a *systematic* policy of lockouts, blacklists, labor espionage, and legal prosecution. The *widespread* use of blacklists and Pinkerton labor spies caused labor to organize *more or less* secretly and *undoubtedly* helped bring on the violence that *characterized* labor strife during this period.[4]

One historian asserts: "Employers *everywhere* seemed determined to rid themselves of 'restrictions upon free enterprise' by smashing unions."[5] The *"typical* [labor] organization during the seventies," writes another scholar, "was secret for protection against intrusion by outsiders."[6] Such seemingly final judgments are questionable: How *systematic* were lockouts, blacklists, and legal prosecutions? How *widespread* was the use of labor spies and private detectives? Was the secret union the *typical* form of labor organization? Did violence *characterize* industrial relations?

It is widely believed that the industrialist exercised a great deal of power and had almost unlimited freedom of choice when dealing with his workers after the Civil War. Part of this belief reflects the weakness or absence of trade unions. Another justification for this interpretation, however, is more shaky—the assumption that industrialism generated new kinds of economic power which immediately affected the social structure and ideology. The supposition that "interests" rapidly reshaped "ideas" is misleading. "The social pyramid," Joseph Schumpeter pointed out, "is never made of a single substance, is never seamless." The economic interpretation of history "would at once become untenable and unrealistic . . . if its formulation failed to consider that the manner in which production shapes social life is essentially influenced by the fact that human protagonists have always been shaped by past situations."[7]

In postbellum America, the relationship between "interest" and "ideology" was very complex and subtle. Industrial capitalism was a new way of life and was not fully institutionalized. Much of the history of industrialism is the story of the painful process by which an old way of life was discarded for a new one, so that a central issue was the rejection or modification of a set of "rules" and "commands" that no longer fitted the new industrial context. Since so much was new, traditional stereotypes about the popular sanctioning of the rules and values of industrial society either demand severe qualification or entirely fall by the wayside. Among questionable commonly held generalizations are those that insist that the worker was isolated from the rest of society; that the employer had an easy time and a relatively free hand in imposing the new disciplines; that the spirit of the times, the ethic of the Gilded Age, worked to the advantage of the owner of industrial property; that workers found little if any sympathy from nonworkers; that the quest for wealth obliterated nonpecuniary values; and that industrialists swept aside countless obstacles with great ease.

The new way of life was more popular and more quickly sanctioned in large cities than in small one- or two-industry towns. Put another way, the social environment in the large American city after the Civil War was more often hostile toward workers than that in smaller industrial towns. Employers in large cities had more freedom of choice than their counterparts in small towns, where local conditions often hampered the employer's decision-making power. The ideology of many nonworkers in these small towns was not entirely hospitable toward industrial, as opposed to traditional, business enterprise. Strikes and lockouts in large cities seldom lasted as long as similar disputes outside urban centers. In the large city, there was almost no sympathy for the city worker among the middle and upper classes. A good deal of prolabor and anti-industrial sentiment flowed from similar occupational groups in the small towns. Small-town employers of factory labor often reached out of the local environment for aid in solving industrial disputes, but diverse elements in the social structure and ideology shaped such decisions.

The direct economic relationships in large cities and in small towns and outlying industrial regions were similar, but the social structures differed profoundly. Private enterprise was central to the economy of both the small industrial town and the large metropolitan city, but functioned in a different social environment. The social structure and ideology of a given time are not derived only from economic institutions.[8] In a time of rapid economic and social transformation, when industrial capitalism was relatively new, parts of an ideology alien to industrialism retained a powerful hold on many who lived outside large cities.

Men and their thoughts were different in the large cities. "The modern town," John Hobson wrote of the large nineteenth-century cities, "is a result of the desire to produce and distribute most economically the largest aggregate of material goods: economy of work, not convenience of life, is the object." In such an environment, "anti-social feelings" were exhibited "at every point by the competition of workers with one another, the antagonism between employer and employed, between sellers and buyers, factory and factory, shop and shop."[9] Persons dealt with each other less as human beings and more as objects. The *Chicago Times*, for example, argued that "political economy" was "in reality the autocrat of the age" and occupied "the position once held by the Caesars and the Popes."[10] According to the

New York Times, the "antagonistic . . . position between employers and the employed on the subject of work and wages" was "unavoidable. . . . The object of trade is to get as much as you may and give as little as you can."[11] The *Chicago Tribune* celebrated the coming of the centennial in 1876: "Suddenly acquired wealth, decked in all the colors of the rainbow, flaunts its robe before the eyes of Labor, and laughs with contempt at honest poverty." The country, "great in all the material powers of a vast empire," was entering "upon the second century weak and poor in social morality as compared with one hundred years ago."[12]

Much more than economic considerations shaped the status of the urban working population, for the social structure in large cities unavoidably widened the distance between social and economic classes. Home and job often were far apart. A man's fellow workers were not necessarily his friends and neighbors. Face-to-face relationships became less meaningful as the city grew larger and production became more diverse and specialized. "It has always been difficult for well-to-do people of the upper and middle classes," wrote Samuel Lane Loomis, a Protestant minister, in the 1880s, "to sympathize with and to understand the needs of their poorer neighbors." The large city, both impersonal and confining, made it even harder. Loomis was convinced that "a great and growing gulf" lay "between the working-class and those above them."[13] A Massachusetts clergyman saw a similar void between the social classes and complained: "I once knew a wealthy manufacturer who personally visited and looked after the comforts of his invalid operatives. I know of no such case now."[14] The fabric of human relationships was cloaked in a kind of shadowed anonymity that became more and more characteritic of urban life.[15]

Social contact was more direct in the smaller post–Civil War industrial towns and regions. *Cooper's New Monthly*, a reform trade union journal, insisted that while "money" was the "sole measure of gentility and respectability" in large cities, "a more democratic feeling" prevailed in small towns.[16] "The most happy and contented workingmen in the country," wrote the *Iron Molders' Journal*, "are those residing in small towns and villages. . . . We want more towns and villages and less cities."[17] Except for certain parts of New England and the Middle Atlantic states, the postbellum industrial towns and regions were relatively new to that kind of enterprise. Men and women who lived and worked in these areas usually had known another way of life, and they contrasted the present with the past.

The nineteenth-century notion of enterprise came quickly to these regions after the Civil War, but the social distance between the various economic classes that characterized the large city came much more slowly and hardly paralleled industrial developments. In the midst of the new industrial enterprise with its new set of commands, men often clung to older "agrarian" attitudes, and they judged the economic and social behavior of local industrialists by these values.

The social structure of the large city differed from that of the small industrial town because of the more direct human relationships among the residents of the smaller towns. Although many persons were not personally involved in the industrial process, they felt its presence. Life was more difficult and less cosmopolitan in small towns, but it was also less complicated. This life was not romantic, since it frequently meant company-owned houses and stores and conflicts between workers and employers over rights taken for granted in agricultural communities and large cities.[18] Yet the nonurban industrial environment had in it a kind of compelling simplicity. There the inhabitants lived and worked together, and a certain sense of community threaded their everyday lives.

The first year of the 1873 depression sharply suggested the differences between the large urban center and the small industrial town. There was no question about the severity of the economic crisis. Its consequences were felt throughout the entire industrial sector, and production, employment, and income fell sharply everywhere.[19] The dollar value of business failures in 1873 was greater than in any other single year between 1857 and 1893.[20] Deflation in the iron and steel industry was especially severe: 266 of the nation's 666 iron furnaces were out of blast by January 1, 1874, and more than 50 percent of the rail mills were silent.[21] A New York philanthropic organization figured that 25 percent of the city's workers—nearly 100,000 persons—were unemployed in the winter months of 1873–1874.[22]

"The simple fact is that a great many laboring men are out of work," wrote the *New York Graphic*. "It is not the fault of merchants and manufacturers that they refuse to employ four men when they can pay but one, and decline to pay four dollars for work which they can buy for two and a half."[23] Gloom and pessimism settled over the entire country, and the most optimistic predicted only that the panic would end in the late spring months of 1873.[24] James Swank, the secretary of the American Iron and Steel Association, found the country suffering "from a calamity which may be likened to a famine or a flood."[25]

A number of serious labor difficulties occurred in small industrial towns and outlying industrial regions during the first year of the depression, revealing much about the social structure of these areas. Although each had its own unique character, a common set of problems shaped them all. Demand fell away and industrialists cut production and costs to sell off accumulated inventory and retain shrinking markets. This general contraction caused harsh industrial conflict in many parts of the country. "No sooner does a depression in trade set in," observed David A. Harris, the conservative head of the Sons of Vulcan, a national craft union for puddlers and boilermen, "than all expressions of friendship to the toiler are forgotten."[26]

The *New York Times* insisted that the depression would "bring wages down for all time," and advised employers to dismiss workers who struck against wage reductions. This was not the time for the "insane imitations of the miserable class warfare and jealousy of Europe."[27] The *Chicago Times* stated that strikers were "idiots" and "criminals." Its sister newspaper, the *Chicago Evening Journal*, said the crisis was not "an unmixed evil," since labor would finally learn "the folly and danger of trade organizations, strikes, and combinations . . . against capital."[28] *Iron Age* was similarly sanguine. "We are sorry for those who suffer," it explained, "but if the power of the trade unions for mischief is weakened . . . the country will have gained far more than it loses from the partial depression of industry." Perhaps "simple workingmen" would learn they were misled by "demagogues and unprincipled agitators." Trade unions "crippled that productive power of capital" and retarded the operation of "beneficient natural laws of progress and development."[29] James Swank was somewhat more generous. Prices had fallen, and it was "neither right nor practicable for all the loss to be borne by the employers." "Some of it," he explained, "must be shared by the workingmen. . . . We must hereafter be contented with lower wages for our labor and be more thankful for the opportunity to labor at all."[30]

In cutting costs in 1873 and 1874, many employers found that certain aspects of the social structure and ideology in small industrial towns hindered their freedom of action. It was easy to announce a wage cut or refuse to negotiate with a local trade union, but it was difficult to enforce such decisions. In instance after instance, and for reasons that varied from region to region, employers reached outside their environment to help assert their authority.

Industrialists used various methods to strengthen their local positions with workers. The state militia brought order to a town or region swept by industrial conflict. Troops were used in railroad strikes in Indiana, Ohio, and Pennsylvania; in a dispute involving iron heaters and rollers in Newport, Kentucky; in a strike of Colorado ore diggers; in two strikes of Illinois coal miners; and in a strike of Michigan ore workers.[31]

Other employers aggravated racial and nationality problems among workers by introducing new ethnic groups to end strikes, forcing men to work under new contracts, and destroying local trade unions. Negroes were used in coal disputes.[32] Danish, Norwegian, and Swedish immigrants went into mines in Illinois, and into the Shenango Valley and the northern anthracite region of Pennsylvania. Germans went to coal mines in northern Ohio along with Italian workers. Some Italians also were used in western Pennsylvania as coal miners, and in western and northern New York as railroad workers.[33] A number of employers imposed their authority in other ways. Regional, not local, blacklists were tried in the Illinois coalfields, on certain railroads, in the Ohio Valley iron towns, and in the iron mills of eastern Pennsylvania.[34] Mine operators in Pennsylvania's Shenango Valley and Tioga coal region used state laws to evict discontented workers from company-owned houses in midwinter.[35]

The social structure in these small towns and the ideology of many of their residents, who were neither workers nor employers, shaped the behavior of those employers who reached outside local environments to win industrial disputes. The story was different for every town, but had certain similarities. The strikes and lockouts had little meaning in and of themselves, but the incidents shed light on the distribution of power in these towns and on those important social and economic relationships which shaped the attitudes and actions of workers and employers.

One neglected aspect of the small industrial town after the Civil War is its political structure. Because workers made up a large proportion of the electorate and often participated actively in local politics, they influenced local and regional affairs more than wage earners in the larger cities. In 1874, few workers held elected or appointed offices in large cities. In that year, however, the postmaster of Whistler, Alabama, was a member of the Iron Molders' International Union.[36] George Kinghorn, a leading trade unionist in the southern Illinois coalfields, was postmaster of West Belleville, Illinois.[37] A local labor party swept an election in Evansville, Indiana.[38] Joliet, Illinois, had three workers on its city council.[39] A prominent official of the local union of iron heaters and rollers sat on the city council in Newport, Kentucky.[40] Coal and ore miners ran for the state legislature in Carthage, Missouri, in Clay County, Indiana, and in Belleville, Illinois.[41] The residents of Virginia City, a town famous in Western mythology, sent the president of the local miners' union to Congress.[42] In other instances, town officials and other officeholders who were not wage earners sympathized with the problems and difficulties of local workers or displayed an unusual degree of objectivity during local industrial disputes.

Many local newspapers criticized the industrial entrepreneur, and editorials defended *local* workers and demanded redress for their grievances. Certain of these newspapers were entirely independent; others warmly endorsed local trade union activities.

The small businessmen and shopkeepers, lawyers and professional people, and other nonindustrial members of the middle class were a small but vital element in these industrial towns. Unlike the urban middle class they had direct and everyday contact with the new industrialism and with the problems and outlook of workers and employers. Many had risen from a lower station in life and knew the meaning of hardship and toil, and could judge the troubles of both workers and employers by personal experience. While they invariably accepted the concepts of private property and free entrepreneurship, their judgments about the *social* behavior of industrialists often drew upon noneconomic considerations and values. Some saw no necessary contradiction between private enterprise and gain and decent, humane social relations between workers and employers.

In a number of industrial conflicts, segments of the local middle class sided with workers. A Maryland weekly newspaper complained in 1876: "In the changes of the last thirty years not the least unfortunate is the separation of personal relations between employers and employees."[43] While most metropolitan newspapers sang paeans of joy for the industrial entrepreneur and the new way of life, the *Youngstown Miner and Manufacturer* thought it completely wrong that the "Vanderbilts, Stewarts, and Astors bear, in proportion to their resources, infinitely less of the burden incident to society than the poorest worker."[44] The *Ironton Register* defended dismissed iron strikers as "upright and esteemed . . . citizens" who had been sacrificed "to the cold demands on business."[45] The *Portsmouth Times* boasted: "We have very little of the codfish aristocracy, and industrious laborers are looked upon here with as much respect as any class of people."[46]

In 1873 when the depression called a temporary halt to the expansion of the Illinois mining industry, Braidwood, Illinois, was less than a dozen years old.[47] Coal mining and Braidwood had grown together, and by 1873, 6,000 persons lived in the town. Except for the supervisors and the small businessmen and shopkeepers, most residents were coal miners. Braidwood had no "agricultural neighborhood to give it support" and "without its coal-shafts" it would have had "no reasonable apology for existing." The town had three coal companies, but the Chicago, Wilmington and Vermillion Coal Company was by far the largest, and its president, James Monroe Walker, also headed the Chicago, Burlington and Quincy Railroad. This firm operated five shafts and employed 900 men—more than half the resident miners. Most of the owners did not live in the town. The miners were a mixed lot, and unlike most other small industrial towns in this era Braidwood had an ethnically diverse population. About half the miners came from Ireland. Another 25 percent were English, Welsh, and Scottish. A smaller number were Swedes, Italians, and Germans, and still others came from France and Belgium and even from Poland and Russia. There were also native-born miners. "The town of Braidwood," a contemporary noted, "is . . . nearly akin to Babel as regards the confusion of tongues." Although they came from diverse backgrounds, they were a surprisingly cohesive social community. A trade union started in 1872 was strong enough to extract a reasonable wage agreement from the three coal firms. A hostile observer complained that nearly all the voters were miners and that a majority of the aldermen and justices of the peace "are or have been miners."

The depression cut the demand for coal and created serious problems for the operators. By March 1874, at least 25 percent of the miners were unemployed, and the town was "dull beyond all precedent." In late May the operators, led by the Chicago, Wilmington and Vermillion firm, cut the rate for digging coal from $1.25 to $1.10 a ton and cut the price for "pushing" coal from the work wall to the shaft nearly in half. They announced that the mines would close on June 1 unless the men accepted the new contract for a full year. The miners' efforts to compromise and suggestions of arbitration were summarily rejected, and the mines closed.

The Chicago, Wilmington and Vermillion company approached private labor-contracting agencies in Chicago and recruited a large number of unskilled laborers, most of whom were Scandinavian immigrants and were not miners. Three days after the strike began, sixty-five Chicago workers arrived. More came two weeks later, and a few arrived daily until the end of July, when the number increased sharply. At the same time, anticipating trouble in putting the new men to work, the operators brought special armed Chicago Pinkerton police to the town.

Difficulties plagued the operators from the start. The miners realized they had to check the owners' strategy in order to gain a victory. As soon as new workers arrived, committees of miners explained the difficulty to them. "We ask the skilled miners not to work," the leader of the strikers explained. "As to green hands, we are glad to see them go to work for we know they are . . . a positive detriment to the company." All but three of the first sixty-five new workers decided to return to Chicago and, since they lacked funds, the miners and other local residents paid their rail fare and cheered them as they boarded a Chicago-bound train. By mid-July one shaft that usually employed two hundred men had no more than ten workers. At the end of July, only 102 men worked in the mines, and not one of them was a resident miner. The disaffected miners also met the challenge of the Pinkerton men. The miners appointed a seventy-two-man committee to prevent violence and to protect company property. The mayor and the sheriff swore in twelve of these men as special deputies, and, with one exception—when the wives of certain miners chased and struck the son of famed detective Allan Pinkerton—the miners behaved in a quiet and orderly manner.

Braidwood's tiny middle class "all back[ed] the miners." They denied complaints by the owners that the miners were irresponsible and violent. One citizen condemned the coal companies for creating "excitement so as to crush the miners" and declared that "public sympathy" was "entirely" with the workers. The operators wanted Pinkerton and his men appointed "special deputies" and made "merchant police" with power to arrest persons trespassing on company properties, but the mayor and the sheriff turned down and deputized the strikers. Mayor Goodrich forbade parading in the streets by the Pinkerton men, and the sheriff ordered them to surrender their rifles and muskets. He did not want "a lot of strangers dragooning a quiet town with deadly weapons in their hands," and feared the miners "a good deal less than . . . the Chicago watchmen."

The operators faced other troubles. Local judges and police officials enforced the law more rigorously against them and their men than against the resident miners. Two new workers who got into a fight one Sunday were arrested for violating the Sabbath law and fined $50 and court costs. Unable to pay the fine, they were put to work on the town streets. Another, jailed for hitting an elderly woman with a club, was fined $100 and court costs. A company watchman was arrested four times, twice for "insulting townspeople."

Frustrated in these and other ways by the miners and the townspeople, the operators finally turned for help to the state government, and E. L. Higgins, the adjutant general and head of the state militia, went to Braidwood to see if troops were needed. Higgins openly supported the mine owners. He tried to prevent union men from talking with new workers, and although he asked the mayor to meet him in the office of the Chicago, Wilmington and Vermillion firm, he "never went to see the officers of the city . . . to gain an unprejudiced account of the strike." "If this is what the military forces and officers are kept for," one miner observed, "it is high time . . . such men [were] struck off the State Government payroll and placed where they belong." Mayor Goodrich reminded Higgins that neither the Braidwood nor the Will County authorities had asked for state interference. In a bitter letter to the *Chicago Times*, Goodrich wondered whether Higgins had come "in his official capacity or as an agent of the coal company," and firmly insisted that "the citizens of this city were not aware that martial law had been proclaimed or an embargo placed upon their speech."

Unable fully to exercise their authority in the town and worried about the possibility of losing the fall trade, the operators surrendered to the strikers fourteen weeks after the struggle began. The final agreement pleased the miners. They were especially amused when the Chicago, Wilmington and Vermillion company agreed to send all the new workers back to Chicago. A spokesman for the operators, however, bitterly assailed the Braidwood mayor and other public officials for their failure to understand the meaning of "peace, order, and freedom." Surely the operators had further cause for complaint in 1877 when Daniel McLaughlin, the president of the miners' union, was elected mayor of Braidwood, other miners were chosen aldermen, and one became police magistrate.

Manufacturers in the small industrial iron towns of the Ohio Valley such as Ironton and Portsmouth, Ohio, and Newport and Covington, Kentucky, had similar troubles.[48] Several thousand men and fifteen iron mills were involved in a dispute over wages that lasted for several months. The mill owners who belonged to the Ohio Valley Iron Association cut the wages of skilled iron heaters and roller men 20 percent on December 1, 1873. After the workers complained that the manufacturers were taking "undue advantage" of them "owing to the present financial trouble," their wages were cut another 10 percent. The valley mill owners worked out a common policy; they decided to close all the mills for a month or so in December and then reopen them under the new scale. Hard times would bring new workers.

Although the mill owners in large cities such as St. Louis, Indianapolis, and Cincinnati found it easy to bring in new workers from the outside, it was another story in the small towns. They could hire new hands in Pittsburgh, Philadelphia, and other Eastern cities, but the social environment in Covington, Portsmouth, Newport, and Ironton made it difficult to keep these men. Fellow townspeople sympathized with the locked-out workers. In such an environment they were a relatively homogeneous group and made up a large part of the total population of the town. When workers agitated in small towns, paraded the streets, or engaged in one or another kind of collective activity, their behavior hardly went unnoticed.

The difficulties small-town iron manufacturers faced especially beset Alexander Swift, owner of the Swift Iron and Steel Works in Newport, Kentucky. Although his workers suffered from almost indescribable poverty after the factory closed, they would not surrender. When Swift reopened the mill, he hired armed "special policemen." Some of the new workers left town after they learned of the conflict, and the "police" accompanied the rest to and from their work. The old workers made Newport uncomfortable for new hands. There was no violence at first, but many strikers and their wives, especially the English and Welsh workers, gathered near the mill and in the streets to howl at the "black sheep" going to and from work. The Newport workers exerted pressure on them in "the hundred ways peculiar to workingmen's demonstrations." Swift was embittered, for by the end of January only a few men worked in his mill.

He was not alone. Mill owners in Covington, Ironton, and Portsmouth faced similar difficulty. Early in February, therefore, the Ohio Valley Iron Association announced that unless the men returned to work on or before February 20 they would lose their jobs and never again be hired in the valley iron mills. When most of the workers refused to return, they were fired. New workers were quickly brought to the towns, and Swift demanded special police protection for them from the Newport City Council, but it assigned only regular police. Crowds jeered the new men, and there were several fights. A large number of new workers again left Newport. "We never went any further with those fellows," a striker explained, "than calling them 'black sheep' and 'little lambs.' " Swift vainly appealed to the police to ban street demonstrations by the workers and their families, then armed the new men with pistols. When the strikers and their supporters gathered to jeer them, one of the imported laborers shot wildly into the crowd and killed a young butcher's helper. The enraged crowd chased Swift's men out of the city. After blaming the shooting on the failure of the Newport authorities to guard his men properly, Swift closed the mill.

These events did not go unnoticed in the Ohio Valley. The *Portsmouth Times* leveled a barrage of criticism at Swift and the other manufacturers. It asked whether or not they had a "right" to circulate the names of strikers in the same manner as "the name of a thief is sent from one police station to another." Such action was "cowardly . . . intimidation," and the *Times* asked: "Does not continued and faithful service deserve better treatment at the hands of men whose fortunes have been made by these workmen they would brand with the mark of CAIN? . . . Is this to be the reward for men who have grown gray in the service of these velvet-lined aristocrats? . . . Out on such hypocrisy!" After the shooting in Newport, the *Times* turned on Swift and called him a "blood-letter." Violence was wrong, the *Times* admitted, but "if the gathered up assassins from the slums and alleys of the corrupt cities of the East are brought here to do deeds of lawlessness and violence, the stronger the opposition at the beginning the sooner they will be taught that the city of Portsmouth has no need of them."

Immune to such criticism, Swift continued to try to break down the strength of the Newport workers. In the end he succeeded. He realized that the only way to weaken the strikers was to suppress their power of public demonstration and therefore urged the Newport mayor to enforce local ordinances against dangerous and "riotous" crowds, asked the Kentucky governor to send state militia, and even demanded federal troops. Although the mayor banned "all unusual and unnecessary assemblages" in the streets, Swift still asked for state troops, and on March 5, the Kentucky governor ordered twenty-five members of the Lexington division of the state militia to Newport. Their arrival weakened the strikers and created a favorable environment for Swift. Street demonstrations were banned. The police were ordered to arrest "all persons using threatening or provoking language." When a number of unskilled strikers offered to return at the lower wage, Swift turned them away. He also rejected efforts by a member of the city council to effect a compromise with the old workers. A week after the troops arrived and three and a half months after the start of the lockout, Swift was in full control of the situation. New men worked in his factory, and the strikers admitted defeat.

The use of troops, however, was bitterly condemned in the Ohio Valley. A reporter for the *Cincinnati Enquirer* found that the "general opinion" in Newport was that Swift's maneuver was "little else than a clever piece of acting intended to kindle public sentiment against the strikers and . . . gain the assistance of the law in breaking up a strike." A Newport judge assailed the Kentucky governor, and a local poet sang of the abuse of public power:

> Sing a song of sixpence
>> Stomachs full of rye,
> Five-and-twenty volunteers,
>> With fingers in one pie;
> When the pie is opened
>> For money they will sing,
> Isn't that a pretty dish
>> For the City Council Ring?

There was less drama in the other Ohio Valley iron towns than in Newport, but the manufacturers in Portsmouth, Ironton, and Covington faced similar trouble. The old workers persuaded many new hands to leave the region. When fourteen men from Philadelphia arrived in Ironton and learned of the troubles for the first time, they left the city. Strikers paid their return rail fare. The same happened in Portsmouth, and the departing workers declared: "A nobler, truer, better class of men never lived than the Portsmouth boys . . . standing out for their rights." Nonstrikers in these towns also acted contrary to the manufacturers' interests. Each week the *Portsmouth Times* attacked the mill owners. "We are not living under a monarchy," the *Times* insisted, and the "arbitrary actions" of the employers were not as "unalterable as the edicts of the Medes and Persians."

A Covington justice of the peace illustrated something of the hostility felt toward the companies. Three strikers were arrested for molesting new hands, but he freed one and fined the others $1 each and court costs. A new worker, however, was fined $20 for disorderly conduct and for carrying a deadly weapon. He also had to post a $500 bond as a guarantee that he would keep the peace.

In the end, except in Newport where Swift had successfully neutralized the power of the workers, a compromise wage settlement was finally worked out. Certain mills brought in new men, but some manufacturers withdrew the blacklist and rehired striking workers. A friend of the Ohio Valley iron manufacturers bitterly complained: "Things of this sort make one ask whether we are really as free a people as we pretend to be." This devotee of classical laissez-faire doctrine sadly concluded: "If any individual cannot dispose of his labor when and at what price he pleases, he is living under a despotism, no matter what form the government assumes."

Although hardly any Negroes worked in coal mines before 1873, soon after the depression started mine operators in the Ohio Hocking Valley recruited hundreds from border and Southern cities. Some had been sparingly employed in certain Indiana and Ohio mines, but attracted little attention. It was different in the Hocking Valley in 1874. A large number of white miners struck and showed an unusual degree of unanimity and staying power. They found support from members of the local middle class, and the operators, unable to wear down the strikers, brought in Negroes. Although the miners were defeated, the problems they raised for their employers indicated much the same social environment as that in Braidwood and the Ohio Valley iron towns.

The railroad opened new markets for bituminous coal, and the years between 1869 and 1873 were a time of great prosperity. In 1870, 105,000 tons left the valley, and in 1873 just over 1,000,000 tons were shipped. Two years later, more than 20 percent of the coal mined in Ohio came from the Hocking Valley. Although entry costs were low, the ten largest firms in 1874 employed nearly two-thirds of the valley's miners.[49]

The miners fell into two social groupings. Those born in and near the valley had spent most of their lives in the mines and often held local positions of public trust and esteem. A Cincinnati reporter found that miners held "a good position in society . . . as a class" and filled "a fair number of municipal, church, and school offices." These men had seen their status depersonalized as they quickly became part of a larger labor force, dependent on a distant and uncontrollable market. They unavailingly complained when operators brought in many more miners than needed for full-time work. A perceptive observer found that many of the older miners "have worked in these mines since they were boys and feel they have an actual property right to their places." Most of the new men who flocked to the valley after 1869 came from distant areas, and a good number were from England, Wales, and Ireland. The rapid growth of the industry made it difficult to support trade unions in the valley.[50]

Economic crisis in 1873 suddenly punctured the region's prosperity. At best, miners found only part-time employment, and cash wages were less common than usual, for working miners were paid mostly in 90-day notes and store credit. The operators complained that labor costs were too high and made the selling price of coal in a competitive but depressed market prohibitive. Talk of wage cuts, however, turned the miners toward trade unionism, and in December 1873 they founded several branches of the newly established Miners' National Association. The operators in turn formed a regionwide trade association, and each of them posted a $5,000 bond as proof he would follow its directives. They also announced a sharp wage cut effective April 1, 1874, and entirely proscribed the new union.

Prominent union leaders lost their jobs. One operator closed his supply store "for repairs," and another locked his men in a room and insisted that they sign the new wage agreement. But the union thrived. Only nine "regular" miners favored the new contract, and no more than twenty-five or thirty regulars refused to join the union. The union men agreed to the lower wage but refused to abandon their organization. The operators remained adamant and insisted that the "progress or decay" of the region hinged on the destruction of the new union—"a hydra too dangerous to be warmed at our hearth." A strike over the right of labor organization started on April 1.[51]

The strike brought trouble for the operators. Except for the *Logan Republican*, the weekly valley newspapers either supported the strikers or stood between them and the operators.[52] No more than thirty regular miners accepted the new contract on April 1, and only seventy men entered the mines that day. Local public officials declined to do the bidding of prominent operators. The New Straitsville police deputized strikers, and after Governor William Allen sent the state inspector of mines to investigate reported miner violence, country and town officials assured him there was no trouble and a committee of merchants and "other property owners" visited Allen "to give him the facts."

New Straitsville town officials joined the miners to check the effort of operator W. B. McClung to bring in from Columbus "a posse" of nine special police armed with Colt revolvers and Spencer rifles. The miners felt it "unnecessary" for armed police to come to "their quiet town," and men, women, and children paraded the streets in protest. They made it uncomfortable for McClung's police, and he promised to close his mine and return the men to Columbus. But the mayor, on the complaint of a miner, issued a warrant for their arrest for entering the town armed, "disturbing the peace and quiet." Ordered to stand trial, the nine left town after McClung's superintendent posted their bond.

Except for the Nelsonville operators, other owners closed their mines on April 1 for two months and waited out the strikers. Toward the end of May, the operators divided among themselves. A few settled with strikers, but the largest rejected arbitration and rebuked the union.[53] Compromise was out of the question, insisted the more powerful operators, and they attacked the governor for not sending militia. The triumph of the union would soon lead to the "overthrow" of "our Government and bring upon us anarchy and bloodshed that would approach, if not equal, the Commune of Paris."[54]

Unable to exert authority from within, the owners brought in between 400 and 500 Negroes in mid-June. Most came from Memphis, Louisville, and Richmond; few were experienced coal miners. They were offered high wages, were told nothing of the dispute, and were generally misinformed about conditions. One employer admitted that "the motive for introducing the Negro was to break down the white miners' strike." Another boasted of his "great triumph over Trades-Unions" and called the use of Negroes "the greatest revolution ever attempted by operators to take over their own property." Gathered together in Columbus, the Negroes then were sped by rail to one of the mines, which was turned into a military camp. The county sheriff, twenty-five deputies, and the governor's private secretary were also there. Apparently with the approval of these officials, the operators armed the Negroes with "Government muskets," bayonets, and revolvers, and placed them on "military duty" around the property. No one could enter the area unless endorsed "by the operators or police." In the meantime, state militia were mobilized in nearby Athens, in Chillicothe, and in Cincinnati.[55]

Anger swept the Hocking Valley when the strikers learned of this. The first day 1,000 miners and their families stood or paraded near the Negro encampment. No violence occurred, but the men called across picket lines of armed Negroes and urged them to desert the operators. The second day even more miners paraded near the encampment and urged the Negroes to leave. The miners succeeded in "raiding" the operators with an "artillery of words," and around 120 Negroes went back on the operators. Two of the defectors admitted they had been "led by misrepresentations to come North" and "wouldn't interfere with white folks' work." They defended unions as "a good thing" and advocated "plenty of good things" for everyone. The strikers housed the Negroes in union lodge rooms, and with the help of local citizens raised about $500 to help them return South. But this was only a small victory for the strikers. Enough Negroes remained to

POWER & CULTURE

strengthen the hand of the operators and to demoralize the union men. Negroes went to other mines, even though strikers begged them not to work and "mothers held their children in their arms pointing out the negroes to them as those who came to rob them of their bread."[56]

Outside the Hocking Valley, the press applauded the operators. The *Cleveland Leader* thought the strikers were "aliens"; the *Cincinnati Commercial* called them drunkards, thieves, and assassins. In the Hocking Valley, however, some residents complained of the "mercenary newspaper men and their hired pimps." The valley newspapers especially criticized the owners for using Negroes. Some merchants and other business folk also attacked operators. Certain Nelsonville businessmen offered aid to the strikers and unsuccessfully pleaded with the operators to rehire all the miners. The police also were friendly, and the New Straitsville mayor prevented the sending of militia to his town.[57]

Destruction of the union and the introduction of Negro workers did not bring industrial harmony. There were strikes over wage cuts in 1875 and 1877, and conflict between Negro and white miners. In 1875, when the men resisted a wage cut, the employers tacitly admitted that their power in the valley still was inadequate. Two of them, W. F. Brooks and T. Longstreth, visited Governor Allen and pleaded that he "restore order" in the valley towns. The governor was cautious, however, and sent no troops. But their pleas revealed the employers' anxieties and need for outside power.[58]

Nothing better illustrated the differences between the small town and large city than attitudes toward public works for the unemployed. Urban newspapers frowned upon the idea, and relief and welfare agents often felt that the unemployed were "looking for a handout." The jobless, one official insisted, belonged to "the degrading class . . . who have the vague idea that 'the world owes them a living.' " Unemployed workers were lazy, many said, and trifling.[59]

Native-born radicals and reformers, a few welfare officers, ambitious politicians, responsible theorists, socialists, and "relics" from the pre–Civil War era all agitated for public works during the great economic crisis of 1873–1874. The earliest advocates urged construction of city streets, parks and playgrounds, rapid-transit systems, and other projects to relieve unemployment. These schemes usually depended on borrowed money or fiat currency, or issuance of low-interest rate bonds on both local and national levels. The government had aided wealthy classes in the past; it was time to "legislate for the good of all not the few." Street demonstrations and meetings by the unemployed occurred in November and December of 1873 in Boston, Cincinnati, Chicago, Detroit, Indianapolis, Louisville, Newark, New York, Paterson, Pittsburgh, and Philadelphia. The dominant theme at all these gatherings was the same: unemployment was widespread, countless persons were without means, charity and philanthropy were poor substitutes for work, and public aid and employment were necessary and just.[60]

The reaction to the demand for public works contained elements of surprise, ridicule, contempt, and genuine fear. The Board of Aldermen refused to meet with committees of jobless Philadelphia workers. Irate Paterson taxpayers put an end to a limited program of street repairs the city government had started. Chicago public officials and charity leaders told the unemployed to join them "in God's work" and rescue the poor and suffering" through philanthropy, not public employment.[61]

The urban press rejected the plea for public works and responsibility for the unemployed. Men demanding such aid were "disgusting," "crazy," "loud-mouthed gasometers," "impudent vagabonds," and even "ineffable asses." They were ready "to chop off the heads of every man addicted to clean linen." They wanted to make government "an institution to pillage the individual for the benefit of the mass." Hopefully, "yellow fever, cholera, or any other blessing" would sweep these persons from the earth. Depressions, after all, were normal and necessary adjustments, and workers should only "quietly bide their time till the natural laws of trade" brought renewed prosperity. Private charity and alms, as well as "free land," were adequate answers to unemployment. "The United States," said the *New York Times*, "is the only 'socialistic,' or more correctly 'agrarian,' government in the world in that it offers good land at nominal prices to every settler" and thereby takes "the sting from Communism." If the unemployed "prefer to cling to the great cities to oversupply labor," added the *Chicago Times*, "the fault is theirs."[62]

None of the proposals of the jobless workers met with favor, but the demand by New York workers that personal wealth be limited to $100,000 was criticized most severely. To restrict the "ambition of building up colossal fortunes" meant an end to all "progress," wrote the *Chicago Times*. The *New York Tribune* insisted that any limitation on personal wealth was really an effort "to have employment without employers," and that was "almost as impossible . . . as to get into the world without ancestors."[63]

Another argument against public responsibility for the unemployed identified this notion with immigrants, socialists, and "alien" doctrine. The agitation by the socialists compounded the anxieties of the more comfortable classes. Remembering that force had put down the Paris Communards, the *Chicago Times* asked: "Are we to be required to face a like alternative?" New York's police superintendent urged his men to spy on labor meetings and warned that German and French revolutionaries were "doing their utmost to inflame the workingman's mind." The *Chicago Tribune* menacingly concluded: "The coalition of foreign nationalities must be for a foreign, non-American object. The principles of these men are wild and subversive of society itself."[64]

Hemmed in by such ideological blinders, devoted to "natural laws" of economics, and committed to a conspiracy theory of social change so often attributed only to the lower classes, the literate nonindustrial residents of large cities could not identify with the urban poor and the unemployed. Most well-to-do metropolitan residents in 1873 and 1874 believed that whether men rose or fell depended on individual effort. They viewed the worker as little more than a factor of production. They were sufficiently alienated from the urban poor to join the *New York Graphic* in jubilantly celebrating a country in which republican equality, free public schools, and cheap Western lands allowed "intelligent working people" to "have anything they all want."[65]

The attitude displayed toward the unemployed reflected a broader and more encompassing view of labor. Unlike similar groups in small towns, the urban middle- and upper-income groups generally frowned upon labor disputes and automatically sided with employers. Contact between these persons and the worker was casual and indirect. Labor unions violated certain immutable "natural and moral laws" and deterred economic development and capital accumulation.[66] The *Chicago Times* put it another way in its discussion of workers who challenged the status quo: "The man who lays up not for the morrow, perishes on the morrow. It is the inexorable law of God, which neither legislatures nor communistic blatherskites can repeal. The fittest alone survive, and those are the fittest, as the result always proves, who provide for their own survival."[67]

Unions and all forms of labor protest, particularly strikes, were condemned. The *New York Times* described the strike as "a combination against long-established laws," especially "the law of supply and demand." The *New York Tribune* wrote of "the general viciousness of the trades-union system," and the *Cleveland Leader* called "the labor union kings . . . the most absolute tyrants of our day." Strikes, insisted the *Chicago Tribune*, "implant in many men habits of indolence that are fatal to their efficiency thereafter." Cleveland sailors who protested conditions on the Great Lakes ships were "a motley throng and a wicked one," and when Cuban cigar makers struck in New York, the *New York Herald* insisted that "madness rules the hour."

City officials joined in attacking and weakening trade unions. The mayor forbade the leader of striking Philadelphia weavers from speaking in the streets. New York police barred striking German cigar workers from gathering in front of a factory whose owners had discharged six trade unionists, including four women. Plainclothes detectives trailed striking Brooklyn plasterers. When Peter Smith, a nonunion barrel maker, shot and wounded four union men—killing one of them—during a bitter lockout, a New York judge freed him on $1,000 bail supplied by his employers and said his employers did "perfectly right in giving Smith a revolver to defend himself from strikers."[68]

Brief review of three important labor crises in Pittsburgh, Cleveland, and New York points out different aspects of the underlying attitude toward labor in the large cities. The owners of Pittsburgh's five daily newspapers cut printers' wages in November 1873 and formed an association to break the printers' union. After the printers rejected the wage cut and agreed to strike if nonunion men were taken on, two newspapers fired the union printers. The others quit in protest. The *Pittsburgh Dispatch* said the strikers "owe no allegiance to society," and the other publishers condemned the union as an "unreasoning tyranny." Three publishers started a court suit against more than seventy union members, charging them with "conspiracy." The printers were held in $700 bail, and the strike was lost. Pittsburgh was soon "swarming with 'rats' from all parts of the country," and the union went under. Though the cases were not pressed after the union collapsed, the indictments were not dropped. In 1876, the *Pittsburgh National Labor Tribune* charged: "All of these men are kept under bail *to this day* to intimidate them from forming a Union, or asking for just wages." A weekly organ of the anthracite miners' union attacked the indictment and complained that it reiterated "the prejudice against workingmen's unions that seems to exist universally among officeholders."[69]

In May 1874, Cleveland coal dealers cut the wages of their coal heavers more than 25 percent, and between 400 and 500 men struck. Some new hands were hired. A foreman drew a pistol on the strikers and was beaten. He and several strikers were arrested, and the coal docks remained quiet as the strikers, who had started a union, paraded up and down and neither spoke nor gestured to the new men. Police guarded the area, and a light artillery battery of the Ohio National Guard was mobilized. Lumber heavers joined the striking workers, and the two groups paraded quietly on May 8. Although the strikers were orderly, the police jailed several leaders. The strikers did not resist and dispersed when so ordered by the law. In their complaint to the public, they captured the flavor of urban-industrial conflict:

> The whole thing is a calumny, based upon the assumption that if a man be poor he must necessarily be a blackguard. Honest poverty can have no merit here, as the rich, together with all their other monopolies, must also monopolize all the virtues. We say now . . .

we entertain a much more devout respect and reverence for our public law than the men who are thus seeking to degrade it into a tool of grinding oppression. We ask from the generosity of our fellow citizens . . . to dispute [*sic*] a commission of honest men to come and examine our claims. . . . We feel confident they will be convinced that the authorities of Cleveland, its police force, and particularly the formidable artillery are all made partisans to a very dirty and mean transaction.

The impartial inquiry proved unnecessary; a few days later several firms rescinded the wage cut, and the strikers thanked these employers.[70]

Italian laborers were used on a large scale in the New York building trades for the first time in the spring of 1874. They lived "piled together like sardines in a box" and worked mainly as ragpickers and street cleaners. They were men of "passionate dispositions" and, "as a rule, filthy beyond the power of one to imagine." Irish street laborers and unskilled workers were especially hard on Italians, and numerous scuffles between the two groups occurred in the spring of 1874. In spite of the revulsion toward the Italians as a people, the *New York Tribune* advised employers that their "mode of life" allowed them to work for low wages.[71]

Two non-Italians, civil engineers and contractors, founded the New York Italian Labor Company in April 1874. It claimed 2,700 members, and its superintendent, an Italian named Frederick Guscetti, announced: "As peaceable and industrious men, we claim the right to put such price upon our labor as may seem to us best." The firm held power of attorney over members, contracted particular jobs, provided transportation, supplied work gangs with "simple food," and retained a commission of a day's wages from each monthly paycheck. The company was started to protect the Italians from Irish "adversaries," and Guscetti said the men were willing to work "at panic prices." The non-Italian managers announced the men would work for 20 percent less in the building trades. Employers were urged to hire them "and do away with strikes."[72]

Protected by the city police and encouraged by the most powerful newspapers, the New York Italian Labor Company first attracted attention when it broke a strike of union hod carriers. Irish workers hooted and stoned the Italians, but the police provided them with ample protection. The *Cooper's New Monthly* complained that "poor strangers, unacquainted with the laws and customs and language of the country," had been made "the dupes of unprincipled money sharks" and were being "used as tools to victimize and oppress other workingmen." This was just the start. The firm advertised its services in *Iron Age*. By the end of July 1874, it had branched out with work gangs in New York, Massachusetts, and Pennsylvania.[73]

There is much yet to learn about the attitude toward labor that existed in large cities, but over all opinion lay a popular belief that "laws" governed the economy and life itself. He who tampered with them through social experiments or reforms imperiled the whole structure. The *Chicago Times* was honest, if callous, in saying: "Whatever cheapens production, whatever will lessen the cost of growing wheat, digging gold, washing dishes, building steam engines, is of value. . . . The age is not one which enquires when looking at a piece of lace whether the woman who wove it is a saint or a courtesan." It came at last almost to a kind of inhumanity, as one manufacturer who used dogs and men in his operation discovered. The employer liked the dogs: "They never go on strike for higher wages, have no labor unions, never get intoxicated and disorderly, never absent themselves from work without good cause, obey orders without growling, and are very reliable."[74]

The contrast between urban and rural views of labor and its fullest role in society and life is clear.[75] In recent years, many have stressed "entrepreneurship" in nineteenth-century America[76] without distinguishing between entrepreneurs in commerce and trade and those in industrial manufacturing. Reflecting the stresses and strains in the thought and social attitudes of a generation passing from the old preindustrial way of life to the new industrial America, many men could justify the business ethic in its own sphere without sustaining it in operation in society at large or in human relationships. It was one thing to apply brute force in the marketplace, and quite another to talk blithely of "iron laws" when men's lives and well-being were at stake.

Not all men had such second thoughts about the social fabric which industrial capitalism was weaving, but in the older areas of the country the spirits of free enterprise and free action were neither dead nor mutually exclusive. Many labor elements kept their freedom of action and bargaining even during strikes. And the worker was shrewd in appealing to public opinion. There is a certain irony in realizing that small-town America, supposedly alien and antagonistic toward city ways, remained a stronghold of freedom for the worker seeking economic and social rights.

But perhaps this is not so strange after all, for preindustrial America, whatever its narrowness and faults, had always preached personal freedom. The city, whose very impersonality would make it a kind of frontier of anonymity, often practiced personal restriction and the law of the economic and social judge. As industrialism triumphed, the businessman's powers increased, yet he was often hindered—and always suspect—in vast areas of the nation which cheered his efforts toward wealth even while condemning his methods.[77]

Facile generalizations are easy to make and not always sound, but surely the evidence warrants a new view of labor in the Gilded Age. The standard stereotypes and textbook clichés about its impotence and division before the iron hand of oppressive capitalism do not quite fit the facts. Its story is far different when surveyed in depth, carrying in it overtones of great complexity. And even in an age often marked by lust for power, men did not abandon old and honored concepts of human dignity and worth.

2

JOSEPH P. MCDONNELL
AND THE WORKERS' STRUGGLE
IN PATERSON, NEW JERSEY

THIS ESSAY considers a single individual in order to assess his career, but more important, to reexamine certain general views of the Gilded Age American radical and of the Gilded Age itself. An Irish immigrant, Joseph Patrick McDonnell was a socialist, a trade union organizer, a lobbyist for protective and reform legislation, and a New Jersey newspaper editor. Orthodox labor history relates these facts and little more. Standard historical works of a broader sort entirely ignore men like McDonnell. Yet he was a figure of some importance between 1873 and 1893 and typified an entire generation of Gilded Age labor radicals. Men like McDonnell played dominant roles in the labor and radical movements of that time. They were harsh critics of the emerging industrial society. They pioneered in early legislative efforts to humanize a changing and an insensitive social order.

These are significant facts. Why, then, is so little known about radical and working-class leaders like J. P. McDonnell? Re-creating the past is an ongoing and a selective process. But the principles that guide such selection are not objective and are often shaped by a particular overview (a general interpretation) of a past era. The dominant view of Gilded Age America allows little room for radicals like McDonnell and much else of importance. At best, such men are counted as nagging and ineffective reminders that conscience and moral purpose did not entirely wilt in that American Dark Age. At worst, such men exist beyond the fringe or simply are forgotten by a collective memory cramped by certain crude and misleading stereotypes that give conceptual shape to the Gilded Age. Men like McDonnell are misunderstood, minimized, or entirely neglected. Their role as critic escapes the historian. Their successes and failures confuse the historian. The Gilded Age radical lives outside the mainstream of his times. Even his own historians emphasize this fact and often study the radical and his movements as little more than exercises in exposure. Historians of the

This essay is reprinted from *Work, Culture, and Society in Industrializing America* (New York: Alfred A. Knopf, 1976), 260–92, where it appeared under the title "A Brief Postscript: Class, Status, and the Gilded Age Radical. A Reconsideration."

working class accept this larger view, too, and their writing records mainly bitter industrial conflicts as well as the tiresome inner struggles between working-class leaders over principles of organization and over strategy and tactics. Together with the more general historians, they concede that the age belonged to Andrew Carnegie. Disaffected workers, moralists like Henry George, Edward Bellamy, and Henry Demarest Lloyd, agrarians like the Populists, and scattered mugwump intellectuals were eloquent but powerless censors. Displaced craftsmen, rural folk, and utopian intellectuals, they were overwhelmed by a national ethos that thrived on an ugly materialism, deified the dollar, and worshipped in the marketplace. There is some truth in this perspective, and much has been learned from it. But it is defective in essential ways.

In examining McDonnell's role and influence, we do more than just study a single man. We reconsider the status of the Gilded Age radical and the character of the Gilded Age itself. The reason is important: careful assessment of his radical efforts challenges some of the comfortable clichés about the Gilded Age that saturate our historiography and obscure our past.

I

WE FIRST consider the dominant view of the Gilded Age more closely. Historians correctly emphasize indisputably significant themes such as industrialization, urbanization, and immigration and see the post–Civil War decades as a time (in Sigmund Diamond's words) when the "nation" was "transformed." Certain widely held assumptions affect their treatment of these themes and should be summarized (perhaps too simply, but this is a short paper). Industrialism was still new to most Gilded Age Americans—new as a way of work and new as a way of life. Its norms were not yet internalized, institutionalized, or legitimized. Yet the Gilded Age is described as a time when industrialization generated new kinds of economic power which, in turn, immediately altered the older social and political structure. Much follows from this flawed assumption. In another connection, I have summarized some of its implications. Studying Gilded Age social conflict as reported by most historians is to learn

that the worker was isolated from the rest of society; that the employer had an easy time and relatively free hand in imposing [new] disciplines; that the spirit of the times, the ethic of the Gilded Age, worked to the advantage of the owner of industrial property; that workers found little if any sympathy from nonworkers; that the quest for wealth obliterated nonpecuniary values; and that industrialists swept aside countless obstacles with great ease. The usual picture of these years portrays the absolute power of the employer over his workers and emphasizes his ability to manipulate a sympathetic public opinion as well as various political, legal, and social institutions to his advantage.

No one has expressed this view more cogently than Louis Hacker. Writing in 1966, he insisted:

> The end of the Civil War . . . cleared the way for the triumph of American industrial capitalism. . . . Far from being sharply critical of the capitalist processes of private accumulation, investment, and decision-making, Americans, *almost to a man*, veered to the opposite position; what before had been rejection now became assent. This new climate produced new institutions (values and attitudes) to support and strengthen industrial capitalism; in the law-text writers . . . ; in the writers of economy texts; . . . in the acceptance by the clergy of a market economy with its unequal distributive shares; in the programs and formulations of the labor organizations. *Americans, almost universally, during 1865–1900, when industrial capitalism made its swiftest progress in the United States, looked upon a market economy founded on the rules of laissez-faire . . . as the normal, more the right, way of life.* [Italics added.]

So bold a statement exaggerates what others often accept in more quiet and subtle ways. J. P. McDonnell's career allows us to examine this view.

II

WHEN JOSEPH MCDONNELL crossed the Atlantic in December 1872 to settle permanently in the Great Republic of the West (first in New York City and then in Paterson, New Jersey), he already was a radical. Then just twenty-five years old, he carried unusual baggage with him. Four arrests and three prison terms suggest that he was not typical of the immigrant millions pouring into post–Civil War America. Militant Irish nationalism and socialism had shaped his formative years. Never a worker, he was born into a middle-class Dublin family in 1847, attended Dublin's schools and its university, and prepared for the priesthood. Irish nationalism ended his formal education. He refused to take the Maynooth Oath, joined the National Brotherhood (the Fenians), helped edit Irish nationalist newspapers, and soon spent ten months in Dublin's Mount Joy Prison. Just twenty-one, he quit Ireland in 1868 to live in London for five years. Lectures and impressive public demonstrations that he organized urged amnesty for Irish political prisoners and independence for Ireland. In 1869, to cite one example, he led several thousand persons in a July 4 march from London to Gravesend. They carried Irish and American flags. London street demonstrations twice resulted in his arrest.

More than the cause of Ireland attracted McDonnell's concern and support during his London years. Working-class social movements won his allegiance. In 1869, the *Sheffield Journal* called McDonnell "a full-fledged Republican—disloyal but highly talented." He went to Geneva to an International Peace Congress, stayed in London for an International Prison Congress, and helped organize the Anglo-Irish Agricultural Union. The Franco-Prussian War caused yet another arrest after McDonnell formed an "Irish Brigade" that hoped to leave England illegally to support the French Republicans against their German enemies. McDonnell publicly endorsed the Paris Commune, won nomination to Parliament from London, and organized massive street parades and demonstrations to test the right of public assembly and free speech. He also joined the International Working Men's Association, associated with Karl Marx, became a socialist, and served as Irish secretary of the International's General Council. McDonnell brought these experiences and values with him to the United States. Few other immigrants carried to industrializing America so full and so complete a set of radical credentials.

His five years in New York City followed a predictable pattern. Socialist and labor agitation consumed his time. On his arrival, McDonnell's bitter letters filled long columns in the *New York Herald* as he exposed steerage conditions on immigrant vessels. "Better accommodation is provided for cattle . . . than . . . for human beings," fumed the new immigrant. Challenged in print by a less angry passenger, socialist McDonnell exploded:

> He evidently has more money than heart and belongs to that intelligent class of Englishmen who delight in discussing the qualities of dogs and horses over their punch and pipes. It is a well known fact that such men are very humane when horses or dogs are concerned, but their eyes are blind and their ears deaf to the miseries of the poor and toiling.

McDonnell told American readers he had "allied" himself "permanently with the great proletarian movement throughout Europe," and that steerage abuses of immigrants proved once more "that there is one law for the poor and another for the rich, even on the ocean."

Between 1873 and 1878, McDonnell involved himself deeply in the faction-ridden, tiny New York City socialist movement. These were busy but not fruitful years. Calling himself a "journalist and orator," McDonnell lectured widely and traveled the East Coast to spread socialism and to strengthen existing craft unions and build collective strength among the unskilled factory workers. After 1876, he gave much time to editing the *New York Labor Standard*, a Marxist weekly. His public lectures revealed a large but not total debt to Marx: "The modern State has given them [the workers] perfect freedom to go whither they list and die when they please. It is that system which has turned earth into a Hell for the toiler and a Heaven for the idle monopolist." A second lecture told that the promise of America remained unfulfilled: "The despot Poverty seizes our noblest intellect by the throat and stifles out its genius. . . . Law which the founders of the Republic meant to be Justice is now only a farce when invoked for the protection of innocence or humanity." Althought the *Labor Standard* survived a difficult birth, factionalism aborted the socialist movement that had given it life. McDonnell himself attracted little notice outside radical and labor circles. During the 1877 railroad strikes and riots (which McDonnell called a "a sort of guerilla warfare" by workers "for their rights"), he pleaded with New York City workers: "The laziest hog can grunt; if we are Men we shall not grunt any more, we shall act. . . . We must organize; unorganized we are a mob and a rabble; organized in one compact body we are a power to be respected. . . . Union is your shepherd." A similar speech in Baltimore (the scene of much bloodshed and industrial violence) finally caused the *New York Times* to notice McDonnell but only to warn that he preached "disorganizing doctrines" and "the unadulterated gospel of communism" to "loafers and ruffians." That was in August of 1877. A year later, McDonnell moved himself and his newspaper from New York City to Paterson and settled permanently in that New Jersey industrial city.

Failure and factionalism pushed the radical McDonnell from New York City. But the condition of the silk and other textile workers (the largest number of them women and children) together with his desire to organize them into the International Labor Union pulled McDonnell to Paterson. By then, he and a few other socialists had made common cause with New England labor radicals like Ira Steward and George McNeill, hoping to organize unskilled factory workers and to spark a movement among them for shorter hours that would end by abolishing the "wages-system." Before that time, McDonnell had occasionally lectured to the Paterson workers. In 1876, he had helped some Paterson radicals celebrate bitterly the nation's centennial at an open-air meeting at the Passaic Falls. A general strike by Paterson silk ribbon weavers in 1877 had commanded sympathetic attention in his New York newspaper. A year later, a nine-month strike by unorganized women and girls against the nation's largest cotton mosquito-net manufacturer convinced McDonnell that Paterson was fertile ground to plant his radicalism. He moved there, helped organize the cotton strikers, and

POWER & CULTURE

renamed his newspaper the *Paterson Labor Standard*. Across its mast-head, he emblazoned the words of Karl Marx: "The Emancipation of the Working Classes Must be Achieved by the Working Classes Themselves." In its columns, he defended the Paterson workers and scorned their employers. McDonnell addressed the cotton strikers:

> All hail! Your struggle is the struggle of humanity for humanity. Your warfare is the warfare of human hearts against a heart of stone. Your contest is that of human flesh against the Dagon of gold. . . . Those who serve a lordly autocrat to cut down the living of full grown human beings without a word do sell themselves for slaves. . . . Whoever holds his food at the will of another, he is the other man's slave.

McDonnell minced no words in demeaning the factory owner:

> Sir, you are a man born to the image and likeness of your Creator. . . . You ought to remember that you have sprung from poverty, that you are nothing, and that in the natural order of events, death will close your eyes in a few more years. What will all your ill-gotten wealth then avail you? Your mills will stand as monuments of your cruelty. . . . The greatness that is won by shattering the health and happiness of thousands, driving young men to crime and young women to prostitution is the greatness of Lucifer. Be just and fear not. . . . Descend from the pedestal of your sinful pride, and wipe away some of the stains from your past life.

Paterson residents got a different message. In its first issue, the *Labor Standard* warned:

> After a century of Political independence, we find that our social system is not better than that of Europe and that labor in this Republic is not better than that of Europe, and that labor in this Republic, as in the European monarchies, is the slave of capitalism, instead of being the master of its own products.

McDonnell argued that to save "the Republic . . . from monarchy and ruin"—even from "a dreadful revolution"—"steps" had "to be taken and at once to prevent the march of poverty and the growth of industrial despotism."

Such severe printed words were new to Paterson and shocked and worried otherwise uneasy manufacturers and their supporters. From his start, therefore, McDonnell faced critics who wanted to stamp out the growth that he and his newspaper nurtured. Soon after his arrival, in October 1878, loyal nonstrikers convinced a county grand jury to indict McDonnell because the *Labor Standard* had called them "scabs." A citizens' jury found McDonnell guilty of libel, and a judge fined him

$500. A year later, McDonnell angered a local brick manufacturer. His newspaper published a letter from Michael Menton, a young, itinerant common laborer, which exposed working and living conditions in his Passaic River brickyard. The manufacturer charged McDonnell and Menton with libel. A court found them guilty. They were fined, and in early 1880 McDonnell and Menton spent nearly three months in the Passaic County jail.

III

NOTHING YET in McDonnell's career challenges the general view sketched earlier of Gilded Age America. Quite the contrary. His two trials and his imprisonment illustrate and strengthen that view. But these few facts are not the full story. McDonnell left prison in 1880. Despite much difficulty, his newspaper survived its early troubled years and remained a weekly labor paper until McDonnell's death in 1908. More important, less than four years after his release from prison a New Jersey governor appointed McDonnell as the state's first deputy inspector of factories and workshops. Although he held that position for less than a year, in 1892 he was chosen to head New Jersey's short-lived State Board of Arbitration.

Even these appointments lose significance beside other information about McDonnell's post-1880 career. McDonnell and a few other trade unionists, labor reformers, and radicals founded the New Jersey Labor Congress in 1879 and a few years later changed its name to the Federation of Organized Trades and Labor Unions of the State of New Jersey. Between 1883 and 1897, McDonnell headed the Federation's legislative committee. The Federation never was a powerful body. Its constituent organizations never represented more than 65,000 workers and less than a third of that number in the 1890s. For a few years, the dispute between the craft unions and the Knights of Labor severely weakened it. Its annual expenditures rarely exceeded $250 before 1900.

And yet, between 1883 and 1892, much of the spirit and pressure that resulted in remedial laws to check the freedom of the industrialist and to improve the condition of working people and other citizens came from this small group. Each year, McDonnell and other members of the Federation's legislative committee drew up laws and organized campaigns to prod Trenton legislators for their support. Not all of their efforts were successful. A factory inspector and several deputies were empowered to enforce these laws, but some laws were badly written. Few of these laws passed without bitter legislative battles, and some became statutes only after amendments had weakened them. But their range was impressive and their intent clear. McDonnell believed that the state's major duty was to satisfy "the wants of those who by their toil are the architects of the State's greatness," and the laws satisfied that objective. The list of laws passed after 1883 is too long to be catalogued fully but deserves brief summary. In 1883 and 1884, the state checked contract convict labor and child labor for the first time. A year later, the first of eight general factory laws passed between 1885 and 1893 took effect. These laws began civilizing primitive factory working conditions. Some provided for fire escapes and adequate factory ventilation; others required protective covering on dangerous machinery, belts, and gearing. Another limited the employment of children in dangerous occupations; factories were required to provide seats and suitable dressing rooms for women. Other laws incorporated trade unions, cooperatives, and working-class building and loan associations. Archaic conspiracy legislation was repealed. Nonresidents, often Pinkerton police, were prohibited from serving as public officers. Labor Day became a legal holiday first in New Jersey. So did the fifty-five-hour week for workers engaged in manufacturing. McDonnell and the Federation drew up and won even broader social reforms including ballot reform, the protection of tenants from landlords, the founding of public libraries, and, most important, the state's first comprehensive compulsory education law. "No better measure ever passed a legislative body," argued McDonnell, "and no state in the United States can boast of having a better system of compulsory education." Reviewing this law and others like it enacted between 1883 and 1892, McDonnell concluded: "The interests of the wage earners have been promoted through legislation. . . . No other state in the United States can show greater accomplishments by legislation for the welfare of the wage class during a like period."

After 1892, McDonnell's efforts were much less successful and he and others like him despaired greatly, but McDonnell deserved much credit for the earlier successes. "Every labor law on the state statute books of New Jersey owes its birth to the fostering care and indefatigable work of McDonnell," said the *Boston Post* in 1897. "Not a tithe can be told of all he has done for the betterment of mankind." But to say only this is to miss the larger significance of McDonnell's career. He could not have done this much alone. And it is here that we return to the larger view of Gilded Age America. McDonnell survived despite his Paterson critics; he won two state-appointed offices; he engineered significant legislative victories that industrialists bitterly opposed. Why was this possible? Why was this radical critic able to affect the political system in ways that promoted pioneering reform legislation? Answers to these questions require that we examine neglected but important aspects of the Gilded Age social, economic, and political structure.

IV

SO BRIEF a paper cannot entirely alter the larger view of Gilded Age America, but it can suggest new ways of looking at that world so that McDonnell's career and much else fall into place better. We must first put aside the view that the industrialist had authority as well as power because his ownership of "things" (machinery and a new technology) together with a widely shared set of beliefs that sanctified property, entrepreneurship, and social mobility gave him unexampled social prestige and exceedingly high status.

Many persons new to the urban-industrial world did not settle easily into a factory-centered civilization. McDonnell was one of them. More significant, however, is the fact that McDonnell's survival, much less his success, depended on such tension and conflict. Certain elements in the preindustrial American social structure and in older patterns of popular ideology persisted strongly into the post–Civil War urban world, profoundly affected behavior, and served as a source of recurrent opposition to the power and status of the new industrialist. At times, they narrowed the industrialist's freedom of action and widened McDonnell's opportunities. Four such "factors" deserve brief note and then illustration:

First: Not all urban property owners and professionals shared common values with the industrialist. Older patterns of thought and social ties persisted among such persons and often alienated them from the new industrialist. Some became his severe critics. Others supported men like McDonnell.

Second: Vital subcultures among the immigrant and native-born poor as well as among the more substantial craftsmen and artisans thrived in Gilded Age America and were sustained by particular norms that shared little with the industrialist and his culture.

Third: Such subcultures were especially important in the Gilded Age industrial town and city and gave its social structure a particular shape and its quality of life a special tone.

Fourth: Politics in the industrial city was affected by these subcultures and an awareness of a potential (and, at times, active) working-class political presence. Many industrial-city politicians had special ties to working-class and immigrant voters that usually filtered through a political machine but nevertheless affected the style of politics.

McDonnell's status and power rested on this world. Without support from it, his efforts would have failed, and he would have earned the anonymity that historians undeservedly have assigned to him.

V

IT IS UNFORTUNATE that so little is yet known about the Gilded Age industrial city because most of the significant changes that altered traditional American society occurred in such places. Tensions between the old and the new social structure were sharpest there. Immigrant and working-class subculture was most vital there. To say this is not to minimize all else but to locate just where the factory, the worker, and the immigrant intersected. New Jersey was the nation's sixth largest industrial state in 1880. Ten years later, five major manufacturing cities (Camden, Jersey City, Newark, Paterson, and Trenton) counted one-third of the state's population and more than half of its 150,000 factory workers. Immigrants (90 percent of them in 1890 still from Ireland, Germany, and Great Britain) settled overwhelmingly in these and smaller industrial towns. Because its main industries were diverse (especially boots and shoes, jewelry, thread, shirts, scissors, felt hats, and leather goods), Newark, the state's largest city, was untypical. One or two industries characterized the usual New Jersey industrial city. The dock and railroad workers of Bayonne, Hoboken, and Jersey City gave those towns a special character, but large sugar refineries and the huge Lorillard tobacco factory centered in Jersey City and the mammoth Standard Oil refineries towered over Bayonne. Iron miners and iron mill workers lived in the Sussex and Morris county towns. Trenton had important iron and steel works, and its potteries made it the center of the American whiteware (common table dishes) industry. Camden was best known for its iron factories and shipyards. Orange specialized in the manufacture of hats. Southern New Jersey towns such as Bridgeton, Minatola, Millville, and Glassboro made that region a major producer of varied glass products. Paterson's silk and other textile factories caused it to be called the Lyons of America, but its workers also labored in locomotive, iron, and machine shops. Although the social history of such towns has not yet been written, sufficient scattered evidence indicates the presence of vital clusters of urban working-class subculture, a diversity of attitudes among nonworkers toward industrial power, and unique patterns of protest and politics essential to understand the larger developments of that time.

Let us turn first to McDonnell's trials and his imprisonment to see what it was that protected him from his early critics and allowed him to make Paterson his permanent home. It is necessary to repeat some of the evidence used in the preceding essay but to view it from a different perspective. Paterson was a model industrial city. Some of its nearly 50,000 inhabitants (in 1878) were radicals like McDonnell, but only a few. Campbell Wilson had been a Scottish radical before working as a Paterson silk weaver and then running a working-class boardinghouse and saloon. A Lancashire Chartist, Samuel Sigley had fled England in 1848 after a threatened treason trial. He made out nicely as a Paterson house painter. Another Lancashire worker, Simon Morgan, had settled in Paterson after being blacklisted for leading a Fall River cotton strike. Irish and German radicals also befriended McDonnell, but by themselves they lacked the power to protect the socialist editor against his local critics.

Others in the city sustained McDonnell, and their behavior reveals much about the industrial city's inner structure. We consider first his supporters among nonworkers. Twenty "agents," including nearly every stationer and newsdealer on the city's main thoroughfares, sold the *Labor Standard*, and early issues earned advertising revenue from forty-five retail shopkeepers and other vendors of goods and services (among them eleven clothing and drygoods stores, ten saloons, eight boot and shoe makers, and eight grocers). Ethnicity varied among these petty retailers: the group included German, Irish, French, Dutch, and ordinary "American" names as well as an Italian bootmaker and three Jewish clothing dealers. Such support may have been just good "business sense," but the sympathy McDonnell evoked during his first trial rested on other causes. His lawyer was a pioneer manufacturer who later grew wealthy as a real estate speculator. He had broken with the Whig party over slavery and later quit the Republicans to protest the "money power." A jury of shopkeepers and successful independent artisans agreed that McDonnell was guilty, but only after unusual pressure by a presiding judge. Even then, another judge, himself a poor Lancashire immigrant who then owned a small bobbin factory, convinced the presiding judge to fine McDonnell and not send him to prison. Some storekeepers and merchants helped McDonnell pay his fine. Aid also came from a prominent coppersmith and alderman as well as a third-generation Yorkshire blacksmith who then headed a small bolt and screw factory. Orrin Vanderhoven also cheered McDonnell. Vanderhoven had traveled a long route from Jacksonian Democracy to Greenback reform and soon would return to the Democracy. "A scab," Vanderhoven wrote in his own newspaper, "is a man who deserts his fellows. . . . The name of 'scab' is not degrading enough for such a person. It ought to be a 'villainous, shameless, sneakthief traitor.' . . . God bless the laboring classes. . . . May the God of fortune favor them through life. . . . May their beds be roses and their bolsters banknotes."

Others of local prominence joined editor Vanderhoven to side with McDonnell during his second trial. Two respected lawyers defended the troubled socialist. The son of a New Hampshire blacksmith, Socrates Tuttle was then sixty-one and Paterson's most revered Republican leader—a lawyer who had served as school commissioner, city clerk, state assemblyman, and mayor. William Prall, the son of a former Democratic mayor and cotton manufacturer, helped Tuttle defend McDonnell. A few years later, Prall went to the state assembly; after that, he gave up politics and became an Episcopal clergyman. Just before his trial, McDonnell had complained loudly that Paterson's clergy prayed to "that Trinity of Power, 'the Almighty Dollar, the Golden Eagle, and the Copper Cent,'" but two prominent clergymen protested publicly in his behalf. One of them, a Baptist, worked among the Paterson poor and later played a significant role as a Midwestern antitrust propagandist. The other, John Robinson, was an Irish Protestant, a Primitive Methodist, for a time Republican state senator, and Paterson's most esteemed clergyman. Nor was this all. Two former silk factory foremen (one English and the other German), soon to become prosperous businessmen, organized McDonnell's sympathizers. Thomas Flynn, then a saloonkeeper and ten years later speaker of the state assembly, posted bond for Menton, and a contractor financed the young man in a well-drilling business. Several aldermen, former aldermen, and county freeholders visited McDonnell in prison. On McDonnell's release, a committee of seventy-five arranged a celebration. Not only workers organized the fete. The committee included a band leader, a contractor, a clothier, a doctor, five grocers, and twelve saloon and hotel keepers.

His first night in jail, McDonnell angrily confided in his diary: "Here in Jail for defending the poor in their Rights! Alas, for American Liberty." Yet his prison stay was made less harsh than expected by a county jail warden, John Buckley, who would himself soon head the county Republican organization. McDonnell's imprisonment apparently upset Buckley. He made his guest as comfortable as circumstances allowed. McDonnell spent some of his prison days writing letters for illiterate fellow prisoners and himself appealing to the New Jersey governor to enforce a moribund ten-hour law. Buckley also let him edit his newspaper and organize a national protest campaign from his cell. Visitors (twenty-one came on a single day, and children often called on McDonnell) met the editor in the warden's office. Meals came regularly from outside the prison. So did cigars, wines, and liquors supplied by friendly saloon and hotel keepers. Others brought fresh fruit, cakes, and puddings. Shamrocks came on Saint Patrick's Day and two fancy dinners on McDonnell's birthday. On his release, Buckley commended McDonnell as a model prisoner.

Scores of ordinary working people supported McDonnell in their own way. They crowded the jail to console him and raised the money to pay his fines. But their support came in more significant ways. After his first trial, working-class sympathizers (and even some shopkeepers) jammed Democratic political rallies to humiliate the Democratic county prosecutor. On his release from prison eighteen months later, working people (organized mostly by skilled silk workers) arranged Paterson's greatest celebration to that time. Quite possibly more than half of the city's residents filled its streets and "almost mobbed" their hero. A band played; a carriage awaited McDonnell to carry him through the jammed streets; American flags decorated the parade route; a rally followed the street march; then came a festive banquet at which three young girls presented the socialist editor with a gold watch—a gift from "the ladies of Paterson." "No one ever purchased the title of martyr at so slight a cost," sneered a hostile Paterson newspaper. A sympathizer disagreed. "Paterson," he insisted, "is redeemed by the suffering of the innocent for the guilty." Such varied opinions did not matter as much as the fact that Paterson residents made it possible for McDonnell to survive in a social setting usually identified with little more than hopeless poverty, disorganized and ineffective protest, and God-like industrial power.

McDonnell's 1878–1880 Paterson experiences were never exactly repeated in other New Jersey Gilded Age industrial cities, but events like them occurred with sufficient frequency to suggest that the Gilded Age worker was more than "a factor of production," that he was the sum of a total culture that has been scarcely recognized and little studied. That culture differed between groups of workers. Ethnicity and levels of skill counted for much in explaining these diversities. Despite them, however, Gilded Age workers had distinct ways of work and leisure, habits, aspirations, conceptions of America and Christianity, notions of right and wrong, and traditions of protest and acquiescence that were linked together in neighborhoods by extensive voluntary associations and other community institutions. Not all of this entirely separated the industrial city's workers from the larger community, but these strands wove together in ways that shaped a particular subculture.

Evidence of convincing support from nonworkers is drawn from an Orange hatters' boycott (1885). Nearly 2,000 men and women worked in more than twenty Orange hat factories. The Knights of Labor won much sympathy from them, but a single manufacturer named Berg discharged women employees who wanted to join the Knights, refused to negotiate, and brought in new hands. A citywide boycott followed, and a labor journalist reported the attitude of the boycotters and their supporters toward Berg and the nonstrikers ("the foul"):

> They will not trade with any person who has any dealings with the boycotted foul or with any one who furnishes goods or supplies to Berg himself. Brewers refuse to furnish beer to foul saloonkeepers; bakers refuse to furnish bread to the fouls; and the knights of the

razor turn them out of doors. One fair manufacturer discharged a man because he lived with his brother who is a foul, and two female trimmers were refused admission to the roller-skating rink because they were foul. . . . The foul cannot even find lodging places, and are compelled to resort to adjacent localities at night for bed and board. . . . One beer seller who has been threatened says he may be forced to sell beer to a foul, but he cannot be prevented from charging him a dollar a glass for it.

Although this reporter's enthusiasm caused some exaggeration, he insisted that the boycott had "the sympathy of nearly everybody in Orange."

What, finally, was politics like in the industrial city? The ballot gave the industrial city worker a presence, if not a power, that has been little studied. Political machines often disciplined the worker-voter and narrowed his choices. Votes were even purchased by "bosses" for cash and favors. That is an old story, but it is not the full story. Working-class voting behavior took many forms as a protest device. Camden and Phillipsburg had workers as mayors in 1877 and 1878. Some southern New Jersey counties sent glassblowers to the state legislature. Paterson elected two workers as state assemblymen in 1886 and two more in the early 1890s. A Paterson machinist and outspoken socialist twice served as city alderman. The direct election of workers on independent tickets, however, was not common. More typical was the elected official who was not a worker but nevertheless sympathized with the workers or feared alienating working-class electoral support. During the 1877 general silk strike, Paterson's Republican mayor (a Lancashire cotton worker who became a Paterson banker, manufacturer, and popular politician) and the Board of Aldermen publicly rebuked efforts by the Paterson Board of Trade to enlarge the police force and to deny strikers the use of the streets for their effective public demonstrations. Ten years later, Jersey City's Democratic mayor, a former congressman and also a manufacturer named Orestes Cleveland, declined to deputize Pinkerton police during a violent coal handlers' strike. After the *New York Times* condemned Cleveland as "a demagogue," the mayor fired back: "It is not the business of Jersey City to interfere between the great monopolies and their workmen. . . . If it were proper for Jersey City to interfere at all, we should interfere to assist and protect the men who are fighting for the right to live, instead of for the protection of the great monopolies. . . ."

The Jersey City mayor may have been a "demagogue." It is also possible that he learned from the bitter experiences of other urban politicians who had sided with employers or broken promises to organized workers. Here a third pattern—punishment—emerged.

During the 1877 potters' strike, Trenton's Republican mayor condemned the potters in the *New York World*. Their response was to vote him out of office that spring. Such flashes of independent political anger among urban workers recurred in the 1880s. A Camden Republican state assemblyman promised McDonnell's Federation his help but turned back on his pledge after the election. Aided by two Camden newspaper editors (one of them German), McDonnell organized Camden workers and prevented his reelection. The 1887 coal handlers' strike saw similar results. Bayonne aldermen and a Jersey City police official opposed the strikers and suffered defeat at the polls. These few examples suggest some of the ways in which working-class political presence affected industrial-city politics. Such a presence also was felt on the state level and helped explain McDonnell's legislative victories.

VI

MCDONNELL WON reform legislation between 1883 and 1892 by playing "pressure politics." Not enough is yet known to tell that story fully, but its outlines seem clear. For one thing, two state officials—one elected and the other appointed—supported McDonnell and eased his way in Trenton. One was Leon Abbett, twice-elected Democratic governor (1883–1886 and 1889–1892), and the other was Lawrence Fell, the chief factory inspector from 1883 until 1895 when a hostile state senate finally rejected his reappointment and began undoing his pioneering work. Fell's support was the more unusual, and Abbett's was the more important.

The available evidence allows us to say no more than that Leon Abbett supported the efforts of McDonnell and the Federation. Just why remains obscure and is entangled in bitter controversy over his motives and his career. But it is sufficient in these pages to know only that McDonnell had a powerful friend in Abbett, New Jersey's most significant nineteenth-century governor. During his two terms, Abbett gave much time battling the New Jersey railroads to tax them fairly, and in doing so he attacked the state's most well-organized private interest. Abbett won a public victory but twice lost a United States Senate seat as his reward. Abbett's methods aroused much public criticism. That he built "a machine" to fight "a machine" worried many, as did his continued public appeal for electoral support from urban workers and immigrants. The son of a Philadelphia Quaker journeyman hatter, Abbett was a wealthy Jersey City lawyer and state legislator. Even then (in the late 1860s and the 1870s), his actions showed a concern for the lower-class vote. As president of the state senate (1877), he worked hard to abolish scrip money and company stores then common in the southern and western New Jersey iron and glass towns. That same year, he represented workers in a successful suit for back wages against a bankrupt railroad and also defended strikers arrested in the aftermath of the 1877 railroad riots. Abbett accepted no fees in these cases. As candidate in 1883 (his Republican opponent was the judge who had sentenced McDonnell to prison in 1880), Abbett appealed to immigrant and working-class voters. After his election, the governor proclaimed: "Every citizen of this State, whether he be high or low, whether he be rich or poor, can always see me personally without the intervention of any man." Abbett was not a John Peter Altgeld, but McDonnell and the Federation found him sympathetic to their proposals. Historians, incidentally, have credited his administration's labor legislation solely to Abbett and not realized that it first came from men like McDonnell. But Abbett's response should not be neglected.

Lawrence Fell is easier to explain than Abbett and is, in some ways, more interesting. His career suggests how new experiences remade even grown men. The 1883 legislature allowed the governor with the state senate's approval to pick a chief factory inspector to enforce the new laws. Fell was not the governor's first choice. Instead, a Newark hatter and outspoken trade unionist, Richard Dowdall, was nominated. But the senate turned him down because, according to the *New York Times*, it felt him to be "a labor extremist, a demagogue identified with the [Irish] Land League, and altogether an unfit person." An Orange hat manufacturer and real estate dealer, Fell was his replacement. If the conservative senate thought him a "safe" choice because of his background, Fell disappointed it. He became a vigorous proponent of enlarged and more effective labor legisltion. He worked diligently under difficult circumstances to enforce the school and factory laws, and he cooperated openly with McDonnell and the Federation. When the opportunity existed, Fell urged the appointment of McDonnell and a Newark trade unionist as his deputies. After their appointment and work angered industrialists and caused their removal, Fell praised them: "The manner in which they have acted is sufficient proof that the advocates of labor interests are fitted to fill the highest [public] labor offices."

What Fell learned as chief factory inspector made him a reformer and an advocate of extensive remedial and protective legislation. "Old faces and dwarfed forms are the offspring of the Child Labor System," his first report concluded. "In a country where life is so intense as it is in this, where so much is expected in a little time, childhood and youth should be a time of free physical growth." Fell's second report detailed widespread illiteracy among "factory children." His description

is a neglected classic of its kind. Fell told of his experiences with twelve-
to fifteen-year-old boys and girls in the New Jersey factories:

> Nearly all the children examined were naturally bright and intelli-
> gent, but neglect, years of work and their general surroundings had
> left sad traces upon their youthful forms and minds. It is not possible
> in this report to enter into the details of every case, either of factory
> or child examination; to do so would be to fill the largest volume
> that the State has ever published. . . . There is no exaggeration in
> saying that three-fourths of the work-children know absolutely
> nothing. The greatest ignorance exists on the most commonplace
> questions. Most of these children have never been inside of a
> schoolhouse, and the majority have either been at school for too
> short a period to learn anything or have forgotten the little instruc-
> tion they received.
>
> Not two percent know anything about grammar or have ever
> been taught any. One of the few children who professed to know
> something about grammar said that the word "boy" was "a comma,"
> when asked what part of speech it was. The vast majority could not
> spell words of more than one syllable, and very many could not
> spell at all. About ten percent could answer questions in simple
> multiplication. Of the remaining ninety percent, the majority know
> absolutely nothing about simple geographical and historical ques-
> tions. The number able to read and write, in a distinguishable way,
> was shockingly small, and very many could neither read nor write
> even their own names.

Fell illustrated his experiences concretely:

> Very few of these children, the large majority of whom were born
> in the United States, ever heard of George Washington. Amongst
> the answers given about Washington, by those who heard of him,
> were the following: "He is a good man." "He chased the Indians
> away." "He died a few years ago." "He is President." "I saw his
> picture." "He is a high man in war." "He never told a lie." "He
> discovered America." "The best man who ever lived," and so forth.
> Over ninety-five percent never heard of the revolutionary war,
> Abraham Lincoln, the Civil War, Governor Abbett or President
> Arthur.
>
> At least sixty percent never heard of the United States or of
> Europe. At least thirty percent could not name the city in which
> they lived, and quite a number only knew the name of the street
> where they housed. Many who had heard of the United States could
> not say where they were. Some said they were in Europe and others

said they were in New Jersey. Many big girls and boys were unable to say whether New Jersey was in North or South America. Girls were found in Jersey City and Newark who never heard of New York City. In Newark and Jersey City this was, of course, the exception, but in other parts of the State it was the rule. Some who had heard of New York said it was in New Jersey, and others answered that Pennsylvania was the capital of New Jersey. Not ten percent could tell what an island was. Very few had heard of the city of Washington, and not three percent could locate it. A girl aged fourteen years said Europe was in the moon. A few were found who never heard of the sun, or moon, or earth, and a large number who could not tell where or when they were born. . . . Children, who had been brought to this country before their sixth year, in some cases, never heard the name of their native country, and others could not locate them.

One finding especially concerned Fell:

Boys and girls who had been brought to this country from Great Britain, Ireland and Germany, between the ages of twelve and fifteen years, were better educated and knew more about the geography and history of America than children born and reared in the State. . . . This sad tale of illiteracy is not overdrawn in the slightest degree. It is, alas, too true. . . .

Such evidence caused legislative critics in 1885 and again in 1886 to try to abolish Fell's office. But McDonnell and the Federation frustrated such efforts, and Fell continued his work for another decade.

VII

ALTHOUGH FELL and Abbett provided important help, McDonnell's legislative success depended on more than their support. It came only when McDonnell and the Federation could make a majority of the state's elected officeholders conscious, if not fearful, of the presence and potential power of the industrial city's workers and immigrant poor. This was not an easy task. The New Jersey legislature was a jungle of competing special interest groups, the railroads king among them. In addition, the state senate increasingly underrepresented the growing industrial cities and became a choice nesting ground for well-organized interest groups opposed to the Federation and its legislative programs. McDonnell scorned the typical state legislator, advising workers: "Leave him to himself and his surroundings, and he will forget all about you and his promises." So harsh a judgment was not unfair. Despite the Federation's important legislative gains, in

1897 New Jersey spent $222,400 for its National Guard ("our tin soldiers," McDonnell called the militia), a sum that nearly equaled the state's educational expenditures and was almost ten times the amount allotted to the Bureau of Labor Statistics and the Bureau of Factory Inspection.

In such a world, a single belief informed McDonnell's legislative efforts. His radicalism together with his experiences convinced McDonnell that neither rhetoric nor "right" won legislation. Only pressure worked, and the worker's weapons was the organized but "independent" vote. McDonnell preached and practiced this point for twenty-five years. As early as 1878, he advised *Labor Standard* readers: "Heaven help the laborers who rely upon their public officers to legislate for the good of labor. But honest legislation can be forced by labor unions." He regularly published the names of antilabor legislators with the frequent admonition: "If there is courage, intelligence, and Manhood in the people, not one of these enemies will ever again be elected to a legislative position. Men of New Jersey, kick them out." McDonnell explained in 1882: "It is Power that men in office fear, and it is because the wage workers have not had organized Power that they have been treated with the grossest contempt." Legislative victories came because workers had "commenced to think and to act." "Politicians," he said in 1893, "are as a rule what we make them or what we permit them to be." Five years of decline in the Federation's influence (1893–1897) caused a similar outburst: "We should not forget that if we won't aid ourselves, no one else will, and that we shall get just as much as we fight for, *and no more*." Nothing, McDonnell insisted, "of importance will be obtained from our Legislature unless they hear the workingman's and workingwoman's growl. We can get anything we want *by growling loud enough*."

A "growl" unaccompanied by a "bite" was hardly enough, and that potential "bite" was the electoral power that rested in the industrial cities and their diverse but dense clusters of working-class subculture. McDonnell and men like him therefore cut the Federation loose from all formal political ties to enable it to apply nonpartisan local pressure. The Federation supported Abbett when he favored its program, but it also gave its blessings to sympathetic Republican legislators. "The political policy of the Federation," a spokesman said in 1884, "has been and is to identify itself with no party but to support men of all parties favorable to their objects." In this way, McDonnell hoped to create effective working-class pressure and cement "natural" alliances with its legislative representatives. The regular procedure was simple. Each year the Federation convention established legislative priorities. Just before the fall election, it circulated a pledge among all candidates for public office:

I pledge my word of honor that if elected to the Legislature, I will support the bills introduced for the benefit of the wage class by the Legislative Committee of the New Jersey Federation of Trades and Labor Unions, whether said bills were approved or opposed by the political party to which I belong, provided that said bills are of a purely labor character; and I will support no measure, whether of a private or party nature, which may be introduced in opposition to labor measures and against the wishes of the organized wage-workers of New Jersey.

Approval of the pledge won Federation endorsement together with Federation scrutiny and pressure while the legislature met. For fifteen years, McDonnell spent the winter months largely in Trenton working this risky strategy. It depended for its success almost entirely on the Federation's ability to mount pressure from outside the party system. A Federation without close ties to the industrial-city working class was weak and lacked such strength. Between 1883 and 1892, such connections were sufficiently strong to win significant legislative achievements. And so in this neglected fashion, social reform came from "below." Such successes angered conservatives and those who found comfort in the ever-increasing gross national product. These victories so upset the *New York Herald* that it accused many New Jersey legislators of lacking in "courage." "Fear of the loss of the labor vote," moaned the *Herald,* "drives public men and parties into concessions against which their conscience and better judgments often rebel. . . . The law of supply and demand is offended at every tack and turn. The philosophy of trade is set at defiance." McDonnell did not share the *Herald*'s rhetorical remorse.

Just what kind of industrial-city legislators supported McDonnell and the Federation is difficult to tell. These men differed in social background and seemed to share only the fact that their constituents were mostly wage earners. Take the cases of two quite different Paterson legislators: Thomas Flynn, a Democrat and for a time state assembly speaker, and Robert Williams, a Republican state senator.

Tom Flynn was a model Gilded Age ward politician. He started as a machinist, drove a horsecar, fooled with firehouse politics, studied for the law, opened a saloon, built a personal political machine among the Paterson Irish, traded favors for votes, and went to the assembly several times starting in 1881. He became a Trenton power and critics identified him with corruption and the "racetrack lobby." The *New York Tribune* complained of his "unscrupulous conduct and aggressiveness." "A product of the slums, endowed by nature with more than an ordinary amount of acuteness, . . . and utterly without moral scruple or finer feeling," the *Tribune* saw in "Flynn's life from the first to the last . . . what any careful student of human nature might have predicted." But Flynn supported the Federation's legislative program from the very start. McDonnell often praised him and with good reason. He helped abolish an antilabor conspiracy law and pushed the regulation of prison labor. He tried to get the legislature to lower utility rates and regulate insurance companies. Flynn worked so diligently for the fifty-five-hour law that Paterson silk workers renamed him "Fifty-five Hour Flynn." A candidate for reelection, he emphasized his ties to the workers and his efforts in their behalf. Working-class voters learned that Flynn still "ranks among his friends the men who were then his comrades at the bench." A Democratic leader urged Paterson workers to reelect Flynn: "You have named him Fifty-five Hour Flynn, and he deserves the title. He fought your battle and kept the faith."

A graduate of the Columbia College Law School and a Republican newspaper publisher, Robert Williams was the antithesis of Tom Flynn. Democratic opponents mocked his upper-class style when Williams sought election to the state senate:

> Robby Williams. Nice boy, sweet little beard, dreamy way and langorous expression, long wavy hair. . . . Robby's a real nice fellow, but what does he know about labor? . . . He was born with a silver spoon in his mouth and never did anything but dandle it round his mouth. . . . Starvation has never stared him in the face . . . and [he] cannot legislate for something of which he knows nothing.

Williams disappointed his political enemies: he knew his constituents well and regularly voted for Federation legislation. He even introduced bills drawn up by McDonnell. When Williams quit the senate, McDonnell had only words of praise: "This county has never had a Senator who more faithfully represented the interests of the common people." The real test for McDonnell was neither man nor party; only the issues counted. "Robby" Williams had also "kept the faith."

Just how McDonnell and other Federation leaders worked with men like Abbett, Fell, Flynn, and Williams can be illustrated briefly in 1884 and 1893. A fairly complete record relates McDonnell's Trenton experiences in 1884. He and the Federation's legislative committee met twice in December 1883 to discuss proposed labor legislation with a sympathetic Newark assemblyman and Abbett. After that, McDonnell drew up the several laws. Between mid-January and late March, he spent thirty-four days in Trenton and conferred with, cajoled, and pressured Democratic and Republican legislators from such industrial cities as Paterson, Jersey City, and Newark. He and other Federation spokesmen testified before legislative committees and brought pressure to bear in other ways. "We had hard work getting the child-labor bill through the Senate," reported McDonnell, "as they were trying to kill it by amendments, but several Senators were brought to terms by delegations of workingmen waiting upon them in their respective districts." When the Assembly Committee on Revision of Laws held back a strengthened factory inspection law for two weeks and then allowed only a brief public hearing, McDonnell accused it of "discourtesy toward the labor organizations" to force it to hear him and Fell. The commitee stalled again, so Federation leaders conferred with Abbett. But the committee quickly won assembly support for a badly amended bill. A labor journalist reported what followed:

> [McDonnell first] succeeded through Assemblyman Flynn . . . in having the vote on the report reconsidered and the bill recommitted. The members of the Federation Legislative committee then went to work gallantly among the members, until they made things very unpleasant for the Committee on Revision of Laws. Mr. McDonnell at once telegraphed to the absent members in various parts of the State, urging them to come to Trenton at once, which they did early on Thursday morning. By this time, the aspect of things had changed. It was rumored among the Assemblymen that the labor men and their friends were swarming into Trenton like bees, and that their power was not to be made little of. The forenoon's work produced good results.

The factory inspection bill left the committee without its crippling amendments and soon became law. "What a change in twenty-four hours!" enthused McDonnell. "Would it have taken place if the labor men were not alive and doing?"

A different tactic prevented repeal of the fifty-five-hour law in 1893. It had passed the year before, the first of its kind in the United States. Inadequately enforced, it was nevertheless bitterly opposed by manufacturers. Some went to the courts to test its constitutionality. Others mounted a campaign for its repeal, and in 1893 sent such circulars together with instructions to factory superintendents to get the signatures of workers. McDonnell quickly responded. A public appeal to the state's legislators defended the law, and a circular (entitled "Danger Ahead") urged every New Jersey trade union to elect delegates to attend a special Trenton convention on twenty-four hours' notice. The response was gratifying. Nearly all picked delegates and flooded Trenton with resolutions favoring the law. The manufacturers backed away from full repeal, but their supporters pushed two bills to emasculate the law. McDonnell worked for their defeat. The night before final adjournment, the senate passed one of them. Then, Tom Flynn and others from the industrial cities stepped in. "Thanks now and forever to Speaker Tom Flynn and other friends," McDonnell explained, "neither . . . bill went through."

VIII

THIS JOURNEY has taken us from Dublin, to London, to New York, to Paterson, and finally to Trenton. That was the route McDonnell traveled, and we have followed it to fit the Gilded Age labor radical into the mainstream of that era's history. To do so, several detours were necessary to avoid the roadblocks set up by certain misconceptions concerning the Gilded Age itself. Some of the larger implications of that trip through America's Dark Age deserve summary. For one thing, McDonnell's New Jersey career was not isolated and unique. Similar patterns of working-class political pressure for reform were found in such states as New York, Massachusetts, Pennsylvania, Ohio, Indiana, Michigan, Illinois, and Connecticut. Their success varied, but the men who led these movements shared a common moral purpose with radicals like McDonnell. "The foundation of the Republic," McDonnell insisted in 1882, "is men not things, and to attend to the welfare of man, knowing that things will take care of themselves is the true wisdom of statesmanship." McDonnell believed in the 1880s that strong trade unions and legislative reform would open the way to more radical changes, but a little-studied conservative political backlash in New Jersey after 1892 that made it a one-party state for more than a decade blocked such possibilities and began weakening the ties that had given power and status to men like McDonnell. After that McDonnell faded in significance, and his last fifteen years were filled with much personal and political disappointment. It remains to be said, however, that the modern "welfare state" was not just the child of concerned and sensitive early twentieth-century upper- and middle-class critics of industrial capitalism. A generation earlier, working-class leaders, including radicals like McDonnell, had helped give birth to a premature "welfare state." They had arranged a marriage between the industrial city's workers and immigrants and their political representatives. Such men, not the Progressive reformers of a later time, were the founding fathers of modern movements to humanize industrial society.

"What a comment upon our civilization it is that you who have given so much of yourself have received so little for yourself," George McNeill wrote of McDonnell in 1896. A worker who had matured in the world of the New England abolitionists, McNeill was McDonnell's counterpart in Massachusetts. His letter reassured his Irish friend by quoting a poem McNeill had written some years before when another neglected American radical, Ira Steward, had died:

> Even now I see the coming day, the dawn
>   appears,
> The thoughtless brain will some day think
> And at thy fountain pause and drink,
> And praise thy name.

Although men like McDonnell deserved such recognition, it was not just because they gave so much and got so little. In 1873, McDonnell's first American letters had appeared in the *New York Herald*. The young socialist denounced steerage abuse of poor, powerless European immigrants. He explained his concern for them by quoting John Milton, not Karl Marx:

> Not to know at large of things remote
> From use, obscure and subtle, but to know
> That which before us lies in daily life
> Is the prime wisdom. What is more is fume
> Or emptiness or fond impertinence,
> And renders us in things that most concern
> Unpracticed, unprepared and still to seek.

Milton's words belong in this final paragraph. As more is learned of the world and the culture that bred men like McDonnell, more is revealed about the larger "forces" that have shaped modern American society. And that reason, not mere sentiment, is why we look with care at the life and times of radicals as obscure as Joseph P. McDonnell.

3

LABOR IN THE LAND
OF LINCOLN

Coal Miners on the Prairie

THE TRANSCONTINENTAL railroad was completed in 1869. That same year, two Scottish immigrants, both labor reformers in their homeland, penned private letters to friends back home that found their way into the *Glasgow Sentinel*, a working-class weekly. The two men played different but important roles in shaping the American coal-mining industry after the Civil War, and both had been closely connected with Alexander McDonald, the famed Scottish leader of the British Miners' National Association. McDonald, incidentally, made his second trip to America in 1869, met with miners everywhere, visited with President Ulysses S. Grant in Washington and General Philip H. Sheridan in New York City, and traveled to California on the Union Pacific Railroad. His stay was temporary, but his two former associates made America their home and never returned to Great Britain. One, a barrel maker, fled Scotland in 1842, possibly (the evidence is not conclusive) to escape persecution as a radical Chartist agitator; the other, a coal miner, came to America for less dramatic reasons, seeking a better life for himself and the family he left in Scotland. One came as a youth, the other as a man. the cooper, Allan Pinkerton, later headed a Chicago detective agency that specialized in protecting railroad and express companies from thieves and dishonest employees. Pinkerton had given up cooperage after winning election as an Illinois deputy sheriff, but he still boasted of his Chartist youth and reminded McDonald in a letter of his connections with "the Coopers' Trades' Union of Glasgow" and "the Chartist party." "My feelings are still, and always will be, with the working population," he told the Scottish trade unionist. McDonald, in turn, remembered Pinkerton well, calling him "the great American 'detective'" and finding his letter proof that "though no longer a worker, he has all the feelings of a son of toil yet."[1]

Another Scottish immigrant, in entirely different circumstances, also wrote old friends that year. On August 27, just after his thirty-eighth birthday, coal miner Daniel M'Lachlan, born in Lanarkshire of Irish Catholic parents (his father was a stonecutter), left the Broomielaw for

America. As a child and a youth, he knew only the coal mines. He started working underground at age nine or ten; as a twelve-year-old, he engaged in a twenty-two-week strike; five years later, he gave his first speech defending trade unionism. M'Lachlan grew into an active trade unionist and became a close associate of McDonald. The struggle by Scottish miners for shorter hours between 1865 and 1867 found him among their leaders, and before leaving for America he held office as secretary and president of the Mary Hill District of the Scottish Miners' Association. M'Lachlan traveled with more than five hundred other Scottish and Irish migrants headed for New York, and his diary notes of the ship voyage, later printed in the *Glasgow Sentinel*, told how severe storms made an otherwise uneventful trip exciting and revealed much about the hopes and fears and pleasures of immigrant workers in steerage. Passing the Clyde shipyards "reminded us of how we had cheerily and honestly toiled in the land we are leaving in sorrow, perhaps, to some, but with regret to all." The ocean before and behind them, M'Lachlan mused: "Yes, Scotland was disappearing from our view; again our thoughts are directed to scenes of our old haunts and pleasant associations to the many true friends we have left behind us, to our dear wives and children who are mourning and sorrowful at our parting."

The trip was not without its pleasures and amusements—especially those involving M'Lachlan's friend "Willie"—and the diary told of many small diversions each day:

My companion Willie is very amusing; he is quite happy, taking fun where he can find it. In the very height of the storm, he was hard making love to a fine young girl. All at once she got frightened, and all William could do she would not be consoled till some one came to her assistance. However, he got a scare, and I don't think they will catch him in the same well again during the voyage. . . .

Willie sported his figure to-day. There was fiddling and dancing, and he was foremost in the ring, taking good rises out of the young girls. . . .

During this forenoon, there was consternation [in the midst of a severe storm] among the women. One old woman who was sure we were going down, kept shouting as loud as she could—"Holy, J——s, is there not a man among you will go and tell the captain to make the ship stop pitching!" Another called out, "Biddy, agra, light a candle, for God's sake, and let us see where we are going, anyway." . . .

We had no sermon today [Sunday], but were supplied with new Testaments and some tracts. . . . We pass the time on deck when the weather is fine, and there is always some one to keep music to the great crowd of people. Fiddles, concertinas, singing, and dancing for those disposed to amuse themselves; others amuse themselves by watching the numerous ships passing within sight of our vessel.

On September 5, M'Lachlan landed in New York. "Hurrah!" the newcomer wrote, "here we are once more on *terra firma.*"[2]

M'Lachlan stayed only one night in New York before leaving to spend time with a brother-in-law in Boston. New York City depressed him: "the streets are dirty and the buildings look like prisons." Boston was another matter: his kin and other Scots were "all vieing [*sic*] with one another who will be kindest to me." And the prosperity of the Boston Scots stunned him. M'Lachlan saw "the look of plenty in every house I have visited" and learned that "the worst-paid laborer in Boston lives better and has a more comfortable home than the best tradesman in Scotland can get for his wages." "Everyone," he wrote home, "tells me that if you are willing and able to work, and inclined to be steady and sober, you can at least rear your family comfortably." But M'Lachlan moved on. He had come to America to make money, and the Western coal mines promised high wages. "It is money I want," he unashamedly wrote, "if I can get it for the earning honestly, I will have it." M'Lachlan found work in Braidwood, a new mining town sixty miles to the south of Chicago, that had among its residents a friend, John James.

James was a Renfrewshire miner who had also worked with McDonald and twice been blacklisted for his outspoken trade union activities before crossing the Atlantic "in search of better fare and peace of mind . . . in the young Republic." Arriving in America in 1865, James was hired first as a strikebreaker in a West Virginia coal mine, but when he realized this he went to work for a farmer instead. Then he signed on in a Pennsylvania mine; went to Illinois on false promises of high wages; returned to Pennsylvania; and finally settled in Braidwood at the urging of James Braidwood, a Scottish pit boss.

M'Lachlan had better fortune than James. "I am still enjoying good health and am in good spirits," he wrote in October from Braidwood to his friend John Barnes. "Taking all things into consideration, I must say I like this country well." He found a week's work in Braidwood in place of a man "badly off." Then, without employment, he decided to leave and, after paying his board, found he had saved two pounds. "Not bad, you will say," he wrote to his friend. James and other Scottish miners had shared openly with M'Lachlan: "there was plenty of meat and drink for me—for nothing if I liked—and a good bed to lie on until I could get work." But M'Lachlan had come to America for the money. "I wanted work; or if I could say it right, I wanted the

POWER & CULTURE

pay, no matter about the work." On his way to the railroad station, he stopped to thank James for his kindness. But James would not let him leave.

> He pressed me to stay; but it would not do—I must get employment. He and his two brothers were working together. He went and got two or three of the men from the old country together, and the result was that two of the men took one of his brothers, and I got in [a work group] with John himself, and the two pounds I sent home to Bridget [his wife].

Important personal ties—Old World friendships—kept M'Lachlan in Braidwood. "Pope says, 'Whatever is is right,' " he concluded. "So be it."

M'Lachlan, his name soon Americanized to McLaughlin, stayed in Braidwood and became a powerful figure in the weak and disorganized Illinois miners' unions. His early reactions to the Illinois mines, however, foretold little of his future career and suggested that he had put aside his trade union past and planned a life to honor Samuel Smiles and Horatio Alger. Because he brought so much practical experience to his work, McLaughlin's early comments deserve additional attention. In 1869, Braidwood miners earned $1.25 for digging a ton, 5 cents for every fifty yards they "drew it," and 15 cents a ton for "brushing the road." Like most other Midwestern miners, the Braidwood men had full-time work in the fall and winter months and half-time work at best the rest of the year. Such seasonal employment did not bother McLaughlin: a miner working full time in the winter ("if you be fortunate") could "make over one hundred dollars a-month, . . . and forty dollars, I am informed, can keep a very large family." In the summer, the miners worked half time but might average each month as much as $60. Work was irregular: "Some weeks you may get good work, and the next you may get hardly anything." The pace of work, too, proved especially irksome.

> No man likes to lose his turn, as you are not sure but it might be half a-day the next day; and if your side-road should fall through the day, if you cannot stow it at the face it must lie there till night, and then you have to come out and draw it. You will see what I have said that there is neither eight nor ten hours a-day here for the miner. All the day men, above and below, work ten hours. The truth is, John, when the work is brisk every miner in the place works as long and as hard as he can—digging and drawing coals all day and repairing your [*sic*] place three or four hours every other night; but this is only when the work is running brisk five or six months in the winter.

Hard work, however, did not deter McLaughlin. The probability of material improvement made such disadvantages mere obstacles to be overcome.

A few weeks after he arrived in Braidwood, McLaughlin joined the other miners there to celebrate Alexander McDonald's second visit to their village. McDonald had come again to America to "learn the institutions and . . . study the habits of the people." Much had changed since his first visit to Braidwood in 1867. McDonald saw many new faces among the Scottish miners and said of them, "They know best if the changes were for the better." Less than five years later, McLaughlin's and Allan Pinkerton's paths would cross in ways that told much about how New World experiences both altered and reaffirmed many immigrants' attitudes.[3]

In 1869, Braidwood, located in Reed Township, was only a few years old and already a booming industrial frontier village. While digging for a well on a newly settled tract in 1864, a farmer, William Henneberry, had accidently discovered a coal bed. Although successful coal mining had started in the 1850s in LaSalle County to the west, and Joliet was a thriving city to the north, the Wilmington coal bed lay under a desolate land mass "considered worthless with only a few farmers who were almost starving." Except for William Smith, a Vermont Yankee who hunted and whose home was "wherever his dog and gun could be found," most early settlers were Irish immigrants— men like Dennis Glenny, who worked first as a stonecutter on the Illinois and Michigan Railroad, and James Curmea, the first farmer, who traveled as a peddler before purchasing land for $1.25 an acre in 1849. The region attracted few others until the discovery of coal. "Nothing," said a Chicago mining engineer, "could be seen but a bleak prairie, dotted here and there by small groves of stunted trees, the monotony being broken occasionally by a chain of sand hills." The Wilmington field reached west from the southwest corner of Will County into Grundy and Livingston counties, and together with the LaSalle County mines made up the northern Illinois coalfield. The Scot James Braidwood, in America since 1863, sank the first coal shaft in 1865 and gave the town its name. The Chicago *Workingman's Advocate* called him "the pioneer of the prairie."* C. D. Wilbur, the Illinois state

---

* Braidwood became a pit boss and later ran a small mining company that carried his name. He was not connected with the larger absentee firms in any "pooling" arrangements and apparently sold most of his coal to Chicago's Bridgeport Rolling Mills. The entire city mourned his unexpected death in 1879. Daniel McLaughlin joined the *Joliet Sun* in celebrating his importance. "He built the first house in Braidwood," said McLaughlin of his fellow Scot, "sunk the first coal shaft, his wife had the first child born, and the first child to die in Braidwood was his." (*Joliet Sun*, 3 Feb. 1879; *National Labor Tribune*, 15 Feb. 1879; August Maue, *History of Will County, Illinois* [Indianapolis, 1928], 347.)

geologist, and four associates leased some Wilmington coal land but sold it in 1866 to the Chicago and Wilmington Coal Company, a firm composed of Chicago and Boston capitalists. The C & W bought a section of land for $120 an acre and in 1867 started active mining. A town grew so rapidly that a Will County historian called its development "a wonder," even "a marvel." Andrew Cameron, the Scottish editor of the Chicago *Workingman's Advocate*, visited there the first year and found only "a few scattered cottages." But rapid exploitation of the coalfield soon had so transformed the empty prairie that in 1873 the *Advocate* could tell of "the almost marvelous growth of this thrifty village (beg pardon, city)."

Building its own branch railroad to connect the mines to the Chicago, Alton and St. Louis Railroad, the C & W invested $475,000 in its Braidwood operations in twenty-four months. "Other men of capital" saw promise in its "extraordinary profits," and a second company, the Diamond Coal Company, started in 1870. In the following five years, three other firms—the Eureka (soon the second largest), the Wilmington Star, and the Braidwood Coal Company—commenced operations. The Wilmington coal bed promised quick returns to investors. A mining engineer figured that the soft nature of the measures and the moderate depth of the coal seam meant that "a vigorous prosecution of operations" would allow operators to pay expenses, if not show a margin of profit, within six months from the date of breaking ground. Little villages—Coal City (buildings went up "like magic" there in 1874) and Diamond City—sprang up a few miles west of Braidwood. The entire field thrived because no other was as near to the expanding Chicago market, and Wilmington coal went there and to other markets in northern Illinois, Iowa, Michigan, and Wisconsin. Of inferior quality to the Eastern coal that was shipped west mainly across the Great Lakes, the Wilmington product, though it had less generating power, was nevertheless useful as steam coal and in locomotives, and much went to Chicago to be "sold uncleansed of sulphur and slate" to those not able to "afford the better qualities of Pennsylvania coal." Contemporaries called it "the poor man's coal," but production boomed and, almost overnight, Braidwood became a major Midwestern mining field. Its rate of expansion was phenomenal: in 1866, the Braidwood mines shipped 10,000 tons; in 1869, 265,000 tons; in 1872, 460,000 tons. Two thousand tons left Braidwood each day in 1873.[4] In less than a decade coal mining had transformed the prairie.

In 1871–1872, the Chicago and Wilmington Coal Company secured control of the Vermillion Coal Company in Streator (LaSalle County) and was reorganized as the Chicago, Wilmington and Vermillion Coal Company, capitalized at $2,000,000 and by far the largest Illinois mining corporation (and quite possibly the largest mining corporation west of Pennsylvania). The CW & V drew capital and corporate leadership from the East and dominated coal mining in Will, Grundy, and LaSalle counties. In 1873, its Braidwood and Streator mines produced just over half a million tons of coal. Its five Braidwood shafts gave work to more than half of the city's 1,665 miners in 1876, and of the nearly $1 million invested in local mining enterprise, more than half belonged to the CW & V. In 1874, all of the CW & V decision-makers lived in Wilmington, a pleasant nonmining town a few miles from Braidwood. James Monroe Walker, who headed the company from 1866 to 1880, busied himself with many other corporate matters. A Chicago resident since 1853, Walker served as attorney for the Michigan Central Railroad, later acted for Boston investors in purchasing the Chicago, Burlington and Quincy Railroad right-of-way, served as that company's president between 1870 and 1875, and helped organize the Chicago and Kansas City stockyards. Walker even found time to serve as president of Chicago's Union Stock Yards Company. His financial support came from the East, from those Boston financiers who invested heavily in Western railroads, coal mines, and other new industrial enterprises. A Boston capitalist, Francis Bartlett, replaced Walker as CW & V president in 1881, and the Nathaniel Thayers, father and son and major managers of the Boston banking house later called Kidder, Peabody and Company, served as company directors for thirty-six years. Such connections later caused an angry Henry Demarest Lloyd to charge that Braidwood "babies and men and women wither away to be transmigrated into dividends of a millionaire coal-miner of Beacon street, Boston."

Alanson W. Sweet, the CW & V general superintendent, who also lived in Chicago, came not from Boston but from the Michigan Central Railroad, where as superintendent in 1862 he had imposed a wage cut and altered traditional methods of paying engineers and firemen. Before then, the "time" they put in, not the distance they traveled, had determined their pay, but Sweet preferred payment according to the "run" ("piece rates"). Disaffected engineers and firemen accused Sweet of encroaching upon "established rights and usages," but he fired them and even hired some black firemen in their places (causing a small number of railroad engineers in 1863 to found the Brotherhood of the Footboard, a craft organization soon renamed the Brotherhood of Locomotive Engineers). When he became CW & V general superintendent, Sweet brought with him experience as a manager of men and helped order and discipline the expanding labor force of a new mining corporation with a power that amazed contemporaries. "In traveling over this great coal prairie," a *Chicago Tribune* reporter (1877) felt it was "impossible to escape the [Chicago,] Wilmington, & Vermillion Coal Company, which haunts every one everywhere with a persistence equal to the albatross in the 'Ancient Mariner.' Unlike that celebrated fowl, however, the omens are tangible."[5]

Little is known of the men, mostly Scots immigrants, who pioneered as coal miners on the Illinois prairie. A few letters and some poems (these mostly from leaders among the miners between 1867 and 1870), along with the descriptions of isolated meetings, survive to tell something of their thoughts, their feelings, and their aspirations, and it is hazardous to infer too much from these scant sources. But they do make it clear that the "frontier" experience did not cause a sharp break with the past. The reverse may have been the case. Because the miners lived in relative social isolation but dealt each day with a powerful modern corporation, Old World traditions—a curious mixture of Chartist ideology, post-Chartist "new model" trade unionism, pride in craft, and an ethic that emphasized benevolence, self-help, and mutuality and drew heavily on perfectionist and postmillennial Protestantism—became more intense and deeper to them. Their experience in a changing America, the Great Republic of the West, sharpened these feelings.

John James, a leader among the Braidwood miners, fancied himself something of a poet. He had been a ten-year-old with but four years of formal schooling when he entered the mines in Scotland. His poems have a simple meter and a commonplace structure, but they tell much about the thoughts of a Scots miner fresh to the prairie. In one poem, James celebrates ties to the "old country" and "friends left behind":

> Our spirits when bent 'neath the burden of life,
>   And the many reverses we find,
> That are still to be met 'midst the trouble and strife
>   Of the world far from friends left behind.
>   .   .   .
> Good bye, then, dear friends, although absent
>   from thee,
>   And between us the wide ocean's foam,
> Still it cheers us to hear, or by letters to see,
>   That 'tis well with you all left at home.

Another poem, penned during Braidwood's first, bitter strike in 1868—which resulted in the eviction of James and other miners from company-owned houses—is entitled "An Address to Hope." It makes no reference to the strike, but betrays in every stanza a deep-felt tension between hope and despair, expectation and frustration:

> . . . I must
> Still pursue thee, even thou doest
> Repel, reject, and cuckold make of me.
>
> . . . For thou are my life,
> And I must hang upon the veriest fold
> Of thy most holy robe. And though aware
> That thou has't played me false, and oft
> Hath led me in the paths, which thou didst say
> Would lead to truest happiness.
>
> . . . Thus thou dost
> Still play the double part:
> A ministering angel, yet an arch deceiver,
> Leading me on promised joys. And when
> Their realization seems within one's grasp,
> They prove to be illusions.[6]

A perfectionist Protestantism emphasizing secular good works, self-sacrifice for others, and a continued concern for the common good (all men were the children of God and therefore brothers) saturated James's prose and poetry. His prose sentences, often Biblical in structure, emphasized duty to man and urged organization: "Put ye into motion the one, the five, the ten talents, God has given you. . . . Then might you reform the world so as never to allow the oppressor's heel once raised to fall"; "Gird ye on your armor and be ye as one also; let there be no divisions amongst you. For in that lies your destruction." Millennial hope offered solace after the death in 1869 of William Sylvis, then America's leading trade unionist and head of the National Labor Union. Biblical example promised that others would take up where Sylvis, "The Fallen Chieftain," had left off.

> But on some Joshua may
> The heavenly command,
> Devolve to lead the way
> Into the Promised Land.
> Or, as on Elisha, may
> The inspired mantle fall
> Upon some *one* to-day
> Designed to lead us all,
> Unto that great and
>   happy goal
> That SYLVIS meant was
>   for the whole.

POWER & CULTURE

The failure of the British miners to help Alexander McDonald win election to Parliament caused James to warn: "A day of retribution I fear will soon overtake them." Another time, anxious to spur self-esteem among the Illinois miners, James advised: "God himself labored six days and rested on the seventh day, and . . . our blessed Savior plied his time as a carpenter."[7]

William Mooney and an unidentified miner's wife, writing in the *Workingman's Advocate* in 1868, shared James's perfectionist imperatives. "The line of duty," said Mooney, a miner soon to become a lawyer, "is visibly marked that all may see it." In Mooney's view, strong trade unions would allow miners to "realize what every honest working man has hoped and prayed for, and what Burns, the poet, has beautifully said in a seemingly prophetic language: 'Let us pray that come it may,/ For come it will for a' that, /That man to man O'er a' the land/ Will brothers be for a' that.' " Christian methods offered concrete ways to workers. "As the Catechism precedes the practice of Christianity," Mooney argued, "so must the necessity to organize precede the organization itself." And to one miner's wife, Christian ethics meant to "strive to do what we can to help our sisters and our brothers while we have an opportunity." She could even encourage her husband to "overthrow . . . politicians, land sharks and speculating gamblers, and [then] shine as pure gold."[8]

The religion and ethics of the immigrant miners had new meaning in America, and were expressed in several ways. The Civil War and the abolition of chattel slavery loomed large in their minds. "Slavery," a miner worried, "is planting itself in the North before it got cold in the South." James answered critics who called miners "*ignorant, quarrelsome, drunken*, and *reckless*" by cleverly accepting their judgment to compare this supposed condition of the miner to that of the freedman and then ask for help from "the Christian and the philanthropist to lead us out of our blinded state, [and] to make us partakers of all the privileges that a people's government can bestow." Congressional support for the freedman was seen as a precedent for similar aid to white workers:

> Can we not feel the consequences of the late rebellion in our unbearable taxation and debt; and was not the negro the cause? Can we not see the interference of Congress in their behalf that they might have justice done them—and why? Is it not because of their ignorance and inability to take care of themselves? Why was it that thousands of lives were sacrificed in their behalf? Was it not to cleanse a stain from the nation's honor?

A second theme insisted that impoverishment and unreasonable working conditions had no place in America. Bitter because he worked "long, long hours," James saw his condition as a betrayal of national ideals:

> I get up in the morning at 6 A.M., gets to work at 7, and don't return home again till about 6 P.M., sometimes later. Many there are who go to work at a much earlier hour, and don't return until 8 or 9 o'clock at night. . . . All this, too, in free America. . . . Yea, confined in the bowels of the earth and hardly ever to see the light of day, from Sabbath to Sabbath, was there ever greater serfdom? was there ever worse slavery?

"No," James answered, "never."[9]

James had paradoxical feelings toward America, but their origins are neither inexplicable nor obscure. In the United States less than three years, he nevertheless identified fully with its past and its patriotic heroes. But the world about him betrayed this idealized past. He transformed the mythic national heroes in ways that revealed much about his conception of America. In 1867, he worried that so many miners "consoled" themselves into "inactivity, apathy, and inaction" by saying, "I am but a workingman." James offered examples of workers who had "overstepped the narrow limits of custom and of superstition and . . . demonstrated to the world that the workingman saw with the same eyes, heard with the same ears, and felt with the same feeling" as those who enjoyed "the benefits of affluence and of state." "Our great men were but workingmen," James argued, and he cited Francis Bacon, James Watt, George Stephenson, Alexander McDonald, and Jesus Christ. America had its worker-heroes, too, and James's selection suggests how an immigrant miner and a labor reformer transformed national myths into class myths:

> We forget that George Washington left the plough to fight the battles of his country. . . . We forget that "Old Abe" Lincoln split rail fences, yet did he steer the helm of the nation through one of the most gigantic civil wars in the annals of history. We forget that "Ben." Franklin was but a workingman, yet does he stand as an ornament in literature and philosophy.

It hardly matters that James entirely misunderstood the careers of Washington, Franklin, and Lincoln; what is important is that he made special models of the nation's great heroes. Some months later, James penned a tribute to Washington on the anniversary of his birthday. In his poem, the career of the "noble Washington" typified the eternal struggle for "equality and right." James contrasted men like Washington with the "money-changers" who later betrayed the Republic, in order to argue that only "honest working men" could complete the work begun by the Founding Fathers and hasten the return of "the happy days of yore."

> Arise, corruption's in your halls,
> Usurpers settled there;
> While money-changers gold enthralls
> And binds them in its lair;
> Where legislation once so pure,
> From forth their portals roll'd—
> But now your interest's insecure—
> And bartered there for gold!
>
> Oh, for the pearly streams that flowed
> Through those old heroes veins;
> Whose honest hearts with ardor glowed,
> To break tyranic [*sic*] chains.
> Whose highest aim was but to serve
> Their country and mankind,
> And raise a structure to preserve,—
> All toiling sons should mind. . . .
>
> [James then described "gaunt destitu-
>   tion everywhere."]
>
> Republican and Democrat
> Are both within the house
> And in like manner as the cat,
> Treat you as the mouse.
>
> Arise, and round your platform, then,
> Come flock you, every one;
> Erect ye honest working men,
> Complete the work begun—
> So shall the happy days of yore
> More speedily return;
> When poverty is known no more,
> And fewer hearts shall mourn.

A secular myth paralleled the Christian myth, and though the young Republic had been betrayed, workingmen could assure its redemption. Such views about the Republic's decay were not unique to James and the miners. Five years after he wrote his poem, the *Joliet Signal*, a Will County Democratic and reform weekly and the county's oldest newspaper, lamented that radical changes in the "national life and character"—"the subtle but potent influence of wealth"—might cause America "to join the historic march of republics to the grave." An editorial entitled "The Olden Times and Now" expressed fears similar to those of James and also idealized the early Republic: "The Calf of Gold has been set up for public worship, and its devotees swarm through our marts and streets and capitols. Men are weighed by the weight of their purses. Old time ideas of happiness and domestic life have faded, like the mysterious disappearance of a dissolving view." Madison and Jefferson—and even Clay, Calhoun, and Webster—would have scorned Gilded Age America.

> Our country politically and socially is changing rapidly. Old forms, old manners, old ideas and old principles are being lost in the dimness of the past, and though they may there be entwined with beautiful and holy traditions, they serve little useful purpose now, except as landmarks to show the wide departure from them that we have made and are making.

The *Signal* urged readers to draw upon "the time honored forms of liberty . . . yet ours" to reverse these trends. A Braidwood coal miner said what mattered was the awareness that "the spirit of freedom is surely on the wane, as the once proud workman of America is fast becoming the slave to filthy lucre and the selfish propensities of his tyrannical and unscrupulous fellow man."[10]

Just as letters and poems told something of the Illinois coal miners soon after they arrived on the prairie, so did the special celebration— almost a ritual—that greeted Alexander McDonald on his first visit to Braidwood in October 1867. Braidwood was no more than a village, and its immigrant miners were still new to America. The gathering had religious overtones. About three hundred miners and their families, many of them old friends of McDonald's and all seeming admirers of the Scottish trade unionist, heard John James, William Mooney, James Braidwood, and six others (some with Irish names) offer a formal tribute to their visitor. Their statement attributed to McDonald values and ideals they cherished:

> It is not alone amongst the high in life, the titled and the wealthy that we are to seek for true nobility of soul. . . . Neither is it in the haunts of these only that we do find Benevolence, Charity, and Brotherly Love exercised to the greatest degree of perfection. No. Providence in that, as in her dispensations of the Seasons, sends them in her wisdom, in her justice, and in her equality, alike upon the lowly as upon the exaulted. Upon the unjust as well as upon the just. Upon the plain John with as much grace as upon My Lord Duke, and upon a son of Lazarus with as much honor as if bestowed upon heirs of a Rothschild, or of the Princes to a throne. We have seen these in the possession of a son of the mine, who peering up from the bottom of his shaft, through the clouds of obscurity, to

the pinnacle of fame . . . struggled and obtained the highest eminence. . . .

McDonald filled his response with allusions to broken family ties. He mourned their absence from Britain "as the loss of a brother, whose friendship I valued above all price." "Imperious necessity" had driven them from the old country; most, having "formed new habits and associations," would never return.

You from Ireland have left the traditions of your fathers; you from Scotland have left her glens, her heather and her mountains, and have found yourselves virtually strangers in a strange new land. Yet I trust you will become in your new homes a band of brothers and sisters, and raise a new colony which shall be known by your probity and good works; known equally as citizens of the land of your adoption, and the dear old land of your birth.

McDonald urged an ethic of mutuality and organization for self-protection. A strong benefit fund made every miner "a husband to the widow and a father to the fatherless." A strong union was "a bond of brotherhood." Cooperatives made possible "higher considerations than the mere acquirement of wealth—viz., the greatest happiness to the greatest number."[11]

The miners needed little urging from McDonald, since men among them had worked from the start to institutionalize that ethic of mutuality. "Benevolence," James argued in 1867, "thou bright gem of all the attributes of man—how much good might the world not derive from a more healthy exercise of thee; how much suffering might be allayed. . . . Ah, that the world could feel the truth of the poet when he exclaimed: 'By pride and envy we have been/ But strangers to each other;/ Yet nature meant that we should lean/ In love on one another.' "
Soon after settlement started, the miners set up a "sanitary fund" to aid the sick and disabled. They put aside 1 percent of their gross earnings each month to allow those "who from sickness or accident should be rendered unable to work" to be paid five dollars a week. The men later cut the contribution to fifty cents a month, and when they had sufficient funds to pick a physician "to attend on them exclusively," they dissolved it and turned over the surplus money to help finance construction of a schoolhouse. One time, the sanitary fund gave five dollars a week to a miner severely injured in a pit accident. The men helped him in other ways. One or another miner stayed with him day and night to see him through his recovery, and for a time, they hired a man to nurse him. When it became clear that he could not return to the pits, they raised nearly $500 to allow him to open a small business and thereby "make a livelihood and be

independent." Another time, the miners raised special funds for the widow of a murdered fellow. The spirit of mutuality that shaped these voluntary efforts also spurred trade union organization. Workers without unions, James argued, were "as a ship without its rudder, driven hither and thither with every wind and wave." Trade unions allowed men to "steer on direct to the grand object, moral and intellectual improvement." "With these," he believed of unions, "[the miners] fear not tyranny or oppression; without them, they live in continual dread. With these, harmony, love and kindness prevail; without them, discord, envy and selfishness is the ruling order of the times." James had a clear vision of the meaning of human existence:

> The end—the greatest happiness to all mankind on earth—
> No matter what his country be, or how obscure his birth;
> No matter what his color is, if he the impress bear
> Of man upon his forehead, let him each comfort share.[12]

The ideals workers expressed in prose and poetry were more than rhetoric. They were the outcropping of a complex system of social values, itself resting on the bedrock of a distinctive social structure. Work patterns, leisure habits, a network of voluntary associations, and much else knit together a common culture. Devices for self-protection were important, but by themselves did not give coherence to life. The social structure in Braidwood felt the miners' presence at all times and reflected it. First a village, Braidwood quickly became a town, even a small city. In its earlier years, many Chicago and Wilmington miners lived in company-owned houses, and the resident superintendent and his brother ran a general store, expecting employees to patronize it. Four independent shopkeepers failed because they could not entice away C & W miners. But rapid growth over a five-year period profoundly altered the early "paternal" village structure, and in 1873 Braidwood was anything but a company town. When the journalist Andrew Cameron revisited the region, the contrast after six years astonished him. Churches, schools, hotels, and retail stores had risen "as if by magic"; even a local bank serviced between 5,000 and 6,000 inhabitants. "This settlement," another visitor said a year later, "is quite populous and decidedly thriving over a large area. . . . The main street presents a solid aspect and shows that the people have come here to stay." Coal mining, of course, gave the town its distinctive character. A *Chicago Tribune* reporter stated: "This is emphatically a mining town. Without its coal shafts, it would have no reasonable apology for existing, since there is no agricultural neighborhood to give it support, as in the case with nearly all Western towns of its size." Even the town's architecture told that it was mining that counted most.

POWER & CULTURE

The coal firms sold land to miners and shopkeepers, but reserved the right to mine the coal beneath the lots. As a result, houses and stores were built entirely of wood. "Light balloon frames, which a settling of the earth would not injure, are universal," said a contemporary. In 1878, the city had only two stone or brick buildings: a schoolhouse and a bakery. Life and work centered about the mine shafts and along a single long business street with frame buildings and wooden sidewalks on either side. "Back of this street," a contemporary noted, "stretches an unregulated scene of cabins, cottages, and patches of prairie." By 1877, settlement had spread irregularly to the north and west of the main business street. To the west were "discernable the roofs of Diamond [City] and Coal City, clustered around the horrible black structures reared above the shafts that furnish a livelihood to the inhabitants." Although its majority worked in and around the coal shafts, the town had a thriving middle class. "The town proper—the business portion," noted the *Chicago Tribune*, "is garrisoned by a small army of shop and saloon keepers, grocers, tailors, shoemakers, and others, who may be called the camp-followers of labor." In the 1870s, the town counted at different times six newspapers: the *News*, the *Journal*, the *Republican* ("an earnest, live, and unterrified Republican journal, free and outspoken . . . and death to political stealings and unprincipled doings in general"), the *Herald*, the *Daily Phoenix*, and the *Daily Siftings*. So active a press in so small a city suggests a high level of literacy among its residents. Some of the newspapers had a brief life, but others survived for a longer time; none are extant. In 1874, the city had four schools and even more churches.* A single Catholic church was the city's largest, claiming (although it had a rapid turnover in parish priests) nearly 500 families and by 1875 a permanent church and parsonage. The oldest and largest Protestant sect was the Methodist Episcopal, which held its services in a schoolhouse in 1867, and two years later built a church capable of seating 250 persons and had a thriving Sunday school superintended by a prominent local merchant, L. H. Goodrich. A traveling missionary had sparked the establishment of the Presbyterian church in 1871–1872, and like the Methodist church it had nearly 150 members (one of them John James) and a Sunday school. A tiny Welsh Congregational church attracted twenty-five communicants to hear its Welsh sermons. The Primitive Methodists had a Sunday school and "a small house of worship, neatly furnished." Although a young city, Braidwood by 1878 already had an empty church building, erected and then abandoned by Welsh Baptists. Some residents were Mormons, Protestants who "cleaved to

* In 1876, the Braidwood schools and those in the west part of Custer Township nearby enrolled 1,188 students. (W. W. Stevens, *Past and Present of Will County, Illinois* [Chicago, 1907], 112.)

Joseph Smith" but disclaimed ties to the Salt Lake Mormons and "their pecular beliefs and practices." Except that they found the Book of Mormon "an additional divine revelation," a contemporary said these Mormons hardly differed from other evangelical Protestant sects.

The details of religious influence inside and outside formal church organization are difficult to discern, but the churches were active social organizations. In the fall of 1874, for example, the Presbyterian Church Society ladies gave a festival that raised $100, and regular Methodist meetings were "awakening the religious sentiment of the community." A reporter found the miners "not quite so noted for [religious] orthodoxy" but detected strong formal religious ties among their wives. The city as a whole, he insisted, had "seen and recognized the light of the Cross."[13]

The coal miners shaped Braidwood's style of life. It was not merely that the miners were the majority; most were also recent immigrants. In Will County in 1880 foreign-born adult males outnumbered native-born adult males by a few hundred.* Commenting on that era's Boston Irish, Oscar Handlin has written: "Unable to participate in the normal associational affairs of the community, the Irish felt obliged to erect a society within a society, to act together in their own way. In every contact, therefore, the group, acting apart from other sections of the community, became intensely aware of its peculiar and exclusive identity." Braidwood's immigrant miners also had their own distinct group consciousness and separate institutional life—as miners and as immigrants—but these separate strands were not swallowed up by the hugeness and diversity of an urban metropolis. Instead, Braidwood's modest physical size made them so significant compared to other local institutions that the miners' social organizations were often those of the city itself. Miners' children filled its schoolrooms, and miners' wives crowded its churches. A heterogeneous group, the British predominated among the miners: in 1874, about 50 percent of the 1,665 miners were Irish and another 25 percent came from England, Scotland, and Wales. The Irish at first were mostly Catholics, but then an increasing number of Ulster Protestants settled in Braidwood—enough to form "a strong Orangeman's lodge." Smaller numbers were French, Belgian, and Bohemian, and still others came from Bavaria and Baden, Italy, and the Scandinavian states; even Russia and Austria-Hungary caused a reporter to describe the town as "nearly akin to Babel of old as regards the confusion of tongues." Native-born miners,

---

* The 1880 census figures for Will County were: native adult whites, 6,802; native adult colored, 366; foreign adult whites, 7,764. Only in Cook (59,395) native, 107,718 foreign) and in St. Clair (6,800 native, 8,600 foreign) counties was the ratio of the adult foreign-born to the adult native-born higher than in Will County. (Illinois Bureau of Labor Statistics, *Second Biennial Report, 1882* [Springfield, n.d.], xxi–lvi.)

including a few blacks, added to the unusual diversity of the prairie labor force, but were a distinct minority. A visitor found in Braidwood every nationality "except the 'heathen Chinee,' " and William Mooney excluded only the Chinese, Japanese, and Turks from his list. Bohemian and German miners mainly inhabited Lower Braidwood. The Bohemians and Italians had supposedly come there first during the 1868 strike. But the British majority predominated. Local language patterns astonished visiting reporters. The *Chicago Times* reporter observed:

> It is curious to hear the "long roll" of Cork, racy of the shamrock, mingling in brotherhood with the damnable patois of Lancashire, the harsh tones of Llewellyn's countrymen, the liquid sounds of Italy (which melt like kisses from a female mouth), . . . the guttural of Germany, and the rasping utterances of Bohemia and the rest of the Slavonic nations. They are a picturesque, if rather poverty-stricken, mosaic pavement of far-assembled humanity.

A *Chicago Tribune* journalist found Braidwood had "a dialect peculiar to itself," and he had "some difficulty in understanding it." He called it "a cross between Scotch, South of Ireland, and Yorkshire . . . at times very broad and at others very flat." "But few, if any, of the local citizens," he concluded, "spoke straight English."[14]

Work inside the mines tightened family ties but weakened ethnic distinctions. The longwall advancing system of mining practiced in the northern Illinois coalfield meant that two miners and a "pusher" worked as a team in a particular "room" in the vein. Information on how miners related to one another in the pits is scant, but scattered evidence suggests significant patterns. In 1879, about 150 "children"— 10 percent of the total labor force—dug in the mines. A list of seventy-four miners killed in a severe flood in the Diamond pits in 1883 illustrates interesting ethnic and family patterns. Twenty-three of the seventy-four were related to one another in various ways: the list includes a father and three sons, a father and two sons, a father and his son and son-in-law, three brothers, two brothers, and four sets of men with the same surnames. The disaster took lives without regard to ethnic origin: of thirty-four married miners who drowned, sixteen were German, nine Scottish, six Polish, two English, and one Irish. The Diamond mine was the least productive in Braidwood, and this helps explain the relative preponderance of Germans and Poles among the dead. But the heterogeneity of the list also indicates that if the Diamond managers were typical, Braidwood white miners were not segregated ethnically in the pits. Work patterns therefore intensified family ties, not ethnic differences.[15]

Fraternal lodges based on ethnicity further cemented relations between Braidwood's miners. As in nearby Streator, "Each nationality has its society. The English have the St. George's, the Scotch the St. Andrew's, the Welch the St. David's, and the Irish the St. Patrick's." But whereas the voluntary associations of Streator fought continually, Braidwood was without such troubles. Lodges of the Ancient Order of Hibernians and Father Matthew's Total Abstinence and Benevolent Society also thrived, and in 1874 on Saint Andrew's Day the Scots formed a Caledonian Club "to keep alive and perpetuate the characteristics and genius of Scotland." The Caledonians celebrated Robert Burns's birthday by first listening to a lecture about the poet, then hearing recitations and songs by men and women, and finally dancing to a string band "with great glee and spirit till the wee sma' hours." The Scandinavians and Italians had their fraternal lodges, too. But not all fraternal and benevolent societies depended on ethnic ties. Braidwood had its Masons, three Odd Fellows lodges, branches of the Knights of Pythias (one called Saint Andrew's Lodge, another the Talmud Lodge), the Ancient Order of Foresters, the Free Gardeners, the Phil Kearney Post of the Grand Army of the Republic, and other societies called the Miners' Friendly Lodge, the Sons of Liberty, the Golden Rule Lodge, and the United Order of Honor. Miners belonged to all these organizations, and men of different ethnic origins often mingled in them. Although they organized impressive funeral rituals, these societies served festive as well as benevolent purposes. The Odd Fellows had a gala ball; a Free Gardeners' parade attracted much notice, its fifty members "wearing a regalia of blue and red, and white gloves, and carrying bouquets of beautiful flowers." These societies helped bind together the community. Despite its "incongruity of race," noted an astounded *Chicago Times* reporter, "interest unites the otherwise antagonistic community in one solid body." A *Chicago Tribune* writer agreed. "There is a remarkable unanimity among the miners," he concluded, because they viewed themselves as "members of a rude Republic . . . disposed to foster international sentiment to the extent of tolerating each other."[16]

Other ties knit the miners together, weakening the pervasive economic power of the Chicago, Wilmington and Vermillion company. The songs and poems that they shared were almost ritualistic in their function. In 1867 and again in 1869 when McDonald visited their city, they ended celebrations with men among them giving individual renditions of traditional songs. In 1869, a doctor joined eight miners in singing separate songs. Five years later, when John James left Braidwood to work for a new national miners' union, a celebration in his honor ended with songs and poems—miner John Young "sung 'Twelfth of April' [and] Mr. McLaughlin . . . gave in magnificent style 'The Workingman.' " Organized sports also meant much to the miners.

Quoiting matches regularly spurred rivalry among them, and in 1868 a Braidwood team, including miners, defeated Chicago quoiters to win $1,000 and the championship of the "northwest." Rivalry ended each year in early fall with a gala festival and competition for which leading townsmen contributed prizes (a silver jug, a table castor, a box of cigars, a fancy pipe, a can of oysters); "all enjoyed themselves and parted in the best of friendship." During a strike in 1874, the Stars of the Grove defeated the Nameless of Lower Braidwood 39 to 24 in a six-inning baseball game. Other miners found pleasure in pigeon and prairie-chicken shooting. A Fourth of July celebration in 1874 included baseball, football, quoiting, horse racing, leaping and vaulting, and footraces for old men, young men, and boys and girls. "None who witnessed the sports will doubt the patriotism of our foreign-born population," noted the *Joliet Signal*. Occasional newspaper notes told of cricket matches, but footracing attracted the most attention. In 1881 a 150-yard race between two miners brought out a large crowd of coal diggers. "It was a splendid race," McLaughlin wrote, "both men being in good trim and doing their best." The miners gambled heavily on its outcome: "Thousands of dollars changed hands. Some men are poorer but wiser, while others are richer and may act foolishly some other time." When one of the footracers, James Dinsmore (the miners called the young Scot "Dinger"), was killed by falling stone in a mine, McLaughlin said he "took great delight" in "a manly sport" but "never allowed it to interfere with his daily labor in the mines." If sports counted a great deal among the miners, and so did organized temperance. The Good Templars had three lodges and several hundred miners as members, including John James, the Worthy Chief. The Templars did more than preach moderation; they held dances. The miners had their own band, too. William Patterson founded the Braidwood Band in 1873, made up entirely of miners and "a feature of the town." Its members, Cameron boasted, "are all self-taught and have devoted every spare time to their studies."[17]

Relations between the miners and the merchants, shopkeepers, and professionals were neither distant nor difficult, and for several reasons. "It is asserted by friends and foes [of the miners]," reported the *Chicago Tribune*, "that very little unpleasantness has ever occurred between the miners and the trades people, although the latter manage to tax their customers pretty heavily." Miners and other workers entered the local middle class in such numbers as to dominate it, and many maintained ties with their fellows in the pits. Of thirty-five men known to be shopkeepers and professionals (most of them listed as "prominant citizens" in a Will County history published in 1878), twenty-five had started in life as wage earners, twenty of these as coal miners. In 1873, most were young men or just entering their middle years. The ages of thirty-two are known: twenty-four were under forty, and half of these were not yet thirty years old. The shopkeepers were overwhelmingly Northern European immigrants, but there were exceptions such as L. H. Goodrich and Joseph Randeck. A Bohemian immigrant, Randeck was apprenticed to a tinsmith at age twelve, came to Chicago in 1865 to work at that trade for three years, and then labored in the Braidwood mines until 1877, when he opened a saloon. Goodrich, the town's first mayor, was about forty when he arrived in Braidwood in the early 1870s. Born in Chenango County, New York, he had crowded much into these four decades. His father was a carpenter and joiner as well as a farmer, and Goodrich worked on his farm until he started teaching school at age seventeen. In 1855, he moved to Illinois and taught school there. He farmed in Grundy County near Braidwood for seven years between 1861 and 1868, and then superintended a mine for six years. Grundy citizens elected him several times as justice of the peace and town supervisor before he moved to Braidwood to open his store. Four other merchants had agricultural backgrounds: Pennsylvanian John Shenk, who became a butcher, and three Irish immigrants—Thomas Hennebry, Robert Huston, and Cornelius O'Donnell. Hennebry and O'Donnell farmed with their fathers in Illinois before opening a Braidwood boot and shoe store and a saloon. Huston's father was a weaver in Ireland and a farmer in Illinois. Young Huston worked on the farm, taught school, and weighed coal before opening his store. Of the thirty-five merchants and professionals for whom biographical information exists, only five came from merchant or professional backgrounds. Two were physicians: one a Canadian (his father a lawyer), and the other a Frenchman (his father a "speculator") who had left his homeland to fight in the American Civil War, studied medicine in Chicago and Detroit, and actively aided the Fenian rebels. Ira Marsh and Joseph Donnelly were the sons of merchants and grew up as clerks in Attica, New York, and Durham, England. Both opened stores in Braidwood, as did French Canadian Moses Peletier, whose father had settled in Illinois in the 1830s to become a baker for a canal company, the owner of a hotel, and then a defeated canal contractor. Peletier's son began as a shopkeeper in Wilmington, shifted to Braidwood as a butcher, and then ran a boot and shoe store that also marketed flour and feed.

Most Braidwood merchants and shopkeepers in the 1870s came from the lower classes. Some workers opened stores, and one, a Michigan blacksmith, started a foundry that supplied coal miners and made stove castings. English baker William Carlisle had worked in Canada, Chicago, and Wilmington before opening a bakery in Braidwood. Another English immigrant, Henry Parkinson (born in London), had also traveled widely before settling there. Apprenticed to a printer at age eleven, he worked at the craft in St. Louis, Joliet, and other Illinois cities and edited the *Bloomington Anti-Monopolist* (a Granger weekly) before purchasing the *Braidwood Republican* in the mid-seventies. Irish immigrant John Ward had worked as a mason (like his father, who had labored on the Erie Canal) and also as an agent for national insurance companies; his fellow countryman Thomas Connor had had many jobs before becoming a Braidwood butcher, having worked on a Vermont railroad, in a Joliet woolen factory, as a canalboat driver and station agent, as a coal miner, and finally as a farmer who specialized in butchering. An urban retailer, he nevertheless owned 800 acres of land. Among the twenty miners in retail enterprise not one was native-born: two were English, one Welsh, a few Irish, and the rest Scottish. Seven had started in the mines between the ages of eight and ten. Their careers varied: some came directly to the Braidwood mines; others worked their way West from mine to mine. John James (who opened a general store and steamship agency in the early 1870s) and William Steen and John Young (they started stores in 1877) went directly from the mines into retail enterprise. Peter Barr ran a saloon and then a drugstore. Robert Burt went from a restaurant to a saloon. Andrew Benny opened the first hotel (probably a boardinghouse for single miners) and then moved to Missouri. Another hotelkeeper ("doing well") had been a coal miner in Connellsville, Pennsylvania. Physical impairment forced some miners to become merchants. John Bambrick dug coal until 1872, when a steam car cut off his right arm; he then opened a saloon. Nine years later, Dennis Dougherty quit the mines for health reasons and started a grocery "well patronized by his fellow workmen." A shrewd shopkeeper, Dougherty kept a wagon to deliver goods. He also kept close ties with the miners' union; this miner-*cum*-grocer accompanied two Indiana union miners on a trip to seek strike funds from Braidwood workers and merchants.[18]

The county and city courts as well as the local political structure were dominated by the immigrant coal miners and their merchant and professional countrymen. The 1874–1875 Will County grand jury panel included the name of Finley Littlejohn, an Ayrshire Scot who worked five years as a miner in Braidwood, and many other men with British surnames. William Mooney, a lawyer, remained an active labor reformer and trade union enthusiast and was elected justice of the peace in 1870. Four years later, he gained office as Reed Township supervisor. The miners called him Squire Mooney. Not all the miners who became storekeepers remained as close to the pits in sentiment and politics as Mooney, but when Greenback-Labor politics stirred the miners between 1873 and 1882, they found friends and candidates among miners who had become successful shopkeepers. Saloonkeepers Bambrick and Randeck, furniture dealer Patterson, and shopkeeper Wakefield, among others, supported them and got their votes when they stood for local office. An observer said of the miners that they "eschew political prejudices for the common good." A critic, however, complained that merchants, often candidates for public office, needed their votes and competed crudely to "secure and retain the good will of the miners." Whatever the truth, no one doubted that miners affected the style of political rhetoric as well as day-to-day political decisions. Braidwood was incorporated as a city in March 1873, and the next month saw its first election for city (not township) officers. L. H. Goodrich, the Republican candidate, won as mayor by twenty-seven votes. In that context and others like it, the individual decisions of immigrant miners counted for much. And the miners did not back away from exercising political duties. According to one contemporary estimate, about 1,000 Braidwood residents (mostly miners) were eligible to vote in the mid-1870s; in one crucial election, no less than 940 ballots were cast.[19]

Besides their involvement in business and civic affairs, widespread home ownership also rooted the coal diggers in their new community. According to one contemporary, the CW & V "offered each man with a family an acre of ground and encouraged them to build houses on the land." In this way, the company "permanently *staked* down" its labor force. Miners resisted this, however, and instead purchased house lots, and the *Chicago Tribune* praised them for having "succeeded in saving enough from their hard earnings to buy . . . little homesteads." Some married miners lived in company-owned houses and single men found lodging in private or company boardinghouses, but larger numbers of married miners either owned their own homes outright or made mortgage payments regularly.* Miners' houses varied: some

---

* Home ownership among miners also was widespread in Streator, and a careful report to the Illinois Bureau of Labor Statistics (*Third Biennial Report, 1884* [Springfield, 1884], 432–4) suggested patterns of home ownership that probably applied to Braidwood:

> The type of miner's house most frequently met with is a one-story frame, painted and plastered cottage, standing on a lot 50 × 150 feet deep. The house is commonly about 16 × 24 feet, with an addition about 12 × 14 feet. This class of homes will perhaps have an average value of about $500. The number of miners who own their homes here is very large, and an observant stranger would deem it very remarkable. It is partially accounted for by the system of buying lots by installments which prevails here, and which allowed early settlers to purchase before land became too high. This practice of the early miners has become a custom, and now most industrious miners try to get a home of their own, and stop paying rent as soon as they can. Out towards the suburbs the lots are larger, some miners having two or three acres which they cultivate during the summer. There are also miners' homes which would sell for $1000 or $1500. Their furniture usually consists of tables, chairs, bedsteads, sewing machine, bureau or stand, sometimes a rag carpet, and pictures and other

were "quite comfortable" and "beyond mere shanties"; others were "rough, unhewn tenements, bearing a striking resemblance to log-houses in the backwoods." Small produce gardens attached to many of these "homesteads" added supplementary income to unsteady wages. The importance of land and home ownership among the miners cannot be overstated. A list of property-tax payers for Reed Township in 1882 or 1883 included the names of almost all important leaders of the miners' union and other important figures in the miners' community between 1869 and 1880. Real estate ownership gave these men a stake in their community, freed them from total dependence on the companies, and encouraged stability by tieing the community's working-class leaders more firmly to the town. But it did not make them more conservative, as property ownership sometimes does. It is quite possible that home ownership had the opposite effect because these miners had more to preserve than just wages or working conditions.*

Other evidence of material well-being impressed contemporaries. The "typical" resident miner also seemed well-fed; at least, a careful reporter thought so and concluded: "The average miner keeps a very fair table—not many luxuries, but plenty of wholesome, solid food." Only his habits of dress disturbed the journalist: "He neglects his wardrobe with almost barbaric indifference." Clothing remained a visible badge of working-class status: "He has no use for fine clothes, and is satisfied after his hard work is over to put on fresh, dry, coarse underclothing and the common blue blouse, which is the favorite uniform of most laboring men."[20]

Braidwood's social environment and its Scottish and English miners encouraged the slow and at first ineffective development of trade union organization. A combined lockout and strike in 1868—when Braidwood still was a tiny village, and the Chicago and Wilmington did not yet own the Streator mines—showed the miners' early weak-

---

common household goods. There are cabinet organs in a number of miners' houses, and two or three pianos. . . .

Streator also had a building and loan association. Sixty-eight miners out of 2,000 men employed in and about the mines belonged to it. The Bureau of Labor Statistics also noted that in one bank eleven miners had favorable balances ranging from $10 to $400 and that a second bank listed about fifty miners with balances from $15 to $400.

* Quite origi l and important evidence on property ownership by workers is found in Stephan Th strom, *Poverty and Progress: Social Mobility in a Nineteenth-Century City* (Cambridge, Mass., 1964), 115–65. I am not sure that such ownership automatically encouraged "social stability" and tied workers to the American Dream in the ways that Thernstrom brilliantly suggests. We remain in debt to Thernstrom, however, for posing for the first time the critical relationship between working-class mobility patterns and ideology.

nesses. On December 1, 1867, C & W president Walker agreed to pay the miners $1.50 a ton for the entire year and extra monies for "pushing" (moving) the coal to the mine face. The following March, however, the C & W superintendent closed the mines for three weeks and announced a cut in ton rates to $1.25, a drop in payments for "pushing," and a larger screen. About 150 men refused to return to work, and a strike followed the lockout. "Capital," John James complained to the *Workingman's Advocate*, "is fully arrayed against labor . . . the whole system is rotten to the bottom." James complained with reason. The company refused to compromise, brought workers from Chicago (mostly Germans, whom James called "Dutchmen" and "nothing more nor less than BOILS, *scabs*, and putrifications, that afflict the toiling masses of every clime and every nation"), and served eviction notices on miners living in company-owned houses. A lawyer advised the men that such eviction was "entirely illegal," and the miners refused to quit the houses. A court order, however, upheld the company because the miners had not signed house leases even though the C & W deducted rent from their monthly wages. In early August thirty miners were still holding out, but they found little support and finally accepted company terms. The C & W refused them work and evicted James and eight others. "I have to-day everything packed, and . . . am now only waiting for the arrival of the officer of the law to have us turned on to the streets," James reported, and he made his feelings clear. Although opposed to strikes as wasteful strategy, he would not give in to the company's demands. "Let me tell the Chicago & Wilmington Coal Company," he publicly announced, "that they may drive me from their services—they no doubt can do without me, and I without them—but whether I work for them or not, they can never control my opinions, nor stay my tongue, my brain, nor pen." James stayed on in Braidwood and a few years later opened his general store. Men like him joined with southern Illinois miners (the American Miners' Association had thrived briefly there during the Civil War) to lobby vigorously against well-organized operator opposition for the passage of Illinois's first mine safety law in 1872.* A year before,

---

* The southern Illinois miners were most responsible for the first mine safety laws. In 1870 the St. Clair miners sent John Hinchcliffe to the Illinois Constitutional Convention, where he argued successfully for a constitutional clause obliging safety legislation for miners. Then the miners elected Hinchcliffe to the state assembly and the state senate. In 1872, Hinchcliffe pushed through a weak mine-inspection law. Organized pressure against safety legislation came from the operators, including the CW & V. In early January 1872, the operators jointly petitioned the legislature against such regulations because they were "burdens and restrictions to cripple if not destroy" the Illinois mining interest. They called systematic mine inspection and escapement shafts "unjust and oppressive" regulations that would "work financial ruin to the owners of mines." The state, they argued, needed to "nurture," not regulate, "an infant industry." Their pressure resulted in a weak safety law. Mine inspectors were not examined by mining

POWER & CULTURE

Braidwood miners and the southern Illinois men had organized for Illinois, Indiana, and Missouri miners the weak Miners' Benevolent and Protective Association of the Northwest. John James, elected its first secretary, held that position until January 1874, when he left Braidwood following his unanimous election as national secretary of the new Miners' National Association. Three Braidwood miners (McLaughlin, Frank Lofty, and John Keir) accompanied James to the MNA founding convention in Youngstown, Ohio, and were the only Illinois miners there. McLaughlin won a place on the executive board. Before that time, he had helped James spur trade unionism among the Braidwood miners. James represented them in all district and regional meetings and was "always . . . the mouthpiece of the miners." McLaughlin worked closely with James and presided over District Four, a region that covered Will and La Salle counties. When James departed for Cleveland, the miners packed a new schoolhouse to lament his loss and to celebrate his place in their community. "Squire" Mooney, district president McLaughlin, and Chicago editor Cameron told of his "seven year's service to the miners." The large gathering expressed regret at "his loss (socially) to this community," and said James had earned their "esteem" for "his moral and social qualities as a citizen and for his steady and persevering effort in behalf of labor and especially . . . [the] miners." James responded that he had only done his "duty" and that his "heart was in the movement."[21]

In its first years, the Braidwood union made little headway against the Chicago, Wilmington and Vermillion, a powerful and uncompromising adversary. Although it paid high wages by contemporary standards, the CW & V demanded absolute compliance from its workers and rejected all efforts at collective self-protection. The complex environment of the town protected the miners from absolute social domination by the company, but company officials rigorously enforced harsh and arbitrary work rules and struck down efforts at self-help. In 1869, the miners started up their sanitary fund again, and each miner contributed one dollar a month to pay sickness and funeral

engineers but chosen by county supervisors. John James called the final law "nothing short of a gigantic humbug, a huge injustice . . . and a grand farce." On March 30, Braidwood miners heard Hinchcliffe and thanked him publicly for his efforts in their behalf. The miners urged the election of laborers to the legislature and demanded improvement of the faulted law. Hinchcliffe, a West Riding Yorkshireman, had worked as a tailor in his youth before coming to America. The English Chartists influenced him profoundly. In America, he studied for the law, finally settled in Belleville, Illinois, edited the *Weekly Miner*, and espoused the cause of the American Miners' Association during the Civil War. In 1866, he presided over the first congress of the National Labor Union. (*Workingman's Advocate*, 3, 28 Feb., 30 March 1872; Andrew Roy, *A History of the Coal Miners in the United States* [Columbus, Ohio, 1906], 137–40; Edward A. Wieck, *The American Miners' Association* [New York, 1940], 14–16, 173–80, 193–203.)

benefits. The CW & V undermined their efforts by itself deducting a dollar a month from wages, and had its resident superintendent administer the fund. A miners' committee protested to President Walker and Superintendent Sweet, but found no satisfaction. The miners asked to see a monthly statement on how these monies were expended and to be allowed to administer the fund, but Walker and Sweet felt they could not be "entrusted with its control." The miners fumed. One called the action "a piece of petty tyranny" and "a high handed outrage." "He is it," this miner said in 1870 of the superintendent, "who says whether we shall have any money when we are sick or not, and even if our claims are admitted to be valid, we have sometimes to wait four and six weeks before we get them paid."* In addition, each spring the CW & V gave its men an annual contract to sign that lasted from June 1 to May 31. The other Braidwood firms did the same, but the CW & V had an advantage over them because it negotiated the Streator annual contract a month before the Braidwood contract and could play the men against each other.

The 1873–1874 Braidwood CW & V contract was illustrative of the attitudes of the company's managers and owners. Contract clauses required the miners to obey appended work rules and "all other rules and regulations promulgated [by the firm] from time to time," and allowed the firm "the privilege . . . of closing the mines at any time, or of reducing the number of miners by discharging them, or such of them as the Superintendent or persons having charge of the miners . . . may think proper." Miners might quit at any time, but had to vacate company houses and get their pitrooms "in good order and repair" before being paid. If the company fixed a working miner's "room," it deducted the cost from his monthly wage. Daily absence demanded approval from a company official. The men had to "perform a full day's work of ten hours" unless ordered to work less by their superiors, and no one would be lowered into the mines after seven in the morning without special permission. To quit during the working day was "positively forbidden . . . as such practices materially increase the company's running expenses and result in no practical good to any one." Arbitrary grievance procedures gave absolute authority to the company: miners could complain to the superintendent, but if they felt his judgment wrong "on any disputed point," they would be "required to quit the works at once." The company retained all control over the job.

---

* The miner complained of other deductions: "Two dollars per month is deducted from each miner to pay men whom they never employ, one dollar for blacksmithing, one dollar for physicians, whom they never appointed, and last of all one dollar for this sanitary fund over which they have no control, and a thousand other grievances I could mention."

No person will be allowed to interfere with the employers' just right of employing, retaining, and discharging from employment, any person or persons whom the Superintendent may consider proper; nor interfere in any way by threats or menace, or otherwise, with the rights of any employe[e] to work, or to engage to work, in any way, and upon any terms, and with whom he think proper and best for his interests, or the benefit of his family.

Furthermore, the contract included an explicit refusal to deal with "any committee purporting to represent any league, organization, or combination of workmen."[22]

Because the miners had inadequate bargaining power, the CW & V enforced its rules without difficulty until 1874. "I have lived a long time," a miner lamented four years earlier. "I have been in England, I have been in Scotland, I have been over a large part of this continent, and the treatment the men suffer at the hands of the Chicago & Wilmington Coal Company, I have never seen equalled." Petty abuses made work rules even worse, according to another miner:

It is humiliating to see how thing are managed in the works of the largest company operating here. One of the underground managers has an interest in two whisky shops in the place, one of which is kept by his son-in-law. Men who bestow patronage on these places are furnished steady employment, and good at that, while the good fellow, should he be Templar and Unionist, is ousted to make them room. . . . A fellow must needs only spend his surplus money in one of these "hell holes," denounce the Union, its leaders and its motives, and he is sure to get a place, should a noble-minded man who has done no wrong require to be turned away.

The absence of effective union power meant that the enforcement of company rules depended on the will of company foremen and pit bosses. It is not necessary to rely only on the subjective complaints of miners to reveal company attitudes toward the men. In 1877, a *Chicago Tribune* reporter could not restrain his shock and anger after a visit to Braidwood. The attitudes of company officials stunned him. Even if we discount his rhetoric, the essence of his observation remains:

It would indeed be a serious and awful error for the companies to admit that these miners were men, or that they were to be treated like human beings. A miner, according to official ideas, is a certain sort of mechanism gotten up by the Creator especially for the use of coal companies, not designed to be furnished with anything except physical powers, and whose duty in life is to dig coal, and be properly grateful for the inestimable privilege. He may eat and sleep, get married and raise children, be in every way an industrious and honest citizen, but all such little eccentricities are kindly ignored by the companies as long as he is promptly to work with the other mechanisms for that noblest of all achievements—keeping the coal market supplied.

"To barely intimate that the miner is a man who has rights that might be respected," the journalist concluded, "is to cause the cheek of the average Director to blanche with astonishment, and his hair to rise up on his head with fright."[23]

In late spring of 1873, the simmering disputes between the miners and the operators boiled over. At issue was the proposed CW & V contract for that year. About one thousand miners, many already members of the new regional union, gathered on May 1 to hear district president McLaughlin, Joliet labor reformer Obediah Hicks, and Richard Trevellick, the wandering Cornish ship carpenter, trade union organizer, and popular labor lecturer, urge the eight-hour "system." The miners shared their views and asked for even more. They challenged the established contract procedures and work rules in two ways: asking, first, for a board of arbitration made up of three district union men, three operators, and an "umpire" to deal with grievances and make "final and binding" decisions, and suggesting, second, that a joint committee of miners and operators draw up the 1873–1874 contract. The miners publicly opposed strikes, calling a labor walkout "a *dernier resort* . . . injurious to the best interests of the employer and employ[e]." But they firmly pushed the eight-hour day. "Experience . . . in the Old and New Worlds," their resolution argued, proved that "too long hours of toil" meant "social and moral degradation." A miner working twelve out of twenty-four hours lacked "the opportunities for social and mental improvement" and was without "the companionship of his family." Reform ("the rights of the producing classes") demanded "united action" because "individual effort can accomplish little." Not "sympathetic" to strikes, the miners took even bolder action: "Eight hours in actual work is sufficient for any man to labor, and we, . . . in mass meeting, pledge ourselves that from this day forth we will work eight hours only." No man would descend the mines before 6:30 A.M. or come up after 3:30 P.M. A special committee of five, including McLaughlin, Frank Lofty, and John Keir (names that would appear regularly in union activities in the following years), received instructions to report on the enforcement of this "edict." And the union planned weekly meetings. Fifty men joined the union that day; a week later, another thirty-nine came in. And, most important, all the mines worked eight hours. Without striking, but with an unusually firm degree of unanimity, the miners seemed to have won a victory.[24]

Their success, however, lasted only two weeks; the miners had not anticipated the CW & V's response. On May 17, just before announcing the new contract, the company suspended operations for a week so the miners could consider it. The contract included a ten-hour clause. "No deviation will be made from these terms," a posted company announcement made clear. "Don't subscribe to them with any mental reservations to violate them the first time an opportunity presents itself, as the company expect to enforce the agreement with every one." The miners resolved to stand firm and talked of resisting "by all honorable means." A committee told the company they would abide by the contract if they worked only eight hours. CW & V president Walker rejected its plea that he intervene, and the company reopened its mines. The miners divided sharply over returning: some quickly signed the new contract and started digging; others stayed away from a mass meeting called to consider strategy; the rest voted by ballot in support of eight hours and "no contract." But the vote was close, and many abstained. Divided in sentiment, the miners agreed to resume work on company terms. A few weeks later, the Eureka, Braidwood's second largest firm, ordered its men to work ten, not eight, hours, and they too gave in. The movement for shorter hours had failed. In the summer, the companies cut the men to five hours a day. A disillusioned miner admitted the union's inability to put "a muzzle" on the "tyrant." CW & V policies convinced him that large mining corporations meant to deny miners "the freedom the founders of this free Republic intended for all classes." These firms, "slowly but surely riveting the chains of slavery around us," were successfully eroding traditional rights "day by day, month by month, and year by year." George Kinghorn, a Belleville miner and president of the Miners' Benevolent and Protective Association of the Northwest, made the same point to the Braidwood miners. On August 9, the Braidwood Band led Kinghorn and McLaughlin through the main street to a grove, where the MB & PA president warned a throng of the deterioration of its status:

> Let me point out to you the standing of your craft in the old world, and ask you to compare with them yours. There, they have worked themselves up from a mental state of serf-dom—by the power of their Association. . . . Their government and the customs of their upper classes had assigned them . . . the lowest place in the structure—the Social Fabric. Here, under a system of Government, the justest, the best, and when properly administered admits of no inequalities, you, by your own conceit that your rights are secure, have slept until your names are mentioned only with contempt by those who employ you and those outside of you. Such is the place which this society has assigned you in this land which we are

accustomed to call "The Glorious Republic of the West"—"the Land of the Free."

McLaughlin and Lofty joined Kinghorn in pleading for strengthened organization and in reminding the recent immigrants that "our fore-fathers" struggled through a "dark, dreary winter" and then "won the glorious victory, placing the Banner of Freedom in the soul of this great land."[25]

Although the depression that followed soon after their defeat brought severe hard times to the miners, it did not destroy their union or their community. In the winter of 1873–1874, the demand for Braidwood coal dropped sharply, and the companies laid off some men and worked the rest half time. By March 1874, at least 25 percent lacked work, and the city was "dull without precedent." In May, the *Joliet Signal* reported from Braidwood: "The one universal cry in our midst is dull times." But the union held its strength. In October 1873, District Four voted unanimously to join the Miners' National Association. Nine lodges counted nearly 600 members. Three hundred others owed dues, but the lodges had a treasury of more than $500 in late December 1873. The district sanctioned a strike against a small operator who cut wages and whose mine lacked adequate escape shafts. It visited a hostile state attorney to press legal action against the operator for violating state law and advertised in the *Workingman's Advocate*: "Do not go to Braidwood unless you want to take the bread from the mouths of your fellow men." Increased unemployment led union partisans to urge collective solutions. James, not yet in Cleveland, advised men out of work not to drift around the country but to stay among friends and neighbors: "The money that will take you from Pennsylvania to Illinois or Indiana, or *vice versa*, will support you, if you are single, a couple of months; if married, something less, where you are. Where you are now, you are known, and have friends and acquaintances. Where you go to, you possibly have none. How can you hope to make things better—a stranger in a strange place?" James suggested "cooperation" as an alternative; miners needed to share work and unemployment in their time of trouble.

> Some men may ask "what would Mr. James have us do? We have no work—we have no money—we cannot steal—we must have bread. Yet he asks us to stay still where we are." To this dilemma I believe there is a solution, if the proper spirit be felt by the men. . . . The bosses, . . . as the sales decrease, . . . discharge so many men to correspond . . . giving all the work that is going to a portion of their workmen. I have suggested that the portion thus favored give a full share of their work to those of themselves who have none. . . . If they have four days work to do in the week . . . they

will arrange to let those who are idle work in their places a full share of the time. In times past, this has been done, and served the purpose well. . . .

McLaughlin picked up where James left off. He traveled to other prairie mining towns, urging firmer organization and more cooperation among the miners. In January, he chaired a miners' meeting that heard Trevellick plead for labor politics and compare the status of the Illinois miner to that of the antebellum slave. Less than three months later, McLaughlin arranged a great celebration to greet Miners' National Association president John Siney, then organizing in the prairie towns. Siney, McLaughlin, and Mooney urged the men to support the national union. And their pleas echoed those of an anonymous Braidwood miner who appealed to Illinois coal diggers to flock to the union:

It seems to be that the majority of our men to-day have no ambition whatever, no desire to better the class to which they belong, no wish to leave the world better than they found it, no desire that their posterity should cherish their memory by having them bless them for the good they would live to enjoy, if their parents would only unite with others. . . . They are dead to everything that tends to elevate themselves and others, dead to everything except the desire to obtain (at whatever cost to their health) the almighty dollar.

Too many miners lived only for themselves and wore out in a "weary round of life" that made "an old man" of a worker "in the prime of life." The miner was not "a beast of burden," but "a being . . . made in the image and likeness of his Creator," and his life and work demanded a different ethic. He urged his fellows to "come forward and assist in the glorious work of reformation."[26]

Opportunity for reformation arrived sooner than expected. After eight months of depression, the annual contract came up again for negotiation. The year before, the miners had suffered a severe defeat. Although they expected a wage cut for 1874–1875, notices posted on the pitheads by the CW & V and two smaller companies surprised them. A few days before June 1, the companies announced that the digging rate would be cut from $1.25 to $1.10 a ton and the rate for "pushing" coal from the work wall to the shaft entrance nearly by half. Rejecting negotiation, the companies promised to close their mines on June 1 if the men turned down the new one-year contract. But the miners overwhelmingly pushed it aside, and at a huge open-air meeting angrily accused the operators of taking advantage of the depression. In good times under the old rates, the men had trouble earning $1.50

a day; now, they said, it would be much worse. They nevertheless proposed a compromise: the stated reduction for digging but no change in the "pushing" rates. "While we concede that the exigencies of the present times may demand a reduction to some extent and for some time," their union said, "we do not admit nor cannot think it reasonable to make the present temporary lull in business the pretext for so large a reduction." The men feared a strike—"it is dreaded by all," reported the *Joliet Signal*—but many felt they might "as well . . . starve in idleness as . . . starve by oppression." The coal companies felt no reason to compromise and closed the mines on June 1. That day more than one thousand miners gathered in what was Braidwood's greatest meeting ever to hear John Siney—again organizing in Illinois— counsel patience, compromise, and arbitration, and to pick committees of miners to consult with company officials. The miners also heard speeches in French, Italian, and Bohemian from local leaders. A visit by the miners' committee to the Chicago residence of President Walker found him "out of town," and a conference with Superintendent Sweet disappointed the men because he rejected arbitration and offered only a blanket reduction of 25 cents a ton. The *Chicago Times* said Sweet showed "a haughty indifference as to whether the mines 'run' or not."[27]

Bitter at the closing of the mines and angry with Sweet's obstinate attitude, the miners withdrew their offer and voted, 552 to 93, to strike. Although Daniel McLaughlin warned that their walkout would last five or six months (until the brisk fall trade came), the men overwhelmingly favored quitting. The *Joliet Signal* found in their firmness proof that the strike bid to "far exceed anything of this kind ever before recorded in the history of the coal mines of this prairie," and a Chicago reporter predicted "one of the stubbornest" strikes ever among Illinois coal miners. McLaughlin defended the men and blamed the CW & V for the entire difficulty and for forcing the smaller firms to support its policies. Calling the Chicago company "right up and down monopolists," the Scottish miner complained, "They treated us with contempt." The men would not have received "worse treatment in the old country." Yet despite their anger, the miners continuing pressing for a settlement. The operators, hoping that the depression would wear them down quickly, rejected several compromise offers. They were silent when the *Chicago Tribune* advised arbitration, and an official, pushed by a *Tribune* reporter, said, "If we propose new terms, they shall be even lower." He denied the miners' complaints about inadequate wages: "That is all gammon. They can [live on the new wage scale] but they want too much." When Sweet offered his 25-cent reduction, McLaughlin accepted it if the rate would rise 5 cents the following winter. Sweet rejected this suggestion, arguing that high wages prevented Braidwood coal from selling in the competitive

Chicago market. "Let him show us the facts, and we will give him the prices that will enable him to sell as cheaply as any other," McLaughlin wrote the *Tribune*. Sweet did not answer. Instead, he labored to restrain the smaller operators. Alexander Crombie, the Scottish superintendent of the Wilmington Star mines, for example, favored "any rational arrangement" but was helpless because Sweet was "pretty obstinate."[28]*

Soon after the strike started, it became clear that more than wages blocked agreement between the men and their employers. The CW & V felt the time appropriate to weaken the new miners' union and brought strange workers and "special police" to the prairie town. Thousands of Illinois and Indiana miners were without jobs, and Sweet made "strong efforts to induce workingmen from other localities to . . . fill the places of the strikers." Private Chicago labor-contracting agencies also supplied workers from among the many Chicago unemployed, particularly unskilled laborers—most of them recent Scandinavian immigrants and none of them miners. Unaware of the dispute and unfamiliar with the *Workingman's Advocate*, which printed numerous strictures against "blacklegging," these men came, enticed by the high wages promised. Three days after the strike started, sixty-five Chicago workers arrived. More came two weeks later, and from then on a smaller number arrived each day until the end of July, when the number increased sharply. Other strangers poured into Braidwood. Even before the miners voted to stay out, the CW & V had hired twenty armed "police" from Chicago's Pinkerton National Detective Agency. William Pinkerton, the son of Allan Pinkerton, the firm's founder, accompanied them. The day after the walkout began, an old CW & V boardinghouse mysteriously burned to the ground. The cause of the fire was unknown, and a deputy sheriff absolved the miners, who blamed the company for starting the blaze to "excite the country" against them. The *Joliet Signal* agreed, insisting that the fire furnished a pretext for hiring more private police. Thirty additional Pinkerton men came, making fifty in all, armed with rifles and muskets to earn four dollars a day and board.[29]

The strike raised many difficulties for the miners. They needed funds to survive the crisis, and they had to neutralize their adversary's abilities to bring in new workers and special police. At first, committees went to mining towns nearby for money and goods, but so little material aid was forthcoming that the union organized a local relief committee made up of men from each of eight ethnic groups. "There is perfect unity among the different nationalities," reported the *Joliet*

---

* McLaughlin called Crombie "a good fair man." "God knows," Crombie, a former miner told a reporter, "I have no desire to tyrannize over these poor fellows. I worked underground for many a long year, and know how hard it is." Crombie's relations with the miners, however, deteriorated soon after the strike ended.

Signal. The new workers, for whom the CW & V build a special barracks, posed another problem. How could the Braidwood strikers prevent them from coming without violence that might cause state intervention? Peaceful street demonstrations successfully drove off many new hands. As soon as men arrived, McLaughlin sent committees of miners to call on them and explain the dispute. "We ask the skilled miners not to work," he said. "As to green hands, we are glad to see them go to work for we know they are . . . a positive detriment to the company." A committee met the first sixty-five the day they arrived, and all but three quit. The men lacked return fare, so the strikers and their supporters paid it. The miners' brass band accompanied them to the railroad station, and as they boarded a Chicago-bound train, "cheering and hurrahing [came] from a thousand lips." During the first weeks, the miners persuaded most new hands to leave their town. In mid-July, a shaft that usually needed 200 men counted 9 or 10 workers, and at that month's end only 102 men worked the mines. Not a single resident miner was among them.

The Pinkerton police offered a different challenge. Used rarely in the Illinois coalfields in these years (this may have been the first time), the presence of private police was new and unusual and viewed as a menace to the new town's social order. "The Wilmington Company," McLaughlin charged, "got up a 'hurrah,' just as if we were a lot of cut-throats, in order to get public sympathy with them and have a pretext for putting police over us." The miners found an answer: appointing a seventy-two-man committee to prevent violence and protect company property, they offered its services to the Braidwood mayor and county sheriff. These local officials, in turn, swore in twelve miners as special deputies, and the *Signal* said of this decision: "The lawfully constituted authorities . . . rule a police force selected from the miners, and maintain excellent order." And the rest of the strikers— except in one instance—were quiet and orderly. "Our police magistrate is obliged to sit in idleness, and our calaboose is empty," said the *Signal's* Braidwood correspondent. Another time, he insisted that only "an old sermon and a flock of geese" menaced the Chicago Pinkertons and that the city was "indulging in a long sleep." A *Chicago Tribune* reporter said Braidwood looked "as if it were tenanted by Quakers," and Crombie agreed. He did not hire watchmen to guard his shafts: the miners, he insisted, would "not harm anything" and "behaved admirably, all things considered." "I would not be afraid to trust them any time," Crombie affirmed, and local businessmen (even those whose credit arrangements suffered during the strike) and other nonminers joined him to testify that the strikers were engaged only in peaceful protest.[30]

A single serious incident marred the miners' orderly record, and it involved their wives and detective William Pinkerton. On July 7, the CW & V induced two pit bosses and two roadsmen to repair a mine shaft, and they agreed after assurance they would not be required to dig coal or "in any way . . . teach or assist the newcomers in mining." Pinkerton helped guard them. A crowd of women, mostly miners' wives, marched down Main Street ("merrily . . . with many a friendly whoop" according to the *Signal*), and then surrounded the shaft to denounce the four men. Correspondents for the *Chicago Times* gave different versions of the women's behavior but agreed about their anger. "On that evening," said one report, "the women of the city turned out with an American flag and martial music, and parading the streets expressed their indignation and disgust for the quartette in question. . . . When the storm of indignation burst upon the heads of these poor fellows, they grew penitent and have since respected the public feeling." Another *Times* correspondent told a more graphic tale:

> During the day, a large number of women surrounded the mine in question, and gave no icy expression to their indignation at the action of the said "bosses." Toward evening the amazons' mob increased, and when the offending bosses ascended from the mine a frenzied yell went up. . . . The bosses, of course, realized the situation, and beat a hasty retreat for their respective homes, closely followed by the modern "Florence Nightingales" of the coal city. Clubs were trumps, and the women held full hands. Some of the bosses escaped the wrath by taking leg bail; two were overtaken, caught, and severely beaten; one of them, a Mr. Hunter, was knocked down with a stone and then pounced upon and dragged some distance. Mr. Pinkerton, of your city, was on guard at the shaft and strove to stay the storm. He was struck several times.

The skillful sleuth "fought back by using the butt of his revolver and discharging one chamber." Later that night, Pinkerton boarded a Joliet train, "avowing with blood in his eye" to bring his assailants before the grand jury. A deputy sheriff dispersed the women, and they "quietly resumed . . . the celebration of the Fourth of July." A few days later, the sheriff arrested five male and thirteen female "rioters" and brought them before the Joliet circuit court. The sheriff rejected an offer of militia from the governor to help round them up, and in Joliet, the *Signal* noted, the arrested men did not "look like desperate characters, while the women were generally too delicate in appearance and of too modest demeanor to be classed as 'Amazons,' as has been done by certain correspondents and editors." No record has been found of their trial, and no other violent incidents occurred. The strikers and their wives regularly jeered, hooted, and cajoled new workers but restrained themselves in other ways with unusual discipline and much success.[31]

Braidwood's tiny middle class also affected the course of the strike in ways that frustrated the coal companies. It did not mediate between the disputants; instead, time and again, a small but influential group of merchants, storekeepers, and public officials interceded to strengthen the strikers. A Chicago newspaper said that local businessmen and saloonkeepers "all back the miners." Property owners denied dispatches that called the miners an irresponsible and dangerous "mob." One prominent citizen blamed the coal companies for creating "excitement so as to crush the miners" and said "public sympathy" rested "entirely" with the men. Braidwood's mayor agreed. "In fact," a special correspondent wrote the *Chicago Tribune*, "Braidwood is with the strikers root and branch." Readers of the *Joliet Signal* learned from its Braidwood reporter that "the universal opinion is that the men are in the right" and that "all . . . conversant with the true state of affairs" viewed the CW & V's action "as nothing short of tyranny." The Democratic but antimonopoly *Signal* regularly published Braidwood reports that entirely favored the strikers, and Braidwood's city and town officials weakened the coal firms in many ways. They let the miners talk freely with incoming workers, and the mayor and county sheriff refused a request by the operators to make the Pinkertons special deputies, "merchant police," with power to arrest persons trespassing on the companies' properties. A Braidwood reporter explained, "We have good material for policemen among our own citizens." Mayor L. C. Goodrich would not allow the Pinkerton men to parade in the streets, and the sheriff made them surrender their rifles and muskets. Fearing the miners "a good deal less than . . . the Chicago watchmen," the sheriff did not want "a lot of strangers dragooning a quiet town with deadly weapons in their hands." Goodrich supported the sheriff. "The miners," he wrote the *Chicago Times* in late July, ". . . have to a remarkable degree preserved the peace, and order has been maintained in our midst." A CW & V supporter especially condemned the police Goodrich appointed:

> They have . . . abused the power claimed by them, by overrunning the private property of the company, by going to all of the passenger trains . . . to either persuade or hire them [the new workers] to leave, and in several instances they have ordered them to leave, and otherwise attempted to intimidate them. We now refer to men *wearing the police badge of the city* whose duties are to protect all the legitimate industries of the place. . . . "City stars" have been numerous among the hooting crowds. This is what the mayor calls "peace and order," while the miners claim this is a "free country."

> We think the public will hardly agree with them in regard to what
> constitutes peace, order and freedom.

Other troubles plagued the operators, their "special police," and the
new workers who stayed on as "blacklegs." Judges and police officials
enforced local ordinances more rigorously against them than against
resident miners. Once three new workers, disorderly on a Sunday,
were arrested for violating the local Sabbath law and fined $50 and
court costs. Unable to pay, they went to work repairing streets, and
then Goodrich released them, finding their offenses "trivial." Another
time a new hand struck a miner (also a special deputy) and paid $10
and court costs. In other instances, Pinkerton men got fined "for
pushing intruders off the private property they were employed to
guard." One, jailed for hitting an elderly woman with a club in the
July 7 "riot," was charged with "murderous intent," found guilty, and
fined $100 and court costs. A company watchman, Michael Budd,
suffered most. Arrested four times—twice for "insulting" townspeople
and a third time for holding a revolver to the face of an Italian miner
(the court ordered him to post a $200 bond to keep the peace)—Budd
"ran away like a hired hand" after his fourth arrest.[32]

Frustrated by the public authorities and the miners in its efforts to
bring in new workers, the CW & V unavailingly shifted its strategy in
mid-July. Twenty-five Chicago men, mostly Danes and Norwegians,
arrived in an unusual manner: their train stopped at the depot and
their cars, shunted off to a side track and coupled onto a switch engine,
took them directly to a mine shaft. A few strikers met them and
induced seven to leave. According to a union miner, the defectors
complained: "When they came to the depot and saw so many idle men
around, they wished to get out, but . . . the company . . . had the
doors locked, and told the men . . . that if they did [get out] . . . the
men of this place would kill them." "You see what the company is
doing," said this miner, "bringing men under false pretenses, and
locking them in the cars . . . what I call kidnapping."[33]

An unfriendly mayor and a noncompliant police authority finally
forced the coal operators to seek help from the state government. At
the urging of the CW & V, Governor John Beveridge sent the state
adjutant general, E. L. Higgins, to survey the scene. Early rumors of
his coming caused the *Signal* to insist he would find a peaceful town
"with the majority of its inhabitants smoking or whittling wood."
Higgins arrived on July 13. Three days later, eight men climbed from
a closed boxcar at the CW & V's G shaft, and Higgins prevented
strikers from talking with them. Higgins angered town residents. One
joked that he came as the company superintendent's "guest." Although
he asked Mayor Goodrich to meet him in the CW & V office, he "never

went to see the officers of the city . . . to gain an unprejudiced account of the strike." Nor did he approach the union miners and their leaders. "He seemed to act as if in the pay of the companies," McLaughlin asserted, "and his mission appeared to be to assist in running in 'blacklegs' as we call them." The operators, however, found his presence "more valuable than a company of soldiers as the miners know he represents state authority." Higgins left the city on July 16 but returned three days later on a train that brought forty-two new workers. Twenty-seven went to the CW & V's G shaft, and the rest worked at the Diamond mines. But Higgins's presence proved of little value: the next day, seven G shaft workers quit, and fifteen Diamond laborers "skedaddled" after breakfasting with the superintendent. In addition, the miners and the town authorities lashed out at Higgins. One miner called him "Agitating General Higgins," and another blustered: "If this is what the military forces and officers are kept for, it is high time . . . such men [were] struck off the State Government payroll and placed where they belong." Goodrich reminded Higgins that neither town nor county authorities had requested state interference and assured him that the Will County sheriff would "render . . . any assistance necessary." In the *Chicago Times*, Goodrich berated Higgins for "giving orders that no man should speak with or to the men who come for employment. The citizens of this city were not aware that martial law had been proclaimed or an embargo placed upon their speech." The *Joliet Signal* echoed Goodrich's views: "The truth is the company has put in all the men they could induce to go to work and not one of them has been harmed or molested by the men. It is true they have been asked to stay out, but in this free country this was not supposed to be criminal." Mayor Goodrich worried whether Higgins had come to Braidwood "in his official capacity or as an agent of the coal company."[34]

Higgins's trouble added difficulties to the CW & V's ability to hold out, and in August the operators began weakening. In June, July, and August the company's Braidwood mines produced only 4,800 tons of coal; in these months a year earlier, the figure had stood at 43,500 tons. The dismissal of an unpopular underground superintendent did not appease the strikers, whose ranks increased to include most engineers, "top men," and "bosses." Dispatches emphasized the expenses the company incurred: one figured $500 a day, and a miner said the company lost between $10,000 and $20,000 each month. The inefficiency of many new hands added to this difficulty. Only a small number of the 200 or 300 "blacklegs" had been miners; the great majority, unskilled Chicago day laborers, could not prevent some mine shafts from falling into disrepair. And the new men were not without grievances: some left and others threatened to depart because they got inferior food and harsher treatment from their employers as the conflict continued. Although they suffered much privation, the union miners grew more optimistic. They believed that as the winter trade approached, the operators would need to commence production to hold a place in the shrunken Chicago market. "If we can keep all practical men out," a miner argued, "we will be able . . . to teach that company a lesson they will not forget as long as they are a company." The CW & V would learn its "folly and come to look upon . . . workmen not as slaves but as free men that have rights they are bound to respect." Sensing victory, the miners pleaded with Chicago's Scandinavian community leaders to "stop their countrymen from injuring us." In late August, they unanimously resolved to continue their walkout. But the miners had failed to reckon with the ability of the CW & V to fill its contracts from the Streator mines.* In early September, the miners negotiated a compromise with the Star and the Diamond firms: the wage rate fell to $1.10, but the companies did their own "pushing" from the working face to the pit bottom, thereby relieving the miners of poorly paid hard labor. A few days later, the union made essentially the same agreement with the Eureka and the CW & V, and the fourteen-week strike ended. The miners viewed the settlement as a victory, and drew a final concession: they demanded that all remaining new workers leave, and in mid-September Sweet shipped away the last of his Chicago men. The night of the settlement, the *Signal* reported, the miners paraded the streets and Braidwood was "jubilant." The following weekend beer, ale, and whiskey flowed freely, and the *Signal* just noted: "In fact, last Saturday and Sunday evening were rather wet." "Everything was carried on so smoothly," an elated miner boasted, ". . . that we can almost say it was a pleasure to be in the strike." The *Workingman's Advocate* compared the Braidwood men to ancient Romans and found their wives similar to the "Spartan mother, who told her boy to come home 'victorious or a corpse.' "[35]

Although their success stirred admiration in other Midwestern miners, the Braidwood men had even more power than their success against the Chicago, Wilmington and Vermillion Company and its allies suggested. Streator CW & V miners called their triumph over "a wealthy, powerful, and hitherto invincible opponent . . . a victory unparalleled in the annals of labor in the West." John James and John Siney found it proof that miners of diverse ethnic origins could "fraternize and work together for the general good when all are justly treated." In a circular addressed to miners everywhere they said, "Let

---

* In June, July, and August 1873, the CW & V Streator mines put out 35,500 tons; during the strike months a year later, they produced 62,500 tons. (*Report of the Directors of the CW & V Coal Company, 1881*, 6.)

those who become despondent because the foreign speaking people and the negroes in their regions cannot be made to join hands in the work of raising themselves in the social scale take courage from the Braidwood encounter."[36]

Despite severe obstacles, the Braidwood men increased their strength in many ways during the two and a half years of depression that followed their 1874 victory. And they did so in the face of recurrent unemployment, much plain hardship, and company policies that overstocked the town with men to fill rush orders, weaken fraternal sentiment, and, as a *Chicago Tribune* correspondent put it, "hold workers in constant fear of discharge." CW & V officials hoped that by controlling output they could discipline the miners. In the fall of 1874, the men worked half time at best, and when certain merchants served legal papers to collect debts, the *Signal* told of miners who had "a will but not a way to pay just debts."* Work picked up at the end of 1875, but the operators, hoping to force up Chicago prices, shut down three shafts, adding 600 men to the "already long list of idle men in this place." In January 1876, the nonminers—day laborers, trappers, and drivers—had their daily wages cut by 50 cents. "They have to submit or want of daily bread," said a sympathetic miner. The year 1877 found "many . . . leaving and many more [who] would leave if they could." Overall, the miners worked two-and-a-half days in the summer and four days in the winter. An experienced miner could manage two tons in ten hours of daily labor, so that summer weekly wages came to about $5.50. In the winter, a miner could put away about $8.80 each "week." Two Scottish miners, Charles Duncan and John Young, deplored their condition. Duncan said in 1877:

> I have been in Braidwood two years. I think the men will tell you that no more sober or economical fellow is living here than I am. I haven't got a cent of money today. I have earned $30 a month on the average, and I consider myself a fair workman. Before coming here I sailed on the lakes four or five years. I have tried to work steadily, and can swear that I never lost a day's work from my own neglect. There have been times when I have walked these streets for three months without work. The Wilmington Company has everything in their own hands. A man goes to work for them, and the first thing he knows the Company shut down the shaft, and he is thrown out together with 200 or 300 others. They treat us like brutes.

---

* Unemployment after the strike ended did not mean general stagnation. In the three months following the strike, twelve new retail enterprises, not counting saloons, started, and their presence spurred a price war between merchants that forced the prices of many items "below cost." (*Joliet Signal*, 24 Nov. 1874.)

John Young told a similar story:

> I am 37 years old. At 8 years I began to work in a shaft at Ayrshire, Scotland. I have been in Braidwood ten years. The condition of the men is not nearly as good now as then. . . . I am married and have four children. Living expenses are about the same now as when I came here, but the wages have been gradually going down, down, down, until they have reached a point that does not allow a man to live. . . .

"A bare living with the strictest economy in every household," reported John James in February 1877, a few months after he returned from Cleveland following the collapse of the Miners' National Association.[37]

Depression employment patterns, company production schedules, and the breakdown of their national union in 1875 and 1876 made troubles for the Braidwood miners, but their local union thrived and increased in effectiveness. This unusual paradox made the Braidwood miners the envy of bituminous diggers everywhere. By December 1874, they had separate lodges among the Bohemian, French, and German men as well as four English-speaking lodges; and that month 105 Italians formed their own lodge—"all eager to do what is right," said Dan McLaughlin. The miners worked to strengthen their organization. "Strangers" from distant regions who sought work had to produce a union card or "prove" they had never belonged to an American union and therefore were not fleeing from responsibility. Twice the 1874 contract came up for renewal, and each time the union bargained firmly and won a fair settlement. In 1875, the companies agreed to the 1874 contract, and the *Miners' National Record* cheered their "wisdom and business capacity," suggesting that such policies "always produce good friends." A year later, the operators favored a sharp cut in wage rates, but the miners forced a compromise and got a contract that lasted until May 1, 1877. Between November 1874 and March 1877, Braidwood was without a serious labor stoppage. Organized strength explained the miners' local successes as well as the help they offered less fortunate Western miners. In 1875, each Braidwood miner gave one dollar a month to assist Clay County miners in a long, bitter strike to preserve their Indiana union. In all, the Indiana men got $8,421 in outside help, and $3,143 came from Braidwood. The Illinois miners still found money to aid John Siney and Xingo Parks in their 1875 Pennsylvania conspiracy trial. "Their purse strings have never been drawn when their fellow craftsmen in other sections appealed to them for aid," said the *Workingman's Advocate* of the Braidwood men. "The miners of the prairie have set an example that others would do well to copy after."[38]

Among the considerations that contributed to the increasing strength of the Braidwood miners was the powerful influence exerted by Dan McLaughlin. "He has drilled and organized this conglomeration of races," said Harry Wallace, the *National Labor Tribune*'s traveling correspondent. "God speed you, Daniel—the right man in the right place." McLaughlin went to mining towns nearby and even to Indiana to spur union organization. After he visited the Clay County strikers, an Indiana miner explained: "Our friend has clear and comprehensive views, upon short hours of labor, and how to control the law of supply and demand." In Braidwood, McLaughlin frequently advised the miners of the "hunger and privation" other American miners "endured in the cause of right against might" and called it "the duty" of all to aid every miner engaged in conflict with his employer. McLaughlin had his own troubles. After the "memorable strike," the CW & V refused him work, punishing him, the *Workingman's Advocate* said, because he "had the brains or pluck to advocate the cause of the wronged." But the Scottish miner found jobs at other local mines— first at the Eureka and then at the Star—and earned enough to feed his wife and six children. Practical and moderate in his tactics and short-run objectives, McLaughlin was not an opportunist in his devotion to trade unionism, labor reform, and the ethic of mutuality. He spoke carefully, though from the miner's point of view, of the complexities involved in mining and marketing Illinois coal, and his mastery of such detail partly explained his preeminence among the miners. During a dispute in 1877, for example, McLaughlin told a *Chicago Tribune* reporter:

> The Wilmington and Vermillion Company pay $1.10 for digging, and 70 cents a ton for freighting to Chicago. The average daily production of the shafts is about 500 tons. I think that $100 a day ought to pay their running expenses, such as clerk-hire, etc. That would be 25 cents a ton, making in all a total expense of $2.05 per ton. They have taken several large contracts for delivering coal, that I know of, at the rate of $2.50 per ton. Even at that rate, there is a fair profit, as you see. This does not include the numerous sales made at higher figures, which they undoubtedly obtain. Why, then, should they come back down upon the poor miners? . . . They have got a man for Superintendent at a salary of $2,000 a year, and he is utterly useless. The entire work could just as well be done by Ramsey, the Assistant Superintendent. There is no use for more than one of these officials. . . .

McLaughlin gave no notice to company debts and other costs that plagued enterprises in these years, but his analysis reveals a man of more than ordinary intelligence. And his prose often suggests the influence of evangelical Christian imperatives. "Any man," he told

Wallace, "who starts out with the good intention of aiding suffering and enslaved humanity must be prepared to suffer as much as the Saviour did while sojourning on this earth." McLaughlin was not deluded into believing that trade unionists suffered only from harsh and uncompromising employers. Form the "days of the first reformers," labor leaders had as much trouble from "the calumny and lukewarmedness of the very men" they sought to protect us from "the persecution of the money changers." But neither obstacle deterred McLaughlin. "Hope and fight on," he advised Wallace, "must be the watchword until Labor is emancipated, and should we go down in the struggle, others will take it up, and so on till the day comes, as come it will, when Labor will stand free and unshackled from the power of the monied Kings." McLaughlin was not one to wait for that day to come; he worked carefully in planning stategy. In 1877, the editors of the *National Labor Tribune* urged a convention of soft-coal miners. McLaughlin disagreed: the miners everywhere were too poor and too disorganized to profit from it. Instead, he urged a full airing of the "labor question" through the press and suggested a general suspension of the entire bituminous region for four or five weeks or until the market was entirely cleared of coal. Then, but only then, he said, the miners should resume and "on the *eight hour system*." McLaughlin offered this strategy as one alternative among many others and made it clear that he would support any policy approved by "the will of the majority."[39]

But McLaughlin's leadership alone did not cause the success of the Braidwood union. A spirit of community and an ethic of mutuality extended beyond ordinary union matters and indirectly strengthened the union itself. Although it exaggerated and distorted what it observed, the *Ottawa Free Trader* grasped something of the ties that bound the Braidwood miners together:

> These Braidwood miners are about all foreigners—clannish in their ways and largely imbued with ideas that they bring with them from Europe of the necessity of strikes and violence to maintain their "rights." Decently treated—as they understand it—they are sober, industrious, quiet, and tractable—but imposition, real or imagined, they are ready to resent with uncontrollable fury.

Violence was not common among the miners, but other "clannish" activities found frequent expression. In March 1875, they despaired over ways to provide work for their unemployed and finally agreed that "whatever work was going on should be shared by all—the married and single as well." McLaughlin cheered this expression of "good feeling," but, after urging the men not to seek work in other depressed mining areas, asked the single men to sacrifice for the others by "striking out into the country among the farmers." Farm labor might assure them "good board" and allow married miners "to feed some children who must otherwise suffer for the common wants of life." A year later, "doubling up" was less popular among the men, one of whom reported that "hard feeling and hatred . . . already exist here." But the tradition of shared work lingered on: "some speak of taking all the small boys out and giving the married men their places. Others go in for doubling up, four in a room."

The spirit of mutuality showed among the miners in other forms. Despite their troubles, the miners listened sympathetically as Moses Hooker, the superintendant of the Chicago Newsboys' Home, pleaded for coal to help during the 1876–1877 winter. The operators promised free coal if the miners agreed, and by "acclamation amid great cheers," the men instructed their employers to deduct 1,000 pounds of coal from each workplace in November 1876 for the Chicago refuge. The *Workingman's Advocate* called the 200 tons they mined "a donation of black diamonds." Another time, the miners helped raise $1,500 to build a town library, and by February 1877 it was operating, "well patronized by our citizens." The library was one instance where the men and their employers worked together. Its directors included William Maltby, the Eureka superintendent, Mayor Goodrich, and miners Mooney, Dando, Kier, and McIntyre. John James called the funding and construction of the library "a movement like others in the right direction."* James and other local and state labor leaders also urged distributive cooperatives. Andrew Cameron favored stronger trade unions, but advised the Braidwood miners that such organizations were not "the ultimate objective of the labor movement," but rather "stepping stones in the right direction." The miners needed little prodding to support cooperatives. During the fall and winter of 1876–1877, they formed the Braidwood Cooperative Society and subscribed initially $3,000. In mid-January they opened a cooperative grocery, and James hoped that effort meant "the inception of something beyond the mere matter of a distributive concern only." In its first month, the grocery did $1,300 worth of business, more than even "its most sanguine friends" expected, and James believed it "destined to have a long and successful career before it."[40]

Such optimism was not utopian in Braidwood. Innovation went

---

* In 1881, the library badly needed funds for books and for repairs. A. L. Sweet, the CW & V superintendent, contributed $500, and the library directors urged miners to agree to a 25-cent deduction from the monthly wage for these purposes. The library directors said the miners would find the library "especially beneficial to themselves and those of their families unable to attend school." In 1884 the library counted 1,500 volumes, and Miss Margaret Mooney was appointed librarian. (*National Labor Tribune*, 12 Feb. 1881; *Souvenir of Settlement and Progress of Will County, Illinois* [Chicago, 1884] 443.)

along with the successful preservation of established collective advantages. In 1879, the miners easily prevented the introduction of the "truck system" by Alex Crombie, the Scottish operator who had sympathized with the 1874 strikers but who later persuaded more than twenty men to accept store orders every ninety days in place of cash. An angry miner warned local merchants that if Crombie succeeded they had best "pull up stakes and follow the advice given by Horace Greeley." Crombie's actions astounded this miner: "It seems strange to us that persons who have left the land of their birth, through the oppression and tyranny of their employers, should come to this country and be instrumental in giving birth to these evils." This same miner pleaded with Crombie's supporters to "consider their wicked action and sin no more." McLaughlin reminded the men of the old "evil" in Scotland and warned that "we have many evils to contend with in the prairie, but 'TRUCK' we never had." The miners agreed. They called store orders "vile, cursed, and degrading" because the system made employers "the selectors of our food and raiment as well as the directors of what we shall do with the little pittance we earn." They demanded that storekeepers "refuse and decline to receive store orders issued for pay" and promised not to patronize those who took Crombie's notes. Crombie's men got the message and quit his works. The other miners cheered their action and agreed that "no man go near Crombie's works until he, Mr. Crombie, agrees to pay the same as the other works of the Prairie." Crombie gave in too, and the *Miners' National Record* again commended the Braidwood men for having "risen in their might and repelled the vicious truck system on its first showing." "This is America," said the *Record*, ". . . and such things should not happen here."[41]

In that new industrial city, the Braidwood miners built a community of their own and protected and improved their condition where possible, but theirs was not an isolated frontier village. Visiting labor dignitaries and lecturers came with words of advice and encouragement. In November 1875, soon after his acquittal in the Clearfield, Pennsylvania trial, a parade led by the brass band again brought John Siney to an overcrowded schoolhouse, where he called the 1874 strike "a struggle . . . hailed with delight, not only by American miners but by many of those they . . . left behind on the other side of the Atlantic." Siney's argument that cooperatives were the ultimate answer to maldistributed wealth and economic power was received "with the greatest enthusiasm." Andrew Cameron also visited the miners to tell them that "he who did His Lord's will . . . would be saved." Another time, Sam Cary, the Ohio Democrat who supported financial and labor reforms, lectured there and drew praise from James, who found his talk "learned, eloquent, profound, and impressive." "To hear him speak," James said, "is a perfect feast. He is a power in the land. He is a genius." But the miners saved their greatest applause for Alexander McDonald, the Scottish leader of the British miners, who made his third trip to America in 1876, his first since being elected to Parliament. McLaughlin, who had learned much as a co-worker with McDonald in the Scottish coalfields, introduced him to a great throng, and the British trade unionist urged American miners to build powerful trade unions as well as producer cooperatives. American miners needed to follow "in the footsteps of their brethren in the old world and become their own employers." McDonald's visit kindled memories of the old country and drew the miners together—and not just the Scots. A "sociable" held in his honor featured the singing of Scottish and Irish ballads, and James Barrowman, Robert Meicklejohn, and Peter Dailey "vied with each other in dancing a reel and hornpipe." "Dancing was kept up to the wee, sma' hours," a much-pleased participant remembered, "and after a night of unalloyed pleasures, the company dispersed, after singing 'Auld Lang Syne' with a vim—[and] with hands crossed—wishing their honored friend a safe return to the land of his nativity."[42]

The closely knit community, with its common set of problems and interests, also shared a common political ideology that influenced particularly city and county but also state elections. Politics meant labor reform to Braidwood's union leaders. In 1872, for example, John James urged support for a national labor party:

> The barrier between capital and labor must remain there until it is destroyed by the workingmen, acting on all public questions as a unit, and elect[ing] their own officers to serve them. . . . Reform— pure and simple—we desire; such as will give the laborer the just share of the profits of his labor . . . [and] take off the weights that turn the dice, every time they are thrown, and make the juggler win. . . . "Oh!," say some folks, "we cannot get into this fix in this country; the proud lands of Uncle Sam can never be monopolized." Not so, I think . . . for now they are being monopolized—even now corporations bid defiance to the statute laws of the State by every day violating them.

James wrote of national politics, but the full influence of the miners could best be felt in local affairs. Braidwood was in Reed Township, and elected township offices included supervisor, assessor, justice of the peace, and constable. In 1873, William Mooney won election as Reed justice of the peace and a year later as town supervisor. Miner votes made the difference for Mooney. In February 1874, the Braidwood union urged "independent"—that is, reform—politics: "We recognize no party but the great party who labor for a living . . . [and] we vote for no man who is not pledged to legislate in behalf of the producing classes." Later that month, the union sent delegates to the Illinois State Grange convention, and at other times it urged immigrant miners quickly to become citizens and then use the ballot "to secure the election of men to power . . . in sympathy with the laboring men." In June 1874, Reed sent five delegates to a county antimonopoly convention that nominated reformer Alexander Campbell and a full slate of local candidates for the 1874 elections. At least three delegates— Mooney, McLaughlin, and John Young—were immigrant miners, and the convention, composed mostly of nonworkers, nominated Mooney and a rural German, H. H. Stassen, for the state legislature. The Republicans nominated Braidwood mayor L. C. Goodrich for the same office, and two others also ran for the three available offices. Voters cast three ballots, and those of the miners assured Mooney's election. The Scottish miner won three Joliet wards and Wilmington Township, but in Reed Township Mooney did even better. He got 1,390 votes, Goodrich 616, and three others candidates, including Stassen, 38. The miners wasted no votes on Stassen and apparently most cast three ballots for Mooney, who also led the county vote: Mooney, 6,125; Stassen, 4,759; Goodrich, 3,799. Mooney won the largest majority ever in Will County, and the *Miners' National Record*, boasting that "Braidwood may feel proud of her success," expected Mooney to do "good work not only for the miners but for the Commonwealth."* Meshank Dando, the Braidwood union's financial secretary and the man the Reed reformers pushed as Mooney's successor as town supervisor, praised Goodrich: "Although he is a Republican, he fully appreciates our platform." Miner votes also helped elect a reform county sheriff and coroner and return Alexander Campbell to the national Congress that year. The sixty-year-old Campbell had been a successful Pennsylvania iron manufacturer and later a land speculator in Illinois, and Republican mayor of nearby La Salle. Historian Irwin Unger has argued that Campbell's writings "had a profound emotional and, indeed, almost spiritual significance" for postbellum labor reformers. Miner Dando cheered Campbell as "one of the oldest as well as one of the ablest Labor Reformers of the Nineteenth Century." Soon after the fall 1874 elections, Braidwood miners not surprisingly formed an "Independent Club." They applauded a Chicago "Greenbacker," in-

---

* Mooney was not successful in his efforts to reform the state mining law. Ineffective mine inspection concerned all Illinois miners. Not one Braidwood miner was killed at work in 1875 and 1876, but fifty suffered serious injuries. In February 1877, stone fell from a roof at the Star shaft and killed a miner. A Braidwood coroner's jury blamed the company for not removing "rotten timbers," and friends of the deceased miner talked of suing the firm. In 1875, Mooney introduced an improved-ventilation bill called "Mooney's Pet." It passed the assembly by better than a 2–1 vote, but effective mine inspection did not come until 1883 and only after a severe flood in a mine killed a number of men. (*Workingman's Advocate*, 27 March 1875, 31 March 1877.)

troduced to them by their Republican mayor, and committed themselves to monetary reform and protective state labor legislation."[43]

The spring 1877 municipal election showed that the 1874 political victories rested on a solid network of social and economic ties that bound the Braidwood miners together as a cohesive group. We need not argue that the operators were powerless (they could open or close their mines and set production schedules) in order to understand that in many matters, politics included, the miners affected the flow of everyday events. The miners and their supporters organized a local Greenback-Labor party and captured the township and city elections. In early April, miners David Lofty and John Young won township office as school director and supervisor. A few weeks later the *Chicago Tribune* reporter was in Braidwood on the day of the city election, and his colorful coverage captured fully the flavor of that festive occasion. The Republicans and the Democrats put up separate tickets; "each," said the *Tribune*, "containing a sop to the miners." But the miners "would have none of it." McLaughlin headed their ticket as candidate for mayor. The *Tribune* correspondent described that day:

> It was election-day, an entire municipal ticket was to be elected, and the town was therefore extraordinarily lively. For once the mining population was aroused to the importance of the elective franchise. . . . Along the streets, or rather along the street, of Braidwood, a curious sight was presented. About every able-bodied man in town was there, and it was truly promiscuous and picturesque. Along the edge of sidewalks, which were generally elevated above the street, sat rows of holiday-attired individuals, showing two solid lines of human beings, for the distance of half a mile. In the middle and along the sides of the same street were groups, some standing, and other complacently seated in the sand. The sidewalks were so crowded as to render them practically no thoroughfare.
>
> Yet everything was strangely and inconsistently quiet. In Chicago such a congregation on the streets would mean a riot or a tumult. Here all conversation was in low tones. The saloons were open, but there was no drunkenness. Everybody was thoroughly in earnest. Around the polls the utmost good order prevailed.

The miners swept the election and won every office. Frank Lofty became alderman; Meshank Dando was the new police magistrate; William Mooney, then county mine inspector, took his place as city attorney; and union president McLaughlin was now mayor for two years, replacing Goodrich who had served from 1873 to 1877.* The

* Others elected were John McIntyre, John Cox, Jr., and John Creeley (aldermen), William Steen (city clerk), John Kier (city treasurer), and Patrick Muldowney (city

Workingman's Advocate imagined CW & V superintendent Sweet's reactions to these dramatic political changes and called the election "a
bitter pill for Mr. Sweet to swallow": "Just think of the outrage of being
compelled to live even temporarily under the administration of a man
whom he has ostracized for years, and annoyed by every little petty
meanness." And the *Advocate* joked: "What is the world coming to?"
But Braidwood residents had little to joke about that day. A few weeks
earlier, the miners had quit work to forestall a severe wage cut and a
harsh and repressive new contract, and to prevent the CW & V and
other Braidwood firms from entirely destroying their enclave of
immigrant working-class power on the Illinois prairie. No one then
realized that the strike would become the longest single industrial
dispute in American history to that date.[44]

The 1877 strike involved much more than negotiating an annual
contract, a fact clearly understood by the companies and the miners.
The Braidwood union had gained too much power on the prairie, and
the CW & V sought to repress it and its leaders. The miners were in
poor financial position. Most did not average $22 in wages for March
1877, and the *Braidwood Republican* asked, "What is this small pittance
to pay house rent and keep starvation from the door?" On March 26,
the coal companies together announced a new contract, effective May
1: between that date and October 1 miners would be paid 70 cents a
ton and then 80 cents to April 30. The immediate cut in wages of 25
cents a ton was severe. Wage rates had remained fixed at $1.25 a ton
between 1869 and 1874, years of rapid expansion, but after three
years of depression, the new contract meant a drop of more than 40
percent in money wages. Moreover, for the first time miners had to
sign a contract repudiating strikes and their union. It read:

> [The miner] further agrees that he will not stop work, join any
> "strike" or combination for the purpose of obtaining or causing the
> Company to pay their miners an advance of wages or pay beyond
> what is specified in this contract, nor will be aid in any such "strike,"
> combination, or scheme for any purpose whatever.

Sweet, publicly defending company policies, said nothing about this
new clause and insisted that low wages paid Indiana miners and the
threat of Indiana coal to Braidwood's Chicago market position justified

---

marshal). Remuneration for holding city office was not high. In 1874, the aldermen
fixed the mayor's annual salary at $200, and their own at $3 a night when in session.
The city marshal got $65 a month, the city attorney $30 a month, and the city clerk
$150 a year and fees. (*Joliet Signal*, 31 March, 9 June 1874.)

the severe wage cut. He also charged that McLaughlin was stirring discontent only to win the April election. "I do not deny that the company has made a profit," he told a *Chicago Tribune* reporter, "but not what it ought to make, considering the capital invested. . . . We are paying altogether too much to the miners." The men disputed Sweet on every point, and a committee they sent to Indiana found those coal companies regularly underbid in Chicago by the CW & V.

The day after the announcement of the reduction and new contract, "a vast crowd" of miners packed Odd Fellows Hall to hear McLaughlin and other union leaders denounce the companies and plead against "any immediate resort to violence." The men demanded the 1876–1877 wage rate and the abolition of the annual contract, urging in its place one month of formal company notice of intended wage changes. The miners also promised to resume work as individual firms met their demands. A committee headed by John Keir got instructions to meet with Sweet, and other miners left to talk with CW & V Streator miners. On April 5, Keir reported that Sweet was adamant and offered no compromise. In the meantime, however, the Streator miners had pushed the Braidwood men into a premature strike against their employers.[45]

The Streator miners lacked the firm social organization characteristic of the Braidwood workers and therefore posed difficult problems for the Braidwood men. Streator, founded in 1868, was still a new town. "Not more than four or five years ago," noted an 1874 report, "wild turkeys were shot on the town plot." The CW & V dominated Streator's mining business: one of its shafts, 100 feet deep, once brought up 928 tons in ten hours and gained a reputation as "the champion shaft of the United States." Employing 750 men, the CW & V far overshadowed two lesser Streator shaft mines (the Peanut Shaft and the Streator Company) and numerous tiny "country banks"—drift mines along the Vermillion River. Streator miners belonged to the same district union organization as the Braidwood men, but they lacked effective union leadership and suffered much as a result. In February 1874, a Streator miner complained:

> The company here is a remorseless taskmaster, demanding all that is possible from the laborer for the least amount. . . . They [the miners] have to pay the highest prices for everything they consume not being allowed to purchase at the first price from the farmer, because if the farmer will sell to the miner, none of the city traders will buy from the farmer. So that this keeps a continued barrier between them.

That winter the CW & V fired a number of union men: some found work in the "country banks," but "many . . . left the city." The 1874–

1875 company contract cut wages 20 percent and denied pay for slack, nut, and other inferior grades of coal. The men petitioned against "obnoxious clauses," and one said they had "a decided war feeling" but lacked "the munitions of war."

When the Braidwood miners struck the CW & V in 1874, the Streator men kept working. Despite efforts by McLaughlin, Trevellick, and local union stalwarts, the Miners' National Association made little progress in Streator. The companies cut wages again in 1875–1876 and gave irregular employment. In September 1875, the men worked full time for the first time since the previous winter. The 1875–1876 winter, however, was quiet, and a miner reported: "Things look dark here for the winter. . . . There is no Union." Another miner agreed: "Union is, in the eye of the employer, an unpardonable sin. The Western coal monopoly have ironclad articles. The company is law maker, and the superintendent is judge, jury, sheriff and constable." The CW & V fired all unmarried miners in one Streator shaft in April 1876: men with families could be controlled more easily. In August of that year, CW & V men worked only twelve or thirteen days and averaged between $18 and $25 for the month. "They have slackened in their duties as Union men," said a correspondent, "and they are paying the penalty." Full time in the 1876–1877 winter brought wages as high as $45 a month, but it did not bring the men closer together. Conflicts between the fraternal societies organized by British miners held back union organization: the English, Scottish, Welsh, and Irish miners worked against one another, and a depressed miner lamented their "religious bigotry and intolerance." Streator was not Braidwood. The "societies of the different nationalities of the British Empire . . . created cruelties against one another that would disgrace Blue Beard, and yet they call themselves Christians." This miner could not help but "worry why men flying from persecution in their old homes . . . should bring with them all their old time bigotry to crush the working men of this free land." Even the eloquence of Richard Trevellick was lost amid these ethnic frictions.[46]

But further wage cuts in March 1877 stirred enough resentment among the Streators miners to unite them temporarily against their employers. On the last day of March, the company announced that ton rates would drop ten cents the next day (cumulatively a 30 percent decline since April 1874). The Streator contract came due on April 1, a month before the Braidwood contract, and CW & V officials expected trouble from the Streator men but figured those Braidwood would remain at work through April and allow the firm to fill its contracts. But the Streator men voted to strike only if "the Braidwood men would stand by them through thick and thin," and they agreed to strike together, the Braidwood men quitting work a month early. The

Streator strike started successfully. All the Streator firms except the CW & V withdrew the wage cut, and their miners resumed work at the 1876–1877 rates. The CW & V, however, prepared for a long strike. The night of April 11 it brought two carloads of Chicago "blacklegs" (sixty-five men), promising them one dollar a day and board. Locked in a caboose and guarded by seven Chicago Pinkerton "police," they went directly to a company shaft. The strikers twice filled Streator's streets and, led by a band, paraded to the shaft, but a heavily armed LaSalle County posse denied them permission to talk with the men. Half of the new men, however, "escaped from the mine, sought refuge in town, and speedily fraternized with the strikers, who gladly provided them with food and lodging." Each day, the strikers paraded the streets, and a *Chicago Tribune* reporter found them "sympathized with by the best business men in Streator." A dispatch to the *National Labor Tribune* also reported that the miners "have the good will of all the business men." Streator's leading butcher, "Schaeffenberg and Wheeler, promised the strikers $500 for their relief fund. The *Free Trader* in Ottawa nearby supported the strikers, accused the CW & V of hiring only "tramps and idlers," called the Pinkerton police "peelers . . . armed with pistols and blunderbusses," and said, as in the Braidwood strike of 1874, that local opinion favored the strikers ("the people of Streator . . . say [they] are among the most peaceable and respectable citizens") and feared disorder only from the "foreign cops." LaSalle operator Ralph Plumb, owner of the Penny Shaft and a state senator, read dispatches in the Chicago press of "a reign of terror . . . at Streator," hastened there, and called the reports "without foundation in truth." Proof of successful organization among the hitherto divided miners occurred in the spring municipal elections: four miners won seats on the city council. Despite these encouraging signs, the miners surrendered to the CW & V in early May. A Braidwood union miner blamed their return on a few miners who "frightened" the others back to work and called them men who "whimper and whine around the corner as spaniels are wont to do," and "suck the 'Big Pap' always and procure the cream of all the good work." The evidence does not tell clearly why the Streator men returned, but a Braidwood miner complained of their betrayal and called them "faithless to the cause of labor" because they forced the Braidwood miners "to stand alone" against "the despised company."*[47]

* The CW & V kept on about 100 new workers, and a few weeks after the strike ended severe illness, perhaps poisoning, befell about 60 of them. By mid-May, most of the old hands had returned, and the new workers that stayed on all labored at one shaft and lived together. Meals were prepared for them there. On May 15, 60 fell ill in the mines, and reports told of arsenic in the lunch food. The *Joliet Sun* called this a "dastardly crime," and the *Ottawa Free Trader* suspected "unadulterated 'Molly Maguireism.' " The

POWER & CULTURE

At the time the Streator men gave in, the Braidwood miners had already been out a full month, and had their original grievances compounded several times by the unwillingness of their employers to pay back wages. March wages were due on April 15, but the companies (except for the Braidwood Coal Company, which paid its men the old wage and started up) refused the men March wages because they had violated their contract by quitting on April 1. Payday—April 15—caused great excitement in the coal city. "Thousands of rumors are afloat, which lend fuel to the fires of excitement," said a dispatch. The combination of the electoral victories of McLaughlin and the other miners, the strike, and the dispute over back wages caused the companies to fear an outbreak, and they brought in more than twenty Chicago "Pinkertons." The Will County sheriff sent eight special deputies, and the city authorities added twenty-eight extra local police officers. "No one knows how many 'cops' there are in the city," noted a report. False information that five or six hundred Chicago "blacklegs" and state militia were headed there twice sent crowds of miners to the railroad depot, but the trains arrived empty. In the meantime, according to a preconceived plan, individual miners each asked company officials for the wages due them. Not one miner received his March wages. That afternoon, the Braidwood Band let a parade that packed the main street, and afterwards the miners agreed to continue their strike and to sue as individuals for back pay. Union leaders pleaded that they "do nothing rash" and "keep cool." The day passed without violent incident, and the strike continued. Their behavior, concluded the *Joliet Daily Sun* of the strikers, "gained the sympathy of the community."[48]

At its start and for more than three months, the 1877 strike had both close parallels to the 1874 struggle and important differences. After mid-April, it attracted little attention in the press. Between April 17 and May 18, the *Joliet Daily Sun* printed only one strike report, and that told of troublesome women. The *Sun* worried about the miners' wives as others had in 1874, called them "perfect torments," and concluded: "The coal miners are not to be feared so much as the women." On May 17, a large crowd of women pelted with stones a train filled with new hands and broke a window. A deputy sheriff

---

"poisoning" proved to the *St. Louis Republican* that coal miners were men of "pitiless cruelty." Indiscriminate criticism of the miners caused the *Free Trader* to shift its tone and ask: "Is it certain that the poisoning was not accidental? . . . Has any satisfactory analysis been made to prove that there was any arsenic at all in the case? The cooking was done in the company's own kitchen, by its own servants, and its premises were so guarded that no one else had access to them. When and how was the poison administered?" No one died from the "poisoning," and despite a police investigation, the press failed to report further news on the causes of this trouble.

jumped into the crowd and seized one woman, almost tearing her clothes off. He grabbed the wrong woman, the *Sun* reported, and the others "pitched into him and made things lively." Sheriff Noble and more deputies prevented further trouble, and the *Sun* again concluded: "The wives and daughters of the miners are giving the officers ten times more trouble than the men ever have, and scarcely a day passes without a lively 'brush' between them. . . . Susan B. Anthony, Mary Livermore, and the army of strong-minded females can find a perfect Arcadia in Braidwood. Come West, Susie—Oh, *do* come West." But neither feminists nor dollars poured into Braidwood. Aid for the strikers from outside their city was scant: between May 12 and July 16 the Braidwood men got only $323.20, and all of it from Streator, Bloomington, and Oglesby.

In contrast to 1874, local opinion about the dispute was divided sharply, though there was still strong support for the miners. "The opinion here," said a *Chicago Tribune* reporter in late March, "is that the reduction demanded . . . is too much." A month later, another *Tribune* reporter found "the feeling among the business men of the town . . . strongly in favor of the miners and against the companies." The local courts upheld the miners in their claim for back wages, and the companies appealed to the circuit court in Joliet. A Wilmington resident found the companies "technically right in withholding the pay" but said the men "certainly had a moral right to pay for the value received." One of Braidwood's Protestant clergymen, a Methodist, publicly supported the strikers, and the others remained silent. A lecture by "the Rev. Mr. Rogers" entitled "Work and Capitalists" before a packed hall included passages that strongly "advocated the cause of the miners." Father R. H. Maguire, the city's only Catholic priest and "spoken of with great respect by all classes of the population," joined neither side. "He never interferes in their disputes," said the *Chicago Times*, "but is always found on the side of moderation and obedience to the constituted powers."* A Braidwood newspaper, the *Republican*, joined Rogers and devoted nearly two full pages of a single issue to a

---

* Suggestive but inconclusive evidence indicates that the Catholic church and Father McGuire played an important, if undetermined, role during the strike. Because it was the largest church in the town and because strike leaders McLaughlin and Mooney, among others, were Catholic, the influence of the church was felt. But for reasons unknown, church membership (about five hundred families before the strike) fell by half as a result of the strike. "The strike which occurred in 1877 severely affected the strength of the Church," noted a commentator in 1878. He gave no explanation. (*History of Will County*, 471.) The church suffered further in November 1878 when Father McGuire shot and killed Patrick Muldowney, a miner, then city marshal, and his close friend. Some reports told that the priest was drunk and others hinted that Muldowney and McGuire had quarreled over the affections of the priest's servant girl, but a coroner's jury called the shooting accidental. Full details appear in the *Chicago Times*, 20, 21, 22, 23, 25, 27 Nov. 1878.

denunciation of the companies. "A little daily sheet called the *Braidwood Republican,* published in the interests of the miners by an illiterate and overzealous young ignoramous," said a Wilmington writer, "has done much to widen the breach between the employers and employed." After surveying the crisis in great detail and filing a dispatch that covered its front page and gave fair reports from all sides, a *Chicago Tribune* reporter concluded that the miner "is fighting not alone for justice, but for bread."

But not all Braidwood or Will County residents shared his view. The *Tribune* found many merchants unwilling to extend the strikers credit, and McLaughlin and Frank Lofty pleaded for outside help because "the storekeepers have suspended their custom of giving goods on credit." Will County's sheriff, whom the Braidwood miners had opposed in his election campaign, regularly disputed with the Braidwood city fathers, and the sheriff frequently sided with the coal companies. A correspondent found "no love lost between the Sheriff and the miners." In mid-April, when the county deputies first came, the Braidwood authorities, fearing they might "kick up more of a rumpus than the striking miners," played "a nice joke" on them by appointing "a police committee of citizens to watch over and guard the sheriff's men and see they did no mischief." Six weeks later, a county deputy arrested "an Italian desperado" in Braidwood but brought him to Wilmington for examination. When a Braidwood justice of the peace demanded why he had bypassed the local courts, the deputy called them "frauds and farces . . . [with] no justice in them." This outburst cost him an $8 fine. But the sheriff evened the score by denying McLaughlin and Lofty permission to appeal for funds from the Joliet County courthouse. They spoke, but in a private hall. Public opinion in Joliet finally divided over the strike. The *Daily Sun,* a Republican paper (and the only extant newspaper from Joliet) sided with the operators and scorned efforts to raise funds for the strikers as "humbug," denouncing a supporter of the Braidwood strikers as "a communist of the deepest dye" and the strike leaders as men imbued with the "spirit of the commune" who lived "by bleeding the miner." Little money came from Joliet even though its reform mayor, James G. Elwood, presided at a meeting that heard McLaughlin plead for help. The contrast with 1874 was marked: then, an undivided local middle class aided by city and county officials had frustrated efforts by the coal companies to gain advantages.[49]

The strikes of 1874 and 1877 differed in one additional but essential way: during the first strike, the miners had a sympathetic city government; three years later, they controlled it. Braidwood in 1877 saw one of those rare instances—perhaps the only time—in American history when workers controlled a city government during a severe dispute that involved most local laborers. McLaughlin and the other miners took city office on May 1, a month after the strike started. That same day, miner John Young became a county supervisor. The new mayor's predecessor had appointed twenty-eight special city policemen, and the new common council authorized McLaughlin to retain them and, if necessary, add more. Then, led by miners Frank Lofty and John McIntyre, the council adopted an expanded public works program of street repair and grading that cost $1,500 and gave some work to more than 500 unemployed men (no doubt mostly strikers) in June and July. Although the actual amount each earned was small, the principle their income represented could not be measured. Critics later charged unfairly that city officials also gave monies allocated for poor relief to strikers.

Young also used his power as a county supervisor for the benefit of working people. He began equalizing county taxes on real and personal property. The Republican *Joliet Sun* admitted that "the property of the poor is easily counted but not so that of the rich," and McLaughlin later said that Young, aided by a "good honest" assessor, found that "a great deal of injustice had been done the small property owners." What Young uncovered amazed him. The owners of three-fourths of the railroad flats, eleven miles of railroad track, two-thirds of the "engines," the Chicago and Alton Railroad roundhouse, and certain bank properties paid no county taxes. Other bank taxes he found too low. Young made sure that "all property found, no matter who it belonged to, rich or poor, was listed and assessed," and McLaughlin cheered his effort to see that "the burden of government falls equally on all." The county supervisors gave their assent to many of Young's suggested revisions, including increases in bank and railroad taxes, and even the *Sun* approved some of them. The contemporary record does not tell of the immediate response by local banks, railroads, and coal companies, but in 1878 they fired a full salvo against Young to prevent his reelection.[50]

Although the community remained sharply divided, the first two months of the strike passed without serious incident. A Wilmington correspondent for the *Chicago Journal* later remembered that "to the credit of the miners . . . they behaved themselves personally and in their strike in an honorable and heroic manner, though it called for great sacrifices, extending very frequently to the very necessities of life in hundreds of cases." The city remained "extremely quiet" except for "a few insignificant disturbances between perhaps half a dozen hot-headed fools and discourteous Deputy Sheriffs." Each side became more firm in its outlook. Although the Streator miners weakened their position and John James, perhaps disillusioned by the Miners' National Association's collapse, bitterly opposed the strike, the miners showed strength in other ways. In late April, they struck the Braidwood Coal Company when it too failed to pay back wages as promised. The strikers asked for aid over the entire country. "They will never yield," McLaughlin told the *Chicago Tribune.* "Their cause is just, and they know it." Dando, Keir, and Duncan, strike leaders and public officials, told *Tribune* readers that the miners quit because "a *Sweet* reduction of 25 cents per ton . . . set the men of this place on their ear." McLaughlin and Lofty signed an appeal for funds that appeared in Chicago, Pittsburgh, and New York labor newspapers. "Our employers are strong in wealth and influence; we are strong only in our unity and determination to resist further exactions," they explained in asking for "any sum, however small," from "all fair minded people inside and outside our ranks." The new wage rate made it "impossible to earn our living and pay our way honestly as we go"; the new contract was "a model of its kind"; the denial of back wages seemed only "a desire to irritate and punish us because they think we have been bad boys in refusing to accept the conditions and prices offered." The miners expected to win in the courts but needed funds because "the law delays" and families faced "starvation." Their most revealing phrase hinted at a profound fear of losing independence and status: "Lowered wages means dependence on others for part of our living, even when working all the time we can be employed." The conditions surrounding wage rates counted as much as the income itself. Their appeal found editorial comment only in the *Workingman's Advocate.* Braidwood was too far from Pittsburgh and New York to attract close attention from its labor press. But the Chicago labor weekly, itself in financial crisis and appearing irregularly, jeered Sweet time and again. "Pennsylvania has her Gowen and Illinois has her Sweet (?)": the *Advocate* wondered who was "the biggest petty tyrant." "Satan-like" in his methods, Sweet deserved his reputation as the "champion wage reducer in the middle west." Sparing little invective, Cameron's weekly mocked Sweet as one of those "who wears out the knees of their Sunday pants praying to God to forgive other men for crimes they themselves commit." Withholding wages was a crime "in the eye of an all-seeing God." When the CW & V protested that its profits were inadequate, the *Advocate* retorted that it thrived on special railroad rates, misused funds by hiring "too many jacks of all trades and masters of none," and simply lacked "business capacity and practical knowledge."[51]

Sweet paid no attention to these insults. Despite certain difficulties and the tenacity of the strikers, he remained optimistic, and company president Walker shared his enthusiasm. Stockholders learned in a special circular from Walker on April 27: "To take any other course would simply be destruction to property, and we had better make an assignment at once. We expect, of course, to succeed in breaking the strike." Sometime in May the CW & V successfully brought in at least eighty new Chicago workers. Two Chicago labor contractors (their officers were "prominent in the Chicago Y.M.C.A," complained the *Advocate*) supplied them. But as in 1874, the company had trouble with its new hands, and in mid-June Sweet fired them. "I became so disgusted with my white men that I was trying to learn [*sic*] to mine that I discharged them all in a lump," the digusted Sweet wrote a stockholder on July 2. "We had to feed . . . and pay them $1.00 per day and they eat like a lot of Hoggs and they loafed around for two months and slept and did not work." On June 15, about one hundred white strikebreakers passed through Joliet from Braidwood, men the *Sun* called "the roughest looking set seen in Joliet in many days." Only the police chief and his men could get them on a Chicago train. But the CW & V's failure with these workers and its inability to pay July dividends did not deter it and the other operators from making a new and far-reaching decision. On June 19, four days after the white workers left, a "party" of about 300 black workers, accompanied by the county sheriff, arrived in Braidwood, and the *Sun* predicted Braidwood would "come out from the cloud."[52]*

Although the exact circumstances that brought the blacks to Braidwood remain unknown, by mid-July as many as 600 had arrived. Sometime earlier, a CW & V stockholder in Cambridge, Massachusetts, advised Sweet to hire "half or two-thirds colored miners, if not all." A striker later charged that "recruiting sergeants" sent "into the Southern States," probably Virginia, got the blacks by promising them one dollar a day and board. Some came with families; all were housed on company property, their places of residence "surrounded by high board fences." The companies armed them for self-protection. Only a single letter by a striker dated July 18 survives to tell of the early reaction to the blacks. "Feel as determined as ever," he insisted. "The companies are shipping in negroes by the car loads: tobacco spinners, blacksmiths, tinkers, street cleaners, and corn hoers from the plantation. This kind of rubbage [*sic*] can not hurt us any, and all the companies are finding that out at their expense." The company took another view. "Our colored men are doing nicely," Sweet reported to a stockholder. "They

---

* Sweet early favored bringing in black workers. On June 2, he wrote stockholder Cyrus Woodman, who lived in Cambridge, Massachusetts: "We are bringing Colored Miners from the South, and expect to fill up our mines at Braidwood with regular Colored Miners. This, we think, will obviate the necessity for having any more strikes at that place for some time to come." President Walker, however, early opposed such action. 'I wanted to send darkies when the strike first commenced," Sweet told Woodman on July 2, but Walker did not agree. Disappointment with the new white workers, however, led Sweet to bring in the blacks and then notify Walker. The firm president sanctioned Sweet's action and "recommended active efforts to fill" the Braidwood mines "with colored miners." (A. L. Sweet, Chicago, 2 June, 2 July 1877, to Cyrus Woodman, Woodman Mss., Wisconsin State Historical Society.)

are no expence [*sic*], only for their fair [*sic*] to this place & that they pay back to us." The blacks left no record of their early reactions, but Sweet said they "say they have found the Land of Promise."* Although the evidence told little of the blacks themselves, a circular to CW & V stockholders made clear the reasons for their coming: "With the mines filled with colored men, it is believed the company will not be burdened with the expense of another strike for many years." The strikers, however, showed no signs of giving in, and on July 20, with the dispute well into its fourth month, a Braidwood dispatch told the *Chicago Tribune* that the strike "remains as at the beginning. The miners are still firm and confident of success." The presence of black strikebeakers angered the miners, but no violence against them was reported. "No demonstrations," the dispatch noted, "other than loud talking and threats as yet."[53]

Nothing that happened before July 20 even vaguely hinted that the great railroad strikes that were to stop Illinois trains for several days and bring violence, riot, and even death to Chicago and other railroad centers would force a severe confrontation between the Braidwood strikers and the municipal officers, on the one hand, and the coal companies, the black workers, and county and state authorities on the other. But on the night of the twentieth an ugly mood swept the city. That day the black miners had received their first wages, and according to the *Chicago Times*, some drank heavily. City authorities arrested two black men, and there were rumors that 150 others planned to rescue them. White citizens crowded the streets, and the sheriff and his deputies guarded the "Negro quarters." The night then passed quietly. But a few days later a crisis did come, and it brought troops to Braidwood, leaving much ill feeling and mistrust in its aftermath. "In looking over the history of this place for the past ten or twelve days," a striker wrote on August 12, soon after the troops left, " . . . it seems to me like a huge dream."[54]

Part of the trouble that brought militia to the coal city resulted from a dispute between city and county authorities about maintaining public order, and the rest involved difficulties between blacks and either the strikers or the coal companies (possibly both). It is difficult to reconstruct the precise causes of these frictions because the extant sources are mostly fragmentary newspaper dispatches. The most they tell about the conflict between the city and county authorities is that between July 23 and July 25 a rupture occurred in relations between Mayor

* Sweet said the blacks came mostly from Kentucky and West Virginia. He said they were pleased in "finding such a good company to work for, such fine equipment and easy digging and liberty of work and when they can live so cheaply." (A. L. Sweet, Chicago, 28 June and 2 July 1877, to C. Woodman, Woodman Mss., Wisconsin State Historical Society.)

McLaughlin and the Will County sheriff. On the twenty-third, the *Braidwood Republican* reported "excitement" in the city over the Pittsburgh railroad riots and said of the miners: "Their blood boils to-day, and it would take but very little to cause an outbreak in this place." That day, a county deputy in Braidwood urged the sheriff to take "precautionary measures" to prevent "a riot." After visiting Braidwood, the sheriff telegraphed Joliet for twenty-two additional deputies. At the railroad depot that night, McLaughlin advised them "not to make any demonstration" because "no danger existed except in the minds of a few deputies." The county officers agreed, and most spent the night in Dwight nearby.* A *Chicago Tribune* correspondent said county authorities spoke "very highly of Mayor McLaughlin's evident candor and fairness in stating the situation," and the *Joliet Sun* of July 24 said it knew "nothing . . . as to the real grounds for apprehension in Braidwood." Serious trouble, however, came on the twenty-fourth. It is impossible to reconstruct its causes: the evidence is contradictory, and participants disagreed. According to the *Chicago Times*, which printed the most detailed reports, that morning some strikers seized a commissary wagon filled with bread, milk, and meat to feed the blacks and confiscated it. Then they surrounded the Eureka shaft, and a committee ordered the black miners to leave Braidwood before four o'clock on the twenty-fifth. "The blacks," said the *Times*, "accepted the situation" and agreed to depart. That same day, the Will County sheriff telegraphed the state capitol for 300 soldiers. From Springfield, Adjutant General H. H. Hilliard asked Chicago militia officer General Arthur C. Ducat if his troops were available. Ducat wondered if troops were needed because newspaper dispatches predicted quiet in Braidwood "provided militia [are] not ordered there." Hilliard pressed him. In the meantime, Braidwood remained free of new trouble. Because the railroad strike had disrupted train service, the black miners did not leave as promised. On the afternoon of the twenty-fifth, the county sheriff, saying he had "surrendered his authority to the mayor," refused

---

* A Wilmington dispatch in the *Chicago Times* on July 25 said that "one woman presented a pistol to Sheriff Noble's head, when her arm was grasped by the mayor, and a tragedy avoided." Days later, a critic charged that McLaughlin and "his thugs"—one of them "a man dressed in woman's clothing [who] flourished a revolver about the head of [the] Sheriff"—kept the county officials away on the night of the twenty-third (Stowe to the editor, *Chicago Tribune*, 31 July 1877). That same day, July 25, the *Joliet Sun* printed an unusual "story" that had no basis in fact. It called the story "a magnificent lie . . . in reality a dream, the product of the overheated brain of one of the [Citizen's Militia] Corps."

According to it, "a great riot . . . burst suddenly" in Braidwood and 160 Joliet militia marched there to find "a bloody battle" involving between 2,000 and 4,000 men. Flames threatened to consume the city, and the soldiers entered the city "with bayonets glistening in the lurid light of the burning city." The soldiers charged the "mob" twice, and the "mob" responded once. One hundred soliders and 200 "rioters" lost their lives before peace was restored.

an unidentified request that he go to Braidwood. The twenty-fifth passed without disorder. Troops were not sent. The next day, the blacks, the sheriff's deputies, and the Chicago Pinkerton guards left Braidwood. "Gwinn Back to Ole Virginia," reported the *Times* of the blacks, who left on foot with their families, carrying with them their few belongings, and camped on the prairie near Wilmington. That night the *Times* added: "Complete order and quiet has been restored. . . . No personal violence has been committed on any person, and no disorder of any kind exists to-night." The Pinkertons stopped in Joliet on their way back to Chicago, and one of "the most intelligent" among them told a *Joliet Sun* reporter that the strike had ended: "Everybody is quiet and peaceful . . . and the old miners are going back to work. . . . The removal of foreign restraint seems to have been the one grand desire of the miners. . . . Happiness and peace is restored to this unhappy town."* The *Sun*, surprisingly, praised McLaughlin, called him "amply competent to take care of his city," said the mayor had "proven himself willing to keep within the bounds of the law," and insisted that "the miners' trouble at Braidwood is at an end."⁵⁵

Contemporaries disputed this account in all essentials. "Braidwood," roared a *Chicago Tribune* dispatch, "is now in the hands of the strikers," who had "starved out" the blacks and Pinkertons and forced the "noble" sheriff to "succumb to the inevitable" and "surrender the city" to McLaughlin to avoid a "riot" and the "murder" of many black men. The Illinois adjutant general shared the *Tribune*'s views, as did most contemporary newspaper accounts. According to the adjutant general, after the deputies left, the miners set "all laws at defiance" and "obliged a large number of colored people, . . . peaceably engaged in the work of mining, to desist from their labor and leave with their families." Newspaper accounts added such harrowing details as the strikers taking away the arms given the blacks by the operators and threatening them "in the rear with a howling mob" as they left town. But these same vivid dispatches contained contradictory evidence suggesting that the operators caused the exodus of blacks. The *Chicago Interocean* blamed the miners, but said they "drove out the negroes with the consent and connivance of the owners of the miners and the authorities of Braidwood." No other contemporary source hinted at so fraternal a gesture between the strikers and their employers. A final version put forth by the strikers said the blacks left because the operators fired

---

* A Wilmington journalist said that the miner saw the coming of the blacks as a severe blow meant to "blast their hopes . . . after all their wanting, watching and suffering. This seemed more than flesh and blood could stand and their last hope of success depended on inducing Sambo to leave. He had rights under the law the miners acknowledged, but, they themselves, their families and property were here, and natural antagonism sprung up." (C., Wilmington, to the editor, *Chicago Journal*, 30 July 1877.)

them. "On account of the strike," Braidwood miners told a correspondent in Morris nearby, "the coal Company is in such condition that it cannot carry on its business . . . has stopped all work . . . [and] been obliged to discharge even the colored miners." The fact that the Eureka Coal Company, Braidwood's second largest mining firm and with the CW & V a prime recruiter of black labor, filed a bankruptcy petition that week adds plausibility to this explanation.[56]

After the crisis passed, other miners argued more emphatically that the companies had deserted the black miners and forced them out. The Eureka and the CW & V "put away all their colored men about a week ago," and the Eureka refused them their wages, wrote a miner on August 2. "The bosses discharged all their watchmen and then told the colored men to leave inside of ten minutes! They tried to scare them out of their pay," and the blacks left for towns nearby. Ten days later, another striker gave a similar explanation but in greater detail:

> They succeeded in getting about six hundred genuine Africans to work in their mines. Everything went on quietly, as the older miners knew that the negroes were not producing enough coal to pay for the food consumed by them. This continued up to the time the railroads suspended operations, when the companies, not knowing how long the railroad strike would continue, and seeing that they had an elephant on their hands, gave the negroes twenty minutes to quit the quarters occupied by them and drove them away.

The miner expressed empathy for the departing black miners:

> It was a touching sight to see these poor negroes driven forth, without any means at their command to reach their far away homes, and a great deal of sympathy was expressed by all the old miners as they saw them going forth with all their worldly goods packed in a small valise or handkerchief, some leading and some carrying small infants on their backs. As transportation was stopped at this time, the negroes scattered up and down the railway lines in the small towns within a radius of from ten to twenty miles from the place their cruel employers drove them. Everything was quiet, and Braidwood was completely in the hands of the old miners.

Their departure occasioned no disorder: "Not an angry word was spoken or a stick of property molested by any one." An account of the strike published in 1878 in *The History of Will County, Illinois* lends credence to the insistence that the blacks left voluntarily. Fear drove them from Braidwood. After the railroad strike began, the county history reported, "the spirit of defiance took possession of the strikers, and they determined to drive out the 'blacklegs,' who, upon being apprised of the intention of the strikers, though promised protection

by their employers and the county authorities, fled from the city."
Then the sheriff telegraphed Governor Cullom for militia "to quell
the hourly-expected outbreak."[57]*

Whatever caused the blacks to leave, the Chicago press told blood-
curdling tales of violence by the miners against the blacks, and state
officials in Springfield joined the Chicago dailies in demanding the
punishment of men the *Chicago Times* and the *Chicago Tribune* called
"savages." An unidentified state official described the Braidwood city
fathers as "revolutionary authorities," and a Springfield dispatch told
of "great indignation" there because the blacks had been "left to the
mercy of the mob." Violent rhetoric punctuated editorials in the
Chicago newspapers. The *Times* demanded that the "whole power of
the government . . . be put in motion to send the Braidwood savages
straight from the mouths of cannon to the infernal region," and the
Tribune agreed, calling the miners "mobocratous" and insisting that
unless Braidwood quieted down, its citizens would "receive their quietus
at the point of the bayonet and the mouth of the cannon." The "fugitive
negroes," said the *Tribune*, merited protection; they had "performed
their duties faithfully." "They have a right to work," it added; "they
have stomachs to fill, and their families to care for." And the Braidwood
strikers, the *Tribune* went on, deserved the worst.

> They have shown themselves as brutal, cruel, and inhuman savages
> in their treatment of the colored men, who have as much right to
> work and earn a living as they. . . . [If the strikers interfere again]
> they should be accorded the same punishment that is meted out to
> savages. There should be no temporizing with them. Let it be instant
> submission or instant bullets.

After some hesitation, state authorities ordered troops to Braidwood.
Intervention by L. H. Goodrich, then a state legislator and Braidwood's
former mayor, may have blurred the vision of Springfield politicians.
On the twenty-fifth, Goodrich telegraphed Adjutant General Hilliard
that "no violence has been used against the negro miners, and none
is intended"; a day later, he advised Governor Shelby Cullom that the
blacks, anxious to leave, needed "transportation and protection."
According to a newspaper dispatch, Cullom replied that "if the strikers
interfered with their departure, the miners would be held reponsible."
"It is hard to get the truth here," Hilliard wired Ducat on the twenty-
fifth, but he urged that troops be readied. Ducat seemed to favor

---

* This version was reported *verbatim* in Maue's *History of Will County*, 348–9, but Maue
attributed it to "Maltby's History." William Maltby was superintendent of the Eureka
mines that year. No such history has been located.

sending local militia, not Chicago soldiers, but Hilliard demurred. On the morning of the twenty-seventh, Cullom finally instructed Ducat to move against the strikers. "The Braidwood colored people have been driven away," the governor explained. The "miners and the colored men, when they return," needed protection. Cullom condemned the strikers and feared their power: "The treatment of the colored people is disgraceful. You will have to send a pretty strong force." He instructed Ducat to "be sure and take care of Braidwood." The *Interocean* and other Chicago newspapers cheered Cullom's decision; Braidwood's miners needed "an overhauling."[58]

Ducat worked with dispatch and readied the Illinois National Guard's First Regiment. The arrival of six companies of regular infantry from the West had calmed the Chicago rioters and allowed him to move quickly. On the morning of the twenty-eighth, more than 800 militia, mostly Chicago men but a small number from Sycamore, Creton, Rockford, and Aurora, left by rail for Braidwood. Ducat had maps of the city and its vicinity that located mine shafts and other "points of trouble." The train also carried two officers of the Wilmington Star Coal Company and later picked up officers of the CW & V, the Eureka, and one or two other firms. In Joliet, Ducat added the Joliet Light Artillery armed with two cannon along with members of Joliet Citizens' Corps. The *Tribune* found "the military force . . . large enough to sweep Braidwood from the face of the earth," and the *Times* said the miners had no more chance of winning "than the bull dog has to vanquish the lion. The claws of the king of cats are too many for the monarch of canines." The militia carried instructions to restore order, protect property and person, and "reinstate the negro miners . . . expelled by white strikers." State authorities had determined to return the "colored fugitives . . . to their homes and labor." Ducat exaggerated his mission: he later claimed "information" that striking iron-mill hands and coal miners in towns nearby planned to join the Braidwood miners, who "had received arms, ammunition, money, and men from Pennsylvania" (no doubt the Molly Maguires). When the troop train crossed the Kankakee River, black "refugees" cheered its passing, and the soldiers answered by singing "John Brown," "We'll Rally 'Round the Flag," and "other national melodies." At 5 P.M. on the twenty-eighth, the train halted a mile north of the city. Ducat described his strategy: "The center of advance was the railway line, with two companies on either side deployed as skirmishers." Artillery followed in the rear. The soldiers marched to the railroad depot. Between 200 and 300 miners and their families had gathered there, but Ducat had difficulty distinguishing between a "crowd" and a "mob." "In our front and center," he noted in his official report, "was a strong force of rioters." He asked the crowd to fetch McLaughlin but got no response. Then, a "captain" from "Pinkerton's Preventive Force" conferred with Ducat, and a miltiaman went to get the mayor.[59]

A confrontation between the mayor and the general made it clear that the military ruled the city. Upon arrival, Ducat informed McLaughlin "that riot and disorder, robbery and mob violence, have prevailed and do still prevail in your city, and that your people are armed and disposed to resist by force of arms the officers of the law." He accused the strikers of driving off the county sheriff and then the black miners, who roamed the prairie "without food, shelter, or money, having been robbed of their effects." Ducat blamed the disorder on the failure of the city government and particularly its mayor:

> I am further informed that the mines cannot be worked because of persistent interference from a desperate, armed mob. All of this, sir, would indicate that you are powerless to protect the people or else that you had no disposition to do so. I now call upon you, Mayor McLaughlin, to disperse the mob in my front. You have no use to think of fighting. Warn all women and children away, and warn all men also. If they resist I will at once drive them in with my troops. I also command you to surrender up all arms in your possession at once.

The mayor had half an hour. He advised the crowd to depart, promised Ducat the arms possessed by the city, and did not search the private homes of citizen-miners for weapons. Dissatisfied, Ducat repeated his demands: surrender their weapons, clear the streets. He then "ordered a search for arms, which resulted in the capture of 34 muskets, formerly the property of the colored people, and which I subsequently turned over to . . . the [CW & V?] superintendent of the mines." The search continued the next day and provided an additional thirty-nine "pistols, rifles, and shotguns"—a total of seventy-three weapons, including the arms allegedly stolen from the blacks. A surprised *Tribune* correspondent admitted that "reports as to the possession of arms by the strikers are greatly exaggerated." Years later, a miner recalled the house-by-house search for weapons: "In squads of two, they searched every house for weapons. When they reached my house, they asked my mother if she had any weapons. She said she had and went to the table, picked up the family Bible, and told them that was the only weapon her family needed." Although Ducat later insisted his pickets were fired on once during the night, reporters disagreed: "The town is perfectly quiet; not a blow has been struck nor an insult offered to a man." Ducat telegraphed his successes that first night. "I have dispatched the mob and seized their arms and have full control," he told his chief of staff. "The colored people," he wired Cullom "can return with entire safety." The news thrilled Hilliard: "I know the country will thank you. Hurrah! for the Illinois National Guards! . . . You will of course hold the Fort." Ducat responded, "We *will* hold the fort."[60]

The next day was Sunday, and the blacks returned to Braidwood. Ducat worried for their safety, and early that morning warned Hilliard: "These Braidwood savages all have revolvers and shot-guns, and the mayor has not turned in to me the muskets concealed here. There is no safety for the negroes, or other peaceable people, while these arms are left in the hands of this desperate mob." Ducat's fears, however, proved ill-founded. Two trains took the harried black workers to the city, and the Will County sheriff and militia protected them. A miner wrote: "They were marched up our main street singing 'Hold the Fort,' with soldiers in advance and in the rear, with fixed bayonets." A Will County correspondent for the *Chicago Journal* described the scene:

> Imagine, if you can, some hundreds of these colored fellows filling the air with a grand chorus in one of the most thickly settled points on Main street. Companies of militia extended from one side of the street to the other, while either side was guarded by soldiers in double file. A section of artillery, twelve-pounders, covered the scene, while pickets patrolled their beats, causing citizens of all classes to stand back.

Ducat directed the entire proceeding, which this same reporter called "the unkindest cut of all to the citizens and miners." "They were sent at once to their homes near the mines," Ducat said later of the blacks. "They were cheerful yet destitute, and I ordered rations issued to them for the day, notifying the owners of the mines that hereafter they would have to provide for them.* The bankrupt Eureka company did not take its black miners back, but the CW & V piled them into its quarters. Only once, according to a *Tribune* reporter, did trouble threaten:

> Those darkies were very defiant in their attitude, and went along the street, singing, cheering, and jeering at the citizens of the place assembled along the sidewalks. One very black wretch, more demonstrative than the rest, even went so far in his triumphant indignities as to spit in the face of one of the people—some declared a woman.

---

* Cullom had instructed Ducat to make the mine owners "take care of their employees." "Don't let them suffer," the governor said of the blacks. Ducat explained that the black workers were being fed "at the expense of the State" because "their employees don't seem to have made provision for them." (Collins, *The Riots of 1877 in Illinois*, 12.)

Tempers flared, but the militia "dispersed the assembling and fast-increasing crowd."* The next morning Ducat, instructed to send some militia to other troubled Illinois areas, withdrew 600 soldiers and the artillery. But he left enough men "to protect property until the colored miners are allowed to work unmolested" and issued a final proclamation to McLaughlin:

> The colored people driven from here by your citizens have been returned by me to their work and homes: they are again under your protection. I leave a military force . . . to assist the civil authorities in preserving peace and order, and the lives and property of all peaceable people. It would be well for you to warn your people that should it be necessary to return here to suppress riot, it is certain all rioters will be punished.

Ducat was still concerned for the safety of the blacks. A day before, he had complained to Cullom about the county authorities: "Don't believe [that the] sheriff will make many arrests. The rioters, and nearly the whole population of this place, should be punished." Ducat took it upon himself to prevent disorder. According to a *Chicago Times* reporter, the general warned McLaughlin he would "hold the mayor responsible for [subsequent] overt acts of violence." McLaughlin argued with Ducat that "he did not think it just that he should be held responsible for outrages committed by individuals over whom he could not possibly exercise a personal supervision." Ducat answered quickly and charged that McLaughlin had "threatened Sheriff Noble with death" and "laid himself liable to arrest and severe punishment." Mooney, at the conference as McLaughlin's counsel, urged the general to make the arrest "at once" and do so "quietly." McLaughlin nodded agreement. But because "the town was quiet," the general saw no reason to make the arrest, and he departed from Braidwood.[61]

Although civilian government was restored, troops remained in Braidwood for nearly two weeks and were there when Cullom visited the town on August 2. The governor worried about Braidwood. Before Ducat left, he ordered that force enough be left there to protect property, and "until the colored miners are allowed to work unmo-

---

* The evidence concerning the attitude of the strikers toward the returning blacks is inconclusive. We have only the firsthand dispatches of a *Tribune* reporter. He said the miners were "down on the darkeys," and that the strikers' wives said they were "constantly being insulted by these colored people, who certainly are among the lowest the writer ever saw." The correspondent found that "the most indecent and disgusting morality prevails in common among the colored miners and their families." "The lowest of lewd white women, as well as black," he added, came from the cities to "cohabit" with the black men. The same reporter said the miners would get even with the blacks after the troops left. But the entire absence of any violence, petty or serious, against the blacks in the months that followed casts serious doubt on this observation as well as the on the others made by this reporter. (*Chicago Tribune*, 31 July 1877.)

lested." "The proprietors of the mines must put themselves in shape to defend their mines and men," Cullom wired Ducat on the thirtieth. "I will go up to Braidwood soon." Three days later, Cullom, accompanied by the county sheriff, arrived and conferred with McLaughlin and the aldermen. They reached an agreement to remove all but two companies of soldiers. A week later, these men departed. During their stay, Chicago newspapers reported one exchange of shots at a shaft between strikers ("citizens") and soldiers, but otherwise found the town "very quiet." Braidwood, according to the *Chicago Times*, surprised even Cullom. After hearing all sides, the governor "expressed the opinion that Braidwood had been represented a great deal worse than it deserved to be." Cullom did not doubt that "the representation of the city officials, in effect that no overt act had been committed or was likely to be committed, was true."[62]

The absence of serious violence between the troops and the strikers did not mean that the two groups got along well. Although there were some reports of fraternization between the soldiers and miners, a *Chicago Tribune* dispatch, which otherwise cheered the "glory" of the militia, told of tension between the citizens and those guardsmen from Chicago:

> The rioters manifested a particular aversion to the first [Chicago] regiment. They called them a "regiment of clarks" [*sic*] . . . who would not hesitate—even were anxious to shed gore for the capitalist. But they felt more kindly disposed toward the other organizations. They counted much upon the sympathy of the rural militiamen.

Nothing is known of the relations between the rural soldiers and the miners, but the Chicago troops and the strikers mistrusted and disliked one another.

> The [Chicago] boys were not generally disposed to be very merciful toward the citizens . . . and [made] petty raids . . . of a foraging nature. Chickens, pigs, calves, and the like were furnished to a certain extent, but no very extended damage was done, and there were no excesses in vandalism or destruction of property. . . . The inhabitants were loth to yield their provisions to the boys of the First, although the latter invariably proffered ample payment for everything before taking.

Ducat called the behavior of his men "highly commendable, proving steady under arms and well disciplined," but the hostilty of the citizens weakened their code of honor. A shortage of milk among the Chicago troops caused two or three from each company to be sent with buckets "to purchase milk if they could, [but] with instructions to get it anyhow." The *Tribune* reporter described what followed:

> They would start out like honest boys, go to a house where they
> knew cows were owned, offer their money for the milk, but would
> be met defiantly by the men and reviled by the women, who would
> call them all the hard names they could think of. Then the honest
> boys . . . would go out into the lot, after being refused, and milk
> the cows for themselves.

The soldiers lost admirers in other ways. Anxious to return to Chicago
with "some sort of a trophy," they made sport of stealing miners'
headlights. A Joliet reporter also made much of trouble between the
militia and the Braidwood women ("these Amazons of the Mines").
He said the soldiers feared ten striking women—"those strapping
Welch [sic] women and Bohemian women"—more than one hundred
armed strikers. The women, who carried "stones in their aprons" and
in "bags hung at their sides" and flung them at the militia in slingshots
made from "long, strong" stockings, were "perfectly fearless women"
and would "rather fight than eat." He quoted a deputy sheriff in
Braidwood since April: "I would rather meet the devil, and he with a
two-pronged fork, bent on my destruction, than meet one of those
women with blood in her eye. At night none of us felt safe, and we
never knew when a stone would come whizzing by and light right near
a fellow. . . ."63

Despite the "Amazons," the imposition of martial law, and the return
of the blacks, the strikers and their supporters remained peaceful and
orderly. A *Joliet Sun* reporter said the troops enjoyed "a pleasant
vacation," and the strikers' behavior troubled other on-the-spot observers. All agreed, some in astonishment, that the men, "armed from
the boots to the teeth and eager for blood" before the soldiers came,
behaved quietly. The record showed not a single arrest while the
troops patrolled the city. The *Interocean* credited the militia. "No city
was ever more humbled than Braidwood," it said; the military had
reduced "to perfect quiet the most significant labor strike ever known
in this part of the State." But the orderliness remained after the troops
departed. Other observers credited McLaughlin, and the *Tribune* called
it the "policy" of the strikers to "remain absolutely quiet." The absence
of disorder testified more to the discipline of the strikers than to the
absence of anger among them. If the return of the blacks and the
presence of militia were meant to demoralize them, this did not
happen. Not a single striker returned to work. Instead, the miners
protested the appearance of armed militia in such numbers that "the
old settlers could scarcely recognize their city." Although Mooney
pleaded publicly for an "honest" compromise, the *Tribune* noted that
"the strikers are well organized, and they, one and all, say that the
coal companies will have to come under." The *Braidwood Republican*

agreed, finding the strikers as "determined as ever to hold out till snow falls." "Never in my forty years of existence," complained a striker after the troops left, "have I been witness of such a military force, perpetrated and played at the expense of the taxpayers of this State." A second striker added: "Had they brought all the militia from Maine to Mexico, they could not scare us, as we were doing nothing that the law can take hold of us for." When some Braidwood merchants and bankers pleaded with the strikers to return to work because other firms might join the Eureka company in bankruptcy, a striker replied that the companies, having "miserably failed" in using troops and black workers to dislodge the men, "ask us to try and save them." "The universal reply is *no*! . . . No, they can go into bankruptcy or into a hotter court, but we will never yield."[64]

Opinion among nonminers in and around Braidwood divided over the militia. Although it cheered the soldiers, the *Joliet Sun* complained because the troops did not arrest the "ring leaders," urged that a special county grand jury do so, and especially rebuked Ducat for dealing with McLaughlin, "this leader of mobs," and not putting him and "every recognized leader of the strike" in jail. Some Braidwood merchants, fearing further bankruptcy among the coal companies, joined to condemn the strikers, but others in the community and nearby protested the call for militia. "The leading men of the town," said the *Interocean* on July 30, sent "word to Governor Cullom that there was no necessity for assistance." A Wilmington resident for twenty years filed a long dispatch in the *Chicago Journal* that called the use of troops to return the blacks "a bitter pill of humiliation to the people, many of whom are as respectable, intelligent and law-abiding as can be found anywhere." The *Wilmington People's Advocate* sympathized with the strikers, but urged them to settle the back-pay issue, resume work "so soon as God will let them" at a lowered wage, and then plan to "grapple with the future as their better sense will dictate." Although it felt strikes "erroneous" and "a licentious freedom" at best, the *Ottawa Free Trader* condemned Ducat's "raid" and his "pomposity," calling his capture of a town "as quiet as Sleepy Hollow" an action "hardly adapted to inspire high respect for the law." Evidence of continuing hostility also followed the publication of a letter signed by Caleb Stowe in the *Chicago Tribune*. "Stowe" remains unknown, and there are hints that the name was a pseudonym. Reviewing the Braidwood dispute, Stowe blamed it on "the Irish . . . ruled by about a score of pure Mollie Maguires, and the Bohemians by half a dozen Communists." The "American," English, and Scottish miners "very foolishly" voted with them and "filled every office worth anything with Mollie Maguires exclusively." McLaughlin ("the precious Mayor . . . King Dan," "the lord of the blood of his poor dupes"), John James ("another of the savages" and formerly associated with the Miners' National Association, "that gigantic engine of oppression"), and the aldermen were "personally responsible for the inhuman outrages perpetrated during these four months' reign of terror." Stowe raged at the city authorities:

> We have no gas, nor fire brigade, nor water-works. All of the officers of the law are Mollie Maguires. There is not a pig nor a chicken within miles of Braidwood. . . . O, Mr. Editor, what a dreadful time we have had, and what a disgusting outrage these poor negro women have suffered. You cannot know what a joy it was to see the troops.*

Unless "the rebel crew from Dan down to his henchman, John James," faced trial in Joliet (not Braidwood) for "their crimes," Stowe feared the worst. "It is the first time I have ever invested in a town wholly governed by foreigners," Stowe concluded, "and it will be the last." Stowe's anger prevented him from seeing his unintended humor: it was a bad joke, at best, to make a Scot like McLaughlin the leader of Irish Molly Maguires. But he erred seriously in naming four nonminers (among "other leading citizens") as having urged Cullom to send the militia. The miners did not answer "Stowe," but one of the four, William O'Dell, did, and he called Stowe's allegations "a most unfair statement . . . full of misrepresentations," denied that he and the others had called for troops, described the attack on James as "a slander against a peaceable and law-abiding citizen," and wondered why the *Tribune* allowed Stowe space "to mislead the public." Edward Conley, editor of the *Wilmington People's Advocate* and like O'Dell a former Wilmington elected official, shared O'Dell's anger with Stowe, calling his letter "absurd," "cowardly," "a most damnable tissue of falsehoods and exaggerations from beginning to end," and filled with "infernally mischievous things."[65]

So ended a phase of the dispute between the miners and their employers, but not the strike itself, which dragged on another four months. The state militia left, the blacks stayed on, and the strikers stayed out. The overwhelming display of state power had not shaken the miners' willingness to suffer further for their union. "The men are as persistent as ever, and say they will not concede to the companies," reported the *Chicago Journal* on August 8. Harsh judgments by county and state courts did not weaken the strikers. The day before the last troops left, McLaughlin was arrested on a "state warrant" issued by a

---

* Braidwood citizens organized a fire company in June 1877 (*Souvenir of Settlement and Progress of Will County*, 442).

Joliet judge, and the *Sun* headlined its report "At Last." The Will County sheriff had filed a complaint against McLaughlin and miner-alderman John McIntyre, charging them with "riot." Away fishing that day, McIntyre was not served, but McLaughlin went to Joliet, where he waived examination, was bound over for trial, and was released on $500 bail. John Donahue, an Irish Braidwood grocer whose brother served on the Wilmington City Council in 1876–1877, and who himself won election as county treasurer on the Democratic ticket in 1879, signed McLaughlin's bond. The available record does not tell that McLaughlin ever came to trial, but less than a week after his arrest the Will County courts struck a more severe blow at the miners' efforts to win their disputed back wages. When the militia were still in Braidwood, an operator had insisted that the firms would not pay the wages because the miners would use them to purchase arms "for purposes of terrorism." The lower courts had supported the miners, and the companies had appealed to the circuit court. A single "test case" before that court resulted in a remarkable reversal. The lawyers for the coal companies—a Joliet firm and Chicago's Walker, Dexter, and Smith—produced no witnesses and addressed themselves only "upon questions of law," and a satisfied judge instructed the jury to "bring in a verdict of no cause of action" because the miners, who worked in groups in the pitrooms, could not "recover as individuals under the contracts." The strikers had to start their court action anew. Although the CW & V offered the man fifty cents on the dollar and promised to pay court expenses, the miners returned to the courts. A decision did not come until the late fall, and the lower courts again ruled against the companies.[66]

After the troops departed and the court ordered new trials, the strike settled down.* About 450 black men continued to work in the mines. Sixty left for St. Louis ("a very bad set," said the *Sun*), but 100 more arrived in Braidwood. Most worked for the CW & V and about 100 labored in the Diamond mines. At first, four Chicago militia officers trained the blacks in military matters, and then a black major

---

* "These are terrible times for every one who is handling property of this kind," Superintendent Sweet explained on August 18 to a Massachusetts stockholder who complained that the strike endangered earnings. He comforted his critic by stressing the work of the blacks and the inability of the Braidwood strikers to get the Streator miners to quit work. Sweet made it clear that the strikers deserved defeat and that compromise was unwise: "Our people here have decided . . . that we have no other course to pursue than to 'fight this thing out on the line,' if it takes not only all summer, but all winter to accomplish what we have set out to do. If our coal miners succeed in carrying their points now, the property will be of no value to any one." Sweet remained optimistic: "There is no doubt but what we shall ultimately accomplish what we have decided upon, and should we succeed we will hereafter be in shape to hold our trade and make some money for our Stockholders." (A. L. Sweet, Chicago, 18 Aug. 1877, to Cyrus Woodman, Cambridge, Mass., Woodman Mss., Wisconsin State Historical Society.)

and Civil War veteran took over. The black miners had access to a sizable arsenal (300 Springfield rifles, 45 Belgian guns, 16 Spencer carbines, 30 Union carbines, and 8 "shooters"), and the *Sun* predicted that "should trouble occur there will be no necessity for white troops." The press told of only one riotous incident. After two strikers returned to work, a crowd, again composed mostly of women, threatened them with "death" and "tar and feathers." It frightened off one worker, and the second went to work guarded by an armed escort. But these were exceptional events. The *Sun* said the strikers "pass the time as best they can, pitching quoits, playing ball, and indulging in games of all kinds." McLaughlin found time to campaign in support of Greenback-Labor candidates in Joliet and other northern Illinois towns. More and more, the strikers grew dependent on their own resources for survival. "The farmers for twenty miles around have been very liberal in supplying the miners with food," reported the *Sun* in mid-August, "but 'the free horse' has been about driven to death, and supplies will soon cease." Efforts to get the Streator men to strike failed. Braidwood union leaders went to Streator to plead with its CW & V employees and at first enjoyed success, but on August 19 the Streator men voted to remain at work. Although they sent slight financial aid to Braidwood (on August 16, they forwarded $126.45), their refusal to strike allowed the CW & V to fill contracts normally satisfied with Braidwood coal. A week later, the Braidwood miners voted unanimously to stay out until they won their back wages and their old wage rate. District union secretary James Pettigrew exploded resentfully toward the CW & V:

> The first settlement that can be made with the men . . . [is] "Pay what thou owest." Mtt. 19, 23. Jesus says, "a rich man shall hardly enter the kingdom of heaven," [and] I think it no wonder if they try to get their riches by robbing the poor workman of his hire, or trying to defraud him out of the pay he worked hard for in the mines.

"May the Lord hasten the time," Pettigrew hoped, "when the CW & V Company will have to pay the uttermost farthing."[67]

September passed, and on October 1 the strike entered its seventh month. Outside help fell away, and troubles from within and without threatened the strikers. The *Joliet Sun* gave them scant attention except to call their leaders, particularly McLaughlin, men "with all the luxuries of life, caring nothing for the miseries of their miserable dupes" and deserving only to be "severely punished." Pettigrew defended the strikers and insisted that the "attempt to starve [us] has failed." "Although our diet is light," he cracked, "our work is light also." But as the months dragged on, friction among the strikers threatened their staying power. For the first time, union leaders warned strikers of "pap suckers" and "wily serpents" among them—"hired tools . . . to tell lies and sow seeds of discords."

> Do not give ear . . . to these miserable and detestable creatures, though they profess to be Christians and elders of the Church. Judas professed to be a Christian, yet he sold our Saviour for thirty pieces of silver, just as these miserable fellows would sell you and your families to these soul-less corporations.

The strikers' Central Committee reminded the men that the blacks had come "to supplant you" and troops "to over-awe and scare you" with no success. The company's terms meant "slavery to yourselves and starvation to your wives and families." On October 16, the men voted 546 to 8 to continue the strike and selected a new negotiating committee because the operators would not meet with their old leaders. "This concession," a striker hoped, "gives the company a chance to make settlement if they wish." Instead, the companies sent reports that the strike had ended and invited miners to Braidwood. Men drifted there from as far east as Pittsburgh, and Pettigrew observed, "I have seen tears fall from their eyes when they found out the true state of affairs at this place." Reports that the strike had ended, however, continued to filter East, and the strikers again protested: "We are still in the field. The men are as firm as they were on the first of April." But their statement betrayed a growing need for outside financial support: "The men of Braidwood never refused a helping hand to all who applied to them in their hour of trouble. He who helps quick helps double." In early November, funds were solicited again. An appeal to miners throughout the country reminded them that for more than half a year miners had held out against "one of the most oppressive and gigantic corporations on this side of the Allegheny mountains." They sought a "fair remuneration for our labor" but also wanted to preserve "our rights and liberties as citizens of this free Republic." The strikers feared having to "sign away their birthright and become bonded slaves in this boasted land of liberty." McLaughlin, Pettigrew, and Lofty signed the appeal, appending to it the still-secret symbol of the Knights of Labor. That fall, McLaughlin and others had founded a secret lodge, Local Assembly 876, among the miners.[68]

In mid-November, after more than eight months (a time long enough to make the Braidwood dispute the longest in the nation's history), the miners voted to return to work. For nearly nine months they had stymied the operators. Between April 1 and November 30, the CW & V's Braidwood mines had turned out 38,500 tons of coal,

115,500 tons less than the preceding year.* But the strikers were wearing down. The courts ruled in favor of the strikers on the wages owed them and ordered the men paid by November 26, but the companies once again threatened an appeal. Many miners feared additional delay if this happened, and their Central Committee accused the operators of using the courts to "sink into utter despair those from whom they have derived their good fat living." But winter was approaching, and the miners needed that month of wages. A final plea for help read like an evangelical sermon: "We deem it our duty to appeal as men and brothers in this trying hour to stand as firm as the Rock of Ages." Many had suffered and still suffered.

> But the hour of your redemption has come, for your cries have entered into the ears of the Lord of the Sabbaoth, and the vengeance that he has promised will soon be poured out upon the unhallowed heads of those who now seek our downfall, and a fearful retribution will certainly be meted out to those who have and would again defraud the laborer of his hire.

Appeal to a retributive and just God was insufficient. Expecting defeat in the courts and anxious to corner the increasing winter trade, the companies shifted ground and offered the strikers their disputed wages if they returned to work. The operators promised to rehire all the strikers except for "a baker's dozen of old ringleaders." The miners accepted this settlement. But for a time, it looked as if this "compromise" would not work. A Joliet dispatch, the only extant document that tells of the terms of settlement, reported that the companies "rejected a majority of the English-speaking Welsh, Italians, and Bohemians and nearly every Scot and Irish miner." They also hesitated paying full legal costs. "The companies," the Joliet correspondent noted, "evidently propose to protect their own interests and prevent strikes in the future, by retaining 'the blacklegs,' and re-employing only those of the old miners in whom they have confidence." In ways unknown, however, a settlement was achieved. The miners accepted 70 cents a ton from October 1 to April 1 and 80 cents from April 1 to October 1; an additional 15 cents a ton was paid for "brushing" and "pushing." Their union was shattered and its leaders without jobs. The companies refused work to McLaughlin, John Young, John Kier, Frank Lofty, and John McIntyre—the township's supervisor, and the city's mayor, treasurer, and two aldermen. The miners had suffered

---

* The miners did not realize that the CW & V was in financial difficulty as a result of the strike and was being pressured by stockholders like Boston investor Cyrus Woodman to resume earlier profitable patterns. (See Cyrus Woodman, Boston, 15 Aug. and 12 Nov. 1877, to A. L. Sweet, Chicago, Woodman Mss., Wisconsin State Historical Society.)

too long and spent too much of their collective energies to protect the jobs of their leaders.[69]

Explaining their defeat, the strikers' Central Committee said, "We were exhausted, our families naked and hungry, and the necessities of winter staring us in the face." A bitter but realistic public statement blamed the surrender on the "absence of humanity" among "the people of this State and other parts of the country." The onset of winter barred continued self-protection: "The God of Heaven has smiled on us, and given us a good yield in our gardens, and this has been our main support." Their "struggle for liberty" ended, the miners predicted a grim future: "We feel our defeat to be disastrous for many reasons." "Many of us will be victimized," they forewarned, adding that those promised work most hated laboring alongside men who had done "all they possibly could to assist capital to crush labor." "When will the day come," asked the committee, "when the love of liberty will be more general, so that one poor man will not fight and crush another poor man?" McLaughlin shared this view but found hope in the possibilities of political reform. His experiences in 1877 had deepened his belief in the need for radical social change, and he celebrated the New Year by passing harsh judgment on the Republic's failure and urging the overthrow of "the golden god." A letter supporting the national Greenback-Labor platform suggested only moderate reforms: McLaughlin talked of the need for paper currency, the denial of land to speculators, free education to "rich and poor alike," and a tariff to protect "young" industries. But advocacy of such legislation did not make of McLaughlin a mere moderate or a "money crank." He believed such laws essential to more far-reaching fundamental reforms: "These, once adopted, long hours, prison labor, poverty, and degradation would become things of the past, and with education diffused among the masses, industrial cooperation will soon follow." The "free ballot" allowed workers to "control the causes" of their depressed condition, strike down "evil legislation," and "break the chains of industrial serfdom." "It does not require much logic or reason to prove that the wage workers and wealth producers of the civilized world are defrauded and robbed out of their fair and just share of the wealth they create," McLaughlin insisted. "The basis of our social system requires to be remodeled and founded on industrial equality." The mayor shared the Central Committee's muted optimism: "We are dead, but not defeated. He who conquers by force, only conquers half his foe."[70]

The miners were not yet without power. Although their union had been severely weakened, their victimized leaders still dominated local politics and enjoyed much community esteem. "All good and true men," a miner wrote of them. In late March before the 1878 township and city elections, Braidwood's Greenback-Labor party endorsed the national platform and nominated a full township slate. Two blacklisted miners, one of them the supervisor John Young, whose imposition of taxes on previously untaxed industrial properties had angered the coal companies, headed the ticket. Young's renomination polarized Braidwood politics for the first time. Republican and Democratic leaders joined with coal-company officials (and, according to a scornful miner, "other scales and uclers on the body politic") to form "a combination ticket"—the People's party—with Eureka superintendent William Maltby as Young's opponent.* A brief but bitter campaign preceded the April election. Although Maltby's supporters warned that his defeat would close the mines, and the companies ordered certain miners to "peddle the ticket," the Greenback-Labor candidates had their strongest and most surprising adversary in John James, formerly the town's most esteemed trade unionist and labor reformer. The evidence does not explain James's remarkable shift except to suggest that the 1877 strike divided him from his old supporters. Then employed as an "agent" (probably a salesman) for the companies, James blamed Young's nomination on a "secret conclave," the Knights of Labor, and accused him of having "prostituted his office," overassessed properties, misused tax money to feed strikers, and by his behavior threatened the return of prosperity. James warned on Election Day that a victory for Young would make things worse, but the voters felt otherwise and by small majorities ranging from 57 to 197 votes elected the entire Greenback-Labor slate.† "The city and workingmen's true interests have been ruined," James publicly despaired. But the union miners felt otherwise, calling Young's victory "a terrible blow to the codfish aristocrats," one that "they would not readily forget." James's behavior astounded former friends and co-workers. Although they had labored together for years and James's friendship had caused him to settle in Braidwood, McLaughlin scornfully denounced him after the election:

> Yes, John, it was wrong to put a poor man, a coal miner, into office, who was denied his right to live in this place where he had invested

* Maltby's career made him an ideal candidate. Then thirty-eight, Maltby had come from England in 1862. His father had tended cattle for a large English coal and iron firm, and Maltby worked as a child on the farm before entering the mines. He settled in Braidwood in 1866 as a superintendent, but had traveled widely before then, working in Michigan, Pennsylvania, other towns in Illinois, and even Nova Scotia. A biographical sketch published that year found him a prime example of the American Dream: "Mr. Maltby came to America financially a poor boy; to-day he has risen from the lad that was engaged in driving the mule to the plow to a Superintendent of one of the largest coal companies in the West." (*History of Will County*, 758.)
† Among those elected with Young to township office were Irish saloonkeeper John Bambrick (town clerk), Bohemian saloonkeeper Joseph Randeck (town constable), and English storekeeper Edward Wakefield (justice of the peace). (*History of Will County*, 466.)

all that he had ever saved from his labor, and for what? because he was honest enough to see that the banks, the railroad and coal corporations' property and other monopolists were taxed on the same footing as the other people's property. . . . "Vengeance is mine, saith the Lord," and so say these lordly corporations.

Young's election had important symbolic meaning for McLaughlin and others like him. It blunted the impact of their earlier defeat. "Mose," the *National Labor Tribune*'s regular Braidwood correspondent, felt it proved the miners would not "sell out our birthright for a mess of potage." The coal companies felt differently. A *Chicago Times* correspondent said they despaired because "the leading spirits in the 'nationals' were identified, or at least sympathized, with the great coal miners' strike." And the same source warned: "Now that they are to continue in power, it is said that the coal companies will close the various shafts . . . excepting only those in which negroes are employed. The feeling is bitter." "Mose" showed no awareness of this danger. He cheered because otherwise victorious employers had felt "a glorious rebuke . . . for the coercion and intimidation they brought to bear against us at the polls."[71]

But such enthusiasm was short-lived. In the city election a few weeks later, another Greenback-Labor ticket—this one headed by victimized miner Frank Lofty, a former alderman now seeking election as city marshal—was "completely routed." Lofty and the other jobless miners deserved election, said one supporter: "all of them are good citizens— intelligent, sober, and industrious workmen." Public office rather than private employment would keep them in Braidwood. But in this second election, opponents of the labor slate did more than organize a "combination" ticket. The companies discharged ten miners who had worked hard to elect Young and illegally enfranchised more than 200 black men. Illinois required a year's residence before citizens could vote; the blacks had come in June 1877. A disillusioned miner mocked the anger of the coal companies:

How dare you, our slaves, seek to retain him [Lofty], when we have forbidden his presence in this place? Do you not know that he is too intelligent, and his ideas of freedom are so obnoxious to us that he must not, will not or shall not live in this place? Therefore, we your lord masters, have over two hundred colored men, and, although they are not one year in this State, and cannot legally vote, yet we have men in your midst who for a few dollars and the promise of our favors will perjure themselves, and swear that these colored men are voters, and with their votes and all the other white slaves whom we will bully, bribe and intimidate, we shall defeat his election.

The votes of blacks ensured the defeat of Lofty and his entire ticket in what a miner called "a great fraud committed on a body of free men." According to the miners, all but two of the labor candidates had won a majority of the "white votes," and they demanded that "justice be done, no matter who suffers." McLaughlin and Mooney, still in office as mayor and city attorney, tracked down "some of these villains" and arrested several black voters. Superintendent Maltby gave bond for them, but miner Meshank Dando, then police magistrate, bound them over for a grand jury hearing. Petitions urged an investigation of the disputed election, and some blacks supported the challenge. "Our principal witnesses are colored men," reported a miner, "[men] who came here with those who voted, and of course know where they came from, and how long they are in this State." But the companies fired those blacks who testified for the Greenback-Labor ticket, hoping to force them to leave town, and other obstacles frustrated efforts to reverse the election. John James called the defeat of the labor ticket "a glorious revolution against dark lanterns, passwords, signs, and gripes," but a critic retorted, "My God! John James calls this diabolical outrage a glorious revolution."* A committee of

---

* John James lost his position of esteem among the miners because of his role during the spring elections. Bitter exchanges between James and his critics filled the pages of the *Labor Tribune* and the *Braidwood Republican*. "Mose" joined McLaughlin in attacking their old leader. He accused James of "braying like Whitelaw Reid . . . about communists and communism." A large meeting of miners supported McLaughlin and condemned James for his "treacherous and villainous" role. James did not remain silent. He called his critics "dead-dead communists, conspirators, and men to whom 'the [Knights of Labor] pledge' has been given." He compared "Mose" to "a flea as he hops under one's clothing" and scoffed at McLaughlin as "his excellency." James detailed his criticisms of the labor government and accused Young and the others of "unexampled, unlawful, and disgraceful" management of the city. Detailing alleged examples of fiscal dishonesty, he called his old associates prophets who falsely told of a "promised land that flows with milk and honey." McLaughlin answered James's complaints in detail and concluded, "John, your day of . . . fooling the people, especially the mining classes, is past." "Mose" agreed: James's "sayings and doings at the time of our spring elections will long be remembered." The bitterness against James lingered on. In August 1878, John Siney, a close associate of both James and McLaughlin in the Miners' National Association, visited Braidwood. No one but James knew of his presence. "Mr. Siney," "Mose" wrote after he left the city, "has hundreds of warm-hearted friends here, and they hope he will call again, and that he will make it a little better known when he does come here." The miners did not condemn Siney for his apparent support of James. And they did not make it difficult for Robert James, the brother of their acid critic. Robert James ran for city attorney a few years later on a labor ticket headed by McLaughlin. But John James had lost his position of trust among the miners, and in 1880 he left that city to take work as superintendent of an Ohio coal mine. The contrast between his departure in 1880 and his earlier leave-taking in 1874 to help build the MNA needed no comment. In 1874, the miners welcomed his return; in 1880, a Braidwood miner noted his departure and then added: "He should make a good superintendent, as he has long advocated many useful and needed reforms in and around the mines." James later managed a hotel in Albuquerque, New Mexico, and a coalworks in Carthage, New Mexico. He served as assistant warden in the Santa Fe penitentiary for six years, and

miners (the names listed on their appeal included none of the older leaders) begged for outside funds to right the electoral wrong and keep Lofty, McLaughlin, and the others in their city:

> We are and intend to punish those who perpetrated this outrage. Can you aid us? We are poor, [and] a little from those who love liberty will help. . . . We are crushed and oppressed beyond a hope of redeeming ourselves, and our good men will be banished from their homes and the fires of liberty will be quenched in our midst, unless you Brothers will extend us a helping hand.

The spirit of mutuality was not dead among the Braidwood miners but transformed; the committee also attached the secret symbol of the Knights of Labor to its circular, and Joseph N. Glenn, a Cincinnati Knight, responded by comparing the prairie miners to the "noble and heroic defenders of outraged labor, the so-called Mollie Maguires . . . offered up on the scaffold" by the "prearranged and damnable machinations" of "tyrannical and vicious masters."[72]

The symbol of the Knights of Labor was new and unusual, but the Braidwood miners also used older and more traditional important symbols to express their dissatisfactions. The promise of the Republic and the reality of their condition generated a recurrent and deeply felt tension. More than once, "Mose" contrasted the two:

> We are often reminded by politicians of our glorious Constitution, and how every man is to be protected in his right of "life, liberty, and the pursuit of happiness." . . . Corporations can and do dictate to thousands what they shall eat, drink, and wear, and should any one grumble at their lot, they must be discharged and will not be allowed to work anywhere that the influences of said corporations

---

then, for reasons of health, moved to Santa Monica, California, where he died in 1902. The record tells of no further connections with the labor movement after he quit Braidwood. Frank Lofty also left Braidwood in 1880. He moved to Scranton, Kansas, to work as a coal miner and help build the Knights of Labor. Lofty, who had come from Scotland in 1868 as a twenty-year-old, became a Seventh Day Adventist preacher in Kansas in the 1880s and won election as a Kansas probate judge in the 1890s. He died in 1929. The careers of Lofty and James moved in opposite directions after 1880, but both left a subsequent impress on the United Mine Workers of America through relatives and close associates. Lofty's nephew, Alexander Howat, became a powerful but dissident leader of the UMW in the West between 1910 and 1940. Before he left Braidwood, James hired a widow to wash clothes for his family. Her husband had been killed by a runaway tram. That woman was John Mitchell's stepmother, and as a young man Mitchell moved west from Braidwood to find work. He labored for a time in the New Mexico mines that James watched over as a superintendent. Mitchell, of course, later became UMW president and a figure of great national importance between 1900 and 1910. (*National Labor Tribune* 28 May, 15 June, 6, 13, 20, 27 July, 3, 24, Aug. 1878, 13 March 1880; Pinkowski, *John Siney*, 291, 293, 299.)

will extend. Yet, mark you; every man is to be protected in his right to "life, liberty, and the pursuit of happiness." Oh, my country, what a mockery!

The symbols and rituals that marked the distinctiveness of American civilization for the Braidwood coal miners, however, served as more than devices for protest. In June 1878, the miners planned a "grand picnic" to celebrate Independence Day and included among their guests two Chicago socialists and nearby Joliet's Greenback reform mayor, James Elwood. The son of a pioneer Joliet settler and early railroad builder, and himself a Civil War hero, Elwood drifted through Democratic and Republican politics to the Greenback movement. A real estate developer, Elwood was instrumental in first bringing gas, water, and telephone companies to Joliet. In 1878, the Braidwood miners remembered him as "a very good man, who . . . stood at our backs last year during the great cornmeal strike," and invited him to their celebration. "A grand success," the parade attracted about 5,000 marchers and viewers, and one observer called the labor procession larger, relatively, than any that had ever occurred west of Chicago. The symbols and events that shaped the day pitted the Braidwood miners' actual experiences against their version of the American ideal and served to tie together a weakened, depressed community. An independent military company composed entirely of miners wearing green caps with red bands headed the marchers, and each of three parading divisions was led by a citizen carrying an American flag. Three miners' brass bands marched, too. Although the paraders were overwhelmingly recent immigrants (the Bohemian, French, and Italian miners, for example, marched as a group), a wagon carried thirty-eight "girls" representing each state and the Goddess of Liberty. The mottoes that the miners carried on banners told of their hopes and fears and made much of recent events: "A Republic Forever"; "Never a Monarchy"; "We Use No Coercion to Get Votes"; "The Only Reasoning of Kings Is the Gun and Bayonet"; "Long Live the Republic"; "Greenbacks Paid the Soldier; Why Not Pay the Bondholder?"; "We Are Poor But That Is No Reason Why We Should Be Ignorant"; "Labor and Justice Will Triumph"; "Liberty, Equality, and Fraternity." John Kier, the blacklisted city treasurer, presided in McLaughlin's absence (he was ill, suffering from a recurrent eye ailment), and the Methodist minister who had supported the 1877 strikers gave a sympathetic "oration." The Joliet mayor and I. B. Belopdradsky, a Bohemian socialist from Chicago, also spoke. William H. Steen, city clerk under McLaughlin, read the Declaration of Independence. In the context of that year's dramatic events, the celebration counted for more than mere mawkish rhetoric and ceremonial gesture. The

Braidwood miners, weakened in so many ways, had prepared a vivid symbolic protest.

In November of that year, Ducat, reflecting on the Braidwood "riot" sixteen months earlier, advised the Illinois adjutant general that stern measures, changes in the law and even the Constitution, were essential to prevent meetings by "professed agitators" and "men of dangerous character." Braidwood fresh before him, Ducat worried that his country had changed for the worse:

> The constitution and laws of the United States were framed for patriots, and at a time when almost the whole population was united in its desire for the welfare, success and peace of the new republic. Since then, many agitators, and advocates of theories, dangerous to the peace of the country and to society, have drifted to our shores, invited, perhaps, by the liberty so freely offered and which they are disposed to abuse. . . . If law and order and peace are to be maintained, there must be power and force. Laws are of little value without the power to enforce them.

"Our country," Ducat now believed, "is no longer new." The Braidwood miners also had learned this lesson and showed it in their struggles, and in their celebrations. Theirs was no longer an industrial frontier city.[73]

Even the miners' worst expectations did not match the actual deterioration in living conditions that followed their defeat in 1877. The mines did not resume normal production until October 1878: in February, usually a busy month, men got one-and-a-half to two days of work each week. Total CW & V output for the year was less than in 1876, and income suffered accordingly. Frank Lofty gave careful monthly estimates of wages earned in 1878 to a state legislative committee: the average miner's annual income totaled $285—40 percent of it earned in October, November, and December. For nine months, the Braidwood miner averaged a little more than $18.00 a month, and each month the companies deducted $4.30 for house coal, oil, and blacksmithing. "But for our garden patch," said one miner, "we would starve." An appeal for financial aid signed by George Hunter, the new union secretary, and addressed to "all labor organizations and to the . . . [Knights of Labor] throughout the land," told of families "actually starving," and Hunter asked, "How in God Almighty's name . . . [can] a man having a family live properly on such a pitiful sum?" Another miner worried: "It is possible that low wages, poverty and enforced idleness may [be] carried too far. There is a limit to human endurance and it is well for those at the helm of the ship of State to think well.

. . ." Continued and worsened suffering might even cause "an uprising that would startle the world."[74]

The absence of steady employment and a weakened union gave back the coal companies some of the power they had lost. The firms took full advantage of their new strength to bolster their social position, impose restraints and new disciplines on the men, and punish their leaders. Numerous small shops and independent mercantile enterprises existed in Braidwood, and in 1875 the miners had easily prevented the setting up of "truck stores." But in January 1878, their condition had so deteriorated that they could not stop the CW & V from opening such a store in a building previously used to feed black miners. In the next few months, the company opened two more stores, one in Braidwood and the other in Streator. A miner mocked the store as "a New-Year's gift" that promised the men everything "from a cradle to a coffin . . . with a good supply of corn meal and molasses always on hand." Compulsion, however, forced him and others to trade in these stores: those unwilling to take some of their wages in "store pay" learned they could "take up their beds and walk." The company store symbolized deepened dependence and overt exploitation. A miner felt it wrong that men could no longer "handle their money when hard and honestly earned." "A pair of mits for my child which cost in truck forty cents, I bought for twenty-five cents cash," Frank Lofty complained to the legislature. Another worker said that in these stores the men were "so well soaped they never feel the shaving process." CW & V net earnings in 1880 suggested that its Braidwood and Streator stores served as more than just paternal or disciplining devices. Net earnings for the stores came to $33,008.06, seven and a half times the net earnings on land and house rent, and 15.2 percent of the firm's total net earnings for the year.* The miners could not prevent the compulsion that made them trade income for goods on company terms. Their previously successful cooperative grocery failed. A fire in late January 1878 burned the store to the ground, and the men lacked funds to rebuild it. "Poverty," one said sadly, "is too deep-rooted and widespread to reaccomplish this glorious undertaking."†

The company store became more important for other reasons. It weakened the economic position of established storekeepers, and in early February 1878 a miner reported, "Already one of our old business houses has been closed by the sheriff." A shift in policy by a

---

* The CW & V annual report (1880) listed as a liability $16,936.05 for goods purchased, but also counted as an asset $45,500 of inventory in its three stores.
† The store operated in Odd Fellows Hall, and even though it suspended for nine months during the 1877 strike, it made sales for the year totaling $14,651, earned a profit on these sales of $2,135, and paid dividends amounting to $708. McLaughlin was president of the cooperative society in 1877, and Frank Lofty replaced him in 1878. (*National Labor Tribune*, 9 Feb. 1878.)

local bank made the miners more dependent on the store. Before this time, the bank had extended credit to miners needing cash between monthly wage payments. In 1878, it abolished this service. When business picked up in the fall of 1878, store prices increased between 10 and 35 percent, but wage rates remained constant. A miner complained unavailingly, "Our hands [are] tied . . . with the curse called a yearly contract and all the beauties of a 'pluck-me' . . . truck." Prosperity, he worried, "goes past us here . . . leaving us more destitute from its very coming, as everything is rising in prices except our labor."[75]

Discipline was imposed upon the miners in other ways, some petty and mean by any standard, all exacting and effective. McLaughlin and his four co-workers remained without jobs until September 1878, when the operators temporarily abolished their blacklist. A miner scoffed, "Their game of 'starve them out' has not succeeded as well as expected. . . . Very generous, ain't it?" Busy campaigning for the Greenback-Labor ticket that fall, McLaughlin resumed work in December, and a supporter took pride in his return: "Some people think it looks well to see the mayor of a city taking his bread and butter out of the coal face, down in the mine. All honor to him for his independence. It is no disgrace to his honest heart." But the blacklist remained a recurrent instrument for discipline. A year later some men who urged a strike against the annual contract lost their jobs. "They were good, intelligent, practical miners, and married," said a friend. "They had lived a good many years in this place. . . . More are said to be booked for the road." After he criticized company advertisements for new workers in 1881, McLaughlin again could not get work. "The bosses and superintendents have given me 'hail Columbia,' " he wrote.

Blacklisting affected only outspoken company critics, but other company policies operated to the disadvantage of all miners. Men who quit one company to work for another needed a written permit to make the change. In March 1878, the CW & V (as it had done earlier in Streator) fired all white single miners. "This practice of discharging men because they do not take some man's daughter and help bring children into this world to be walked around half clad and half starved," said a critic, "is a disgrace to our civilization." Other miners found fault with new company rules making it more difficult to quit work and collect wages. The most unusual and petty of all new company policies concerned a shift in attitudes toward unused but privately owned prairie lands. "Hundreds of workmen," said a miner, "when times were good, bought a cow, that they might have milk for the use of their families. The coal companies had hundreds of acres of land, and all were at liberty to pasture their cows thereon free of charge." After the spring 1878 elections, the companies rented these lands to two miners who had supported the "combination ticket" and whom their fellow miners "and all other poor men . . . pay from seventy-five cents to one dollar for the privilege of allowing their cows to roam over the prairie." "This," the same miner complained, "is another blow to the poor of this place, and one that will be keenly felt by many a poor family that is striving to keep hunger from the door."*

Home ownership, a benefit to the miners when their union had power, worked to their disadvantage in the new context. In March 1879, a miner figured that about one-third of the men owned their homes outright or were paying off mortgages. These men became more dependent on the companies. "We have four or five hundred good men here," a miner observed, "who had all they ever saved from their labor invested in the little homes of their families, and if they could get one-third of its cost for it, they would not stay twenty-four hours in the accursed place." And he added: "As it is, many are going, and leaving their property behind them."[76]

Three recurrent "issues"—the continued dispute over the 1877 wages owed the miners, the presence of the black strikebreakers, and the renewal of the annual contract—regularly reminded the Braidwood miners that times had been better in their town. Although the companies had promised the back wages to end the 1877 strike, all but one firm refused to pay its men, and court cases dragged on for more than three years. The miners turned back an offer of seventy-five cents on the dollar and went again to the courts. In February 1878, a local court ruled in their favor. "At last," said an overjoyed miner, "Divine Providence got mad and interfered." The companies stalled, went to the court of appeals, lost again, and then asked the state supreme court to hear their arguments. In 1879, the highest state court ruled in two test cases involving $22,000 of black wages. It ordered payment to those miners not on annual contract in 1876–1877 and returned the case of the contract miners to the lower courts. Two years later, the miners were still in litigation, and McLaughlin complained of "those dreary law suits." But even then the noncontract miners held back dividing the monies awarded them and elected a committee that instructed lawyer Mooney to keep the cash until a final court ruling decided the status of the contract miners. The men felt

---

* The importance of the cow as a source of supplementary income for prairie workers should not be minimized. In 1877, reform aldermen in Joliet exempted cows from an ordinance designed to prevent animals from running through that city's streets at will. They banned horses and hogs but not cows because so many of the Joliet "poor," like those in Braidwood, kept cows and could not afford to purchase private feed. This ordinance infuriated the *Joliet Sun*: "Parties owning lawns, gardens, and garden fences should add to their personal property rifles, and when a cow commits a trespass she should be shot the same as a burglar or any other trespasser. A few dead cows lying around loose would have a most excellent effect." (*Joliet Sun*, 6 June 1877.)

that too much energy had been spent for some miners to go without a share of the wages won back.[77]

The continued dispute over back wages told of renewed power held by the coal companies. So did the presence of the black strikebreakers. Most blacks stayed on after the strike ended, daily reminders of the defeat suffered by the union. In December 1877, they worked the CW & V's "best shaft." "Just scratching away," said an embittered white miner. In June 1878, some blacks left the city, but others came in their place. "Just to keep the white men in subjection, you know," noted another white miner. That year a small number left, armed, to break a strike in Coal Creek, Indiana, and sixty others went to Tazewell County to the southwest where operators and miners disputed the price of powder. The blacks had a hard time in Braidwood: only two companies—the CW & V, in its G shaft, and the Diamond mines— employed blacks, and the Diamond mines were the region's poorest with regard to monetary remuneration.

Little is known of the relations between the white and black miners. Letters written by white miners record their presence, but tell little about the black community. Black miners started a Colored Baptist Church in 1877, a fraternal lodge the next year, and in 1880 a Colored Odd Fellows Lodge. These separate institutions suggest a separate social existence, but scattered evidence tells of frequent contact between white and black miners. The data hint at a mixture of friction and friendship. In 1880, a small number of black and white miners disputed over the annual contract that the blacks had quickly accepted, some shooting occurred, and a riot nearly erupted.* At the same time, isolated items told of fraternal feeling toward the black miners. Some blacks lost their jobs for supporting the white miners in the 1878 election, and that was not forgotten. William Cunningham told the state legislature a year later: "We have no hard feelings toward the colored miners. We blame those who brought them here." In 1880, a white miner cheered the black ones for refusing the overtures of agents seeking black miners to break a strike in Rapid City, Illinois. "Most of the colored men in this place," he insisted, "are wide awake to these foul fellows, who act as agents for those bloodsucking companies."

Only one document survives to tell us of the attitudes of Braidwood's blacks: it is a letter from Moses J. Gordon, a black miner and union

* Early in May 1880, according to a black miner, John Woods, a black man, went into a saloon, where three or four white miners cursed the blacks for signing the 1880–1881 contract. A fight resulted, and Wood left the saloon brandishing a revolver. A police officer took his gun from him, and Wood fled but was shot by the officer. A crowd gathered, and four black men picked up Wood. The whites threatened Wood with more harm, and the other blacks protected him. A few days later several blacks, including Wood, were arrested in Joliet. (*Joliet Sun*, 3, 4 May 1880.)

advocate, to the *National Labor Tribune* in December 1881. Worried because of recurrent attacks by white miners on black strikebreakers, Gordon saw the cause in the unwillingness of white miners to let black men work with them.

> A rule that will not work both ways will not work. They [the blacks] could no more get work here until the year 1877 than they could fly. Why was this? Was it capital that prohibited them from working here? Not by any means; it was the miners themselves, who would come out on strike before they would allow the negro to earn his daily bread. Was that not taking the bread out of the mouth of the negro? or would my fellow miners consider the negro unworthy of earning his bread?

Gordon reminded readers of black miners who joined the union, lost their jobs, and had to leave town. Because only two companies offered them work, black miners had less freedom than white miners. "If he is discharged from the G shaft," Gordon said of the black miner, "he must go to the Diamond and work in an inferior room, or else he must move [away]." Until they could work freely in all the mines, few blacks would join the union. Gordon advised the white miners that their self-interest required cooperation in spreading job opportunities for blacks to all the mines:

> Every nationality on the face of the globe can come here and go to work wherever there is work to be had, except for the colored man, and in nine cases out of ten the miners are to blame for it. A house divided against itself cannot stand. If the laboring class fights capital for their rights, they have enough to do without fighting against six millions of people that have got to earn their bread by the sweat of their brow.
>
> Many men went to war and fought for the liberation of the slaves, and after they were liberated they did not want them to have a chance to make a living, which is a contrast with Ireland. In Ireland, the landlord don't want the people to have pay for their work, and in America the [white] people don't want the colored people to have a chance to work.

Gordon did not condemn all the white miners but made subtle distinctions among them. Singling out McLaughlin as "the most liberal reasoner I have ever met," the black unionist was convinced that "if Mr. McLaughlin had his way matters in regard to labor would soon be at a better standpoint than they are to-day." The evidence is too scanty to show what influence black miners like Gordon had on other blacks and on the white miners. But in 1883, when the weakened union selected representatives from each shaft for a central organization, it picked a black miner as delegate from the CW & V's G shaft. No evidence exists of protest by white miners. His name was listed along with those of the other delegates: "Elijah Roey (colored)."[78]

Neither Roey, the other black miners, nor the more numerous white miners had adequate organized power to affect the annual contract between 1878 and 1883. A miner scorned those who called it a "mutual agreement": a family man competing with five others like him had few choices. He "has no alternative. . . . He feels the pangs of hunger; his family is naked and hungry; capital has him by the throat. . . . And this is a mutual agreement!" The 1878–1879 and 1879–1880 contracts gave the miners the same low wage rates fixed after the 1877 strike. Coal production boomed everywhere in 1880, and Braidwood was no exception: the CW & V mines broke all past records (150,000 more tons than in 1876, 361,607 tons in all). That year, the companies tightened work rules but raised the wage rate 10 cents (to 80 and 90 cents a ton) and offered the miners a "sliding scale" arrangement that promised them 40 percent of all profits when coal sold for more than $1.60 a ton in Braidwood or $2.50 a ton in Chicago. "The old, the young, the lame, and the lazy" among the miners voted to accept the increase, and it was renewed without change in 1881–1882 and 1882–1883. Although McLaughlin said the miners did not gain much from the sliding scale, details on its effects are lacking.* In May 1883 the miners, prodded by McLaughlin, voted to accept a 5-cent cut in the wage rate. The 1883–1884 rates (75 and 80 cents a ton) showed that the miners had lost much in ten years. In 1873–1874, they earned $1.10 a ton. The absence of a powerful local union together with intensive competition from other nonunion coal operators in the Chicago market entirely weakened their bargaining power.† No one

---

* In 1880, the companies offered the men a flat 12½-cent increase, or 10 cents and the sliding scale. McLaughlin and other mine leaders favored the latter arrangement. Under it, whatever the selling price of coal during the year, the men got 80 or 90 cents a ton, depending on the season. McLaughlin worried that the base price was too low but said that in the previous winter Braidwood coal sold for $4 a ton in Chicago. That price included 85 cents for "teaming and screening" and 90 cents for freight charges. Adding these figures to the $1.60, McLaughlin estimated company costs at $3.35. If the miner had earned the promised 40 percent, he would have gotten an additional 26 cents a ton. Much depended on the price of coal in Chicago. Braidwood coal, however, was only a small part of the total consumed in that city, and the quantity of coal shipped there hardly affected its price. Interesting to note in McLaughlin's estimates is that teaming and screening costs together with freight charges came to $1.75 a ton, and that miners earned either 70 or 80 cents a ton for digging that winter. These costs were twice the rate paid the miner for digging coal. (*National Labor Tribune*, 1, 15 May 1880.) Two years later, McLaughlin still favored the sliding scale and criticized as an alternative "striking at every turn of the industrial wheel." But he complained that the Braidwood firms often made long-term contracts with coal purchasers when the market price was low so that the men did not benefit from the sliding-scale arrangement. (*Ibid.*, 27 May 1882.)
† The CW & V managed its accounts well in these years. In 1880, for example, it listed

realized this more than McLaughlin, who argued that strikes under such conditions were fruitless and faulted efforts. In 1883, for example, he opposed striking against the wage cut. The companies argued that low wages paid Ohio and Indiana miners threatened their position in the Chicago market and even offered to send four Braidwood miners to study Chicago market conditions. Some Braidwood miners favored a strike, but McLaughlin felt such protest meaningless until the miners "are better educated, better unified, and thoroughly understand the selfish laws of competition that control the trade and commerce of our country." For McLaughlin, strikes were means, not ends; their success or failure was shaped by their particular contexts.

> Strikes are all right when we have a rising market and the supply not equal to the demand, but when the supply is greater than the demand, and the particle produced becomes a drug on the market, and hundreds of men [are] in idleness and thousands on short time, then strikes are a curse and should not be encouraged or tolerated among us. They are not a cure, and if a remedy, they are worse than the disease.

McLaughlin looked to the time when the miners would hold enough power "to grapple with that selfish monster, Competition, the curse of the coal miners and the wealth producers generally." At a mass meeting on May 1, 1883—as in earlier years, the men paraded to the meeting grounds led by brass bands—McLaughlin argued against a strike. He reviewed the many strikes and lockouts they had known (telling even of Scotland and England in the 1830s and 1840s) and called them "causes" that fill "the hearts of many of the old and middle aged men present with joyous and sometimes sad recollections of the years that are past." But to strike in 1883 was a futile act, an illusory rejection of reality. "If you want to stop these reductions, you must join your brothers in the East, as that is where reductions in most cases have their beginnings. You must be more liberal in your thoughts, and more liberal in your pockets." A national market for coal had convinced McLaughlin and others that local economic power could not shape wage rates. McLaughlin often idealized the past, but he had also learned from it and saw no reason to return to it.[79]

That McLaughlin and miners like him favored more moderate trade union strategy meant they had grown more realistic, not more conservative. But despite frequent efforts, the Braidwood miners' union did

---

as "net earnings" $216,829.14. The same year, it twice paid 3 percent dividends to stockholders, totaling $120,000. Incidentally, the company paid a total of $4,911.34 in taxes. (CW & V, *Annual Report, 1881*, 4–5.)

not regain its former strength betwen 1878 and 1884. Still, trade union sentiment did not disappear. The secret Knights of Labor, whose symbol had mysteriously appeared on the miners' petition in 1877, gained support and some miners openly espoused socialist doctrine. Most remained trade unionists committed to Greenback-Labor ideology. Protests came to little, however, and union organization and sentiment fluctuated severely for seven years. In the fall of 1878, widespread "feeling" for a strike for higher wages was calmed by "prominent leaders" among the miners. The following summer, the men elected committees to enforce a new ventilation law and reorganized their union as the Miners' Mutual Protective Association. Nearly 500 joined the union, but it faltered. Many meetings in the spring of 1880 could not convince the companies to alter oppressive work rules, and four months later a Belleville union leader reported from Braidwood, "To my astonishment, [I] found no union there." Three years later, the miners again had an organization, but it was too weak to prevail upon the companies to alter the screen size, allow them free choice in selecting a checkweighman, give them wages every two weeks (instead of once a month), and let a miner together with the resident superintendent hear individual grievances.

Efforts to strengthen union organization among the northern Illinois miners also failed. In 1879 and 1880, the LaSalle miners spurred regional organization and raised funds for organizer Cornelius Curtin, who had some success, including the start of a new union among the Minonk miners with "a colored gentleman as president." McLaughlin took over from Curtin in 1881 and agreed to "a twelve-month" as organizer. That spring he traveled through northern Illinois, making as many as five speeches a week to miners. Other union partisans spurred his work and raised funds to help McLaughlin. The miners learned they needed him in the field to keep "shooting ideas into your brains, stirring you up, and making you alive to your own best interests." Richard Trevellick, then in Illinois, joined LaSalle's John McLaughlin (not related to Daniel McLaughlin) in appealing for money. "His services will prove beneficial to you as a class, if you stand by him," Trevellick advised. John McLaughlin added:

> If you are pinching his family for bread, are you not driving your own into slavery? . . . I know his name is almost a household word in the villages of this State. . . . Supply the living with bread and butter. It is much better than raising empty, living marble columns to the dead organizer. Organize yourselves, then! Let us have a general resurrection day!

But the miners contributed only $350 to support McLaughlin, and he quit as organizer after six months. Not until 1885 did the miners reorganize successfully, and then it was with Daniel McLaughlin as president of the Illinois Miners' Mutual Protective Association.[80]

Despite their frequent frustrations between 1878 and 1885, the Braidwood miners did not entirely surrender the ethic of mutuality so important in their early years. The commitment among their traditional leaders to their *own* notions of the common good deepened. They renewed pride in craft. During the bitter 1882 Pennsylvania and Ohio miners' strike, McLaughlin scorned newspaper opinion that advised the miners to take "half a loaf":

> That may be for those seeking alms, but miners are not alms-seekers. They gave their labor and skill for the wages they ask. . . . No miner or other workingman who has the spirit of true manhood in his breast will accept half a loaf when he believes himself justly entitled to a whole one.

Concern for the common good found expression in these troubled years. In 1878, a CW & V miner said that "there was more coal mined" than the days men worked indicated because the men "divided up" the work offered. Another time, McLaughlin argued that piece-rate payments divided the miners from one another and weakened the social fabric.

> The miner in performing his labor is doubled up and twists about his body like a serpent from the time he goes to work in the morning till the time he comes out at night. . . . This is the curse of piece work, and if it has any good or redeeming feature it might be excusable. But it has none whatever. It blunts the intelligence of youth, and creates a desire for stimulants that too often lead to drunkenness. It brings on disease of the body and premature old age.

Cooperation flavored pleas for political reform. Testimony by Braid-wood miners before the state legislature in 1879 emphasized protective legislation, but John Crooley added: "The land, mines and all natural wealth belong to the whole people." Frank Lofty agreed. Asked why he favored a reduction of hours by law (in busy season the miners worked twelve to fourteen hours a day), he responded: "It would increase wages by lessening competition among workingmen, but co-operative production would cure all these ills. I believe the people should own the land and all natural wealth. Land should not be bought and sold. A co-operative system of industry would abolish poverty among the working class." Some months later, another miner urged restriction of output and a maximum daily wage of $1.50 for all miners to "stop the competition . . . carried on by our employers." "The present system of production and distribution is false," he argued.

"Death to competition among ourselves and death to competition . . . now carried on by the capital that employs us. The capitalist only recognizes us as a ware in the market, and not as human beings or Christians." He signed his letter "Progress."[81]

"Progress" meant more than higher wages to the leaders of the Braidwood miners. It also meant preservation of the ideals of the Republic. McLaughlin admitted that he and other immigrant miners "find themselves better here than in the land of their birth" (a fact that could "hardly be disputed"), but he and others worried over the perversion of the American egalitarian spirit. A miner feared that the absence of union strength threatened "all the liberty left to us by the founders of our government." Unemployment, said another, was "a sad and sickening picture to look upon in a free country where the responsibilities of the government rest in the hands of the people." McLaughlin asserted: "We live in a country the Constitution of which guarantees equal rights to each and every man." The nation's organic law obliged employers to meet "their workingmen on the principle of equality." But new laws did not escape McLaughlin, and he worried that repressive legislation and the "shackles of party" worked to deny "the rights and liberties guaranteed by the Constitution of the United States to the sons and daughters of toil." "Boards of Trade and such places," he believed, "are made lawful, while trade unions are outlawed. Corporations are made and fostered by law. Laws to foster true co-operation . . . [are] denied to the people." The miners further expressed the connection between their rights and the health of the Republic during their third annual Independence Day celebration in July 1880. McLaughlin introduced Albert Parsons, a Chicago socialist and organizer for the International Labor Union, an organization that brought together immigrant socialists and Yankee eight-hour-day reformers. Parsons told three thousand miners and their families of the need for strong trade unions, higher wages, and shorter hours. The miners approved the resolutions he offered, but added their own: "We declare that the sacredness of the elective franchise, free from the destructive influence of bribery, intimidation, and corruption, is wholly dependent upon the material condition of the wage receiving class. . . . The struggle to maintain freedom of speech, free ballot and free elections is the battle . . . for eight hours." Miners insisted that the welfare of the Republic depended on the welfare of its workers.[82]

Braidwood miners retained their political opinions and some of the social cohesiveness that had developed in the town's early years. Without these social underpinnings, it is difficult to explain the regularity with which the miners voted as a group for their own candidates in the decade following the disputed 1878 spring election. The fact that the Republican *Joliet Sun* denounced Greenback-Labor ideology as "a cover lid" for leaders of the "commune" and a crass appeal to "the baser natures of men" and to the "murderers and thieves of the county" did not deter the miners. The bitter 1878 congressional election stirred Braidwood as the Republicans worked hard to win the city: they fed $1,000 of campaign funds to local Republicans, and a miner complained that Republican "pimps and tools [are] at work trying to stir up religious animosities among the workingmen." McLaughlin refused to reenter the mines until after the election, and the *Braidwood Republican* ("that common sewer," a miner called it) condemned his busy campaigning for the national Greenback-Labor ticket all over northern Illinois. John Young supplemented McLaughlin, and they worked well together: "Dan is well liked, well known, a good speaker. . . . Young is a number one Greenback singer and has some good songs. They are a good team." "It is with the old man," a miner said of McLaughlin, "not money [but] principle. He is not a reformer to-day and the tool of oppression to-morrow. . . . Old Dan stands on the same platform to-day [that] he did when I was a boy, and I do not think there is enough money in the country to buy him. He will die as he lived, fighting in the interests of labor." Many miners shared McLaughlin's reform zeal. All the Greenback-Labor candidates won in Reed Township, and their votes outdistanced Republican and Democratic votes combined. Will County sent a Greenbacker to the state legislature in 1878, and in 1880 the Greenback-Labor party nominated McLaughlin for the state legislature. Although he ran last among four candidates in Will County, he ran far ahead of his ticket. In Reed Township, moreover, no one doubted his appeal: McLaughlin had more votes than the total netted by all three opponents. The miners nominated him for mayor again in the spring of 1881. Traveling then through northern Illinois as a union organizer, McLaughlin resisted the nomination and did not campaign against a strong Republican candidate. Nevertheless, "the Old War Horse," as the miners called him, won the election with ease and carried the entire labor ticket into office. Once again, miners held most elected city offices, and a former miner, the brother of the despised John James, served as city attorney. McLaughlin's most severe critic, the *Joliet Sun*, ignored his reelection, but the *Joliet News*, a Greenback paper founded in 1877, remembered how "his wise and cool management" had done much to "preserve peace and order" during the 1877 strike and called his return to office "the highest compliment ever paid to a citizen of Will county." Meshank Dando, a close associate for years and once more police magistrate, went even further. Praising McLaughlin for the "strength" that allowed him to withstand "the tempest of years," he saw his victory as a step toward "industrial emancipation." The 1881 city election gave Dando and others like him no little pleasure, and evangelical, perfectionist rhetoric flowed easily from his pen: "As 'Old Dan' often says, 'We know where we are but we know not where we may be going when we leave this world. Then, why should we not do our best to make this world a heaven while we remain here, and leave it better for our posterity?' " Others, miners and nonminers, shared this view. After the miners reorganized and strengthened their union in 1884, and while he served as president of both the Illinois Miners' Mutual Protective Association and the National Federation of Miners and Mine Laborers of the United States, Will County voters twice (in 1884 and 1886) sent McLaughlin to the state legislature.[83]

McLaughlin was not a newcomer to the state capitol. As a representative of the Illinois miners, he had lobbied there in 1879 and again in 1883 for protective labor legislation, and he knew the state legislative process well. In 1879, Braidwood miners, supported by other Illinois coal diggers and some Chicago workers, sparked a brief but intensive campaign of labor pressure politics. In March, they urged a state legislative committee (the first of its kind in Illinois) to pass laws improving mine safety; abolishing company stores, child labor under fourteen, and contract prison labor; regulating working hours; making education compulsory; and establishing a state bureau of labor statistics to show (a miner said) "who it is that does the work and thus makes civilization possible." A month before they testified, other Northern miners urged similar legislation, and then a state miners' convention sent McLaughlin and William E. Owens, a Belleville miner, trade unionist, and St. Clair County mine inspector, to Springfield to push for improved ventilation and mine inspection and the abolition of company stores. Helped by Chicago trade unionist John McGilvray, McLaughlin and Owens prodded the legislature for three months. Special circulars explained the reasons for particular labor reforms. Partly as a result of their work, and despite vigorous opposition from coal operators, the legislature passed an improved ventilation bill, abolished company stores, and set up a Bureau of Labor Statistics.* In May, McLaughlin reported: "Up to date we have been able to 'hold the fort.' " At the session's close, he said: "We had a long and hard fight, and although we have not accomplished all we would have liked, yet our friends think, all things considered, we have done well." McLaughlin especially praised "our many friends outside and inside the legislature" who resisted "all and every kind of temptations." Governor Cullom's veto of the company-store bill disappointed but did not surprise him. Remembering 1877, an angry McLaughlin

---

* McLaughlin also boasted that the legislature had put aside "the infamous tramp law" by burying it in a committee "where it 'sleeps the sleep of death.' "

exploded: a politician who sent soldiers to "compel poor men at the point of a bayonet to go to work at a reduction in wages" could not be expected to "sign a bill to save them from being robbed by soulless corporations and other tyrannical employers." Workers could "expect nothing better from him."

Despite McLaughlin's dismay, his small legislative successes counted for much, for these were the start of three decades of similar pressure by workers and others sensitive to the failure of the commonwealth in an industrial society. In 1883, McLaughlin lobbied again in Springfield to help pass a much-improved mine inspection law. When he took his seat in the legislature a few years later, the *Springfield Monitor* remembered his earlier efforts: "He was the active, urgent, and almost the only one who fought for the establishment of a bureau of labor statistics." The *Monitor* neglected an essential fact: McLaughlin's presence in Springfield in 1879 depended on his community position in Braidwood. In part, McLaughlin's successes on the state level were those of the Braidwood miners. A curious paradox, even an irony, resulted from the fact that the prairie miners, without bargaining power against absentee employers and suffering for that reason, retained sufficient social sense and organization to encourage state sensitivity to the "labor problem." A jagged line connected Springfield to Scotland, and the crucial link was the culture that sustained the Braidwood miners and nurtured their spirit through the varying fortunes between 1865 and 1885.[84]

A jagged line from Springfield to Scotland traced the course of Daniel McLaughlin as he rose from immigrant miner to champion of labor in the Land of Lincoln. But no place on that course was as important as Braidwood. In Braidwood, McLaughlin shared the miners' culture, imbibed their ethos, joined their organizations, and helped to shape their politics. It was that experience which joined him to some newly arrived immigrants—made him not merely a representative but the embodiment of the miner's travail—and separated him from others, like his illustrious countryman Allan Pinkerton.

4

THE LABOR POLICIES
OF THE LARGE CORPORATION
IN THE GILDED AGE
The Case of the Standard Oil Company

THE BEHAVIOR of the Gilded Age industrialist has long been a subject of heated controversy. But critics of the "robber baron" and defenders of the "industrial statesman" have both neglected important features of American industrialization in the years immediately following the Civil War. For one thing, they have often taken for granted the existence of a sort of Golden Age of near-perfect competition between relatively homogeneous manufacturers, and have therefore ignored the dramatic emergence of the large manufacturing firm in the late 1860s and the 1870s. An equally serious shortcoming is that in studying the rise of the industrial elite, historians and economists have given almost exclusive attention to its relations with competitors, shipping companies, consumers, politicians, and the "public." The labor practices and policies of the robber baron/industrial statesman have been largely ignored, so that his attitudes toward modernizing technology and his many *external* relationships have become the main measures of his historical performance. Only the labor policies of the large railroad corporations have been scrutinized intensively.[1] Careful review of the voluminous secondary literature on so important an industrialist as John D. Rockefeller and on so pioneering an enterprise as the Standard Oil Company, for example, suggests that the man did little more than manage money and other managers and that the firm was fully automated from its very start.[2] Muckrakers as well as serious business and labor historians have made little of the fact that in the 1870s the Standard Oil Company employed several thousand workers.[3] And although its size was not "typical," firms nearly as large existed in other industries. This essay attempts to correct these oversights in two ways. First, in a selective fashion, it calls attention to the prevalence of the "large factory" in the early 1870s, and second, it comments in a more

I am very much in debt to Professor Harry N. Scheiber for his helpful comments on and criticisms of this paper.

detailed way on the labor policies of one of the largest and best known of these firms, the Standard Oil Company of Ohio.

Too often, economic historians date the start of "big business" in the late 1880s, when so much public concern was voiced about the "trusts."[4] As a result, the early economic and social roles of the large manufacturing enterprise have been neglected. Certainly the "average" manufacturing unit in 1870 was smaller than in 1890 or 1900, and the late eighties and nineties witnessed the organization of large, integrated enterprises with manufacturing units in more than one geographic location,[5] but failure to study the large factory of the 1860s and 1870s has masked the extent to which entrepreneurs *within* particular industries took advantage of the new industrial technology and the economies of scale. Because of this neglect, economics historians have underestimated the imperfect structure of the wage and price markets, and labor historians have fussed in excess over craft workers and laborers in small workshops. The large factory, its labor policies, and the composition and behavior of its work force remain unexamined. In describing factory life following the Civil War, inferences have been drawn mainly from the prewar New England textile towns. Little is known of the ways preindustrial Americans and European immigrants confronted the large Gilded Age factory.[6] It is hazardous therefore to guess who worked in these factories, how their owners recruited and disciplined workers, how these workers responded to factory conditions and new work norms, and how the surrounding community felt toward the large factory, its owners, and its workers.

One may reasonably ask first what the term "large factory" meant in the 1870s. The most useful indicator in a study of a factory's labor policies and its workers is the size of the labor force it employed. Esoteric and fanciful econometric formulas are not needed to establish the fact that by the 1870s there were great variations in the size of the labor force from factory to factory within particular industries. We are concerned here only with the large factory.[7] The Standard Oil Works in Cleveland employed nearly 2,500 hands.[8] The Singer Sewing Machine Company gave work to almost as many New Yorkers.[9] The best integrated iron and steel mills employed large labor forces; the Cambria Iron Works in Johnstown, Pennsylvania, employed 6,000 men and boys in its huge complex of mills and mines,[10] and the largest Pittsburgh rolling mills each employed several hundred men and boys. "Some . . . are small towns in themselves," a contemporary wrote of the Pittsburgh iron mills. "One of them covers an area of twenty acres and contains forty-four puddling furnaces, two blast furnaces, hot and cold rolling mills, iron and brass foundries, a nail mill, [and] pattern and machine shops."[11] Four New York ironworks together hired 2,650

TABLE ONE

Fall River, Massachusetts, Print Cloth Mills, 1877

NUMBER OF WORKERS IN EACH MILL	NUMBER OF MILLS
0–99	0
100–399	7
400–599	15
600–799	0
800–899	1
900–999	3
1,000	1

laborers in busy seasons.[12] Three locomotive factories in Paterson, New Jersey, gave jobs to a total of more than 3,000 machinists and other ironworkers.[13] Philadelphia also had large iron factories: the Baldwin Locomotive Works counted 2,800 full-time hands; a large rolling mill had 1,200 workers; and the Keystone Saw and Steel Works listed 900 employees.[14] Midwestern cities also housed sizable iron mills. A huge Cleveland rolling mill needed 2,700 workers, and the North Chicago Rolling Mill had 1,500 employees.[15]

Nor were large labor forces in textile mills unusual. A New York City carpet factory employed 1,500 persons, and numerous Philadelphia woolen, worsted, carpet, cotton, and hosiery mills each hired as many as 600 or 700 workers.[16] The twenty-seven Fall River print cloth mills gave work to 12,810 persons, but 35 percent of these workers found employment in the five largest mills (table 1).[17] The same was true in the Paterson silk factories, fourteen of which employed 8,000 persons in 1876 (two-thirds of them women and one in four under sixteen years of age).[18]

Other industries had large firms in the early 1870s. New York City's biggest sugar refinery employed more than 500 workers.[19] The more important Philadelphia shoe factories gathered as many as 500 or 600 workers, and two Cincinnati shoe factories each gave work to between 250 and 300 persons.[20] In the furniture industry, some large steam-powered factories had between 500 and 1,000 hands; 750 worked for Cincinnati's Mitchell and Ramelsburg.[21] A New Jersey underwear and hosiery plant counted 581 employees, and in that same state a hollow-glass factory had 500, a rubber shoe factory 275, and a trunk and bag factory 205.[22] Even in industries where smaller units of production were "economical" and entry costs not prohibitive, large factories already existed. Krebs and Spiess, New York's major manufacturer of cigars, had 800 employees, and another local competitor, Bondi, Jacobi and Company, listed 450 workmen.[23] Spence and Company hired more than 200 Cincinnati workers, and although that city claimed 400 cigar "factories," this particular company employed 5 percent of the city's cigar workers.[24] Tiny contract shops cluttered the clothing industry in every large city, but custom and wholesale manufacturers had workrooms crowded with more than 100 employees.[25]

Similar patterns are found for Cincinnati, Chicago, and Cleveland, where a large proportion of the local factory population worked for a small number of firms. Two large Cleveland factories, the Cleveland Rolling Mill Company and the Standard Oil Works, hired approximately half of the lake city's factory workers.[26] The 1870 federal census listed 4,400 "manufacturing" units that gave work to 61,000 Cincinnati workers. A simple and misleading "average" tells that each firm had about 14 workers. But seventeen Cincinnati factories, a few years later, had an average labor force of 310 workers. In other words, roughly one of every twelve Cincinnati factory workers labored in seventeen of the city's few thousand "factories."[27] A survey by the Chicago Relief and Aid Society in February 1874 found that 112 of the city's leading iron, lumber, and furniture factories normally employed 12,000 persons. But nearly 50 percent of these workers, 5,895 persons, were employed by only eleven firms. Excluding the North Chicago Rolling Mill, which alone hired 1,500 hands, six of the largest factories had an average of 463 employees.[28]

The relationships between large and small manufacturers within particular industries has been little explored, and it is sufficient for the purposes of this study just to indicate its character. The size of the labor force in various Ohio industries shows a sharp demarcation between firms[29] (table 2). In the Philadelphia carpet industry hand-looms far outnumbered power looms. Handloom weavers worked in tiny shops, often in the rear of their residence. They filled orders from large manufacturers, who supplied them with yarn.[30] New York custom shoemakers gathered in groups of from 2 to 12. Factory shoeworkers in the same city labored with as many as 500 employees.[31] It is well known that the cigar mold revolutionized that industry and spurred bigger manufacturing units.[32] In twenty-four Cincinnati shops without the mold, the average number of skilled workmen was 9 or 10; twenty-three factories that used the tool averaged 41 workers.[33] And although it is well known that industrialists who feared techno-logical innovations often fell by the wayside, it has not been sufficiently appreciated that laborers and employers in small workshops and large factories in the same industry inhabited different worlds. These distinct milieus are not as easy to grasp as the differences in labor force, but

TABLE TWO

Differentiation in the Size of the Labor Force
in Selected Ohio Industries, 1878[a]

INDUSTRY	"SMALL" FACTORIES			"LARGE" FACTORIES		
	NUMBER OF FIRMS	NUMBER OF WORKERS	AVERAGE LABOR FORCE	NUMBER OF FIRMS	NUMBER OF WORKERS	AVERAGE LABOR FORCE
Agricultural implements with foundries	22	650	29.5	6	1,401	233.5
Stove foundries	21	776	37.9	7	782	110.7
Furniture	28	702	25.1	5	942	188.4
Carriages and wagons	41	669	14.9	4	850	212.5
Cigars	12	181	15.0	2	282	141.0
Barrels	26	347	13.3	6	725	120.8
Boots and shoes	9	240	27.4	2	375	187.5

[a] The firms included in this table were those that answered questionnaires sent them by the Ohio Bureau of Labor Statistics. Not all manufacturers responded to the bureau, so these are by no means a complete listing of the firms in particular industries.

they affected such matters as labor recruitment and discipline, working conditions, methods of payment, the power of workers relative to their employers, and the relations among workers and between them and their employers. Some idea of the world of labor in the great corporations can be gained by a closer view of John D. Rockefeller's Standard Oil Company and the coopers who made Rockefeller's barrels.

The controversial relations of John D. Rockefeller and the Standard Oil Company with producers, fellow refiners, and shippers have been chronicled in great detail; here we give attention only to Standard's role as employer.[34] Rockefeller entered the refining business in 1863, and less than ten years later the Standard Oil Company was the nation's largest and most powerful oil manufactory. By 1870, it controlled more than 25 percent of the nation's total daily refining capacity and from then on moved steadily to control a rapidly expanding and chaotic industry.[35] Despite early technological improvements in other areas, oil barrels remained essential and refiners purchased barrels in the open market from independent cooperages, built their own barrel shops and factories, or did both.[36] Little is known of just when Standard first built its own barrel shops, the particular relations between Standard and barrel manufacturers nearby, or the wages, hours, and working conditions of Standard employees.* In 1867 and 1868, Rockefeller and his partners significantly cut costs by building modern, machine-run barrel shops; as Allan Nevins observes:

> Rockefeller and his partners . . . began buying tracts of white-oak timber and seasoning part of their own [barrel] staves. They bought their own hoop-iron, and installed machines for barrel-making. Thus they cut the cost of the finished barrel from the $2.50–$3.50 rate usually charged to about half those figures; and the barrels, strongly hooped, tightly glued, and painted blue, were exceptionally good.[37]

Standard continued to hire skilled coopers, but most of its barrel workers were unskilled and semiskilled hands called "hoopers-off." Samuel Andrews, a Wiltshire Englishman and an early Rockefeller partner, was plant superintendent in the 1860s and 1870s, and Ambrose McGregor, the son of an old Cleveland barrel maker,

---

* I have not been able to uncover useful data about the size of the cooperage industry and the economic functions of cooperage in Cleveland before 1870. Published census material is inaccurate, so it is hard to tell how many barrel shops and factories thrived in Cleveland and how many workers they employed. The histories of the petroleum industry and of the Standard Oil Company give inadequate information on the changing cost structure in oil refining. It is therefore impossible to estimate accurately the relationships between the cost of manufacturing barrels and other costs.

managed the cooperage shops.[38] But a memorandum book Rockefeller kept in 1869 shows the attention he gave to the cost and manufacture of barrels. On August 24, he noted: "Not over 10,000 good barrels on hand and coopers must work *more*"; an undated entry is even more specific: "Barrels in sheds cost 12 to 15¢ to repair. 6 mo. storage & 6 mo. Int. 10¢. Chgs to bbl houses 1⅜¢—some of the H. S. barrels were in *very bad* condition and nevver were fixed of any account."[39] No description has been found of the actual operation of Standard's barrel works, but a skilled cooper's 1872 account of the St. Louis Barrel Works illustrates the effects of contemporary mechanization:

> The [St. Louis] stockholders were men of means, and money was not sparingly used to furnish the factory with all the modern improvements. The barrels were raised by boys, clamped and trussed by machinery, the heads were turned by machines and put onto the barrels by boys, and there was nothing left for the coopers to do but plane, shave up, and hoop the package.[40]

In this factory, the cooper no longer was a skilled craftsman. He was an adept, an easily trained factory worker—"semiskilled" at best. Although the details differed, the quality of work demanded of men and boys in the Standard barrel works must have been the same.

In 1872, Standard added significantly to its barrel shops when it gained control of competing Cleveland refineries. Largely through the exchange of stock or controversial cash payments, and with the aid of three important local banks and two trunk-line railroads, all but five of twenty-six Cleveland refineries had given in to Standard before the spring. That summer, Standard merged and reshaped these disparate firms, and by January 1873 it commanded one "six-plant organization, by far the most efficient in the country."[41] Standard was also one of the nation's largest employers. Although little is known about the employees, at least 2,000 men and boys—and possibly as many as 3,000—worked in its Cleveland shops.[42]* Reorganization surely meant efficiency: Standard closed the less-valued Cleveland refineries and still more than doubled its overall output in 1873 over 1872.[43] Three years later, an awed observer described Standard's physical properties: "There are shops and covered ways, and tanks and paint houses, and cooper shops, and more covered ways, and more shops, and stills, and

---

* Sometime in the early or mid 1870s, Standard introduced a special training department, the "cub shop," in its barrel factories to teach new workers the simple tasks of working barrel machinery and performing the few hands operations still necessary to complete a barrel. After an unspecified period of training, these men were transferred to the "hooping-off" department, and new workers entered the "cub shop." Although it was dealing with easily trained workers, Standard, in effect, had assumed the traditional role of an old guild or craft union. (Franklin E. Coyne, *The Development of the Cooperage Industry in the United States, 1620–1940* [Chicago, 1940], 24.)

more tanks." The entire operation covered twenty acres and the "buildings and tanks appear[ed] to be without number."[44] The start of the 1873 depression brought protracted crisis to the petroleum and other manufacturing industries, but Standard Oil already held a strong position in relation to its workers and its competitors. Mechanization had already reduced the old craft of barrel making to insignificance in Cleveland. It was another story in East Coast cities, where so much kerosene was barreled for shipment to Europe. Skilled coopers had an effective union in many Eastern refineries, and barrel machinery was not yet as important in New York and Philadelphia as in Cleveland. But Standard Oil was already a power in the Eastern cities.

The ability of large firms such as the Standard Oil Company to adopt modern technology and machinery depended on more than their wealth or the innovative energies of particular men. Such changes were dependent on complex social factors. Processed goods had been shipped in barrels for centuries, and the skill of a "hand cooper" was greatly valued. The transportation revolution before and after the Civil War increased the flow of goods and made the barrel more important, but in fact created the conditions that destroyed this traditional skill. This great increase in the movement of goods after 1815 stimulated the first improvements in the manufacture of "tight" barrels for liquids and "slack" barrels for solids. As early as 1811, new technology had altered the coopers' skills, but without destroying artisanship. That year, a Kentuckian patented a stave and shingle machine (driven by one or two horses), which allowed a man and a boy to dress and joint staves for 100 barrels, hogsheads, or casks in twelve hours. A barrel "factory" started in Cincinnati in 1815, and in other food-, drink-, and meat-processing centers in the three following decades, as the spread of the railroad network made it unnecessary for cooperage shops to locate on or near rivers. In the late 1830s, Massachusetts and New York firms marketed improved stave knives and stave and chamfering saws, but only the 1850s saw the first major mechanical change: the invention of the Benson bucker, a powerful machine that made the laborious handwork of "hollowing out" and "backing" barrel staves unnecessary. "Bucked staves" were the first of many such mechanically produced changes. Still, on the eve of the Civil War, cooperage was essentially a craft industry. Artisans worked in both small shops and large "factories"; machinery had not yet deprived them of the power and status associated with their traditional skills.

The invention of several barrel-making machines in the decade after the Civil War quickly—almost abruptly—revolutionized barrel manufacturing. At first, the increased need for barrels, particularly well-made tight oil barrels, brought onto the market too many imperfect barrels made by inexperienced workers, and this consideration among others sparked the search for simplified machine processes to expand barrel manufacture. Just after the Civil War, James Crossley successfully marketed a wheel stave jointer and a heading jointer, so that now the hand cooper worked with machine-made jointed staves and heading blanks. A Massachusetts firm marketed a new cylinder or drum stave saw that produced staves quite different from the older bucked staves, resulting in considerable savings in lumber used, and this saw was widely adopted by oil barrel manufacturers. In the early seventies a heading turner and a heading planer greatly simplified the work of barrel making, and Michael Heiseman, a Cleveland manufacturer of barrel machinery who later built plants in Oil City and Titusville, developed a number of machines and improvements that furthered manufacturing processes, including a windlass made of iron, not wood, a trusser known widely as the "Yankee cooper," a crozing machine that cut a small groove in the stave ends, and a hoop-flaring machine with an attached hoop punch that made unnecessary the driving down of barrel hoops by hand onto an iron tub or mandrel to secure the proper flare. Heiseman also used iron truss hoops in place of the older hickory hoops. The same years saw E. B. Holmes, a manufacturer in Buffalo, New York, perfect machinery to level and truss barrels and to make headings. Together, these inventions profoundly altered barrel manufacturing: "staves and headings could be made ready for the barrel, and the barrel itself completed [by machines] up to its being chamfered and crozed." An ordinary laborer could be quickly taught to operate machines that now performed tasks which under "the old hand-system required genuine skill and craftsmanship derived from years of training and experience." In the early 1870s, a well-equipped barrel factory asked its hand workers only to "insert the heads, spoke shave the barrel, [and] rivet and drive down the thin hoops." The hoops supplied these workers were already punched and flared by machine. The remaining hand operations could be learned easily by unskilled workers, and in mechanized plants skilled coopers took jobs repairing leaks and defects in machine-made barrels or joined the semiskilled laborers who finished the barrels when they came from the crozer. From that time on, according to the historian of the cooperage industry, barrel workers had "the lowly name of 'hoopers' instead of 'coopers,' or sometimes . . . 'hooper-coopers.' "

In ways as yet little understood, machines profoundly altered the structure of the barrel industry and of those processing and manufacturing industries dependent on barrels to ship solid and liquid goods. Where possible, these latter firms shifted to machine-made barrels, and those with sufficient capital, like the Standard Oil Works, built or bought their own barrel factories. In Cleveland, for example, Martin

Snyder produced machine-made barrels, sold them to Standard Oil, and soon sold his skills and his factory to the great refinery. In addition to stimulating the development of mechanized factories, these changes made manufacturers of barrel machinery important. Cleveland's Heiseman and Buffalo's Holmes, among others, innovated in developing and marketing barrel machinery. The rapid spread of barrel machinery opened opportunities for investment, created economies of scale, and gave new jobs to unskilled laborers otherwise employed.

But in less than a generation, mechanization also destroyed the craft of the hand cooper. In *The Development of the Cooperage Industry in the United States*, Franklin Coyne says that the old hand cooper saw the machine as "hard [and] insensible," "not a blessing" but an evil that "took a great deal of joy out of life." The machine-made barrel threatened more than his traditional skills and income. Pride in workmanship and a way of life, perhaps best described as the particular culture of particular groups of American artisans, disappeared when challenged by the Yankee cooper and other innovations. Without idealizing this culture, it is sufficient to note that it existed and was deeply felt, and that its destruction involved more than the obliteration of outdated methods of barrel making. Hand coopers, men of "obstinate and carefree manner," had a style of work and leisure that, paradoxically, did much to bring on the introduction of machinery. Because Saturday normally was their payday, hand coopers "lounged about" all day, so that employers considered that day lost. Nor was the following Monday a productive day.

Early on Saturday morning the big brewery wagon would drive up to the shop. Several of the coopers would club together, each paying his proper share, and one of them would call out the window to the driver, "Bring me a Goose Egg," meaning a half-barrel of beer. Then others would buy "Goose Eggs," and there would be a merry time all around. . . . Little groups of jolly fellows would often sit around upturned barrels playing poker, using rivets for chips, until they had received their pay and the "Goose Egg" was dry.

Saturday night was a big night for the old-time cooper. It meant going out, strolling around the town, meeting friends, usually at a favorite saloon, and having a good time generally, after a week of hard work. Usually the good time continued over into Sunday, so that on the following day he usually was not in the best condition to settle down to the regular day's work.

Many coopers used to spend this day [Monday] sharpening up their tools, carrying in stock, discussing current events and in getting things in shape for the big day of work on the morrow. Thus, "Blue Monday" was something of a tradition with the coopers, and the day was also more or less lost as far as production was concerned.

"Can't do much today, but I'll give her hell tomorrow," seemed to be the Monday slogan. But bright and early Tuesday morning "Give her hell" they would, banging away lustily for the rest of the week until Saturday, which was pay day again, and its thoughts of the "Goose Eggs."[45]

This habit of labor and leisure—a four-day workweek and a three-day weekend—surely angered manufacturers anxious to ship goods in barrels as much as it worried Sabbatarians and temperance reformers. Hand coopers worked hard, but their pace was distinctly preindustrial, and so machine-made barrels and the enormous scramble for barrels in the late 1860s and early 1870s pitted modernizing technology and modern habits against traditional ways of work and life. To the owners of competitive firms, struggling to ensure efficiency and cut costs, the "Goose Egg" and "Blue Monday" proved the laziness and obstinacy of craft workers and the tyranny of craft unions that upheld preindustrial traditions. To the skilled hand coopers, their long weekend symbolized a traditional way of working and living. In the America of the 1870s, compromise between these conflicting interests and values was not possible. The hand coopers in Eastern cities who belonged to the Coopers' International Union learned that lesson in the spring and summer of 1874, in their conflict with the region's powerful oil refineries.

Founded in Cleveland in May 1870, in part to protect traditional skills from the machine, the Coopers' International Union was not yet four years old when the 1873 depression began, but it counted more than 8,000 makers of flour, oil, whiskey, beef and pork, cement, sugar, and syrup barrels.[46] The union made no provision for factory hands working with barrel machinery, and this eventually proved a fatal flaw. The union leaders, men of more than ordinary abilities, included the Pennsylvania-born president, Martin A. Foran, and the vice-president, Robert Schilling, a German immigrant. Foran was also a lawyer and a labor novelist, and in the 1880s Cleveland voters sent him to the national Congress. Schilling followed a different path that led from the Coopers' Union to editing Midwestern labor and reform newspapers and involvement in the Industrial Congress, the Knights of Labor, and the Greenback and Populist movements.[47] In the early 1870s, those men, able craft unionists in the tradition of William Sylvis, supported far-reaching labor and social reforms and also built a "new model" union that offered strike benefits during labor troubles and death benefits to widows and orphans, upheld narrow apprentice regulations, and paid the travel expenses of members to limit the supply of craftsmen in particular local markets. The New York union's standard regulations illustrated the traditions of the craft, its efforts to restrict the supply of skilled coopers, and its desire to protect urban workers against the competition of casual rural labor:

> Hours of labor: 9 hours per day, being from 7 A.M. to 5 P.M. with one hour for lunch. . . . No member shall be allowed to use country shaved hoops or straps. . . . No members are allowed to use borrowed or old hoops. . . . Wages for steady men, $4 per day; transient men, $4.50 (if discharged before Saturday night). . . . For overtime, 80 cents per hour. . . . Each shop employing one man steadily shall be entitled to one apprentice and no more. . . . No person shall allow himself to be borrowed out from one employer to another. . . . No member shall be allowed to work with any man who is not a member of the Cooper's Union. . . . No member shall charge any more work for the bosses than was actually done under penalty of $25. . . .[48]

In 1873, branches thrived in many large cities and small towns. Cleveland, the national headquarters, had three separate locals.[49] Five hundred of the 700 or 800 skilled Philadelphia barrel makers were union men.[50] The New York City region (including the city proper, Brooklyn, Long Island, and Weehawken, New Jersey) had fifteen lodges, about 2,000 members, and a local treasury of $40,000.[51] In addition, the *Coopers' New Monthly* rated as one of the best-edited contemporary labor journals.[52] Overall, few craft unions appeared as organized as this one.

But by the mid-1870s the severity of the depression, the introduction of machine technology, and the hostility of organized employers— particularly the Eastern oil refiners—transformed the Coopers' International Union into a pale shadow of its former self. By early 1876, membership was less than 1,500 and *Coopers' New Monthly* had ceased publication.[53] Although its old national treasurer, Thomas Henneberry, reorganized it, the union never regained its early strength.[54] In 1872, 900 men made pork and whiskey barrels in Cincinnati, mostly by hand, but in 1876 in this former union stronghold, only about 600 men worked, mostly on machines, laboring as many as sixteen hours on busy days and taking home as little as $6 or $7 a week.[55] An entire craft was in decline and with it a union that could not hope to retain its vitality.

Another blow hastening its collapse was struck in 1874 by leading Philadelphia and New York refiners. Although Standard Oil was prominent among these firms, the available published sources do not assign it an especially unique or innovating role. It simply worked together with other large Eastern refiners to destroy the union's power. Between 1872 and 1874 Standard's importance in the New York petroleum market had grown spectacularly. The firm had its troubles with producers and transporters, but it moved steadily eastward from dominance in Cleveland alone to dominance on the eastern seaboard. William Rockefeller, John's brother and the company vice-president, had lived in New York City since 1866 and managed export sales from the great metropolis. In 1872 Standard already owned extensive warehouses and transfer facilities at Hunter's Point on the Long Island side of the East River. That year it purchased Bostwick and Company, probably the largest New York export marketing agency, took control of the New York Central Railroad's oil docks in New York City, and added tugs and barges. In January 1873, the beginning of a year that saw almost 5.5 million barrels of refined oil and naphtha exported, Standard gained control of the Devoe Manufacturing Company, a Long Island can manufacturer and an important exporter of "case oil." Charles I. Pratt and H. H. Rogers, owners of the Pratt Astral Oil Works in Brooklyn and powerful refiners in their own right, aided the Rockefeller firm, and formed a "quasi-alliance with Rockefeller." By the end of 1873, the Standard Oil Company had "obtained an important share of New York's manufacturing capacity."[56]* In the fall of 1874, Standard secretly bought the Pratt works and William G. Warden's Atlantic Petroleum Refining Company, Philadelphia's largest refinery. The firm also leased the Erie Railroad's oil terminal facilities in Weehawken, New Jersey. By then, Nevins observes, "the Standard Oil Company was Leviathan."[57]

Prior to these secret purchases (but several months after the depression started), the Eastern oil refiners had turned against the Coopers' International Union. In March 1874, Philadelphia coopers struck against Warden's Atlantic refinery rather than sign an "iron-clad" contract, and police arrested strikers seeking to parade to the Delaware River plant.[58] In mid-May, the Philadelphia strike became more general—this time because the "iron-clad" ordered the withholding of from $30 to $75 of a cooper's wages, to be forfeited if he joined a union, quit his job without proper notice, or was fired. More than 250 coopers, joined by 300 stevedores and longshoremen who moved oil barrels along the Delaware River docks, struck to defend their "rights as free-born Americans." James L. Wright and Uriah S. Stephens, leaders of the still-secret Knights of Labor, publicly supported the coopers and dock hands.[59] But by the end of June, the aggrieved men had failed to win concessions, and even more serious struggles had begun in New York.

Although its national officers lived in Cleveland, the center of the

---

* No evidence has been found as to the number of workers Standard Oil employed in the New York City area.

Coopers' International Union was in New York City and its environs and it was there that the union's fate was determined. In April 1874, union men who struck when Pratt's Astral Oil Works purchased 1,000 machine-made barrels were fired. Pratt hired nonunion hands. The strikers thought twice, quit the union, and returned.[60] A month later, the *New York Sun* reported that the largest oil refiners in the New York area had "concocted a systematic plan to kill the Coopers' Union." Pratt was joined by A. T. Briggs, a prominent oil barrel manufacturer, the Kings County Oil Works, the Weehauken Oil Company, Sone and Fleming, and William Rockefeller of the Standard Oil Company.[61] Although the evidence is indirect, these manufacturers apparently saw the union as an obstacle to introducing efficient barrel-making machinery; in addition, the depression made them place a premium on lowered costs.

The New York refiners expected the severe depression to assure an easy victory over the union. In early May, they cut their barrel workers to two-thirds time and then to half time. A few days later, coopers making oil barrels learned that unless they signed an "iron-clad" contract and took a Bible oath renouncing the Coopers' International Union, they would be without jobs. From that moment, as a condition of employment, barrel makers would deposit $50 (coopers earned between $2.50 and $4.00 a day, but their employment was seasonal and highly irregular) to be kept if they rejoined the union or failed to give thirty days' notice before quitting. A lockout followed, and petroleum buyers and sellers met at the New York Producer's Exchange to support the refiners.[62] The *New York Tribune* called the Coopers' International Union "not only arbitrary but almost tyrannical," and the *New York Times* agreed, describing the union as a "simple and exclusive monopoly." The *Times* urged the refiners and barrel manufacturers to resist union "dictation by all lawful means."[63]

Despite the depression, the Coopers' Union called a general strike against the oil refiners. On May 4, 3,000 journeymen met and condemned the Bible oath. Foran came from Cleveland to charge the refiners with attacking the "right of combination." The strike soon spread to pork and flour barrel makers, and when the city's leading sugar refinery, Havemeyer, Eastwick and Company, tried buying nonunion barrels, its employees quit work. By mid-May syrup and cement barrel makers had also joined the strike. But the oil barrel coopers and their employers were central. "It requires pluck to strike in these hard times, but we're all holding together, and we're bound to win through thick and thin," boasted a hopeful union man. He and the other strikers met every morning; and union funds ($8 a week for married strikers; $6 for single men) fed those out of work. The union turned aside several smaller firms that accepted its terms, fearing they would supply the larger refineries. "This fight involves the life of the union," a cooper said. Defeat meant "the sacrifice of years of mutual organization."[64]

The strikers issued local and national appeals for help. Circulars were spread throughout the country asking for funds and begging coopers to stay away. Union barrel workers in Belgium and Lorraine sent assurances that they would refuse to repair nonunion New York barrels. The strikers got support closer to home as well: the New York Knights of Saint Crispin and Journeymen Tailors' Union each gave $500, and building trades workers promised aid. Funds flowed from Boston, Chicago, and Cleveland coopers; San Francisco coopers sent the proceeds from a benefit ball. The *Iron Molders' Journal* said the strikers needed $6,000 for weekly relief and pleaded with ironworkers to put aside the troubles caused them by the depression: "We cannot, as men, turn a deaf ear to the appeals for help from those even poorer than ourselves." "Would-be tyrants" had to learn that "workingmen sympathize with each other."[65]

In early June the dispute took a turn for the worse. Some nonunion men took their jobs, and some union men quit the union and returned to work. Briggs, a major oil barrel supplier, imported barrels from Boston, Philadelphia, and Poughkeepsie and threatened to open a machine barrel factory in Yonkers, New York, and employ only Chinese laborers to turn out 1,500 barrels a day. But the employers had difficulties, too. New hands often proved inefficient. William Rockefeller found their work of poor quality. New men at Pratt's Astral Oil Works finished only two barrels a day; a skilled craftsman could make as many as twelve or fourteen. Some hands brought in from distant cities left their new jobs, and strikers paid their return fares. In one instance, nonunion hands quit an employer who held back their tools. Lacking machinery, the refiners needed able craftsmen, but did not want them with their union intact.[66]

As the strike progressed the stakes became higher, and angered strikers posted this classic warning at the Standard Oil refineries:

> There is George More, our Union
>   he did ignore
> For the sake of a paltry job.
> Nicholas Burgundy went on Monday
> And our holy cause betrayed.
> But soon he will find the rod
>   in the hands of an angry God;
> Likewise Jew Charley and Mike Spade,

> Toomey, and the Cavenaughs, too,
> And all the rest of the perjured crew
>   that from us withdrew;
> I pity their sad fate before they go to
>   ———— they'll go,
> For now they're standing at the gate.[67]

Tension increased. Police accompanied nonunion men to and from the Standard Oil Works, and some anxious employers armed nonunion workers. One nonunion cooper drew a ten-inch knife on several strikers and was arrested on their complaint. Peter Smith, expelled from the union a few weeks earlier, shot at four strikers, critically wounding and perhaps killing John Cunningham. Smith was not without friends: Charles Pratt and another prominent refiner, Stephen Jenny, went to court and posted his $1,000 bail. A judge released Smith, insisting his employers "did perfectly right in giving Smith a revolver to defend himself from the strikers." The jurist found the only substantive issue to be whether or not Smith had made "a proper use" of the weapon.[68]

In late June, the coopers surrendered. Their union, according to the *Toiler*, a New York socialist weekly, was "somewhat shattered." Any Coopers' Union leader in the New York area thereafter was "a marked man." "He must leave the city or starve," the *Toiler* complained. "The blow struck against the union was more than *malicious*—it was FELON-IOUS! Every action of the employers to *prevent* a man from earning his bread because he is a *unionist, should be punishable by law!*" The *Coopers' New Monthly* used similar language and called the contract "highly unjust and malicious," but its rhetoric could not substitute for effective power.[69] In the fall of 1874, the principal "boss" coopers making other than oil barrels adopted the "iron-clad" too. The weakened union called another strike and planned a cooperative barrel factory. In $50 shares, union supporters raised $8,000 of the $20,000 needed to start the cooperative.[70] But there is no record of its actual operation—only evidence that the union was no longer an effective force in New York City and elsewhere.

Although the destruction of the Coopers' International Union made 1874 a memorable year for most barrel manufacturers and all coopers, other doings made it a banner year for the Standard Oil Company. By its end, Standard so dominated the nation's refining industry that the major New York, Philadelphia, and Pittsburgh competitors had joined it, finally accepting "consolidation as a Gibraltar rising out of the stormy sea." From then on, when Standard "called the tune, nearly all refiners had to dance." The firm was even more powerful by 1877, "an imposing structure . . . one of the soundest and strongest industrial organizations in the world, making money even in years of depression, and growing steadily and inexorably."[71] By then, a barrel worker figured, the Cleveland, New York, Philadelphia, Pittsburgh, and Titusville Standard refineries gave work to nearly 7,000 persons.[72] Even if this estimate were twice too large, it would still mean that the Standard Oil Company was one of the leading American employers of wage labor—comparable to the Cambria Iron Works or the largest railroads—and that its barrel makers worked in an industry dominated by men with unprecedented power. All had much to learn. The independent refiners already understood the cost and the value of submissiveness to the great Ohio firm. The skilled coopers in Eastern refineries paid a price but received no value in return in 1874. Standard's semiskilled Cleveland factory workers and Pittsburgh's independent skilled coopers and their employers were to learn the cost in 1877.

Native workers and German and Irish immigrants labored for Standard Oil, but the largest group among the unskilled and semiskilled Cleveland barrel workers was of recent Bohemian immigrants. Before the 1873 depression, large numbers of immigrants had passed through Cleveland on the way West; some stayed. In 1873, for example, 35,000 foreigners arrived by rail, and 3,600 remained. Only scattered information has been found about the Bohemians among them, but two significant social characteristics seem clear. Most were unskilled or semiskilled wage earners already living in an established immigrant community. Apart from the many who worked at the Standard Oil Works, other Bohemians obtained employment as cigar makers and tailors or as unskilled day laborers. Family income, the rule for most married postbellum unskilled workmen, was important to the Bohemians. Their wives and daughters often held jobs at the Cleveland Paper Mill, as washerwomen, or on farms near the city. That they were so recent an immigrant group and largely working class did not mean a disorganized social order.

Although it was rather new to America, the Bohemian community was stable. Bohemians lived together in three wards (the Sixth, Thirteenth, and Fourteenth), and, according to the Ohio Bureau of Labor Statistics, in 1873 fully a quarter of Bohemian families owned homes valued at about $500 each. But unsteady depression employment and lowered wages made mortgage payments difficult and some lost their property. Still, other ties held the community together. Churches and a network of fraternal and benevolent associations thrived together with weekly newspapers and even four theaters. The Bohemian brass band, reputedly Cleveland's best, featured Standard Oil employees among its finest soloists.[73] Little is known of Bohemian political interests, but in 1877 the tiny socialist Workingmen's party had Bohemian branches and published a weekly newspaper, *Delnicke Liste*, edited by Leopold Palda and Francis Skarda. Early that winter, J. Benes and V. Votova organized the Bohemian Tailor's Union. German and Bohemian socialists met together to jointly petition the national Congress to amend the Homestead Act and "allow a sufficient loan to all those unemployed workmen . . . willing to make use of it [the Homestead Act] to buy the necessary implements and provisions for the first year."[74] How deeply socialist radicalism penetrated the Bohemian community is not clear, but a Bohemian community with a separate identity existed and protected itself as best it could against the outside world and against occasional nativist abuse. In 1875, for example, a nativist in the *Cleveland Sunday Morning Voice* crudely slurred the local Bohemian community. He made much of their poverty and the fact that their women worked in factory, field, and home.* The officers of all Cleveland Bohemian fraternal and benevolent societies publicly and eloquently responded. They admitted the poverty of many recent Bohemian immigrants and added, "If the poverty of an American working man is a sign of disgrace and a target of abuse, then in God's name we have no objection to make." The Bohemian workers were an "industrious and honest people."[75] In the spring of 1877, the Bohemian workers faced a different challenge, and again responded. It came from the Standard Oil Company and pitted against one another two groups significant in reshaping nineteenth-century America: the new large, integrated, and mechanized corporation and the "new" unskilled and semiskilled immigrant worker.

Although the Standard Oil Company had moved systematically and with much entrepreneurial skill and daring to almost total dominance of the oil-refining industry during the 1873–1878 depression, its more than 2,000 Cleveland employees suffered great hardship. It is difficult to fix accurately the wage trends of Standard employees; the evidence is scanty. But one contemporary figured that between 1872 and 1878 money-wage rates (not actual income earned) fell 16½ percent for hoopers-off, 24 percent for skilled coopers, between 38 and 43 percent for "laborers," and between 40 and 50 percent for "mechanics."[76] These data are fuzzy at best, but the following information is hard and firm. In January 1875, the *Coopers' New Monthly* said Standard's ordinary laborers earned $1 a day if they worked full time.[77] That month, the officers voted a dividend of $115 on each $100 share.[78]

---

* This attack on Bohemian immigrants was not peculiar to Cleveland. In 1876, the *Chicago Post and Mail* called that city's Bohemians "a band of thieves and paupers . . . squalid, wretched, depraved beasts; harpies decayed physically and spiritually, mentally and morally." (*Chicago Post and Mail*, n.d., reprinted in the *Chicago Tribune*, 25 July 1876.)

The year 1875 was a "very dull" one for the oil industry (the average selling price of refined standard white in New York City was 12.99 cents a gallon, the lowest ever to that time), and the men worked only half time.[79] One barrel shop ran for a full week; another remained idle; the next week, this pattern was reversed.[80] In March 1876, the managers laid off about 1,000 men.[81] In September of that year, the pay of hoopers-off—the semiskilled factory barrel workers—rose from 10 to 11 cents a barrel; the men worked half time; all were employed.[82] The fluctuations in hours worked and wages paid were the result of large-scale maneuvering in the market. "The centennial year," Nevins writes, "witnessed the first striking demonstration of the power of the Standard Oil combination to deal with petroleum prices." In the three previous years, refined and crude oil prices had been lower in the last six than in the first six months of each year. European speculators expected a similar pattern in 1876 and went "largely 'short' of oil for the fall and winter of 1876." What followed surely destroyed their confidence in making predictions and handsomely enriched the American combination headed by Standard Oil. Nevins graphically reports the details:

> But in July the market for kerosene turned up sharply two and a half cents a gallon, in August it rose two cents more, and September found it up almost another six cents! December brought a marked additional advance, the New York price then being 29.26 cents as against [the] 14.02 of January [1876]. In brief, the "combination" had practically doubled the price of kerosene during the half year in which the bears expected it to drop.

The Standard group "reaped golden profits," and a writer for the New York Chamber of Commerce cheered: "Great credit is due to the boldness and wisdom of the gentlemen composing the 'combination.' . . ." But Standard's success could not continue for long, and after this masterly stroke prices again fell. Refined oil brought an average price in New York City of 24 cents a gallon in January 1877. By July the price had fallen to 13⅜ cents, and in November it fell to 13¼ cents.[83]

Despite its 1876 triumph, Standard found the subsequent price drop sufficient reason to cut wages in the refineries, and a strike resulted. In early March 1877, and without any recorded complaint from the workers, the piece rate paid hoopers-off fell to 10 cents. Six weeks later, on April 19, the company lowered it to 9 cents. The cut affected between 1,000 and 1,500 workers, but they only learned of it on reporting to work that morning.[84] The workers were aware of the firm's 1876 triumph but did not know what only the secret minutes of stockholders' and trustees' meetings could tell: in January 1877, Standard Oil declared a $30 dividend; on April 3 (less than three weeks before the second wage cut), it announced a $25 dividend; and on July 10 gave $25 more—$80 in all on each $100 share in half a year.[85] The most conservative estimate shows that Standard's largest stockholder, John D. Rockefeller, earned in dividends at least $561,680 in these six months, a figure that does not count any salary paid him or dividends earned from subsidiary and allied corporations.[86]* But such secret information would only have added fuel to a fire already blazing. That morning the barrel workers in Shops Two and Three joined in a spontaneous walkout. Some of the strikers were German and native workers, but the Bohemians made up the greatest number. They were without a union and came mostly from the mechanized barrel shops. The *Cleveland Leader* found them sufficiently distressed to "behold absolute starvation at no long way in the future at the present state of affairs." Some skilled hand coopers joined the strike, too. But apparently most of them remained at work, and one condemned the "unskilled" immigrant laborers:

> Why should we strike? . . . We fought the introduction of machinery a few years ago in the construction of barrels. The work which these workers do is not cooperage. We don't recognize them as mechanics. They were imported here when we refused to do the work they are now doing. For my part, I shall work as long as I can find anything to do, and don't feel that this case touches me at all.

The evidence does not tell how widely skilled coopers shared this view, but the machine barrel workers' walkout stymied production and called attention to the troubles at the Cleveland refineries.[87]

Although John D. Rockefeller was "out of town" to the press, Superintendent Samuel Andrews "cheerfully" explained company action to *Cleveland Leader* and *Plain Dealer* reporters. Of the hoopers-off, he said: "It is only necessary to shave off the barrels with a draw-shave after they have been put together by machinery. And then [they] put on the hoop." Andrews minimized the importance of skill and called their labor "easy." He insisted that the company had the interests of the workers at heart. If it employed only half its men full time, the company would save two cents on each barrel. Instead, Standard gave work to all its men half time "to do the greatest good to the greatest number." In fact, orders were so few that the company was "really

---

* This estimate is based on Rockefeller's ownership of 7,021 $100 shares in 1872. In 1879, he held 8,984 shares, but no information is available for the middle years. The 1872 figure has been used for the 1876–1877 estimate. If we assume that Rockefeller, like his machine barrel workers, labored half time between January and July, he received in dividends $43,200 each week he worked. Machine barrel workers put in sixty hours a week. If Rockefeller did the same, his dividends per *hour* between January and July (working half time) came to $720. Rockefeller, of course, worked "full time." But few if any Standard Oil workers earned *an annual income* of $720 in the 1870s.

running . . . at a loss." A convinced *Plain Dealer* reporter concluded: "They would rather close up . . . but out of justice to the men have kept the works open at half time." Andrews opened the firm's payroll books "for any reasonable investigation," and a hasty look by a *Plain Dealer* reporter resulted in the publication of inflated and entirely misleading wage statistics.* Finally, Superintendent Andrews argued that Standard barrel makers earned 10 percent more than Pittsburgh barrel makers—even after the second wage cut.[88]

The strikers told a quite different story. Insisting that the company paid unusually high dividends in 1876, they complained mostly about low wages and half-time work. The *Plain Dealer* and the *Leader* interviewed men at random and learned of their determination to hold out. A few threatened violence and one even talked of arson, but the normal response to reporters' questions was moderate and firm. One striker said an adult hooper-off could finish only seven barrels in a full day. Another said four men in his family worked in the Standard shops, and at 9 cents on full time each could bring home about $2 a day. Half time meant only 70 cents. Other workers insisted the new rate meant as little as 30 cents a day. The *Plain Dealer* reported:

> The man working on Stand No. 2067 says that with the help of two full grown men he has only made $70.85 since the first of January. The superintendent says in reply to this that these men probably didn't work a full month in that time. Another, a good man, on repairing work . . . states that he made $449.10 for the year ending December 31st, 1876. Since the first of January [1877] he made $82.65. . . .

The workers also denied Andrews's assertion about lower Pittsburgh wages. But they worried most about the relation between lowered wages and short time. The barrel makers earned piece rates, and so less hours meant harder work to increase take-home pay. Even extraordinary diligence and strength had its limits when the hours were fixed; a worker could "hoop" just so many barrels. Young "boys"— often the sons of these same workers—therefore were more important

---

* The *Plain Dealer* reporter found that men's wages before the March cut ranged from $20.35 to $45.32 a week. But a day or two later, the newspaper admitted that its published account was inaccurate. "The superintendent showed our reporter the payrolls for some months past with the remark, 'You can see for yourself what the men draw each week,' and read the figures without mentioning the fact that they represented two weeks' work." The strikers insisted that even this correction was inadequate. The wages cited for two weeks of work were for "groups" of barrel makers, not single men. Another *Plain Dealer* survey showed that 37 men in Shop Two, working *full time*, made 827 barrels a day, or an average of 22½ barrels a man. A Standard paymaster said this was "a fair average of the several shops." At half time, this meant 10 or 11 barrels a man per day—and at 9 cents a barrel, a daily wage of between 90 and 99 cents. (*Cleveland Plain Dealer*, 20 April 1877.)

under the piece-rate system than if paid an hourly or daily wage rate. One worker despaired:

> Why, there's lots of talk about free education and the advantages to the working man of our public school system. Do you suppose, sir, at the wages we have to work for now-a-days, we can afford to send our children to school? No, sir! Every man who has a child wants him with them and then can't make a living. There's a boy (pointing to a lad standing by), he's fourteen years old, shouldn't he be at school? Well, he's not. Every morning he has to go to the works and help his father. Even then they hardly make sufficient to keep the family from actual starvation.

Unmarried workers also complained. "I haven't bought a suit of clothes for a year," said one, "and am behind in my board for some months. I know plenty of single men in the shops who can't make their board at the present rates and time working." A barrel worker who joined staves did not complain of his wages but said of the hoopers-off:

> These poor "hoopers-off" have a very hard time to live. They get but the smallest pay, even smaller than what has been represented by the papers. And with flour at $12 a barrel, as it is today, and potatoes at $1.50 what can a poor man with a large family on his hands do better than to strike? He will starve if he don't and only do so if he does.

A *Plain Dealer* reporter warned a striker that Standard might close its doors entirely: "They are rich and can stand the loss better than you." The striker answered: "Well, let 'em do it. When we get to starving they can send us to the workhouse. We'll get bread for our work there anyhow."[89]

In its first few days, the strike caused much excitement and attracted citywide attention. After the men in Shop Three had put down their tools and the Shop Two men joined them, they congregated in a hollow between the shops. Andrews arrived and closed the shops for a week to allow time to consider the complaint. About 1,500 strikers formed a procession and marched several abreast through the city streets. They first halted in front of Standard's Euclid Avenue headquarters and then marched to the offices of *Delnicke Liste*. Editor Leopold Palda directed them to a vacant street lot nearby, and he and Francis Skarda addressed them. Skarda spoke at length in German and then more briefly in English. Palda talked only in Bohemian. They urged the men to stand together and counseled against violence. Palda found their discontent proof that "workingmen were oppressed by the capitalists" and needed to "rise and assert their rights." The Czech socialists called a meeting for that evening in the same place so the strikers might better prepare themselves through formal organization. Little more was spoken, and the strikers resumed their march, returning to the refineries before dispersing. "Their appearance on the street," observed the *Plain Dealer*, "was the occasion of considerable excitement and curious questions. Business men, clerks and customers, rushed to the doors of their stores. In private houses windows were thrown open and frightened children and amazed women gazed on the unusual scene." That night, a few thousand persons crowded at the corner of Broadway and Forest Street, where from "a rude platform among . . . torch lights" Palda spoke in Bohemian for nearly an hour and Skarda in Bohemian, German, and English, urging the election of a strike committee of fifteen, with equal representation for the three dominant nationalities. The crowd voiced agreement, elected the committee to negotiate with the company, and made Skarda, apparently not a Standard employee, its chairman. Then the assembled workers voted to stand for 12 cents a barrel, shouting assent after Skarda made this demand in all three languages. The gathering quietly adjourned after the committee promised to meet Andrews the next morning.[90]

Andrews received Skarda, Palda, and the committee courteously, but held firm to 9 cents. He insisted that most other machine barrel workers got only 8 cents and promised a return to 10 (not 11) cents when conditions improved. The committee asked for 12 cents.[91] The meeting lasted an hour, without agreement, and afterwards the strikers again paraded the streets. That night, in the same vacant lot, a much larger crowd, including many wives and children, joined the strikers, heard the committee, and restated the 12-cent demand. The following day, the strikers paraded in the morning and at night. A Bohemian brass band headed 4,000 evening marchers. In addition, strikers stuck posters on lampposts throughout the city demanding the 12-cent rate. Through all this physical movement, the *Plain Dealer* found the strikers' demeanor "orderly and peaceable."[92]

After this flurry of marches and meetings, the dispute settled down to a more normal pattern. But the strikers seemed strong and united. The Cleveland press reported regularly on daily strike occurrences but made few editorial comments. The *Leader* early dismissed the strikers' argument that the high 1876 dividends made the Standard wage cut unjustifiable. Standard had taken enormous risks in 1876 and "reaped the reward" of its enterprise. But two days later the *Leader* shifted its argument:

> If any working people ever had fair reason to quit work and appeal to popular sympathy, they had such reason. Their behavior on the

streets was peaceable and orderly, and they showed beyond question that with the limited work and reduced wages offered them they are unable to support their families.

The wage cut was indeed without excuse. The "present depression in the oil trade" resulted from "the deliberate management of the Standard Oil Company itself," which had "produced a glut and depression . . . for the deliberate purpose of gaining future advantages." The strikers therefore deserved "an unusual degree of sympathy and moral support" from the public.[93] Although there is little concrete evidence of other such "public" support, the strikers gained strength in the early days. Groups of strikers urged nonstrikers working for less than $1 a day to quit Standard, and some coopers in smaller contract shops joined the walkout for a few days. On April 25, Palda and Skarda met with Standard's hand coopers and urged them to quit. It is not known how many coopers left, but that day about 400 Standard yard hands left work. Skarda was optimistic. When "imposters" sought strike funds from the public, an open letter from Skarda advised "not to give anything to anyone, as the coopers have not authorized anybody yet to ask the kindness of our fellow-citizens." Committee members dismissed rumors that the strike was failing, and doubtless felt encouraged by the behavior of other disaffected Cleveland workers.[94]

Unexpectedly, the example of the Standard Oil strikers spread to other Cleveland workers, particularly German and Bohemian immigrants, and much parading and agitation followed. "Strikes are fashionable and all branches of trade have caught the fever," remarked the *Plain Dealer*.[95] City sewer workers struck against a contractor for higher wages and paraded through Cleveland's streets. A brief skirmish between strikers and nonstrikers brought police, who protected nonstrikers for several days.[96] Some masons and carpenters quit work, too, and a large number of striking brickmakers paraded for higher wages.[97] On April 23, about 100 cigar makers joined the troubled workers and marched from shop to shop, persuading others to join them.[98] Skarda and Palda were busy those days. They met regularly with Standard strikers and also addressed the cigar makers and sewer workers, arguing against violence and advising elected grievance committees to meet with employers.[99] The "strike fever" finally spread to the iron mills. Since January, steelworkers at the giant Cleveland Rolling Mill Company had been out of work in protest against a large wage cut. On April 24, thirty Cleveland Iron Company employees and sixty men at an axle factory demanded higher wages. Police rushed to guard nonstriking iron workers.[100] Except for the nearly four-month dispute at the Cleveland Rolling Mill, which ended in complete defeat for the workers on April 30, none of the other disputes assumed serious proportions. But these minor strikes added to the troubles at Standard cast a grim shadow over the city and suggested widespread disquiet among its workers.

Even though the striking Standard Oil workers gave the impression of increasing strength, they were weak from the start. The "strike fever" outside the oil refineries dissipated the effectiveness of their own protest, and suggesting a possible general strike may have frightened off those sympathetic to the particular complaints against Standard Oil. The *Leader* curtly dismissed the grievances of the sewer workers, brickmakers, masons, and cigar makers. Because they "overdid the matter," they endangered the legitimate distress and complaint of the Standard strikers.[101] Significant public support for Rockefeller's striking employees never materialized. Instead, Cleveland's mayor and police officials acted quickly to protect Standard's interests. The barrel workers hoped to gain support by parading the streets and gathering near the refineries to persuade nonstrikers to join them, but the public authorities frustrated them. The *Plain Dealer* felt "no anxiety" that the strikers would do "any violence" to the plant and its loyal employees, but city officials feared otherwise and as early as April 19—the first day of the strike and before the other strikes—ordered a special police force to guard Standard properties. Two days later, after several parades and public meetings, the city fathers made "every precaution for an outbreak," put nearly the entire police force on duty, and even alerted the local militia. Several militia companies waited "under arms . . . ready to respond at the first sign of trouble." That same day, a reporter toured the refinery neighborhood and saw no one there except police and "occasionally two or three persons returning from places of amusement in the city." But soon after the discontent had spread from the barrel workers to the others, the authorities clamped down vigorously. On April 24, after admitting that "large numbers of laboring men" felt "aggrieved at the low wages paid them by employers" and complaining that disaffected workers "interrupted the progress of work on various public improvements . . . and . . . interfered with the conduct of private business," Mayor William G. Rose issued a proclamation limiting the strikers' use of the streets and other public areas. Rose allowed the strikers "all orderly, unobtrusive action to maintain their rights and promote their welfare," but severely cramped effective protest.

> I . . . warn all citizens of Cleveland against in any way violating or invading the rights of any others either by actually obstructing them in the prosecution of their various avocations or by intimidating them with threats to their person or property. I also advise that the assembling together in large numbers and marching through the

streets of the city be at once discontinued, as its effect is in every way pernicious, tending only to disorder and discontent.

The law would be "strictly enforced" and "leaders in acts resulting in breach of the peace or infringement of the rights of citizens . . . promptly arrested and punished." The police acted with dispatch. Strikers near the refinery gates learned from the police superintendent, Captain Hoehn, and a squad of bluecoats that their "assemblage" violated the "law of the city." The men dispersed quietly, and did not congregate there the following day. Standard had won an important early advantage.[102]

Other significant considerations strengthened the Standard Oil Company. Its size, the complexity of its total operation, and its available capital resources allowed it a freedom of action denied to all but the largest postbellum manufacturers. Few firms, for example, operated factories in more than one section of the United States, but the Cleveland giant exploited its ownership of the refinery in Hunter's Point, New York, so that on April 27 the *Plain Dealer* said the strike had caused "the Standard Oil Company to move their [barrel] shops from this city . . . [and] hereafter to make their barrels at Hunter's Point." The company already was shipping staves there and building 250 tank cars to transport refined oil from Cleveland. The *Leader* called this an "absurd story." Superintendent Andrews agreed, but took advantage of the "rumor" and explicitly warned that the barrel shops would not be removed "unless the strikers force it."[103] Standard had no reason to face so drastic a choice. Other alternatives existed. Threatening to close down the barrel shops permanently was not nearly as effective or economical a policy as keeping the rest of the refinery open, purchasing barrels from independent suppliers, and counting on the protection of loyal workers by sympathetic city authorities. Standard chose wisely. The dispute, after all, affected mostly the machine barrel workers, and the company had sufficient capital reserves to keep its refineries open and make special arrangements for needed barrels. An unknown number of skilled coopers (displaced when Standard had mechanized its barrel shops) offered the firm their cooperation and found the strike "a very godsend." In addition, Standard received "many applications for barrels at a very low price" from coopers all over Ohio and also ordered "second hand" barrels from other parts of the country. Standard's powerful market position as a large consumer of barrels paid off well. On May 7, for example, three ships—the steamer *Egyptian*, the bark *Pelican*, and the barge *Sanilac*—arrived in Cleveland carrying more than 2,100 barrels to the struck refinery.[104]

Smaller postbellum manufacturers could do nothing of this kind;

they lacked the capital to practice the strategy of large firms like Standard. When confronted with a dissatisfied but less specialized and more homogeneous labor force, the small manufacturer usually closed his plant and tried bringing in new workers. In a period of intense competition, falling prices, and rising costs, such a decision cut off needed revenue and caused enormous difficulty. More than this, in seeking new workers the manufacturer took enormous risks that might, and all too often did, end in disaster for him. Standard was in a much stronger position. Its size and complexity together with its capital reserves and enormous market power permitted it to keep its refineries running and to bring in new supplies, rather than new workers. So long as barrels could be purchased, the sale of refined oil continued and the company earned income. That the plant remained open told the strikers production could continue without their labor. This additional pressure weakened the strikers and showed the ineffectiveness of their major weapon: a strike by one group of specialized but semiskilled workers, even as many as 2,000 persons, could not halt the operations of a large, complex enterprise and cut off its revenues. Standard's labor strategy, therefore, derived in part precisely from its size. It could defend itself without introducing the intangible and often volatile human elements involved in bringing new workers to a disputed mill. Standard wisely purchased new barrels, not new barrel workers.

Superintendent Andrews made yet another decision that weakened the strikers. Before the dispute the barrel shops had run on half time. But this policy had angered the workers by giving many men a lower weekly wage than would have gone to a smaller number at full time. Moreover, the firm had grown rapidly, and as a consequence, its overhead costs had risen. When it ran at half time, the company carried unnecessary additional costs, and its unit costs rose. During the strike Andrews announced a drastic change in company policy:

> The company has not yet decided just when we shall start the [barrel] shops again, but we have decided a few things very fully. One of these is that when we do start it shall be on full time. The half time plan has been a sad failure. We see it and we are free to admit it. We believe that it is the fruitful cause of all the trouble. But the meaning and intention was all right from the start. . . . We were obliged to keep and pay twice as many engineers, foremen, and kiln men, keep twice as much machinery in repair, etc., as we would have needed under the other plan. But when we start again we shall only engage half as many men as we did before.
>
> We shall pay them at nine cents per barrel for hooping off, and if the men who have formerly worked do not wish to be engaged with us again at that price, there are plenty who are offering every

day to do so, whom we shall employ. We shall start at nine cents, but shall increase that figure as soon as sales will warrant us in doing so, to ten, eleven, twelve, and so on. Again, we shall put good men in each berth next time. We are done with boys' work. . . .[105]

The strikers learned from this that not all would be rehired when the shops started again. Standard might even hire new workers. The strike committee's protests did not affect Andrews. They addressed a bitter appeal to the public and accused Standard of a "treacherous movement . . . to divide the coopers."

It promised to employ half of the men at full time and pay them at the reduced wages, . . . the [other] half to become a burden to the city. The company ought to have acted that way when they were asking for 2000 men, knowing very well they could not employ any more than half of them. This scheme won't work, gentlemen.

The committee promised that the strikers would remain firm and urged Standard to comply with "the just demands of the poor men who helped you to the fortunes you now have."[106] Andrews must have known the weakness masked by these warnings. The strikers had lived through nearly four years of depression and had worked for meager wages for some time before the strike. Few could have put aside sufficient savings to tide them through an extended dispute, and they lacked a permanent union to supply essential strike benefits. Outside support proved negligible: there is evidence of aid only from the socialist Workingmen's party in New York City.[107] And even more important, the worker tending a barrel-making machine needed little skill and therefore had limited bargaining power. Standard had mechanized its barrel works and the individual hooper-off could be easily replaced. When the shops reopened, Andrews's policy meant greater competition for fewer jobs.

At the end of April, Standard announced its decision to reopen Shops Two and Three and discharge those unwilling to return at 9 cents. Although a small number had already gone back to work at the reduced wage, the *Plain Dealer* estimated that 2,000 men and boys were still holding out. The company issued a circular printed in English, German, and Bohemian:

NOTICE TO "HOOPERS OFF." All men who have tools in the berths of Number 2 and Number 3 shops who are not ready to go to work at nine cents per barrel for "hooping off" are hereby notified to come and get their tools on or before Saturday [May 5] of this week. . . . After that date, we will not reserve berths for any man who has not commenced work during the week.

According to the *Leader*, the management planned to retain only "those whom they know are competent hands." Worried about possible "violence" and fearing that the strikers would "probably attempt to prevent the men going back to work," Standard decided to open each shop on a different day, and took extraordinary precautions to protect its properties and its loyal workers.[108]

Active support from the Cleveland city authorities permitted Standard Oil to reopen its barrel shops as planned. Even though no violence had occurred to that time, police officials worked closely with company officials, and direct telegraphic communication existed between the refinery and the central police station. Standard believed the regular city police force inadequate, and at a "protracted secret conference" with Mayor Rose, the police superintendent and the police commissioners got permission to "swear in . . . special policemen at the expense of the company." Standard would "furnish each . . . with the necessary outfit to do duty while the strike lasted." Regular police also would serve. On May 1, the day before the reopening of Shop Two, Andrews had drawn up a list of loyal workers willing to serve as "special police." That afternoon, ninety-eight men, sworn in by the city police clerk, received regular metal police badges and orders to report at five the next morning. The following day, Andrews summoned additional workers, mostly from the boiler shops, and the police clerk "deputized" them, too. Equipped with clubs, these men got only printed ribbon badges identifying them as "specials"—the city had run short of metal badges. The combined regular and special police at the refineries came to 338 men. "At ordinary times," observed the *Plain Dealer*, "the men in the company's employ are under almost military discipline, and the grounds are guarded . . . as strictly as a war camp. At present, extraordinary precautions are taken and everything is on a regular war basis." A police sergeant renamed the plant "Fort Standard."[109]

Early on May 2, the regular and special police led by Captain Hoehn confronted 400 strikers as unknown numbers took up work in Shop Two. Hoehn ordered the crowd dispersed, and the police moved forward slowly. Except for a middle-aged man (who opened his vest as the police approached, striking his breast with his hand and shouting in broken English, "Shoot! Shoot! You will thus free me of my trouble and keep me from starving!"), the strikers obeyed, and before eight o'clock the refinery was operating normally. Later that day, police arrested cigar maker I. M. Drucker. He had urged the strikers on at the factory gates, and was charged with "menacing in a threatening manner." Shop Three, guarded by Hoehn, the police superintendent, and their men, reopened the next day. The *Plain Dealer* said that the strikers, "many . . . carrying clubs and sticks," gathered near the main entrance to persuade men from going in, but that "no violence was attempted" nor were "any threats used." More hands returned that day, particularly Germans, and the *Plain Dealer* expected "no further trouble."[110]

But the *Plain Dealer* misjudged the strikers. Even though the barrel shops resumed, a large number of old hands stayed away, and at a well-attended May 2 evening meeting (after entertainment by a Bohemian brass band) Skarda urged them to stand firm and obey the law because violence or the arrest of strikers would lose them "the sympathy of the good [Cleveland] people." The Committee of Coopers unanimously rejected the company's terms, and the strikers agreed— to a man. After that, day after day and early each morning, several hundred strikers, mostly Bohemians, gathered near the refinery gates to urge their demands. But Standard, its refineries working and its supply of barrels assured, did not listen. "It is still nine to twelve," reported the *Plain Dealer*, "the company offering nine cents and the strikers demanding twelve." The same paper joked: "Their daily visits remind one of the ancient couplet—The King of France with 40,000 men / Went up a hill and so came down again."[111]

After their wives and daughters joined the strikers' demonstrations, the dispute took a much uglier and grimmer turn. On May 9 between 50 and 150 women argued near the mill with returning workers. The *Leader* observed:

> The women with their shawls pulled closely around their heads to keep out the cold damp of the early morning were very active, and appeared even more determined than the men. They urged firm adherence to the path [the strikers] had at first taken. At one time, the women started in a body for the main entrance but upon getting about half way from the street they suddenly stopped as though their courage had failed them.

No disturbances occurred, but the women made their presence felt— seventy-five fewer men returned to work. The *Plain Dealer* said the strike was "changing front" and "becoming an Amazonian contest." That night, Skarda addressed an enthusiastic meeting and again advised holding out for 12 cents. If additional workers stayed away, sentiment might shift toward the strikers. The next morning, the adversaries mustered maximum strength. City authorities and company officials had determined to end the "intimidation" of returning workers. The strikers had found their wives and daughters unusually effective allies, and the company managers, supported by the city fathers, sensed this, too. One hundred regular police and about 300 "specials" guarded the works at five that morning. The fire department waited on call. Between 500 and 1,000 workers and their female supporters gathered near the gates.[112]

Besides agreeing that a "riot" had occurred, eyewitness accounts of the battle of "Fort Standard" on May 10 varied. The "men had sticks and the women . . . clubs," reported the *Plain Dealer*. The women, "much more stubborn and aggressive than the men, . . . stopped a number of men going to work and handled them very roughly tearing the clothes off of some and badly beating others." Police action followed. The *Leader* told another story. From the start, the police had orders to drive back the crowd and make "the highway clear to passersby":

> The officers advanced, the men at the same time falling back slowly and sullenly. The women, however, became infuriated, and determined on attacking the officers, and before they could reach them the men came on in a crowd as reinforcements. Obeying orders, the officers pulled their clubs and went for the attackers, making a point of sparing the women and cracking the male heads as fast as they could reach them. It was a lively fight for a moment but was soon ended. The strikers retreated up the street closely followed by the men in uniform. A shower of sticks, stones, and clubs came flying over the head of those in front of their comrades in the rear and did some execution among the police among whom the missiles fell. A couple of officers were struck. . . .

At the moment the police action started, a prearranged signal reached the fire department and three or four steam fire engines together with two hook-and-ladder companies arrived "ready to set up and douse the rioters." But effective police work made the firemen unnecessary. The crowd fell away rapidly. "Some women were pretty badly beaten by the police," and the authorities arrested two twenty-year-old married Bohemian women. For the entire day and through the night, police carefully guarded the refineries.[113]

That evening, the strikers and their women supporters bitterly condemned the police actions. Skarda insisted that the strikers threw stones only after the police moved on them, and the crowd shouted approval. He especially attacked using city police to "uphold the interest of any private citizen or business firm" unless "a breach of the peace was imminent or the destruction of property almost certain." The strikers had not damaged company property, so that "officers paid for by the public and intended for its protection" had served "a private citizen, without the least cause." "Begging for work for their husbands that their children might have bread," women had been "clubbed and trampled." Skarda also questioned the use of the fire department. He urged the strikers to heed police orders and said "the law is all-powerful and right or wrong must be obeyed." Skarda feared that additional violence would bring the militia. "But," he insisted, "you have a perfect right to talk with the men now at work for the

Standard Oil Company and tell them they are taking bread out of your mouths."[114]

Skarda's fears were real. The *Leader* reported that the May 10 "riot" proved to city authorities and company officials that even more serious troubles lay ahead, and that they said among themselves, "The peace must be preserved at all hazards; private property must be made secure, regardless of the right or wrong that originally underlay the difficulty." The night of May 10, three Cleveland militia companies— the Grays, the Emmetts, and the Light Artillery—"slept on their arms." "A show of force, if not of force itself, might be desired," quipped the *Leader*. The city authorities readied the regular police and instructed the fire department, "Keep up the steam and be ready, for at any time we may need you." Standard added new private police that night, bringing its total to about 400 "specials," and the *Leader* said "the Standard Oil Company spared no expense to make their defenses strong." Regular police gathered in stationhouses at 4 A.M. and marched to the refinery to meet the "specials" already guarding the gates, each of them carrying "a club—some borrowed of the police, but the greater part rough and heavy as though hurriedly manufactured by a draw-shave." Detective roamed the area. The police board, the police superintendent, Captain Hoehn, and two Standard officials (Superintendent Andrews and Treasurer Payne) directed the operation. The refinery "looked like a citadel under defense."[115]

But the strikers stayed away. Perhaps they feared this awesome display of private and municipal power, or were obeying the ancient adage that discretion is the better part of valor. Walking to work at the paper mill nearby, some Bohemian women passed the refinery. A few male strikers came, "stood as mute as a stone fence," and there was "not even [a] hint" at interfering with those returning to work. That was all; the resistance of the strikers, conspicuous by its absence, had ended. At 7 A.M. the "danger" was ended. A small number of police regulars stayed on to help the "specials." The next morning, no demonstrations occurred and the police superintendent said if the strikers gathered again his men planned "active operations."[116]

Standard now took the initiative. The *Plain Dealer* reported: "Mr. Andrews says the pass at which this nonsense must stop is about reached. The company have kept these men's berths open for them for nearly three weeks now and unless they return to work in a day or two he will fill them up with numerous applicants who present themselves every day." On May 12 the Committee of Coopers waited on Andrews and called off the strike. It accepted the 9-cent rate, and Andrews promised to increase wages when business "picked up" and not to hire any more "boys." The settlement involved other terms about which the evidence is contradictory. According to Skarda and the Chicago *Workingman's Advocate*, all the strikers were rehired and none victimized. But the *Plain Dealer* reported that the men resumed at full time, and this made it improbable that all would be taken back. When the strikers returned on May 15, the company had "more applications for labor" than it "could accept." Whatever the exact final settlement, Standard had defeated the hoopers-off. Skarda made much of the promised higher wage and even called the final agreement "a compromise," but begged the issue. Actually, the strike convinced Skarda, a socialist follower of Ferdinand Lassalle, that only cooperatives and working-class politics would settle the "labor question."[117]

Others drew different lessons from the debacle. The *Workingman's Advocate* worried over the power large corporations held and, scoffing at Standard's promise of higher wages, predicted:

> The Standard Oil Company has made more money in sixty days this last winter than it has done since it came into existence. Did their employees get any benefit from it? Not at all. If they got one dollar per gallon for their oil, they wouldn't voluntarily advance wages one penny.

The New York *Labor Standard* emphasized another point. It drew attention to Standard's ability to import barrels to Cleveland and argued that only "a thorough system of national and international labor organization" could prevent wealthy capitalists from winning industrial disputes "by transferring their orders from one locality to another." The press in Cleveland came to quite different conclusions about the settlement. The *Leader* admitted the strikers "behaved with unusual decorum" at the start but then "got more desperate," so that only police action prevented "serious riot." It came down heavily on Skarda and Palda and found the Bohemian strikers "ignorant of the English language" and "limited in general intelligence." The strikers were "like wax in the hands of their leaders." The Cleveland daily found no other explanation for the discontent and nothing unusual in the fearsome display of civic authority in behalf of a private corporation.[118]

In Pittsburgh and Allegheny City during the late summer and early fall of 1877, Standard Oil gave additional and quite convincing proof of its enormous power to discipline discontented workers—even men it did not directly employ. In 1874, the Standard Oil Company had purchased (secretly at first) seven Pittsburgh refineries, and within a year, it had made other purchases to own more than 50 percent of the city's refining capacity. By the end of 1877, only a few small refiners remained independent.[119] Standard reorganized the Pittsburgh refineries, dismantling and closing the less efficient plants.

Some of the Pittsburgh refineries had their own cooperage shops at that time, but were without large, mechanized barrel shops of their own and had to purchase barrels as needed in the open market. Standard was the largest user of oil barrels in the Pittsburgh region, and its decisions affected all local oil barrel manufacturers and their employees. A large number of Standard's orders were filled by the local market, where barrels were made either by skilled workers laboring in traditional ways in shops of varying sizes, factory hands in a few small machine-run shops, or convicts working machines in the Allegheny County prison. In the mid-1870s, contractors in the Western Penitentiary had made for them such items as shoe leather, ladies' and children's shoes, brooms, whips, cigars, tin cans, and oil barrels. Standard purchased some of the few thousand barrels the convicts made each week, and Pittsburgh coopers formally complained to a committee of the Pennsylvania legislature in early June 1877 that this arrangement weakened their bargaining position. Without effect, they argued that few if any prisoners became barrel workers on leaving the jail, and that competition from within the prison had so depressed the local barrel trade that it drove away all young barrel workers. They accused Standard Oil of playing off the convicts against the coopers. "Our State and county officials," an embittered cooper wrote, helped Standard Oil "to the full extent of their power, in putting in and maintaining barrel machinery at the workhouse." Among coopers, it was "the popular belief" that "this machinery was put in, not for the purpose of rescuing from crime and turning into a lawful pursuit the thieves and vagrants of our community, but for profit."[120]

That Standard Oil benefitted from its purchases of prison-made machine barrels was only one grievance against the firm by Pittsburgh and Allegheny City coopers. In 1877 Rockefeller and his associates were engaged in a fierce struggle with the Empire Transportation Company, a powerful competitor aided by Thomas A. Scott and the Pennsylvania Railroad. Empire and its ally threatened the hard-won hegemony recently attained by Standard Oil, and the Ohio firm responded vigorously. In March—a month before Standard Oil cut the wages of its Cleveland barrel workers—the Ohio company canceled its 1875 shipping contract with the Pennsylvania Railroad, cut the price of its kerosene in all markets reached by the Empire firm, and, most significantly for the Pittsburgh barrel workers, closed the Standard Pittsburgh refineries. Scott and his associates fought back hard, with little success. The 1877 trunk-line rate wars and the destruction of much Pennsylvania Railroad property in Pittsburgh during the July railroad-strike riots weakened Scott and his allies. In the fall, they surrendered to Standard and sold it the Empire assets. Much of these doings have been recorded in close detail by Allan Nevins, who calls

Rockefeller's triumph over the Empire Transportation Company and Tom Scott "a victory that was literally epochal."[121] Forgotten entirely in this tale of the struggle for control over refining capacity is the way Standard Oil disciplined the Pittsburgh barrel manufacturers and workers.

The struggle between Standard Oil and the Empire-Pennsylvania group had nearly ended when the barrel manufacturers and their employees became locked in a dispute over wage rates. By late August, when the demand for oil barrels suddenly rose sharply in Pittsburgh, local oil barrel shops had been without orders for nearly six months, leaving many coopers unemployed. In addition, wages of skilled oil barrel coopers had fallen steadily for several years. "To say [the coopers] have been brought down to starvation prices would not be just," observed the *National Labor Tribune*, Pittsburgh's important labor weekly, "for they have been brought even below that." The "boss" manufacturers offered the journeymen coopers 14 cents for handmade oil barrels. But between 400 and 450 journeymen, many of them Germans, quit work and closed all but one shop. They first demanded 16 cents, and then raised the rate to 20 cents for handmade and 11 cents for machine-made barrels. At the 20-cent rate, a hand cooper working full time on oil barrels figured to earn between $9 and $10 a week. From this wage, the worker deducted the cost of his tools.[122] Although the journeymen struck against the "boss" coopers and not against Standard Oil, their employers blamed the low piece rate on the huge refinery. The *Labor Tribune* said the strikers laid all their troubles "at the doors of the Standard Oil Company, who have persistently, for the last six or seven years, by every means within the power and scope of that corporation made reduction after reduction until at last the coopers have been forced to strike." An Allegheny City striker condemned the 14-cent rate and accurately pinned it on the conflict between the great refineries for market power.

> Just think of making a barrel for fourteen cents, and work one half of the time, and bring up a family, and keep the wolf from the door. We could have living wages if the oil refineries only would not try to ruin each other, and sell oil so cheap, for the sake of carrying on a war between themselves, seeing which can sell oil cheapest to consumers in Europe, while we workingmen in this country work fourteen to sixteen hours per day, and have no living at that.

All would benefit if only the refineries "would act right and hold up the price of oil." Then barrel workers "would make a better living" and refiners "would make more money."[123]

In late September the "boss" coopers surrendered and agreed to the 20-cent rate. Despite their desperate condition, the strikers had remained firm and taken advantage of the increasing demand for oil barrels. They turned aside suggestions of compromise, reorganized the weakened if not defunct Coopers' Protective Association, and even found time to play a football game. Although machine-made barrels from the prison and from a few small private shops placed on the market about 2,500 barrels a week, the strikers successfully cut the supply of local barrels and forced their employers to concede.[124]

Standard Oil was not directly involved in this phase of the conflict, but its presence loomed large over the scene and its ability to secure barrels elsewhere did not escape attention. A few years earlier, during a similar strike, Standard had sent barrels from Cleveland to Pittsburgh, and this time Standard hinted that it again would ship large numbers of barrels, when needed, from its Cleveland machine works. The *Labor Tribune* called this a "game of bluff," and a striker said his "brothers in Cleveland" promised to quit work if barrels were sent. But the arrival of secondhand barrels from Eastern cities was not illusory, and the *Pittsburgh Evening Chronicle* called these the first to make "the grand tour to Europe and back to the Smoky City—to the very place of their birth.[125] A striker, calling himself "Evigena" and warning that "it is this company that the coopers are really fighting, and [it] is not the employers," advised fellow strikers not to underestimate the effective power of Standard Oil during labor disputes. Although he did not cite the Cleveland strike of that spring, Evigena saw that Standard's wealth and diverse holdings allowed it to bring barrels in from the outside during local strikes and thereby pit geographically dispersed workers against one another. He called this "standard" company practice.

> This company thought to arrange affairs so that they would beat down every striking locality in detail, and it has done so heretofore. The method is: For instance, a strike occurs at Titusville, [and] barrels are forthwith shipped from Pittsburgh, Cleveland, Oil City, and other points to Titusville until the men there yield compliance to their terms through sheer starvation.

The blacklisting of strikers followed their defeat. "They keep a blacklist of the strikers," Evigena insisted, "so that a [Standard] cooper being discharged for striking in Pittsburgh, would be refused employment in Cleveland, Oil City, Titusville, and even in Pittsburgh and New York."* Evigena's rhetoric reached back to the Age of Jackson, but the content of his warnings presaged the McKinley years and the

---

* No additional evidence has been found of a Standard Oil blacklist in 1877, but this disciplining device was used by Rockefeller and other employers of barrel workers during the great strikes and lockouts of union coopers in Eastern cities in 1874.

power of the large, geographically dispersed industrial corporation. The strikers would not tolerate interference by that "lustful, greedy, overgrown corporation, the Standard Oil Company." The men were "determined to do . . . everything rather than yield." The image of the burning and mangled equipment from the July railroads strikes before him, Evigena even suggested that Standard Oil might yet "share the fate of the Pennsylvania Railroad."[126]

Evigena was both right and wrong. He understood fully the strength of Standard Oil as a direct or indirect employer of barrel workers, but entirely misjudged the holding power of the hand coopers when confronted by that firm. A second dispute in October and November illustrated the mortal inability of the journeymen *and* their employers when challenged by the great Rockefeller firm. In early October, the selling price of handmade barrels rose from $1.35 to $1.40, and flushed with their earlier victory, the journeymen asked first for 2 and then 3 cents out of the 5-cent increase, for a total of 23 cents a barrel. Rebuffed, they struck a second time. A number of boss coopers closed their shops. Then, Standard Oil intervened directly. During the week of October 1 it paid only $1.35 for local barrels. In mid-October it made an even more dramatic move and stopped buying local barrels entirely. "It seems," the *Pittsburgh Evening Chronicle* reported, "that the Standard Oil Company, with a desire to break the market, and lower the selling price per barrel, did, as it had often done before, cease purchasing in this market." No less than 15,000 "foreign barrels" (new or used barrels bought outside the Pittsburgh region) flooded the city. Standard had supplied its needs, and more.[127]

The *Labor Tribune* admitted the hopeless condition of the journeymen and their employees. Standard Oil, "the most complete monopoly that ever existed on a large scale in the United States," was giving the Pittsburgh cooperage interest "a hard squeeze." "Employer and employe[e] are in the same boat—neither making enough to buy salt, and this through a chartered company whose privileges should never have been granted," charged the *Tribune*. Standard could "at any time say to barrel makers, 'we will give you only one dollar per barrel,' " and the boss coopers could do no more than refuse to sell and close shop. Standard was too powerful; it could "dictate the same way to oil producers" as it did to journeymen and their employers. Then, it could "soak" kerosene users.[128]

The boss coopers protested ineffectively against Standard's action and forced the company to an even more drastic decision. On October 23, the bosses unanimously resolved not to sell barrels for less than $1.40 and suspended work in the few shops still open, hoping Standard would buy at that price when it had used up its supply of "foreign" barrels. They also shut down to prevent the journeymen from striking effectively for higher wages if demand rose, or if in the end the bosses had to give in and "make barrels at the price offered by the Standard Oil Company." Standard responded in kind. Though the "market price" for local barrels was $1.40, it now offered $1.30. At the lower price, journeymen's rates could go no higher than 18 cents—2 cents lower than the rate they had won in the September strike. The boss manufacturers offered Standard a $1.35 "compromise," but the company held firm and then pulled from its sleeve a master trump card. It announced plans to build a machine barrel factory in Pittsburgh, a blow that struck down both the bosses and the journeymen. Faced with this drastic alternative, one that only as rich a firm as Standard Oil could pose, the boss coopers gave in, agreed to $1.30, and fixed the journeymen's rate at 18 cents. The journeymen stayed out for 23 cents, but with no chance for success. On November 8, the shops still closed pending acceptance of the 18-cent rate, the *Evening Chronicle* predicted that when work resumed it would be at 14 cents. Even though the bosses had surrendered to Standard's price, the refinery went ahead with its plans for the new factory, "a mammoth cooper shop" turning out daily between 5,000 and 7,000 machine-made barrels. The bosses offered Standard several thousand barrels each day at a fixed price, but the company turned them down because the bosses had rejected a contract clause that read "whenever the company needed barrels." The introduction of a new factory utilizing advanced technology was Standard Oil's means of disciplining the Pittsburgh barrel market. The experience in the Western Penitentiary (and in Cleveland as well) proved that even labor of the "poorest" quality could work a barrel machine. Skill would lose its premium and its power as the machine took over. *Iron Age* drew a single conclusion: "This is another case in which workmen by their foolishness have hastened the introduction of labor-saving machinery."[129]

"This is too much power to be in the hands of any one corporation," an Allegheny City cooper wrote of Standard Oil soon after multiplant ownership and machine-run factories doomed the Pittsburgh barrel makers and made ineffective the complaints of Cleveland factory workers. He urged fellow coopers to protect their skill by building a strong national craft union. But such a union could not thwart the construction of a new, modern factory or the use of capital to introduce new technology, and this Allegheny City cooper never thought to suggest organizing unskilled and semiskilled factory hands.[130] Standard had done more than render the journeyman cooper's skills obsolete: it had made a union composed exclusively of skilled barrel craftsmen virtually powerless in its plants. Henceforth labor and capital would face each other in a new arena.

Although technological improvements and innovations in themselves often doomed older skills and the protective associations built on them, the introduction of those innovations and their impact in post–Civil War America was shaped by the absence or presence of a competitive entrepreneurial structure. In the oil industry in 1874 and 1877, a single firm with enormous market power and large capital reserves used these advantages to rationalize its inner operations, cut costs, and wipe away traditional skills along with the voluntary associations and ways of life associated with them. Technological change never occurred in the abstract; particular circumstances shaped its impact. Technology altered power relationships inside the factory, but power relationships always affected the introduction of technology and its consequences. What mattered in the case of the Standard Oil Company was the fact that the firm and its managers were sufficiently powerful to determine the context that, in turn, affected certain technological changes. There was nothing "inevitable" about the impact of technological change in industrializing America. Standard's successes in the 1870s were unusual for that time. So far as its workers were concerned, market power and technological innovation had joined together, destroyed a traditional craft, and turned the powerful skilled craftsman into a powerless factory laborer.*

Technology and market power eroded the barrel worker's status further in the 1880s. The Standard Oil Company was even stronger in that decade, and its wage earners, whatever their material condition, were less able to resist the firm's decisions. During those years, new technology and machinery entirely displaced the hooper-off. He had served briefly as a transitional figure in a process that ended in the mechanization of barrel making from beginning to end. A heading-up machine improved the old "Yankee cooper" and together with a barrel planer, a hooper riveter, and a thin hooper driver permitted the completion of a barrel "entirely with the aid of machinery, even to boring the bung holes." By the end of the 1880s, the modern barrel works in an oil refinery had no place for the hooper-off, and like the old-time hand cooper he too "became only a memory."[131] The semi-skilled hooper-off working for the Standard Oil Company was in no position to resist his own destruction. In July 1887, for example, 300 employees at the refinery at Point Breeze, Philadelphia (the old Atlantic in 1874), struck for unknown reasons, quickly lost their jobs, and got

---

* Coyne writes that "many old-time coopers were firm in the belief that many of the early labor-saving machines introduced in the cooperate industry were developed and brought out through the financing of the John D. Rockefeller interests." No evidence has been found to substantiate this suspicion, but the policies of Standard in the 1870s surely encouraged such explanations. It is not hard to believe that old-time coopers identified the Standard Oil Company with the rapid decline of their craft. (Coyne, *Development of the Cooperage Industry*, 21–2.)

no support from other Standard workers. The *National Labor Tribune* called the walkout "a mistake": only "absolute necessity" justified challenging so powerful a firm. Standard was "immensely wealthy and most thoroughly organized"; it had "ruled great lines of transportation, [and] bought legislatures." Small numbers of dissatisfied workers could not hope to defeat it. "If the company has, when its interests dictated, successfully 'knocked out' the states of Pennsylvania and Ohio, and made the federal government assistant to its system of distribution of refined oil in Europe and Asia," the *Tribune* warned, ". . . it is passed whipping in a strike." "An enthusiastic boycott . . . by the whole country and a big end of the oil consumers of Europe" might work, but this was a mere dream. "There are disagreeable things men must 'grin and bear' in this wicked world," the *Tribune* despaired, and one was the seemingly unassailable position of firms such as as the Standard Oil Company.[132]

Here, however, the focus has been on the 1870s, not the later decades. Every large Gilded Age industrial firm faced common problems in adopting new machine technology and systems of factory organization, and in recruiting, disciplining, and transforming preindustrial workers, "old" craftsmen, and "new" immigrants. Each firm had its own inner "labor history." How that of Standard Oil differed from or was similar to those of its contemporaries is not yet fully clear. But enough is known to reverse the judgments of Nevins that "material upon Standard's labor relations is scanty" and that "all observers agreed that Rockefeller insisted upon good wages and kindly treatment, and that labor troubles were rare; also that unions were discouraged."[133] For the 1870s, only the last point is accurate. Even more important than such judgments is recognition of the uncommon power Standard Oil had by 1878 in dealing with its workers. What followed in the 1880s and the 1890s resulted in part from these earlier developments, particularly the multiplant organization in a time of rapid communication and transportation.

Extensive research has uncovered only two contemporary examples of similar power. In 1872, when about half of its 2,300 New York City employees struck for the eight-hour day, the Singer Sewing Machine Company hardly felt threatened. The company had in hand a huge inventory, and its branch in Glasgow, Scotland, produced 1,400 sewing machines each week.[134] In 1874, the Erie Railroad successfully broke a strike in its railroad repair shops in Susquehanna Depot, Pennsylvania, by promising to move the shops to another city. This gesture converted a hostile surrounding community into a friendly one.[135] But these are isolated examples of multifirm power. Even the gigantic Cambria Iron Works could not make such a move to end the determined resistance of employees in Johnstown, Pennsylvania, in 1874.[136]

Multiplant organization was only a part of Standard's early strength; there also was the support it got from the Cleveland municipal authorities. So close a tie between a firm and civic authorities was not enjoyed by all Gilded Age industrialists. Small manufacturers did not command the "respect" that Standard did in 1877, and even the larger ones—in a social context quite different from that in Cleveland—had their troubles with local civil authorities and political officeholders. In 1874–1875, a western Pennsylvania operator was convicted by a jury of fellow citizens after bringing armed Italian strikebreakers to his coal mines, and the mayor of an Illinois town frustrated a local mining corporation by disarming Pinkerton police brought there to protect its properties.[137] In 1877, a mayor and an entire common council rebuffed the pressures of silk and iron manufacturers in Paterson, New Jersey, to enlarge the police force to put down an industry-wide silk strike.[138] And there is the tale, as yet unchronicled, of the indictment for murder of William W. Scranton and fifty-two of Scranton's local leaders ("all of them bearing good characters, and belonging to the best society and business associations of Scranton," according to a contemporary defender) during the bitter railroad troubles in July and August of 1877.[139]* These events occurred simultaneously with those detailed in these pages. But Standard Oil found a helpful ally in the local civic authorities, and the others found only trouble from men with similar power and prestige.

So far as shaping an efficient and disciplined labor force was concerned, by 1878 Standard Oil seemed free of the nagging and often quite severe internal and external pressures that plagued other industrialists. Its form of organization and its market position allowed it a freedom of action denied most contemporary manufacturers. Standard therefore could innovate in many ways. The Bible oath against union membership of 1874 was not a Standard first; that strategy Standard shared with the other New York City petroleum refiners. But Standard's early rapid development as a multiplant firm allowed it to innovate in ways that later came to characterize "big business."[140]

These pages are not meant to rekindle the still-smoldering dispute about "robber barons" and "industrial statesmen." Too often that controversy has shed heat rather than light. But two final points will

* The *Scranton Times*, a Democratic newspaper, supported the indictment and warned: "God help the Judges in Luzerne County that undertake to treat this matter in any other manner than the law provides. . . . We want them to understand, and the corporations, too, that there is but one law in this country for the rich and the poor. 'Hell on earth' would be nothing compared to what will take place in this country if the Judges fail to do their whole duty in this matter." (*Scranton Times*, n.d., reprinted in Samuel D. Logan, *A City's Danger and Defense* [Scranton, Pa., 1877], 136.)

help refine understanding of the Gilded Age industrialist and his early critics. The first is a problem of historical analysis. In studying a particular Gilded Age industrialist it is essential to analyze in particular the scope of his freedom of action. The possibilities and limits shaped the labor policies of Standard Oil differed markedly from those operating on lesser industrialists. Recognition and then comparison of these differences should illuminate previously unexplained variations in industrial labor policies and social behavior. Second is a problem of historiography. Defenders of Gilded Age industrialists have scored heavily by arguing that muckrakers, journalists, and professional historians later imposed the image of "robber baron" on the business giant. Actually, this was not the case. Contemporary critics of Gilded Age industrial power often identified it with feudal Europe. A Standard Oil worker called himself and other Standard employees "serfs" to illustrate their helplessness,[141] and a Cleveland writer named Pickleburg (surely a pseudonym) ascribed feudal attributes to Standard Oil. In 1877, a Young Men's Christian Association branch in Buffalo, New York, published wise maxims for the time. One read: "Take pleasure in your business, and it will become your recreation." Pickleburg scorned such "capital advice," asked, "How about the pleasure a workingman can take in his business?" and said of Standard Oil: "Your chaps who run huge monopolies like the Standard Oil Works . . . crush out of existence all smaller rivals . . . by underhanded treachery that should scout them from the presence of fair-dealing men. They find their business as full of pleasure and jolly recreation as did those jovial maurading barons of old, who waylaid weaker brethren with a very simple formula—'stand and we'll deliver, or we'll run you through.' "[142] The validity of Pickleburg's judgment is not at issue. What matters is that his condemnation of Standard Oil was not the metaphor of an angry individual but the common language of countless critics of Gilded Age industrial power. This language reveals a fear that republican institutions would decay when challenged by distant, inaccessible industrial-"feudal" power, and helps explain the intensity of so much disorganized but deeply felt Gilded Age social protest.

There is finally the matter of John D. Rockefeller himself. His particular role in 1874 and 1877 remains shadowy. It is well known, however, that he was a devout Baptist and a Sunday school teacher. Although Mrs. Rockefeller purchased a variety of books, "the husband cared little for any literature outside the Bible."[143] Rockefeller knew his Bible as well as he knew his refinery, and we must wonder what he thought and felt when reading 1 *Kings* 17:12: "I have not a cake, but a handful of meal in a barrel, and a little oil in a cruse."

5

A NOTE ON IMMIGRATION HISTORY, "BREAKDOWN MODELS," AND THE REWRITING OF THE HISTORY OF IMMIGRANT WORKING-CLASS PEOPLES

NOT MUCH is known yet about the migration of various European peoples to the United States in the post–Civil War era. I believe that our lack of knowledge is caused by more than mere neglect. Partly, of course, it results from the inadequate study of working-class, or labor, history in general. The intersection of immigration and working-class history can be illustrated with two brief examples. First, after the Civil War industrial development made rapid strides in large American cities. In 1880, between 78 and 87 of every 100 residents of San Francisco, St. Louis, Cleveland, New York, Detroit, Milwaukee, and Chicago were either foreign-born or the children of foreign-born parents. These were mostly Northern and Western European immigrants, but there were also significant numbers of foreign-born Chinese and Canadians.

Second, the sources of immigration shifted greatly starting in the 1890s, but not the relationship between the immigrants and the American working class. By 1910, most foreign-born residents of the United States were Southern and Eastern Europeans, and that year, two of three workers in America's largest manufacturing and mining industries were either immigrants or American blacks. The great Carnegie steel mills, for example, then owned by the United States Steel Corporation, employed 14,359 common laborers, 11,694 of them Southern and Eastern Europeans. To study these persons solely as "immigrants," on the one hand, or "workers," on the other, makes an artificial distinction. Much of importance in their lives and behavior will be either neglected or misunderstood.

But our study of the immigrant experience has been misshapen by more than just a failure to identify the immigrants as workers. The theory that continues to dominate immigration history is old and limited. The model conventionally used in writing immigration history flows from what the anthropologist Clifford Geertz calls the "theoretical dichotomies of classical sociology—*Gemeinschaft* and *Gesellschaft*, mechanic and organic solidarity, and folk and urban cultures." An emphasis on such dichotomies has led immigration historians to give inadequate attention to what Geertz describes as primordial—as contrasted with civic—attachments. Historians have underplayed "the 'assumed' givens . . . of social existence: immediate contiguity and kin connections mainly, but beyond them, the givenness that stems from being born into a particular religious community, speaking a particular language, and following particular social patterns." That failure in the study of immigrant history has resulted in a deemphasis on the *adaptive* capacities of diverse immigrant groups. We know much too little about *how* the "old" became the "new." Instead, it has been assumed that "breakdown" of all sorts occurred as a consequence of migration, and that anomie and alienation characterized the movement of peoples from farm to factory and from rural setting to urban community.

My own research in recent years bears only indirectly on immigrants, but casts much doubt on the adequacy of the "breakdown" model as a way of understanding the behavior of migrant and immigrant populations. I have been working on a history of the Afro-American family, and part of that study focuses on the migration of black families to the North between 1880 and 1930, and uses vast quantities of federal and state manuscript census data to reconstruct black households. Such data allow us to test the "breakdown" thesis as applied to American blacks, by first examining the occupational structure of various black communities, and then studying the composition of black households in diverse Northern communities. In addition, comparisons have been made to white community and household structures. I have also studied Irish, British, and German immigrants in Paterson, New Jersey, in 1880, and Jews and Italians in New York City in 1905. A brief summary of some of the findings reveals the utter inadequacy of the conventional models in explaining immigrant and working-class behavior. Let us see why.

1880

PATERSON, New Jersey, was an immigrant city in 1880, and its economy was sustained by the manufacture of iron, locomotives, machinery, and a variety of textiles, especially silk products.

British, German, and Irish men were the largest ethnic communities in that town, and were predominantly working class. Of the 5,858 British, German, and Irish men studied, about nine of ten Irish, five of six British, and three of four German men were either skilled or unskilled workers. The distribution of skills differed among these groups: three of four British and two of three German men were skilled, and the Irish workers were divided evenly between skilled and unskilled. Large numbers of women and children in all three communities also labored in the textile mills.

Nearly all of these working people lived in kin-related households, that is, households in which two or more residents were related by blood or marriage. The typical household was nuclear in composition—containing only members of an immediate family—for all groups: British, 74 percent; Germans, 78 percent; and Irish, 73 percent. One measure of the "breakdown" thesis is the presence of a significant number of broken families, or male-absent households. Such households exist in all cultures but were not abundant among these immigrant workers. Nine of ten German households, and nearly the same proportion of British households, had in them either a husband and wife or two parents and their children. That was also true in four of five Irish households.

The three immigrant groups compare favorably with native white Patersonians with roughly the same occupational distribution as the Paterson British community. Most native white men were also skilled workers. Extended households (those with kin) and augmented households (those with lodgers) were more common among the native whites than among the immigrants. Most important, male-absent households were more common among the native whites than among the British and Germans, and just as frequent as among the Irish. That finding serves as powerful evidence that the "breakdown" model tells very little of importance about immigrant and working-class adaptive capacities between 1840 and 1890. These immigrant groups were not similar culturally, but they all revealed a similar adaptive capacity, and that capacity did not distinguish them from native whites.

1905

WORKING-CLASS immigrant family distruption was just as uncommon among Lower East Side Jewish and Greenwich Village Italian immigrants in 1905 as among the Irish, British, and German immigrants of Paterson in 1880.

The occupations of 6,250 Jewish and 4,518 Italian men have been examined, and again, these men resided in predominantly working-class communities. One of four Jews and one of seven Italians had non-working-class occupations; nearly all engaged in petty trades. Clothing workers, with various levels of skill, predominated in the Jewish community but had less importance among the Italians. Overall, about 50 percent of Italian and 30 percent of Jewish men were unskilled.

POWER & CULTURE

The composition of 3,584 Jewish and 2,945 Italian households have been examined, and kin-related households predominated in both of these early-twentieth-century ethnic communities. Only about one in twenty-five residents of each group lived outside such a household. About half of Jewish and three of five Italian households contained just the immediate family. Two of five Jewish households took in boarders, and extended kin lived in one of four Italian households.

This evidence, once again, raises serious questions about the "breakdown" model. Working-class families did not collapse in these two early-twentieth-century ghettos. In fact, more than nine in ten Jewish (93.2 percent) and Italian (92.9 percent) families contained a husband and wife or two parents and their children.

1905 AND 1925

ALTHOUGH I have focused on the immigrant family in 1880 and 1905, it is useful for comparative purposes to summarize briefly the findings on New York City blacks in 1905 and 1925.

The occupational structure among New York City blacks in 1905 differed greatly from that of either of Jews or the Italians. Twenty-four of twenty-five black men were laborers, and among those about nine in ten were unskilled laborers and service workers.

Furthermore, though men outnumbered women in the Jewish and Italian migrations, the opposite was true among black migrants to New York City.

Yet migration to Northern cities did not cause massive breakdown among Southern blacks. Poorer black household heads took in relatives and nonrelated boarders more often than better-situated Jews and Italians, and the nuclear family unit was also less important among blacks. But their disadvantaged economic and demographic position did not mean that they lived in disorganized families. Four of five blacks lived in kin-related households, and about five of six black New York City households had in them either a husband and wife or two parents and their children. And an examination of nearly 15,000 black Harlem households shows that no significant changes occurred in the composition of the black household between 1905 and 1925.

The data reported have their limitations. They describe powerful adaptive capacities among working-class migrant and immigrant groups between 1880 and 1925. But they do not explain the origins of those capacities. Nothing reported is meant to deny the severe inequalities that these groups knew in their daily lives. And surely the data do not dispute the conventional emphasis on suffering and strain. But "suffering" and "strain" are not synonyms for "breakdown." The point emphasized here is a quite simple one. An inadequate "breakdown" model has prevented us from understanding the diverse ways in which migrant and immigrant groups—new and old immigrants, blacks and whites—have dealt with the problems imposed upon them in new and strange settings. We need to put aside that model once and for all.

6

SCHOOLS FOR FREEDOM

The Post-Emancipation Origins of Afro-American Education

"THE PRINCIPLE of schools, of education," said James T. White, a black delegate to the 1868 Arkansas Constitutional Convention, "is intended to elevate our families." The role former slaves and other blacks such as White (an Indiana-born minister and Union Army veteran) played in bringing schools to their children offers a rare insight into the values of the black community as it emerged from slavery. Blacks voluntarily paid school tuition, purchased schoolbooks, hired, fed, boarded, and protected teachers, constructed and maintained school buildings, and engaged in other costly (and sometimes dangerous) activities to provide education for their children. To expect such sustained efforts from men and women fresh to freedom, poor by any material standard, and entirely without political power is, perhaps, much to ask. But evidence disclosing such efforts is indeed abundant.

The former slaves themselves, not the schools per se, remain the center of this study. Historians of American (and particularly Southern) education have reconstructed in close detail the work of Northern white schoolteachers and missionaries in the postbellum South. While making it clear that articulate freedmen and freedwomen enthusiastically welcomed education for their children, the existing literature—even by "revisionist" historians of the Reconstruction—emphasizes the energy sympathetic Northern whites expended in helping freedpeople establish schools. In actual fact, the former slaves themselves played the central role in building, financing, and operating these schools, a fact that adds to our understanding of the family sensibilities and parental concerns of these men and women. It also indicates some of

This essay originated as a draft chapter of *The Black Family in Slavery and Freedom* and was not included in the finished volume. Never having received final editing, it was somewhat unwieldy, and in preparing it for publication certain repetitious passages have been eliminated. The footnotes, derived largely from the records and publications of the Freedmen's Bureau and Northern freedmen's aid societies, supplemented by newspaper accounts and by reminiscences of blacks of the Civil War era, were not yet in finished form and have, of necessity, been omitted here. The essay in its original, unedited form, complete with footnotes, may be found with the Herbert G. Gutman Papers in the New York Public Library.

the ways in which reciprocal obligations operated beyond the immediate family and bound together former slaves living in rural and urban communities.

Postwar educational efforts by blacks built on a firm base of educational activism during slavery. Scattered but nevertheless convincing evidence reveals that secret slave schools had existed in a number of antebellum Southern cities. A black woman named Deveaux began a secret school in Savannah, Georgia, in 1835 and taught in the same room for the next thirty years. After the war, a visitor talked with her (she still taught in that room but to "the children of the better class of the colored people") and learned how she had eluded "for more than a quarter of a century the most constant and lynx-eyed vigilance of the slaveholders of her native city." She was not alone in this work. James Porter, a free black from Charleston, South Carolina, arrived in Savannah in 1856 and established a similar school. A tailor, Porter had "won some distinction in music, which led the Bishop of the Episcopal Church in Savannah to have him come there to train a choir for the St. Stephen's Episcopal Church." Porter taught piano and organ to white and free black children, kept his secret school, and taught many "private pupils," who in turn "kept the secret with their studies at home." Charleston also had secret schools. "Miss L" used a sewing school as a cover to teach young blacks, who "always had a piece of sewing in hand" while learning to read and write. Blacks guarded her premises from suspicious whites.

Mrs. Milla (Lila) Grandison (Granson), a slave woman, taught secretly in Natchez, Mississippi; she had learned to read and write from the children of her "indulgent owner" in Kentucky. His death had caused her to be sold to Mississippi, where she labored first as a field hand and then as a house servant. Slaves on the plantation used to "study in her house from eleven until two o'clock at night," Union Army chaplain Joseph Warren wrote in 1864. "From this school," he added, "others of a similar character sprung up." Laura Haviland, a Michigan abolitionist, added details:

> Every window and door was carefully closed to prevent discovery. In that little school hundreds of slaves learned to read and write a legible hand. After toiling all day for their masters they crept stealthily into this back alley, each with a bundle of pitch-pine splinters for light. . . . Her number of scholars was twelve at a time, and when she had taught these to read and write she dismissed them, and again took her apostolic number and brought them up to the extent of her ability, until she had graduated hundreds. A number of them wrote their own passes and started for Canada, and she supposes succeeded, as they were never heard from.

Discovery caused Mrs. Grandison to close her school, but she reopened it, so that it continued for seven of her twelve years as a Mississippi slave.

Other Southern cities with secret schools included Richmond, Virginia, where an unnamed black woman managed such a place for slaves, and Augusta, Georgia, where Edwin Purdy, a black clergyman, started a school in "a small room of his house" in the middle of the Civil War. Soon discovered, Purdy paid a $50 fine, suffered sixty lashes, and was sentenced to prison for an undisclosed time (friends, apparently whites, won his release after twelve days). These secret efforts begin to explain why white missionaries who went to Savannah soon after General William T. Sherman captured that city found, to their surprise, that "a goodly number" of former slave children could "read and spell" and that some even "evinced considerable knowledge of arithmetic, geography, and writing." Northern schoolteachers in Richmond shared their surprise. Seventeen days after the Union Army took the city, they opened schools and soon had enough students ("a sufficient base") to "grade the schools." Among some 1,000 pupils, teachers found 80 "good readers," 200 "good spellers," 100 boys and girls familiar with the alphabet, and between 500 and 600 who had "picked up a letter or two."

The efforts of blacks to educate themselves expanded greatly during the Civil War, especially in locales that fell to the Union Army. "One of the first acts of the Negroes, when they found themselves free," observed the American Freedmen's Inquiry Commission, "was to establish schools at their own expense." A pay school—the first school for wartime runaways—was opened in Alexandria, Virginia, on September 1, 1861, by two black women. Later that month, one of them joined Mrs. Mary Smith Peake, the daughter of an English father and a free black woman who had taught at an antebellum Hampton, Virginia, school (and had her black stepfather among her pupils), to start a second contraband* school at Fortress Monroe, Virginia. White teachers did not work with the Alexandria contrabands until October 1862. By that time, blacks managed three other schools. Before the war's end, at least sixteen other black men and women taught or directed Alexandria schools for runaway slaves. By April 1863, about 2,000 former slaves had congregated in Alexandria and 400 children attended their schools. "The first demand of these fugitives when they come into the place," observed a *New York Evening Post* correspondent,

---

* In May 1861, fugitive slaves entering Union lines were denominated "contraband of war" by General Benjamin F. Butler, who gave them refuge but had no power to grant them legal freedom. The name stuck and became a generic term for former slaves even after the passage of the Confiscation Act of 1862 and announcement of the Emancipation Proclamation legally freed those who reached federal lines.

"is that their children may go to school." "Another surprising fact," he went on, "is that the poor negro women had rather toil, earn and pay one dollar per month for their children's education, than to permit them to enter a charity school." The contraband blacks also built, by voluntary labor, a school worth about $500, and later enlarged and improved it, making it "well lathed and plastered."

But there was more to establishing a school than bricks and mortar. At the start, a dispute over whether white or black teachers should be "the superintendents" threatened this Alexandria school's future. The blacks called a meeting. "I wish you could have been at that meeting," reported North Carolina fugitive slave Harriet Jacobs, who had come to Virginia to teach. "Most of the people were slaves until quite recently, but they talked sensibly and . . . put the question to a vote in quite parliamentary style. The result was a decision that the colored teachers should have charge of the school." The school opened in January 1864 with 75 pupils; two months later, it had 225, and the following August it was "the largest school and schoolhouse in the city." Once it had opened, blacks maintained their support. "My table in the school room," an early Hampton teacher reported, "is loaded, morning and noon, with oranges, lemons, apples, figs, candies, and other sweet things too numerous to mention." Such gift-giving was common in many parts of the South.

Wartime Virginia and Maryland refugees also crowded Georgetown and the District of Columbia, and these places soon had their complement of black-run schools. William Slade, the president of the District's black Social, Civil, and Industrial Association, told the American Freedmen's Inquiry Commission in 1863 that District blacks paid tuition to support 14,000 children at twenty different schools. Joseph Ambush (the son of a slave but himself a free black) opened a school in July 1862, and later that year a black teacher managed a classroom for a Northern benevolent society. In February 1864, William J. Wilson, a well-known Brooklyn black teacher, and his wife started a school that soon had as many as 400 pupils. That same year, the African Civilization Society (founded in New York in 1858 by Henry Highland Garnet) opened its first District school. By January 1866, the society supported ten day and two night schools, attended by 961 students. The society spent $3,000 in 1865, and its leaders (Garnet among them), together with District of Columbia black clergymen, also supported efforts in 1864 by the National Freedmen's Relief Association to establish the Washington High School for Colored Youth, a free school that would especially train black teachers. Evening schools for adult blacks (voluntary teachers, some of them blacks, gave lessons to 1,080 pupils in May 1864) used black churches rent-free, and some churches also supplied free light and fuel. The capital's first public

TABLE ONE

School Statistics, Military Districts North and
South of the James River, December 1864

	DISTRICT SOUTH OF THE JAMES RIVER	DISTRICT NORTH OF THE JAMES RIVER
Number of children under 14[a]	11,170	5,032
Number of day-school pupils (6–14)	3,772	1,652
Number of night-school pupils	1,228	802
Number of teachers	81	35

[a] It is estimated that half of this population was between the ages of 6 and 14.

school for blacks opened on March 1, 1864, in the "colored Ebenezer church," and had two teachers, one of them Miss Emma V. Brown, a black woman. Although the New England Freedmen's Aid Society paid her salary as a public schoolteacher and sent her an assistant, a tax on District of Columbia black residents paid all other expenses.

Schools grew with the arrival of the federal army. Norfolk's first black schools met in the city's black churches in April 1863. Indeed, so many Norfolk blacks wanted schooling that after the first week white teachers hired fifteen "colored assistants." In January 1864, the Norfolk and Portsmouth schools together counted 2,600 pupils drawn from a contraband population of about 19,000. A careful survey in December 1864 revealed that about two-thirds of contraband children between the ages of six and fourteen attended day schools in the military districts south and north of the James River (table 1).

According to the American Missionary Association, seven blacks were "connected" with the Norfolk and Portsmouth schools. One, Mary Watson, described an evening school with "parents and children, side by side, and [the] grandparents of some who attend the day school." At the war's end, Norfolk also had tuition schools "conducted by enterprising colored persons of both sexes," and a white observer found their "zeal in teaching . . . truly commendable." Rural and town missionary-sponsored schools on the peninsula between the York and James rivers also had black teachers in the winter and spring of 1864–1865. Nancy Battey taught the first day school at the Darlington farm outside Fortress Monroe and had help from two black men, "formerly teachers." A Yorktown woman teacher had as her assistant "one of my best night scholars, Washington Phillips, our head carpenter." And at Acretown, a contraband settlement, Quaker schools were taught by ten persons, "five from among the people." Blacks "frequently express their good will by offers of assistance and by little presents of whatever their means afford," remarked a white teacher. A *"very poor* woman . . . brought some eggs to school and shyly dropped them into the pockets of her teacher, and many are the partridges and eggs that have been offered to us."

North Carolina contrabands knew their first school in the spring of 1862, taught by a white man in the New Bern African Methodist Episcopal Church. Army officers also gave a Baptist missionary two Beaufort churches in which to teach. He found them "very filthy and sadly out of repair," but Beaufort blacks soon agreed to raise funds for their improvement. A Sabbath collection produced $84.88 ("to my surprise," said the white missionary), and in five weeks the blacks had gathered $200. In the winter and spring of 1863, New Bern blacks also established their own small schools. A *New York Tribune* reporter visited a school near the Camp Trent contraband "huts" built by the former slaves. "In one of the huts," he related, "a school was in progress, kept by a black man. He has thirty scholars, who he told me were learning quite fast. He himself has a fair education; could read, write, and cypher. He had learned all this, while a slave, from a school-boy." Later that year, New Bern had twenty-four teachers, three blacks among them. James O'Hara, a West Indian mulatto, ran a "self-supported school." O'Hara's institution, New Bern's "most advanced colored school," included among its subjects "Geography, Grammar, and Arithmetic."

In *Rehearsal for Reconstruction*, Willie Lee Rose fully described the schooling given South Carolina Sea Island blacks by Yankee missionaries and schoolteachers. Sea Island blacks contributed mightily to that effort. A white Boston Baptist clergyman started Beaufort's first school in early January 1862. "Both teachers and pupils are negroes," said one report. This school, called "the Billaird Hall school," had four black "assistant" teachers: Paul Johnson, Thomas Ford, Peter Robinson, and Ephraim Lawrence, "themselves not far advanced but able to read and spell one-syllabled words." Missionaries spent an hour each day giving them special instruction, and a weekly contribution of five cents from each pupil (both boys and girls attended the school) helped pay their salary. The five-cent contribution, a white teacher wrote, "is cheerfully made, but not enforced in exceptional cases of orphanage or extreme poverty." Sixteen pupils attended the first day; two months later, school enrollment had reached 101. Indeed, three of every five Beaufort youths regularly attended the wartime schools.

POWER & CULTURE

Beaufort was the only town of size on the Sea Islands, but schools also flourished in rural areas, some maintained by Northern benevolent societies like the National Freedmen's Relief Association (which had established twenty-two schools by 1864) and others by the blacks themselves. A former slave woman named Hettie (she had "stolen a knowledge of letters from time to time") began a day school in March 1863 and kept up her work after the Edisto blacks became war refugees on St. Helena's Island. Even before that time, white missionary-teachers arrived at the Smith plantation to find that "the children were all assembled by Cuffy, and he was teaching them when we went in." Another black, a crippled former slave named Bacchus, assisted the teacher on the Coffin's Point plantation and took over the class when the teacher left for a time. "Uncle" Cyrus, then about seventy years old, along with another black taught 150 children as much as they could until the Northern societies provided additional white teachers. In January 1863, the missionary-teacher E. W. Williams pleaded with New England friends for small contributions to help this man out: "He has taught seven months gratuitously, and is of great help in the school every day. The Government has rationed him, and he has, perhaps, had some charitable clothing, but no money." Shortly afterwards, the old man died.

In other places, Sea Island parents shared in the supervision of the schools. Northern teachers encouraged St. Helena's blacks to form visiting committees to help manage that island's school. One person from each plantation served on the committee, which Robert Chaplin headed. The school visiting committee did its work every Friday, and once thanked New England friends for "helping us to drop the scales from our eyes." Chaplin, then seventy-three, composed the report that went North, explaining that the committee visited the schools to "see that everything go regular among the children" and to help the teacher "so far as our understanding goes." "All books and property that belong to the school," he added, "is in our charge."

Farther west, blacks exhibited the same concern for wartime schooling. When Union Army recruiters first arrived in Nashville, Tennessee, they found that blacks had started "without any assistance" schools in which more than 800 children "received instruction from teachers paid by their parents—the slaves but just emancipated." A *New York Times* correspondent found it "a remarkable fact" that the blacks "at once" had "opened schools for themselves." A Nashville bookseller remarked that he had "sold more spelling books in a short time than he has done for years." The first school had opened in the fall of 1862 in the First Colored Baptist Church. Its teacher was Daniel Wadkins, an antebellum free black whose school for free black children had twice been closed by worried whites in the 1850s. By the fall of 1863, several schools had "sprung up, taught by colored people who have got a little learning somehow." Students paid between one and two dollars each month. By the summer of 1864, the schools had "become so numerous, and the attendance so large, that all open opposition to them has ceased." That year, more black than white Nashville children attended school, and some black students established "schools on their own as soon as they were able to read."

Similar efforts flourished throughout Tennessee. Northern whites taught in several schools at Clarksville, a river town sixty miles northwest of Nashville. So did two blacks. "Here," said one visitor, "there is a school of the lowest grade, taught by a colored girl, herself but a primary scholar, and a feeble colored man, of similar attainments. They do not receive compensation." At Columbia, Tennessee, a free black named Jordon started a school in the spring of 1864, but Tennessee Union soldiers broke it up, and after Jordon reopened it, these same men (one of them a local constable) seized him, held a mock trial, and punished him (even though the school had been sanctioned by other federal army officers) with twenty-five lashes.

Former slaves also played an important role in wartime education in the Department of the Tennessee, a military district that included western Tennessee, northern Louisiana, and all of Arkansas and Mississippi. One National Freedmen's Relief Association official, noting the zeal for schooling among the blacks in Vicksburg, Mississippi, promised them a free school "instead of compelling the blacks to pay *sixty cents per month*." "They will starve, and freeze themselves in order to attend school, so highly do they value the privilege of learning to read, write, and reckon . . . ," he added. Army officers initially withheld support, but finally offered two vacant lots without secure title, causing the blacks to construct movable school buildings. "The colored people," reported missionary Joseph Warren, "have subscribed liberally to aid in building these houses, and are giving personal attention to the business."

Blacks also established schools deep in the hinterland of the Mississippi Valley. Elizabeth Bond, a white teacher at Young's Point, Louisiana, opened one "in a rough log house, thirty feet square, and so open that the crevices admitted light sufficient without the aid of windows. The furniture consisted of undressed plank benches without backs, from ten to twelve feet long, and in the centre of the room stood an old steamboat stove, four feet long, which had been taken out of the river." Her only teaching materials were "some old charts, very inferior, which [she] picked up in camp." Despite these dismal conditions, black teachers soon followed in Bond's wake. During 1863, when Young's Point was filled with despair and death, black refugees had "a colored teacher who could read some and taught school for a short time out of doors." He used the "old charts." James Yeatman, president of the Western Sanitation Commission, also found blacks teaching near Goodrich Landing. Rose Ana, "a colored girl," taught a school for fifty blacks at Groshon's plantation, Uncle Jack had eighty-nine students at another estate, and thirty learned from Uncle Tom at the Savage plantation. "He is infirm and teaches them remaining himself in bed," said Yeatman of Tom. Then there was William McCutchen, who had a school on the Currie plantation. Its sixty-three students were "greatly in want of books . . . using books of every kind and description, scarcely any two of them alike. Some even were using scraps of paper. One had a volume of Tennyson's poems, out of which he was learning his letters. . . ."

Overall, Northern whites taught most Mississippi Valley black children in 1863 and 1864. But their parents, by paying tuition and giving help in numerous other ways, had played an indispensable part in the process. Early educational efforts in the Department of the Tennessee proved fruitful. John Eaton, the department's superintendent of freedmen, estimated that in July 1864 the Union Army supervised 113,650 former slaves and that 13,320 of them (almost 12 percent) had been "under instruction in letters." About 4,000 could read "quite fairly" and about 2,000 could write.*

Between April 1865 and the advent of Radical Reconstruction two years later, educational opportunities for blacks expanded dramatically

---

*Eaton did not indicate whether or not his estimates included former slaves then serving in the Union Army. The first school for black soldiers in the Vicksburg area started in late December 1863. It opened in a tent, and 10 or 15 men attended. A few months later, over 200 persons were enrolled, but military duty caused irregular attendance. Some among these soldiers learned to read and even to write. We have as striking evidence letters written by William Lee McGinnis to Maggie A. Smith, his former teacher. Sometime in 1864, ill health had forced her to quit Vicksburg, and former students, McGinnis among them, urged her to return. The *Freedmen's Bulletin* printed three of his letters and insisted they had not been altered in any way. (*Freedmen's Bulletin* 1 [Nov. 1864], 47–8.)

1. Miss maggi. A. Smith you will pleas bring your sister with yow we have mooney a naugh for yow and her both and Sloobars for yow and her we are bilding Baracades on Chery street two squares from the jail onn the left in a hannsome place beautifly Shaded and we will have a haus Sutable for yow and your Sister if She will come with yow and a bove all things do not fail to bring your Self when you get this note give my Respects to your parence I hope to be better er quainted with them if we should live to meet a gane Now I shal cloze my letter Saying Send your Sister and dont forget to bring your Self Miss Maggi A Smith I Remain your Schollar

WILLIAM LEE McGINNIS
Co. B 48th Regt.

2. Miss Maggie I. am not well I have been very sick with Fever and I am unable to write So I. got my Friend Ordle Sergt Wm Lee McGinnis in my Co to write you may Come Just as Sune as You Can we have Mooney Anuft to Spare Just as long as you will Stay with us
I still remane your Scholar

Richard F. Griggs.

throughout the South, thanks in part to the work of Northern benevolent societies and the newly established Freedmen's Bureau. But as during the war, initiative often rested with the blacks themselves. The process can best be examined in four states: Virginia, South Carolina, Louisiana, and Georgia.

The general public and private policies that affected the education of blacks deserve brief notice. Except for Florida, where the legislature imposed a special education tax on blacks, no Southern state made provision to educate the former slaves. In establishing the Freedmen's Bureau, Congress did not include funds for education in 1865; not until the summer of 1866 did the federal government authorize the bureau to spend half a million dollars for the rental, construction, and repair of schoolhouses. Some additional money for the education of former slaves came from funds appropriated by several Northern states to purchase black substitutes in the South and thereby help to fill draft quotas. Bureau policies and a shortage of funds obliged the former slaves to take the initiative in establishing schools, and in this they were encouraged by the Northern benevolent societies. The New England Freedmen's Aid Society, for example, only offered funds to blacks who erected, repaired, and cared for schools, furnished board for teachers, and paid small tuition fees. Edward Everett Hale explained the guiding assumptions shared by many who managed these benevolent societies: "The policy . . . has not been to make these people beggars. 'Aide-toi et Dieu t'aidera' is their motto. The black people know they must support themselves, as they have always done." Hale admitted that such policies assured "suffering" but went on: "Where is there not suffering in this world? We have never said that the black man's life should be raised above suffering. We have said that he should

3.   Camp 48th U. S. Col'd Infty Sept 9th 1864
                                              Vicksburg Mississippi
    Dear Teacher your kind note came to hand this morning and your Schollars were glad to hear from yow and thur nevr ware a letter met with that give aney one so much tiden of Joy as to hear your letter Red and yow may Just depend onn what I Say to yow Miss maggi A. Smith yow have friends a nough in the 48 that will give yow a life time Serport less more a year Serport all we want is yow to come to us we will Carey yow throw this ware and yow Shall be made Comfortable the Balance of your life if yow wish to make this your Home we know that the Copper heads have to be comd biterly a ginst yow and for this reason we want yow to Come to us. Mr Griggs have benn unwell but when he heard from yow his fever left him Miss Maggi A. Smith yow will pleas tell the Copper heads for me that I Say the fall of the year has made its er pear ance in the South and the leaves are falling and we will commence thrashing green Backs for yow tell them tha need not put ther Selves to any troble for when we are don fiting for uncle Sam we will lend them a hand if tha wish it this is from a Camp mate of Mr Griggs I expect Miss Smith yow have forgotten me as I did not come to Schoold much ec cuis my Bad Spelling I hope this may fine you in Joying your Self yours
                                     WILLIAM LEE McGINNIS.

be free to choose between inevitable hardships. This promise we perform."

In fact, blacks did not wait for state authorization, the advent of the bureau, or the advice of Northern societies to establish schools in 1865 and 1866. In the late fall of 1865, John W. Alvord, superintendent of education for the Freedmen's Bureau, toured the South. Everywhere he traveled, he informed General O. O. Howard, the bureau commissioner, he found "a class of schools got up and taught by colored people, rude and imperfect, but still groups of persons, old and young, *trying* to learn." They lacked "the patience to wait for the coming of a white teacher." Alvord estimated that the South knew "at least five hundred" such schools, many of them never before visited "by any white man." "In the absence of other teaching," he said, "they are determined to be self-taught." Alvord supplemented this official report with an even more enthusiastic statement to the *Freedman's Journal*, the monthly periodical of the American Tract Society. "All our party have been surprised by this unusual face," he said of the black teachers and schools started by blacks. "A cellar, a shed, a private room, perhaps an old school-house, is the place," he went on, "and, in the midst of a group of thirty or forty children, an old negro in spectacles, or two or three young men surrounded by a hundred or more, themselves only in the rudiments of a spelling-book, and yet with a passion to teach what they *do* know; or a colored woman, who as a family servant had some privileges, and with a woman's compassion for her race—*these* are the institutions and the agencies." Schools taught by whites had ended in the summer, but some black teachers continued through that difficult season. "In truth," Alvord added, "these spontaneous efforts of the colored people would start up everywhere if books could be sent them."

Virginia and South Carolina blacks typified the early postwar concern for education. Richmond and Charleston deserve special attention. Quite different in many ways (Richmond, for example, had more black factory workers than any other American city), both cities had fallen to the Union Army just before the war's end. It should be kept in mind that schooling for blacks in these and other Southern places was entirely voluntary. No external compulsion forced the former slaves to attend school or to contribute to the success of educational institutions. A school for Richmond blacks started in mid-April at the First African Baptist Church, and 1,025 students (50 of them sixteen or older) showed up. Their enthusiasm for schooling stunned one observer: "I never before imagined it possible for an uneducated class to have such zeal of earnestness for schools and books. . . ." On a visit to Richmond in 1866, William Hepworth Dixon, the editor of the

London *Athenaeum,* agreed, noting that the city had forty black schools. Dixon toured some of them with Eli Brown, the headwaiter at a Richmond hotel. "Last night," Dixon reported, "I went with Eli round this city; not to see its stores and bars, its singing-rooms and hells; but bent on a series of peeps into the negro schools." Dixon found them "mostly in garrets or down in vaults; poor rooms with scant supplies of benches, desks, and books." "These men," he said, "are not waiting for the world to come and cheer them with its grand endowments and its national schools; they have begun the work of emancipating themselves from the thraldom of ignorance and vice." The waiter Brown proved this to Dixon. As a slave, he had "learned to read in secret," and since his freedom, he had learned to write, too. None of this came easily. "Many of our children" explained a Quaker teacher, "have been driven from their homes because they came to school; and, in some instances, *whole families* have been turned into *the streets* because they were represented in the school-room."

In these early months, "by far the largest proportions of Richmond children" paid for "their books, slates, etc." The teachers received gratification in yet other ways. Once, at least, schoolchildren brought "beautiful boquets" to their homes. That winter individual black children, most from families living on the edge of poverty, contributed to or collected for a "fuel fund" to heat their schools in sums ranging from two cents to one dollar. When the Second Baptist Church burned in March 1866 (some suspected "rebel malice"), it also meant the destruction of an important school facility. "All were for action," said a leader of the affected blacks. They hired rooms to continue the school and planned to rebuild a brick building. About then, a British traveler attended a concert at Richmond's Ebenezer Baptist Church that raised funds to erect a school. "It was believed," he reported, "that the school would get burned down if erected, but they were disposed to go on with the erection." Similar contributions continued for a few years, so that in the winter of 1868 the teacher, Lizzie Parsons, could still write that "the struggle they have made to meet the tax [tuition?] and purchase books is almost painful." She visited one family whose father had "twice lost a situation, first, on account of voting, and then in consequence of the snow and ice." The couple had four children and had "taken an invalid sister and her son to care for." "The mother," Parsons went on, "has striven in every way to get along without aid, till, at last, one of the children told me she had eaten nothing for two days. Yet they have never once failed to bring me their wood money. I gave them tickets for soup, and now they have work again."

Charleston blacks took similar initiatives. Schools there opened in

POWER & CULTURE

early March 1865 and immediately served (in separate rooms and on separate floors) between 200 and 300 white and 1,200 black students. At least that number of black students waited for additional school places. A *New York Tribune* correspondent noted that "the loyal white people—the Irish and German population"—allowed their children to attend school with the freed blacks but would not "tolerate" mixed classes. Five days after the schools opened, James Redpath, their superintendent, counted forty-two teachers, nearly all local residents and twenty-five of them blacks. At first, whites were not permitted to teach the black children. "Some of the colored teachers," said George Newcomb, "passed a good examination, and will, I doubt not, prove excellent." "Colored South Carolinians" also taught in the night schools. These teachers included women "very light in complexion" and members of "the aristocracy of the colored community," who, a white teacher noted, were "advanced enough to pursue intelligently all the common branches of English education." Among them was Miss Weston, an "accomplished and talented colored lady" once jailed "for teaching a little school." Early in 1867, several young Charleston black men ("most of them, though quite well educated, had never taught before") quit that city to spread literacy in "the country districts." A reverse process brought black teachers to Charleston: the Old Zion Church School included on its staff women graduates of the Philadelphia Institute for Colored Youth. A Northern observer who described the "typical" Charleston teacher as "a Yankee woman . . . a God-made teacher, a sort of steel-trap spring" and therefore "irresistable" in her "mode of instruction," failed to notice the number of black teachers.

Charleston blacks did not just staff their schools and fill them with their children. They purchased books and, after a time, paid "a school tax." "I will make them pay for their own school-books," insisted Redpath in March 1865. A year later, students at Francis Cardozo's school (three-fourths of them former slaves) still paid for their books. In January 1867, parents contributed $95 to the school "tax" and purchased books and stationery worth $77 in a single month. "Of course," explained one teacher, "there are very many who must be excused from the tax (twenty-five cents a month), and who have their books given to them. Only about one-half of the children pay the tax every month, and I have to give away a good many books."

Blacks also sustained schools outside these two large cities. Wartime schools continued in portions of southeastern Virginia that had been occupied early in the war. Norfolk evening students paid five cents each week for "light," and both day and evening students purchased their books, some paying regular small installments. Acretown teachers continued to receive "little presents" from black parents: one told of getting "pieces of fresh pork and eggs," and another revealed that "many of them have presented us with fresh pork, sausages, &c." In 1865 and 1866, most Tidewater Virginia blacks could not manage even these small gestures. The Virginia legislature put a tonnage tax on vessels in the oyster-fishing business that badly hurt black fishermen. "I see nothing but poverty and suffering for them," said a Quaker relief and school official, "until they are more distributed over the country." Some rented patches of land, but had "no money to buy seed." And yet these same blacks managed schools through the winter of 1865–1866. A black clergyman, William Harris, who had helped found a school in wartime Williamsburg, taught forty students on the Tinsley farm near Yorktown that winter. He charged 50 cents a month tuition, but only twelve or fifteen students could pay that sum, and Harris himself lacked adequate private means to manage on $6 or $7 a month. The Tinsley farm blacks went to Quaker relief officials to ask for help for Harris and their school. "I found him very smart and active," said missionary Jacob Vining. Philadelphia Quakers agreed to pay Harris $15 a month; Harris promised to board himself, and a free school opened.

Letters sent by teachers working for Northern benevolent societies help illuminate Virginia blacks' educational activities. Just after the war, Farmville blacks applied at Petersburg for a teacher, and despite some threats of violence, a school started and remained open two years later. (A Farmville teacher noticed black shoemakers there who "not unfrequently," during their employer's "absence from his shop, indulged in stolen readings.") Three teachers started Petersburg schools in May 1865: chased from their first building, they taught 200 students next in a railroad station; when a tobacco company claimed that place, the school was moved to a warehouse. Less than a year later, Petersburg and its vicinity counted twenty-two schools and 2,769 registered pupils. Just outside the city, a young black woman taught a school in a log house "built by our soldiers during the war, and . . . on land owned by a colored woman." Much farther west, Pocahontas blacks agreed to contribute to a building fund to purchase a school lot. "Some pledged themselves for twenty dollars, some ten, some five, and so on," reported a teacher. "I soon found I could raise the money, not all at once, but by installments, the last to be paid before the first Monday in next June [1866]." The Pocahontas blacks formed a committee to find an appropriate school lot. "The people are building houses all over the district which . . . answer for both school and church," reported teacher James Stradling from Lynchburg in April 1867. "In some cases, the white people render them some assistance, but principally [the blacks] are doing their own work, and relying entirely upon their own resources."

Official Freedmen's Bureau reports for 1866 and early 1867 fill in the Virginia picture. The bureau took notice of 136 teachers in January 1866 and 225 twelve months later. By March 1867, the number had risen to 278 (81 of them blacks). In January 1866, Rolzo M. Manly, then superintendent of the bureau's Virginia schools, reported: "Every week since the first of October, new schools have been opened in some part of the State. It has been essentially a period of organization." Manly did not give much credit to resident whites, claiming that "practically all our progress, with rare exceptions, is in the face of actual opposition." "Milder modes of resistance" included "refusing the use of all churches or vestries which the whites can possibly control, refusing to rent room or charging exorbitant rates, refusing to board teachers, forbidding colored tenants sending their children to school on pain of being turned out of doors." "The more forcible forms of resistance," Manly felt, "such as mobs and conflagrations, are restrained by occasional hints from the military arms." Later that same year, Manly added that "in more than a score of places, the colored people have erected schoolhouses with their own hands, and employed either some poor white person, or someone of their own people, who has some small attainments, as a teacher. . . . They lack books, and have not a penny of money, their wages of the farm being received in the form of food and clothing."

Local bureau officials filled in precise details. From Westmoreland and Richmond counties came word that "churches and schools are going up in every direction." "Colored preachers are exhorting their race to push forward the work of education," said a bureau officer. "Freedmen throng my office daily for papers or something to read. We want a few teachers." In May 1867, another bureau officer visited schools in and near Culpeper County, and sent a detailed report:

> I paid a visit to the more remote part of my district last week. . . . The school at Springville, Rappahannock County, Virginia, is taught by Peter Lawson (colored). He is a man who possesses very good qualifications, for the advantages he has had, and is deeply interested in the work. . . . The school at Woodville, Rappahannock County, Virginia, is taught by L. W. W. Manaway (colored). . . . I arrived at Washington, Rappahannock County . . . and found that my coming had been announced already. I was not long at the hotel before several of the leading colored people called upon me . . . and wanted to know if I would help them . . . and [I] asked them how much they could do. They replied, "We'll do all we can." I called them

together the next evening, and got up a subscription paper for them, and in a short time raised $125 (pledged) for the building; and, before I left, I saw the list, and found that several of the white citizens had also subscribed nearly enough to bring the amount up to $150. This looks quite encouraging. . . . This school will, with a little assistance in the way of books, be entirely self-supporting. . . . I hope to get a church and school building up at Crooked Run, Culpeper County, Va., by next fall. Colored teachers can be had for this place, and can all be supported without outside assistance. Four hundred dollars is already subscribed for that place. . . .

The energy of the Virginia blacks worried some bureau officials, particularly Manly, who showed a persistent concern for the quality of education in private schools established and operated by blacks and not supervised by the bureau. Manly estimated that about 1,500 pupils attended them in the spring of 1867, and felt these schools (with few exceptions) to be "only better than none at all." Teachers there could read "very imperfectly" and knew "nothing of writing or arithmetic." Manly's fears revealed something about these "less qualified teachers." Some had learned to read after escaping from slavery during the war. Others had gained literacy after the war ended. Many were discharged black soldiers, their "first and only" education having come in "their regimental schools." Moreover, the bureau's decision to disband refugee settlements and to scatter "surplus" urban blacks meant that many young persons educated in white-sponsored wartime schools now became "informal teachers upon the plantations." Little is yet known about these black-run "plantation schools" of 1865 and 1866, but a study of education in Albemarle County hints at what remains to be uncovered. "When the Bureau did not establish schools in the county districts in the fall of 1866," writes Joseph C. Vance, "local Negroes themselves attempted to found three." A former slave, Lindsay Smith, taught one of these schools, instructing thirty-three pupils at "the African Church near Carter's Bridge." The county bureau head reported the following spring that "several schools . . . supported by the freedmen alon[e]" existed in Albemarle County. He knew so little about them that he did not include them in his official report.

The detailed letters of two white Quaker teachers in Danville, Eunice Congdon and George Dixon, allow us to examine with greater precision the ways Virginia blacks sustained schools for their children and protected white teachers. Eunice Congdon and another white woman teacher arrived in Danville to teach early in the fall of 1865. Their early experiences were disheartening. "The first few days," Miss Congdon reported in October, "we tried boarding ourselves, getting our food cooked as best we could, and eating it off a trunk." Soon, a Union Army surgeon let them eat in the officers' mess, but charged them five dollars a week. Their funds quickly ran out, and the teachers lacked money to pay the carpenters who were building school benches. For a time, they ran classes in an army hospital. After promised money from Philadelphia Friends arrived, the school managed better. Yet throughout, the blacks played an active role. "I think the people will see to furnishing wood," wrote Miss Congdon. "We are going to suggest that they take up a contribution now and then among themselves to buy kerosene for the night school." By early February 1866, the Danville teachers had enrolled 299 day-school pupils and employed "a young colored girl to assist" in "the lowest division."

The Danville school taught more than reading and writing. In 1866, blacks crowded densely into it to hear the Civil Rights Bill of 1866 read and discussed. Miss Congdon called the discussion "rich and significant beyond description." Another time, the Northern teachers distributed seeds to Danville blacks. And when some black men formed a voluntary association called "The Mechanics' Society for Mutual Aid," they met in the schoolhouse and their president asked Miss Congdon to "send North and get for him the book containing the names of the different *trades*, coming under the head of mechanics." Such community efforts suggest that schools had become more than mere educational institutions. And for that reason, among others, they provoked bitter opposition.

Opposition by whites to the Danville school increased after the Union Army withdrew from the town. The school remained there, however, owing to the courage displayed by Eunice Congdon, George Dixon, and Danville blacks. When Congdon fell ill, Dixon, who was then teaching English in Greensboro, North Carolina, came to help. Soon after his arrival, a white man attacked Eunice Congdon. "He attempted to 'finish' me," she reported. Dixon offered additional details, claiming that "a rebel" had awakened Congdon at one o'clock at night, "seizing both her arms and grasping them tightly." She asked who it was, and "the fellow muttered something which she did not understand." Congdon shouted, and a black servant overheard the commotion and hastened for Dixon, causing the intruder to flee through a window. A Union Army officer later learned that the man had planned to kill Miss Congdon, plunder the place, and then "set fire to the buildings." Threats against Miss Congdon were overheard in the streets. "A white woman," Dixon insisted, "told a colored child she need not go to school on Monday morning, because Miss Eunice would be dead." Danville blacks protected the teacher and the school. Dixon explained: "The colored men are kind in coming to keep a watch in the dead of night, but we are fearful of their coming in collision with the citizens, and blood being shed, as they will bring firearms with them and feel very desperate." "The colored people are our friends," Congdon confirmed. "They guard us every night." After Dixon arranged with a black carpenter to make school repairs and had bricks brought from an army arsenal to build a fireplace and flue, he left Danville. But before he left, he arranged "for a colored man to sleep in the house during my absence." Miss Congdon herself left Danville after the school year ended. "The first day school," she explained, "will be continued by four colored men whom we have initiated." More than this, other blacks promised to protect school property and records. When the Danville school closed for the summer, it had a full enrollment: 237 children had registered for its day classes.

Evidence also abounds of the black zeal for education in rural South Carolina. The Sea Island schools established during the war continued, and still received aid from local blacks. Blacks at Edgerly and Union Point joined together to build a new schoolhouse. "The island has gone wild to have a school on every plantation," reported Laura Towne from Port Royal in November 1865. Enthusiasm did not wane in the next two years. When Elizabeth Botume opened a schoolhouse at the Old Fort Plantation, some men came unannounced to "white-wash the interior of the building." "New school-houses are being erected in various places on these Islands," said another teacher in November 1867. "One has just been completed on the Walker plantation." And when Laura Towne's school building showed signs of dry rot, a black minister let her use his church nearby until the school was repaired. In March 1867, Beaufort blacks "inaugurated their new building for a free high school, bought and secured entirely by their exertion."

Throughout South Carolina, blacks pressed for schools and contributed to their success, and their efforts deserve particular notice because, unlike Sea Island blacks, they had not experienced wartime contact with Northern soldiers, missionaries, and schoolteachers. The war had hardly ended before Simon Miller, a returned soldier, along with several other Columbia blacks, formed a Committee on Education to start schools in that war-devastated city. Miller thanked the New England Freedmen's Aid Society for some books it had sent. "A large number of parents," he explained, "wish to send their children to school, but were unable to purchase [books] at the present high price." Miller's committee distributed the books free to the children of these poor families. Some could not even raise the fifty to seventy-five cents monthly tuition charged at their school. The school had another difficulty. "Columbia," Miller explained, "has been the greatest sufferer, I think of any other place. The colored people were burnt out as well as others, and the spoil hunters did not regard color in the late raid; and, work being scarce, many of our most liberal citizens have not the means to help this important step of erecting churches, school-houses, etc." Miller wanted Northern teachers and ended his letter appropriately: "You will perceive from this letter, that I am not grammarian, but I can certainly make a beginning for those teachers who, I hope, will soon appear."

The National Freedmen's Relief Association sent Dr. T. G. Wright (an army surgeon in the Mississippi Valley during the war) and three women teachers to Columbia in early November 1865, and Wright's reports in the six months following detailed how local blacks sustained their efforts. The first school opened in November in the basement of a black church. Government buildings also served as classrooms along with the Odd Fellows Hall (although its owners would not formally rent the place to the blacks). In early December, Columbia blacks put down $100 on a building lot worth $700. Reverend Henry McNeil Turner, soon to become a powerful leader among Georgia blacks, gave several lectures to gather additional funds, raising $101 the first night. "I am surprised," Wright admitted, "at the amount they have contributed, when I see the great destitution that prevails." By February 1866, 905 pupils attended the Columbia schools and two small schools in Hopkins and Lexington nearby.

Other South Carolina blacks made efforts on behalf of education. "Father Haynes, a colored man of the genuine African type," reported a schoolteacher of a man who lived some miles from Charleston, "has for several months been trying unweariedly to have a teacher . . . from Charleston. . . . His love for the children and interest in their improvement amount to an enthusiasm." A school started by Haynes lasted just for a week, but after it closed "children came two or three days from a distance of seven miles hoping to find the teacher to receive them." Another former slave could not sustain a day school, but taught in other ways. The head of the South Carolina Freedmen's Bureau described him as "a native African . . . a thoroughly educated man and a distinguished linguist, conversant in several languages, and at home with the Greek Testament and the Koran." "This man," he added, "is now laboring as a field-hand, and he devotes his evenings to teaching his fellow-laborers."

Elizabeth Doggett worried about her school in the "Edgefield district." We do not know when this black woman, herself apparently new to literacy, started teaching, but in February 1868 she explained to a bureau official: "I am teachen Still on the ridge al tho I ant at the Same place. . . . the bush whackers says I should not keep School thare. . . . So Have move my school 3 mils from thar. . . . thar wars but one name as I heard of that wars a ganst me and thar fore it looks quare and if no acedent takes place I will con tin ure here al the year."

Even more dramatic were developments in northeastern South

Carolina, a rich cotton region that was home to nearly a third of the state's former slave population. Benjamin Franklin Whittemore—an Amherst College graduate, Methodist clergyman, and former Union Army chaplain—supervised education there for the Freedmen's Bureau between 1865 and 1867. Despite their economic troubles and local white opposition, he reported that black men and women contributed handsomely to their children's education. They moved an old "Confederate building" ten miles from Florence to Darlington to start the district's first school. By April 1866 six schools existed, and a month later eleven. Northern soldiers had burned a Marion schoolhouse, so its teacher met classes in the woods.

Summerville got its school sometime before July. Two white women offered two acres of land for $200 as school property. Local blacks, many among them poor and destitute, crowded into an army barracks they used as a church to agree that if the Northern societies paid for the land and the government supplied lumber, they would build a school to open in October. "A good carpenter," Dan Meyers, spoke first: "I is a plain man and alers does what I agree, and I say that I will stan' by the good work till it's done finished." Another black man boomed: "I is called a good carpenter; I has no children of my own to send to the school; but I want to see the house build, and I gives two weeks work for it." Others offered their labor, and some, including young boys, gave small sums of money. In all, $60 was raised and twelve weeks of labor pledged. "The women," enthused schoolteacher Esther Hawkes, did "their part, offering to board or lodge the workmen as they best could." "These destitute people," she mused, "living, some of them, in rude huts made of mud and palmetto, one might suppose that all their interest was necessary [just] to keep them from starving. . . ." But this was only the start. By October, the burned Marion school had been rebuilt ($200); Darlington black men and women gave their labor and money for a school ($500); Simmonsville blacks ditched and fenced and then built a home for the teacher ($150); Sumter blacks moved a building forty miles and then reconstructed it ($250). Lynchburg blacks also moved and repaired a building ($150), and so did those in Florence ($350). In Camden, black muscle and money meant a new schoolhouse ($800), and Camden blacks also rented an old building for $30 a month. Schoolhouses also went up on the Mulberry Plantation ($100) and in Springville ($100).

In Camden, most blacks worked crops on contract and saw no cash until they had gathered the full crop. Teachers, however, did not suffer discomfort. "They furnish us with beds, bedding, and furniture for our rooms free, though they do not pay the rent," reported one teacher. "They sell articles to teachers at under price, and bring in gratuitously articles of food. The girls at the night school have made me some presents." "There is no lack of 'a disposition to do all in their power *now*,' " the teacher added. "Indeed I think they *have* done it." The obstacles faced by these former South Carolina slaves seeking education for themselves and their children, however, should not be obscured by this enthusiasm. In June 1867, Darlington residents appealed to Boston's mayor: "We are on the eve of Starvation. Only through our Friends North. . . . If there is any chance in the world to get anything to eat in your city, do for Heavens Sake Send us some and save us from Perishing." This was not their first such appeal, and efforts continued throughout 1867. Between September 1866 and January 1867, Camden blacks raised $120 to pay the school rent, heat the school building, and furnish the schoolteachers' rooms. "They have performed *all they have promised*," reported Jane Smith from Sumter. "They were to pay a certain sum toward the erection of their church which they have done. They were to whitewash it, to buy a bell, build a belfrey, furnish lamps, lumber for the pulpit, and several comforts for the teacher. All this, *they have done*." Overall, South Carolina blacks had done much to educate themselves. For the entire state in the year starting July 1866, $106,797.73 was expended to educate South Carolina blacks. Northern societies gave $65,087.01, while the Freedmen's Bureau advanced $24,510.72. South Carolina blacks contributed cash to the amount of $17,200.00 (16 percent), and more in kind and labor. Only where poverty prevented such self-help efforts did blacks request assistance.

A similar commitment to education could be found among the freedpeople in postwar Louisiana. Here, however, events took a course different from that in other states and therefore deserve brief examination. Louisiana blacks had known free public schools in 1864 and 1865 and then had witnessed their destruction. Prior to secession, free people of color—who paid property taxes that helped fund white Louisiana educational institutions—independently built schools on their own. New Orleans free blacks knew such schools, as did those in Pointe Coupee, Opelousas, and Baton Rouge. In 1850, about 1,000 free blacks attended New Orleans schools. The Point Coupee school dated back more than half a century. But formal education for nearly all Louisiana blacks did not come until the Union Army occupied New Orleans in 1862.

With federal occupation, the number of schools for blacks multiplied rapidly. Some antebellum free blacks supported schools which made "no distinction . . . in regard to the former status of pupils." In the fall of 1863, their efforts received additional support when federal officials, apparently at the request of local blacks, appropriated $3,000 to educate indigent children. New Orleans soon had seven schools, twenty-one teachers, and 1,240 pupils. Common-school education made additional strides in February 1864, when General Nathaniel P. Banks, the commander of the Department of the Gulf, imposed a property tax to finance free schools for blacks throughout his southern Louisiana command. Banks's appropriation provided schools for slave children on the great plantations of the sugar parishes.

The education of blacks made unusual progress in these parishes between April and December 1864. Unlike blacks in New Orleans and Plaquemines, few in these outlying parishes had been free before the war. In fact, outside New Orleans the wartime schools drew their pupils largely from a population of field laborers. By the end of August 1864, schools existed in 67 of 174 separate school districts over the entire region and enrolled 7,203 pupils (average attendance, 5,343). During 1864, increases averaged ten new schools per month, fifteen new teachers, and 850 new pupils. Such progress pleased school officials. "The country schools are prosperous and thronged," said one. And children in the New Orleans schools came from poor families— "most of them very poor, owning not even themselves till that ever memorable day in April 1862." About half the New Orleans pupils did not know the letters of the alphabet before starting school, but "average attendance fully equalled that of white schools." An army census taken in the spring of 1864 fixed the number of school-age children (black youngsters five to twelve years old) at 15,840. Fully one of every three black children attended school in June 1864. Six months later, 44 percent were enrolled. Ninety-five of the 174 districts had schools in December 1864.

The fact that local whites (many of them no doubt loyal Unionists) taught most Louisiana blacks did not make the common schools more palatable to the white majority. A Northern school official said that white women among the teachers "quietly bore the load of calumny, sneers, and social ostracism," and the schools themselves had other difficulties. Schoolrooms were hard to find in the city, and classes were held in "confiscated houses, the attics of untenanted stores, and, in two instances, the basements of churches" (the church facilities "grudgingly given, or rather, not given at all, but taken"). Outside New Orleans, there were greater troubles. The absence of available buildings led provost marshals to seize needed facilities: "Cabins, sheds, [and] unused houses were appropriated, roughly repaired, fitted with a cheap stove for the winter, [and] a window or two for light and air." Teachers outside the city had difficulty finding adequate housing. Students were not free from troubles in some places. The Thibodeaux parish schoolhouse was "broken open on successive nights for months . . . the furniture defaced, the books destroyed and the house made untenable by nuisance." "Bricks and missiles" had been "hurled through the windows," but "complaint after complaint had not yet afforded relief or protection."

The experience of one parish teacher revealed the nature of white opposition and black commitment to education. A plantation manager let her start a school on a place owned by "a gentleman of Northern extraction said to be a Unionist, but who, to some extent, is an absentee proprietor." The owner returned and ordered the school removed. Soon after, the head teacher—a New Orleans resident her entire life— had a visit from "rebels" who carried an order that she close the school. B. Rush Plumly summarized what followed:

> The teacher defied and shamed them, so that they left. On a day or two following they returned, broke up the school, borrowed a buggy, captured the teachers, and prepared to leave with them for Dixie, amid the clapping of hands and general acclamation of the lady spectators. The more timid of the two teachers was alarmed and distressed, but the Principal chided her companion for her fears, and vented her scorn and hatred of the cowardly ruffians in no measured terms. Laughing at her spirit, they ordered the girls into the buggy and set out, a black man driving, and a Confederate Captain and Lieutenant riding on either side of the vehicle.
>
> The colored people were greatly agitated at the prospect of the rebels taking their teachers, and gladly obeyed the Principal's injunction to "ring the bell" and alarm our pickets. The sympathizing and vigilant Africans had already sent a messenger to the pickets, but he was stopped and ordered back by somebody.
>
> Many threats were made by the rebel officers against the negro driver for his tardy pace, which he could not be induced to hasten. . . .

Some miles along and nearing the "rebel pickets," the principal noticed "a weak spot in the harness, snatched the lines from the driver's hands and struck the horse smartly." The harness snapped. In the delay that resulted, Union soldiers arrived to free the teachers. The teachers moved their school to an abandoned plantation, but it was raided and broken up again. Plumly insisted that the assistance given by these blacks to the teachers was not unusual. He gave much credit to the former slaves for the survival of the army-sponsored common schools: "Despite all the efforts of our agents, the assistance of the Provost Marshals, and the devotion of the teachers, many of these schools would have to be abandoned but for the Freedmen themselves."

A single document, William M. Harmount's account of a trip to Ascension Parish in September 1864 to enforce the army schooling edict, provides a detailed view of the world of rural Louisiana slaves and their children. Ascension lay between New Orleans and Baton Rouge. Donaldson, where Harmount stayed, was its most important town. In 1860, two-thirds of the parish population had been slaves, and four of every five had lived on units of at least fifty slaves. Free blacks represented less than 2 percent of the parish population. Harmount carried orders to establish a free school in Ascension "district" and found help from some Donaldson whites, among them a refugee physician from Texas and a French woman, long an open critic of slavery. But the Northern white learned to his great surprise that the former Ascension slaves "were ahead of us in organizing schools." Two had already been started, one by Washington Daggs, who "intended to teach it himself, but finding himself in deep water" hired a young Philadelphia "colored man." "After a time," Harmount went on, "one of Daggs' students, a young man about twenty years of age, withdrew and started another school." Harmount visited both schools, found them "well conducted," and was "exceedingly gratified with the school of young Fobbs, Daggs' former pupil." Children whose parents were unable to pay, "orphan children, and those whose parents were in the army" attended these schools free of charge. Daggs had sixty-five pupils in his school, and Fobbs had twenty-seven. What especially amazed Harmount was that persons who had been slaves "at the beginning of the war" now practiced "the generous philanthropy that gives free schooling to the children of our country's defenders and [to] the little orphan."

The Unionist Louisiana legislature failed to appropriate funds to educate blacks in 1864 and 1865. A bill to authorize the use of state monies to educate blacks failed although it required that white and black parish schools be separated by at least half a mile. When the war ended, Louisiana blacks knew that little support for education would come from the loyal whites who dominated state politics. The education of their children depended on their own efforts, the willingness of the army to maintain the special tax, and the support of federal officials.

As blacks suspected, they soon had only themselves to rely upon. The Freedmen's Bureau took over an ongoing public school system. In July 1865, Louisiana blacks had 126 schools and 230 teachers. By that time, 19,000 blacks had attended (5,000 adults, including 1,000 soldiers, among them). In the fall and winter of 1865–1866, this entire program of public education was dismantled. Andrew Johnson's desire to conciliate Southern whites caused the revocation of the special tax in November 1865. The restoration of confiscated lands also eliminated an essential source of supplementary revenue and took away school buildings.

Louisiana blacks protested these reversals of federal policy that destroyed the army-sponsored free school system. Angry blacks crowded the Abraham Lincoln School in New Orleans to support resolutions that approved taxation to be borne "cheerfully . . . to the extent of our abilities." East Baton Rouge blacks opposed losing their schools "at any cost." "True manhood and education go hand in hand," they said, and declared their willingness to pay a head tax to defray all school expenses. Others even petitioned to pay a special tax in addition to the regular school tax. "Petitions," John Alvord observed, "began to pour in." He saw "one from the plantations across the river, at least thirty feet in length, representing ten thousand negroes" and found it "affecting to examine it, and note the names and marks (-X-) of such a long list of parents, ignorant themselves, but begging that their children might be educated; promising that from beneath their present burdens and out of their extreme poverty, they would pay for it."

Not all Louisiana blacks, however, favored so discriminatory a tax. The *New Orleans Tribune*, the organ of the antebellum free black community, reminded readers that free blacks had paid property taxes to educate whites for decades and urged instead an increased general tax and mixed schools for all children. It opposed a special tax on blacks: "Do not make the colored people ridiculous by begging—themselves—to be re-taxed and over-taxed, while the whites put the money into their pocket[s], and use it for the white children exclusively." Instead, the *Tribune* urged blacks to "organize, and take the whole management in our own hands. . . . Let the schools come out of the hands of the government . . . and . . . come entirely under the control of the colored population, since the colored population has to exert themselves to support these schools." The *Tribune* favored the establishment of a "School Aid Association" in every parish to sustain the schools by collecting "a kind of voluntary poll tax." This proposal did not mean to exclude the very poor unable to manage such a cost: "Let each colored man who has no children, pay for one . . . pupil—twenty cents per month—and our schools are safe." Blacks' own efforts, said the *Tribune*, would "make up, by all means, the shortcomings of the governing class."

Nothing came of their proposal. "A temporary demoralization has ensued, producing a sort of chaotic period from which it will take time to recover": so wrote John Alvord about the Louisiana schools in July 1866. By that time, however, Louisiana blacks and some local bureau officials had begun to patch together the shattered free schools. "Almost immediately," said Alvord, "large numbers of private schools were started, most of them of inferior grade, and usually taught by colored persons." The bureau itself tried to restore "public" education to Louisiana blacks in 1866 and 1867, but its policies shifted nearly the entire burden onto the blacks. Urban blacks paid for the "public" schooling of their children by purchasing "tuition tickets" costing $1.00

or $1.50 a month, and the bureau imposed a 5 percent school tax on the monthly wages of plantation families. The revenue was meant to pay the salaries of teachers and the rents for schoolhouses. Blacks had to start nearly from scratch to reconstruct the school system.

Black teachers played a special role in this effort. Although the black teacher who established the log-cabin school may have been, as one Louisiana bureau officer complained, "utterly incompetent to advance the pupils further than a, b, c," advance them they did. And this was hardly the full story. John Alvord visited a private New Orleans school in 1865 "wholly taught by educated colored men, . . . a free school . . . supported by the colored people of the city, . . . the children from the common classes of families." The next spring, readers of *Harper's New Monthly Magazine* learned about fifteen or twenty private New Orleans schools. Some had teachers educated in France or Saint-Domingue. Some, quite exclusive, admitted only light-skinned persons or children whose families revealed a better "social condition" than the mass of New Orleans blacks, but most followed a democratic admission policy. A bureau inspector glowed after visiting "the institute of which Mr. Armand Lanatter (colored) is the principal." It had a regular attendance of 250 male and female students. "They speak, read, and write both English and French fluently, and are also well advanced in arithmetic, geography and history," said the same person. "The pupils pay their tuition fee promptly," he added, "and the discipline is perfect." Lanatter had six assistants, "two . . . Americans and all colored men." "We could multiply similar testimony," he insisted; "it shows that colored instructors can succeed."

Schooling for blacks advanced significantly in the winter and spring of 1866 and 1867. "The freedmen," wrote bureau superintendent Frank E. Chase, "are forming church and club associations for the purpose of raising the amount necessary to pay the salaries of teachers. . . . Quite a number of churches, to be used for school purposes, are either nearly finished or in the process of erection."

In January 1866, the bureau had supported 104 schools and 232 teachers; 11,134 students had attended these bureau schools. Nine months later, tuition and tax payments sustained 106 schools, but the number of teachers and students had dropped by more than 50 percent. Those that remained were supported almost entirely by the blacks themselves. In 1867, blacks owned 17 school buildings and helped sustain 198 schools. In the last six months of that year, the bureau expended $3,694.55 to educate Louisiana blacks, and blacks themselves paid in tuition $28,943.10. Louisiana blacks did much more than either the Freedmen's Bureau or the benevolent societies to support the public tuition schools.

Still the efforts of Louisiana blacks pale in comparison with those of

Georgia blacks. Between 1865 and 1867, black people in Georgia did more to educate their children than those in any other Southern state. When white missionary teachers arrived in Atlanta, they found that two former slaves, James Tate and Grandison Daniels, had started a small school in an old church building. "On the first Sabbath" after their arrival, Atlanta blacks "put windows in their house, the African church, so as to have one school there." In Augusta, illiterate blacks filled a meeting place and helped pick a committee to aid the white teachers. That committee raised more than $100 and received promises of more money. Augusta blacks also repaired a schoolroom in an old Confederate shoe shop. "We found one colored man and two colored women . . . willing to do the best they could in teaching," said a missionary. A school opened on June 12: 500 children showed up the first day, and 100 more came in the days that followed. Quitman, Valdosta, and Thomasville blacks also started schools in 1865, using former Confederate properties and agreeing "readily to furnish the requisite labor" to fix up these places. A "colored" Thomasville resident also opened "a small school," but could not find a suitable building for it. Richard R. Wright started learning in a Cuthbert school in 1865. It "scarcely had one of its sides covered or weather-boarded," Wright remembered. "It was about twenty by thirty. . . . The house was packed as tightly with dusky children as a sardine box. . . ." (In Atlanta, Wright's second schoolhouse was "an abandoned box car.") Macon freedpeople paid for schoolbooks and fuel and light for the school building; Calhoun blacks owned a schoolhouse and raised a teacher's salary; Sanderson blacks made an old church available and offered support to a teacher; Newton blacks held their first classes in a kitchen.

Georgia blacks made phenomenal advances in educating their children in 1866 and 1867. A March 1866 survey found fifty-two black schools in ten Georgia cities and towns. In a four-month period (December 1865 to March 1866), blacks in seven of these places contributed $5,060 in cash for their schools, causing a Northern missionary to note that "the benevolent efforts among the Freedmen *themselves* for their education are considerable." One of every three Georgia teachers (102 men and women in all) received funds from that state's blacks. Schools existed in out-of-the-way Georgia places. Rome and Marietta had black teachers, and the Rome teacher held his classes "in a church with no windows." Tuition payments supported other black teachers in small Dalton, Deep Valley, Cartersville, and Red Clay schools. Milledgeville blacks could not give much and their schools faltered, so they met and appointed three men to appeal for financial help to "establish a *Free School* in this city." "We are dependent upon our daily labor for the support of our families," these men

TABLE TWO

Sources of School Support, Georgia, June 1867

	FREEDMEN'S BUREAU	FREEDMEN	NORTHERN SOCIETIES	TOTAL
Number of schools	44	104*	84	232
Number of teachers	50	104	78	232
Number of pupils	3,093	3,045	7,125	13,263

* Georgia blacks also "sustained in part" another 45 schools

explained, "and have nothing to spare wherewith to school our children."

Opposition from hostile whites, especially in 1866, made the work of these blacks and their few white allies especially difficult. Two former Confederate soldiers taught Elberton and McDonough blacks until pressure from white mobs forced them to seek bureau protection. From Henry County came "frequent complaints" to federal officials "that the inhabitants attacked the scholars and teachers of freedom schools—stoned them on the way home and threatened to 'kill every d——d nigger white man' who upheld the establishment and continuation of the 'nigger schools.'" A black teacher in Newman was so harassed that he quit that place. Despite these troubles, twenty-one Georgia schools remained open in the summer of 1866. The Freedmen's Bureau supported three of them, and the freed men and women the rest. More than 2,000 children attended these summer schools. Overall, the number of school increased from 79 in June 1866 to 147 in December 1866 and then to 232 in June 1867. Enrollment jumped from 2,755 to 13,263. Blacks contributed much to these schools; during the 1867 winter quarter, they paid $7,224 in tuition. In June 1867, a bureau report showed that 45 percent of the schools and 23 percent of the pupils were entirely supported by the freedmen themselves (table 2). In part, these successes derived from the organization of the Georgia Educational Association in January 1866. But its work cannot be understood without first examining events in Savannah between December 1864 and January 1866.

Prodded by James Lynch, a missionary for the African Methodist Episcopal Church, Savannah blacks entered on a massive program of school organization in the years immediately following the war. Lynch himself deserves notice. Born in 1839 to a Baltimore free black father and a slave mother, Lynch drove a delivery wagon as a boy to help his father's mercantile business, attended a New Hampshire college, preached for a time in Indiana and then in Illinois, and helped to edit the AME's *Christian Recorder*. When Union troops entered the slave South, he followed as one of the African Methodist Episcopal Church's first missionaries. He labored for a time among the South Carolina Sea Island blacks. In late 1864, he taught a St. Helena's Island school sponsored by the National Freedman's Relief Association. That agency then supported eighteen Sea Island schools, which enrolled 1,178 black pupils. Lynch's school was third largest among them and enrolled over 10 percent of the students on the island. Lynch had early advocated the placement of black teachers in black schools. Color, he insisted, did not entirely shape his estimate of other human beings, but—he explained to the readers of the *Christian Recorder*—he could not "see the entire work of the education of our black brethren being carried on entirely by the whites." Savannah allowed Lynch a good place to test out this belief.

General William T. Sherman's army had conquered the city in December 1864, and Savannah blacks, led by their resident clergy and helped along by Lynch, quickly set up their own schools. "I hurried here," Lynch wrote in early January, "expecting much to do, [and] I have not been disappointed." The same clergy and church officials met on January 12, 1865, with General Sherman and Secretary of War Edwin M. Stanton, to promise their support for the Union, to press for land and protection for the freedpeople, and to spark the Savannah educational effort. Twenty men, Lynch among them, talked with Stanton and Sherman. Four had been born free; three each had gained their freedom either through manumission or by self-purchase; and nine had been slaves until Sherman's arrival in Georgia. Their spokesman, Garrison Frazier, had been a North Carolina slave until 1857, when he had purchased his freedom and that of his wife. An ordained Baptist minister, he had tended his duties for thirty-five years, but declining health no longer permitted him to lead a congregation. Others among these clergymen worked as barbers, pilots, and sailors or had been overseers on cotton or rice plantations.

Even before they met with Stanton and Sherman, Savannah's "principal colored men" had formed the Savannah Educational Association and started schools for their children. Help came from Lynch and three white missionaries, John Alvord, Mansfield French, and William Richardson. In either late December or early January, Savannah blacks filled Campbell's church to overflowing; hundreds could not gain admission. Garrison Frazier chaired the meeting, which opened with the hymn "Blow Ye the Trumpets, Blow." They also sang "The year of jubilee has come,/Return ye ransomed *bondsmen* home." ("You see," said Lynch, "we altered it a bit.") The blacks also sang "My Country,

'Tis of Thee," and heard Alvord (who had spent time in Savannah before the war, and now represented the American Tract Society) insist that the freed slaves were "not babes to be carried or rocked in cradles but men who could develop themselves." Lynch, Alvord, and French spoke, calling for the establishment of schools for former slaves. Lynch asked that the local clergy remain afterwards and assured Alvord that "persons could be found among the colored people who would teach [the] schools if organized." He proved true to his word.

Later that day, the cleric Abraham Burke, a Georgia slave who had purchased his freedom sometime in the 1840s, moved that the governing boards and clergy of Savannah's black churches constitute the Savannah Educational Association. A second mass meeting, in early January, heard members propose the names of teachers and saw a constitution adopted requiring all members to pay three dollars a year and twenty-five cents each month in dues. A resolution invited the cooperation and support of the American Missionary Association, and its representative promised such aid. Contributions were then solicited from the crowd, and a white observer reported to the secretary of the American Missionary Association that "the scene was novel and intensely interesting." "Men and women," it was noticed, "came to the table with a *grand rush*—much like the charge of union soldiers on a rebel battery! Fast as their names could be written by a swift penman, the Greenbacks were laid upon the table in sums from one to ten dollars, until the pile footed up the round sum of *seven hundred* and *thirty dollars* as the cash receipts of the meeting."

Soon after, Lynch and Alvord examined prospective teachers and found fifteen suitable black teachers, ten women and five men. "The teachers," Lynch said, "are the best educated among our people here." According to Lynch, the teachers themselves asked for a normal school under "a competent person from the North." James Porter, the musician who had secretly taught slaves, agreed to teach the more advanced students and to serve as school principal. An officer of the National Freedmen's Relief Association found Porter "quite an accomplished gentleman" and said he took "great pride in his work." Monthly salaries ranged from $35 each for two principals to $15 each for the women teachers, so that the SEA's monthly wage bill came to $300.

Local Union Army officers (Lynch found General John Geary, the federal commander in Savannah, "*sincerely* willing to encourage anything that will elevate the freed men") gave the Savannah Educational Association four buildings for schoolrooms, including Oglethorpe Medical College and Bryan's Slave Mart, a three-story building that fronted on Market Square and had till nearly that day served as a meeting place for slave traders and owners. Buildings, however, are not schoolhouses. "Their school rooms," Alvord noted, "had been

fitted up with much care and labor by the colored people themselves."
A few days later, the schools opened. About 500 children gathered in
the First African Baptist Church's lecture room to parade to their new
schoolrooms. An observer felt that the street procession excited "feeling
and interest second only to that of Gen. Sherman's army." "Such a
gathering of Freedmen's sons and daughters that proud city had never
seen before," said this same witness. "Many of the people rushed to
doors and windows of their houses, wondering what these things could
mean! *This* they were told is in *onward march of freedom.*"

Savannah's blacks, Lynch wrote on January 4, 1865, were "growing
every day, and seem to lose that dread which slavery had made a
second nature." The Savannah Educational Association plan, he went
on, did not mean to undercut the Northern benevolent agencies. "Of
course," he explained, "teachers wil be needed from the North and
will be welcomed by the Association, but the more intelligent of the
colored people are determined on using, as much as possible, their
own instrumentality for their elevation." Savannah blacks, according
to Lynch, meant to test the intentions of the Northern societies. "It is
often said," Lynch declared, "that the Freedmen's Aid Societies will
not encourage colored teachers who are willing to give themselves to
the work of educating the Freedmen, though they are ever so competent. We intend to fairly test that in Savannah, as well as make the
trial of having our folks rely on themselves to the fullest extent
possible." The Savannah blacks did not wait long. Soon after their
schools started, they encountered just the trouble they feared.

It came from the American Missionary Association. S. W. Magill, a
missionary, arrived in Savannah to head the association's educational
work and schemed to subvert what the local blacks had started.
"However good men [they] might be," he said of the Savannah
Educational Association leadership clergy, "they know nothing about
education." None had "much more in the way of education than [the]
ability to read & write & cypher a little." "I sympathize most deeply
with the Apostle in his desire not to build upon another man's
foundation," said Magill, but such awareness did not deter him from
his mission. "I fear," he wrote of the Savannah black clergy, "they will
be jealous & sullen if I attempt to place t[he] management in t[he]
hands of our white teachers. But this must be done in order to make
[the] sch[ools] effective for good."

Magill blamed Lynch for these troubles and accused him of drunk-
enness. Lynch, he said, had advised the Savannah clergy that the
American Missionary Association as well as some other white benevolent societies "discriminated unfavorably against colored people, in
respect to employing them as teachers, &c." Magill had quite specific
complaints. Leaders of the Savannah Educational Association expected

to hire white teachers only as "assistants" and hoped the American Missionary Association would lend financial support. "The whole thing in this aspect of it is preposterous," Magill warned. When he first met with the Savannah Educational Association's executive committee, he learned that it controlled four school buildings, had already enrolled 600 pupils, and had appointed fifteen "colored teachers." More than this, his request that the Savannah blacks allow him to start a school for adults did not get a prompt reply. They "gave me the cold shoulder," complained Magill. The entire operation disturbed him: former slaves and free blacks had preempted his mission. "Here," he moaned, "instead of finding a clear field to work in, we find it preoccupied by this radically defective organization."

Magill pressured vigorously for a federal appointment as the head of Savannah's educational work. Even after Savannah blacks allowed him to use a building for his school, he remained dissatisfied and urged the American Missionary Association to withhold promised funds and not to praise the Savannah blacks too excessively in print. A letter dated February 16 (which, incidentally, noted that Savannah's blacks had already raised perhaps $1,000 for their schools) explained that when he took over he would "be obliged to relieve many of their teachers, some of whom are not professors of religion, and are very lavish in the use of the strap & to diminish the salaries of others, some of whom receive from $25 to $35 per month." Magill expected "trouble," but promised to "proceed with great caution and kindness."

The zealous evangelical finally had his way, as Union officials appointed him to supervise the government's educational efforts in the city. Magill soon reported that the executive committee of the Savannah Educational Association had surrendered the principle of "excluding white control." Magill seemed pleased. Managing Savannah's black schools, after all, required "more head than these colored people yet have." Another Northern white cleric, a visitor to Savannah, made the same point somewhat differently. "They have several interesting schools of their own starting and maintaining there," J. W. Fowler reported in June 1865. He found the black clergy and teachers "gifted with a large share of common sense," but worried because "their expression is very bad" and urged that some Savannah black children be sent North to live in the homes of refined whites and study there to become teachers and ministers.

Despite their defeat, Savannah blacks continued to support their own schools. Financial help came from the New England Freedmen's Aid Society after prodding by William C. Gannett, who visited Savannah in the spring of 1865 and thought the Savannah Educational Association's leaders "men of real ability and intelligence" who had "a natural and praiseworthy pride in keeping their educational institutions in their own hands." "What they desire," he observed, "is assistance without control." By late July 1865, Savannah blacks had spent more than $20,000 for salaries and other educational costs. Crude estimates fixed the number of school-age children in Savannah at 1,600, and three-quarters of them were in school. When the schoolteachers Harriet Jacobs and her daughter arrived in mid-December to work in the schools, they found nineteen of them "principally sustained by the colored people." Another visit to Savannah about that same time convinced John Alvord that the Savannah Educational Association had improved over the year. But he worried over its fiscal condition: "Their association is now, with the high price of everything, falling in debt." In March 1866, Savannah still had eight schools, the largest with 300 students. Savannah blacks boasted of their schools, calling them "self-supporting" and insisting that such was "the only true road to honor and distinction." Alvord agreed. He accepted as "fact" that such "self-made efforts may not be perfect" nor "perhaps as good as those taught by men and women from the North." But Alvord pointed out that the Savannah blacks had revealed "a vitality *within themselves*," showed that "*opportunity* will induce *development*," and made it clear that black people "are not always to be dependent on white help and Government charity."

Savannah's blacks did more than start schools on their own in and near their city. In January 1866, together with other Georgia blacks and some friendly whites, they founded the Georgia Educational Association to encourage the state's former slaves to form local associations that would build schools supported "entirely by the colored people." At first the Georgia Educational Association advanced political as well as educational objectives, but at an October 1866 convention attended by blacks from more than fifty counties it renounced its political role and, while defending equal rights under the law, restricted its work to educational matters. By then, the association had established county organizations in different places in the state. Augusta had five subassociations, each with its own officers and a special school committee to "establish the schools and employ and pay the teachers. The scholars pay the expenses. All persons are allowed to attend the schools." The association, however, suffered for want of funds, and John E. Bryant, a Maine-born Union Army officer, and others pleaded for help from the North: $7,000 would sustain its work so well that the Georgia Educational Association would "never need further assistance from friends outside of the State." The full story of the association's local work remains to be studied in detail, but its larger impact seems clear. It helped Georgia blacks organize schools and pressured for a free public school system that would serve whites as well as blacks. When the Radical Constitutional Convention met in 1868, more than half the members of the Georgia Educational Association's state executive board served as delegates. These blacks helped draw up a constitutional provision that assured free public education to black as well as white children. Their work between 1865 and 1868 had prepared them well for this task. "Great good has already been accomplished by this association," noted John Alvord's January 1868 report. "In a very important sense," the association had "developed and stimulated the self-reliant spirit of the freed people."

Blacks throughout the South voluntarily built and sustained schools in ways similar to those in Virginia, South Carolina, Louisiana, and Georgia. Although their work cannot be detailed here, John Alvord's published semiannual reports allow a brief summary of that work before 1868. His reports contain serious flaws but nevertheless retain general value. In the fall of 1865, school attendance, as a percentage of all children eligible to attend, ranged from 43 percent in New York State to 93 percent in Boston. That same fall, 41 percent of eligible white children and 75 percent of eligible black children attended District of Columbia schools. An equally high percentage of black children attended the Memphis (72 percent) and Virginia (82 percent) schools. In the three years following the war, General O. O. Howard estimated that nearly one-third of black children over the entire South had some formal education. Not all of these former slaves and free blacks studied with Yankee schoolmarms. In December 1866, 37 percent of teachers in the South known to the bureau were blacks. The percentage increased to over 40 in June 1867, and was even higher a year later. The bureau noted in June 1868 that 2,291 men and women were teaching blacks, and that 990 (43 percent) of them were blacks.

In the fall of 1866, moreover, blacks sustained in full or in part the operation of at least half of the Arkansas, Florida, Georgia, Kentucky, Louisiana, Maryland, and Texas schools. In five states (Alabama, North Carolina, South Carolina, Tennessee, and Virginia), between 25 percent and 49 percent of the schools received financial support from resident blacks. Six months later, at least half of the schools in ten Southern states received assistance from black parents and in six states (Arkansas, Delaware, Kentucky, Louisiana, Mississippi, and Texas) at least three of every four schools were partially financed in this way (table 3). The significance of these financial payments can best be realized by comparing the dollars paid in by blacks for tuition with the money expended by the Freedmen's Bureau between January 1 and June 30, 1867 (table 4). In two states, Alabama and Florida, blacks paid in less than $25 for every $100 spent by the bureau, but in seven others, tuition payments ranged between $25.00 and $49.99 for every $100 of federal money. Tennessee blacks paid in $59.20 and Georgia

TABLE THREE

Schools Sustained Entirely or in Part by Freedmen
and School Buildings Owned by Freedmen, December 1866 and June 1867

| | DECEMBER 1866 | | JUNE 1867 | | SCHOOL BUILDINGS OWNED BY FREEDMEN | |
STATE	NUMBER OF DAY AND EVENING SCHOOLS	PERCENTAGE SUSTAINED IN PART OR IN FULL BY FREEDMEN	NUMBER OF DAY AND EVENING SCHOOLS	PERCENTAGE SUSTAINED IN PART OR IN FULL BY FREEDMEN	DEC. 1866	JUNE 1867
District of Columbia	94	13.9%	122	35.5%	17	15
Delaware	n.g.	n.g.	20	100.0	n.g.	8
Maryland	98	59.8	107	71.0	45	53
Virginia	192	26.5	229	32.3	25	61
North Carolina	118	36.4	147	47.6	22	23
South Carolina	69	33.3	90	42.2	n.g.	n.g.
Georgia	127	75.6	236	64.4	57	39
Alabama	51	41.2	175	18.9	11	27
Florida	60	50.0	56	58.9	n.g.	11
Mississippi	43	7.0	66	78.8	n.g.	14
Louisiana	111	100.0	246	84.6	15	28
Texas	34	100.0	55	12.0[a]	19	25
Arkansas	12	100.0	24	91.7	7	10
Tennessee	105	34.3	128	53.1	28	38
Kentucky	67	97.0	96	91.7	32	33
					Total 278	465

[a] This percentage indicates an obvious typographical error in the printed report.

TABLE FOUR

Expenditures for Education by the Freedmen's Bureau and by Resident Blacks by State, January 1–June 30, 1867

STATE	TUITION PAID BY BLACKS	EXPENSES FOR CONSTRUCTION, RENTAL, TEACHER TRANSPORTATION	TUITION PAID BY BLACKS FOR EVERY $100 SPENT BY FREEDMAN'S BUREAU
Maryland-Delaware	$ 5,800[a]	$13,594	$ 42.66
Virginia	5,125	19,198	26.69
North Carolina	1,761	5,526	31.86
South Carolina	8,000	22,551	35.47
Georgia	17,224	22,306	77.22
Alabama	1,543	2,868	5.38
Florida	304	4,815	6.28
Mississippi	2,020	4,787	42.19
Louisiana	25,734	14,391	178.82
Arkansas	2,308	8,078	28.57
Texas	2,472	9,790	25.25
Kentucky	7,107	5,413	131.29
Tennessee	7,814	13,208	59.16

[a] Tuition payments by blacks from both states are included in the $5,800, but we have only the bureau expenditures for Maryland.

blacks $77.20. In two states, Kentucky ($131.20) and Louisiana ($178.80), resident blacks, nearly all former slaves there as elsewhere, put more money into the schools than the bureau itself.

Innumerable obstacles, which should not be minimized, hampered the voluntary efforts made by former slaves to educate their children before the start of Radical Reconstruction and the coming of free public education to the South. But neither should these difficulties be emphasized so as to divert our attention from the extraordinary energy and social purpose revealed by these men and women. Theirs was a magnificent effort. We study it in detail because of what it tells about important and little-understood historical processes. In examining how men and women fresh to freedom built and sustained schools, we find much more than simply a desire for schooling. It is inconceivable, for example, that former Memphis slaves would have paid more than $5,000 in tuition between November 1864 and June 1865 without preexisting notions of parental and responsibility and kin obligation. Yet it is erroneous to find in their quest for education "proof" that the former slaves held "middle-class" values. The ways in which former slaves built and sustained schools, for example, were quite alien to the "middle class." Yankee shopkeepers and successful artisans favored education, but did not move buildings ten miles and then reconstruct them as schoolhouses. Ohio and Indiana farmers paid school taxes, but did not stand guard over teachers threatened with violence. Former slaves did. The freedpeople's early post-emancipation craving for and defense of schooling for themselves, and especially for their children, rested in good part on values and aspirations known among them as slaves. "The daily job of living did not end with enslavement," the anthropologist Sidney Mintz comments, "and the slaves could and did create viable patterns of life, for which their pasts were pools of available symbolic and material resources." That was true for the blacks after emancipation, too. At an 1865 ceremony that celebrated the opening of a Baltimore school named for him, Frederick Douglass related the quest for schooling to the historical experiences of the former slaves:

> Our history has been but a track of blood. . . . The question forced upon us at every moment of our generation has not been, as with other races of men, how shall we adorn, beautify, exalt, and ennoble life, but how shall we retain life itself. The struggle with us was not to do, but to be. Mankind lost sight of our human nature in the idea of our being property.

Schooling, Douglass said, allowed "boys and girls" for the first time to "hold themselves in higher estimation." Douglass hinted at what W. E. B.

Du Bois made explicit seventy years later—the larger meaning of the thrust for education by those still new to freedom: "They built an inner culture which the world recognizes in spite of the fact that it is still half-strangled and inarticulate."

Not all the schools freedpeople established between 1861 and 1867 succeeded. The poverty of most Southern blacks, the early decline in interest (and in money and teachers) on the part of Northern benevolent societies, the federal government's shifting policies, and white violence closed many schools. Teachers everywhere noticed the strains that poverty caused among schoolchildren and their parents. Near Darlington, South Carolina (where former slaves had done so much to build schools in 1866 and 1867), a teacher said that students came to school "very badly dressed and barefooted, though the winter has been very cold and the ground frozen." Farm laborers there had been offered one-third of the crop (hardly enough "to keep their families from starvation"), and many suffered "for food." "The best of the women get only four or five dollars a month," she added, "and work for nothing but their poor and scanty food." These observations were made by Frances A. Keigh, who had been a student at the new Darlington black school two years before, in 1866. Now she was a teacher.

Another black teacher, Harriet Jacobs, had returned to her Southern birthplace to teach. A single sentence in her narrative, published in 1861, explains why she, a fugitive slave, and so many other Southern blacks had done so much to bring education to their children and those of other former slaves so soon after their emancipation. "There are no bonds so strong," Jacobs insisted, "as those which are formed by suffering." Slaves and freed blacks did not forget the sacrifices they had made for one another. Ferebe Rogers had grown up a slave and labored as a field hand in Baldwin County, Georgia, had married and had several children before emancipation. "Young marster," this woman recollected in the 1930s, "was fixin' to marry us, but he got cold feet, and a nigger by name o' Enoch Golden married us." Golden, a slave, held a special place among the Baldwin County blacks. "He was," Ferebe Rogers remembered, "what we call a 'double-headed nigger'—he could read and write, and he knowed so much. On his dyin' bed he said he been de death o' many a nigger 'cause he taught so many to read and write." It was because of the daily efforts of many Enoch Goldens ("double-headed niggers") and other blacks in the American South between 1861 and 1868 that black and white schoolteachers were able to spread literacy among their children.

7

ENSLAVED AFRO-AMERICANS AND THE "PROTESTANT" WORK ETHIC

WE CONSIDER first the most important new "finding" in *Time on the Cross* (hereafter referred to as T/C): the conclusion that Southern slave farms and plantations were much more efficient than Southern free farms and Northern farms because of the "quality of black labor." Summing up what they consider "some of the principal corrections of the traditional characterization of the slave economy," Fogel and Engerman (hereafter referred to as F + E) assert: "The typical slave field hand was not lazy, inept, and unproductive. On an average he was harder-working and more efficient than his white counterpart."[1] All earlier historians of slavery—writers as different as U. B. Phillips, Stanley Elkins, and Kenneth Stampp—are severely criticized for failing to understand the "fact" that most *ordinary* slave workers had internalized what F + E call the " 'Protestant' work ethic." This proposition about the "quality of black labor" is much, much more important to the general theme of T/C than F + E's discussion of slave material conditions such as food, clothing, shelter, and medical care and their discussion of "the slave family." F + E explain: "Material treatment is [not] the issue on which the economic analysis of slavery turns. Indeed, the resolution of none of the other issues depends on the resolution of the question of material treatment. Slavery could have been profitable, economically viable, highly efficient, and the southern economy could have been rapidly growing under either a cruel or a mild regime."[2] It is instead the productive labor of slaves that "explains" the relative efficiency of the plantation system.

Efficient Slave Labor Is Not the Same as an Efficient Plantation. The authors of T/C do much more than describe the relative efficiency of the antebellum plantation system. They attribute that efficiency to the

This essay is reprinted from *Slavery and the Numbers Game: A Critique of "Time on the Cross"* (Urbana: University of Illinois Press, 1975), 14–41. An earlier version of that work, entitled "The World Two Cliometricians Made: A Review-Essay of F + E = T/C," was published in the *Journal of Negro History* (January 1975).

"quality of black labor" and, therefore, are describing the social character of the enslaved themselves. David and Temin put it well:

> Superior "efficiency" is . . . said to have characterized the work performance of the individual slaves, as well as the class of production organizations that utilized them.
>
> While they are analytically distinct, it is important to notice that the two types of statements involving comparisons of efficiency are *not empirically unconnected.* Fogel and Engerman have not developed *any independent quantitative support for their propositions regarding the comparative personal efficiences of the typical slave and free worker* in agriculture. Instead, they have arrived at these conclusions essentially by the process of *eliminating some other conceivable explanations* for the measured factor productivity advantage of slave-using agriculture—such as differential economies of scale, technical knowledge[,] or managerial ability. . . . [Italics added.][3]

Econometricians are examining with care the measures by which F + E figure that "slave farms" were X percent more efficient than free Southern or Northern farms. David and Temin have begun that discussion and have suggested a number of biased estimates and erroneous assumptions that greatly exaggerate the productivity of slave farms as opposed to free farms.[4] The following pages examine in detail the evidence used by F + E to reveal the "comparative personal efficiencies of the typical slave . . . worker in argiculture" but do not discuss the relative efficiency of productive organizations worked with slave labor. David and Temin's point that the "two types of statements involving comparisons of efficiency are not empirically unconnected" is important, but they neglect the critical quantitative data the F + E have assembled on the rural and urban slave occupational structures, the only new quantitative data meant to explain why slaves worked so hard and so well.

The Transformation of Slave Work Habits and the "Protestant" Work Ethic. F + E's most crucial arguments about the quality of slave labor and much of their least convincing evidence are found in a brief portion of chapter 4 entitled "Punishments, Rewards, and Expropriations." A short but controversial section, it has attracted the attention of nearly all reviewers and contains data essential to some of F + E's most startling conclusions.[5] It also uses evidence in ways that strikingly reveal the utter inadequacy of the old-fashioned model of slave society that tarnishes T/C. David and Temin vigorously dispute the low rate of expropriation estimated by F + E, insisting that inaccurate estimates indicate a bias.[6] The focus here is different. It is on F + E's arguments and their use of evidence to show that enslaved Afro-Americans worked hard and diligently because they wanted to and because profit-maximizing owners skillfully mixed a few punishments with many rewards to encourage productive slave labor. We examine "punishments" and "rewards"—the positive and negative incentives used by slaveowners, especially planters, to improve slave labor and to increase productivity.[7] F + E do not deny that slaveowners used physical punishment, but they greatly minimize its significance in relation to the prevalence of positive labor incentives. The carrot counted more than the stick: "While whipping was an integral part of the system of punishment and rewards, it was not the totality of the system. What planters wanted was not sullen and discontented slaves who did just enough to keep from getting whipped. They wanted devoted, hard-working, responsible slaves who identified their fortunes with the fortunes of their masters. Planters sought to imbue slaves with a 'Protestant' work ethic and to transform that ethic from a state of mind into a high level of production. . . . Such an attitude could not be beaten into slaves. It had to be elicited."[8]

Convinced that a system of positive planter-sponsored labor incentives existed, F + E also insist that most slaves responded positively to the rewards offered them. The very last paragraph in T/C emphasizes this point. A high level of slave productivity resulted in the production of cotton, tobacco, sugar, and rice. But the "spikes of racism"—that is, "myths"—hid this "fact" from contemporaries and later historians. Racist beliefs turned slave high achievers into Uncle Toms.[9] The biased beliefs of antislavery advocates and so-called neo-abolitionist historians kept hidden from the American people, and especially from black Americans, truths about how the ancestors of twentieth-century Afro-Americans had been transformed as slaves into nineteenth-century "economic" men and women. Sambo really was Horatio Alger with a black skin.

Evidence supporting such a transformation is not found in T/C. If such a transformation actually occurred, *that* would be a social fact of great importance in understanding the behavior and beliefs of enslaved Afro-Americans and of their emancipated descendants. But most of the evidence in T/C about this important conclusion is not impressive. Much of it is circumstantial; none of it is substantial; most of it is quite traditional; hardly any of it comes from new sources; and, when used, such sources are often imprecisely presented and sometimes wildly exaggerated. To transform means "to change something to a different form," a change "in appearance, condition, nature, or character." Transformation, therefore, is a social process and has to occur over time. Something happens to someone. Slaves are made into "efficient" workers. The F + E model, however, is static and ahistorical. F + E never consider who was being transformed. Because there is no discussion of who the slaves were and how well they worked at the beginning of this social process, it is hardly possible to describe a transformation. Instead of that kind of needed and useful analysis, important evidence—especially that dealing with punishments, rewards, and mobility—is so badly used that it casts considerable and disturbing doubt upon the entire argument.

Scant Evidence on Negative Labor Incentives (or Slave Punishments). Negative labor incentives, or punishments, are treated with a single and greatly misinterpreted quantitative example: Appendix C ("Misconduct and Punishments: 1840–1841") in Edwin Adams Davis's *Plantation Life in the Florida Parishes of Louisiana, 1836–1846, as Reflected in the Diary of Bennet H. Barrow.*[10] The historian Davis apparently gathered cases of slave misconduct and punishment from the cotton planter Barrow's diary.[11] The Davis study contains one of the few easily accessible quantitative sources used by F + E. Cliometric theory is not needed to examine it. Analysis does not depend upon computer technology. Ordinary readers of T/C should examine these data, and draw their own conclusions about how accurately they have been used. My own analysis follows.

The Barrow punishment record serves to create a pseudostatistic that diminishes the importance of slave whippings. This record is the only evidence dealing with slave punishment, so it serves to trivialize planter-sponsored negative labor incentives. After a brief paragraph which tells that "whipping could be either a mild or a severe punishment" (an indisputable but hardly original generalization), a critical four-sentence paragraph based entirely on the Davis appendix follows: "Reliable data on the frequency of whipping is extremely sparse. The only systematic record of whipping now available for an extended period comes from the diary of Bennet Barrow, a Louisiana planter who believed that to spare the rod was to spoil the slave. His plantation numbered about 200 slaves, of whom about 120 were in the labor force. The record shows that over the course of two years a total of 160 whippings were administered, an average of 0.7 whippings per hand per year. About half the hands were not whipped at all during the period.[12] Figure 40—entitled "The Distribution of Whippings on the Bennet H. Barrow Plantation during a Two-Year Period Beginning in December, 1840"—which accompanies these few sentences, and which is reproduced here as table 1, merely illustrates what the written word reports.

The two brief paragraphs which follow the one quoted above do not enlarge upon these "findings" but examine whipping generally and offer some "comparative" observations.[13] The data drawn from

TABLE ONE

Distribution of Whippings on the Bennet H. Barrow Plantation
During a Two-Year Period Beginning in December 1840

WHIPPINGS PER HAND	ESTIMATED PER- CENTAGE WHIPPED
0	45%
1	18
2	14
3	7
4	11
5	3
6	1
7	1

the Barrow diary, then, are the only items of hard data dealing with negative labor incentives.

How the Historian Measures the Frequency of Slave Whippings: Figure 40. The sentence—"The record shows that over the course of two years a total of 160 whippings were administered, an average of 0.7 whippings per hand per year"— is examined first. Several questions come to mind. Is "0.7 whippings per hand per year" a useful average? Have the Barrow diary data and the appendices which accompany them been properly used? Have the right historical questions been asked of those data? It is assumed for the moment that Barrow owned 200 slaves, of whom about 120 were in the labor force. (It shall be seen below that each number—200 and 120—is wrong.) To report "an average of 0.7 whippings per hand per year" using these numbers is accurate. That is not, however, the significant average. The wrong question has been asked. The logic producing this average is socially flawed along with the inferences suggested by it. The same logic could just as easily calculate the average number of whippings per hand per week (0.013). It is known, for example, that "on average" 127 blacks were lynched every year between 1889 and 1899.[14] How does one assess that average? Assume that 6 million blacks lived in the United States in 1889 and that 127 of them were lynched. Is it useful to learn that "the record shows an average of 0.0003 lynchings per black per year, so that about 99.9997 percent of blacks were not lynched in 1889"? An accurate average, that is a banal statistic. Lynching as a form of social control cannot be evaluated by dividing the number of blacks (or whites) lynched into the number of living blacks (or whites). The absolute number of lynchings in a given time period and whether that number rose or fell later in time are important numbers. They measure the changing frequency with which this particular instrument of social violence was used. It is then possible to study that instrument's relative significance.

The same is true with slave whippings. Southern law permitted slaveowners to punish their chattel, and most historians agree that whipping served as the most common form of physical punishment, figuring as a central device in imposing order over troublesome slaves and in revealing the source of authority in a slave society. The essential statistic, therefore, is not the average number of whippings per hand per year.[15] Whether by the week or the year, such an average does not measure the utility of the whip as an instrument of social and economic discipline. It is much more relevant to know how often the whip was used: on Plantation X with Y slaves in Z years, how frequently was the whip used? That information is available in the Davis volume. In 1840–1841, Barrow's slaves were whiped 160 times. A slave—"on average"—was whipped every 4.56 days. Three slaves were whipped every two weeks. Among them, sixty (37.5 percent) were females. A male was whipped once a week, and a female once every twelve days. Are these averages "small" or "large"? That depends. And it depends upon much more than whether one is a "neo-abolitionist" or a "quantitative" historian. These are quite high averages, and for good reason. If whipping is viewed primarily as an instrument of labor discipline and not as the mere exercise of arbitrary power (or cruelty), whipping three slaves every two weeks means that this instrument of physical discipline had an adequate social visibility among the enslaved. Slave men and women were whipped frequently enough—whatever the size of the unit of ownership—to reveal to them (and to us) that whipping regularly served Barrow as a negative instrument of labor discipline. Imagine reading the following argument:

> While whipping was an integral part of the system of punishment and rewards, it was not the totality of the system. What planters wanted was not sullen and discontented slaves who did just enough to keep from getting whipped. They wanted devoted, hard-working, responsible slaves who identified their fortunes with the fortunes of their masters. Planters sought to imbue slaves with a "Protestant" work ethic and to transform that ethic from a state of mind into a high level of production. . . . *Reliable data on the frequency of whipping is extremely sparse. The only systematic record of whipping now available comes from the diary of Bennet Barrow, a Louisiana planter who believed that to spare the rod was to spoil the slave. Over the course of two years,*

> *Barrow whipped a slave every 4.56 days. Women were whipped less frequently* *than men. On average, a male slave was whipped every 7.3 days and a* *female slave every 12.2 days.* [The "Protestant" work ethic] . . . could not be beaten into slaves. It had to be elicited.

A schoolboy would not take such an argument based on this evidence seriously. There is a *real* social difference between a slave being whipped every 4.56 days and "an average of 0.7 whippings per hand per year." And it rests on more than a mastery of long division.

Constructing a Whipping Table: Numerical Errors in Figure 40. So far, it has been pointed out that F + E asked the wrong question. That error is common among historians. But F + E also have inaccurately used the Barrow diary and the accompanying appendices. "His [Barrow's] plantation," they write, "numbered about 200 slaves, of whom about 120 were in the labor force." Both numbers are wrong. Whipping data are available for 1840–1841, but the Davis volume, including the diary itself, does not tell how many slaves Barrow owned in 1840–1841. An "Inventory of the Estate of Bennet H. Barrow," printed as an appendix, gives by name and age the slaves he owned when he died. About 200 men, women, and children are listed. But Barrow died in 1854, fourteen years after the recorded whippings, and it appears that F + E assume that Barrow owned "about 200 slaves" in 1840–1841. No data in the Davis volume warrant that assumption. Additional appendices—birth (1835–1846) and death (1831–1845) lists (pp. 427– 31)—show that slightly more than twice as many slaves were born as died in these years. Since Barrow apparently sold few slaves, these records suggest that he owned far fewer than 200 slaves in 1840–1841. F + E, therefore, measured the actual number of recorded whippings against a total slave population far in excess of its real size. As a result, the frequency with which *individual* slaves were whipped is greatly underestimated. (After the publication of the journal version of this review-essay, Professor William Scarborough of the University of Southern Mississippi kindly supplied me with the number of slaves Barrow owned in 1840, a statistic drawn from his own research into the 1840 federal manuscript census. That document reveals that Barrow owned 129 [not 200] slaves in 1840. F + E estimate that 90 Barrow slaves were not whipped; the actual number is closer to 19, a drop of about 80 percent. Their inaccurate reckoning shows that 1 out of 2.2 Barrow slaves escaped the whip. Actually, only 1 out of 6.7 was not whipped. The ages of the Barrow slaves in 1840 are not known, but if they fit the typical age distribution given by F + E, then 89 were at least ten years old. F + E tell that Barrow whipped 110 individual slaves. If all slaves at least ten years old were whipped one or more times, we still would have to account for 21 slaves [110 − 89 = 21]. These 21 slaves had to be children under the age of ten. That means that half of slave children under ten were whipped at least once. If Barrow did not whip children under the age of five, and if children under the age of ten were fairly even distributed, that means that every child aged five to nine probably was whipped one or more times in 1840–1841. F + E's argument about relative absence of negative labor incentives would have been greatly strengthened if they had assumed that Bennet Barrow never lived rather than that he owned 200 slaves in 1840.)

Barrow's Diary Entries Compared with the Whipping List. The Barrow diary entries are just as valuable as the Davis whipping list.[16] There is one question whether the diary is complete.[17] The same volume also includes several valuable appendices and a sixty-seven-page essay on Barrow, his family, and his business, plantation, and social doings. Written in the Phillips tradition, the essay has some of the severe shortcomings characteristic of that genre but still contains much useful information. F + E rely heavily on the essay and Davis's list, "Misconduct and Punishments: 1840–1841," but for an unexplained reason none of the rich details describing plantation management and especially slave disciplining that stud the ten-year diary found their way into the pages of T/C. F + E possibly felt that this material was irrelevant to T/C's central themes. Extracts from the diary follow:[18]

1836

Dec. 26   House Jerry & Isreal chained during Christmas Jerry for general bad conduct—for a year and better—Isreal bad conduct during cotten picking season

1837

Sept. 4   . . . had a general Whiping frollick

Oct. 2   More Whiping to do this Fall than alltogether in three years owing to my D mean Overseer

Dec. 31   ran two of Uncle Bats negros off last night—for making a disturbance—no pass—broke my sword Cane over one of their skulls

1838

Jan. 23   my House Servants Jane Lavenia & E. Jim broke into my store room—and helped themselves verry liberally to every thing— . . . I Whiped [them] . . . worse than I ever Whiped any one before

Sept. 28   Dennis and Tom *"Beauf"* ran off on Wednesday— . . . if I can see either of them and have a gun at the time will let them have the contents of it . . .

Oct. 12	[Tom ran off again] will Whip him more than I ever Whip one, I think he deserves more—the second time he has done so this year . . .
Oct. 20	Whiped about half to day
Oct. 26	Whiped 8 or 10 for weight to day—those that pick least weights generally most trash . . .
Oct. 27	Dennis ran off yesterday—& after I had Whiped him
Nov. 2	Dennis came in sick on Tuesday—ran off again yesterday—without my ever seeing him—will carry my Gun & small shot for him—I think I shall cure him of his rascallity
Nov. 7	Dennis came in last night—had him fasted—attempted to Escape. ran as far as the creek but was caught—the Ds rascal on the place
Dec. 30	Demps gave his wife Hetty a light cut or two & then locked her up to prevent her going to the Frollick—I reversed it turning her loose & fastning him
1839	
Jan. 4	Whiped every hand in the field this evening commencing with the driver
April 27	My hands worked verry badly—so far general Whipping yesterday
July 19	Gave L. Dave a good Whipping for some of his rascallity intend chaining him & Jack nights & Sunday till I think they are broke in—to behave
Sept. 9	Whiped G. Jerry & Dennis for their shirking
Sept. 30	Had G. Jerry T. Fill & Bts Nat up here washing all yesterday as punishment—generally dirty & ragged
Oct. 2	Lewis still out. no doubt but he is down at Uncle Bats Where his Father lives—which proves the impropiety of having slaves off the plantation
Oct. 3	told Dennis I intended to Whip him. [Dennis fled] . . . started Jack after him—to give him $50 if he catches him—I had rather a negro would do anything Else than runaway. Dennis & his Brother Lewis & G. Jerry the only ones that gives me any trouble to make do their part
Oct. 4	Boy Lewis came in last night—gave him the worst Whipping I ever gave any young negro. I predict he will not runaway *soon*. Building a Jail for him Dennis & Ginny Jerry—intend jailing them for Saturday nights 'till Monday mornings
Oct. 13	Put Darcas in Jail last night for pretending to be sick, repeatedly—the first one ever put in the Jail & G Jerry
Oct. 20	Gave my negros about my lot the worst Whipping they ever had

Oct. 23   Gave every cotten picker a Whipping last night for trash & of late my driver has lost considerable authority with them

[Dec. 23   Dennis caught]

Dec. 24   intend exhibiting Dennis during Christmas on a scaffold on the middle of the Quarter & with a red Flannel Cap on

Dec. 25   Let Darcas out of Jail—Dennis confined in Jail

1840

Jan. 9   Darcas began to sherk again—let her out of Jail Christmas she promised to do well &c.

April 18   gave my driver a few licks this evening, not knowing Who had done bad work

April 19   had a general Whipping among the House ones & two Carters for stealing, &c.

July 5   had Jack rigged out this evening with red flanel on his years [*sic*] & a Feather in them & sheet on, "in the Quarter." every negro up. Made Alfred and Betsey ride him round the Quarter dismount and take a kiss, for quarreling, Jack & Lize, Frank & Fanney the same.

July 30   [The cook Lavenia had run away and was found] Lavenia thought she had been whipped unjustly owing to Jane (the Cook), let Lavenia gave her a good *drubing*, &c.

Oct. 13   I think my hands have Picked cotton worse this year than in several years picked it verry trashy & not better weights nor as good as *common*, intend Whipping them *straght*

Oct. 15   am sattisfied the best plan is to give them every thing they require for their comfort and never that they will do without Whipping or some punishment

1841

Jan. 3   [Barrow gave the Negroes a dinner] and afterwards inspected their manners in the Ballroom several acted very rude as usual. put them in Jail

Aug. 16   Ginney Jerry has been sherking about ever since Began to pick cotten. after Whipping him yesterday told him if ever he dodged about from me again would certainly shoot him. this morning at Breakfast time Charles came & told me that Jerry was about to run off. took my Gun found him in the Bayou behind the Quarter, shot him in the thigh

Sept. 16   Ginney Jerry ran off Last Thursday to day a week, after being shot, Will shoot to kill him should I be fortunate enoughf [*sic*] to meet him, Will sell him &c.

Oct. 2   More hands attempting to sherk for two weeks past than I ever knew, Gave a number of them a good *floging*

1842

June 15   [Ginney Jerry ran away again] will shoot to kill him if an opportunity offers. . . . has not been touched this year, nor have I said a word to him, pray for a shot at him

Nov. 6   Friday night Jack Let Jerry slip for purpose of getting a pig thinking as Jerry was Jailed at night there would be no suspicion of him—for some reason told Alfred Jerry had a pig in his house A. went and found it as Jack thought. put him in Jail & in the stocks in the morning there was nothing of Jerry stocks Broke & door—no doubt some one turned him out—one concerned in the Pig—gave about a dozen severe Whipping in the Yard & all—Jack old Jenny & Darcas the most severe hand sawing

1844

Nov. 28   Whiped all my grown cotten pickers to day

Nov. 29   [Dennis ran off and was then caught] gave him the worst Whipping he ever had—& ducking

1845

May 27   [Darcas cut her husband with a hatchet in the hip] Very dangerous cut—will make her sick of the sight of a Hatchet as Long as she Lives

June 4   missed several of my young Hogs, found 8 or 10 Guilty, ducked & gave them a good thrashing. Mr. *Ginney* Jerry next morning Felt insulted at his treatment & put out, would give "freely" $100 to get a shot at him

Sept. 6   The negro hunters came this morning, Were not out long before we struck the trail of Ginny Jerry, ran and trailed for about a mile *treed* him, made the dogs pull him out of the tree, Bit him very badly, think he will stay home a while

Oct. 18   Fell quite unwell for two days past, effect of negro hunting

Oct. 27   Went with the negro Dogs to Hunt Ruffins runaways, & his small house boy Ed. ran off still out, 12 years of age—no Luck—negro dogs here—tired of them

Nov. 11   the negro dogs to Mrs Wades Quarter. . . . dogs soon tore him naked, took him Home Before the other negro & made the dogs give him another over hauling, has been drawing a knife & Pistol on persons about Town

It is surprising that as rich a source as these diary entires was entirely neglected. It reveals much about the labor incentives Barrow used with his slaves. More than once, for example, Barrow penned suggestive diary notations such as "had a general Whiping frollick," "whiped about half to day," "general Whipping yesterday," "intend Whipping them *straght*," "whiped all my grown cotton pickers to day." None of these general whippings counted in the list of whippings. The diary, in fact, reveals that general whippings of productive Barrow male and female slaves occurred quite regularly: there were at least six collective whippings—1837, 1838, twice in 1839, 1840, and 1841—between 1837 and 1841. The diary also listed other punishments. In his fine dissertation on the slave family, Bobby Jones concluded that Barrow resorted to "practically every known form of chastisement slaveholders used." Jones pointed out: "During his career, Barrow resorted to chains; extra work; whipping; humiliation, such as making a man wear women's clothing and parade around the quarters; imprisonment; stocks; 'raked several negro heads to day'; 'staking out'; 'hand-sawing'; and dousing or ducking in water which occurred in October and November." Jones figured that "hand-sawing" probably meant "a beating administered with the toothed-edge of a saw."[19] The diary extracts reprinted in these review-essay pages include yet other punishments, including the occasional shooting of a runaway. It is not inappropriate to ask—especially in a study which assesses the relative importance of slave physical punishments—why F + E failed to weigh the full punishment record reported in the diary. That source, after all, serves as the single piece of evidence on slave punishments.[20]

Barrow's Cotton Pickers (Field Hands) Were Frequently Whipped. The Davis appendix, it turns out, can measure the frequency with which an owner used a whip and, more important, suggest the relationship between whipping and slave labor "efficiency," even hinting that Barrow's field hands—the women as well as the men—had not internalized either Barrow's or F + E's conception of the "Protestant" work ethic. Only the Davis appendix "Misconduct and Punishments: 1840–1841" is used in their arguments that follow. Other methods of negative labor discipline (such as ducking, jailing, and even "hand-sawing") are put aside, and it is assumed that the list is the full record of all slaves whipped. Slave misconduct and whippings are examined, but just for those slaves listed as cotton pickers by Barrow in other appendices published by Davis (two cotton picking lists dated November 3, 1838, and September 10, 1842). This analysis does not account for the misconduct and whipping of slaves who were not cotton pickers, particularly house servants. But it tells a good deal about those slaves who picked cotton, an activity of some importance on the Barrow plantation. Their misconduct and subsequent whipping indicate a pattern of slave and planter behavior entirely contradictory to the F + E thesis about slave punishments and slave work habits.

Table 2 indicates the frequency with which Barrow whipped his cotton pickers. Three out of four were whipped at least once during 1840–1841. Seven out of ten women felt the whip at least once. In all,

TABLE TWO

Frequency of Whippings of Barrow Male and Female Cotton Pickers,
1840–1841

NUMBER OF TIMES WHIPPED	MALE COTTON PICKERS		FEMALE COTTON PICKERS		ALL COTTON PICKERS	
	Number	Percentage Whipped	Number	Percentage Whipped	Number	Percentage Whipped
0	7	19.4%	9	30.0%	16	24.2%
1	8	22.2	5	16.7	13	19.7
2	10	27.8	6	20.0	16	24.2
3–4	8	22.2	8	26.6	16	24.2
5+	3	8.3	2	6.7	5	7.6
Total	36	100.0%	30	100.0%	66	100.0%

fifty of sixty-six male and female cotton pickers were whipped at least
once in this brief period. These fifty slaves together were whipped no
fewer than 130 times during 1840–1841. The cotton pickers, incidentally, accounted for four out of five of the 160 whippings listed by the
historian Davis. If we add to these data the names of women who gave
birth to children during 1840–1841 (they were listed in a separate
appendix), it is learned that twelve female cotton pickers gave birth to
fourteen children in these years, and that seven were whipped in this
period (two of them twice and a third no fewer than four times). Some
cotton pickers, men and women alike, were not whipped at all. Let us
consider them—about one in four of the Barrow cotton pickers—
"efficient" field laborers. One in ten of the rest was whipped at least
five times. Slightly more than two in five felt the whip at least three
times.

The Reason Barrow Whipped Most Slave Men and Women: Inefficient Labor.
The same appendix in which Davis listed whippings also includes
evidence indicating the varieties of slave "misconduct" detected by
Barrow, misconduct that led to physical punishment. Most of Barrow's
slaves were whipped for not conforming to the Protestant work ethic.
It is hardly a complete list of incidents of slave misconduct in 1840–
1841, but it serves, nevertheless, as a most useful document bearing
directly on the F + E thesis that slaveowners had successfully transformed the work ethic of their slaves. Barrow sometimes listed a
disorderly slave but failed to describe the particular "disorder." Nevertheless, 267 individual disorderly acts were described, 80.9 percent of

TABLE THREE

Frequency of Individual Acts of Misconduct
by Barrow Plantation Male and Female Cotton Pickers,
1840–1841

NUMBER OF ACTS OF MISCONDUCT PER COTTON PICKER	MALE	FEMALE	TOTAL
0	5	7	12
1	2	2	4
2	4	3	7
3–4	9	4	13
5–6	7	6	13
7–9	6	6	12
10+	3	2	5
Total Slaves	36	30	66

all those listed. Women committed slightly more than two in five (43 percent). A variety of disorderly acts were recorded, including familial quarrels, child neglect, theft, "impudence," visiting town, and running away. Failure to keep the evening curfew fixed by Barrow was a frequent disorder. But—most significantly—nearly three in four (73 percent) of the acts listed related directly to inefficient labor: "for not picking as well as he can," "not picking cotton," "very trashy cotton," "covering upon cotton limbs with ploughs," "for not bringing her cotton up," and so forth. A slight but not significant difference existed between the slave males and females: two in three acts of misconduct by females related to labor behavior, as contrasted to nearly four in five (78 percent) acts by males. The frequency of whippings among the cotton pickers has been examined, and now the frequency of recorded acts of misconduct among these same persons is studied. (table 3). In all, the 66 cotton pickers engaged in no fewer than 181 disorderly acts during 1840–1841. The average per hand did not differ between men (4.3) and women (4.2). Men (86.2 percent) more commonly engaged in misconduct than women (77 percent), but the difference should not have greatly pleased Barrow. Over all, four in five cotton pickers engaged in one or more disorderly acts in 1840–1841. Once again, we do not include the twelve men and women who did not commit a detected disorderly act. Among those with disorderly records, four out of five committed three or more disorderly acts as shown in Table 4. As a group, a slightly higher percentage of women than men committed seven or more disorderly acts. Is it possible to

TABLE FOUR

Frequency of Recorded Acts of Misconduct
Among Male and Female Cotton Pickers
Who Committed One or More Acts of Misconduct,
Barrow Plantation, 1840–1841

NUMBER OF DISORDERLY ACTS	PERCENTAGE OF COTTON PICKERS COMMITTING DISORDERLY ACTS		
	MALE	FEMALE	TOTAL
3 or more	80.6%	75.3%	79.7%
7 or more	29.0	34.8	31.5

describe these male and female slave cotton pickers as members of a well-disciplined, orderly, and efficient slave laboring class? To characterize them so distorts the historical record kept by the planter Barrow.

The Most Productive Cotton Pickers Were Whipped More Frequently and Were More Disorderly Than the Least Productive Cotton Pickers. In 1838 and 1842, lists also gave the amount of cotton picked each year by individual slaves, and much of social importance is learned by examining the relationships among the most productive cotton pickers, whippings, and acts of recorded misconduct during 1840–1841. Twelve men and twelve women were counted as Barrow's best field laborers. It is quite revealing to compare them with the least productive cotton pickers as illustrated in table 5. The more productive cotton pickers—both the male and the female pickers but especially the females—were much more disorderly and were more frequently whipped than the less productive cotton pickers. Given their absolute and relative record of misconduct (nearly all of it is related to "inefficient" labor), is it possible to hint that these slave men and women had drunk deeply of the "Protestant" work ethic? If the main thrust in the arguments of F + E is sound, the least productive workers should have been more disorderly and should have received more frequent whippings.

Why the Barrow Cotton Pickers Had Not Internalized the "Protestant" Work Ethic. That the Barrow cotton pickers had not internalized the "Protestant" work ethic is further suggested by their ages and the moment in time for which a record exists of their behavior. The approximate ages of fourteen male and sixteen female cotton pickers in 1840 can be learned from the 1854 inventory. All except three of the males whipped were between the ages of 19 and 26. The others were older, the oldest among them aged 37. Betsey was 45, and another of the female cotton pickers was a 13-year-old, but nearly all of the other women whipped were between the ages of 15 and 26. The median age of cotton pickers whipped was nearly the same for men (23.8 years) and women (23.2 years). That means that these men and women had grandparents probably born in the 1760s and great-grandparents who probably were native Africans enslaved in the New World. These men and women were a few generations removed from initial enslavement. Nevertheless, three out of four among them had to be whipped— nearly always for labor inefficiency—during 1840–1841. Internalizing any new ethic (work or otherwise) is a social process and takes time. New attitudes toward work are not learned overnight. These same cotton pickers, moreover, were members of the last generation of adult Afro-American slaves. Upon emancipation, some were grandparents, and most were in their middle forties. Surely if any generation of enslaved Afro-Americans had internalized the work ethic prized by their owners, it had to be this one. It was not.

Barrow himself knew why. On April 16, 1840, he wrote in his diary: "am directing them to make a slow & sure lick in one place & to cut the full width of the hoe every time—unless reminded of it they would stand & make 4 or 5 licks in one place, tire themselves & do no work, have several grown ones that work harder & do less work than any in the field." He added disgustedly two days later: "—there never was a more rascally set of old negroes about any lot than this. Big Lucy Anica Center & cook Jane. the better you treat them the worse they are, Big Lucy the leader, corrupts every young negro in her power . . . gave my driver a few licks this morning, not knowing Who had done bad work."[21] There is much to learn from just these two diary entries. Barrow complained bitterly about the older slaves, the most "rascally set" he knew. And he regularly whipped the younger slaves during 1840–1841. If what F + E call the "Protestant" work ethic had been successfully internalized by the Barrow slaves, the values associated with it would have passed along from slave generation to slave generation. In this instance, that means from slave parents born in the late eighteenth or early nineteenth centuries to their children who lived into the Civil War. But, according to Barrow, the opposite happened. Too many of the young slaves listened to Big Lucy, and her message quite obviously differed from that emphasized by Barrow. Barrow, therefore, had an unusually difficult task and was kept busy "transforming" different generations of enslaved Afro-Americans. That fact may explain the frequency with which he used the whip. We have come a long way from the thoroughly misleading sentence that "the record shows that over the course of two years, a total of 160

TABLE FIVE

Acts of Misconduct and Whippings Compared to Rank of Cotton Pickers, Barrow Plantation, 1840–1841

MALES

| NAME | RANK AMONG ALL COTTON PICKERS | | 1840–1841 | |
	1838	1842	DISORDERLY ACTS	WHIPPINGS
Atean	1	1	3	2
Ben	3	4	5	2
Dave B	2	2	12	8
Demps	8	6	6	2
Lewis	10	10	6	3
D. Nat	9	3	8	4
Randall	7	7	10	2
L. Tom	11	9	3	3
Levi	4	8	2	1
Dennis	–	5	8	2
Thornton	4(5)	–	1	0
Kish	4(6)	–	0	0
N			64	29
Highest pick	622	520		
Lowest pick	413	385	*(Table continued at right.)*	

whippings were administered, an average of 0.7 whippings per hand per year." That pseudostatistic fails to explain Barrow's behavior, the behavior of his cotton-field hands, and the relative importance of physical punishment as a form of negative labor incentive.

Reviewing T/C, the historian David Rothman complains that F + E have made too much of the Barrow whippings:

> Fogel and Engerman offer a very weak analysis of physical punishments on the plantation. In part, this is a result of a paucity of quantitative data on whippings. One owner, Bennet Barrow, did keep some records, and these are tabulated—an average of 0.7 whippings per hand took place each year. But Barrow was a very special sort of a planter, self-consciously dedicated to the proposition that the plantation should run as a factory. He fits the Fogel-Engerman model *too* well to stand as representative of the system.[22]

TABLE FIVE (continued)

FEMALES

| | RANK AMONG ALL COTTON PICKERS | | 1840–1841 | |
NAME	1838	1842	DISORDERLY ACTS	WHIPPINGS
Betsey	1	3	5	2
Darcus	5	7	6	2
Fanny	10	6	6	2
Creasy	9	9	8	3
Hetty	4	8	2	1
L. Hannah	3	4	3	1
Luce	8	9	7	4
Oney	6	–	9	4
Patience	7	–	12	6
Lize	2	1	4	2
Milley	12	2	6	5
Sidney	11	5	0	0
N			68	32
Highest pick	443	425		
Lowest pick	273	300		

| | AVERAGE NUMBER OF DISORDERLY ACTS | | AVERAGE NUMBER OF WHIPPINGS | | NUMBER OF SLAVES | |
	MALES	FEMALES	MALES	FEMALES	MALES	FEMALES
Most productive pickers	5.3	5.7	2.4	2.7	12	12
Least productive pickers	3.7	3.1	1.9	1.1	24	18

Rothman is right in calling the analysis "very weak" but wrong in suggesting that Barrow "fits the Fogel-Engerman model too well." Barrow, it has been seen and shall soon be seen again (because F + E return to this Louisiana cotton planter two more times), hardly fits the F + E model at all. That poses three different questions. Was Barrow untypical? Is the F + E model inadequate? And, most important, why did Barrow behave in the ways revealed by the data in these pages?

Why Barrow Whipped Slaves So Frequently and Whether Barrow Was "Typical." The third question, of course, is the most important. Unless

Barrow's actions merely reflected a personal satisfaction in whipping slaves so frequently, we must look elsewhere than to his psychic needs or makeup to begin to comprehend his behavior. And the only place to start is with his slaves and their behavior. The whippings on his plantation make social sense primarily in relation to the misconduct among his slaves and to Barrow's conception of misconduct. The essential flaw in the F + E model is its failure to make a place in the historical process for slave behavior not directly determined by the policies and practices of their owners. Slaves "behave" in their model, but only in response to master-sponsored stimuli. They work hard when promised rewards or threatened with physical punishment. The Barrow slaves, of course, did not have to read their owner's diary or major in college algebra to know how frequently and why he used to whip. Ordinary vision and common sense made that clear. More than this, they surely had enough familiarity with Barrow and his whip to realize how their owner defined slave misconduct. And yet their acts of misconduct during 1840–1841 were by any measure numerous. Those acts of misconduct—mostly variants on the theme of not working hard enough—provoked their owner to use the whip. A model that fails to take into account the behavior of the slaves cannot explain the behavior of their owners.

Whether or not Barrow's response to the behavior of his cotton-field hands was "typical" is a more difficult question to answer. Too little, for one thing, is yet known about the everyday behavior—especially in the fields—of slaves like those who lived on the Barrow place. More is known, of course, about Barrow himself. He was born in 1811, and, according to his biographer Davis, his "mode of living was that of a well-to-do planter." "A substantial and respected man in his community," observed Kenneth Stampp, "Barrow inherited lands and slaves from his father; he was in no sense a crude parvenu." (Stampp, incidentally, hardly cited the Barrow diary in *The Peculiar Institution*. Barrow is only mentioned twice in the index.) There are more substantial hints that Barrow was not unusual among Louisiana cotton planters. At least one planter nearby copied Barrow's plantation "rules." Bobby Jones points out that those rules, reprinted as an appendix in the Davis volume, were not original to Barrow. He had copied them verbatim from a "restrictive" system of plantation management advocated by the *Southern Agriculturalist* and then reprinted in the *Southern Cultivator* (March 1846). His biographer, Davis, insists that in his "general outlook on the institution of slavery" Barrow was "typical of his time and section." Davis adds: "In general, Barrow treated his slaves better and took more time in the organization of his labor system than did many of the neighboring planters. He was in the planting business for the sole purpose of making money and evidently believed that a contented black would work far better than one who was dissatisfied with his surroundings." When a favored slave died, Barrow could say that "a more perfect negro never lived." But such sentiments should not be exaggerated. Barrow believed—according to his diary—that "negroes are not Capable of self-government—want of discretion—judgement &." The historian Davis understood Barrow somewhat better than he understood the Barrow slaves. With the 1840–1841 record of slave misconduct before him, Davis nevertheless concluded: "On the whole the Negro was a tractable individual. Barrow's slaves gave him very little trouble. That they were not mean or vicious is evident; but that they often needed punishment for the breaking of plantation rules must be admitted."

We need waste little time with the tone of gentle apologetics that marred the abilities of the historian Davis. Despite this shortcoming, he had some insight into Barrow's management policies. "As a rule," observed Davis, punishments were "designed to be only severe enough to be conducive to good discipline." Brutal whippings were exceptional. "Barrow," Davis goes on, "was constantly devising ingenious punishments, for he realized that uncertainty was an important aid in keeping his gangs well in hand." The range of punishments—aside from whippings—has been indicated. Duckings followed brutal whippings. And, according to Davis, for the most "flagrant violations the Negroes were 'staked down.' This was apparently the old punishment of staking them to the ground on their backs, spread-eagle fashion. Periods of staking were usually short." But especially troublesome slaves were staked down for as long as between twelve and fifteen hours.

Barrow, nevertheless, also conformed in important ways to the managerial pattern emphasized by F + E. According to Davis, the slaves lived in "comfortable frame buildings." Their owner spent a "sizable" amount of money each year for clothing. Field hands ordinarily got four or five pounds of meat each week. The Barrow slaves enjoyed regular holiday celebrations and even dinners and dances. Their owner built a dance hall, but he also built a jail. In describing his conception of the plantation, Barrow used metaphors more appropriate to Yankee New England. "A plantation," he insisted, "might be considered as a piece of machinery, to operate successfully, all of its parts should be uniform and exact." That was an economic aspiration, not an economic or social reality. The slave Dave Bartley is a case in point. He was one of Barrow's best cotton pickers. At Christmas in 1839 he and the slave Atean were singled out for "their fine conduct." Each received a suit of clothes from Barrow. During 1840–1841, Dave Bartley committed more acts of misconduct and received more whippings than any other Barrow slave: twelve instances of misconduct and eight whippings were recorded. Only one other slave committed as many as twelve acts of misconduct. Her name was Patience. She was whipped six times. Neither Bartley nor Patience was "uniform and exact." That was their trouble. They were factors of production but did not exactly fit into Barrow's definition of the plantation as "a piece of machinery." That was so even though Dave Bartley had been given a suit of clothing by his owner.[23] Columbia University economist Peter Passell, who reviewed T/C in the *New York Times Book Review*, would have benefitted from knowing Dave Bartley. The data in T/C describing the relatively decent treatment of enslaved Afro-Americans did not shock Passell. "All not very surprising," he said, "for a society that treated slaves as capital; good businessmen oil their machines."[24] Passell apparently does not know the difference between men and women like Dave Bartley and Patience and a steam engine or a cotton gin.

Negative Labor Incentives and the Ubiquitous Words "More" and "Most" in T/C. We are finished for the moment with Bennet Barrow and his slaves, but not yet with F + E on negative labor incentives. A brief paragraph follows the "summary" of the Barrow whippings to remind the reader once again that whipping was common in many places before the nineteenth century—even quoting from what is called "the Matthew's Bible," the English translation by John Rogers under the pseudonym Thomas Matthew. The next paragraph "generalizes" about whipping and contains ten sentences which indicate that none of the evidence used is "quantitative." The sentences are numbered *seriatum*:

[1] To attribute the continuation of whipping in the South to the maliciousness of masters is naïve. [2] Although *some* masters were brutal, even sadistic, *most* were not. [3] The *overwhelming majority* of the ex-slaves in the W.P.A. narratives who expressed themselves *on the issue* reported that their masters were *good men*. [4] *Such men* worried about the proper role of whipping in a system of punishment [*sic*] and rewards. [5] *Some* excluded it altogether. [6] *Most* accepted it, but recognized that to be effective whipping had to be used with restraint and in a coolly calculated manner. [7] Weston, *for example*, admonished his overseer not to impose punishment of any sort until twenty-four hours after the offense had been discovered. [8] William J. Minor, a sugar planter, instructed his managers "not [to] cut the skin when punishing, nor punish in a passion." [9] *Many* planters forbade the whipping of slaves except by them or in their presence. [10] *Others* limited the number of lashes that could be administered without their permission. [Italics added.][25]

Sentence 1 is left aside for the moment. The other nine sentences are a curious mode of argument in this work, mainly because the imprecision in language and the use of isolated examples (sentences 7 and 8) are styles of historical rhetoric and argument usually scorned by cliometricians when used by noncliometricians. How typical were Weston and Minor?[26] What methods were used to establish their typicality? Sentences 2, 5, 6, 9, and 10 contain favored imprecise quantitative words such as *some* and *most* (2, 5, and 6), *many* (9), and *others* (10). It is surprising to see how often such ambiguous words are used. It is, of course, difficult to generalize without using words meant to describe the presence or absence of regularities, and such words are essential to the social and economic historian. But neither volume 1 nor volume 2 of T/C contains any evidence indicating how F + E uncovered such regularities in planter behavior. Sentences 3 and 4— at least as written—do not bear at all on the question of planter patterns of punishment. The point under discussion is the regularity and frequency of slave punishment, not whether elderly former slaves, who were mostly between the ages of eight and twelve when the general emancipation occurred and, therefore, had probably never been beaten or whipped, felt their old owners to be "good" or "bad" men. Where, furthermore, is the evidence that the planters as a social class or group "*worried* about the *proper* role of whipping in a system of punishment and rewards" (italics added)? *Worry* has a fairly precise meaning, but *proper* is an ambiguous word. To worry means "to feel uneasy, or anxious; fret; torment oneself and suffer from disturbing thoughts." Did men like Bennet Barrow, William Minor, and Weston fret over the use of the whip and suffer disturbing thoughts? *Proper* has several meanings, and it is unclear which one is implied in this sentence. Do F + E mean that planters worried about how to adapt whipping to the purposes of enslavement? Do they mean that planters worried about conforming to established standards of behavior? Or do they mean that planters worried about whether or not whipping was right? These are quite different kinds of worries, and each has a social importance of its own.

Kenneth Stampp on Whipping and F + E on Kenneth Stampp. Sentence 1 concerns historiography. "To attribute the continuation of whipping in the South to the maliciousness of masters is naïve," insist F + E. No historians are mentioned, but this barbed sentence is aimed at so-called neo-abolitionist historians. Later in the first volume, the authors of T/C make it unnecessary to guess the target of their criticism: "[Kenneth] Stampp provided testimony that cruelty was indeed an ingrained feature of the treatment of slaves. . . . Cruelty, Stampp said, 'was endemic in all slaveholding communities'; even those 'who were concerned about the welfare of slaves found it difficult to draw a sharp line between acts of cruelty and such measures of physical force as were an inextricable part of slavery.' For Stampp, cruelty arose not because of the malevolent nature of the slaveholders but because of the malevolent nature of the system. . . ."[27]

Stampp's arguments have not been fairly summarized. Here are Stampp's sentences from which F + E drew these extracts:

> Although cruelty was endemic in all slaveholding communities, it was always most common in newly settled regions. . . . [And then two paragraphs later] Southerners who were concerned about the welfare of slaves found it difficult to draw a sharp line between acts of cruelty and such measures of physical force as were an inextricable part of slavery. Since the line was necessarily arbitrary, slaveholders themselves disagreed about where it should be drawn. . . . But no master denied the propriety of giving a moderate whipping to a disobedient bondsman. . . By [the] mid-nineteenth century . . . [the whip] was seldom used upon any but slaves, because public opinion now considered it to be cruel. Why it was less cruel to whip a bondsman was a problem that troubled many sensitive masters. That they often had no choice as long as they owned slaves made their problem no easier to resolve.[28]

Stampp's explanation for the decline of whipping ("public opinion") is hardly satisfactory, but neither is the summary of Stampp's analysis as quoted by F + E. In Fact, Stampp's analysis of whipping is as good as any we yet have and deserves to be read in full:

> [T]he whip was the most common instrument of punishment— indeed, it was the emblem of the master's authority. Nearly every slaveholder used it, and few grown slaves escaped it entirely. . . . The majority seemed to think that the certainty, and not the severity, of physical "correction" was what made it effective. While no offense could go unpunished, the number of lashes should be in proportion to the nature of the offense and the character of the offender. The master should control his temper. . . . Many urged, therefore, that time be permitted to elapse between the misdeed and the flogging. . . .
>
> Planters who employed overseers often fixed the number of stripes they could inflict for each specific offense, or a maximum number whatever the offense. . . . The significance of these numbers depended in part upon the kind of whip that was used. The "rawhide," or "cowskin," was a savage instrument requiring only a few strokes to provide a chastisement that a slave would not soon forget. . . . Many slaveholders would not use the rawhide because it lacerated the skin. . . . How frequently a master resorted to the whip depended upon his temperament and his methods of management. . . . Physical cruelty, as these observations suggest, was

always a possible consequence of the master's power to punish. Place an intemperate master over an ill-disposed slave, and the possibility became a reality.

Not that a substantial number of slaveholders deliberately adopted a policy of brutality. The great majority, in fact, preferred to use as little violence as possible. . . . The public and private records that do survive suggest that, although the average slaveholder was not the inhuman brute described by the abolitionists, acts of cruelty were not as exceptional as pro-slavery writers claimed.[29]

Stampp's illustrative evidence has not been included in this extract, but it strains the imagination to suggest that Stampp's quite balanced analysis can be characterized as representing little more than either crude neo-abolitionist bias or innocent naiveté. Stampp explicitly denied that "a substantial number of slaveholders deliberately adopted a policy of brutality," insisting that "the great majority, in fact, preferred to use as little violence as possible." Quite interestingly, Stampp emphasized that rational "economic" calculations often restrained the use of the whip. And the reasons given by this so-called neo-abolitionist historian hardly differed from those put forth two decades later by F + E.

F + E on the Economic Cost of Whipping, and James Hammond on the Social Utility of Whipping: The Inadequate Economic "Model." The brief discussion of whipping in T/C is followed by a still briefer discussion of other slave punishments. F + E soundly remind readers that whipping as an instrument of labor discipline declined "with the rise of capitalism" when "impersonal and indirect sanctions were increasingly substituted for direct, personal ones." Hiring labor in the marketplace "provided managers . . . with a powerful new disciplinary weapon." "Workers who were lazy . . . or who otherwise shirked their duties could be fired—left to starve beyond the eyesight or expense of the employer." These summary sentences hardly differ from the classic indictments of early capitalism. "Interestingly enough," F + E add, "denial of food was rarely used to enforce discipline on slaves. For the illness and lethargy caused by malnutrition reduced the capacity of the slave to labor in the fields." The jailing of slaves is mentioned, but only to be dismissed as a common form of slave punishment. Nothing, however, in these findings is new. Stampp, for example, insisted that cases "of deliberate stinting of rations were fortunately few," and that hardly any slaveholders "built private jails on their premises" because "they knew that close confinement during a working day was a punishment of dubious value.[30] F + E have not demolished yet another "myth" but simply confirmed (without adding new evidence) what is well known. Nevertheless, there is a need for more study about the relationship between control of the food supply, planter-sponsored labor incentives, and slave social behavior. Prolonged denial of food obviously causes malnutrition, just as prolonged overeating causes obesity. And that the "illness and lethargy caused by malnutrition" impair labor efficiency is self-evident. But the social issue is not whether owners denied slaves food; it has rather to do with how control of the food supply affected the life-chances and the behavior of slaves. The denial of a weekly meat ration on occasion did not cause illness and malnutrition, but it served by example to make clear that owners controlled the food supply. The presence of slave gardens where slaves often grew foodstuffs for family consumption does not alter the essential point. It simply makes it more complicated. Slaves did not own these garden plots, and such places could be taken from them. We need to study the relationship between control of the food supply, social dominance, and labor efficiency.

Much more is involved in slave punishments than an "economic" equation or an emphasis that does no more than stress the rational decisions of "economic man." F + E explain: "When the laborer owns his own human capital, forms of punishment which impair or diminish the value of that capital are borne exclusively by him. Under slavery, the master desired forms of punishment which, while they imposed costs on the slave, did so with minimum impairment to the human capital which the master owned. Whipping generally fulfilled these conditions." They say further: "Whipping persisted in the South because the cost of substituting hunger [sic] and incarceration for the lash was greater for the slaveowner than for the northern employer of free labor."[31] So simple an "economic" explanation hardly does justice to the complex motivations that shaped planter behavior. "Remember," the articulate proslavery advocate James Henry Hammond insisted, "that on our estates we dispense with the whole machinery of public police and public courts of justice. Thus we try, decide, and execute the sentences, in thousands of cases, which in other countries would go into the courts." Hardly a detached observer, Hammond was anxious to minimize the harshness implicit in master-slave relationships. He wrote in answer to British critics of enslavement:

If a man steals a pig in England, he is transported—torn from wife, children, parents, and sent to the antipodes, infamous, and an outcast forever, though probably he took from the superabundance of his neighbor to save the lives of his famishing little ones. If one of our well-fed negroes, merely for the sake of fresh meat, steals a pig, he gets perhaps forty stripes. . . . Are our courts or yours the most humane? If Slavery were not in question, you would doubtless say ours is mistaken lenity. Perhaps it often is; and slaves too lightly dealt with sometimes grow daring.

A South Carolina planter and lawyer who served in the United States Senate and felt both Northern free laborers and Southern plantation slaves to be "the very mudsills of society," Hammond had doubts about the social utility of whipping. "Stocks are rarely used by private individuals, and confinement still more seldom," said the planter, "though both are common punishments for whites, all the world over. I think they should be more frequently resorted to with slaves as substitutes for flogging, which I consider the most injurious and least efficacious mode of punishing them for serious offenses. It is not degrading, and unless excessive occasions little pain. You may be a little astonished, after all the flourishes that have been made about 'cart whips,' &c., when I say flogging is not the most degrading punishment in the world."[32] How do we fit Hammond's plea that stocks and jails be used more frequently than the whip into a model of planter behavior which measures the utility of diverse punishments only by their "cost" to the planter in "labor time"? Hammond suggests the limitations of so cost-conscious a model when he writes that whipping was insufficiently "degrading." We are back to the meaning of words and to the inadequacies of the central F + E model. To degrade, according to the *Oxford English Dictionary*, means to lower in "rank, position, reputation, [and] character." Why did Hammond feel whipping to be the least effective mode of punishing especially troublesome slaves? It seems clear that the whip—at least in Hammond's estimation—did not have its intended social effect. It failed to lower the troublesome slave in "rank, position, [and] reputation." Rank, position, and reputation among whom? Hammond and his fellow planters? Or the enslaved themselves? Hammond surely meant the enslaved. And if that is so, it is imperative that in measuring the utility of whipping we understand how the enslaved interpreted the act of being whipped. On the Barrow plantation, at least, whipping did not deter misconduct. Barrow himself built a private jail. And the South Carolinian Hammond proposed that jails and stocks be used more commonly than the whip. Was it because the enslaved felt incarceration to be more degrading than whipping? And if so, why? A narrow economic calculus cannot explain so important a social distinction.

Bennet Barrow's Perception of Inefficient Plantation Labor and the Distortion of That Perception in T/C. We shall turn next to the treatment of incentives meant to reward slaves for efficient labor, but first we shall summarize briefly what has been learned about slave punishments. The single piece of numerical evidence (the Barrow diary) tells the

POWER & CULTURE

opposite of what F + E report in T/C. The supplementary evidence on punishment is slight at best, and the *general* details hardly differ from those emphasized in *The Peculiar Institution*. (The tone of the analysis, of course, is quite different.) The discussion of planter-sponsored rewards to encourage productive slave labor is hardly more satisfactory. Portions of the critical paragraph used by F + E to make the transition from negative to positive labor incentives have been printed earlier in these pages, but here I record the entire paragraph:

> While whipping was an integral part of the system of punishment and rewards, it was not the totality of the system. What planters wanted was not sullen and discontented slaves who did just enough to keep from getting whipped. They wanted devoted, hard-working, responsible slaves who identified their fortunes with the fortunes of their masters. Planters sought to imbue their slaves with a "Protestant" work ethic and to transform that ethic from a state of mind into a high level of production. "My negros have their name up in the neighborhood," wrote Bennet Barrow, "for making more than any one else & they think Whatever they do is better than any body Else." Such an attitude could not be beaten into slaves. It had to be elicited.[33]

Barrow entered that sentence in his diary on October 15, 1840, and it was extracted first by Davis in his essay and then by F + E.[34] By lifting the sentence from the full diary entry, Davis and then F + E completely distort its meaning. Barrow was not praising his slaves for identifying their fortunes with his fortunes. The full diary entry, together with the entries that preceded it, is as follows:[35]

Oct. 1   Made all hands stop & trash cotten this morning. . . .

Oct. 2   . . . Women trashing cotten men doing little of every thing, *not much of any thing*

Oct. 5   . . . the trashyiest stuff I ever saw, some of my young Hands are doing verry Badly Ralph Wash E. Nat E. Jim Jim T. Henry Israel Harriet Sam&Maria Lewis & Randal

Oct. 6   . . . bad news from the Cotten market

Oct. 9   . . . never saw more cotten open to the Acre. & verry trashy . . .

Oct. 11   . . . Gave the negros shoes. . . .

Oct. 13   . . . I think my hands have Picked cotten worse this year than in several years picked it verry trashy & not better weights nor as good as *common*, intend Whipping them *straght*

Oct. 15   Clear verry pleasant, Never have been more dissatisfied with
my hands all Excepting 'Lize I [L?] Hannah Jensey Atean
& Margaret, am sattisfied the best plan is to give them every
thing they require for their comfort and never that they
will do without Whipping or some punishment. My negros
have their name up in the neighborhood for making more
than any one else & they think Whatever they do is better
than any body Else.

These diary entries cannot be read as evidence that the Barrow
slaves had become "devoted, hard-working, responsible slaves who
identified their fortunes with the fortunes of their masters," or that
Barrow had managed to "transform" the " 'Protestant' work ethic . . .
from a state of mind into a high level of production." It may be
possible to read the single sentence extracted in T/C that way, but not
the full October 15 diary entry and surely not the full sequence of
diary entries between the first and fifteenth of October. Read in the
context of the full diary entry and in relation to recorded general
whippings in 1837, 1838, twice in 1839, and again in 1840, as well as
in relation to the frequency of punishment (whippings) during 1840–
1841, it is quite clear that Barrow's single sentence meant to scorn the
self-image that Barrow's slaves had of themselves and that others,
including perhaps whites nearby, had of them. Barrow knew better;
that is plainly and incontestably made known by the surrounding diary
entries and by Barrow's behavior. A single sentence in the diary has
been transformed in meaning to bolster a thin argument. The same
rules of evidence, however, should apply to literary sources as to
quantitative data. Barrow, of course, used positive labor incentives to
elicit good work from his slave men and women, and Davis adequately
summarizes them: "He devised many ways to increase their labors and
to make them more contented; they were well fed and well housed;
they received gifts of money at Christmas time; they were divided into
rival gangs at cotton-picking time with the losing side giving dinners
to the winners; and individuals sometimes raced down the cotton
row. . . ."[36] But this summary of positive labor incentives in no way sus-
tains the October 15 diary entry extracted so inaccurately by F + E.
And that is because the full entry told that Barrow believed he had
failed to elicit adequate productive work from his slaves. "The better
you treat them," Barrow had written earlier that same year, "the worse
they are." And why now? Barrow saw to it that the most productive
slaves were better fed than the least productive slaves. But they were
also the slaves whipped most frequently, and, when better fed, it was
the least productive field hands who fed them.

8

LABOR HISTORY
AND THE "SARTRE QUESTION"

SOME MAY be surprised to find American working-class history defined as part of the humanities. What, they may wonder, can the study of changing employment patterns, work processes, employer practices, and trade union activities tell us about the human condition?

Humanists, of course, vary in their interests. But their concerns often focus on those aspects of everyday experiences which deal with the quality or condition of being human. The changing work experiences of ordinary Americans are central to such discourse.

Jean-Paul Sartre tells us why. "The essential," he observed, "is not what 'one' has done to man, but what man does with what 'one' has done to him." Sartre's emphasis redefines the important questions we should ask in studying the history of dependent American social classes: slaves and poor free blacks, immigrant and native-born wage earners, male and female blue- and white-collar workers, and union and nonunion laborers.

What such men and women experienced (that is, what "one" has done *to* them) retains interest, but how they interpreted and then dealt with changing patterns of economic, social, and political dependence and inequality becomes our major concern. Studying the choices working men and women made and how their behavior affected important historical processes enlarges our understanding of "the condition of being human."

That has become very clear to me in the past few summers when I directed a National Endowment for the Humanities seminar ("Americans at Work: Changing Social and Cultural Patterns") for trade union officials, mostly local and regional staff and officers. This summer, men and women from seven states representing workers in chemical, nuclear, textile, and steel factories, in the building trades and on the docks, and in government employment (teachers and unskilled public service workers) examined the "Sartre question" by studying American working-class history.

This essay is reprinted from *Humanities* 1 (September–October 1980).

Discussions ranged from examining seventeenth-century English and African work processes and cultures to the late-twentieth-century worry over the decline of the so-called Protestant work ethic. Earlier patterns of working-class life and labor became vivid after visits to Pawtucket, Rhode Island, Paterson, New Jersey, and New York City's Lower East Side. The unionists explored the autobiographies of Frederick Douglass and Nate Shaw, the poems of John Greenleaf Whittier, William Carlos Williams, and e. e. cummings, and the short stories of Lowell, Massachusetts, mill women, Herman Melville, I. L. Peretz, and Mario Puzo. A regular fare of historical writings fed each day's discussion, including works by Susan Benson, David Brody, Alan Dawley, Nathan Huggins, Lawrence Levine, Edmund S. Morgan, and E. P. Thompson.

These and related materials illustrate how laboring men and women survived and sometimes triumphed in changing American work settings. We learn how new workers use old cultures, and how changing conditions of work and life cause working men and women to reexamine and change settled ways. These processes have been a constant in our history, but have often been experienced anew by different racial and ethnic groups.

For many reasons, we know too little of the processes that helped shape the American working class and the nation. Excessive emphasis in the popular culture and in academic history on "assimilation" and on "achievement" trivializes explanation and meaning. So does the failure to probe "what man does with what 'one' has done to him."

Resistance to dependence and inequality has been an irregular but constant theme in our national history. "Dependence," Thomas Jefferson warned, "begets subservience . . . and suffocates the germ of virtue." Americans, however, especially in this century, have associated the escape from dependence much too narrowly with possessive individualism.

Addressing the Sartre question and reexamining American working-class history reveals a constant if shifting tension inside and outside the workplace between individualist and collective ways of achieving autonomy.

Sometimes a single individual revealed the shifting tension within himself. Abraham Cahan captured that splendidly in his novel *The Rise of David Levinsky*. Levinsky had come to America in 1885 to seek and find his fortune. A man of wealth, Levinsky feared for himself as he aged:

I can never forget the days of my misery. I cannot escape from my old self. My past and present do not comport well. David, the poor lad swinging over a Talmud volume at the Preacher's Synagogue, seems to have more in common with my inner identity than David Levinsky, the well-known cloak manufacturer.

Evidence of cooperative ways of achieving independence regularly dots the national experience. The Philadelphia Journeymen Carpenters explained their opposition to their employers in 1791:

> 'Tis one of the invaluable privileges of our nature, that when we conceive ourselves aggrieved, there is an inherent right in us to complain. . . . Self-preservation has induced us to enter into an indissoluble union, in order to ward off the blows which are threatened us, by the insolent hand of pampered affluence:—We mean hereafter, by a firm, independent mode of conduct, to protect each other. . . .

That theme was not a new one in 1791, and it would be echoed in later generations by men and women as different as Samuel Gompers, Eugene Debs, the young Tom Watson, Aunt Molly Jackson, Carlo Tresca, Nate Shaw, Fanny Lou Hamer, and César Chávez.

The recovery of this historic tension among working people—individual versus collective solutions—should not be misinterpreted. It does not teach "lessons." Nor does it mean that the past should be ransacked for new heroes. Instead, it calls attention to the diverse and competing traditions that have shaped the American working-class experience. "Groups," the British writer and historian David Caute points out, "who lack a sense of their past resemble individuals without knowledge of their parents—stranded, half-invalidated, insecure. The rediscovered past furnishes us . . . with a diachronic pattern which provides an alternative context for thought and action."

Far more important than a "lesson," a context allows us to transform the given in our lives into the contingent. Past and present then merge in new ways and strengthen our capacity to overcome many of the inequities of late-twentieth-century America.

9

INTERVIEW WITH
HERBERT GUTMAN

Mike Merrill, at the time of this interview, was codirector of the Institute for Labor Education and Research in New York City.

Q.   You have made original and influential contributions to both U.S. labor history and Afro-American history, but let's start with your work in labor history, since it was your first research interest. When did you begin to think systematically about the way labor history ought to be done?

GUTMAN   My interest in working-class history flowed first out of my youth and my early politics. My parents were immigrant Jews and belonged to the International Workers Order. They were not Communists, but I grew up very much influenced by that branch of the Jewish Old Left. As an undergraduate I campaigned vigorously for Henry Wallace, flirted briefly but intensely with the Communist movement, read the Marxist classics, and soon grew wary of and then disgusted with vanguard leftist politics. I remained a socialist—an egalitarian and a democrat. I drifted into American working-class history out of this world. My M.A. thesis at Columbia University (1950) was conventional labor history, and I'm sure it bored my supervisor, Richard Hofstadter—and for good reason! Later, in 1952–1953, as a graduate student at the University of Wisconsin, I first confronted problems in writing working-class history as the result of one question: What caused the vast amount of disorder and property destruction during the 1877 railway strikes? Nothing in the secondary literature explained this extraordinary, nationwide disrespect for private property and the law. It was as if the strikes had occurred outside American history, as if they did not belong to—or in—America!

Dissatisfied with what had been written, I devised a simple strategy. I divided the country into several regions and read one or two major newspapers from each [for the years] 1873 to 1878 to find out what

This interview is reprinted from MARHO, the Radical Historians Organization, *Visions of History*, edited by Henry Abelove et al. (New York: Pantheon Books, 1983), 185–216.

Americans, and especially working people, were doing and thinking. I did that for three years looking for labor news, reconstructing working-class experiences from the middle-class press.

The strategy worked well. I began to pick up stories. A brief dispatch in a Cincinnati paper reported: "Special to the *Cincinnati Commercial*. Hocking Valley miners' strike has entered its fifth month." Or in the *New York Sun*, which had very, very good labor reporting: "The 'long vacation' in Fall River continues. It's now August, and the textile strike started in May." Or in the Philadelphia paper: "To the great surprise of everyone, the Scranton jury freed the miners."

What surfaced everywhere were dozens of events—whole class experiences—over the entire country that had never made their way into the consciousness of historians. The evidence raised important and little-studied questions. How did this evidence conform to the common historical belief that the Robber Barons had it all going for them in Gilded Age America, and that they found it relatively easy to transform their new power into authority?

What first struck me was the length of strikes and lockouts. Conventional labor historians insisted that the Gilded Age trade union movement ("organized labor") was very weak. What, then, explained the length of these protracted working-class struggles? Given the absence of powerful unions, benefits, and much else assumed to be necessary to maintain long strikes, what made such intense struggles possible? That's where I started.

I answered such questions in an essay entitled "The Workers' Search for Power." Published in a book on the Gilded Age,[1] it distinguished between workers living in small towns and those living in large cities. I had done most of my research on small towns and very little on large cities. So I argued that face-to-face relationships in small towns created more cross-class solidarities than the seeming anonymity of large cities. The argument would work, I later realized, if Chicago and Pittsburgh didn't exist! Chicago, after all, probably had as large a percentage of its ethnic male work force in trade unions as any other city in the world in the early twentieth century. (Such evidence, incidentally, makes hash of so many fashionable arguments that ethnicity and high rates of social mobility militated against American working-class self-organization.) Rightly or wrongly, these essays argued that the class structure in small towns, coming out of residual or older forms of class relations, gave little-noticed strengths to diverse workers.

I had studied several towns to deal with two questions. First, how and from where did mid- and late-nineteenth-century workers without permanent forms of collective organization derive their strengths? I argued that these strengths came primarily from elements within the class structive unsympathetic to the changing needs of the rising manufacturing class. That seemed a radical explanation to some historians in the late 1950s and early 1960s, when the studies began to appear. It attracted notice. Second, if the power of the manufacturing class was not quickly accepted as legitimate, then another interesting process was at work. How does a powerful new class achieve authority? It always takes time, and it took time for American industrial capitalism to be legitimized, for the power that came with the ownership of new factories to be transformed into authority. Here were clues to the prevalence of violence and corruption in Gilded Age America. New property relations had not yet been fully legitimized.

Q.   All this work you are discussing is pre-Thompson, isn't it?

GUTMAN   Yes, of course. These essays were finished as part of my dissertation in 1959. Some were soon published. *The Making of the English Working Class* appeared in 1963.

Q.   You also published an essay on blacks and the United Mine Workers and one on labor and American Protestantism in the mid-1960s.[2] What was the occasion for writing each of these pieces?

GUTMAN   They were published a few years later. I signed a book contract in the Bobbs-Merrill series edited by Alfred Young and Leonard Levy to be called *The Mind of the Worker in the Gilded Age*. It was to be a book of writings by workers from the 1850s to the election of 1896 that would show that more than just a handful of intellectuals wrote critiques of how Gilded Age capitalism was developing. It showed that a wide-ranging critique appeared every week in the diverse labor press and pamphlet literature that addressed bread-and-butter issues. These critics challenged the lurid assumptions of laissez-faire capitalism and social Darwinism.

In reading the *United Mine Workers Journal*, which I did as research for that book, I ran into weekly letters by R. W. Davis. It took me about a month to figure out he was a black. Those letters astonished me. By the time I finished copying them I had a pile about a foot high, and so when Julius Jacobson asked me to write about black workers for a book to be called *The Negro and the American Labor Movement*, I proposed to publish a few of the letters with a short introduction. That short introduction became a very long essay.

As I studied those letters a whole world came apart and had to be reconstructed. A little arithmetic applied to the bituminous coal industry showed that in the early years of the UMW, black unionists were proportionately more important than whites. Into what could we incorporate *that* fact and the wonderful, wonderful letters of this fellow, born a slave and victimized by racism on all sides? I could find no place for him or his letters in conventional labor and Afro-American historical writing. He simply didn't fit. Neither did all those other black coal miners.

POWER & CULTURE

Q. In the beginning of the Protestantism essay, you mention two influences on working-class consciousness that historians had neglected. The first was religion, and you go on to deal with that dimension in the essay. My only problem with this discussion is that you did not say more about Catholicism.

GUTMAN That's true. I failed to explore the Catholic dimension. But my concern was with the way workers legitimized their protests. My central focus was legitimacy, not religion as such. I had Catholic material. Some local priests, for example, in the anthracite mining regions supported the men hung in the Molly Maguire executions.* The Philadelphia bishop excommunicated the Molly Maguires, but the local priests knew better. Letters from them to New York newspapers in the summer of 1877 declared the Mollies innocent. One was signed by a Father Sheridan.

Q. The second influence historians had neglected, you charged, was the ideology of radical republicanism and the heritage of republican political institutions. Republicanism offers a small-scale, egalitarian vision. It is individualistic, not in the sense of self-interested but in the sense of self-reliant. Unfortunately, you have not had much to say about this influence in print. What do you make of Alan Dawley's recent argument in *Class and Community* that republicanism, for all its importance in the early part of the nineteenth century, was a dead end for the American working class?[3]

GUTMAN Alan's book is very important and original one. I disagree with the last third of it, but it is a fine work. Alan was grappling with the false-consciousness issue when writing *Class and Community*. He sought reasons why a mass socialist movement did not develop and sustain itself. He couldn't find them where Stephan Thernstrom had, so instead he located them in increasingly archaic postbellum republican beliefs.[4]

I would argue differently. If you look at the behavior of workers and the ideological criticism of capitalism that they developed in the 1870s, 1880s, and early 1890s, social and political republicanism was at the heart of their critique. That was so even though most workers and their spokesmen were foreign-born or the children of immigrants. If you read J. P. McDonnell, who had been the Irish secretary of the First International before coming to this country in the early 1870s and in his early years was an uncompromising socialist critic of

---

* In a series of trials from 1875 to 1877, a group of militant miners, known in the press as the Molly Maguires, were convicted of murdering coal company officials and of committing other acts of sabotage in the anthracite region of Pennsylvania. Responding to the trials and executions, labor organizations across the country charged that the coal companies, using Pinkerton detectives, had fabricated evidence of a labor terrorist conspiracy in order to intimidate the miners and remove militant labor leaders.

developing American capitalism, his rhetoric was bathed in working-class republican ideology. Saturated by it. He believed in America and also believed it was being ruined. He was a typical radical unionist, and if I had written a companion piece to the Protestantism essay it would have dealt with individuals like McDonnell. Developing capitalism tarnished—perhaps destroyed—the republican promise, but organized workers, among others, sought to retain that promise. That is quite a different emphasis from arguing that republicanism blocked a mass socialist movement before 1900.

Basic to Gilded Age working-class republican ideology was the belief in a relative equality of means. Workers experienced the 1870s and 1880s! They saw John D. Rockefeller earning more in a minute than a molder or a barrel maker in his factories earned in a year. And that was only his stated salary, [it did not include] his income from stocks and bonds. They saw that and much else. They weren't socially blinded. What did that mean for America? they asked. And to happen so rapidly? A four-hundred-page manuscript I have written and rewritten on Paterson and its workers deals with those questions. So does a soon-to-be-published book containing three long essays on Gilded Age workers and their America.[5]

And are you familiar with James Holt's fine essay in *Labor History*?[6] He seeks to explain why mass unionism failed to develop in the United States between 1890 and the First World War. It is the most probing recent piece on the subject. By most measures, American ironworkers and steelworkers were better organized and more militant in the 1880s than their British brothers. Yet mass unionism took root more quickly in England than in the United States. Why? It cannot be explained by the underdevelopment of the American working class in the 1880s. Holt suggests that failure in the United States is not adequately explained by factors internal to the class, such as upward mobility, ethnic division, and make-it-yourself ideology. Instead, he argues that political changes in the late 1880s and early 1890s weakened workers' organizations.

The really critical year, I think, was 1892. If you locate events that tell us something about essential changes that shaped and reshaped the consciousness of working-class leaders and radicals, of trade unionists, on a time continuum, then 1892 was a big year. The Homestead lockout, the Buffalo switchmen's strike, the Tennessee coal strikes, the New Orleans general strike, the Idaho mining strikes in Coeur d'Alene. The use of state power in the early 1890s against these workers was staggering! In the late 1880s and early 1890s there was a growing awareness among workers that the state had become more and more inaccessible to them and especially to their political and economic needs and demands.

You see what I am saying? These repressive political developments were responses to the workers' upsurge in the mid-1880s. And then, the workers' awareness of these developments revealed itself in their new behavior. Eugene V. Debs, for example, moved to the left and became a socialist, believing that the ultimate solution was political. And Samuel Gompers moved to the right, making the argument that workers could not engage in independent politics because they were too weak to influence the political parties. Gompers turned inward to build strength. Debs turned outward. Both were authentic working-class responses.

David Montgomery, incidentally, told aspects of this larger story in *Beyond Equality*,[7] which was so original that few conventional historians understood it when it was first published. He demonstrated how workers' movements in Northern and Western towns and cities in the Civil War and Reconstruction years raised fundamental questions about prevailing middle-class notions of equality and middle-class definitions of the state. He demonstrated how workers' movements profoundly affected ideology in national politics. That was "history from the bottom up." Go back and read the reviews of *Beyond Equality*, and you will see where the historical profession was at in the good old days. "A curious book about textile workers' strikes and ten-hour movements. What can they have to do with Andrew Johnson and the politics of Reconstruction?" Many historians simply could not grasp the connection.

Montgomery wrote about working-class presence prior to 1873. It resurfaced, more powerfully, in the mid-1880s, and we are just now making sense of this intercession by American workers. It was not predominantly socialist in outlook, but it was anticapitalist. Leon Fink has pieces of this story in his splendid forthcoming book.[8] The rhetoric these movements and their leaders used to legitimize their attack on developing capitalism drew upon premillennial Christianity and republican ideology. The new inequality had no place in a Christian country (as they understood Christianity) and especially no place in a republican country. Workers in large numbers believed that. Even— indeed, especially—immigrant workers. They hadn't come to America to be proletarianized. "What in hell is going on in America? What kind of country is this becoming?" they asked. In the 1880s a deep struggle over the meaning of America took place. In a recent article, Montgomery insists that the struggle was fought again thirty or forty years later.[9] He is probably right. And a similar struggle had been fought in the 1830s by artisans. These struggles have erupted irregularly in our history and are evidence of powerful lower-class responses to changes in the structure of class inequality. In turn, these struggles shape the ongoing historical process and the redefinition of democratic institutions. Theodore Roosevelt and Eugene V. Debs knew that. So should late-twentieth-century American historians, especially those who call themselves radicals.

But let me go on for a moment. The full history of subordinate groups—all of them—involves far more than studying these irregular outbursts of collective, democratic protest. A central tension exists within all modern dependent groups between individualist (utilitarian) and collective (mutualist) ways of dealing with and sometimes over-coming historically specific patterns of dependence and inequality. That tension changes over time. It differs from group to group. It reveals itself in very diverse ways, reflecting regional, racial, ethnic, gender, and other differences. It is little understood, but it always is there and awaits thoughtful historical analysis.

Q. What about socialism? If you look at America in 1840, it seems to me that the republicans are still justified in believing their world is possible. But if you look at America in 1880, if you look at Standard Oil and the other trusts being formed, it seems to me socialism was a much more viable and promising response to the capitalist order than republicanism was. Socialism is much more collective than republican-ism. It is a large-scale egalitarianism, with the emphasis on people working together, in contrast to republicanism, with its emphasis on people working for themselves. I don't see how one can say, in retrospect, that Americans should still be republicans in the 1880s.

GUTMAN   Socialism was only one expression of collective resistance to the dependencies associated with wage labor and modern capitalism. I would argue this way: in the 1880s—a period of intense debate over the ways in which capitalism had transformed America and threatened democratic practices—workers began to develop sets of working-class, or alternate, institutions and beliefs. I shouldn't say "workers" because that is too facile. Working-class movements developed alternative institutions and beliefs. The cooperative, for example, was a very important central institution in that period. There were thousands of working-class cooperatives. Most of them failed, but that is not the point. If you look at the scale of enterprise, the cooperative was an appropriate response to wage-labor dependency. The Knights of Labor, for example, argued that "natural" monopolies such as railroads should be owned by the state. They were too big to be run cooperatively, but everything else should be run on a cooperative basis, everything else should be produced cooperatively. The cooperatives were anticap-italist but have often been treated as spurious and utopian working-class efforts. That's a mistake. Theirs was an anticapitalist and a democratic critique, but socialist movements did not thrive between 1873 and 1896. (Socialists, however, were very important leaders of popular class movements.)

Q. Granted there was no powerful socialist movement before 1896. But it is also important to remember that there was no important working-class republican movement *after* 1896; working-class republicanism collapsed. And while I know this is an argument largely due to hindsight, still it is because of that collapse that I think we can say— as historians—that republicanism was not an appropriate response to capitalism in the 1880s.

But it would also be a mistake to assume that socialism merely took up among workers where republicanism left off. As your work especially has shown, republicanism was a cross-class movement through the 1890s. The workers enunciated an ideology that many classes could accept. But when workers begin to talk socialism in the early 1900s, they break those cross-class links, which are only going to be re-formed much later, if at all, on a different basis.

GUTMAN That is well put. We also need to make allowances for changes in the class structure and in the composition of the working class. That gets us into the twentieth century, a very different world from the one I studied.

Q. Let's change the subject a little. What was the occasion for writing the essay "Work, Culture, and Industrializing America," published in the *American Historical Review* in 1973?

GUTMAN The original version of the paper was prepared for the first Anglo-American colloquium on working-class history in 1968, several years before the revised version was published. My intent in writing it was to go to England, sit down with colleagues whose work I admired, and say to them, "Look, you've been doing so much original and important work, and there is much that American working-class historians can learn from this work. But what you have been doing must first be Americanized." What these British colleagues—Thompson, Hobsbawm, Rudé, Pollard, the several Harrisons, among others— had done was far more than simply study the whole worker. They had begun to reexamine the processes by which new subordinate classes are formed, how they develop. They were studying class conflict and social change in new ways. That, after all, is at the heart of Thompson's work. It is an analysis of the ways in which who workers *had been* affected who they *became*. Our task was to Americanize—so to speak— that insight for wage earners and, of course, other dependent classes in this country such as slaves. What, after all, are the distinctive, much less the universal, problematics essential to understanding changing class relations and behavior in the United States?

Q. Let me lay out a critical reading of the *AHR* article. The focus is almost one century, a long period of disruptive industrial violence. This goes back to your earliest concerns, clearly. The overarching scheme is to try to figure out why the history of American industrial relations had the violent character it had. If we look at Britain during the same century, the violent period seems to have been much shorter. Why? Your response, in this reading, is to say that there is a need to season a new work force in the United States over and over again. The history of American industrial relations is more violent, you seem to say, because of the continual infusion of new masses of workers coming from premodern and preindustrial backgrounds into this increasingly modern industrial society.

I have two questions about this scheme. First, it seems to me to underestimate the role of indigenous American values in opposing capitalism. If readers didn't know anything else about American labor history, they might walk away with the impression that peasants came to the New World and weren't able to adjust to the factory so they revolted or resisted. Such a reading places an emphasis on external opposition, on opposition to industrialism as being un-American.

Second, there seems to be a deemphasis in the essay on internal contradictions within the industrial order itself, a deemphasis of any idea that the industrial order might produce its own internal opposition. After all, you don't need to be a peasant in order to hate factory work.

GUTMAN The essay did not emphasize those internal contradictions, and for good reason. The words *premodern* and *preindustrial* bother me now, but I used them—and this may surprise some readers—as a way of dealing with long-term changes in the American class structure, as a way of enlarging our understanding of changing American class relations and working-class behavior, as a way of reconceptualizing archaic conflict models used to explain diverse working-class responses to changing patterns of inequality. Of course, the use of the terms may have been misleading. The concept of preindustrial covers so much that it can really mean very little. It mixes together very different men and women. Pocahontas, Thomas Jefferson, Nat Turner, and Josiah Wedgwood, after all, were all preindustrial. Precapitalist might have been more appropriate, but it has its problems too.

The most important part of the essay, I think, is not the evidence dealing with recalcitrant work habits, but the argument about periodization and changing class relations. What puzzles me is that even the article's most cogent critics—and I include David Montgomery among them because his remains the most thoughtful discussion of the essay[10]—failed to address that issue. The language I used may have been inappropriate and therefore misled some readers. So let me try a different language to summarize its main points. Differences exist between studying the formation of a new subordinate class and the development of that class, and then the behavior of a well-developed subordinate class. E. P. Thompson's *The Making of the English Working Class*, for example, reshaped our understanding of class formation in the early industrial revolution, and the recent writings of Alan Dawley, Thomas Dublin, Paul Faler, Bruce Laurie, and Gary Kulik, among others, have Americanized Thompson's methods in examining class formation prior to 1840.[11] (We should keep in mind, however, that in 1840 only 11 percent of America's 17 million inhabitants lived in towns or cities with more than 2,500 residents and that among the gainfully employed seven of ten labored in agriculture.) Other labor historians have dealt with a very different *moment* in class relations and working-class history. David Brody's study of immigrant steelworkers examined changes in a *developed* working class.[12] So, too, did Montgomery's essays on shop-floor struggles over control of the work process.[13] The *AHR* essay emphasized the differences in the class structure over time—its central point—and then examined behavior and conflicts involving workers new to wage labor in distinct periods. The analysis may have been incomplete. But it had nothing whatever to do with modernization theories and certainly was not intended to explain the full range of working-class behavior between 1815 and 1920.

The *AHR* essay called attention to three distinct periods. In the years before 1843 (the exact date hardly matters), wage labor came unevenly to the United States. The profound transformations associated with the coming of wage labor were not experienced nationally; that happened between 1840 and the turn of the century. In these decades the preindustrial class and social structure were transformed. That transformation occurred unevenly. But it was that transformation in those decades that made the United States the world's preeminent industrial capitalist nation. And the widening importance of wage labor in those decades was experienced mostly by foreign-born workers and their children. David Montgomery correctly criticized my essay for failing to emphasize that many new *American* workers in that period had been wage laborers prior to their emigration. That fact gave special character to class relations in those decades and is the reason, incidentally, why it is so difficult—indeed, erroneous—to deal with American working-class history and immigration history as discrete subjects. I dealt with the transatlantic (and transpacific) connections too simply. And the third period? The decades after the 1890s? It was different again. Working-class behavior then occurs in the most developed of all capitalist settings. Important changes in the class structure occurred between 1890 and the First World War, but the basic structural changes associated with the spread of wage labor took place in the so-called middle period.

Periodization remains a little-studied question. Alan Dawley's *Class and Community*, of course, moved us light-years ahead on this subject. He was the first so-called new labor historian to reperiodize working-class history in a detailed study that covered a long time-span. No one had done so before Dawley's book on the Lynn shoemakers. Montgomery didn't do it. Brody didn't do it. Neither did I. Dawley rushed through the full process much too hastily, but he nevertheless indicated important linkages between the formation of a new subordinate class (period one), its subsequent development (period two), and the behavior of a well-developed class (period three). My own essay failed to make these important connections.

Q.   Is the violence characteristic of U.S. industrial relations necessarily associated with the need to season new workers?

GUTMAN   Not at all. The issue is not violence, but conflict and its changing nature over time. Conflict does not disappear after the first generation. It is redefined and takes new forms. In the period from the 1840s to the 1880s it was not merely that most workers were new to the factory, but also that the structure of American society changed radically and therefore redefined the sources of new conflict.

Q.   I still worry that we are left with the sense that opposition to capitalism was external to America.

GUTMAN   What do you mean by external? So few old-stock, white Americans labored in factories and mines after 1870 that it becomes essential to study the remaking of the American working class in transoceanic ways. But the foreignness of the working class after 1870 does not make American opposition to capitalism external. It means that much of American working-class history between 1840 and 1920 has a transoceanic dimension that cannot be neglected. My current research focuses on this question. Ira Berlin and I have completed an essay on the composition of the Southern free working class in 1860 that shows the neglected great importance of urban immigrant male workers there and casts new light on the very low status of urban slaves.[14] My own larger research interest now is on the ways in which immigrants and their children were the critical link between working-class formation prior to 1840 and working-class development between 1840 and 1890. Outside the building trades in nearly all parts of the country, white male workers of old stock were relatively unimportant. Immigrants, their children, and Afro-Americans played central roles in the reproduction of the working class and the development of working-class institutions. It could not have been otherwise in places like Leavenworth, Kansas, where blacks, immigrants, and the children of immigrants composed about 90 percent of the working class in 1880. And the Leavenworth pattern was typical for the country at large.

Q.   You placed great stress on a distinction between "culture" and "society" in the essay we have been discussing. What part does the distinction play in your thinking about working-class history?

GUTMAN   The distinction seems to be especially appropriate for dealing with transitional periods—when there is an active tension between old and new, when new class institutions and class relationships are being created. It is a more difficult distinction to use in periods of relative tranquillity. The distinction draws upon the work of the cultural anthropologists Eric Wolf and Sidney Mintz, and it makes good sense.[15] Just how that distinction is useful in studying third- or fourth-generation wage earners in a developed capitalist society remains to be worked out. I'm sure it can, but it means studying the rules by which working men and women organize their everyday lives in a well-developed capitalist society. Those rules change over time as do the constraints operating on a developed subordinate class. These are subjects that should concern students of the twentieth-century American working class. Compare Thompson's *Making* with Gareth Stedman Jones's splendid essay on the remaking of the London working class after the mid-nineteenth century.[16] The developed class differs from the one that engaged the formative experience, but it has not been fully integrated into the new social order. It has its own rules and experiences—its own culture—and sometimes challenges its subordination in new class-specific ways.

My *AHR* essay did not deal with third- or fourth-generation American workers. Such a study involves a different emphasis than the examination of first-generation workers. Amercan capitalism was well developed by 1900. The working class was not new *in America* by then. But large numbers of American workers were new *to American capitalism* in 1900, and the culture/society dichotomy remains very useful in studying how they became American workers. The dialectic, however, is far more subtle than I suggested in the 1973 essay.

Q.   I have problems with the usefulness of the culture/society distinction, even for the 1840 to 1880 period in which you are saying it makes the most sense. From what you were saying earlier, you clearly agree that capitalism is still relatively new in this period. Moreover, because it was new, a different history was still possible. The history we got was not inevitable at any point in that period.

GUTMAN   Quite right. It was not foreordained. It was open, of course, and working-class critics of the developed system acted on that belief.

Q.   Well, it seems to me that the distinction you draw between culture and society closes off the possibility of understanding those historical possibilities. Society comes in as already formed, as finished, complete and single-minded. It comes in as Thompson's windscreen against which the bearers of culture are squashed.[17]

GUTMAN   Put that way it is a static formulation. That is right, and a very fine point. Not only that, the trouble with that formulation is that nothing new is formed among the workers, leaving the impression that what is being described is merely a generational phenomenon. Go on.

Q. That is the society side of my problem. There is also a culture side. The conception of culture in the essay, especially with the emphasis on culture as inherited belief, is also static. I would contrast it to Thompson's more dynamic conception, which focuses on consciousness a great deal more. Tradition and all that is there in Thompson, but the difference between culture in the sense of tradition and culture in the sense of consciousness is that traditions are slow to change. At one point you say as much, describing culture as the things that change slowly, the things that persist or endure. For Thompson, in contrast, culture—as consciousness—is a volatile thing: it is always under pressure of change; it is always making new discoveries; it is always coming up with new things. That is the source of the electricity to *The Making of the English Working Class*. Traditions do not disappear in such a conception, but instead of simply enduring there, they are thought, they are spoken, and ultimately they are lived.

GUTMAN Yes, that element is inadequately treated. That is a fine criticism.

Q. If you put these two criticisms together you get a different emphasis—both on society as something that can be changed and on culture as something always being formed—that avoids the problems I have with the culture/society distinction. Instead of a notion of society as being distinct from culture we get an emphasis on culture as a way of life, in Raymond Williams's terms (or as "social being," in Thompson's terms), embedding culture and society together. One then asks how at each point everything is being formed and is changing. Furthermore, one gets an emphasis on consciousness as active thought. The advantage of working with a distinction between culture and consciousness (or social being and social consciousness) in place of a distinction between society and culture is that the former distinction includes more historical experience and has built into it, at both ends, historical openings and possibilities for change. Thompson, for example, is now saying that we can, simply by virtue of alerting the public mind to the dangers of nuclear war, turn around the greatest juggernaut that humankind has ever faced.[18] That is the possibility of consciousness, that is what its volatility makes possible. (Unfortunately, it doesn't make it certain.) Thompson is saying that we can change the way we think about our history, and if we do, we can change that history itself—at least we can if enough of us change the way we think about it.

In your later book on the black family, by the way, I think consciousness is there. The book is obviously part of an enormous renaissance in Afro-American studies, but it is different from most other contributions in the area—despite all the work on African traditions and slave traditions—because in the book you can watch the people discovering things for themselves, in their own language, and mulling them over. They are meeting challenges—1861, 1863, 1865— things change and the people are thinking about the changes and that is in the book. That is what is good about it, in my opinion.

GUTMAN Your distinction between culture and consciousness is a splendid one, and your criticism is on target. The essay dealt with a long period of time, but it lacked movement. That may be the reason so little attention has been given to the issues of periodization it raised. My emphasis on culture at the expense of consciousness meant freezing a series of different moments in time and thereby ignoring the crucial connections between historical being and becoming

Q. What is the difference between the new labor history and the old labor history?

GUTMAN There were really two "old" labor histories: that of the Old Left—such as the work of Philip Foner—and that of John R. Commons and his school.[19] At the core of the labor history of the Old Left was a critique of the traditional leadership of the American labor movement. The labor leadership, it was argued, consistently misled well-intentioned workers and thus was responsible for the failure of a sustained socialist movement to emerge in the United States. This "essentialist" critique was made not simply of the craft unions but of the earlier, so-called utopian unions as well. The Knights of Labor, according to the Old Left, were as much the bearers of false consciousness as the American Federation of Labor. This explanation of the absence of a socialist movement in the United States was inadequate and misleading. But it rested on a certain politics and a deterministic philosophy of history. So, too, the history associated with John Commons and Selig Perlman rested on a certain politics. They sought to defend the liberal view of the trade unions as institutions essential for balancing inequalities in capitalist society without transforming that society. Commons and his associates shared assumptions about the nature of American society and American politics, most centrally that the narrow craft union fitted American conditions.

The new labor history also rests on a certain politics and is inspired by a distinctive philosophy of history. Much of it, in this country and in Western Europe, developed in response to and out of the decomposition of classical Marxism. One thinks of someone like Thompson. His work comes out of the Marxist tradition while it reacts against Stalinist historiography. This new labor history rejects the deterministic models that the labor history of the Old Left rested on. But it does not reject the vision of a more egalitarian and democratic society. Nor does it reject democratic socialism. I suspect that most of the new labor historians who have done significant work are men and women who define themselves, in one or another fashion, as socialists. The kinds of questions they ask—forgetting about how they go about answering them, which is often technical—come out of a politics broadly associated with the redefinition of socialism, freeing up socialist theory and practice from the totalitarian shroud it has lived in through most of this century.

Much of the new labor history—at least the best of it—rejects what is essentially the Old Left's version of the Whig fallacy of history. It refuses to look at a period of history simply as a precursor of the moment that we currently are living in. Freeing ourselves from the present in that way brings to life movements, brings to life a politics in the past, that were submerged by the crude presentism of the older labor history, whether of the left or the center.

Q.   How does the new labor history answer the question, Why has there been no mass socialist movement in the United States?

GUTMAN   I don't think that is a well-put historical question. We need to put aside notions that workers' movements have developed properly elsewhere and in the United States they developed improperly. We need to put aside the English model, the French model, and the Cuban model, and then ask a set of very, very tough questions about what American workers actually thought and did—and why. Once we free ourselves of the notion that it should have happened in one particular way, then we stop looking for the reasons why it didn't happen that way. If we don't, then we end up offering explanations like the high rate of social mobility or that workers had the vote in America or a whole series of other single-factor explanations, as answers to what is a nonhistorical question.

Q.   Based on your work for before 1900 and on Montgomery's for the period after 1900, can you make judgments about whether or not workers' movements in these periods were adequate to the historical tasks they faced if they were to achieve their political goals?

GUTMAN   I don't think that way as a historian. What does it mean to talk about historical tasks that workers faced? We are letting in through the back door a notion of fixed and predetermined historical development. We are measuring the American worker (or the French worker or the Polish worker) against an ideal type. That is the Whig fallacy of history once again.

Q.   It is not just the Whig fallacy. Some would call it the Marxist fallacy.

GUTMAN   Yes, there is a Marxist variant of the Whig fallacy. It comes from an essentialist view of workers or the working class, one that emphasizes a predetermined pattern of historical development.

Q. But some would argue that such a notion is central to classical Marxism.

GUTMAN   And it contains within it dangerous notions of vanguard leadership and vanguard parties.

Q. Not necessarily. C. L. R. James, for example, rejects the idea of a vanguard party, but still believes in historical progress and a direction to history; he believes in an essentialism of sorts.

GUTMAN   There is direction, and historians study it. And while I am not so sure about the notion of historical progress, I strongly reject the notion of any vanguard party. As I read James, he has a profoundly anti-Leninist position. Rejection of the vanguard party—and of the problematic out of which it emerged—comes out of the politics of this century. It is not simply a philosophical question. It is based on the real historical experience with what vanguard parties meant to the lives of tens of millions of people.

Q. But vanguard parties are not central to the vision of classical Marxism, the Marxism of Marx. What is central is some notion of historical progress and some direction to history. What is left of Marxism, in your view, when you have stripped away this aspect?

GUTMAN   What is left when you clear away the determinist and teleological elements is good questions that direct your attention to critical ways of looking at ongoing historical processes. A fundamental contribution of nineteenth- and twentieth-century Marxist thinking is a set of questions having to do with the way in which one examines class relations and how they change, the way in which one examines the institutionalization of power, the way in which one examines popular oppositional movements, the way in which one examines the integration of subordinate or exploited groups into a social system. These are some of the very useful questions.

I can put it more concretely. What is going on in Poland, for example, poses a whole series of questions for historians dealing with Poland in the 1950s, 1960s, and 1970s. A central question historians should be examining is what was it in the experience of the Polish workers in the period since World War II—and maybe even before— that gave rise to the Solidarity movement?

That is a useful historical question. Look at any given set of class relations. Most of the time subordinate populations live with their exploitation. They make adjustments. They create institutions to deal with inequality, to deal with the unequal distribution of scarce resources and wealth. They do so without seeking to transform the conditions that create or sustain that inequality. Then, under certain circumstances—none of them predictable—that acceptance is transformed into opposition: Chicago in the 1880s, St. Petersburg in 1905, Gdansk in the 1970s. One subject of great interest to democratic socialists—given the collapse of deterministic models—is the study of the historical conditions under which popular opposition emerges. Why does oppositionality emerge in a particular way? Why not in another way? What are the circumstances that give rise to such movements? Explain their successes or failures?

Q. So, you are saying that while we can't predict a future outbreak of resistance or revolt, historians can study past outbreaks and try to understand why they happened at that particular moment. What is the point?

GUTMAN Opposition movements surface irregularly. They help shape historical process, sometimes radically. A classic, recent example from the United States is that of the civil rights movement. If one reads the literature from the 1930s and 1940s on race relations, little in it gives a clue to the movement that would challenge aspects of an oppressive racial and class structure in the 1950s and 1960s.

Once a movement has emerged, its tenaciousness, its successes, its limitations, are all questions for historians of popular movements, especially if we put aside notions of an elite, vanguard leadership. What sustained the movement? How did the rank and file of the civil rights movement, for example, use everyday (nonpolitical) institutional arrangements that they had developed prior to the 1950s to transform oppressive circumstances in their everyday lives? The same kind of analysis can be made about the rise of the CIO. This kind of history teaches us something genuinely important about everyday struggles and historical change, about human agency. What gives the civil rights movement its great historical importance is the way in which black and white people in the South—but especially blacks—transformed traditional institutions that were mechanisms of adaptation and survival into instrumentalities meant to alter radically the structure of Southern society.

Q. Do you think that a student of popular movements in the past will have something to say about how popular movements should conduct themselves today? Are there lessons to be learned from the past?

GUTMAN Of course, there is a value in studying history. But it surely does not take the form of practical lessons for today. Class and social relations are constantly changing. That is why there is no direct lesson learned out of, say, Homestead.* Events illuminate changing structures and processes at work over time. We also study competing traditions

* Homestead, Pennsylvania, was the company town of the Carnegie Steel Company. During the bloody Homestead strike of 1892, the Amalgamated Association of Iron and Steel Workers controlled the town and succeeded in defeating 300 Pinkerton guards hired to keep the mills operating with scab labor. The strike was subsequently crushed by the state militia, and the steelworkers' union was broken for nearly forty years.

(more than two) over time. And we study the history of popular movements: what gave rise to them, why they went in one direction as contrasted to another. But we don't ransack the past for lessons.

Historical study is liberating for other reasons. The central value of historical understanding is that it transforms historical givens into historical contingencies. It enables us to see the structures in which we live and the inequality people experience as only one among many other possible experiences. By doing that, you free people for creative and critical (or radical) thought. I could give you many examples from the teaching I have done with trade union people in the last few summers. Things that people had assumed were normal in their lives (like smog, or speed-up, or television, or clocks, or racism) are seen to have a beginning, a middle, and sometimes an end. When people come into contact with that perspective, they are better able to think analytically about the structures that impinge upon them.

How ordinary men and women engage those structures—then and now—should concern us. In his argument with Stalinism and determinist Marxism, Jean-Paul Sartre put it very well. He said that the essential question for study—this is a paraphrase—is not what has been done to men and women but what men and women do with what is done to them. That is also a Thompsonian formulation. And this is precisely what the best black writers have been writing for the past fifty years. W. E. B. Du Bois argued for this approach when he wrote *Black Reconstruction*, and it is what C. L. R. James's historical writings are about.

Once you surrender the fixed older forms of historical explanation and process, the future becomes open. It then becomes even more important to analyze and examine the history of those structures and ideologies that shape our lives.

Q. When you drop what you call essentialism, don't you run the risk of the meaning disappearing from the history? Don't you run the risk of encouraging a history where people are studied without any judgments being made about what they are doing and whether it makes sense?

GUTMAN No, I don't think so. We need to be asking ourselves in what ways, if any, working-class presence affected the historical process at changing moments in time. These are important and difficult historical questions. George Rawick, for one, has been asking them for years.[20] They are questions for any country, not just the United States. And the answers to them vary over time. There are so many good examples of work of this sort. Alfred Young's magnificent ongoing study of late-eighteenth-century artisans and crowds addresses such questions.[21] So did David Brody's book on immigrant steelworkers. And there are so many others among the younger historians whose ongoing work continually examines these questions.

The real problem with the new labor history is not a lack of essentialism.

Q. What is the real problem?

GUTMAN There is a compelling need for a new national synthesis. Work in labor history and other areas of social history—indeed, much of the so-called new history—is often quite narrow. We need to pull it all together and see how it makes our politics, our national experience, look different. The old Progressive synthesis collapsed long ago, and the so-called corporate liberal synthesis certainly won't do. It simply projects a disillusionment with the New Deal and with the Old Left's uncritical relationship to Roosevelt backward to other movements and moments. If the New Deal successfully incorporated the working class—and that is an open question—and brought them back into the system with the cooperation of the Communist party, that is no reason to create a historical tradition that has its roots in the National Civic Federation.* The corporate liberal synthesis of twentieth-century American history is an expression of the political pessimism of the 1950s and early 1960s, which is simply being projected backward.

Any adequate new synthesis has to grapple with the problems of periodization and social class. The strength of large synthetic work depends upon appropriate periodization. But that question has hardly been discussed. The new work in labor history—and in women's history and Afro-American history—all poses very subtle problems for those concerned with rewriting the *national* experience. Why haven't those problems been confronted? We need to do so.

This need has become very clear to me in my recent teaching. I continue teaching graduate students. But each summer from 1977 through 1980 I also taught an NEH [National Endowment for the Humanities] history seminar for trade unionists entitled "Americans at Work." And in the past three years I also directed an ongoing, NEH-sponsored semester-long seminar on recent American social history for community college teachers in the metropolitan New York City region (CUNY and SUNY faculty). These colleagues teach history and history-related subjects. The new historical works that engage so many of us in intense research and writing and sometimes even in

---

* Founded in 1900 as an alliance of major industrialists, labor, and the public, the National Civic Federation advocated the reconciliation of capital and labor through the avoidance of strikes, compulsory arbitration, and welfare capitalism. Organized in reponse to the growing strength of the socialist movement, the NCF appealed to Samuel Gompers and conservative trade unionists in the American Federation of Labor and was rejected by new unionists involved in fighting the open-shop movement and in organizing unskilled workers.

sharp controversy have failed to reach these very different audiences. That is evident to me. We write for each other too often. What might interest these and other audiences never gets to them.

Teaching trade unionists and community college colleagues—men and women so different from each other in so many ways—has taught me that there is an audience willing to read American history afresh and, more important, to grapple with historical thinking. We are reaching out to that audience.

A general social history of the American people, incorporating the best recent scholarship, is one way to reach such audiences. And I am involved in such a project—the American Working-Class History Project—and working with a group of historians, filmmakers, and graphic artists: Steve Brier, Bruce Levine, Josh Brown, Kate Pfordresher, Dorothy Fennell, and Dave Brundage. We are funded by the NEH and the Ford Foundation and are well under way to making the best of the "old" and the "new" history accessible to community college students and to out-of-school adults, especially trade unionists. We are putting separate strands together in a multimedia social-history curriculum that includes a two-volume general history of American working people and a series of innovative slide presentations and short documentary films. The first documentary, which we are now producing, sets the nationwide railroad strikes and riots of 1877 in the larger context of America's economic, political, and social transformation after the Civil War.

Q.   In *The Black Family in Slavery and Freedom*, it seems to me that you deal most completely with the kinds of questions about the difference between a developed class and a class in formation that we have been discussing. How do you see the book in relation to other contributions to the history of slavery in the United States?

GUTMAN   One of the central assumptions—perhaps the most central—about slavery by historians before 1960 was that, unlike other exploited groups, the slaves could do very little for themselves. That assumption, ultimately, rested on a common view of the slave family. What made slaves different from other exploited groups was not simply that they were owned (which was, of course, central to their experience) but that they were incapable, because of the fragmented nature of the family experience, of transmitting a changing culture over time. The fragmented nature of the family was the reason offered to explain why diverse African practices and beliefs disappeared so quickly. It was offered as the reason "Sambo" really existed.

The slaves, in this view, carried little into relationships with their owners. How could they? Tradition and experience, especially in an illiterate population, are transmitted orally. What was missing in the slave experience, as contrasted to the experience of peasants or wage workers, were the passageways through which class and cultural beliefs could travel. That is what *The Black Family* is about. It shows how the slaves could transmit and develop their own experiences and general beliefs across generations and over time. It is not about the family as such. At the heart of the analysis is an argument about the structure of the slave experience. The seemingly endless comparative data on naming practices was a way of demonstrating—proving—that slaves as a developing class could transfer beliefs between generations. It wasn't simply that they knew their grandparents' names, though that is important for some purposes. The significance of slave naming practices is that events that had occurred sixty or a hundred years earlier had remained part of their life experience.

What I uncovered, in other words, were the passageways through which the experiences and beliefs of these people traveled. Some other historians may have assumed that such passageways existed. But the evidence in *The Black Family* demonstrated their existence. Suddenly, therefore, the same kind of historical questions can be asked of slaves that historians ask about any other exploited population. The *very same* questions! On the first page of *The Black Family* I noted that it was a book about a special aspect of working-class history: the methods, the questions, they were the same. That was not mere rhetoric. I meant it, for better or worse. The answers, of course, would be different because the exploitative relationships differed, but the questions were similar because a similar historical interaction had been uncovered. The slaves could affect historical process. It is precisely what Jean-Paul Sartre was writing about, what Ralph Ellison was writing about, what E. P. Thompson was writing about.

Without these passageways the history of slavery lacked a time dimension. It was impossible to describe changing structures and beliefs. As a result, no one could explain what many very good historians (such as W. E. B. Du Bois, Joel Williamson, and Willie Lee Rose) had discerned about the behavior and beliefs of black people after emancipation.[22] We could not understand that behavior because of the way slavery as a social system had been conceptualized by at least two generations of historians and social scientists.

Let me be more precise. Historians of slavery in the 1950s and early 1960s explained variations in slave behavior by emphasizing variations in their treatment by their owners. In other words, variations in slave behavior were attributed to external factors. Did the slave live on a plantation? Did the slave live on a farm? Did the slave live in a town, a city, or a rural area? Did the slave live in the Upper South or the Lower South? Did the slave have a decent owner or a harsh owner? All the "variables"—to use that ugly word—that historians used to explain slave behavior were external stimuli. The slave did no more than react to these stimuli. Variations in slave behavior were a function of their treatment. The study of slaves, not surprisingly, became largely the study of their owners. It was "top-down" history at its worst. The slaves were acted upon. They could only be acted upon! That flowed from the assumptions most historians made about either the slaves or the structure of slave society.

In *The Black Family* these assumptions were shown to be entirely mistaken by studying slave behavior in areas very different from the usual concerns of labor historians—household arrangements, naming practices, marriage rules, sexual practices, and related matters. Such class behavior was studied among groups of slaves who *experienced their enslavement differently*. That is the essential point. The case studies in the book emphasized diverse types of slave class experiences, a point many critics ignored. There were slaves who lived in the Upper South and in the Lower South. There were slaves who had decent, paternalistic owners (among the nicest owners one could ever want, I guess), and there were slaves who had cruel owners. There were slaves who worked for men born plantation owners, and slaves who worked for farmers who became plantation owners. There were slaves who suffered relatively little family breakup, and slaves who suffered such breakup regularly. The types of slaves missing from the analysis were rice-plantation slaves and urban slaves. Every other kind of nineteenth-century slave setting was in the analysis. Thus, nearly all the variables were studied.

And then, in spite of the differences, there were regularities in familial and sexual behavior. How could we explain that? It could not be explained by the relationship of these slaves to their immediate owners because those relationships were so varied. The explanation had to start with who these slaves had been before they entered into that immediate relationship (or with who their parents and grandparents had been and what they believed), and it had to go on to who they became. Generational (family) linkages, at least for these diverse Afro-American slaves, connected up the era of class formation to that of the more developed slave class. This hard evidence forced me back into the eighteenth century to argue in *The Black Family* that understanding nineteenth-century slave behavior and belief (the developed class) required a reexamination of the process by which Africans first became a social class in North America (the new class). You see, we find ourselves asking the same questions we would ask if we were studying about any other subordinate population.

Kin and quasi-kin connections served at least two functions for the developing slave class early in the Afro-American experience. They served first as passageways into which and through which experiences and ideas flowed (such as Toussaint l'Ouverture, the Declaration of

Independence, the colonization and abolition movements, and even the difference between a nice and a bad owner). The existence of these passageways makes it possible to uncover how slave ideas changed over time, not just ideas about the family. Second, kin networks and concepts of kin obligation functioned as the basis of larger communal relationships and beliefs. Who took care of slave children when their parents died? Owners? Not in the records I read. We learn how the real uncle and aunt became generalized uncles and aunts. When teenagers were sold into the Deep South, for example, they were sold into newly developing slave social networks filled with generalized slave notions of quasi-kin obligation. They experienced deep pain but were not sold to a foreign country.

We have redefined the changing structure within which Africans and Afro-Americans experienced slavery. Without such structures the slaves would have been crushed by the experience; Stanley Elkins was probably right about that.[23] But the slaves were neither crippled nor made totally dependent. The reason my book focused on the family was that the *assumptions* historians made about the family affected how they explained slave behavior. The assumptions were wrong. That much is clear. So we have to look at the evidence afresh, starting in the eighteenth century. When that is done, some of the arguments in my book will be put aside and others modified. That's as it should be. But I very much doubt that the essential arguments in *The Black Family*, the ones that restore structure and process to the study of Afro-American slaves, will be seriously undermined. A changing set of class relationships has been shown to exist. All aspects of that master-slave relationship need to be restudied, and restudied over time—that is, historically.

Q. What do you think historians of slavery and the slave experience ought next to be turning their attention to?

GUTMAN The formation of the North American slave class is perhaps the most important untold story in Afro-American history and in eighteenth-century American history. The only book that seriously addresses the issue is Peter Wood's *Black Majority*, a very good book.[24] How was that new class formed? The suggestion by some reviewers of *The Black Family* that I argued that slaves learned nothing from whites is ridiculous. The argument I made was that the behavior of slaves in the 1830s, 1840s, and 1850s was not determined simply by their immediate relationship with their owners. And then I went on to suggest, on the basis of scattered evidence, that the formative eighteenth-century period involved the creation of a new subordinate class and culture. Ira Berlin and I have studied mid- and late-eighteenth-century plantation records comparable to those used in *The Black Family*, and we can sketch the beginnings of common Afro-American slave familial cultural patterns in diverse South Carolina, North Carolina, Maryland, and Virginia settings prior to the War for Independence. It is possible to talk about a new class (Afro-American slaves) that is reproducing itself and transmitting a distinctive but changing culture. Old African cultures changed in North America, and African slaves and their immediate descendants borrowed heavily from the mainstream white culture. That happened between 1720 and 1770 (ironically, when the largest number of Africans were sold to North America).

That story has yet to be fully told. What did the slaves encounter when they arrived here? Who bought the slaves? What did it mean to an English Midlands farmer who had emigrated to North America and bought a slave? And what did it mean to the slave? What religion did he or she come into contact with? (If Rhys Isaac is right—and he is one of our very best historians—the kind of religious experiences slaves came into contact with in the eighteenth century would make a great deal of difference.[25]) We don't have answers to these questions now. But we can answer them, and there is a spectacular story to be worked out.

We also need fresh study of the interregional slave trade and what it did to the *developed* Afro-American culture. We should start by defining the interregional slave trade as the Second Middle Passage, one experienced primarily by the children and grandchildren of Africans who had experienced an earlier Middle Passage of their own. How did the distinctive slave culture, hammered out by the early generations of slaves, prepare people to deal with the terrible experience of the Second Middle Passage? With the pain of separation? A big book needs to be written just on this subject.

When one looks at the behavior of victims of the Second Middle Passage during the Civil War and immediately afterward and then compares it with the behavior of slaves in other parts of the South who were spared that ordeal, the behavior doesn't look very different. I am not talking about family matters, but about serving in the Union Army, about fighting to keep one's children from being apprenticed and reenslaved, about refusing to sign unfair labor contracts (or going to military court to get claims on contracts). When we look at ex-slave behavior in East Texas, in Mississippi, and in Louisiana, it doesn't look very different from that in North Carolina and Virginia. Ten years ago I would have argued that it *had* to be different. But it wasn't different. That means that the interregional slave trade following upon the industrial revolution facilitated the spread and then the change of late-eighteenth-century and early-nineteenth-century Upper South Afro-American culture. That is why it is so important to know *when* that distinctive culture was formed. And if that makes me a "culturalist," so be it.

This is the context, I think, in which we can best understand Eugene Genovese's work. He posed some important questions. My difficulty is with how he went about answering them. A central question raised in *Roll, Jordan, Roll: The World the Slaves Made* is the effect slaves had on their owners.[26] A splendid question. To answer it one needs to know who the slaves were early in time and how the master-slave relationship was formed and developed.

Think of it this way. Suppose one was writing a book on ironworkers and steelworkers in Pittsburgh called *Roll, Monongahela, Roll: The World the Steelworkers Made*. How would that book begin? It is not a book about the steel industry. It is not a book about class relations in the steel industry. It is subtitled *The World the Steelworkers Made*. Would it begin with a 150-page essay quoting from and explicating Andrew Carnegie's *Autobiography* and his letters? If one writes about the world the steelworkers *made*, the book should begin with the men before they were steelworkers and study how they *became* steelworkers. It would begin with them before they experienced Andrew Carnegie and then watch a world being made as they become steelworkers and interact with Andrew and his factories. Obviously this is precisely the innovative and bold structure of *The Making of the English Working Class*. We don't begin with industrial capitalism already imposed and study strands of upper-class ideology. We begin with the world of the artisan. We begin with the world of the handicraft weaver. We begin with the world before modern capitalism. Then the interaction is intense, painful, sometimes violent, and even creative.

The way in which you examine a world people make is to show that world in formation. A major conceptual problem in *Roll, Jordan, Roll* is that it ignores class formation. A static class relationship is probed for several hundred pages, sometimes imaginatively and brilliantly. We are presented with a fully developed slave system. Class relations and ideologies are described only in the late slave period, the decades immediately prior to emancipation.

The problem with such an approach is that when you freeze a moment in time to examine a structural relationship, you cannot neglect the process by which that relationship was formed, how it developed. If you either ignore or misunderstand that process, then you can give almost any meaning you want to the relationship and to its constituent parts. What struck me on rereading *Roll, Jordan, Roll* is that it is so very functionalist. It is as if we are being told, "This is the way that society worked, why there was so little rebellion, and why slaves and their owners made it through the day and night."

This analysis rests upon a central assertion. Genovese insists that the slaves took the prevailing ideology of the plantation class (paternalism) and transformed it into its opposite, a very interesting idea. It is the heart of the analysis. In much the same way, other historians argue that the Lynn, Massachusetts, shoe workers, for example, took eighteenth-century republican ideology and transformed it in ways appropriate to their new condition as dependent Yankee wage earners. There is fine evidence illustrating that transformation in the works of Paul Faler and Alan Dawley. But Genovese's insight is never made concrete. There isn't empirical evidence showing that it happened, showing how it happened, or showing when it happened. In 1730? In 1770? 1800? 1830? The *dates* are important. We don't know. It just happened!

Q. Genovese does present evidence *that* it happened. The problem may be that most of it was indirect.

GUTMAN What is indirect evidence? And where is it in the book? Given the book's structure, this argument itself cannot be made. You cannot use a static model to explain a transference and transformation of ideology between a superordinate and a subordinate class. It is that simple. The book lacks a time dimension. Ruling-class ideology therefore cannot be transformed. Class relations and ideologies do not develop and change over time.

Q. Aren't your criticisms of the work of Robert Fogel and Stanley Engerman in *Time on the Cross* very similar?[27]

GUTMAN Yes. The argument in *Time on the Cross* hinged on whether Fogel and Engerman could demonstrate the superior efficiency and productivity of the slave economy. Once convinced that they had demonstrated the slave system's efficiency and productivity, they sought an explanation for it. And they argued that the efficiency and productivity of the system resulted from a positive incentive system constructed by the slaveowners. The slaves did the best they could in such a system, and in the process a different slave emerged from the one we knew if we had read about slavery in the 1950s and early 1960s. Sambo became a black Horatio Alger. Fogel and Engerman made the slaves look different but only by first making their owners look different. That's not the way to write the history of a dependent class, any dependent class!

Genovese did the same thing, only differently. Resident ownership and the relatively early need to reproduce the slave labor force, he argued in *The World the Slaveholders Made* (1969), created the material conditions that encouraged the spread of paternalist ideology among nineteenth-century planters. He asserted the prevalence of that new ideology, but he never demonstrated that it was widespread. These are not trivial points, because in *Roll, Jordan, Roll* the central thesis rested on the capacity of the slaves to transform popular paternalist notions of duty and obligation into common slave notions of right. Remaking the owners into paternalists served Genovese in the same way making the owners into profit-maximizing industrial relations specialists had served Fogel and Engerman. Genovese made the slaves look different but only by *first* making their owners look different. The central argument in both books does not rest on evidence so much as on abstract theoretical models, albeit different ones. And that meant either ignoring or minimizing important lived historical experiences that do not fit into those models.

Take the case of the interregional slave trade in North America. The movement of slaves in North America, between 1790 and 1860, from the Upper South to the Lower South was probably the largest single internal forced migration in the world in the nineteenth century. That's real lived historical experience. How many moved with their owners? How many moved in family groups? The best evidence we have demonstrates that for older slaves living in Mississippi and northern Louisiana perhaps as many as one out of every three or four marriages was forcibly broken by the interregional slave trade. A staggering percentage. No one, to my knowledge, has challenged it.

To someone interested in slave society, or the world the slaves made, a central question is, How did slaves experience so high a rate of marital breakup? These data were available to Genovese and to Fogel and Engerman before their books appeared. They cited its publication in the *Annales* in 1972, but never considered it. The models that each had constructed to explain slave behavior and slave society were not compatible with a high level of slave family breakup.

Such evidence is central in *The Black Family*. The first chapter considered the contradictory nature of important slave social experiences among the *last* generation of slaves. It demonstrated that a slave's experiences with his or her owner was, on the level of family mainte- nance, profoundly contradictory. If that was so, a second question quickly followed: Did their beliefs and practices as slaves prepare them to deal with and understand those contradictions? If so, why? The next two-thirds of the book dealt at length with how slaves developed certain common institutional arrangements and beliefs to mediate the owner's abuse and exploitation. If none had existed, as Elkins shrewdly argued, the slaves would have been crippled by their oppression. There is no question about it. An isolated slave (or family) could not sustain himself (or itself) in such a setting. However difficult, the slaves, especially in the eighteenth century, had to forge new institutions and beliefs to sustain them in their oppression. That happened, and *The Black Family* showed how some—not all, by any means—of those institutions and beliefs were formed and transmuted.

In other words, there had to be connectedness. The important discovery in the book, I think, is not that slaves lived in families that were frequently broken, but that the family could serve the slaves as a way of creating social and class connections far more important than the family. Call these connections what you will! Once you know such connections exist, then you can also find out when, why, and how they came together. We know those connections began well before the invention of the cotton gin. That is very clear. These new connections, occurring so early in time, make the entire Afro-American experience look different. And they make the slaves look different. And, of course, they make the master-slave relationship look different, too. Just how these new slaves dealt with their owners over time is still unstudied. I didn't study that changing relationship. No one has done that yet. And without such study, the last thing I was going to do, in *The Black Family*, was to put what I had uncovered back into the conventional picture. To do that would have been ridiculous. If one essential part of the picture is changed, then the other parts of the picture also change. It becomes a different picture, a very, very different history.

10

THE BLACK FAMILY IN SLAVERY
AND FREEDOM
A Revised Perspective

I

IT WAS only in the 1960s and the 1970s that historians began seriously to question the legacy bequeathed them by E. Franklin Frazier's influential social history of the Afro-American family. Before the 1960s, of course, a generation of historians, in part influenced by the sociologist Frazier, explicitly rejected the racial assumptions common in pre-1940 historical scholarship and significantly rewrote the history of Afro-American slavery. Their pathbreaking works shared Frazier's antiracist and harsh environmentalist assumptions. Exceptional (or privileged) slave men and women were shown to have triumphed over the system, but the system's exploitative severity molded most ordinary slaves into a classic *Lumpenproletariat*, a powerless aggregate of displaced African and Afro-American men, women, and children. Before the 1960s, others than historians, the novelist Ralph Ellison prominent among them, disputed Frazier's environmental determinism and its underlying reactive assumption that interpreted slave belief and behavior as little more than an imperfect imitation of the dominant culuture and as evidence of adaptation to a crude "opportunity" model. Ellison asked whether enslaved Africans and their Afro-American descendants could "live and develop over three hundred years simply by reacting." In the 1940s and the 1950s, few North American historians were even asking such questions, much less examining historical evidence to answer them.

The shift among students of Afro-American history in the 1960s and the 1970s to the "Ellison question" did not occur in a vacuum. Nor was it simply a response to the civil rights and black power movements. In these same years, historians studying subordinate social classes other than Afro-Americans grew increasingly dissatisfied with the prevailing reactive models used to explain their belief and behavior. That mode of historical analysis was found to be incomplete, mislead-

This essay is reprinted from Gene D. Lewis, ed., *New Historical Perspectives: Essays on the Black Experience in Antebellum America* (Cincinnati, 1985), 7–36.

ing, reductionist, and overdetermined. The so-called Ellison question therefore was quite similar to the questions that increasingly concerned those European and American labor and social historians who had gone beyond reactive models in seeking to understand lower-class formation and development, patterns of lower-class belief and behavior, and the changing relations between subordinate and dominant social classes. New and often contradictory evidence directed their attention to what Jean-Paul Sartre defined as "the essential." "The essential," Sartre wrote, "is not what 'one' has done to man, but what man does with what 'one' has done to him." Sartre had reformulated the Ellison question. The two called attention to the limitations of reactive models in studying the history of all exploited groups. That mode of anaysis distorted the history of white workers as well as that of black slaves and poor ex-slaves. But no group's history had been more completely twisted than that of slaves and poor ex-slaves.

Such misunderstanding rested, in good part, upon a profound misperception of the historical development of the slave family, and especially the enlarged slave kin group, in the century and a half preceding the general emancipation. Important *assumptions* about the slave and the poor ex-slave family affected the questions historians asked about slaves and poor ex-slaves in general. With notable exceptions, a vast and often useful historical scholarship prior to 1960 studied either what was done for slaves or what was done to them because it was assumed as a given that most slaves could do little more than react to diverse external stimuli. It followed that the study of slaves became mostly the study of what owners did to and for them. The assumptions historians made about either slavery or slaves, not the availability of evidence, dictated the questions that deserved study.

The notion of the inability of most slaves to do much more than react to diverse external stimuli rested on the widely held belief that fragmented and discontinuous slave family experiences either increased slave dependence upon their owners or created the condition of slave or slave-family social isolation. Each circumstance narrowed the choices slave men and women could make. A widespread discontinuous family experience over time made it nearly impossible for slaves to retain, to accumulate, and to transform and then transmit distinctive but changing slave (or class) experiences and beliefs from one generation to another. Unlike other, far less constrained subordinate social classes, slaves could not sustain cumulative traditions: evolving rules, social norms, and cultural beliefs esential to organizing their everyday work and life; interpreting and then dealing with their oppression; socializing and protecting their children; interacting with owners, overseers, and other nonslaves; and developing enlarged social networks called institutions. The absence of such traditions severely limited choices slaves could make, and not surprisingly, the choices slaves regularly made—clues to their beliefs—went unstudied.

The major legacy this generation of scholars bequeathed to historians had far less to do with such "controversial" subjects as the stability of slave marriages, "matrifocality," and "African survivals" than with the assertion that an incapacity rooted in recurrent family fragmentation made it impossible for ordinary slave field hands and laborers to interact with mainstream cultural practices and beliefs and simultaneously develop and sustain historically derived values and behavior patterns of their own. That incapacity—whatever its cause—isolated the slaves from the mainstream of historical analysis. Social class, E. P. Thompson reminds us, is a historical concept, "arising from the analysis of diachronic process, of repeated regularities of behavior over time." "Class," he adds, ". . . is (or ought to be) a historical category, describing people in relationship over time, and the ways in which they become conscious of their relationships, separate, unite, enter into struggle, form institutions, and transmit values in class ways." The generational fragmentation of slave families made it seem unncessary for historians of slavery to study process and to probe how slaves transmitted "values in class ways." The historian asked different questions about slaves than about other exploited social classes. Such groups managed to accumulate new historical experiences and transform them into institutional arrangements and alternative belief systems through which they interpreted their oppression and interacted with their oppressors. Enslaved Afro-Americans could not do so.

II

WE NOW know that this entire view of the enslaved Afro-American is mistaken. The study of slave behavior over time has demonstrated the inadequacy of the assumptions on which earlier reactive models of slave belief and behavior rested. Studying some of the common choices slave men and women made has uncovered cumulative Afro-American traditions that developed over time and spread over space. Studying slave domestic arrangements and household formation on six developing and very different plantations in the century preceding the emancipation reveals two important uniformities in these settings. First, at all times and on all six plantations the typical slave household was double-headed. Over the full family cycle, most slave children grew up in such households, including those sold or separated from their families of origin for other involuntary reasons. Second, and equally important, at all times and on all six plantations households headed by a single parent—the mother—existed over the full family cycle. These households had not been broken by the sale or death of a father; a male parent had never resided in them. The relative importance of these different domestic arrangements varied on the plantations studied, but these variations are far less significant than the coexistence of different (and possibly competing) types of slave households in all plantation settings. Such diversity suggests that the fact that most slaves settled into double-headed arrangements is evidence of owner indifference and of slave preference. Owners surely did not sponsor competing types of slave domestic arrangements. No evidence exists, moreover, that slaveowners either prevented slave women from heading single-parent households over the full family cycle or punished them for doing so. Slaves often chose between alternate types of domestic arrangements. The choices they made are clues—nothing more—to their beliefs.

Yet other regularities associated with their family life are found among the slaves on these six plantations. What is now known about their families—and I mean the families headed by field hands and laborers—can be briefly summarized. Unless broken by an owner, usually by sale or following an estate division (that happened, according to the best available evidence, to about one in six or seven marriages and even more families), most slave marriages lasted until the death of a spouse. This was true even though slave divorce was permitted. Most slave children grew up knowing a slave mother and a slave father. Prenuptial intercourse and childbirth occurred often, but most unmarried slave mothers later took husbands and remained with them until death. Some slave mothers never married. A slave father often had a son named for him, but it rarely happened that a slave daughter was given her mother's name. Slave blood cousins rarely married. Slave children—at least 40 percent in the third and fourth generations—were named for kin, usually blood kin (paternal and maternal aunts and uncles, grandparents, and even great-grandparents). The slave surname usually served to connect a slave to his or her distant slave family of origin, not to an immediate owner. Obligations based on blood and marital ties, finally, became the basis of enlarged slave conceptions of social (or class) obligation.

Some of the common practices associated with slave family life differed from those found in the mainstream culture. Although white marriage rules in general were retained intact, it seems clear that blood-cousin marriages were sanctioned among large plantation owners. Slave exogamy contrasted sharply with planter endogamy. Slave sexual beliefs and practices also differed from those of their owners. No evidence shows that slaves internalized the so-called Victorian ideal which subordinated sexual intercourse to marriage, though slaves scorned marital infidelity as did mainstream cultural norms. By the second quarter of the nineteenth century, if not earlier, Anglo-American cultural norms no longer sanctioned prenuptial intercourse among white women, much less childbirth prior to marriage. But contemporaries—slaves and former slaves among them—observed the prevalence of prenuptial intercourse among slaves. Evidence of childbirth prior to marriage, moreover, is found in all plantation slave birth registers. Its relative importance remains unclear, but perhaps as many as three in ten married slave women had one or more children prior to marriage.

Slaves and their owners differed in their attitudes, toward women who had all their children outside of marriage. The dominant culture rejected such women. Slaves did not. Some slave mothers never married and had as many as eight children. Their families of origin did not reject such women. Children born to these women regularly had the names of maternal kin. During the Civil War, moreover, such women (who described themselves as "single" mothers) regularly accompanied their parents and grown siblings to federal refugee camps.

The ways in which slaves and their owners named newborn children for members of their immediate family differed. Owners and other whites regularly named a son for his father and a daughter for her mother. A slave father often had a son named for him, but it almost never happened that a daughter had her slave mother's name. Sometimes a daughter had her father's given name and might be called Josephine or Georgeanna. A slave child's legal status followed that of its mother, and slaveowners rarely recorded a father's name in plantation birth lists. But slaves regularly named sons for fathers. Fathers were more likely to be separated from children than mothers. Naming a child for its father therefore confirmed that dyadic tie and gave it an assured continuity that complemented the close contact that bound the slave child to its mother.

Important choices slave men and women made affecting their domestic lives have been briefly described. The common choices so far reported come almost entirely from studying six plantation communities over time. Six is not a small number because each of these developing plantation settings differed from the others in significant ways. The differences are usually those emphasized by historians who find variations in owner behavior sufficient to explain variations in slave behavior. They include location, type of ownership, size, economic function, the age of a slave community ("time"), and slave sale, purchase, and gift-transfer. On some plantations, the slaves grew cotton. Others labored in the tobacco and sugar fields. Some had resident owners; others were absentee-owned. Owners included Southern-born whites and Yankee migrants to the South. Some owners were descended from planters; others started as farmers and became planters. Some of the plantations started in the Deep South after 1830; others had a longer life-span. Some of the slaves had decent owners;

others lived in less favorable circumstances. The slaves in these settings differed in many ways from each other, but similar domestic arrangements, kin networks, sexual behavior, marriage rules, and naming practices existed in all six settings. Such evidence in no way means that the slave family was—as some have suggested—"autonomous." The institutional arrangements that exist among all subordinate groups and classes, and especially among slaves, cannot be autonomous. These distinctive practices in diverse settings in which enslaved men and women experienced their oppression differently do no more than reveal the limitations of even the most sophisticated reactive models.

Even more is known than these important (and incomplete) details about slave domestic arrangements and about certain distinctive slave family beliefs and practices. Studying what slave men and women did shows why durable Afro-American domestic institutions and norms sustaining them developed in diverse slave settings in the century before the emancipation, and did so despite the severe constraints imposed among the slaves, the frequent involuntary breakup of their marriages and families, and the absence of any legal protection for their families. That happened because the slaves as a developing social class (made up mostly of field hands and common laborers) forged a widespread, adaptive, and distinctive kinship system out of their African and American experiences, processes (as we shall soon see) that began well before the invention of the cotton gin and even before the American War for Independence. Uncoverng the enlarged slave kin group—not the isolated slave "nuclear family" but the relations between slave families of the same and especially of different generations—tells us something new about Afro-American slaves and something of paramount importance about the Afro-American historical experience. This evidence does not mean that slaves lived in "stable" families. Nor does it mean that mainstream cultural beliefs and practices were either unknown to the slaves or unused by them. Intead, this evidence tells us how it was possible for cumulative slave traditions— rules for everyday living—to develop. It allows us to study the process by which Africans became Afro-Americans and by which a new distinctive social class emerged and developed. It redefines the *context* that shaped the choices slave men and women regularly made.

That slave men and women attached great importance to relations between families or different generations and to extended kin is revealed in historical sources other than reconstructed plantation birth lists. Three letters indicate these attachments and cast grave doubt on the arguments of those historians who identify affection with affluence. The first was written in 1807 and sent by the Virginia slave Gooley to her former owner who had moved to Kentucky and taken some of Gooley's children and other blood kin with her:

You will please to tell my Sister Clary not to let my poor children Suffer & tell her she must allso write & inform me how she & my children are. . . . Mr. Miller is now on the brink of death, & is about to sell 40 of his Negroes and it is likely Joshua may be one. I wish to stay with him as long as possible as you must know its very bad to part man and wife. I should be glad to no what sort of life Clary leads . . . be pleased to inform me how my little daughter Judith is & if she is now injoying health. . . . P.S. . . . old Granny Judy goes about and that is all. . . .

The second letter was written fifty years later, in 1857. The Georgia rice planter Charles C. Jones sold Cash, Phoebe, and some of their children. A letter arrived from them postmarked New Orleans:

Please tell my daughter Clarissa and Nancy a heap how a doo for me Pheaby and Cash and Cashes son James. . . . Please tell them that their sister Jane died the first of Feby . . . Clarissa your affectionate Mother and Father send a heap of Love to you and your husband and my GrandChildren Phebea. Mag. & Cloe. John. Judy. Sue. My aunt Aufy sinena and Minton and Little Plaska. . . . Give our love to Cashes Brother Porter and his wife Patience. Victoria gives her love to her Cousin Beck and Miley. . . .

A former slave wrote the third letter a year and a half after the general emancipation. His sister had written seeking funds to return to their home in Maryland.

My dear Sister
I take my pen in hand to write a few lines to inform you i received your leter and was so glad to hear from you. This is the third leter i have wrote to you since i heard that i had a sister in the land of of [sic] the living; and i dont know wheather you got my letters or not. i am living in Maryland at Miss Nancy Jones with my relatives. Your Father is living and well. all your cousins send love to you. i am sory that your husband has left you in distress. you must write to me and tell me the news, how all is getting on out where you are and what you are doing, and when i get a letter from you i will try (to) help you to get here with me. and tell me who you are living with. i have been sole too to virginia and to North Caryline for E(i)gt(h)een yeers. u have been Back three years to Maryland. i am well at this time. i shall close by saying write as soon as you can and believe me

Your loving Brother
John Rone

That slaves attached such importance to the enlarged kin group (as contrasted with the immediate family) escaped the attention of most owners. No record survives indicating that owners noticed that slaves did not marry blood cousins. Indeed, no record survives indicating an awareness of general slave marriage rules. A single birth list—that recorded in 1773–1774 by Charles Carroll—indicates kin ties beyond the immediate slave family. Owners rarely if ever recorded the naming of a slave child for its slave aunt, uncle, or grandparent. Such naming occurred frequently. A single source records the concern of an overseer for the extended slave family. The slave James Williams fled Alabama in the 1830s. He had been a driver on a cotton plantation and reported: "It was the object of the overseer to separate me in feeling and interest as widely as possible from my suffering brethren and sisters. I had relations among the field-hands, and used to call them my cousins. He forbid me doing so, and told me that if I acknowledged relationship with any of the hands I should be flogged for it. . . ."

III

THE ENLARGED slave kin network served the slaves in two distinct ways. Structure and process, and the relationship between the two, are essential for understanding how all exploited and subordinate social classes are formed, develop, and change over time. That perspective has been absent in most studies of enslaved populations. We now know that intergenerational slave kin and quasi-kin linkages served as slave passageways through time, connecting changing structures and allowing the historians to compare slave belief and behavior over time. What filled these passageways requires careful study, but their presence is indisputable and therefore restores the slaves to the mainstream of historical analysis. Their presence also supports the appropriateness of a bicultural model for studying all aspects of slave behavior over time. Changing but nevertheless historical slave notions of right and wrong as well as slave notions of legitimate slave social and cultural practices were taught to children by immediate and distant older kin. Such an enlarged perspective allows us to see the slave family as far more than an owner-sponsored device to reproduce the labor force and maintain social control. If owners encouraged family formation to either reproduce the labor force or discipline the adult male worker (and these two processes are not necessarily similar), that decision had profound, if unanticipated, social and cultural consequences among the slaves. Intergenerational linkages developed. Passageways for a developing slave culture shaped the beliefs of the new subordinate class. "I suspect," Frederick Olmsted said of slaves and their owners in the 1850s, "that the great trouble and anxiety of Southern gentlemen is—How, without quite destroying the capabilities of the negro for any work at all, to prevent him from learning to take care of himself." Most slaves were learning to "take care" of themselves from kin and quasi-kin.

The kin nework served other functions than that of passageway. Obligations rooted in kin ties developed over time into obligations between slaves unconnected to one another by blood or marital ties. It is well known that slaves and their owners often addressed older slaves by kin titles, such as "aunt" and "uncle." No evidence has been found indicating that whites used such terms of address prior to 1800. Slaves (and I mean Africans, not Afro-Americans) did so before that time. On slave ships, according to Orlando Patterson, "it was customary for children to call parents' shipmates 'uncle' and 'aunt' " and even for Middle Passage adults to "look upon each other's children mutually as their own." Later in time, kin terms of address toward non-kin-related slaves were used frequently by slaves and their owners. Owners used such nonreciprocal terms of address to show personal attachment to favored slaves and to define essential status differences between slaves and nonslaves. Slaves did so for very different reasons. They had real aunts and uncles and had reason to address such men and women by appropriate kin titles. But parents and other adult slaves also taught slave children to address *all* older slaves as "aunt" and "uncle."

Making children do that socialized them into the enlarged slave community, not the family. "They show great respect for age as is manifest from one custom of theirs," said a Yankee teacher in wartime Virginia; "they always call an older person Aunt or Uncle. We had two servants living with us. One was a boy and the other a girl. The boy who was younger always called the girl Aunt." Years before, a Northern white met an elderly Mississippi plantation slave whose owner said, "Uncle Jacob was the regulator on the plantation; . . . a *word* or *look* from him, addressed to younger slaves, had more efficiency than a *show* from the overseer." Kin terms of address taught young slaves to respect older ones, kin and non-kin alike. Such persons had authority within the slave community and were given status by being invested with symbolic, or fictive, kin titles. Socializing children in this way, moreover, also bound them to fictive kinsmen and kinswomen, preparing them in the event that death or sale separated them from parents and other blood kin.

Fictive kin, or quasi-kin, played yet other roles in developing slave communities, binding unrelated slave adults to one another and thereby infusing these groups with conceptions of reciprocity and obligation that had initially flowed from kin obligations. Over time, obligations toward a brother or a niece became obligations toward a fellow slave or that slave's children. Fictive aunts and uncles bound children to quasi-kin outside the immediate slave family, and the ties between a slave child and its fictive aunts and uncles bound that child's parents to such persons. That much is suggested by Sidney Mintz and Eric Wolf's study of ritual coparenthood and Esther Goody's study of proparenthood.[1] In modern Western societies, Goody observes, "all parental roles are concentrated within the nuclear family," but such roles "are potentially available for sharing among kin or even with unrelated neighbors or friends." Such sharing often serves other purposes than caring for deprived children. It is also a way of "forging links between adults," a way in which "many societies make use of bonds between parent and child." Mintz and Wolf suggest that ritual coparentage created quasi-kin ties between a child's parents and that child's ceremonial sponsors, ties that made "the immediate social environment more stable." According to them, the type of class and social structure affected the choice of quasi-kin. A relatively uniform social and class structure meant that coparenthood was "prevailingly horizontal (intra-class) in character," but the presence of "several interacting classes" meant that coparenthood might also be structured "vertically (inter-class)."

Afro-American slaves were never a self-contained social class, a fact that affected how individual slaves sought protection for themselves and especially for their children. Some, usually privileged slaves and especially those belonging to a family over more than one generation, found such protection in modified reciprocal coparental relationships with owners. But not all slaves could (or wanted to) have the protection resulting from such cross-class linkages. And most owners felt no such obligation toward their slaves. Slaves developed alternative, if fragile, means for protecting themselves and their children. Fictive kinsmen and kinswomen—the generalized slave uncle and aunt—served as very important instrumentalities in furthering group solidarities and in ordering a daily life regularly disordered by the choices slaveowners made. Fictive kinship complemented exogamous marriage rules in distancing slaves from their owners and thereby weakening dependence based upon ownership.

Eighteenth-century Africans lived in diverse social settings in which shared kinship beliefs and practices bound an immediate family to its family of origin and assigned significant roles to adult siblings in newly formed families. That is why slave children's calling their parents' shipmates aunt and uncle is so important. It is entirely improbable that these were "real" kin. Initial enslavement shattered kin ties for all but a few Africans. The conversion of kin relationships into symbolic (or quasi-) kin ties on slave ships is evidence of active survival strategy and cultural change. The old was used to deal with the new, and in turn, the old was transformed. Let us shift from the slave ship to the slave plantation, from the enslaved African to the Afro-American slave, and from the mid-eighteenth to the mid-nineteenth century. Teaching Afro-American children to call all adult slaves aunt and uncle converted plantation non-kin slave relationships into quasi-kin relationships, binding slave adults in networks of obligation that extended beyond primordial blood groups. Communal ties based on quasi-kin connections emerged, flowing outward and upward from adaptive Afro-American domestic arrangements and kin networks that developed among all slaves. The sale of children from immediate families as well as the breakup of marriages increased the importance of quasi-kin obligations. A young slave sold from the Upper to the Lower South between 1800 and 1860 (and between 750,000 and 1,000,000 men, women, and children were moved in that migration, the largest internal forced migration in the nineteenth-century Western world) was cut off from his or her immediate Upper South family but found many fictive aunts and uncles in the Lower South. During the Civil War, the consequences of quasi-kin obligations also revealed themselves dramatically. Despite the wartime devastation, the disruption of the plantation system, and the emancipation, Northern soldiers and missionaries found very few orphan children among the slaves and ex-slaves. Children cut off from their parents and other older kin were being cared for by neighbors.

An overall historical process associated with class formation and development has been suggested in these few pages. The process should not be misunderstood. Fictive kin are not distinctive to slave cultures. But they probably had a distinctive importance in Afro-American slave culture. The reality of actual or potential sale and other forms of involuntary family breakup threatened all slave families, putting a high premium on active quasi-kin connections. And because slave society so constricted general associational life, fictive kin probably served as more important devices for enlarging social networks among slaves than among dependent social classes with relatively wider choices.

Obligations rooted in beliefs about ties between adult brothers and sisters and other kin served as models for affective obligations binding together larger groups of slaves, a development that involved a special tension distinctive to slave society. That tension changed over time and varied from place to place. But it was always present. The choice between forming a reciprocal relationship with an owner ("massa") or with a fellow slave ("aunt" or "uncle") caused this tension. It was a tension that had its roots in the conflict between duties based upon ownership and obligations based upon kinship and quasi-kinship.

IV

THE ENLARGED kin group accompanied ordinary Afro-American slaves into legal freedom. It, not the isolated nuclear family, formed the core of all poor Afro-American communities in the full century and a quarter that separate us from Afro-American enslavement. Much remains to be known about the enlarged kin group and its changing functions over time and space. Anthropologists studying the contemporary black poor—Carol Stack and Demitri Shimkin and his associates, among others—have demonstrated that the kinship system forged under slavery retains unusually positive functions among poor rural and urban blacks living in the last quarter of the twentieth century.[2] These outstanding works, however, lack a historical dimension and are too functional in their emphasis. They move the past into the present quickly, and radically alter our understanding of the contemporary black poor. They make it clear that the poor black family cannot be understood in isolation from the enlarged kin group. And they demonstrate how exchanges between kin and quasi-kin based upon principles of reciprocity and obligation allow the poor to deal with severe deprivation. Shimkin and his associates describe the extensive "gamut of rights and obligations" associated with membership in a rural Mississippi black extended family:

> It runs, in general, from pressures for solidarity in public decisions . . . to cooperation in work, aid in job hunting, co-residence privileges, child fosterage, care in old age . . . and gifts and inheritance.

The social scientist Raymond T. Smith finds similar patterns among the urban poor: "The dominant impression is of people helping other people, whether it be by lending, by looking after children, by giving gifts of various practical kinds, or by transfers of money."

V

THE IMPRESSIVE work by Stack and by Shimkin and his associates on the positive functions of the extended family among late-twentieth-century poor blacks is not matched by detailed historical analysis of the poor black person and especially the rural black extended family between 1865 and 1960. Gutman's work, for example, neglects the post-emancipation and extended black family and focuses excessively on the composition of poor black households in the rural and urban South in 1880 and 1900 and in the urban North in 1905 and 1925. Except for Elizabeth Hafkin Pleck's fine *Hunting for a City: Black Migration and Poverty in Boston, 1865–1900* (1979), little useful historical work exists on the black extended family after emancipation.

Studying the behavior of ex-slaves between 1861 and 1867 begins to fill in that gap. It enlarges our understanding of the slaves as a social class upon their emancipation by revealing something about slave beliefs that had been transmitted from generation to generation prior to the emancipation. The reason is simple. Neither the American Civil War nor the general emancipation had transformed Afro-American slaves into a new race of men and women. These external events enlarged the arena in which they could make choices. But too little time had passed by 1867 for us to think that underlying slave cultural beliefs had yet been radically transformed. Studying what ex-slaves did between 1861 and 1867 allows the historian to reexamine two separate but related questions. First, what in their experiences as slaves explains common patterns of behavior among them as ex-slaves? And second, what does their behavior as ex-slaves reveal about the relationship between inward slave beliefs and outward slave behavior? The ex-slave could do and say what often could not be done and said in slavery times. That was so despite their poverty and widespread illiteracy and increasing evidence of insensitive and even brutal abuse by the federal authorities. It had been nearly impossible for many slaves—perhaps for all but a small minority—to get through the business of daily life without seeming to assent to the dominant value system. Associational life had been narrow. So had the range of choices available to slaves.

VI

HOW SLAVE passageways sustained an ethic of self-help as well as an ethic of mutuality and generalized obligation (what the historian Michael Anderson describes as "non-calculative commitment" in another connection) is revealed in the behavior of wartime "contraband" men and women in and near Alexandria, Virginia. Their early condition was deplorable. Between mid-June and early December of 1862, 3,354 contrabands passed through the Alexandria camp. A visit among them by New York Quakers in October 1862 revealed that sometimes as many as ten or twelve persons were quartered in rooms no more than twelve feet square. The runaway North Carolina slave Harriet Jacobs noticed that the "little children pine like prison birds for their native element." Smallpox ravaged the refugees that first winter. D. B. Nichols, the superintendent of contrabands, distressed the refugees. He allowed several dead blacks to be buried in a "box," angering resident runaways who had a "great respect for the dead." A District of Columbia black said the contrabands believed Nichols "better suited to be an overseer of a Southern plantation."

But the condition of the Alexandria refugees improved, and largely because of their own individual and collective efforts. In the fall and winter months of 1863–1864, they built several hundred one- and two-room cabins (ranging in value from $40 to $100) for themselves. They paid an annual ground rent. Government teamsters among them had five dollars taken from each monthly wage payment for "public" support of disabled refugees and helpless women and children. About 7,000 refugees lived there in August 1864; 25 received public assistance. "Hundreds . . . in the last twelve months," said an army physician among them, "built houses of their own, and paid every dollar for them, besides supporting their families." About 1,000 houses had been built by the refugees. "All they need," they physician concluded, "is protection, plenty of work at a fair price, and punctual payment."

Schools started quickly among the Alexandria refugees. "The first demand of these fugitives when they come into a place," observed a reporter, "is that their children may go to school. Another surprising fact is that the poor negro women had rather toil, earn, and pay one dollar a month for their children's education than permit them to enter a charity school." A white teacher did not work with the Alexandria contrabands until October 1862. By that time, blacks were managing three other schools. Before the war's end, at least sixteen other blacks taught in or ran Alexandria schools. In April 1863, about 400 children attended such schools. The total contraband population then numbered about 2,000. One school started in a former "slave pen." Another (a "self-sustaining" school with about 150 pupils) was housed in a building put up as a Lancastrian school at the bequest of George Washington and meant to be "forever free to the poor of the city."

That the Alexandria contrabands were not unusual in their beliefs and behavior is learned by comparing them with rural ex-slaves living in northwestern South Carolina, a rich cotton-producing region that was home to about 100,000 blacks, nearly a third of the state's former slave population. Benjamin Franklin Whittemore, a Massachusetts resident, an Amherst College graduate, a Methodist clergyman, and a former Union Army chaplain, supervised education there for the Freedmen's Bureau between 1865 and 1867 before entering Republican state politics. After he toured the region in January 1866, he pleaded for outside help: "The negroes are willing to deny themselves and do all they can to obtain knowledge, but they can not do much." The Freedmen's Bureau, moreover, was powerless "in many particulars, inoperative because of its poverty," and very much in need of congressional monies. A year later, Whittemore remembered the region in early 1866 as "a wilderness in every particular." Nearly all blacks there farmed, and on January 1, 1866, they celebrated Emancipation Day by "besieging" bureau headquarters to complain about poorly drawn contracts that defrauded them and about inadequate food supplies. Such behavior spread fear of insurrection, and bureau officers worked hard to arrange settlements with white employers. "Mutual dependence," Whittemore worried, had to be "taught, felt, and acknowledged." Afterwards, store orders remained common and cash payments few. A crop failure in 1866—just one-third of the normal crop was harvested—caused even worse troubles. In June 1867, Darlington ex-slaves addressed Boston's mayor: "We are on the eve of Starvation. We have no way in God's world to get provisions. Only through our Friends North. . . . If there is any chance in the world to get anything to eat in your city, do for Heavens Sake Send us some and save us from Perishing."

Despite their increasingly difficult economic circumstances and some local white opposition to schooling for their children, former slaves over the entire region contributed significantly to their children's education. An ethic of mutuality similar to that among the Alexandria blacks shaped their behavior. They moved an old "Confederate building" ten miles from Florence to Darlington to start the district's first school. By April 1866, six schools existed, and a month later eleven. Northern soldiers had burned a Marion schoolhouse, so its teacher met classes in the woods where blacks had put together a makeshift school. In Sumter, blacks first built "a rude shelter in the yard of a Mr. Williams, one of the most enterprising of its colored citizens." Summerville got its school sometime before July. Two white women offered two acres of land for $200 as school property. Local blacks, many among them poor and destitute, crowded an army barracks used as their church to agree that if the Northern societies paid for the land and the government supplied lumber, they would build a school to open in October. Dan Meyers, "a good carpenter," spoke first: "I is a plain man and alers does what I agree, and I say that I will stan' by the good work till it's done finished." The next speaker added: "I is called a good carpenter; I has no children of my own to send to the school; but I want to see the house built, and I gives two weeks for it." Others offered labor, and some, including young boys, gave small sums of money. In all, the blacks raised sixty dollars and pledged twelve weeks of labor. "The women," said the schoolteacher Esther Hawkes, did their part, too, "offering to board or lodge the workmen as they best could." "These destitute people." Hawkes mused, "living, some of them, in rude huts made of mud and palmetto, one might suppose that all their interest was necessary [just] to keep them from starving. . . ."

Schooling made significant progress among these upcountry South Carolina blacks by the fall of 1866. Whittemore pleaded with the American Freedmen's Union Commission in late September: "I am at present wanting eight teachers, where schools of over sixty pupils each are awaiting them. . . . The parents are begging me to send them the 'school teacher.' " The demand for teachers had outrun the supply. The schools varied in size: that in Timonville was 14 by 24 feet, that in Florence 35 by 45 feet, and that in Darlington 30 by 72 feet. Overall, Whittemore figured that each community had expended an average of $320 by October 1866.

Whittemore summed up the year's work in January 1867. Twenty-two schools had been set up, and over 4,000 children instructed. The blacks owned, unencumbered, more than $12,000 worth of church and school properties, "two-thirds of which" had been "secured by their own industry, skill, and collections."

Much more than either Yankee benevolence or federal largesse made the schoolhouse a reality among further northeastern South Carolina slaves in 1866 and 1867. Communal values and sanctions shaped the activities of ex-slaves there. "He who makes himself prominent in opposing the establishment of a school," Whittemore noticed, "is looked upon as an enemy to the *race*, and worthy of suspicion, or 'to be let alone' when contracting is called for." The success of such community sanctions depended on shared values.

This evidence from Virginia and South Carolina tells us much about the ex-slaves. But what in their experiences as slaves had prepared them for such behavior? And what does their behavior reveal about their inward beliefs as slaves? Attitudes toward work, religion, and family and kin that developed during slavery and were difficult if not impossible to act upon then sustained notions of obligation and mutuality among many ex-slaves. The former slaves on the Georgia plantation Henry Lee Higginson leased in 1866 confused their Yankee employer: "They help each other in picking the different patches of cotton, as it opens. If they receive help for it, they return help, not money." Davis Tillison, who headed the Georgia Freedmen's Bureau that same year, reported: "I know of colored men who work hard all day and into the night, and who give one third of all they earn to the support of the poor of their own race. This I learn, not from their own lips, but from those of white neighbors." A perfectionist Afro-Christianity encouraged benevolence among such men and women. About 1,300 destitute former North Carolina slaves lived at the Camp Trent refuge. Crop failures in 1867 meant that many picked cotton for between a quarter of a cent and a half a cent per pound. It was hard for individuals to make twenty-five cents a day. That fall between three and four hundred children attended a Camp Trent school. Adult refugees formed an educational society and paid ten cents to join it. The clergyman Amos York headed the group and quickly collected eight dollars. The following letter to a private Northern relief agency accompanied the money:

> DEAR SIR we The members of the Educational Society auginized in Trent Settlement NC Do Forward to the Sociation Eight Dollars $8 to aide in Serporting our teacher Rev J W Burghduff. The amount is small But it is the Best we can Do under the Present Circumstancis we are a Poore and Destitute People and the times are wary harde But we feel willing to try to help our selves all we Can of such we hope the small amount will Be accepted
>
> Respectfuly yous
> AMOS YORK *President*
> SOUTHEY HUNTER *Sect*

Former slaves over the entire South shared beliefs with men like Amos York. That happened because class obligation built on kin obligation as well as on Afro-Christian perfectionism. A meeting about their schools among former slaves on St. Helena's Island, South Carolina, in 1868 indicated how some of these separate strands had come together. Hastings Garret spoke first and, according to the Yankee teacher Laura Towne, urged that "rich and poor . . . come forward at once and assist in support of the schools, each putting in according to his means." He asked Towne to speak, and she and another white teacher advised the blacks to rely less on outside financial aid and more on their own resources. The "elders and principal men" spoke, too, and promised to raise money and "contribute themselves as soon as they could." Such beliefs—"each putting in according to his means," setting aside a piece of land for a communal purpose and all working it, and considering free schooling for the "poor neighor widow's children"—such beliefs had nothing to do with the moral paternalism of their former owners or of the Yankee missionaries and schoolteachers.

Reactive models cannot explain the beliefs and behavior of ex-slaves like Amos York. How, then, are the class beliefs and behavior found among such men and women best explained? The alternative to a reaction model is not a romantic one. We are instead directed to reexamine the relationship between class formation, class development, and changing patterns of class belief and behavior. By the 1860s, most Afro-American slaves were descended from a four- or five-generation class experience. Emancipation transformed an established and developed subordinate class, allowing ex-slave men and women to act on a variety of class beliefs that had developed but been constrained during several generations of enslavement. The origins of the beliefs ex-slaves acted upon before 1867 (including those "borrowed" from the mainstream culture) require study, as do the particular ways in which slave class experiences over time sustained these beliefs. Static conceptions of either social class or the relationship between dominant and subordinate social classes prevent us from studying such processes.

VII

MUCH MORE is known now about the earlier and established slave culture than in 1976 when *The Black Family in Slavery and Freedom* was published. That is because of important new research and publication dealing with eighteenth-century North American slaves. Among the plantation slaves studied by Gutman, only one group—those growing tobacco in Piedmont, North Carolina—could be studied in detail during the late eighteenth century. The arguments in that work about the enlarged slave kin group and its functions rested primarily on nineteenth-century records and especially on records for the period from 1830 to 1860. In his brilliant critique of Gutman's work, the Latin American historian A. J. R. Russell-Wood wrote: "The formative period of Afro-American culture preceded by several decades the War of Independence. And yet it is precisely for this pivotal period that Gutman is weak."[3] Russell-Wood poses important questions about the relationship between the enlarged kin network and class formation and class development and suggests: "By the 1760s, Afro-American culture was already in what might be referred to as the late formative period. . . . It could well be argued that Afro-American culture had evolved through to the full manifestation of its major characteristics and by 1760 had reached the stage of development which was no longer formative." Critical questions about culture formation require study of the "origins of the African experience in the Americas, not in a later stage of creolization."

It is possible to respond to Russell-Wood's suggestion and thereby enlarge our understanding of the relationship between the enlarged kin network and slave class formation and development. Eighteenth-century Afro-American kinship networks and domestic arrangements can be seen most clearly in the records of planters who periodically inventoried their holdings, kept birth lists of their bondsmen and bondswomen, or indicated slave family connections in ration rolls, estate censuses, and wills. In 1773, Charles Carroll of Annapolis listed his several hundred slaves and noted their familial relations, age, residence by quarter, and occupation. The heirs of his only son compiled a similar, though less detailed, list after the latter's death nearly a half-century later. There are also Carroll inventories dating

back into the seventeenth century. Similarly, Thomas Jefferson enumerated the slaves on his Piedmont, Virginia, plantations at least once
each decade from the 1770s until his death a half-century later.
Richard Bennehan, an ambitious clerk on his way to establishing North
Carolina's tobacco plantation, began his slave birth register in 1776.
And C. C. Pinckney pieced together a South Carolina estate between
1808 and 1812 that included records reaching back into the 1760s
about bondsmen and bondswomen he had inherited and acquired
through marriage.

Taken together, the domestic arrangements revealed in these diverse
eighteenth-century sources indicate that the arrangements and practices common among slaves between 1830 and 1860 existed among
North American slaves prior to 1770. The data on marriage rules
remain unclear, but the domestic arrangements, kin networks, sexual
behavior, and naming practices among these eighteenth-century African and mostly Afro-American North American slaves are unambig-
uous. These findings are revealed in the joint research of Ira Berlin,
Herbert Gutman, and Mary Beth Norton.

The most significant fact about this new evidence is the moment in
time for which it exists—the 1770s. That moment in time is important
for reasons indirectly associated with the American War for Independence. It is the relationship of this evidence and especially the pervasive
presence of multigenerational family connections among Chesapeake
(Virginia and Maryland) slaves to the social transformation of the
Chesapeake slave population between 1720 and 1750—so ably analyzed
by the historical demographers Russell Menard and Allan Kulikoff—
that gives this date its importance. Menard and Kulikoff have demonstrated that prior to 1710 the Chesapeake slave population hardly
reproduced itself and that its growth depended heavily upon the
importation of African slaves. Significant social, cultural, and demographic changes altered this pattern so that the labor force began
reproducing itself. The details of this analysis need not detain us
except to note that prior to 1720 inventory records listed one slave
child under the age of sixteen for every two slaves aged sixteen to
fifty. Three decades later more slave children than slave adults were
listed in similar records. The reproduction of the slave labor force
meant a declining need for African slaves. (In fact, the largest number
of African slaves—210,000, or fully half of those imported into North
America—arrived in the decades in which the native-born slave labor
force began to reproduce itself. The reproduction of the slave labor
force so early in time had a cultural, social, and even political
importance that paralleled its obvious economic significance. Intergenerational kin linkages—central to the development of all social classes

and to the historical relationship between structure and process—could only develop and become important in a population that reproduced itself.

The preconditions for the development, sustenance, and transmission of a distinctive Afro-American culture rested first on the reproduction of the slave labor force and then on the development of kin networks—not mere families—that connected generations of slaves in space and over time. The awareness among these mid-eighteenth-century slaves of third- and even fourth-generation ancestors tells much more that that they retained a consciousness of their "roots." That fact allows us to relate class formation to class development, to examine changing class beliefs and pratices over time, to study how old slave beliefs became new slave beliefs, and to interpret the ways in which slaves regularly borrowed from the changing mainstream culture (itself class-divided), often redefining what became a part of the new cultural patterns they were developing. The Scottish missionary Alexander Garden who settled in Charleston, South Carolina, in 1726 described the process in 1740:

> They are as 'twere a Nation within a Nation. In all Country Settlements, they live in contiguous Houses and often 2, 3, or 4 Families of them in one House, Slightly partitioned into So many Apartments. They labour together and converse almost wholly among themselves, so that if once their children could but read the Bible to them . . . this would bring in at least a Dawning of the blessed Light amongst them; and which as a Sett or two of those children grew up to Men and Women, would gradually diffuse and increase into open Day.—Parents and Grand Parents, Husbands, Wives, Brothers, Sisters, and other Relatives would be daily Teaching and learning of one another.

In two decades, Garden predicted, such slaves "would not be much inferior to . . . the lower order of white People, Servants and Day Labourers (Specially in the Country) either in England or elsewhere."

The new eighteenth-century data about slave family and kinship affect more than our understanding of the relationship between class formation and development. The Pinckney records, for example, include information about sale, death, transfer, and gift as well as birth, and a full study of these records strongly suggests that slave blood ties (especially those between grown siblings) were more lasting and more significant than marital ties. The Bennehan birth list and related documents, moreover, allow us to make an equally important if different point. The slaves belonging to Jefferson and Carroll were owned by Chesapeake planters of great wealth, men untypical of eighteenth-century slave owners outside South Carolina. It might be argued that the familial arrangements among these slaves depended upon their status as plantation slaves. Most Chesapeake slaves and many low-country ones lived in small, farm-size units. Their circumstances doubtless necessitated distinctive strategies for survival. But by the 1770s, they shared the same kin-related values as plantation slaves. Evidence of this is drawn from the experience of the slaves owned by Richard Bennehan. Bennehan acquired his bondspeople in small numbers and in a nonplantation setting, Orange County, North Carolina. Farms dominated the region, and in 1780, when Bennehan began his climb into the planter class, only 3 percent of the county's slaveholders held more than twenty bondspeople. Most of his slaves were newly arrived in the area, and there is no evidence that any had previous plantation experience. No nearby estates existed that might house complex kin networks similar to those in the Chesapeake. By the turn of the century, Bennehan's slaves had established patterns of marriage, childbearing, and naming common to slaves long accustomed to the plantation setting. Two in five of the 103 slave children born between 1803 and 1830 had the name of either a father or another blood relative. What young Bennehan slaves learned from older kin was not the mere product of "plantation culture": that fact is what gives the Bennehan slaves so much importance. The generation born after 1795 matured enmeshed in kin relations and were plantation slaves. But their immediate forebears had not been plantation slaves. They acted on beliefs that antedated their experience as plantation slaves. Those beliefs—particularly the attachment of such great importance to the enlarged kin group—accompanied the first group of Bennehan slaves into the plantation experience and shaped the ways in which these men and women interpreted and interacted with it.

VIII

AFRO-AMERICAN slaves emerged as a distinctive social class between 1720 and 1750. That class developed over the next century and was transformed during the American Civil War. It is now clear that the enlarged kin network played central role in this long and painful process. But the changing role of the enlarged kin group awaits careful study, as do such subjects as sex-role segregation, the relationship between consanguinity and affinity, the relationship between kinship and coresidence, and slave kin strategies in diverse settings including small farms, villages, and cities. More significantly, what is now known about slave kinship needs to be related to changing patterns of production and to changing patterns of subordination implicit in the master-slave relationship. "Systems of kinship," the anthropologist Stephen Gudeman points out, ". . . both incorporate and mediate impulses emanating from other domains. Abstracting a family system from its context has the merit of underlining its patterned normative basis but the demerit of diminishing our understanding of its functions and meaning."[4]

The restoration of what Gudeman calls "context" promises to do more than enlarge our understanding of the changing ways in which slaves and their poor descendants used kin networks to deal with their oppressive circumstances. That enlarged context deepens our understanding of the Ellison and Sartre questions. It enriches our understanding of the communal ethic that led so many ex-slaves to sacrifice for literacy and to endanger their lives by filing complaints against abusive former owners and other whites. We shall comprehend why a vast number of married and older ex-slave women everywhere withdrew from the labor force following emancipation and even why ex-slave husbands and wives seem to have frequently disputed over to whom the wage belonged. It should become clear why wartime South Carolina Sea Island slaves (then supervised by the federal army) refused to grow cotton, wanted to plant corn, broke the cotton gins, hid the ironwork used for repair, and finally agreed to grow cotton but planted corn between the rows of cotton and then refused to pay the military rent on the land on which the corn grew. Such behavior rested on beliefs embedded in slave kin and quasi-kin networks. So did this petition submitted to the federal authorities in 1866 by former slaves in Liberty County, Georgia. They had worked on rice plantations, and the italicized portions of their petition were underlined in the original document:

> We the People of Liberty County . . . appeal to you asking aid and counsel in this our *distressed condition.* We learned from the Address of *general Howard* that We Were to *Return* to the *Plantations* and *Work for our Former owners at a Reasonable contract as Freemen,* and find a *Home* and *Labor, Provided We can agree. But these owners of Plantations . . . Says they only will hire or* —— the *Prime Hands* and our *old and infirm Mothers and Fathers* and *our Children Will not be Provided for* and this Will See Sir Put us in *confusion . . . We cannot Labor for the Land owners . . .* [while] *our Infirm and children are not provided for, and are not allowed to educate or learn . . . We are Destitute of Religious Worship, having no Home or Place to Live When We Leave the Plantation, Returned to our Former owners; We are a Working Class of People* and We are *Willing* and *Anxious* to worke for a *Fair Compensation;* But to *return to work upon the Terms that are at Present offered to us, Would Be We Think going Backe into the state of slavery that We have just to some extent Been Delivered from.*

We *Appeal* to *you Sir and through you* to the *rulers* of the *Country* in our *Distressed State* and —— *that We feel, unsettled as Sheep, Without a Shephard, and beg your advice and Assistance,* and *Believe that this is an Earnest Appeal from A Poor But Loyal Earnest People.*

E. P. Thompson may have had the Georgia ex-slaves in mind when he wrote that "feeling might be *more*, rather than less, tender or intense *because* relations are 'economic' and critical to mutual survival."

11

CLASS COMPOSITION
AND THE DEVELOPMENT OF
THE AMERICAN WORKING CLASS,
1840–1890

with Ira Berlin

CONTEMPORARY understanding of the American working class in the century preceding the First World War—especially between 1840 and 1890—remains enigmatic in important respects because its historians have given inadequate attention to the relationship between the *formation* of this new subordinate class before 1840 and its subsequent rapid *development*. The nature of the relationship between popular and elite culture in the United States during the last half of the nineteenth century therefore also remains problematic. At the root of these difficulties stands the failure to comprehend the changing composition of the working class and the central role played in it by the children of immigrants. This essay explicates the composition of the American working class in 1880, using that year's federal census as a point of departure. The essay examines a brief moment in order to shed light on the larger processes associated with development of the working class in the United States between 1840 and 1890.

The evolution of the American working class between the American Revolution and World War I took place in two distinctive if overlapping stages. The first—beginning during the Revolution and ending during the decade that followed the Panic of 1837—saw the formation of a working class out of the heterogeneous lower orders and self-conscious artisans that composed the laboring population of preindustrial American cities. Drawing on the magisterial work of E. P. Thompson, especially his *Making of the English Working Class*, students of American workers have shown how this new class came into being in the flux of

This essay was originally published in Hungarian as "Osztályszerkezet és az Amerikai: Munkásosztály Fejlödése 1840–1890 Között (A Bevándorlök és Gyermekeik, mint Bérmunkások.)," *Történelmi Szemle/Historical Review* (Budapest) 26 (1983), 224–36. The original essay was written with Ira Berlin.

political revolution and economic transformation. Viewing the process of class formation from a variety of perspectives—that of shoemakers in the town of Lynn, Massachusetts, mill girls in the great textile factories of Lowell, weavers and spinners in a small Pennsylvania village, and workers of all kinds in the metropolises of New York and Philadelphia—historians of the creation of the American working class demonstrated how the common experiences of workers, in relation to production and in opposition to the rising owning class, created a sense of working-class unity. By midcentury, American workers had become a class to be reckoned with.

In showing how the American working class came into being, students of class formation have also demonstrated how workers transformed the political, social, and economic beliefs and practices they carried from the American Revolution into a distinctive critique of early American capitalism. Central to these beliefs and practices was republicanism. The transformation of American men and women into dependent wage earners in the years before 1840 tested not only their adaptability to specialized labor but also the appropriateness of their republican ideology. Though hardly egalitarian, the Founding Fathers had feared the consequences of excessive power. The public, not the private, sphere worried them most. "Give a man power over my subsistence," Alexander Hamilton had warned, "and he has a right to my whole moral body." Hamilton and his generation did not live into the early industrial capitalist era, but republican ideology survived them and gained a new life among the artisans and laborers of industrializing America.

As preindustrial workers became a wage-earning class, republicanism neither disappeared nor remained a set of stale patriotic pieties. Instead, wage earners in Jacksonian America remade it into a distinctive and radical—but nonsocialist—argument against the pervasive inequalities associated with ninteenth-century capitalism. They identified republicanism with social equality, not with open competition in the race for wealth. New England women laboring in the new cotton mills, for example, attacked their employers:

> We will show these driveling cotton lords, this mushroom aristocracy of New England, who so arrogantly aspire to lord it over God's heritage, that our rights cannot be trampled upon with impunity; that we will no longer submit to that arbitrary power which has for the last ten years been so abundantly exercised over us.

Their beliefs went beyond the redefinition of eighteenth-century republicanism, and sparked and sustained recurrent collective efforts—in the form of trade unions, strikes, cooperatives, a tart labor press, and local politics—to check the increasing power of the industrial capitalist. (It was no accident that the largest strike in American history prior to the Civil War—a struggle involving at least one-third of the 60,000 Massachusetts shoe workers in 1860—began on George Washington's birthday.) In sum, prior to 1840, American wage earners had developed a indigenous ideology independent of and opposed to capitalism.

The decades following the formation of the American working class—roughly 1840 to the first years of the twentieth century—witnessed the rapid development of this new subordinate class. Much less is known about the *development* of the American working class than about its *formation*.* Many of the difficulties in understanding its development stem from a failure to comprehend that although this new class grew older and larger, it did not reproduce itself. The development of the American working class between 1840 and 1880 involved a few of the descendants of those men and women who had earlier come to constitute the American proletariat. Logically, they were the bearers of the initial American working-class critique of capitalist social relations and dependent wage labor. And some—as David Montgomery and other labor historians have shown—did just that. But the presence of native workers and their descendants was insignificant in 1880, especially among common day laborers and among industrial workers in factories, mines, and the processing industries. Few older American workers of native stock were employed as ordinary laborers in 1880. Hardly any older workers of native stock labored in American mines and factories. By 1880, industrial capitalism was well advanced in the United States, but the nation had relatively few older old-stock (that is, native-born, of native-born parents) American factory workers (see tables 1 and 2). For that reason, it is impossible to examine American working-class development between 1840 and 1880 by focusing on native white male laborers and factory workers, as so many historians have tried to do. The urban industrial working class formed in America prior to 1840 did not reproduce itself between 1840 and 1880. Its growth occurred in other ways.

It is thus necessary to recognize the importance of immigrants and their children in the evolution of the American working class during the last half of the nineteenth century. In 1880, foreign-born people made up only 13 percent of the total population of the United States,

---

* Although some studies have attempted to link changes in the nature of the organization of American capitalism, the transformation of production, and the consolidation of the American state with the evolution of the working class, this work remains in a preliminary stage. The best of it, moreover, emphasizes developments in the last decades of the nineteenth and the first decades of the twentieth century.

TABLE ONE

PLACE	TOTAL WAGE-EARNING POPULATION IN 1880	NUMBER OF WHITE LABORERS 30 AND OLDER OF OLD STOCK IN 1880
Leavenworth, Kan.	3,092	91
Galveston, Tex.	3,920	95
Covington, Ky.	6,206	145
Newport, Ky.	3,928	51
Saginaw and E. Saginaw, Mich.	7,168	259
Woonsocket, R.I.	4,093	87
Rock Island, Ill.	2,380	52
Joliet, Ill.	2,980	51
Burlington, Iowa	3,717	80
Dubuque, Iowa	4,198	44
Waterbury, Conn.	4,093	87
Paterson, N.J.	11,929	286

and another 13 percent were native-born Americans of color. In all, three in four Americans in 1880 were native-born white men, women, and children, but the high percentage (75%) of native-born whites in the overall population in 1880 has served American working-class historians badly. It has led them to underestimate the importance of foreign-born peoples in the development of the American working class and has distorted understanding of class relationships as well as the connection between the formation of the American working class prior to 1840 and its subsequent history.

A conventional American history derived from this statistic (75 percent) emphasizes workers of native origins as contrasted with workers of foreign origins (and parenthetically, white workers as contrasted to workers of color). Scholars working in this tradition have characterized the American working class as follows:

1. A very high percentage of nineteenth-century American wage earners were native white Americans.

2. An authentic native white American working class had emerged prior to 1840.

3. Formed prior to 1840, the American working class reproduced itself over the next few decades, but immigrants and their children (along with former slaves) impaired an authentic American process of

TABLE TWO

PLACE	INDUSTRY	NUMBER OF WORKERS IN INDUSTRY IN 1880	NUMBER OF WHITE MALE WORKERS 30 AND OLDER OF OLD STOCK IN 1880
Pawtucket, R.I.	Textiles	2,753	137
Woonsocket, R.I.	Textiles	3,834	93
Scranton, Pa.	Mining	4,502	25
Ohio counties[a]	Mining	6,026	374
Illinois counties[b]	Mining	1,913	8
Paterson, N.J.	Iron/steel	2,350	314
Scranton, Pa.	Iron/steel	1,022	72
Cleveland, Ohio	Iron/steel	4,776	292
Youngstown, Ohio	Iron/steel	1,784	41
Covington/ Newport, Ky.	Iron/steel	1,884	114
Joliet, Ill.	Iron/steel	800	50
Waterbury, Conn.	Brass	4,500	114
Derby/ Ansonia, Conn.	Brass/textiles	2,530	197
Haverstraw, N.Y.	Brickmaking	1,143	35
Saginaw/E. Saginaw, Mich.	Lumber products	1,242	88
Cleveland, Ohio	Oil refining/ barrels	1,050	29
Moline, Ill.	Plows	640	54
Paterson, N.J.	Textiles	9,235	67

[a] Mahoning, Trumbull, Stark, Lawrence, and Perry counties.
[b] St. Clair and Will counties.

class formation and subsequent class development. They were out-siders—appendices to a drama that primarily involved native white American men and women.

4. Those born outside the mainstream culture deserve study. But even as workers, they were outside the mainstream. Although immigrants packed into large American cities like Chicago and New York, and most labored as wage earners, theirs was a distinctive and untypical American class experience.

TABLE THREE

PLACE	POPULATION	PERCENTAGE OF TOTAL POPULATION WHITE AND BORN IN THE UNITED STATES	PERCENTAGE OF WORKING CLASS OF NATIVE WHITE STOCK
ILLINOIS			
Rock Island	11,659	71%	25%
Joliet	11,657	72	18
IOWA			
Burlington	19,450	72	26
Dubuque	22,254	71	13

In fact, with a few important exceptions, after 1840 most American workers were immigrants or the children of immigrants. In every American city and in almost every American craft, the disproportionate and generally the overwhelming majority of workers had been born outside the United States or were the children of men and women who were. A close look at the middle-sized towns of Rock Island and Joliet, Illinois, and Burlington and Dubuque, Iowa, with their diverse working-class populations, reveals the trend. In 1880, the total population in each of these towns conformed to the national pattern. Nearly 75 percent of the residents were native-born whites. But workers of native white stock ranged from only 13 percent in Dubuque to 25 percent in Rock Island. In other words, in 1880, 87 percent of Dubuque, Iowa, wage earners were either foreign-born, the children of immigrants, or blacks (see table 3). A careful analysis of the composition of the working class in every other major American city confirms that the pattern found in these small Midwestern towns holds for the nation as a whole. In forty of the fifty largest American cities— places ranging in size from New York to Atlanta and Denver—at least 75 percent of wage earners were either immigrants, the children of immigrants, or blacks. The list of large cities with the highest proportion of wage earners born to either black or immigrant parents is headed by Charleston, South Carolina. And the next fifteen places are San Francisco, Nashville, Richmond, Chicago, Fall River, Atlanta, New Orleans, Washington, New York, Detroit, Milwaukee, Lawrence, Lowell, Cleveland, and Paterson.

A similar analysis made on a regional basis and including all towns and cities with at least 10,000 residents permits an understanding of regional and local variations within this national pattern. It can be summarized briefly:

1. Native white workers of native-born parents were most common in the New England working class and least important in Far Western, Rocky Mountain, Southwestern, and Southern towns and cities. Half of New England's middle-sized towns and an even higher percentage of its small towns had significant numbers of white workers of native stock.

2. Not a single Far Western, Rocky Mountain, Southwestern, or Southern town had a working class in which native-stock whites made up more than 25 percent of the male wage earners.

3. Only three large Midwestern and Great Plains cities (Indianapolis, Columbus, and Dayton) had significant percentages of native-stock white wage earners. Such workers predominated in the old, small Ohio Valley towns that stretched west from the Pennsylvania border, but not elsewhere in this region.

4. Native-stock white wage earners were numerous in eastern Pennsylvania towns and in the Hudson Valley and Mohawk Valley towns. But immigrants and their children dominated the wage-earning population in most Middle Atlantic cities of size.

Yet these regional variations should not obscure the larger national pattern. Over the entire nation, native white workers of native white parents composed a small percentage of the developing American working class.

The years following the formation of the American working class saw that class remade by an influx of immigrants. If native-born workers of native-born parents were so few as to be nearly invisible, then immigrants have to be understood as a massive and forceful presence. Indeed, an examination of the origins of American workers under age thirty suggests that the immigrant workers who dominated the American working class at midcentury had a continuing impact on the development of that class. By 1880, the *children* of immigrants had become the dynamic element in the working class. They often outnumbered either white workers of native parents or foreign-born workers (see table 4). An analysis by occupation emphasizes the relative insignificance of workers of native white stock in the manufacturing, processing, and mining industries. Such workers remained important in the skilled building trades (especially in the older Eastern and Southern towns and cities) and in the operating railroad crafts, but few labored in the iron and steel industry, the coal mines, and those processing and manufacturing industries that sustained single-industry towns. Since most such industries developed in the North and the West before 1880, Afro-Americans were unimportant in them. But

TABLE FOUR

TOWN OR CITY	PERCENTAGE OF WHITE WORKERS UNDER 30 BORN IN THE UNITED STATES OF FOREIGN PARENTS (1880)	TOWN OR CITY	PERCENTAGE OF WHITE WORKERS UNDER 30 BORN IN THE UNITED STATES OF FOREIGN PARENTS (1880)
Galveston, Tex.	50%	Leavenworth, Kan.	51%
Covington, Ky.	63	Newport, Ky.	71
Saginaw/E. Saginaw, Mich.	35	Rock Island, Ill.	42
		Belleville, Ill.	70
E. St. Louis, Ill.	42	Dubuque, Iowa	64
Burlington, Iowa	43	Waterbury, Conn.	58
Davenport, Iowa	54		
Derby/Ansonia, Conn.	56		

immigrants and their sons and daughters more than made up for their absence (see table 5).

The high proportion of young workers born of immigrant parents poses crucial questions for the historian of the working class studying class relations and class behavior. Is it appropriate to call them "native-born" workers? What point of origin and cultural category should be assigned to these men and women? What does the concept of "assimilation" mean in the context of rapid capitalist development *and* the emergence of new popular urban culture? Answers to these questions will affect our understanding of the processes by which they became adult American workers. Failure to answer these questions has resulted in the neglect and isolation of historical processes after 1880 that shaped political behavior and popular culture, class conflict, and class integration.

The further significance of these questions is illustrated by examining young male workers in Paterson, New Jersey, Scranton, Pennsylvania, and Cleveland, Ohio (see table 6). Lumping together native workers of foreign parents with native workers of native parents creates the impression that two equal streams—one "native" and the other "foreign"—came to make up the developing working class. Two streams existed, but they were unequal. The point is strikingly illustrated by examining the origins of young Scranton miners, young Cleveland

TABLE FIVE

PLACE	INDUSTRY	NUMBER OF WORKERS IN INDUSTRY IN 1880	PERCENTAGE FOREIGN-BORN AND CHILDREN OF IMMIGRANTS
Paterson, N.J.	Iron/steel	2,352	78%
Scranton, Pa.	Iron/steel	1,022	85
Cleveland, Ohio	Iron/steel	4,776	86
Youngstown, Ohio	Iron/steel	1,784	90
Covington/ Newport, Ky.	Iron/steel	1,884	87
Joliet, Ill.	Iron/steel	800	87
Lackawanna Co., Pa.	Anthracite	6,440	97
Clearfield, Mercer, Cambria, and Westmoreland counties, Pa.	Bituminous	8,130	74
Mahoning, Trumbull, Stark, Lawrence, and Perry counties, Ohio	Bituminous	6,062	86
St. Clair and Will counties, Ill.	Bituminous	1,910	98
Waterbury, Conn.	Brass	4,500	79
Derby/Ansonia, Conn.	Brass/textiles	2,530	82
Haverstraw, N.Y.	Brick	1,143	87
Paterson, N.J.	Textile	9,235	87
Saginaw, E. Saginaw, Mich.	Lumber	1,242	85
Cleveland, Ohio	Oil refining/ barrels	1,050	96
Moline, Ill.	Plows	640	81

machinists, and young Paterson textile workers. "Method A," illustrated below, is mistaken (see table 7). To follow it is to misunderstand much of American history between 1840 and 1920. How the development of all aspects of the Scranton mining community is understood differs radically if it is assumed that 69 percent of its young miners were "native-born" when, in fact, 96 percent of its young miners were either

Composition and Development of the American Working Class

TABLE SIX

CITY AND OCCUPATION	WORKERS UNDER 30 IN 1880		
	NATIVE-BORN OF FOREIGN PARENTS	NATIVE-BORN OF NATIVE PARENTS	FOREIGN-BORN
SCRANTON			
Miner, mine laborer	65%	4%	31%
Day laborer	49	12	39
Iron and steel	52	17	31
CLEVELAND			
Day laborer	32%	9%	59%
Cooper	29	3	68
Shoemaker	39	7	54
Tailor	19	4	77
Machinist	50	20	30
Iron molder	47	16	37
Other iron/ steel workers	38	9	53
PATERSON			
Day laborer	28%	19%	53%
Building trades	32	41	27
Urban crafts	40	25	35
Iron crafts	46	22	32
Textile workers	46	16	38

TABLE SEVEN

CITY/OCCUPATION	WORKERS UNDER THE AGE OF 30, 1880			
	METHOD A		METHOD B	
	NATIVE-BORN	FOREIGN-BORN	NATIVE-BORN	FOREIGN-BORN AND NATIVE-BORN OF FOREIGN PARENTS
Scranton miners	69%	31%	4%	96%
Cleveland machinists	70	30	4	80
Paterson textiles	62	38	16	84

immigrants or Americans born to immigrant parents. How the development of trade unionism is understood among Cleveland ironworkers
also differs radically if it assumed that 70 percent of young Cleveland
machinsts were "native-born" when, in fact, 80 percent of its young
machinists were either immigrants or Americans born to immigrant
parents. Working-class cultural and social institutions have a different
texture if it is assumed that 62 percent of young Paterson textile
workers were "native-born" when, in fact, 84 percent of its young
textile workers were either immigrants or Americans born to immigrant
parents.

It is not suggested that immigrant parents and their American-born
working-class sons and daughters experienced American capitalism in
identical ways. That would substitute one blunder for another by
reifying "ethnicity" as a constant factor in a changing set of historical
relationships. Second-generation American workers differed from their
foreign-born parents in much the same way that American capitalism
differed in 1920 from American capitalism in 1880. But those differences remain obscure because the second-generation American workers
have not been studied. Most American immigrant history continues to
emphasize what Marcus Lee Hansen described as the "strange dualism"
into which the children of immigrants had been born. According to
Hansen, they "wanted to lose as many of the evidences of foreign
origin as they could shuffle off." But their presence as a distinct entity
in the developing American working class cannot be obscured by so
simple an analysis of assimilation into mainstream culture. Henry Ford
and the managers of his early-twentieth-century automobile factory
knew otherwise. A Ford factory manager described his dealings with
different groups of plant workers in 1915:

> The American is the past master of bluff, and it takes us a long
> time to teach him that bluff and appearance count for nothing here.
> We find the immigrant substantial, developed physically, which
> helps him in his work, and his mental powers of thinking are right.
> . . . He appreciates all that is done for him. It is the children of the
> immigrant—and his children's children—that cause the most trou-
> ble. They try to domineer and resent authority.

The logic of this observation suggests that any reconceptualization of
American working-class history must include a distinction between
native-born workers of native-born parents and native-born workers
of immigrant parents.*

* Writing about unionization in the 1930s, the labor historian David Brody notes:
"Ethnic identity still exercised a powerful influence on unionization in the mass-
production industries. A detailed study of one Detroit auto-parts plant between 1936
and 1940 reveals this progression: the first to join were the young second-generation

Such a distinction reveals that by 1880 an established American working class of immigrant origins had started to reproduce itself, and that its children were becoming America's industrial workers, especially its factory operatives. Their roots and traditions did not reach back in time to John Winthrop and his Puritan City on a Hill. They traveled instead laterally in space to the peasant and commercial farms and especially to the capitalist labor gangs, workshops, and factories of Europe. Many came directly from farms and rural villages, but others, as David Montgomery has cogently argued, "had been born and raised in the industrial world. . . . The interaction between them in the context of rapidly maturing industrial capitalism shaped the consciousness of the working class."

Wager earners, of course, did not live in isolation. They lived enmeshed in class relations that shaped how they organized their lives and interpreted their experiences. Understanding the composition of a dependent social class merely begins to explain its history, and what is known about the composition of the American working class needs to be fitted into a larger context.

The radical alteration of the composition of the American working class between 1840 and 1880 was a part of the larger transformation of American society. That transformation provides the context for reinterpreting the development of the American working class and the relationship between popular and elite culture in the nineteenth century. In 1840, seven of ten Americans worked as farmers, and only 11 percent of the American people resided in cities of 2,500 or more. In 1880, some 22 percent, over 10 million persons, lived in cities of 10,000 or more (see table 8). These new, expanding metropolises, as the centers of American industry and commerce, became the battlefield of class warfare in the mid-nineteenth century. Almost without exception, the non-working-class residents of these cities confronted a working class 75 percent of whose members were immigrants, the children of immigrants, or blacks. The proportion of urban residents who lived in settings of this description varied from place to place to the region and the size of the city: it was between 98 and 100 percent in the South, Southwest and Far West, and the Rocky Mountain states, and between 67 percent and 79 percent in New England. It was

---

workers; then the older Polish and Ukrainian workers, initially hesitant, but ultimately intensely loyal; next, the scattered Appalachian workers . . . ; and, finally, the skilled workers of Northern European descent, who had to be coerced into the union. The progression was not immutable: at the Detroit plant of Midland Steel, the skilled men of Northern European extraction took the union lead between 1936 and 1939, only to be displaced in a factional battle by the second-generation semi-skilled workers in 1940s."

TABLE EIGHT

DATE	RESIDENTS OF CITIES 25,000+	RESIDENTS OF CITIES 250,000+
1840	935,000	306,000
1880	8,600,000	4,400,000
1900	17,500,000	10,800,000

between 92 and 97 percent in the nation's largest cities and between 54 and 64 percent in towns with 10,000 to 19,000 residents. Overall in 1880, between 82 and 86 percent (about six in seven) of all men, women, and children living in a town or a city with 10,000 or more residents inhabited a setting in which no fewer than three in four wage earners were immigrants, the children of immigrants, or blacks.

Working-class beliefs and behavior developed in this context. The ways in which class and cultural solidarities came together between 1840 and 1890 can be illustrated by the activities of the hard-rock silver miners on the Comstock Lode in frontier Nevada, then the largest mining enterprise in the world. Towns such as Virginia City

TABLE NINE

	POPULATION OF TOWNS AND CITIES WITH 10,000+ RESIDENTS IN 1880	PERCENTAGE OF TOTAL POPULATION LIVING IN TOWN OR CITY WITH WORKING CLASS COMPOSED OF 75% OR MORE IMMIGRANTS, CHILDREN OF IMMIGRANTS, AND BLACKS
REGION		
Far West, Southwest, and Rocky Mountains	490,000	100%
South	1,400,000	98–99
Midwest and Great Plains	2,760,000	80–85
Middle Atlantic	3,652,000	83–89
New England	1,679,000	67–79
SIZE OF CITY		
35,000+	7,070,000	92–97%
20,000–34,999	1,230,000	65–71
10,000–19,000	1,710,000	54–64

and Gold Hill grew rapidly and were filled with immigrant miners. The calendar of the social life of Virginia City miners in 1875 reveals their rich cultural diversity. It began New Year's Day with Germans singing and dancing at their Athletic Hall and the French and Italians joining together at Grégoire's Saloon. It continued through that day with a sixteen-piece Cornish orchestra and the English choral society. During the first part of February, the town's Chinese celebrated their New Year and the Italian and Irish benevolent societies had their annual meetings, so that Emmet's Irish guard mixed with Oriental celebrants on the town's streets. A similar conjoining of nationalities could be found at most any time of the year. In August, the Scots celebrated Robert Burns's birthday with a gathering of the clans, and bagpipe music mixed with fortnightly public concerts given by Professor Varney's German band, the players of Emmet's guard, the Cornish orchestra, and the Italian opera company. By month's end, the Miner's Union Hall was converted into a Polish synagogue for Rosh Hashanah and Yom Kippur, Mexicans celebrated their national independence, and a Canadian relief society met. Yet this whirlwind review of the cultural calendar of Virginia City remains incomplete because it does not mention the powerful industrial union established by the diverse and heterogeneous laboring population. The union they formed in 1863 served as a model for workers over the entire Far West, and the introduction of its constitution was sworn to and signed by new members over the entire mining region.

> In view of the existing evils which the Miners have to endure from the tyrannical oppressive power of Capital, it has become necessary to protest, and to elevate our social condition and maintain a position in society. . . . We should cultivate an acquaintance with our fellows in order that we may be the better enabled to form an undivided opposition to acts of "tyranny." . . . We . . . have resolved to form an association . . . , for without Union we are powerless, with it we are powerful;—and there is no power that can be wielded by Capital or position but which we may boldly defy,—For united we possess strength; let us act justly and fear not.

Cultural diversity and even conflict did not prevent the formation of this union, which remained powerful in the region.

In their social activities, the workers of Virginia City, like those of other American cities, carried the culture of the Old World to the New. Between 1840 and 1890, immigrants and their children dominated the various oppositional movements that reached their peak between 1866 and 1872, and again between 1883 and 1894. They led diverse cooperative movements, including the Knights of Labor, the constituent unions that formed the American Federation of Labor, the small but influential socialist and anarchist movements, and dozens of local labor political parties. In so doing, immigrant workers and their children transported European anticapitalist working-class ideologies to America and rekindled and reshaped the old social critique of acquisitive capitalism developed by the first generation of Yankee wage earners.

Understanding how the two critiques of capitalism merged in America during the late nineteenth century will go far in explaining the forms of American working-class life and ideologies and the relationship between popular and elite culture in the United States. By 1880, in most places studied, between 35 and 45 percent of native white males of old stock no longer had working-class occupations. They worked far more often as clerks, bookkeepers, and salesmen than as day laborers and factory workers. What did it mean for the culture at large and for its politics that so relatively small a percentage of old-stock white American males had experienced wage dependence in manual occupations? And what did it mean to live in new and rapidly growing urban settings in which the vast majority of wage earners were not products of the mainstream culture? That was *the* American pattern. New York was typical. And so were Charleston, Davenport, Leavenworth, and Virginia City. Native white Americans experienced little of the pain associated with the expansion of American capitalism after 1840. That may be one reason the distinguished European historian Frank Manuel complained in 1976 that "much of nineteenth-century American history has been too thoroughly enveloped in the nauseating fumes of official optimism to be tolerable to a human being." Manuel pleaded that American historians use a new rhetoric, one that would "liberate the silent groups of American so long entrapped by assimilationist histories and 'achievement' histories." A careful reading of the 1880 federal census manuscript does more than redefine the relationship between class formation and class development in the United States. It also encourages that long-overdue liberation.

12

HISTORICAL CONSCIOUSNESS
IN CONTEMPORARY AMERICA

IN OCTOBER 1981, I participated in a panel discussion at the American Writers Congress on the nature of historical consciousness in the United States. I was struck by the vast distance between the historians and the writers in attendance, and in my report—published soon after in the *Nation* magazine—I wrote:

> We know much more about the American past as we enter the 1980s than we did when we entered the 1960s. And yet the past is more inaccessible to nonhistorians than it was thirty or fifty years ago. Why that is so cannot be understood simply by leaning on old explanations like the cold war, mass culture, and the long-overdue decline of sophisticated and simple-minded "theories" of unilinear progress.
>
> That became clear at the Congress session. The panelists described how a new generation of historians has started to rewrite American history by asking new questions about such old subjects as the Revolutionary War, slavery and Populism, and by studying afresh changing class, race and gender relations as well as the history of family, work and community. But the questions and comments that followed revealed that two decades of important historical discovery and rediscovery had bypassed most of the people in the audience.
>
> It was as if the American history written in the 1960s and 1970s had been penned in a foreign language and had probed the national experiences of Albania, New Zealand and Zambia.

I wrote at that time in haste, touched with anger and perhaps despair, lamenting the absence of a popular synthesis of the best historical work, and its narrow dissemination. Nothing in the year since the panel met has reduced my deep concern for the present state of historical understanding in the United States. I have, however, reconsidered my emphasis on the lack of synthesis as a source of the vast distance that separates working historians and other American intellectuals—and indeed, ordinary Americans of all kinds. Three examples of popular historical consciousness in contemporary America suggest some of the deeper reasons for this chasm. They also illuminate much about the course of American history in the twentieth century.

The first example comes from Paul Cowan's moving account in the *Village Voice* of his experiences with the descendants of Italian immigrant workers involved in the 1912 textile strike in Lawrence, Massachusetts. Cowan was drawn to Lawrence by his interest in ethnic workers who supported George Wallace. There he learned of Camella Teoli, the thirteen-year-old daughter of Italian immigrants, scalped by a machine for twisting cotton into thread at the giant, absentee-owned Washington Mill in 1911 and hospitalized for several months. She returned home as the strike was beginning, and was one of the Lawrence workers to testify at a Washington congressional hearing. Her testimony, Cowan observes, "had the same shocking effect as Fannie Lou Hamer's would when she talked about her years as a sharecropper before the Democratic Party Platform Committee in 1964. The girl's story became front-page news all over America." Cowan sought out Camella Teoli in 1976, but learned that she had died a few years before. Until her death, she had lived with her daughter, a telephone operator and the wife of a welder. Cowan called Camella Teoli's daughter "Mathilda"—she would not let him use her real name.

When Cowan met Mathilda, she was a grown woman with adult children of her own. His subsequent experiences with her are best reported in his own words, which are haunting and filled with meaning for historians:

> I phoned [Mathilda] at 10 o'clock that night. At first she thought I was a crank—a late-night voice raving incomprehensibly about something that happened 64 years ago. Then I mentioned Camella Teoli's scalp. It was as though I'd unlocked a magic box of trust: furnished proof that there was some sort of link between Camella Teoli and me. The accident at the Washington Mill had left Camella Teoli with a permanent scar—a bald spot toward the back of her head that was six inches in diameter. Practically every day of her life, Mathilda had combed her mother's hair into a bun that disguised the spot.
>
> Suddenly, she seemed eager to see me. She suggested we have breakfast in a shopping mall the next morning.
>
> As soon as we met, I realized why my unexpected phone call had been so very confusing. Without much pause for formalities, I began to ask questions about the 1912 strike. But Mathilda knew nothing at all about Camella Teoli's political past—nothing about her trip to Washington . . . nothing about the sensational impact her mother had made on America's conscience. Neither, it turned

out, did her brother. The subject had never been mentioned in her home.

Cowan emphasizes the family's repression, but makes it clear that Mathilda and her brother learned no more about their mother's "political past" from other kin, older neighbors, or young friends. Cowan goes on:

> I was carrying two books that contained descriptions of Camella Teoli's testimony. Standing in that huge parking lot, she read her mother's account of the old days in [the] Washington Mills. She wanted to know more. So I drove her to the Lawrence library where there was a two-volume record of the 1912 hearing. She read her mother's full testimony, enraptured. "Now I have a past," she said softly. "Now my son has a history he can be proud of."

Cowan then briefly reviewed the strike and its aftermath to indicate that what Camella Teoli and her children had experienced was not idiosyncratic. He described the efforts of radical sympathizers (Margaret Sanger the most prominent among them) to find decent homes in other cities for some of the children of Lawrence strikers. The police tried to prevent their departure with violence—a scene vividly depicted in E. L. Doctorow's *Ragtime*—and the children made their way carrying signs and banners which would later seem unduly ironic. "Some day we shall remember exile!" one banner stated, and another sign insisted, "We never forget." But they did forget—or at least deny. Cowan talked with one of the "exiles," now an elderly man, "a city employee who spends most of his afternoons playing the Italian card game *briscola* with other older men." The journalist described his conversation with him:

> He had vivid memories of his trip away from Lawrence and an enduring respect for the strike and its leaders. But he didn't want to discuss his exile. "You have to understand," he said. "I'm a very popular kid around here. I don't want to go around giving away the city's secrets."

By this reckoning, what a parent hid from her children was also part of the "city's secrets." A connection existed between the private and the public, even the familial and the political, and Cowan rightly emphasized the loss of a greater historical consciousness—of access to the fullness of Italian history and culture—in Camella Teoli's severe act of personal repression. He developed this point well:

> The act of going to Washington must have been the most exciting in Camella Teoli's life. But the mother her children knew was just a mill hand with an odd bald spot on her head, a sweet, silent lady

who bought and cooked the traditional eels on Christmas Eve, who rarely missed a Sunday Mass.

Cowan posited an alternate scenario:

What if she had been able to grow up in the political world that seemed so promising in 1912? She—and dozens of children like her—would have been able to take advantage of the Italian culture that strike leaders like Joseph Ettor and Arturo Giovannitti were so eager to transmit—to retain Italian as a language so that they'd have access to writers like Dante, composers like Verdi, thinkers like Gramsci—to feel that they weren't illiterate peasants but heirs to a culture that was even finer than that of the Yankees who defined them as brutes.

When you realize that Camella Teoli's children would have access to that culture, too, then Mathilda's spontaneous exclamation in the Lawrence library—"Now I have a past, now my son has a history"—becomes as much a lament as a cry of joy.

One need not agree with Cowan's insistence on the retention of the Italian language to share his insight. Mathilda's historical consciousness had been limited in ways that went far beyond the 1912 Lawrence, Massachusetts, textile strike, and affected her personal and cultural history.

One might argue that while Camella Teoli's and Mathilda's experiences may have been typical for immigrant workers becoming American workers in a repressive mill town, their experience was still unusual. But a similar experience of loss and closure in historical memory (or consciousness) occurred in a very different American setting. My second example illustrates that point.

Between 1977 and 1980, I directed a National Endowment for the Humanities seminar ("Americans at Work: Changing Social and Cultural Patterns") for trade union officials. Each summer fifteen local and regional staff workers and officers came from all over the country, where they represented workers in chemical, nuclear, textile, clothing, and steel industries, coal mines, the building trades, dock labor, and government employment (postal workers, teachers, and unskilled public services). Over a month, discussions ranged from examinations of seventeenth-century English and African work processes and culture, to the late-twentieth-century concern over the decline of the so-called Protestant work ethic. We focused on the causes of change in work processes and the struggles for control over these processes. The union men and women read the autobiographies of Frederick Douglass and Nate Shaw, the poems of John Greenleaf Whittier, William Carlos

Williams, and e.e. cummings, and the short stories of Lowell (Massachusetts) millwomen, Herman Melville, the Yiddish writer I. L. Peretz, and Mario Puzo. A regular fare of historical writings included works by Susan Benson, David Brody, Alan Dawley, Nathan Huggins, Lawrence Levine, Edmund S. Morgan, and E. P. Thompson.

The oldest participant in the 1977 seminar came from northern Alabama. His father had been a millworker, and A. S. Lemart, as I shall call him, had become a rubber-factory worker in the late 1930s. He spent his adult years as a worker and trade unionist, building an Alabama industrial union, supporting integration within the labor movement, and serving the state labor movement as an elected official. When we met, he was in his mid-fifties, about the same age as Camella Teoli's daughter Mathilda. Lemart was a quiet, dignified, largely self-educated Southern white trade union leader, democratic in his instincts and demeanor.

One seminar session well into the program was devoted to the "New South." We focused on the spread of industrial capitalism and the emergence of a white and black industrial working class in the South between 1880 and the First World War. We read an essay by Paul Worthman entitled "Black Workers and Labor Unions in Birmingham, Alabama, 1897–1904." An original study filled with information about miners, iron and steel workers, craftsmen, and unskilled labor, the essay examines in particular the relations between black and white workers, their unions, and their employers. Worthman describes the fiercely oppressive and violent methods by which the new corporations imposed their power on the region. He shows how racism often divided the workers, but also explains why interracial trade unionism triumphed if only for a brief moment. He points out that the Birmingham Trades Council increased from thirty-one locals with about 6,000 members in 1900 to more than sixty locals with more than 20,000 members in 1902. "The state's labor movement," Worthman concludes, "struggling to overcome both craft-union exclusiveness and racial conflict in Alabama, organized more than 8,000 black workers and challenged the industrialists' ability to use racial hostility to discipline the class antagonisms of the New South."

The Worthman essay provoked a vivid discussion, during which Lemart, the Birmingham trade unionist, remained noticeably silent. After the seminar, he privately praised Worthman's essay, emphasizing that every single item of information in its was new to him. He was an educated man; he knew more about the differences between the American Federation of Labor and the Knights of Labor than most college history teachers. The northern Alabama labor struggles of the 1930s and 1940s were etched deeply in his mind, but he knew nothing about northern Alabama's working-class history before that period.

POWER & CULTURE

Even the thwarted efforts by white and black workers to build democratic and protective unions during his own father's youth were unknown to him. Lemart was the direct heir of experiences important to his everyday work as a trade unionist, yet those experiences had been totally closed off to him.

Mathilda's and Lemart's backgrounds were quite different. One was the daughter of an immigrant mother who had hidden an act of personal and social heroism from her family. Mathilda remained a working-class woman, but was apparently cut off from Lawrence's working-class institutions and their histories. Lemart, descended from upcountry Alabama whites, spent his entire adult life as a factory worker and a trade union organizer and officer. Though Mathilda and Lemart were workers and shared many of the problems common to working men and women, their experiences differed—not only becasue of gender but because of the distinctive regional traditions from which they emerged: one a declining ethnic enclave in the Northeast, and the other a community of old-stock black and white Americans in the South. But both were the victims of a truncated and shrunken historical consciousness. They had been cut off from the past, deprived of access to the historical processes that had shaped their lives, the lives of their parents, and the nation at large. This amnesia was not peculiar to one or another region. It happened over the entire nation between 1910 and 1940, decades during which the Progressive synthesis framed the writing of American history, but during which mainstream American culture increasingly celebrated "American-ness" by defining it narrowly and identifying it with achievement and assimilation.

A third example of popular historical consciousness joins the larger issues posed in the *Nation* essay with the biographical experiences of Mathilda and A. S. Lemart. The *Nation* essay emphasized the decline of *synthesis* in American historical writing, a process that began in the 1950s and still continues. It praised much of the New History but criticized its narrow scope. I wrote:

By the end of the 1970s, whole segments of American history had a different look. A rich, empirical scholarship cast fresh light on the history of either misunderstood or neglected groups such as blacks, workers and women. . . . At its best, this new history revised important *segments* of the national experience. . . . But the stress on segments also reinforces the disintegration of a coherent synthesis in the writing of American history, a process that started in the 1950s. *Pattern* and *context* are often ignored. . . . Black history has been rewritten in this generation. So has the history of women and that of the working class. . . . But *American history* itself does not look that different. And that is the problem.

The third example begins to explain why so much revisionist social history (the study of neglected groups) has failed to transform significantly our overall view of American history. It is the publication of Alex Haley's *Roots* in 1976, the year Paul Cowan and Mathilda met, and the year before Lemart had his encounter with Worthman's early-twentieth-century Alabama workers. I leave aside the question of the authenticity of *Roots*, the dispute over its authorship, and its unquestioned importance in presenting Afro-American slaves as human beings to so large an audience for the first time. Instead, let me focus on the relationship between the book's success and its mode of historical explanation. In a society in which men and women like Lemart and Mathilda have such limited historical memories, what made *Roots* so popular? Why were so many millions of white and black Americans drawn to it, both as a book and, later as a television "mini-series"? Far more was involved than a new or a renewed interest in either the history of slavery, Afro-Americans, or the family.

The themes that *Roots* dealt with are important, but its popularity, and the ease with which the culture celebrated it, had more to do—I am convinced—with the way it constructed a historical narrative and with its mode of historical explanation. In essence, *Roots* succeeded because it did not make American history look different. It contained all the elements of a successful Western novel or film, but its subjects were the experiences of generations of enslaved Afro-American men, women, and children. *Roots* was an adventure story, a success story that pitted the individual (in this instance a slave family, or several generations of slave families) against society. The isolated family triumphed against overwhelming odds because of its *individual* capacity to remember the name of a distant African ancestor. *Roots* succeeded by redefining the central tensions in slave society in ways that made it possible to integrate the Afro-American slave experience (a metaphor here for much revisionist social history) into middle-class American culture. What was more "American" than a small slave family with meager resources ("memory") making it? *Roots* had succeeded in integrating the slave experience into mainstream American ideology. The dialectic was Hobbesian. The poor and unequal—even the slaves— had their winners and losers. The winners were proud. As Diana Ross told *Time* magazine in 1977: "I love being rich. I love playing tennis and not being cold in the winter. I am the original Horatio Alger story."

In its success, *Roots* illustrates how the study of an oppressed historical

POWER & CULTURE

group (even slaves!) can serve to reinforce what Raymond Williams calls "a version of the past . . . intended to connect with and ratify the present." It confirms what Williams describes as "a selective tradition," offering "a sense of predisposed continuity." The devices Haley used to humanize slaves—his achievement ideology, which pitted the individual against society—ironically reinforced the same American possessive individualism which allowed no place for Camella Teoli and her daughter, or A. S. Lemart and his father.

Roots is not an exception. The absence of new syntheses has meant that popular and academic histories of neglected groups often emphasize the same theme of achievement. Sometimes a group's history is distorted by ignoring its inner class and social divisions, as in Oscar Handlin's essay on "Yankees" in the *Harvard Encyclopedia of American Ethnic Groups*. Handlin's essay is written as if the revisionist writings of younger historians such as Alan Dawley, Thomas Dublin, Paul Faler, and Gary Kulik had never been published:

> In the countryside the characteristic patterns of Yankee agriculture combined production for the market, efforts at improvement that would raise the value of the farm, and a willingness to speculate. In the cities Yankees clustered in commercial and professional callings.

There is room in this brief essay for the names of Timothy Dwight and P. T. Barnum, but not for terms like "working class" or "wage earner."

The poor Irish and Jewish immigrants, in turn, find a place in the recent writings of Stephen Birmingham and Thomas Sowell, historical vulgarizers of far less talent and importance than Oscar Handlin. When *The Manions of America* (an ABC television series broadcast in the fall of 1981) told the story of the Irish in America, Birmingham summarized their history for *TV Guide* readers. It should be kept in mind that Birmingham is describing the Gilded Age Irish and Irish-Americans.

> Almost immediately, the Irish in America . . . began to be successful. They appeared to possess characteristics that other immigrant groups did not have. For one thing, they were willing to work at backbreaking and menial jobs that European Jews—who were arriving during the same period—and even emerging blacks refused to perform. A healthy Irishman would work in a tunnel laying subway tracks for 75¢ a day. A healthy girl would work as a housemaid for room and board and a dollar a week, and the Irish girl made a wonderful maid. Clean and virginal and fond of children, she would work seven days a week, asking only for a half-hour off

on Sundays to go to Mass. (Early-morning Masses were introduced to enable the Irish serving-girl to be back at her job in time to serve her master and mistress breakfast.) At the same time, the Irish serving-girl was exceptionally observant of the ways of her employers. Her room might be an unheated cell under the rafters of a city mansion, but she had all day to study the furniture, silver, and appointments of a rich man's house. She might not be able to afford such luxuries, but she was determined that her children would. . . . The Irish were ambitious. . . . The Irish also were attractive— the women with an alarming tendency to look like Maureen O'Hara and the men to resemble Errol Flynn. Wanting to be liked, the Irish laid great stress on appearance, manners, and etiquette. Also, having experienced the humiliation of indebtedness and living on credit, the emerging "Irishtocracy" were scrupulous when it came to paying bills. All these pleasant qualities helped wear down anti-Irish prejudice. . . .

This unceasingly banal popular history was written in 1981. Birmingham, ironically, writes as if Oscar Handlin had never published his great study of the Boston Irish.

The Irish poor made their way up as hard-working achievers. That was the central theme of their history, just as it was for the successful slaves in *Roots*. And for the immigrant Eastern European Jews, according to Thomas Sowell, whose *Ethnic America: A History* appeared at about the same time as Birmingham's essay and was described by Milton Friedman as "a classic," by Stephan Thernstrom as "a stimulating volume," and by Diane Ravitch as combining "the best of recent scholarship in a readable, compact form." Sowell's Jewish immigrants are interchangeable with Birmingham's Irish ones. Hear his rhapsodical but crass description of ghetto work:

While the nineteenth-century home sweatshop was the bane of reformers then and historians later, it provided a way for Jewish women to work without leaving their children unattended. . . . It had its costs. . . . [But] it was essentially a system by which the mass of Americans obtained brand-new clothing at a price they could afford. The Jewish sweatshop workers were, by contemporary accounts, able to save a substantial portion of their earnings, providing for the future economic rise of themselves and their children. In view of their later success, it would be arrogant of others to claim that they were not making the best of their meager opportunities. . . .

Sowell is certain as to why the "Jews" succeeded: they did not have to struggle to improve their condition and transform their lives. They passed unscathed through their American poverty. "The Jews," Sowell writes in a memorable nonhistorical passage, "had the social patterns and values of the middle class, even when they lived in slums. . . . They took those values into and out of the slums." These sentences would cheer Milton Friedman but would chill Abraham Cahan and David Levinsky. Let us see why.

Sowell, Birmingham, and Haley differ from each other in important ways. But all are popularizers of the aspirations and behavior of diverse exploited, poor, and dependent groups of Americans. What links the three writers is their emphasis on individualism as the sole device used by these groups to overcome their exploitation, inequality, and dependence. Resistance to dependence—based upon class, race, or gender—has been a central theme in the nation's history. Such resistance has been irregular and uneven, but it has been a constant. The Founding Fathers addressed the issue of dependence directly. "Dependence," Thomas Jefferson warned in often-quoted words, "begets subservience . . . and suffocates the germ of virtue." Alexander Hamilton put it slightly differently. "Give a man power over my subsistence," he said, "and he has a right to my whole moral body."

Hamilton and Jefferson feared the corrosive impact of dependence. So did others more critical of the established order of their times. But the history of resistance to dependence is not merely that of men and women freeing themselves in individualistic ways. Haley and these others mistakenly identify independence with individualism and reinforce a central and confused element in popular historical consciousness. This oversimplified relationship explains in part the historical silences experienced by Mathilda and Lemart, and flows from the altogether too easy transfer of values from the dominant culture to the subordinate class, gender, or racial group. "No mode of production and therefore no dominant social order and therefore no dominant culture," Raymond Williams reminds us, "ever in reality includes or exhausts all human practice, human energy, and human intention. . . . Significant things . . . happen outside or against the dominant mode."

Indeed, the full history of any dependent group involves far more than their success through individualist ("mainstream") behavior. Instead, a central tension in all dependent groups over time has been between individualist (utilitarian) and collective (mutualist) ways of dealing with, and sometimes overcoming, dependence and inequality. An awareness of that tension is lacking both in popular historical consciousness and in most academic writing.

My point should not be misunderstood. Yankee workers were go-getters. But their world also involved collectivist ways for achieving independence. Hear the Philadelphia journeymen carpenters explaining their opposition to their employers in 1791:

> 'Tis one of the invaluable privileges of our nature, that when we conceive ourselves aggrieved, there is an inherent right to complain. . . . Self-preservation has induced us to enter into an indissoluble union, in order to ward off the blows which are threatened us, by the insolent hand of pampered affluence:—We mean hereafter by a firm, independent mode of conduct to protect each other. . . .

Or the Lowell mill "girls" in their first strike (1834) rejecting charity from their betters:

> Our present object is to have union and exertion, and we remain in possession of our unquestionable rights. . . . If any are in want of assistance, the Ladies will be compassionate and assist them; but we prefer to have the disposing of our charities in our own hands; and as we are free, we would remain in possession of what kind Providence has bestowed upon us; and remain daughters of freemen still.

Nor was the mutualist or collectivist strand in lower-class behavior stirred only by militant strikes. In his splendid critique of the ideological assumptions on which recent studies of social mobility rest, the historian James Henretta emphasizes the steady flow of remittances to the old country by American Irish, who were not simply go-getters climbing up the social ladder. Henretta explains:

> During the so-called "Scourge of 1847" the Irish in Boston sent back more than $200,000, while between 1851 and 1880, the Emigrant Industrial Savings Bank of New York remitted $30 million to Ireland. Estimates for the overall total of remittances vary widely (one, for the period from 1848 to 1864, is $65 million); but their enormous size is not in doubt. Nor is their significance.

Henretta concludes:

> Whatever their hopes for themselves, these migrants were not atomistic individualists, with an intense and overriding goal of self-advancement, but responsible participants in a trans-Atlantic kinship network with strong family ties and communal values.

An ethic of mutuality and of generalized obligation also existed among the former slaves. The black men and women who built and sustained new schools in the post-emancipation South, despite their poverty, drew upon this ethic of mutuality. For example, in the countryside surrounding Darlington, South Carolina, most blacks farmed. Store orders were common, and cash payments few. A crop failure in 1866 (just one-third of the normal harvest was managed that year) caused even worse troubles. In June 1867, Darlington freedmen addressed Boston's mayor:

> We are on the eve of Starvation. We have no way in God's world to get provisions. Only through our Friends North. . . . If there is any chance in the world to get anything to eat in your city, do for Heavens Sake Send us some and save us from Perishing.

Though their poverty put a limit on how much they could do collectively to school themselves and their children, they moved an old "Confederate building" ten miles from Florence to Darlington to start the district's first school. By April 1866, the region had eleven schools. Summerville got its school sometime before July. Two white women offered two acres of land for $200 as school property. Local blacks, many of them destitute, crowded into an army barracks they used as their church to agree that if Northern benevolent societies paid for the land and the government supplied lumber, they would build a school. Dan Meyers ("a good carpenter") spoke first: "I is a plain man and alers does what I agree, and I say I will stan' by the good work till it's done finished." Another spoke like him: "I is called a good carpenter; I has no children of my own to send to the school; but I want to see the house built, and I gives two weeks for it." Others offered labor, and some gave small sums of money. In all, the blacks raised $60 and pledged twelve weeks of labor. The women did their part, too, said a Yankee teacher, "offering to board or lodge the workmen as best they could." "These destitute people," the teacher mused, "living, some of them, in rude huts made of mud and palmetto, one might suppose that all their interest was necessary to keep them from starving. . . ."

What happened in Summerville happened elsewhere in 1866. Darlington blacks gave their labor and money for a school ($500); Simmonsville blacks ditched and fenced a plot, and then built a schoolhouse ($150); former slaves in Sumter moved a building forty miles and then reconstructed it ($250). That also happened in Lynchburg ($150) and in Florence ($350). The schoolhouse Camden blacks built and paid for cost $800. And there were other places, too. The schools varied in size: Timonville (14 by 24 feet), Florence (35 by 45 feet), and Darlington (30 by 72 feet). The schools were sustained by more than just cash. Freedpeople furnished teachers with beds, bedding, and furniture in Camden, sold "articles" at "under price" to teachers, and gave food without charge. By January 1867, the former slaves had started twenty-two schools in the region, and owned more than $12,000 of church and school properties, two-thirds of which was "secured by their own industry, skill, and collections."

Communal values and sanctions also shaped the behavior of the Sea Island blacks who, in 1868, debated ways to sustain schools in their poverty. Hastings Garret spoke first at their meeting and urged that "rich and poor . . . come forward at once and assist in support of the schools, each putting in according to his means." Yankee teachers urged that the former slaves rely on their own resources. The "elders and principal men" replied, promising to raise money but insisting that cash was short. Garret asked that they "set aside a piece of land, work it fruitfully, and devote all its produce to the schools." Others spoke:

> Uncle Liah . . . said they were all poor, and each could do but little, but this was work for many. It may be as it was at Indian Hill, where the great burial-ground was raised by each Indian throwing just one handful of earth upon it each time he passed. Uncle Aleck said, Should each man regard only his own children, and forget all others? Should they leave that poor neighbor widow with her whole gang of children, and give them no chance for a free schooling?

Such beliefs—"each putting in according to his means" and setting aside a piece of land for a communal purpose and all working it—was far removed from Yankee possessive individualism or Southern paternalist pieties. Neither did these notions of mutuality depend upon a reading of either Tom Paine or Karl Marx.

Sometimes the shifting and uneasy tensions between individualist and collectivist means of achieving independence revealed themselves within a single individual. Nate Shaw was that type of person, and the tension within him over ways of escaping dependence makes *All God's Dangers* a singularly significant American autobiography. Abraham Cahan's novel *The Rise of David Levinsky* also calculates the complex costs of "making it." Contrast Thomas Sowell's banal assertion that immigrant Jews brought middle-class values "into and out of the slums" with the millionaire Levinsky's discomfort over his success as a cloak-and-suiter. Early in the book, he worries:

> Sometimes, when I think of my past in a superficial, casual way, the metamorphosis I have gone through strikes me as nothing short of a miracle. I was born and reared in the lowest depths of poverty and I arrived in America . . . with four cents in my pocket. I am now worth more than two million dollars and recognized as one of the two or three leading men in the cloak-and-suit trade in the United States. And yet when I take a look at my inner identity it impresses me as being precisely the same as it was thirty or forty

years ago. My present station, power, the amount of worldly happiness at my command, and the rest of it, seem to be devoid of significance.

Levinsky questions his decision to "make it," grieving over having chosen "a business career." In a passage that captures the tension so common among dependent persons (not just Jewish immigrants) struggling with themselves, Cahan has Levinsky tell us:

I don't seem able to get accustomed to my luxurious life. I am always more or less conscious of my good clothes, of the high quality of my office furniture, of the power I wield over other men in my pay. As I have said in another connection, I still have a lurking fear of restaurant waiters.

I can never forget the days of my misery. I cannot escape from my old self. My past and my present do not comport well. David, the poor lad swinging over a Talmud volume at the Preacher's Synagogue, seems to have more in common with my inner identity than David Levinsky, the well-known cloak-manufacturer.

That "inner identity," so central to David Levinsky and to Nate Shaw, is uncovered when we address the tension between individualist and collectivist ways of dealing with dependency, inequality, and exploitation by the dependent, the unequal, and the exploited. We are humanized by that encounter and so is American history. That is why that tension needs to be restored to American history. It was, and is, always there. It just needs to be noticed.

Except in the civil rights and women's movements, it has been difficult to notice that tension in American society since the Second World War. Its obscurity helps us comprehend why Mathilda and Lemart knew so little of their history, why mutualist or collectivist ways of dealing with inequality and dependence appeared redundant, why the study of such historical subjects appeared to be of interest primarily to antiquarian leftist "social" historians, and why the distinguished European intellectual historian Frank Manuel complained in 1976 that "much of nineteenth century American history has been too thoroughly enveloped in nauseating fumes of official optimism to be tolerable to a human being."

The receding of this central theme in American history during the postwar decades rested on what the sociologist Paul Blumberg calls the "gospel of classlessness," the theory so common in the 1950s and the 1960s of "class convergence." Blumberg examines the popularity of this theory, and that of its critics (those who argued the view of "class stability"), in a very fine but little-noticed book published in

1980, *Inequality in an Age of Decline*. He sketches the dominant "convergence" theory of class and its critical opposition, "stability theory," in simple diagrams and subtle argument. Blumberg's simple diagrams are indicated below:

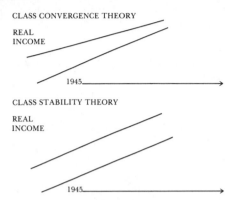

"Dominant postwar opinion held that a growing egalitarianism in American society was narrowing the gap between classes, creating a pattern of class convergence," Blumberg explains. "Other postwar writers disputed this claim and contended that while all classes were moving up that inclined plane, the distance between the classes was not narrowing, producing . . . stability."

The theorists of class convergence won wide attention. That some were liberal and others were conservative hardly mattered. They shared a belief that the "problems of the previous industrial (capitalist) epoch" had been transcended as a consequence of growing abundance and declining material scarcity. According to Blumberg, many of these theorists argued that

> even if wealth and income were not becoming distributed more equally in the postwar period, class conflict over distribution was prevented because of absolute gains for everybody. In the postwar generation relative class harmony was achieved by rapidly rising productivity and economic expansion. Because the size of the pie was constantly increasing, a larger slice for one group miraculously meant a larger slice for other groups as well.

Because the theory of class convergence grew in popularity at the same time that historical study turned its attention to neglected groups (such as workers, persons of color, and women), it began to shape the study of these groups. The very issue—inequality of one sort or another—that defined these groups was trivialized by theorists of class convergence. John Kenneth Galbraith put it best in *The Affluent Society*:

It has become abundantly evident to conservatives and liberals alike that increasing output is the alternative to redistribution or even to the reduction of inequality. The oldest and most agitated of social issues (equality), if not resolved, is at least largely in abeyance, and the disputants have concentrated their attention, instead, on the goal of increasing productivity.

It was almost as if anything was now possible in America. It was almost as if Sholem Aleichem's ironic view of America at the turn of the century had become the real world at midcentury:

We asked her where her husband was.
"He's in America."
"What does he do there?"
"He's got a job as Tsar."
"But how can a Jew be Tsar?"
"Everything's possible in America," she answered.

A world in which everything *was* possible became a world in which everything *had been* possible. The past became a reflection of the present. Historic efforts to overcome inequality and the debates over those efforts became less important, as if "growth" had retroactively solved the problem of "distribution," and the irregular but ongoing debates over historical inequality were granted about the same importance as nineteenth-century debates over the price of public lands or the cost of internal improvements. "Making it"—individual "contributionalist" history—thrived in the world that Sholem Aleichem had mocked. There was a place for Stephen Birmingham's Irish in this world, but not for the aging Camella Teoli, Philadelphia's journeymen carpenters, the sharecropper Nate Shaw or the millionaire Levinsky.

The society of the 1950s and 1960s that the theories of class convergence and class stability disputed does not exist in the early 1980s. Blumberg demonstrates important changes in class relations between the mid-1960s and this moment. The assumption of a permanent "inclined plane of increased benefits for most persons" has indeed proved erroneous. A staggering array of data indicate a marked shift in contemporary American class relations. Real income for nonfarm employees flattened out in the 1970s. The percentage of increase in real gross family income was much lower between 1968 and 1978 (9 percent) than between 1958 and 1968 (42 percent). After accounting for taxes and inflation, median family income hardly changed between 1969 and 1979. The pie is no longer growing.

Blumberg contrasts the old convergence and stability theories with what he now describes as class stagnation or class divergence:[15]

```
CLASS STAGNATION THEORY
REAL          _____
INCOME        _____

       1965_____→

CLASS DIVERGENCE THEORY
REAL          _____
INCOME        _____

       1965_____→
```

These characterizations of current class relations differ greatly, but both assure the reemergence of redistribution as a central political and economic issue. Ronald Reagan's policies have sped up that process, but even before his election Robert Heilbroner observed, "When growth slows down, we must expect a struggle of redistribution on a vast scale." Heilbroner's message is almost the opposite of what John Kenneth Galbraith predicted in the 1950s.

Blumberg offers a bold assessment of recent American history: "The events of the 1970s seemed to involve not merely rapid social change or even the acceleration of social change . . . but a radical discontinuity or break in the direction of social change from the earlier postwar era." He goes on:

> After a generation of moving up that inclined plane, the mass of Americans now find themselves, in a great many dimensions of social class, including jobs, income, housing, and living standards, *locked in* or *bumped down.*

Such a sharp change in class relations promises to affect historical consciousness, although the consequences may not be entirely welcome. The past may yet be ransacked to justify a politics that celebrates inequalities of class, race, gender, generation, and even region. But it is also possible that the politics associated with an era of class stagnation or divergence will again redefine the ways in which people deal with their inequality. The old tensions between alternative ways of overcoming hardship—this time in a stagnant or shrinking economy—should resurface. Historians should be around to explain that the struggle between individual and collective responses is not a new one. As the British historian and novelist David Caute has said, a history which emphasizes the changing character of the tensions and how they differ from group to group "furnishes us not only with heroes, famous and unknown, but also with a diachronic pattern which provides an alternative context for thought and action." It was the absence of such a context, and the narrow identification of the struggle against inequality with possessive individualism, that made history so distant from the lives and sensibilities of men and women like Lemart and Mathilda. They deserve better from us as historians as the twentieth century draws to a close. And as the fullness of their class experience is restored, American history, not just the history of this or that neglected group, should become more coherent and more human. That badly needed new synthesis might even emerge.

PUBLISHED WORKS OF
HERBERT G. GUTMAN

Compiled by Andrew Gyory

* Starred articles were published in Herbert G. Gutman, *Work, Culture, and Society in Industrializing America: Essays in American Working-Class and Social History* (New York, 1976).

* "Two Lockouts in Pennsylvania, 1873–1874," *Pennsylvania Magazine of History and Biography* 83 (1959), 307–26.

"An Iron Workers' Strike in the Ohio Valley, 1873–1874," *Ohio Historical Quarterly* 68 (1959), 353–70.

"The Braidwood Lockout of 1874," *Journal of the Illinois State Historical Society* 53 (1960), 5–28.

* "Trouble on the Railroads in 1873–1874: Prelude to the 1877 Crisis?" *Labor History* 2 (1961), 215–35; reprinted in Daniel J. Leab, ed., *The Labor History Reader* (Urbana, Ill., 1985), 132–52.

"Reconstruction in Ohio: Negroes in the Hocking Valley Coal Mines in 1873 and 1874," *Labor History* 3 (1962), 243–64.

"The Workers' Search for Power: Labor in the Gilded Age," in H. Wayne Morgan, ed., *The Gilded Age: A Reappraisal* (Syracuse, N.Y., 1963), 38–68; reprinted in Herbert G. Gutman, *Power and Culture: Essays on the American Working Class*, ed. Ira Berlin (New York, 1987), 70–92.

Review of *The Origins of Teapot Dome: Progressives, Parties, and Petroleum, 1909 –1921* (J. Leonard Bates), *Choice* 1 (1964), 45.

Review of *Seed-Time of Reform: American Social Service and Social Action, 1918– 1933* (Clarke A. Chambers), *Choice* 1 (1964), 79.

Review of *Carroll Wright and Labor Reform: The Origin of Labor Statistics* (James Leiby), *American Historical Review* 69 (1964), 1167–68.

"The Buena Vista Affair, 1874–1875," *Pennsylvania Magazine of History and Biography* 88 (1964), 251–93.

Review of *The Greenback Era: A Social and Political History of American Finance, 1865–1877* (Irwin Unger), *Ohio History* 73 (1964), 268–9.

Review of *The Nation Transformed: The Creation of an Industrial Society* (Sigmund Diamond, ed.), *Labor History* 5 (1964), 328–31.

"The Tompkins Square 'Riot' in New York City on January 13, 1874: A Re-examination of Its Causes and Its Aftermath," *Labor History* 6 (1965), 44–83.

Review of *Poverty and Progress: Social Mobility in a Nineteenth Century City* (Stephan Thernstrom), *New-York Historical Society Quarterly* 49 (1965), 404–7.

"The Failure of the Movement by the Unemployed for Public Works in 1873," *Political Science Quarterly* 80 (1965), 254–76.

"Peter H. Clark: Pioneer Negro Socialist," *Journal of Negro Education* 34 (1965), 413–24.

Review of *The Seattle General Strike* (Robert L. Friedheim), *American Historical Review* 71 (1965), 334.

Review of *Development of the Labor Movement in Milwaukee* (Thomas W. Gavett), *American Historical Review* 71 (1966), 693–94.

Review of *Labor Revolt in Alabama: The Great Strike of 1894* (Robert D. Ward and William W. Rogers), *Labor History* 7 (1966), 239–45.

"Industrial Invasion of the Village Green," *Trans-Action* 3 (1966), 19–24.

"Documents on Negro Seamen During the Reconstruction Period," *Labor History* 7 (1966), 307–11.

Review of *Labor in Crisis: The Steel Strike of 1919* (David Brody), *American Historical Review* 72 (1966), 324.

* "Protestantism and the American Labor Movement: The Christian Spirit in the Gilded Age," *American Historical Review* 72 (1966), 74–101; reprinted in Alfred F. Young, ed., *Dissent: Explorations in the History of American Radicalism* (Dekalb, Ill., 1968), 137–74; also reprinted in John M. Mulder and John Frederick Wilson, eds., *Religion in American History: Interpretive Essays* (Englewood Cliffs, N.J., 1978), 318–41.

"Labor in the Land of Lincoln: Coal Miners on the Prairie" [1966–67], *Power and Culture*, 117–212.

"The Labor Policies of the Large Corporation in the Gilded Age: The Case of the Standard Oil Company" [1966–67], *Power and Culture*, 213–54.

Review of *Kohler on Strike: Thirty Years of Conflict* (Walter H. Uphoff), *American Historical Review* 72 (1967), 733–4.

* "The Negro and the United Mine Workers of America, The Career and Letters of Richard L. Davis and Something of Their Meaning: 1890–1900," in Julius Jacobson, ed., *The Negro and the American Labor Movement* (New York, 1968), 49–127.

"Labor's Response to Modern Industrialism," in Howard H. Quint, Dean Albertson, and Milton Cantor, eds., *Main Problems in American History* (Homewood, Ill., 1964; rev. ed. 1968), 83–105.

* "Class, Status, and Community Power in Nineteenth-Century American Industrial Cities—Paterson, New Jersey: A Case Study," in Frederic Cople Jaher, ed., *The Age of Industrialism in America: Essays in Social Structure and Cultural Values* (New York, 1968), 263–87.

Preface to Sterling D. Spero and Abram L. Harris, *The Black Worker: The Negro and the Labor Movement* (New York, 1968), vii–xiii.

Introduction to *Labor Age* (New York, 1968), unpaginated.

"English Labor Views the American Reconstruction: An Editorial in The Bee-Hive (London), Sept. 26, 1874," *Labor History* 9 (1968), 110–12.

Review of *The Company Town in the American West* (James B. Allen), *Labor History* 9 (1968), 282–5.

"Five Letters of Immigrant Workers from Scotland to the United States, 1867–1869: William Latta, Daniel M'Lachlan, and Allan Pinkerton," *Labor History* 9 (1968), 384–408.

Review of *A Century of Labor-Management Relations at McCormick and International Harvester* (Robert Ozanne), *American Historical Review* 74 (1968), 301–3.

* "The Reality of the Rags-to-Riches 'Myth': The Case of the Paterson, New Jersey, Locomotive, Iron, and Machinery Manufacturers, 1830–1880," in Stephan Thernstrom and Richard Sennett, eds., *Nineteenth Century Cities: Essays in the New Urban History* (New Haven, Conn., 1969), 98–124.

"Black Coal Miners and the Greenback-Labor Party in Redeemer, Alabama:

1878–1879, The Letters of Warren D. Kelley, Willis Johnson Thomas, 'Dawson,' and Others," *Labor History* 10 (1969), 506–35.

"A Reconsideration of the Labor Problem," in Thomas B. Brewer, ed., *The Robber Barons: Saints or Sinners?* (New York, 1970), 68–74.

Introduction to *Liberty* (Westport, Conn., 1970), unpaginated.

Introduction to *State Labor Reports: From the End of the Civil War to the Start of the Twentieth Century* (Westport, Conn., 1970).

"Industrial Workers Struggle for Power," in Thomas R. Frazier, ed., *The Underside of American History: Other Readings* (New York, 1971), 2: 11–34.

"Marriage Licenses and Registers Among Freed Men and Women, 1865–1866: New Light on the Family and Household Condition of Slaves and Free Blacks," *Historical Methods Newsletter* 5 (1971), 25.

"The Knights of Labor and Patrician Anti-Semitism: 1891," *Labor History* 13 (1972), 63–7.

"New Directions in Black History: A Symposium," with Stanley L. Engerman, Robert W. Fogel, Eugene D. Genovese, *Forum* 1 (1972), 22–41.

"Le phénomène invisible: la composition de la famille et du foyer noirs après la Guerre de Sécession," *Annales: Economies, Sociétés, Civilisations* 27 (1972), 1197–1218.

Many Pasts: Readings in American Social History, ed. with Gregory S. Kealey (Englewood Cliffs, N.J., 1973), 2 vols.

* "Class, Status, and the Gilded-Age Radical: A Reconsideration. The Case of a New Jersey Socialist," in Gutman and Gregory S. Kealey, eds., *Many Pasts: Readings in American Social History* (Englewood Cliffs, N.J., 1973), 2: 125–51.

* "Work, Culture, and Society in Industrializing America, 1815–1919," *American Historical Review* 78 (1973), 531–88; and reply, *American Historical Review* 79 (1974), 256.

"*The International Socialist Review*, Chicago, 1900–1918"; "*The Intercollegiate Socialist*, New York, 1913–1919"; "*The Socialist Review*, New York, 1919–1921"; "*Labor Age*, New York, 1921–1933"; "*Liberty*, Boston and New York, 1881–1908"; "*Alarm*, Chicago and New York, 1884–1889," in Joseph R. Conlin, ed., *The American Radical Press, 1880–1960* (Westport, Conn., 1974), 1: 82–6, 191–7; 2: 373–9, 380–6.

"Moving North" [letter], *Commentary* 58 (1974), 22.

"A Note on Immigration History, 'Breakdown Models,' and the Rewriting of the History of Immigrant Working-Class Peoples" [1974], *Power and Culture*, 255–9.

"Schools for Freedom: The Post-Emancipation Origins of Afro-American Education" [1974], *Power and Culture*, 260–97.

"The World Two Cliometricians Made: A Review-Essay of F + E = T/C," *Journal of Negro History* 60 (1975), 53–227.

Slavery and the Numbers Game: A Critique of "Time on the Cross" (Urbana, Ill., 1975).

"Persistent Myths About the Afro-American Family," *Journal of Interdisciplinary History* 6 (1975), 181–210 [English version of "Le phénomène invisible . . ." in *Annales*, above]; reprinted in Michael Gordon, ed., *The American Family in Socio-Historical Perspective*, 3rd ed. (New York, 1983), 459–81.

Work, Culture, and Society in Industrializing America: Essays in American Working-Class and Social History (New York, 1976).

* "Joseph P. McDonnell and the Workers' Struggle in Paterson, New Jersey," published as "A Brief Post-Script" in *Work, Culture, and Society in Industrializing*

America: Essays in American Working-Class and Social History, 260–92; reprinted in *Power and Culture*, 93–116.

The Black Family in Slavery and Freedom, 1750–1925 (New York, 1976).

Reckoning with Slavery: A Critical Study in the Quantitative History of American Negro Slavery, with Paul A. David, Richard Sutch, Peter Temin, and Gavin Wright (New York, 1976).

"The Black Family Reconsidered: Long Together," *New York Times*, 22 Sept. 1976, 41.

"The Black Family Reconsidered: Durability on the Plantation," *New York Times*, 23 Sept. 1976, 41.

"The Black Family Reconsidered: In the South and in Harlem, Tenacity," *New York Times*, 24 Sept. 1976, A25.

"A New Look at Black Families and Slavery," *Current* 188 (1976), 3–9.

"How Deep Did *Roots* Dig?" with Philip S. Foner and others, *In These Times* 1 (23 Feb.–1 March 1977), 11–13.

Review of *Class and Community: The Industrial Revolution in Lynn* (Alan Dawley), *New York Times Book Review*, 12 June 1977, 29–30.

"As for the '02 Kosher-Food Rioters . . .," *New York Times*, 21 July 1977, A23; and reply, "Disorders of '02 and '77: Readers' Replies," *New York Times*, 3 Aug. 1977, A19.

"The Occupational Structure and the Alleged Social Mobility of Slaves," in Edward Passen, ed., *The Many-Faceted Jacksonian Era: New Interpretations* (Westport, Conn., 1977), 142–56.

"Slavkulturen Oskyldig Till De Svartas Elande," *Familjen Forskning och Framsteg* 5–6 (1977), 73–7.

"Afro-American History as Immigrant Experience," in Shlomo Slonin, ed., *The American Experience in Historical Perspective* (Jerusalem, 1978), 123–46.

"La politique ouvrière de la grande entreprise américaine de 'l'âge du clinquant': le cas de la Standard Oil Company," *Le Mouvement Social* 102 (1978), 67–99.

"Slave Culture and Slave Family and Kin Network: The Importance of Time," in Jack R. Censer and N. Steven Steinert, eds., *South Atlantic Urban Studies* 2 (Columbia, S.C., 1978), 73–88.

"Slave Family and Its Legacies," in Michael Craton, ed., *Roots and Branches: Current Directions in Slave Studies* (Toronto, 1979), 183–99.

"Marital and Sexual Norms Among Slave Women," in Nancy F. Cott and Elizabeth H. Pleck, eds., *A Heritage of Her Own: Toward a New Social History of American Women* (New York, 1979), 298–310.

"The Moynihan Report: Black History Seduced and Abandoned," *Nation* 229 (1979), 232–6.

Introduction to Marc S. Miller, ed. *Working Lives: The "Southern Exposure" History of Labor in the South* (New York, 1980), xi–xvii.

"Moynihan Report" [letter], *Nation* 230 (1980), 98, 116.

"Des voies nouvelles pour l'histoire sociale," symposium with David Brody by Marianne Debouzy, *La Quinzaine littéraire* 330 (1980), 9–11.

"Labor History and the 'Sartre Question,' " *Humanities* 1 (1980), 1–2; reprinted in *Power and Culture*, 326–8.

"Famille et groupes de parente chez les Afro-Americains en esclavage dans les plantations de Good Hope (Caroline du Sud), 1760–1860," in Sidney Mintz, ed., *Esclave = facteur de production: l'économie politique de l'esclavage* (Paris, 1981), 141–70.

"Mirrors of Hard, Distorted Glass: An Examination of Some Influential Historical Assumptions about the Afro-American Family and the Shaping of Public Policies: 1861–1965," in David J. Rothman and Stanton Wheeler, eds., *Social History and Social Policy* (New York, 1981), 239–73.

"Toward a Black Politics: Beyond the Race-Class Dilemma," with Manning Marable, Roger Wilkins, Nathan Huggins, Aryeh Neier, Herbert Hill, and Hulbert H. James, *Nation* 232 (1981), 417, 429–36.

"History Lesson," *Nation* 233 (1981), 366–7.

"The Missing Synthesis: Whatever Happened to History?" *Nation* 233 (1981), 521, 553–4.

"Historical Consciousness in Contemporary America" [1982], *Power and Culture*, 395–412.

Preface, with David Brody, to Dirk Hoerder, ed., *American Labor and Immigration History, 1877–1920s: Recent European Research* (Urbana, Ill., 1983), vii–ix.

"The Afro-American Family in the Age of Revolution," with Ira Berlin and Mary Beth Norton, in Ira Berlin and Ronald Hoffman, eds., *Slavery and Freedom in the Age of the American Revolution* (Charlottesville, Va., 1983), 175–91.

"Interview with Herbert Gutman" [with Michael Merrill], *Radical History Review* 27 (1983), 202–22.

Interview in MARHO, Henry Abelove et al., eds., *Visions of History* (New York, 1983), 185–216; reprinted in *Power and Culture*, 329–56.

"Osztályszerkezet és az Amerikai: Munkásosztály Fejlödése 1840–1890 Között (A Bevándorlók és Gyermekeik, mint Bérmunkások.)," with Ira Berlin, *Történelmi Szemle/Historical Review* 26 (1983), 224–36; reprinted as "Class Composition and the Development of the American Working Class, 1840–1890," in *Power and Culture*, 380–94.

"Trashing a Competitor" [letter], *Nation* 236 (1983), 592.

"Natives and Immigrants, Free Men and Slaves: Urban Workingmen in the Antebellum American South," with Ira Berlin, *American Historical Review* 88 (1983), 1175–1200.

"Afro-American kinship before and after emancipation in North America," in Hans Medick and David Warren Sabean, eds., *Interest and Emotion: Essays on the Study of Family and Kinship* (Cambridge, 1984), 241–65.

"Parallels in the Urban Experience," in Joseph R. Washington, Jr., ed., *Jews in Black Perspectives: A Dialogue* (Rutherford, N.J., 1984), 98–104.

Review of *Chants Democratic: New York City and the Rise of the American Working Class, 1788–1850* (Sean Wilentz), *New Republic* 3,625 (1984), 33–36.

"The Black Family in Slavery and Freedom: A Revised Perspective," in Gene D. Lewis, ed., *New Historical Perspectives: Essays on the Black Experience in Antebellum America* (Cincinnati, 1985), 7–36; reprinted in *Power and Culture*, 357–79.

Introduction, with David Brody, to Daniel J. Leab, ed., *The Labor History Reader* (Urbana, Ill., 1985), xvii–xx.

Foreword to Paul Buhle and Alan Dawley, eds., *Working for Democracy: American Workers from the Revolution to the Present* (Urbana, Ill., 1985), ix–xii.

Introduction to Gutman and Donald H. Bell, eds., *The New England Working Class and the New Labor History* (Urbana, Ill., 1986), xi–xv.

"Learning About America: Memories of Madison in the Fifties," *Radical History Review* 36 (1986), 103–6.

NOTES

Introduction

1. Information on Herbert Gutman's early years is drawn from discussions with Judith Mara Gutman and from interviews with Gutman by Michael Merrill and by Paul Buhle. An edited version of Merrill's interview was later published in the *Radical History Review* and reprinted in MARHO, Henry Abelove et al., eds., *Visions of History* (New York, 1983), and is published below as chap. 9. Professor Merrill was kind enough to allow me to read and quote from the original transcript of this interview, cited herein as "Draft Interview." I have also benefitted from Paul Buhle's interview with Gutman on his years in Madison, "Fresh Air Finally."
2. Merrill, "Draft Interview." Henry David, *The History of the Haymaket Affair: A Study in the American Social Revolutionary and Labor Movements* (New York, 1936). Several recent accounts of the Haymarket Affair have added to our knowledge of events in Chicago in 1886, but David's history remains authoritative.
3. Richard Hofstadter, *The American Political Tradition and the Men Who Made It* (New York, 1948), viii.
4. Ibid.
5. "Interview With Herbert Gutman," below, chap. 9, 329.
6. Herbert G. Gutman, "Early Effects of the Depression of 1873 upon the Working Classes in New York City," unpublished M.A. thesis, Columbia University, 1950, 8.
7. Ibid., viii.
8. Ibid., 135.
9. "Fresh Air Finally." Also invaluable for the Madison years are the interviews with William Appleman Williams in MARHO, Abelove et al., *Visions of History*, 123–46, and with Warren Susman in *Radical History Review* 36 (1986), 106–9.
10. "Fresh Air Finally."
11. "Draft Interview."
12. John R. Commons et al., eds., *A Documentary History of American Industrial Society*, 10 vols. (Cleveland, Ohio, 1910–11), and also *History of Labour in the United States*, 4 vols. (New York, 1918–35).
13. Selig Perlman, *A Theory of the Labor Movement* (New York, 1928). See also

David Brody, "The Old Labor History and the New: In Search of an American Working Class," *Labor History* 20 (1979), 111–26.

14. Perhaps the most vocal of these was another Wisconsin graduate, C. Wright Mills: see *The New Men of Power: America's Labor Leaders* (New York, 1948), and later *The Power Elite* (New York, 1956).

15. "Fresh Air Finally."

16. Herbert G. Gutman, "Social and Economic Structure and Depression: American Labor in 1873 and 1874," unpublished Ph.D. dissertation, University of Wisconsin, 1959, vi.

17. "Draft Interview."

18. "Testimony of Herbert Gutman," in U.S. House of Representatives, *Hearings before the Committee on Un-American Activities*, "Investigation of Communist Activities, New York Area—Part 5 (Summer Camps)," 84th Cong., 1st sess., 1955, 1394–1400.

19. Gutman, "Social and Economic Structure and Depression," v.

20. Ibid., 357–96.

21. Ibid., 199.

22. See "The Braidwood Lockout of 1874," *Journal of the Illinois State Historical Society* 53 (1959), 5–28.

23. Gutman, "Social and Economic Structure and Depression," 115, 128.

24. For a full listing, see 413–17 below for a bibliography of Gutman's published work.

25. See below, chap. 1, 71–2.

26. "Draft Interview."

27. See below, chap. 1, 70.

28. For an early statement of this theme see Jesse Lemisch, "Towards a Democratic History," mimeographed pamphlet (Ann Arbor, Mich., 1967), and also "The American Revolution Seen from the Bottom Up," in Barton J. Bernstein, ed., *Towards a New Past: Dissenting Essays in American History* (New York, 1968), 3–45.

29. E. P. Thompson, *The Making of the English Working Class* (London, 1963). An American edition was published the following year.

30. Ibid., 12, 194.

31. Stephan Thernstrom, *Poverty and Progress: Social Mobility in a Nineteenth Century City* (Cambridge, Mass., 1964).

32. For a critique of the assumptions that undergird the study of social mobility by Thernstrom and others, see James A. Henretta, "The Study of Social Mobility: Ideological Assumptions and Conceptual Bias," *Labor History* 18 (1977), 165–78.

33. Review of *Poverty and Progress* (Stephan Thernstrom), *New-York Historical Society Quarterly* 49 (1965), 404–7.

34. "The Reality of the Rags-to-Riches 'Myth': The Case of the Paterson, New Jersey, Locomotive, Iron, and Machinery Manufacturers, 1830–1880," in Stephan Thernstrom and Richard Sennett, eds., *Nineteenth-Century Cities: Essays in the New Urban History* (New Haven, Conn., 1969), 98–124; also reprinted in Gutman, *Work, Culture, and Society in Industrializing America* (New York, 1976), quotation on 225.

35. See below, chap. 2.

36. Gutman published this essay on McDonnell—reprinted below as "Joseph P. McDonnell and the Workers' Struggle in Paterson, New Jersey" (chap.

2)—as a "Brief Postscript" to the republication of another essay on Paterson in *Work, Culture, and Society.* The "Postscript" essay was published earlier as "Class, Status, and the Gilded-Age Radical: A Reconsideration. The Case of a New Jersey Socialist," in Gutman and Gregory S. Kealey, eds., *Many Pasts: Readings in American Social History,* 2 vols. (Englewood Cliffs, N.J., 1973), 2: 125–51.

37. See below, chap. 2, 101.
38. See below, chap. 2, 111. Gutman's larger historiographic point was that the protective and ameliorative legislation of the Progressive era, which had been laid to a new middle class by Richard Hofstadter and others, had its origins in working-class activism.
39. "Class, Status and Community Power in Nineteenth-Century American Industrial Cities—Paterson, New Jersey: a Case Study," in Frederic C. Jaher, ed., *The Age of Industrialism in America: Essays in Social Structure and Cultural Values* (New York, 1968); reprinted in *Work, Culture, and Society,* quotation on 237.
40. See below, chap. 2, 105.
41. "Protestantism and the American Labor Movement: The Christian Spirit in the Gilded Age," *American Historical Review* 72 (1966), 74–101; reprinted in *Work, Culture, and Society,* quotation on 84.
42. Thompson, *Making of the English Working Class,* 68.
43. E. J. Hobsbawm, *Labouring Men: Studies in the History of Labour* (New York, 1964), particularly chap. 3, and *Primitive Rebels: Studies in Archaic Forms of Social Movement in the Nineteenth and Twentieth Centuries* (Manchester, 1959), chaps. 4–6; Thompson, *Making of the English Working Class,* chap. 11.
44. Center for Advanced Study in the Behavioral Sciences, Stanford University, 1966–1967.
45. "The Buena Vista Affair, 1874–1875," *Pennsylvania Magazine of History and Biography* 88 (1964), 251–93.
46. See below, chap. 3, 124.
47. See below, chap. 3, 134.
48. "Citizen-Miners and the Erosion of Traditional Rights: A Study of the Coming of Italians to the Western Pennsylvania Coal Mines, 1873–1878," Center for Advanced Study in the Behavioral Sciences, Stanford University, 1967, 7, 48.
49. Ibid., 7.
50. Ibid., 10, 40.
51. Ibid., 24, 77.
52. "The Negro and the United Mine Workers of America: The Career and Letters of Richard L. Davis and Something of Their Meaning, 1890–1900," in Julius Jacobson, ed., *The Negro and the American Labor Movement* (New York, 1968), 49–127; also published in *Work, Culture, and Society,* quotation on 124.
53. Ibid., 132.
54. Ibid., 150.
55. See below, chap. 4, 214.
56. See below, chap. 4, 251–2.
57. See below, chap. 4, 251.
58. See below, chap. 4, 251.

59. "Social Structure and Social Conflict in the Industrial City: Paterson, New Jersey," Center for Advanced Study in the Behavioral Sciences, Stanford University, 1967.
60. "Draft Interview."
61. Ibid.
62. For a full listing, see 413–17 below for a bibliography of Gutman's published work.
63. A portion of "The Labor Policies of the Large Corporation in the Gilded Age: The Case of Standard Oil" was later published as "La politique ouvrière de la grande entreprise américaine de 'l'âge du clinquant': Le Cas de la Standard Oil Company," *Le Mouvement Social* 102 (1978), 67–99.
64. "Culture, Conflict, and Violence in American Labor History: Some Comments and Some Evidence," University of Rochester, 1968; "Culture, Work, Conflict, and Discontinuity in American Working-Class History: The Recurrent Tension Between Pre-Industrial Cultures and Industrial Society, 1815–1920," University of Rochester, 1969.
65. "Work, Culture, and Society in Industrializing America, 1815–1919," *American Historical Review* 78 (1973), 531–88; published with slight revision as the lead essay in *Work, Culture, and Society*.
66. *Work, Culture, and Society*, 16–18.
67. Hugh D. Graham and Ted. R. Gurr, eds., *The History of Violence in America: Historical and Comparative Perspectives* (New York, 1969). The violent nature of industrialization played an even larger role in the earlier drafts of "Work, Culture, and Society." See above, note 64.
68. Oscar Handlin, *Boston's Immigrants: A Study of Acculturation* (Cambridge, Mass., 1941).
69. Oscar Handlin, *The Uprooted: The Epic Story of the Great Migration That Made the American People* (Boston, 1951).
70. *Work, Culture, and Society*, 41–3.
71. Handlin had used the word "acculturation" in the subtitle of *Boston's Immigrants*. However, he employed it as a synonym for assimilation. His critics would use the concept of acculturation in a different manner.
72. *Work, Culture, and Society*, 9.
73. Ibid., 41–3.
74. For criticism of "Work, Culture, and Society" see David Montgomery, "Gutman's Nineteenth-Century America," *Labor History* 19 (1978), 416–29, and Daniel T. Rodgers, "Tradition, Modernity, and the American Industrial Worker: Reflections and Critique," *Journal of Interdisciplinary History* 7 (1977), 655–81. Gutman responded to some of the criticism in Merrill's "Interview with Gutman," below, chap. 9.
75. Untitled essay on Buffalo, New York, 1840–1860, State University of New York, Buffalo, 1964.
76. Laurence Glasco, "Ethnicity and Social Structure: Irish, German and Native-Born of Buffalo, New York, 1850–1860," unpublished Ph.D. dissertation, State University of New York, Buffalo, 1973.
77. U.S. Department of Labor, Office of Policy Planning and Research, *The Negro Family: The Case for National Action* prepared by Daniel P. Moynihan (Washington, D.C., 1965), 5.
78. Stanley M. Elkins, *Slavery: A Problem in American Intellectual and Institutional*

Life (Chicago, 1959). Actually, Moynihan took his Elkins at second hand from sociologists Nathan Glazer and Thomas F. Pettigrew. See Glazer's introduction to the 1963 paperback edition of *Slavery*, and Pettigrew's *A Profile of the Negro American* (Princeton, N.J., 1964). *The Negro Family*, 15–16.

79. E. Franklin Frazier, *The Negro Family in the United States* (Chicago, 1939); also Charles S. Johnson, *Growing Up in the Black Belt: Negro Youth in the Rural South* (Washington, D.C., 1941).

80. Moynihan, *The Negro Family*, 47, 30.

81. Lee Rainwater and William L. Yancey brought together much of the debate in *The Moynihan Report and the Politics of Controversy* (Cambridge, Mass., 1967). Also Gutman, "Black History Seduced and Abandoned: The Moynihan Report," *Nation* 229 (1979), 232–6, and see the exchange in *ibid.* 230 (1980), 98, 116; "The Black Family Reconsidered": "Long Together," "Durability on the Plantation," and "In the South and in Harlem, Tenacity," *New York Times*," 22, 23, 24 Sept. 1976; "A New Look at Black Families and Slavery," *Current* 188 (1976), 3–9. See also Gutman, "Mirrors of Hard, Distorted Glass: An Examination of Some Influential Historical Assumptions About the Afro-American Family and the Shaping of Public Policies, 1861–1965," in David J. Rothman and Stanton Wheeler, eds., *Social History and Social Policy* (New York, 1981), 239–73.

82. Herbert G. Gutman and Laurence A. Glasco, "The Buffalo, New York, Negro, 1855–1875: A Study of the Family Structure of Free Negroes and Some of Its Implications," State University of New York, Buffalo, 1966, 22, 20; also Gutman and Glasco, "The Negro Family, Household, and Occupational Structure, 1855–1925, with Special Emphasis on Buffalo, but Also Including Comparative Data from New York, Brooklyn, Mobile, and Adams County, Mississippi," University of Rochester, 1968. Copies of these essays were generously supplied by Professor Glasco along with important information on their intellectual origins.

83. "Le phénomène invisible: la composition de la famille et du foyer noir après la Guerre de Sécession," *Annales: Economies, Sociétés, Civilisations* 27 (1972), 1197–1218; republished as "Persistent Myths About the Afro-American Family," *Journal of Interdisciplinary History* 6 (1975), 181–210.

84. For the policy implications of Gutman's study of the black family see below, chap. 9, and note 81 above.

85. "Persistent Myths About the Afro-American Family," 210.

86. Herbert G. Gutman, *The Black Family in Slavery and Freedom* (New York, 1976), chap. 8.

87. See below, chap. 6.

88. "The Rise of a Marxist Historian," *Change* 10 (1978), 31–5; Jon Wiener, "Radical Historians and the Crisis in American History, 1959–1980," *Journal of American History*, forthcoming, courtesy of the author.

89. Eugene D. Genovese, *The Political Economy of Slavery: Studies in the Economy and Society of the Slave South* (New York, 1965), 3.

90. Eugene D. Genovese, *The World the Slaveholders Made: Two Essays in Interpretation* (New York, 1969).

91. Eugene D. Genovese, "The Legacy of Slavery and the Roots of Black Nationalism," *Studies on the Left* 6 (1966), 3–26. Genovese's views changed

rapidly after the *Studies* article. Five years later, for inclusion in a collection of his essays, he revised it substantially. See *In Red and Black: Marxian Explorations in Southern and Afro-American History* (New York, 1971), chap. 6.

92. Eugene D. Genovese, *Roll, Jordan, Roll: The World the Slaves Made* (New York, 1976).

93. Ibid., 90–1.

94. See below, chap. 9, 353.

95. *Black Family in Slavery and Freedom*, 303–26; quotations on 307, 316.

96. Robert W. Fogel and Stanley L. Engerman, *Time on the Cross: The Economics of American Negro Slavery*, 2 vols. (Boston, 1974).

97. Robert W. Fogel, *Railroads and American Economic Growth: Essays in Econometric History* (Baltimore, 1970); Stanley L. Engerman, "A Reconsideration of Southern Economic Growth, 1770–1860," *Agricultural History* 49 (1975), 343–61, and especially his thoughtful "Some Considerations Relating to Property Rights in Man," *Journal of Economic History* 33 (1973), 43–65.

98. Thernstrom quoted in *New York Review of Books*, 2 Oct. 1975; *New York Times Book Review*, 28 April 1974.

99. Fogel and Engerman, *Time on the Cross*, 1: 4–6.

100. Ibid., 1: 5–6; Herbert G. Gutman, *Slavery and the Numbers Game: A Critique of "Time on the Cross"* (Urbana, Ill., 1976), quotation on 1.

101. For a good summary of the criticism of *Time on the Cross*, see Paul David et al., *Reckoning with Slavery: A Critical Study in the Quantitative History of American Negro Slavery* (New York, 1976).

102. "The World Two Cliometricians Made: A Review-Essay of F + E = T/C," *Journal of Negro History* 60 (1975), 53–227.

103. Fogel and Engerman, *Time on the Cross*, 1: 8.

104. *Slavery and the Numbers Game*, 3.

105. Fogel and Engerman, *Time on the Cross*, 1: 144–8; *New York Times Book Review*, 28 April 1974.

106. See below, chap. 7.

107. "Solidarity and Servitude," *Times Literacy Supplement*, 25 Feb. 1977. The review was signed by Genovese; it was written in concert with Elizabeth Fox-Genovese. Elizabeth Fox-Genovese and Eugene D. Genovese, *Fruits of Merchant Capital: Slavery and Bourgeois Property in the Rise and Expansion of Capitalism* (Oxford, 1983), xii.

108. Eugene D. Genovese and Elizabeth Fox-Genovese, "The Political Crisis of Social History: A Marxian Perspective," *Journal of Social History* 10 (1976), 205–20.

109. *Work, Culture, and Society*, xii. For a general assessment of the professional standing of Gutman's work, see Montgomery, "Gutman's Nineteenth Century America."

110. "Political Crisis of Social History," 212, 214–15.

111. See below, chap. 10, 360, 362.

112. See below, chap. 10, 362, 364, 365–6.

113. "Political Crisis of Social History," 219.

114. See below, chap. 8, 327.

115. Newt Davidson Collective, *Crisis at CUNY* (New York, 1974).

116. Ira Berlin and Herbert G. Gutman, "Slaves, Free Workers, and the Social Order of the Urban South," Shelby Cullom Davis Center for Historical Studies, 1976.

117. Ira Berlin and Herbert G. Gutman, "Natives and Immigrants, Free Men and Slaves: Urban Workingmen in the Antebellum South," *American Historical Review* 88 (1983), 1175–1200.

118. Herbert Gutman, "Whatever Happened to History?" *Nation* 233 (1981), 521, 553–4, and also below, chap. 8.

119. Grant Applications for American Working-Class History Project supplied by Steven Brier.

120. See below, chap. 12.

121. See below, chap. 12, 401.

122. See below, chap. 11.

123. "Draft Interview."

124. See below, chap. 11.

1. The Workers' Search for Power: Labor in the Gilded Age

1. See John R. Commons et al., eds., *A Documentary History of American Industrial Society*, 10 vols. (New York, 1958), 9: i–viii.

2. See Thomas C. Cochran, "The Social Sciences and the Problem of Historical Synthesis," in Fritz Stern, ed., *The Varieties of History* (New York, 1956), 352–6; Frank Tannenbaum, *A Philosophy of Labor* (New York, 1951), 68; John Hall, "The Knights of St. Crispin in Massachusetts, 1869–1878," *Journal of Economic History* 17 (1958), 174–5.

3. The literature is voluminous, if not always accurate or comprehensive; see Harold Williamson, ed., *The Growth of the American Economy* (New York, 1951), 462; Anthony Bimba, *The Molly Maguires* (New York, 1932); J. Walter Coleman, *The Molly Maguire Riots* (Richmond, Va., 1936); George McNeil, ed., *The Labor Movement* (New York, 1892), 241–67; Andrew Roy, *A History of the Coal Miners of the United States* (Columbus, Ohio, 1903); John R. Commons et al., *History of Labor in the United States*, 4 vols. (New York, 1918), 2: 179–80, McAlister Coleman, *Men and Coal* (New York, 1943), 42–4; Arthur Suffern, *Conciliation and Arbitration in the Coal Industry of America* (Boston, 1915), 7–17.

4. Richard Lester, *Economics of Labor* (New York, 1947), 545; emphasis added.

5. Herbert Harris, *American Labor* (New Haven, Conn., 1938), 75.

6. Selig Perlman, "Upheaval and Reorganization Since 1876," in Commons et al., *History of Labor*, 2: 196.

7. J. A. Schumpeter, "The Problem of Classes," in Reinhard Bendix and Seymour Lipset, eds., *Class, Status and Power* (Glencoe, Ill., 1953), 79.

8. Ibid.

9. Adna Weber, *The Growth of Cities in the Nineteenth Century* (New York, 1899), 433–4.

10. *Chicago Times*, 22 May 1876.

11. *New York Times*, 20 Nov. 1876.

12. *Chicago Tribune*, 4 July 1876.

13. Samuel Lane Loomis, *Modern Cities and Their Religious Problems* (New York, 1887), 60–1, 63–6.

14. Massachusetts Bureau of Labor Statistics, *Second Annual Report 1870–1871* (Boston, 1871), 475.

15. See, e.g., Louis Wirth, "Urbanism as a Way of Life," in Paul Hatt and Albert Reiss, Jr., eds., *Cities and Society* (Glencoe, Ill., 1957), 36–63; Bert F. Hoselitz, "The City, the Factory, and Economic Growth," *American Economic Review* 45 (1955), 166–84.

16. "The Distribution of Wealth," *Cooper's New Monthly* 1 (1874), 7–9.

17. *Iron Molders' Journal*, Jan. 1874, 204.

18. See Ohio Bureau of Labor Statistics, *First Annual Report 1877* (Columbus, 1878), 156–92.

19. A. Ross Eckler, "A Measure of the Severity of Depression, 1873–1932," *Review of Economic Statistics* 15 (1933), 75–81; O. V. Wells, "The Depression of 1873–1879," *Agricultural History* 11 (1937), 237–49; Rendigs Fels, "American Business Cycles, 1865–1879," *American Economic Review* 41 (1951), 325–49: Alvin Hansen, *Business Cycles and National Income* (New York, 1951), 24–6, 39–41.

20. T. E. Burton, *Financial Crises and Periods of Industrial and Commercial Depression* (New York, 1902), 344.

21. *Annual Report of the Secretary of the American Iron and Steel Association of the Year 1874* (Philadelphia, 1875), 4–5.

22. New York Association for Improving the Condition of the Poor, *Thirty-first Annual Report* (New York, 1874), 28.

23. *New York Graphic*, 14 Jan. 1874.

24. *American Manufacturer*, 30 Oct. 1873.

25. *Annual Report of the Secretary of the American Iron and Steel Association for the Year 1874*, 12, 81–2.

26. *Vulcan Record* 1 (1874), 12–14.

27. *New York Times*, 27 Oct., 2, 15 Nov. 1873.

28. *Chicago Times*, 3 Oct., 3 Nov. 1873.

29. *Iron Molders' Journal* 1 (1873), 161; *Iron Age*, 26 May 1874, 14.

30. *Annual Report of the Secretary of the American Iron and Steel Association for the Year 1874*, 81–2.

31. See Herbert G. Gutman, "Trouble on the Railroads in 1873–1874: Prelude to the 1877 Crisis," *Labor History* 2 (1962), 215–35; *Cincinnati Enquirer*, Feb.–March 1874; *Chicago Times*, 12 Nov. 1873; *Chicago Tribune*, 10–20 Nov. 1874.

32. *Workingman's Advocate*, 28 March, 27 June–4 July 1874; John James, "The Miner's Strike in the Hocking Valley," *Cooper's New Monthly* 1 (1874), 4.

33. *Chicago Tribune*, 23 April 1874; *Workingman's Advocate* 11–18 July 1874; *New York World*, 23 July 1874.

34. *Workingman's Advocate*, 28 March 1874; *Chicago Times*, 7–9 Nov. 1874; *Cincinnati Commercial*, 11 Feb. 1874; *Iron Age*, 13 Aug. 1874, 14.

35. See Herbert G. Gutman, "Two Lockouts in Pennsylvania, 1873–1874," *Pennsylvania Magazine of History and Biography* 83 (1959), 317–18, 322–6.

36. *Iron Molders' Journal*, Dec. 1874, 138.

37. *Chicago Tribune*, 19 Nov. 1874.

38. *Workingman's Advocate*, 14 April 1874.

39. Ibid.

40. *Cincinnati Commercial*, 18 Jan. 1874.
41. *Workingman's Advocate*, 5–12 Sept., 7, 28 Nov. 1874.
42. *Iron Molders' Journal*, Dec. 1874, 138.
43. *Frostburg Mining Journal*, 25 Nov. 1876.
44. *Cooper's New Monthly* 1 (1874), 16.
45. *Iron Age*, 5 March 1874; *Cincinnati Commercial*, 29 Jan., 3 Feb. 1874.
46. *Portsmouth Times*, 7 Feb. 1874.
47. See Herbert G. Gutman, "The Braidwood Lockout of 1874," *Journal of the Illinois State Historical Society* 53 (1960), 5–28.
48. See Herbert G. Gutman, "An Iron Workers' Strike in Ohio Valley, 1873–1874," *Ohio Historical Quarterly* 68 (1959), 353–70.
49. See Herbert G. Gutman, "Reconstruction in Ohio: Negroes in the Hocking Valley Coal Mines in 1873 and 1874," *Labor History* 3 (1962), 243–64.
50. *Cincinnati Commercial*, 23 May, 4 June 1874; Edward Wieck, *The American Miners' Association* (New York, 1940), 141.
51. *Cincinnati Commercial*, 23 May 1874; *Hocking Sentinel*, 25 Dec. 1873, 8, 22 Jan., 12, 26 Feb., 5 March 1874.
52. *Logan Republican*, 4 April 1874.
53. *Cincinnati Commercial*, 23 May 1874; *Workingman's Advocate*, 23 May 1874.
54. *Athens Messenger*, 7 May 1874.
55. *Hocking Sentinel*, 1 April 1874; *Chicago Tribune*, 30 June 1874.
56. *Cincinnati Commercial*, 13, 14, 15 June 1874; *New Lexington Democratic Herald*, 18 June 1874.
57. *Cleveland Leader*, 7 July 1874.
58. *Cincinnati Commercial*, 3 Oct. 1874, 22 March 1875; *New Lexington Democratic Herald*, 25 March 1875; *Hocking Sentinel*, 4, 25 March 1875; *Ohio State Journal*, 1 April 1875.
59. *New York Graphic*, 10 Nov. 1873; *Chicago Tribune*, 23 Dec. 1873; New York Association for Improving the Condition of the Poor, *Thirtieth Annual Report, 1873* (New York, 1873), 41ff.
60. *New York Sun*, 22 Oct., 4 Nov., 20 Nov.–20 Dec. 1873; *Chicago Times*, 1–31 Dec. 1873.
61. *New York World*, 27 Dec. 1873; see sources in note 60.
62. *New York Tribune*, 12 Dec. 1873.
63. Ibid.
64. *Chicago Times*, 23, 30 Dec. 1873; *Chicago Tribune*, 23–30 Dec. 1873.
65. See *Chicago Tribune*, 29 Dec. 1873; Thurlow Weed to the Editor, *New York Tribune*, 20 Dec. 1873; *Cumberland Civilian and Times* (Maryland), 12 Feb. 1874.
66. *New York Tribune*, 22 June 1874.
67. *Chicago Times*, 26 Aug. 1874.
68. *New York Herld*, 2 Nov. 1873; *New York Times*, 3 June 1874; *Cleveland Leader*, 18 June 1874; *Chicago Tribune*, 15 April 1874.
69. *Pittsburgh Post*, 21–30 Nov. 1873.
70. *Cleveland Plain Dealer*, 7–11 May 1874.
71. *New York Toiler*, 22 Aug. 1874; *New York Sun*, 6 July 1874; Board of Health of the City of New York, *Fourth Annual Report, May 1, 1873 to April 30, 1874* (New York, 1874), 96–7.
72. *New York Times*, 25–30 June 1874; *New York Tribune*, 2–14 June 1874.

73. *New York Sun*, 2, 10 June 1874; *New York World*, 23–24 July 1874.

74. *Chicago Times*, 22 May 1876; *Iron Age*, 27 April 1876, 24.

75. See Gutman, "Two Lockouts in Pennsylvania, 1873–1874," and "Trouble on the Railroads in 1873–1874: Prelude to the 1877 Crisis."

76. Louis Hartz, *The Liberal Tradition in America* (New York, 1955), 110–13, 189–227; Richard Hofstadter, *The American Political Tradition and the Men Who Made It* (New York, 1948), v–ix; John Higham, ed., *The Reconstruction of American History* (New York, 1962), 21–4, 119–56.

77. Cochran, *Railroad Leaders*, 181.

3. Labor in the Land of Lincoln: Coal Miners on the Prairie

1. Allan Pinkerton, National Police Agency, Chicago, 27 Jan. 1869, to Alex. McDonald, Esq., Holytown, Scotland, *Glasgow Sentinel*, 6 March 1869. McDonald appended his comments to this letter. McDonald's trip to America is described in *Workingman's Advocate* (Chicago), 2 Oct., 20 Nov. 1869, 29 Jan. 1870. A brief summary of Pinkerton's early career in Scotland and America appears in Wayne Broehl, Jr., *The Molly Maguires* (Cambridge, Mass., 1964), 133–44.

2. Daniel M'Lachlan, "Narrative of a Voyage from the Broomielaw to New York. By a Maryhill Miner." *Glasgow Sentinel*, 9 Oct. 1869. Scant but useful biographical material on McLaughlin's early life is found in *Journal of United Labor* 4 (June 1883), 484–5; Andrew Roy, *A History of the Coal Miners in the United States* (Columbus, Ohio, 1906), 248–50; *National Labor Tribune*, 16 May 1901; *History of Will County, Illinois* (Chicago, LeBaron, 1878), 758.

3. M'Lachlan, "Narrative," *Glasgow Sentinel*, 9 Oct. 1869; M'Lachlan, Braidwood, 16 Oct. 1869, to John Barnes, ibid., 13 Nov. 1869. A biographical sketch of John James appears in *Workingman's Advocate*, 29 Nov. 1873. McDonald's Braidwood visit is described in ibid., 20 Nov. 1869.

4. John James, "The Braidwood Coal Field System of Mining," Ohio Inspector of Mines, *Fourth Annual Report, 1877* (Columbus, 1877), 118–19; James MacFarlane, *The Coal-Regions of America: Their Topography, Geology, and Development* (New York, 1873), 429–32; Jasper Johnson, "The Wilmington Illinois Coal-Field," *Transactions of the American Institute of Mining Engineers* (Easton, Pa., 1874–5), 3: 188–202; S. O. Andros, "Coal Mining in Illinois," *Bulletin 13, Illinois Coal Mining Investigation* (Urbana) 2 (Sept. 1915), 39–40; August Maue, *History of Will County, Illinois* (Indianapolis, 1928), 345–7; *Souvenir of Settlement and Progress of Will County, Illinois* (Chicago, 1884), 440–1; W. W. Stevens, *Past and Present of Will County, Illinois* (Chicago, 1907), 111–12; CW & V Coal Company, *Annual Report to Directors, 1881* (Chicago, 1881), 6; *Workingman's Advocate*, 20 Nov. 1869, 10 May 1873, 23 May 1874; *Joliet Signal*, 24 Nov. 1874; *Chicago Tribune*, 22 June 1874, 21 April 1877; *The History of Will County, Illinois* (Chicago, LeBaron, 1878), 464–6.

5. Johnson, "Wilmington Coal-Field," 188–202; George B. Harrington, *Coal Mining in Illinois* (New York, 1950), 11–12; MacFarlane, *Coal-Regions of America*, 429–32, 435–6, 658–9; John R. Commons et al., eds., *History of Labour in the United States*, 4 vols. (New York, 1918–35), 2: 61–4; Robert V. Bruce, *1877: Year of Violence* (Indianapolis, 1959), 292–4; Henry D. Lloyd, *A Strike Against Millionaires; or, The Story of Spring Valley*

(Chicago, 1890), 11; biographical data and corporate connections on Walker (15: 381–2) and Thayer (30: 556–7) are in *National Cyclopedia of America Biography*; *Chicago Tribune*, 22 June 1874, 21 April 1877; *Chicago Times*, 28 July 1874; *History of Will County*, 466–8.

6. *Workingman's Advocate*, 8 Aug., 17 Oct. 1868.
7. Ibid., 10 Nov. 1867, 4 July 1868, 21 Aug. 1869.
8. Ibid., 20 Feb. 1869, 12 March 1870.
9. Ibid., 23 May 1868, 6 March, 16 April 1869.
10. Ibid., 10 Nov. 1867, 22 Feb. 1868, 4 June 1870; *Joliet Signal*, 23 Apr. 1873.
11. *Workingman's Advocate*, 3 Nov. 1867.
12. Ibid., 14 Dec. 1867, 18 Jan. 1868, 16 April 1869, 24 April, 4 June 1870.
13. *Chicago Tribune*, 22 June 1874 and 21 April 1877. These two long dispatches gave careful attention to Braidwood's social and economic structure. See also Cameron's report in *Workingman's Advocate*, 10 May 1873; and ibid., 22 Aug. 1868 and 30 April 1870, for early descriptions of company paternalism. Data on churches and newspapers are in *Souvenir of Settlement and Progress of Will County*, 442–3; Stevens, *Past and Present of Will County*, 112; and especially *History of Will County*, 468, 470–6, 763. Formal religious activity is noted in *Joliet Signal*, 3 Nov., 8 Dec. 1874. A detailed description of the social structure in Streator in the early 1880s that suggests striking similarities to Braidwood is found in Illinois Bureau of Labor Statistics, *Third Biennial Report, 1884* (Springfield, 1884), 430–5.
14. *Chicago Times*, 31 July 1874; *Chicago Tribune*, 22 June 1874 and 21 Apr., 31 July 1877; *National Labor Tribune*, 16 Jan. 1875; George McNeill, ed., *The Labor Movement To-day* (New York, 1892), 258; Edward Pinkowski, *John Siney, the Miners' Martyr* (Philadelphia, 1963) 310; *Miners' National Record* 1 (Dec. 1874), 22; Rowland T. Berthoff, *British Immigrants in Industrial America* (Cambridge, 1953), 50, 54, 92–3; Oscar Handlin, *Boston's Immigrants* (Cambridge, Mass., 1959), 176.
15. Full details on the Diamond disaster appear in *National Labor Tribune*, 24 Feb., 3, 10, 17 March, 4, 11 April 1883. Other information is drawn from *Report of Special Committee on Labor* (Springfield, Ill., 1879), 59, and Johnson, "Wilmington Coal-Field," 188–202.
16. *Souvenir of Settlement and Progress of Will County*, 442–3; Stevens, *Past and Present of Will County*, 111–12; *History of Will County*, 472–3; *Chicago Times*, 31 July 1877; *Chicago Tribune*, 22 June 1874 and 21 April 1877; *Joliet Signal*, 5 May, 14 July, 4 Aug. 1874; *Joliet Daily Sun*, 29 June 1876; *Workingman's Advocate*, 28 Feb., 19 Dec. 1874; *National Labor Tribune*, 27 Nov., 4 Dec. 1880, 18, 25 June, 9 July 1881, 4 Feb. 1882.
17. *Chicago Tribune*, 22 June 1874 and 21 April 1877; *Workingman's Advocate*, 3 Nov. 1867, 6 Aug. 1868, 20 Nov. 1869, 30 July 1870, 14 Jan., 26 Nov., 30 Sept. 1871, 10, 26 May, 20 Nov. 1873; *Joliet Signal*, 23 June, 14 July, 1 Sept., 20 Oct., 24 Nov. 1874; *National Labor Tribune*, 18, 25 June 1881.
18. Most of the material in this paragraph is found in the biographical sketches of Braidwood residents printed in *History of Will County*, 751–65. See also *Chicago Tribune*, 22 June 1874 and 21 April 1877; *National Labor Tribune*, 15 Jan. 1875, 13 July 1878, 14 Dec. 1880, 9 July, 10 Sept. 1881, 14 Jan. 1882; Pinkowski, *John Siney*, 113, 310; Roy, *History of the*

Coal Miners, 156–7; *Souvenir of Settlement and Progress of Will County*, 441–2.

19. *History of Will County*, 464–77, 751–65; *Souvenir of Settlement and Progress of Will County*, 441–2; *Joliet Signal*, 15 April 1873.

20. *Chicago Tribune*, 22 June 1874 and 21 April 1877; *Ottawa Free Trader*, 4 Aug. 1877; *Souvenir of Settlement and Progress of Will County*, 443–9.

21. *Workingman's Advocate*, 14 Jan. 1871, 29 Nov. 1873, 17 Jan. 1874. Reports on the Braidwood miners in the regional union are found in ibid., 1, 27 Nov., 20 Dec. 1873, 7 Feb., 11 April 1874.

22. The dispute over the Sanitary Fund is discussed in ibid., 30 April, 4 June 1870. A copy of the annual CW & V contract and its rules and regulations appeared in full in *Chicago Tribune*, 22 June 1874.

23. *Workingman's Advocate*, 30 April, 4 June 1870, 21 March 1874; *Chicago Tribune*, 21 April 1877.

24. *Workingman's Advocate*, 3, 17 May 1873.

25. Ibid., 17 May, 7, 28 June, 16 Aug. 1873.

26. Ibid., 20 Dec. 1873, 27 Dec.–3 Jan. 1874, 7, 21 Feb., 21 March 1874; *Joliet Signal*, 5 May 1874.

27. *Workingman's Advocate*, 21 Feb., 21 March, 6, 20 June 1874; *Chicago Tribune*, 22 June 1874; *Chicago Times*, 4, 28 June, 28 July 1874; *Joliet Signal*, 9, 16 June 1874.

28. *Chicago Tribune*, 17, 22, 30 June, 31 July 1874; *Chicago Times*, 15 June, 28 July 1874; *Workingman's Advocate*, 20 June 1874; *Joliet Signal*, 30 June 1874.

29. *Joliet Signal*, 16 June 1874; *Chicago Tribune*, 22 June, 15 July 1874; *Chicago Times*, 15 June, 28, 29 July 1874; *Workingman's Advocate*, 20 June, 27 June–4 July, 11–18 July, 25 July, 1 Aug. 1874. The new hands were promised $1.50 a day plus board, or $2.25 without board (*Chicago Times*, 28 July 1874). In Chicago, the *Workingman's Advocate* publicized the strike and urged readers to stay: "Don't be deceived by the specious inducements of your oppressors. They are of their father the devil. . . . There is no man—no apology for a man—who can go there and take the bread out of the mouths of honest, hardworking, law-abiding citizens under present conditions" (20 June 1874).

30. *Chicago Tribune*, 22 June, 15 July 1874; *Chicago Times*, 15 June, 25, 28, 29 July 1874; *Workingman's Advocate*, 20 June, 27 June–4 July, 11–18, 25 July, 1 Aug., 19–26 Sept. 1874; *Joliet Signal*, 9, 16, 23 June, 21 July 1874.

31. Disputed reports of this incident are in *Workingman's Advocate*, 11–18 July 1874; *Chicago Times*, 8, 9, 20, 28, 29 July 1874; *Joliet Signal*, 14, 21 July 1874.

32. The state of public opinion is discussed revealingly in *Chicago Tribune*, 22 June 1874. Other details are in *Chicago Times*, 23, 28, 29 July 1874; *Workingman's Advocate*, 20 June, 25 July, 1 Aug. 1874; *Joliet Signal*, 16, 23 June, 21 July, 4 Aug. 1874.

33. *Chicago Times*, 23 July 1874; *Workingman's Advocate*, 11–18 July 1874.

34. *Workingman's Advocate*, 11–18, 25 July 1874; *Joliet Signal*, 4 Aug. 1874; *Chicago Times*, 25, 28, 29 July 1874.

35. *Chicago Times*, 28 July 1874; *Chicago Tribune*, 22 Aug., 11 Sept. 1874; *Workingman's Advocate*, 1, 8–15, 22–29 Aug., 5–12 Sept. 1874; *Joliet*

Signal, 23 June, 11 Aug., 1, 8, 15 Sept., 6 Oct. 1875; CW & V Coal Company, *Annual Report, 1881*, 6.

36. *Workingman's Advocate*, 19–26 Sept. 1874.
37. *Joliet Signal*, 8 Dec. 1874; *Workingman's Advocate*, 14–21 Nov. 1874, 6 Jan. 1876, 31 March 1877; *Chicago Tribune*, 21 April 1877; *Miners' National Record* 1 (Nov. 1874), 15, (Feb. 1875), 61, (May 1875), 122; 2 (Feb. 1876), 60; *National Labor Tribune*, 25 Dec. 1875, 8 Jan. 1876, 17, 24 March 1877.
38. *Miners' National Record*, I (Dec. 1874), 22, (April 1875), 91, (June 1875), 139, 144; *National Labor Tribune*, 28 Aug., 18 Sept. 1875; *Workingman's Advocate*, 27 Nov. 1875; *Chicago Tribune*, 26 May 1876; *Chicago Times*, 23, 26 May 1876.
39. *National Labor Tribune*, 16 Jan. 1875, 15 Jan. 1876, 28 April 1877; *Workingman's Advocate*, 19 June, 24 July 1875; *Chicago Tribune*, 21 April 1877.
40. *Miners' National Record* 1 (April 1875), 91; *National Labor Tribune*, 15 Jan. 1876; *Workingman's Advocate*, 27 Nov. 1875, 30 Dec. 1876, 31 March 1877; *Ottawa Free Trader*, 4 Aug. 1877.
41. *Braidwood Journal*, n.d., reprinted in *Miners' National Record* 1 (June 1875), 138–9; ibid., 143.
42. *Workingman's Advocate*, 27 Nov. 1875, 4 Nov. 1876, 31 March 1877.
43. *Joliet Signal*, 15 April 1873, 14 April, 30 June, 10 Nov., 8 Dec. 1874; *Workingman's Advocate*, 25 May 1872, 7 Feb., 11 April, 6 June, 3–10 Oct., 14–21 Nov., 4 Dec. 1874; *Miners' National Record* 1 (Nov. 1874), 12–13; *Chicago Times*, 29 July 1874; *Souvenir of Settlement and Progress of Will County*, 161; Irwin Unger, *The Greenback Era* (Princeton, N.J., 1964), 97–114.
44. *Joliet Sun*, 16 April 1877; *Workingman's Advocate*, 5 May 1877; *Chicago Tribune*, 21 April 1877; *Braidwood Phoenix*, n.d., reprinted in *Workingman's Advocate*, 5 May 1877.
45. *Joliet Sun*, 4 April 1877; *Chicago Tribune*, 27 March, 21 April 1877; *Chicago Times*, 3, 5 April 1877. The full revised contract for 1877–1878 is in *Chicago Tribune*, 21 April 1877, and *National Labor Tribune*, 5 May 1877.
46. Details on Streator before April 1877 appear in *Workingman's Advocate*, 6 June, 22 April, 22 Oct. 1874, 20 Jan., 24 Feb. 1877; *Miners' National Record* 1 (Jan. 1875), 45, (Feb. 1875), 58; *National Labor Tribune*, 18 Jan., 25 March 1876, 22 Jan., 8 April, 9 Sept. 1877. Faulted efforts to unite the Streator, LaSalle, and Braidwood miners are reported in *Workingman's Advocate*, 6 June, 8–15 Aug., 3–10 Oct. 1874.
47. The best description of the background of the 1877 Streator dispute is in *Chicago Tribune*, 21 April 1877. Further details are in ibid., 20, 24 April 1877; *National Labor Tribune*, 28 April, 5 May 1877; *Joliet Sun*, 21 April 1877; *Ottawa Free Trader*, 21 April 1877; *Workingman's Advocate*, 5 May 1877. But see also the important letter from Braidwood dated 4 May and signed "Nil Desperandum" in *Workingman's Advocate*, 19 May 1877.
48. *Chicago Tribune*, 16, 17, 18, 21 April 1877; *Chicago Times*, 16 April, 31 July 1877; *Joliet Sun*, 13, 14, 16, 17 April 1877.
49. *Chicago Tribune*, 21, 24, 30 April 1877; *Chicago Times*, 24 April 1877; *Chicago Journal*, 30 July 1877; *Joliet Sun*, 16, 17 April, 18, 19, 21, 22, 25,

30, 31 May 1877; *Workingman's Advocate*, 5 May, 16 June 1877; *National Labor Tribune*, 28 April 1877; *Labor Standard*, 12 May 1877. "One of the city's papers," reported the *Chicago Tribune* on 30 April, "devoted almost two pages of last week's issue in denouncing the coal companies, and it is looked upon in some quarters as trying to incite the men to riot, which is very severely denounced by right-minded men."

50. Acrimonious and partisan accounts of the role played by the city government during the strike are found in the exchange of letters between McLaughlin, James, and "Mose" in *National Labor Tribune*, 28 May, 15 June, 6, 13, 20, 27 July, 3, 24 Aug. 1878. See also *Joliet Sun*, 30 June, 12, 13 July 1877.

51. *Chicago Tribune*, 24, 30 April 1877; *Chicago Journal*, 30 July 1877; "Appeal of Frank Lofty, Charles Duncan, and Daniel McLaughlin," *Workingman's Advocate*, 5 May 1877, *National Labor Tribune*, 28 April 1877, and *Labor Standard*, 12 May, 1877. See also the editorial comments in *Workingman's Advocate*, 5 May, 16 June 1877. James's opposition is noted in his letters to the *National Labor Tribune*, 6, 13 July 1878.

52. *Joliet Sun*, 16, 19 June 1877; *Workingman's Advocate*, 16 June 1877; *Labor Standard*, 14 June 1877; J. Walker to J. Joy, 27 April 1877, and Circular to Stockholders of the CW & V Coal Company, Joy Mss., and A. Sweet to Cyrus Woodman, 21 June and 25 June 1877, and Woodman to Sweet, 28 June 1877, Woodman Mss., Wisconsin State Historical Society.

53. A. Sweet to C. Woodman, 2 July 1877, Woodman Mss., Wisconsin State Historical Society; *National Labor Tribune*, 28 July 1877; *Chicago Tribune*, 21 July 1877.

54. Miner, Braidwood, to the editor, *National Labor Tribune*, 18 Aug. 1877; *Chicago Times*, 22 July 1877.

55. *Chicago Times*, 24, 25, 26, 27 July 1877; *Joliet Sun*, 24, 25, 26 July 1877; *Chicago Tribune*, 25, 26 July 1877; Holdridge O. Collins, *The Riots of 1877 in Illinois: An Official History of the Braidwood Campaign* (Chicago, 1879), 3–5.

56. *Chicago Tribune*, 25, 26 July 1877. The *Joliet Sun*, 27 July 1877, gave no notice to the cause for the black miners leaving Braidwood except to deny a report that 150 were approaching that city. The issues of the *Sun* for 28 and 29 July are missing from the microfilm holdings of this newspaper at the Illinois State Historical Society. Hilliard's report is found in Adjutant General of Illinois, *Biennial Report, 1877–1878* (Springfield, 1878), 5. A typical variation of this report is in *Chicago Interocean*, 27 July 1877, and a highly colored version is in J. A. Dacus, *Annals of the Great Strikes in the United States* (St. Louis, Mo., 1877), 351. Dacus (ibid., 347) made the interesting observation that the blacks were "encamped . . . at the Coal Companies expense, waiting until the trouble was settled, so they could resume work." The *Chicago Times*, 29 July 1877, also noted that the blacks camped at company expense. Bruce (*1877: Year of Violence*, 292–4) follows the accounts common to most Chicago newspapers and blames the miners for the black exodus. The observation of the *Interocean* appeared on 27 July. The report by the *Tribune's* Morris correspondent appeared on 27 July, and a similar story was in the *Chicago Journal*, 28 July 1877. Note of the Eureka company's financial difficulty is in Morris

dispatch cited above and in J. P., Braidwood 2 Aug., to the editor, *National Labor Tribune*, 11 Aug. 1877. An "explanation" for the driving out of the blacks that appeared only in the *Ottawa Free Press*, 4 Aug. 1877, said the miners did not "offer forcible opposition" to the blacks until the blacks began to "obtain the larger portion of their provisions by prowling around at night and plundering the gardens, hen-roosts, and pig-pens of the old miners. It was mainly on this account, a Braidwooder will tell you . . . [that] they rose up . . . and ordered the niggers to leave."

57. Braidwood, 12 Aug 1877, to the editor, *National Labor Tribune*, 18 Aug. 1877, and J. P., Braidwood, 2 Aug 1877, to the editor, ibid., 11 Aug. 1877. See also the denials that the miners caused the blacks to leave in the testimony of John Keir and John Creeley, Jr., before a state legislative committee in March 1879. Keir argued that the militia came to "intimidate the strikers," and Creeley said the miners did not "antagonize state or county authorities. "There was no riot," he said. "The Eureka mines refused to pay the wages due the [colored] men." (*Report of Special Committee on Labor, 1879*, 59–60.) See also *History of Will County*, 475–7.

58. Details on the decision to use troops are found in telegrams exchanged by Cullom, Ducat, and Hilliard and printed in Collins, *Riots of 1877*, 4–10. Goodrich's second telegram is summarized in Springfield dispatch, *Chicago Tribune*, 27 July 1877. The *Joliet Sun* is not helpful on the decision to use troops. On 30 July, it reported only that the situation at Braidwood "leaves no room for a large, long, or sensation article." It added, joking, that the Joliet troops in Braidwood had "fought, died, and bled, and are ready to die again." On the particular details before the troops arrived, the *Sun* is not helpful. But many data are found in *Chicago Times*, 28 July 1877; *Chicago Tribune*, 27, 28, 29 July 1877; Springfield dispatch, *St. Louis Republican*, 27 July 1877; Adjutant General of Illinois, *Biennial Report, 1877–1878*, 108–10.

59. *Chicago Tribune*, 29, 30 July 1877; *Chicago Times*, 29, 31 July 1877; A. C. Ducat, 1 Aug., to H. Hilliard, Adjutant General of Illinois, *Biennial Report, 1877–1878*, 109–10.

60. I have followed Ducat's detailed report to Hilliard in *Biennial Report, 1877–1878*, 109–15. But see the telegrams printed in Collins, *Riots of 1877*, 10, and the *Chicago Tribune*, 29 July 1877, which includes Ducat's first address to McLaughlin and much additional information. See also *Chicago Journal*, 30 July 1877, *Chicago Times*, 29, 30, 31 July 1877, and J. M. Donna, *Donna's Story of Braidwood* (Braidwood [?], 1957), 303. A striker's version of the militia coming to the town is in *National Labor Tribune*, 18 Aug. 1877. McLaughlin's later comment is in ibid., 6 June 1879. Nearly two years after the troops left, miners complained to a legislative committee that the firearms taken from them had never been returned. "Col. Stambaugh took a valuable gun from me," said Thomas Dickerson. "It has never been returned. I got a receipt but he gave me the wrong one. The receipt was for a two-barreled gun, when my gun was a single-barreled Damascus gun. I have hired a lawyer, and he can't get it. The gun cost $17 in England, but I would not take any price for it, as it was a present to me, besides being very valuable." (*Report of Special Committee on Labor, 1879*, 67.)

61. *Chicago Tribune*, 30, 31 July 1877; *Chicago Journal*, 30 July 1877; *Chicago Times*, 31 July 1877; *Chicago Daily Interocean*, 30, 31 July 1877; Adjutant General of Illinois, *Biennial Report, 1877–1878*, 109–15, Collins, *Riots of 1877 in Illinois*, 11.

62. *Chicago Tribune*, 3, 9 Aug 1877; *Chicago Times*, 3 Aug 1877; Collins, *Riots of 1877*, 12–14.

63. *Chicago Tribune*, 31 July 1877; *Joliet Sun*, 31 July 1877.

64. *Chicago Daily Interocean*, 30 July 1877; *Chicago Tribune*, 31 July 1877; *National Labor Tribune*, 11, 18 Aug. 1877; *Braidwood Republican* n.d., reprinted in *Kankakee Gazette*, 9 Aug. 1877; *Joliet Sun*, 31 July 1877; *Chicago Times*, 31 July 1877.

65. *Joliet Sun*, 31 July 1877; *Chicago Journal*, 30 July 1877; *Wilmington Advocate*, n.d., reprinted in *Kankakee Gazette*, 9 Aug. 1877; *Chicago Daily Interocean*, 30 July 1877; *Ottawa Free Trader*, 4 Aug. 1877; Caleb Stowe, Wilmington, to the editor, *Chicago Tribune*, 31 July 1877; William O'Dell to the editor, ibid., 2 Aug. 1877; E. D. Conley to the editor, ibid., 3 Aug. 1877. Information on O'Dell and Conley appears in *Souvenir of Settlement and Progress in Will County*, 463–4.

66. *Chicago Tribune*, 9 Aug. 1877; *Chicago Interocean*, 15 Aug. 1877; *Chicago Times*, 31 July 1877; *National Labor Tribune*, 20 Nov. 1877; *Joliet Sun*, 8, 15 Aug., 11 Oct. 1877; *Chicago Journal*, 8, 11, Aug. 1877. Information on Donahue is in Stevens, *Past and Present of Will County*, 541–2, and *Souvenir of Settlement and Progress in Will County*, 162.

67. *Chicago Daily Interocean*, 20 Aug. 1877; *National Labor Tribune*, 25 Aug., 1, 15, 29 Sept. 1877; *Joliet Sun*, 8, 9, 21, 30 Aug. 1877.

68. *National Labor Tribune*, 13, 20 Oct., 3, 17, 24 Nov. 1877; *Joliet Sun*, 26 Sept. 1877.

69. *Chicago Tribune*, 29 Nov. 1877; *National Labor Tribune*, 1 Dec. 1877, 22 May 1878; *Annual Report of CW & V Coal Company, 1881*, 6.

70. *National Labor Tribune*, 15, 22 Dec. 1877, 19 Jan. 1878.

71. *Ibid.*, 25 March, 13, 20 April, 28 May 1878; *Chicago Times*, 4 April 1878.

72. *National Labor Tribune*, 20, 27 April, 4, 11, 28 May 1878; *National Socialist*, 8 June 1878; *Indianapolis Times*, 8 May 1878.

73. *National Labor Tribune*, 13 July, 24 Aug 1878; *National Socialist*, 20 July 1878; A. C. Ducat, Nov. 1878, to H. H. Hilliard, in Adjutant General of Illinois, *Biennial Report, 1877–1878*, 114–15; Stevens, *Past and Present of Will County*, 429–32.

74. *National Labor Tribune*, 1, 15, 22 Dec. 1877, 9 Feb., 28 May 1878; *Indianapolis Times*, 1, 8 May, 3 Aug. 1878; *National Socialist*, 18, 25 May, 1, 8 June, 6 July 1878.

75. *National Labor Tribune*, 12 Jan., 2, 9 Feb. 1878, 22 Nov. 1879; *Report of Special Committee on Labor, 1879*, 59–61; *Annual Report of CW & V Coal Company, 1881*, 4–6.

76. *National Labor Tribune*, 30 March, 13 April, 28 May, 7 Sept., 7 Dec. 1878, 13 Dec. 1879, 27 March 1880, 15 Aug. 1881; *Report of Special Committee on Labor, 1879*, 59–68; *Joliet Sun*, 6 June 1877.

77. *National Labor Tribune*, 12, 19 Jan., 2, 23 Feb., 23 March, 10 Aug. 1878, 8 March 1879, 5 March 1881.

78. *Joliet Sun*, 3, 4 May 1880; *National Labor Tribune*, 15, 29 June, 29 July 1878, 14 Feb. 1880, 3 Dec. 1881, 17 March 1883; *Report of Special*

Committee on Labor, 1879, 62; *Souvenir of Settlement and Progress of Will County*, 443.

79. *National Labor Tribune*, 11 May, 15 June 1878, 10 May 1879, 1, 15 May 1880, 20 Aug. 1881, 29 April 1882, 5, 12 May 1883; CW & V Coal Company, *Annual Report, 1881*, 6.

80. *National Labor Tribune*, 19 Oct. 1878, 5 July, 9 Aug., 22 Nov., 27 Dec. 1879, 13, 27 March, 1, 15 May, 17 Sept. 1880, 2, 9 April, 7 May, 19 Nov. 1881, 15 April 1882, 17 March, 5, 12 May 1883; *National Socialist*, 28 May, 15 June 1878; McNeill, *Labor Movement*, 253–4.

81. *Report of Special Committee on Labor, 1879*, 60–1; *National Labor Tribune*, 6 Sept. 1879, 19 Nov. 1881, 28 March, 22 April 1882; *National Socialist*, 28 May, 15 June 1878.

82. *National Labor Tribune*, 28 March 1878, 31 July 1880, 5 Nov. 1881, 22 April, 10 June 1882.

83. *Joliet Sun*, 28 May, 6 Nov. 1878, 7 April, 8 Aug., 1, 8 Nov. 1880; *National Labor Tribune*, 28 May, 13 July, 14 Sept., 12, 19, 26 Oct. 1878; 13 Nov. 1880, 30 April, 21 May 1881; *United Mine Workers' Journal*, 2 Sept. 1909, 6; McNeill, *Labor Movement*, 253–4; *Souvenir of Settlement and Progress of Will County*, 162–3, 261.

84. *Report of Special Committee on Labor, 1879*, 58–62; *National Labor Tribune*, 22 Feb., 9 March, 12 April, 3, 10 May, 7, 19 June 1879, 10, 17 March, 9 June 1883; *Springfield Monitor*, n.d., reprinted in *United Mine Workers' Journal*, 2 Sept 1909, 6.

4. *The Labor Policies of the Large Corporation in the Gilded Age: The Case of the Standard Oil Company*

1. For an incisive model study see Donald McMurry, *The Great Burlington Strike of 1888* (Cambridge, Mass., 1956). See also Robert V. Bruce, *1877: Year of Violence* (Indianapolis, 1959), 28–48.

2. Examples of this literature include Paul H. Giddens, *The Birth of the Oil Industry* (New York, 1938); Ida M. Tarbell, *The History of the Standard Oil Company* (New York, 1904); Allan Nevins, *Study in Power: John D. Rockefeller, Industrialist and Philanthropist* (New York, 1953) and *John D. Rockefeller: The Heroic Age of American Enterprise*, 2 vols. (New York, 1940); Harold F. Williamson and Arnold R. Daum, *The American Petroleum Industry: The Age of Illumination 1859–1899* (Evanston, Ill., 1959).

3. The authors of the standard history of the petroleum industry, for example, tell us no more than that by the mid-1860s "petroleum refining had already established its permanent characteristic of relatively modest labor requirements in relation to capital investment and value of product." (Williamson and Daum, *American Petroleum Industry*, 283). While this may be accurate, it is not a satisfactory reason for an 864-page study to ignore entirely labor policies and practices in the petroleum industry.

4. Illustrations of the failure to distinguish between the growth of large firms within a particular industry and the development of oligopoly are found in numerous monographs as well as standard economic histories. See W. Z. Ripley, ed., *Trusts, Pools, and Corporations* (Boston, 1905), xi; Thomas Cochran and William Miller, *The Age of Enterprise* (New York, 1942), 140; Louis Hacker, *The Triumph of American Capitalism* (New York, 1940), 430ff.; Edward C. Kirkland, *A History of American Economic Life*

(New York, 1939), 436ff.; E. L. Bogart and Donald Kemmerer, *Economic History of the American People* (New York, 1947), 465–77; Ross M. Robertson, *History of the American Economy* (New York, 1955), 290–313.

5. Alfred D. Chandler, Jr., "The Beginnings of 'Big Business' in American Industry," *Business History Review* 33 (1959), 1–31.

6. See the perceptive criticisms of much postbellum labor history in Henry David, "New Preface to Volumes IX and X," in John R. Commons and et al., eds., *A Documentary History of American Industrial Society*, 2nd ed., 10 vols. (New York, 1958), 9:i–viii. Informal perusal of any standard labor history of that period in America shows how little was written about factory workers and large factories.

7. The published 1870 and 1880 censuses of manufactures do not help in supplying information about large factories. Each census printed only aggregate statistics for particular industries. In addition, the methods employed were, as Allan Nevins says, "scandalously inadequate." See the perceptive criticisms of the 1870 Census of Manufactures in Nevins, *Heroic Age*, 1:287.

8. W. J. Comley and W. D. D'Eggville, *Ohio: The Great State* (Cincinnati and Cleveland, 1875), 407–15.

9. M. R. Werner, *It Happened in New York* (New York, 1957), 226–7.

10. Herbert G. Gutman, "Two Lockouts in Pennsylvania, 1873–1874," *Pennsylvania Magazine of History and Biography* 83 (1959), 307–8.

11. *Boston Commercial*, n.d., reprinted in *Iron Age*, 23 Sept. 1875, 7.

12. *Workingman's Advocate*, 28 March 1874; *Toiler* (New York), 12 Sept. 1874.

13. Herbert G. Gutman, "Industrial Invasion of the Village Green," *Trans-Action* 3 (1966), 20.

14. *Philadelphia Bulletin*, 7 Nov. 1873; *Workingman's Advocate*, 11 Oct. 1873; *Philadelphia Inquirer*, 15 April 1874; *Iron Age*, 7 May 1874, 15; Horace Greeley et al., *The Great Industries of the United States* (Hartford, Conn., 1873), 366–78; Lorin Blodgett, "The Census . . . in Philadelphia in 1870," in Pennsylvania Bureau of Labor Statistics, *First Annual Report, 1872–1873* (Harrisburg, 1874), 434.

15. Comley and D'Eggville, *Ohio*, 406; *Chicago Tribune*, 17 Feb. 1874.

16. *New York World*, 12 Dec. 1874; Pennsylvania Bureau of Labor Statistics, *Eighth Annual Report, 1879–1880* (Harrisburg, 1881), 125–38.

17. Frederick M. Peck and Henry H. Earl, *Fall River and Its Industries* (Fall River, Mass., 1877), 112.

18. Gutman, "Industrial Invasion," 20.

19. *New York Herald*, 6 Nov. 1873.

20. Blodgett, "The Census . . .," 429; Ohio Bureau of Labor Statistics, *First Annual Report, 1877* (Columbus, 1878), 224–6.

21. Ibid.; Greeley et al., *The Great Industries*, 1103; D. J. Kenny, *Illustrated Cincinnati: A Pictorial Handbook of the Queen City* (Cincinnati, 1875), 156–8.

22. New Jersey Bureau of Labor Statistics, *Second Annual Report, 1879* (Trenton, 1879), 104–37.

23. *New York Tribune*, 28, 29 Jan. 1874; *New York World*, 25 Jan. 1874.

24. Kenny, *Illustrated Cincinnati*, 225; Ohio Bureau of Labor Statistics, *First Annual Report, 1877*, 199–200.

25. Massachusetts Bureau of Labor Statistics, *Second Annual Report, 1870–*

1871 (Boston, 1871), 205–21, and *Third Annual Report, 1872* (Boston, 1872), 72–83.

26. Comley and D'Eggville, 406–7; *Ninth Census*, 1870, (Washington, D.C., 1872), 1:784.

27. Ohio Bureau of Labor Statistics, *Second Annual Report, 1878*, 308–14; Kenny, *Illustrated Cincinnati*, 154–8, 225, 237, 239–41, 247, 255–7, 269 –77, 279–80, 284–93.

28. *Chicago Tribune*, 17, 18 Feb. 1874. This survey listed mainly lumber, railroad equipment, and furniture factories as well as rolling mills and iron foundries. It did not include such important Chicago industries as meat packing and the manufacture of shoes and clothing.

29. Ohio Bureau of Labor Statistics, *Third Annual Report, 1879* (Columbus, 1880), 46, 50–2, 132–8, 151–3, 177–8.

30. Pennsylvania Bureau of Labor Statistics, *Eighth Annual Report, 1879– 1880*, 99–101; V. S. Clark, *History of Manufactures in the United States* (New York, 1929), 2:438–9.

31. *New York World*, 12 Dec. 1874; Blodgett, "The Census . . .," 429.

32. John R. Commons et al., *History of Labour in the United States*, 4 vols. (New York, 1918–35), 2:71–4.

33. Ohio Bureau of Labor Statistics, *First Annual Report, 1877*, 204.

34. Nevins, *Heroic Age*, 2:147–217.

35. Williamson and Daum, *American Petroleum Industry*, 353.

36. Exception must be taken to Williamson and Daum (ibid., 285), who insist that by 1870 "receipt of crude in bulk rather than in barrels opened up opportunities for economies of scale" and this "not only wiped out the cost of barrels themselves" but also meant "halving facilities and labor needed for cooperage." Barrel workers remained important in most refineries. In 1870, according to Williamson and Daum, Charles Pratt had so reorganized his New York refinery as to make for the "elimination of nearly all manual operations." But in 1874, as seen below, barrel workers struck against Pratt.

37. Nevins, *Heroic Age*, 1:268.

38. Ibid., 178, 268. Nevins says that Andrews withdrew from the firm in 1874 and McGregor became plant superintendent (ibid., 480–1). This could not have happened that early because in 1877 Andrews was still plant superintendent and served as company representative during the hoopers-off strike described below.

39. Ibid., 271.

40. "What I Know About Machinery," *Coopers' New Monthly*, October 1872, reprinted in Commons et al., *History of Labor*, 2:74–6.

41. Nevins, *Heroic Age*, 1:362–7.

42. Ibid., 392–3. Compare the size of Cleveland refinery labor force with that of ten independent Titusville refiners who in 1874 employed 292 workers. Two employed 155; the other eight 137 (Ibid., 466).

43. Nevins, *Heroic Age*, 1:433.

44. Comley and D'Eggville, *Ohio*, 407–15.

45. Data reported in this paragraph and the three preceding it are to be found in Frankin E. Coyne, *The Development of the Cooperate Industry in the United States, 1620–1940* (Chicago, 1940), 7–26. The description of leisure habits is in ibid., 21–2.

46. *Iron Molders' Journal*, Dec. 1873, 169.

47. Biographical information about Martin Foran is found in George E. McNeill, ed., *The Labor: The Problem of Today* (New York, 1891), 619, and about Robert Schilling in Irwin Unger, *The Greenback Era* (Princeton, N.J., 1964), 227–8, 375–7.

48. *New York Sun*, 25 Nov. 1874.

49. *Chicago Times*, 10 Oct. 1873; *Workingman's Advocate*, 22 Nov. 1873.

50. *Philadelphia Inquirer*, 9 Dec. 1973.

51. *New York Tribune*, 31 Jan. 1874; *New York Herald* , 12 Feb. 1874.

52. Scattered issues of the *Coopers' New Monthly* are in the Wisconsin State Historical Society and the Johns Hopkins Library.

53. *Workingman's Advocate*, 18 Dec. 1875 and 6 May 1876.

54. *Iron Molders' Journal*, Jan. 1877, 199.

55. *Labor Standard*, 25 Nov. 1876.

56. Nevins, *Heroic Age*, 1:437.

57. Ibid., 449, 473–9, 485–8.

58. In December 1873 the Atlantic cut coopers' wages from $3.00 to $2.75 a day. The men did not strike but talked instead of starting a cooperative barrel factory (*Philadelphia Inquirer*, 9 Dec. 1873). The March strike was not over wages but over an onerous contract and was reported in ibid., 7 March 1874.

59. Details of the strike appear in *Chicago Tribune*, 6, 15, 26, 28 May 1874; *Philadelphia Inquirer*, 27, 28 May, 1 June 1874; *Philadelphia North American*, 27, 28 May 1874. This is a significant exception to the widely held view that in these years the Knights of Labor was just a secret society. Although the organization was secret, its leaders were widely known as labor advocates in the Philadelphia area. Stephens called the contract "unjust and despotic," and Wright said that under it the workers were "paying a premium to place themselves under subjection to capitalists." The leader of the Philadelphia Coopers' Union, S. Keith, spoke that day, too. The strike "involved great principles on which depended the rights and liberties of workingmen," he said. The workers had to "conquer the capitalists or be conquered by them."

60. *New York Tribune*, 13, 14 April, 13 May 1874.

61. *New York Sun*, 13, 19, 22 May 1874.

62. Ibid., 19, 22 May 1874.

63. *New York Tribune*, 13 May 1874; *New York Times*, 13 May 1874.

64. *New York Times*, 5, 24 May, 3 June 1874; *New York Tribune*, 5, 15 May 1874; *New York Sun*, 5, 22 May 1874.

65. *Coopers' New Monthly* July 1874, 11; *Toiler*, 23 May 1874; *New York Times*, 3 June 1874; *New York Sun*, 2 June 1874; *New York Tribune*, 6 June 1874; *Iron Molders' Journal*, June 1874, 371.

66. *New York Tribune*, 6 June 1874; *New York Sun*, 5 June 1874; *New York Times*, 5 June 1874.

67. *New York Tribune*, 2 June 1874.

68. Ibid., 5, 6, 9 June 1874; *New York Times*, 6 June 1874; *New York Sun*, 6 June 1874.

69. *Toiler*, 8 Aug. 1874; *Coopers' New Monthly* July 1874, 10–11.

70. Demos, New York, 10 Nov. 1874, to the editor, *Workingman's Advocate*, 14–21 Nov. 1874; *New York Times*, 22, 23, 26 Oct., 25 Nov., 5 Dec. 1874.

71. Nevins, *Heroic Age*, 1:449, 478, 518.
72. R., Allegheny City, to the editor, *National Labor Tribune*, 11 Nov. 1877.
73. Ohio Bureau of Labor Statistics, *Second Annual Report, 1878*, 220–1.
74. *Cleveland Plain Dealer*, 20, 26 Feb. 1877.
75. The full letter from the Bohemian societies appears in *Cleveland Plain Dealer*, 20 Mar. 1875. Further evidence of the ethnic solidarity of the Bohemian community was a petition circulated among Bohemians in 1879 to be sent to the board of education. Its signers urged the teaching of the Bohemian language "in the primary departments of some of the schools in the Sixth, Twelfth, Fourteenth, and Sixteenth wards . . . in addition to other foreign languages already taught there." "We are actuated," the petitioners declared, "solely by the desire to realize that, in common with others, children of our class have opportunity afforded them of acquiring that cementing power of republican governments, a good and sectarian education." Where the languages of the home and the primary schools differed widely, that object was "impeded" and many Bohemian citizens were "compelled to send their children to schools of sectarian character to obviate the difficulty." (*Weekly Advance* [Cleveland], 29 March 1879.)
76. Ohio Bureau of Labor Statistics, *Second Annual Report, 1878*, 220–1.
77. *Coopers' New Monthly*, Jan 1875, 12.
78. Nevins, *Studies in Power*, 208.
79. Nevins, *Heroic Age*, 1:547–9; *Coopers' New Monthly*, Jan 1875, 12.
80. Ohio Bureau of Labor Statistics, *Second Annual Report, 1878*, 220–1.
81. *Workingman's Advocate*, 25 March 1876.
82. *American Manufacturer*, 21 Sept. 1876; *Labor Standard*, 23 Sept. 1876.
83. Nevins, *Heroic Age*, 1:547–9.
84. *Cleveland Plain Dealer*, 19 April 1877; *Cleveland Leader*, 20 April 1877.
85. Nevins, *Studies in Power*, 241.
86. Share ownership by Rockefeller and his partners is listed in Nevins, *Heroic Age*, 1:292, 365, 478, 612. It is difficult to agree with Nevins's judgment that "the wage policy of the Standard was generous" or his observation that "it consistently paid workmen a little more than the ruling rate." (Ibid., 629.)
87. *Cleveland Leader*, 20, 24 April 1877; *Cleveland Plain Dealer*, 19 April 1877.
88. *Cleveland Leader*, 20 April 1877; *Cleveland Plain Dealer*, 19 April 1877.
89. *Cleveland Plain Dealer*, 19, 20 April 1877; *Cleveland Leader*, 20, 21, 25 April 1877.
90. *Cleveland Plain Dealer*, 20 April 1877; *Cleveland Leader*, 20 April 1877.
91. *Cleveland Plain Dealer*, 20 April 1877.
92. Ibid., 20, 21 April 1877.
93. *Cleveland Leader*, 23, 25 April 1877. The strikers claimed Standard paid a 30% dividend in 1876. They said and probably knew nothing of the enormous 1877 dividend payments.
94. Ibid., 21–25 April 1877; *Cleveland Plain Dealer*, 20–25 April 1877.
95. *Cleveland Plain Dealer*, 24 April 1877.
96. Ibid., 21, 24, 27 April 1877; *Cleveland Leader*, 24, 25 April 1877.
97. *Cleveland Leader*, 25, 27 April 1877.
98. Ibid., 27 April 1877; *Cleveland Plain Dealer*, 27 April 1877.
99. *Cleveland Leader*, 25 April 1877.

100. *Cleveland Plain Dealer*, 25 April 1877; *Cleveland Leader*, 25, 27 April 1877.
101. *Cleveland Leader*, 25 April 1877.
102. Ibid., 20, 21, 24, 25 April 1877; *Cleveland Plain Dealer*, 22 April 1877.
103. *Cleveland Plain Dealer*, 27 April, 2 May 1877; *Cleveland Leader*, 28 April 1877.
104. *Cleveland Plain Dealer*, 7 May 1877.
105. *Cleveland Leader*, 28 April 1877.
106. *Cleveland Plain Dealer*, 28 April 1877.
107. *Cleveland Leader*, 3 May 1877.
108. Ibid.; *Cleveland Plain Dealer*, 2, 3 May 1877.
109. *Cleveland Plain Dealer*, 2, 3, 4, May 1877; *Cleveland Leader*, 3 May 1877.
110. *Cleveland Leader*, 3 May 1977; *Cleveland Plain Dealer*, May 3, 1877.
111. *Cleveland Plain Dealer*, 3, 7 May 1877; *Cleveland Leader*, May 3, 1877.
112. *Cleveland Plain Dealer*, 10, 11 May 1877; *Cleveland Leader*, 10, 11 May 1877.
113. *Cleveland Leader*, 11 May 1877; *Cleveland Plain Dealer*, 10 May 1877.
114. *Cleveland Leader*, 11 May 1877.
115. Ibid., 12 May 1877; *Cleveland Plain Dealer*, 11 May 1877.
116. *Cleveland Plain Dealer*, 12 May 1877.
117. Ibid., 11, 12, 14, 15 May 1877. In the fall of 1877, Skarda ran for lieutenant governor on a Socialist ticket bitterly opposed by a Greenback antimonopolist slate whose leading Ohio spokesman was Robert Schilling, formerly a national officer of the Coopers' International Union. Schilling came down hard on Skarda, blamed him for the strikers' defeat, and said that as an employer on *Delniche Liste* Skarda was "tyrannical, despotic and exacting." He had taken control of the strike and denied critics a voice. If the strikers "had held out three days longer, they would have obtained what they demanded." Schilling even hinted that Skarda was paid by Standard Oil to break up the strike. Schilling's charges were serious, but sounded like election propaganda. (*Labor Advance* [Cleveland], 22 Sept. 1877 and 16 March 1878.)
118. *Workingman's Advocate*, 19 May 1877; *Labor Standard*, 26 May 1877; *Cleveland Leader*, 16 May 1877.
119. Nevins, *Heroic Age*, 1:475–8, 489–93, 503; Pennsylvania Bureau of Labor Statistics, *Fourth Annual Report, 1875–1876* (Harrisburg, 1877), 118–9.
120. *Pittsburgh Evening Chronicle*, 20 Oct. 1874 and 13 July 1877; *National Labor Tribune*, 10 Feb. 1877; Ohio Bureau of Labor Statistics, *Second Annual Report, 1878*, 292–300; Evigena, Pittsburgh, to the editor, *National Labor Tribune*, 15, Sept. 1877.
121. Nevins, *Heroic Age*, 1:520–46.
122. *National Labor Tribune*, 1 Sept. 1877; *Pittsburgh Post*, 22–31 Aug. 1877; Evigena to the editor, *National Labor Tribune*, 15 Sept. 1877.
123. Editorial, *National Labor Tribune*, 1 Sept. 1877; A Cooper, Allegheny City, to the editor, ibid., 1 Sept. 1877.
124. *Pittsburgh Evening Chronicle*, 11, 13, 17 Sept., 1, 6 Oct. 1877.
125. Evigena to the editor, *National Labor Tribune*, 15 Sept. 1877; *Pittsburgh Evening Chronicle*, 11 Sept. 1877.
126. Evigena to the editor, *National Labor Tribune*, 15 Sept. 1877.
127. *Pittsburgh Evening Chronicle*, 1, 6, 23 Oct. 1877.
128. "The Coopers and Standard Oil," *National Labor Tribune*, 27, Oct. 1877.

129. *Pittsburgh Evening Chronicle*, 26, 27 Oct., 1, 8, Nov. 22 Dec. 1877; *Iron Age*, 22 Nov. 1877, 14.
130. R., Allegheny City, to the editor, *National Labor Tribune*, 11 Nov. 1877.
131. Coyne, *Development of the Cooperage Industry*, 24.
132. "The Standard Oil Strike," *National Labor Tribune*, 23 July 1887.
133. Nevins, *Heroic Age*, 2:app. 5, "The Standard's Labor Policy," 721. Of the 1877 events Nevins writes only: "Cleveland papers in 1877 reported several demonstrations by discontented employees. But *The Leader* of September 4 explained this by saying that the Standard had found itself with more employees than it needed, and 'rather than discharge some in the hard times, they thought it would be wiser and kinder to keep all, and allot the work so that all could earn at least a support.' The result had been misunderstanding and dissatisfaction." (Ibid.)
134. Werner, *It Happened in New York*, 226–7.
135. Herbert G. Gutman, "Trouble on the Railroads in 1873–1874; Prelude to the 1877 Crisis?" *Labor History* 2 (1961), 215–35.
136. Gutman, "Two Lockouts in Pennsylvania, 1873–1874."
137. Herbert G. Gutman, "The Buena Vista Affair," *Pennsylvania Magazine of History and Biography* 88 (1964), 251–93, and "The Braidwood Lockout of 1874," *Journal of the Illinois State Historical Society* 53 (1960), 5–28.
138. Gutman, "Industrial Invasion of the Village Green," 19–24.
139. Samuel D. Logan, *A City's Danger and Defense: Or, Issues and Results of the Strikes of 1877, Containing the Origin and History of the Scranton City Gaurd* (Scranton, Pa., 1877), 138–44.
140. See, for example, David Brody, *Steelworkers in America: The Nonunion Era* (Cambridge, Mass., 1960), passim.
141. R. to the editor, *National Labor Tribune*, 11 Nov. 1877.
142. Pickleburg, "Wish He Could," *Weekly* [Labor] *Advance*, 8 Dec. 1877.
143. Nevins, *Heroic Age*, 1:641.

7. *Enslaved Afro-Americans and the "Protestant" Work Ethic*

1. Robert W. Fogel and Stanley L. Engerman, *Time on the Cross: The Economics of American Negro Slavery*, 2 vols. (Boston, 1974), 1: 4–5.
2. Ibid., 2: 219–20.
3. Paul A. David and Peter Temin, "Slavery: The Progressive Institution?" *Journal of Economic History* 34 (1974), 739–83.
4. Ibid.
5. *Time on the Cross*, 1: 236–46.
6. David and Temin, "Slavery: The Progressive Institution?"
7. *Time on the Cross*, 1: 144–63; 2: 116–19.
8. Ibid., 1: 147.
9. Ibid., 263–4.
10. Edwin Adams Davis, ed., *Plantation Life in the Florida Parishes of Louisiana, 1836–1846, as Reflected in the Diary of Bennet H. Barrow* (New York, 1943), 431–40.
11. The entire volume includes several other useful appendices, such as a brief but illuminating sketch of Barrow and his planter peers and Barrow's diary entries from 1836 to 1846 (ibid., 72–385).
12. *Time on the Cross*, 1: 145.
13. A few sentences in ibid., 2: 116, tell readers that "an adequate social

history of whipping remains to be written" and that scattered historical writings indicate the persistence (despite a declining frequency) of whippings as a means of disciplining "members of the laboring classes" into the mid-nineteenth century in England, Russia, and even the American North. But what the British historian E. H. Carr calls the "economic whip" steadiliy replaced physical punishment in developing capitalist countries.

14. C. Vann Woodward, *Origins of the New South, 1877–1913* (Baton Rouge, La., 1951), 351–2.

15. Using the same data, interestingly, Eugene D. Genovese makes the same mistake: "Masters who were not slaves to their passions tried to hold corporal punishment to a minimum. The harsh Bennet H. Barrow of Louisiana used his whip more than most: his slaves averaged one whipping a month and many only once a year." (*Roll, Jordan, Roll: The World the Slaves Made* (New York, 1974), 64.)

16. "The only systematic record of whipping now available for an extended period," Fogel and Engerman assert, "comes from the diary of Bennet Barrow. . . ." The sentence more properly should read: "The only systematic record of whipping available to us for an extended period. . . ." Fogel and Engerman have not systematically searched plantation records for similar evidence: that much is clear from their list of sources. No one to my knowledge, including Fogel and Engerman, has yet made a systematic search for such data. It is badly needed.

17. Some of the whippings listed in the Davis appendix, for example, are not found in the published diary.

18. Davis, *Plantation Life in the Florida Parishes*, 85–192 and 202–376, passim.

19. Bobby Frank Jones, "A Cultural Middle Passage: Slave Marriage and Family in the Antebellum South," unpublished Ph.D. dissertation, University of North Carolina, 1965, 57–8. This source is cited in the Fogel and Engerman bibliography, so that if the authors missed such entries in examining the diary itself, they might have noticed them in reading this unusually important study.

20. The fact that this is the single piece of evidence used by Fogel and Engerman to deal with physical punishment does not deter the economist Peter Passell from concluding that "Fogel and Engerman find no . . . pattern of abuse." The "economic" findings in *Time on the Cross* do not surprise this reviewer, but "what is surprising is the general level of dignity accorded the slaves in other aspects of life." (Passell, review of *Time on the Cross, New York Times Book Review*, 28 April 1974, 4.)

21. Davis, *Plantation Life in the Florida Parishes*, 191–3.

22. David Rothman, "Slavery in a New Light," *New Leader*, 27 May 1974, 8–9.

23. Davis, *Plantation Life in the Florida Parishes*, 11, 37–41, 44–8, 52, 406–9; Kenneth M. Stampp, *The Peculiar Institution: Slavery in the Ante-bellum South* (New York, 1956), 186, 189.

24. Passell, review of *Time on the Cross*, 4

25. *Time on the Cross*, 1: 146.

26. It may have been that Minor did not want the skin cut because it lowered the value of a slave in the market. Who wanted to purchase troublesome property? Hardly a detached source, the *New York Tribune* (10 March

1853) reported that whipping scars cut the sale price of an adult male slave from $750–$800 down to $460.

27. *Time on the Cross*, 1: 229–30. The same sentence by Stampp is quoted a second time in *Time on the Cross*, 2: 220: "Where Phillips characterized slaveholders as men of good will whose treatment of slaves was generally 'benevolent in intent and on the whole beneficial in effect,' Stampp responded that 'cruelty was endemic in all slaveholding communities' and 'even those concerned about the welfare of slaves found it difficult to draw a sharp line between acts of cruelty and such measures of physical force as were an inextricable part of slavery." Once more, Fogel and Engerman have twisted the meaning of Stampp's argument.

28. Stampp, *The Peculiar Institution*, 185–6.

29. Ibid., 174–81.

30. Ibid., 172, 289

31. *Time on the Cross*, 1: 146–7.

32. James Henry Hammond, "Letters on Slavery," in *The Pro-Slavery Argument, as Maintained by the Most Distinguished Writers of the Southern States* (Charleston, S.C., 1852), 119–35.

33. *Time on the Cross*, 1: 147.

34. Davis, *Plantation Life in the Florida Parishes*, 41.

35. Ibid., 212–14.

36. Ibid., 41.

9. *Interview with Herbert Gutman*

1. The essay appears in H. Wayne Morgan, ed., *The Gilded Age: A Reappraisal* (Syracuse, N.Y., 1963, 1970).

2. "The Negro and the United Mine Workers of America; The Career and Letters of Richard L. Davis and Something of Their Meaning, 1890–1900" originally appeared in Julius Jacobson, ed., *The Negro and the American Labor Movement* (Garden City, N.Y., 1968). "Protestantism and the American Labor Movement: The Christian Spirit in the Gilded Age" originally appeared in the *American Historical Review*, October 1966. Both have been collected in Gutman's *Work, Culture, and Society in Industrializing America: Essays in American Working-Blass and Social History* (New York, 1976).

3. Alan Dawley, *Class and Community: The Industrial Revolution in Lynn* (Cambridge, Mass., 1976.).

4. The false-consciousness issue addresses the question of why workers did not see their objective interests as an exploited class and act in class-conscious ways to oppose capitalism. In *Poverty and Progress: Social Mobility in a Nineteenth Century City* (Cambridge, Mass., 1964), Stephan Thernstrom argues that workers' opportunities for property and social mobility, though limited, nonetheless contributed to political consensus in late-nineteenth-century Newburyport, Massachusetts.

5. See chaps. 3 and 4 above, 117–254. The third essay, "The Braidwood Lockout of 1874," was published in the *Journal of the Illinois State Historical Society* in 1960 (53: 5–28).

6. James Holt, "Trade Unionism in the British and U.S. Steel Industries, 1885–1912: A Comparative Study," *Labor History* 18 (1977), 5–35.

7. David Montgomery, *Beyond Equality: Labor and the Radical Republicans, 1862–1872* (New York, 1967).

8. Leon Fink, *Workingmen's Democracy: The Knights of Labor and American Politics* (Urbana, Ill., 1982).

9. "The 'New Unionism' and the Transformation of Workers' Consciousness in America" originally appeared in the *Journal of Social History* in 1974. It now appears as chap. 4 in Montgomery's *Workers' Control in America* (London, 1979).

10. David Montgomery, "Gutman's Nineteenth-Century America," *Labor History* 19 (1978), 416–29.

11. See Thomas Dublin, *Women at Work: The Tranformation of Work and Community in Lowell, Massachusetts, 1826–1860* (New York, 1975); Paul Faler, *Mechanics and Manufacturers in the Early Industrial Revolution: Lynn, Massachusetts, 1780–1860* (Albany, N.Y., 1981); Bruce Laurie, *Working People of Philadelphia, 1800–1850* (Philadelphia; 1980); Gary Kulik, "Pawtucket Village and the Strike of 1824: The Origins of Class Conflict in Rhode Island," *Radical History Review*, no. 17 (1978), 5–37.

12. David Brody, *Steelworkers in America: The Nonunion Era* (Cambridge, Mass., 1960).

13. David Montgomery, *Workers' Control in America* (New York and London, 1979).

14. Herbert Gutman and Ira Berlin's essay was read at the Organization of American Historians convention in Detroit, April 1982.

15. See Eric Wolf, *Peasants* (Englewood Cliffs, N.J., 1966) and *Peasant Wars of the Twentieth Century* (New York, 1969); Sidney Mintz, *Worker in Cane: A Puerto Rican Life History* (New Haven, Conn., 1960); and Sidney Mintz and Richard Price, *An Anthropological Approach to the Afro-American Past: A Caribbean Perspective* (Philadelphia, 1976).

16. Gareth Stedman Jones, "Working-Class Culture and Working-Class Politics in London 1870–1900: Notes on the Remaking of a Working Class," *Journal of Social History* 7 (1974), 460–508. See also Gareth Stedman Jones, *Outcast London: A Study in the Relationship Between Classes in Victorian Society* (Oxford, 1971).

17. Thompson links the prevalence of structuralist paradigms of society within contemporary Marxism to the impact of the Cold War upon the left. In a recent essay he wrote: "Voluntarism crashed against the wall of the Cold War. No account can convey the sickening jerk of deceleration between 1945 and 1948. Even in this country [England] the Marxist Left seemed to be moving with 'the flow of the stream' in 1945; in 1948; it was struggling to survive amidst an antagonistic current. In Eastern Europe that same sickening jerk stopped the hearts of Masaryk, Kostov, and of Rajik. In the West our heads were thrown against the windscreen of capitalist society; and that screen felt like—*a structure*." (*The Poverty of Theory and Other Essays* (London and New York, 1978), 73.

18. See E. P. Thompson, *Beyond the Cold War: A New Approach to the Arms Race and Nuclear Annihilation* (New York, 1982); E. P. Thompson and Dan Smith, eds., *Protest and Survive* (New York, 1981).

19. Philip Foner, *History of the Labor Movement in the United States* (New York, 1947–80); John R. Commons, *History of Labor in the United States* (New York, 1918–46).

20. George Rawick, ed., *The American Slave: A Composite Autobiography*, vol 1., *From Sundown to Sunup: The Making of the Black Community* (Westport, Conn., 1972).

21. Alfred Young, ed., *The American Revolution: Explorations in the History of American Radicalism* (Dekalb, Ill., 1976). Young's study of late-eighteenth-century crowds and artisans has not yet been published in a single volume. See "The Mechanics and the Jeffersonians in New York, 1789–1801," *Labor History* 5 (1964).

22. See W. E. B. Du Bois, *Black Reconstruction: An Essay Toward a History of the Part Which Black Folk Played in the Attempt to Reconstruct Democracy in America, 1860–1880* (New York, 1973), originally published in 1935; Joel Williamson, *After Slavery: The Negro in South Carolina During Reconstruction, 1861–1877* (Chapel Hill, N.C., 1965); Willie Lee Rose, *Rehearsal for Reconstruction: The Port Royal Experiment* (New York, 1964, 1976); and William W. Freehling, ed., *Slavery and Freedom* (New York, 1982).

23. Stanley M. Elkins, *Slavery: A Problem in American Institutional and Intellectual Life*, 3rd ed., rev. (Chicago, 1976).

24. Peter Wood, *Black Majority: Negroes in Colonial South Carolina from 1670 Through the Stono Rebellion* (New York, 1974).

25. Rhys Isaac, *The Transformation of Virginia, 1740–1790* (Chapel Hill, N.C., 1982); "Evangelical Revolt: The Nature of the Baptists' Challenge to the Traditional Order in Virginia, 1765–1775," *William and Mary Quarterly* 3rd ser., 31 (1974), 345–68.

26. Eugene D. Genovese, *Roll, Jordan, Roll: The World the Slaves Made* (New York, 1974).

27. Robert W. Fogel and Stanley L. Engerman, *Time on the Cross: The Economics of American Negro Slavery* (Boston, 1974); Herbert G. Gutman, *Slavery and the Numbers Game: A Critique of "Time on the Cross"* (Urbana, Ill, 1975). See also Herbert Gutman, Paul David, Peter Temin, Richard Sutch, and Gavin Wright, *Reckoning with Slavery* (New York, 1976).

10. The Black Family in Slavery and Freedom: A Revised Perspective

1. Sidney W. Mintz and Eric R. Wolf, "An Analysis of Ritual Co-Parenthood (Compadrazgo)," *Southwestern Journal of Anthropology* 6 (1950), 341–68; Esther N. Goody, "Forms of Pro-Parenthood: The Sharing and Substitution of Parental Roles," in Jack Goody, ed., *Kinship: Selected Readings* (Baltimore, 1972), 321–45.

2. Carol B. Stack, *All Our Kin: Strategies for Survival in a Black Community* (New York, 1974); Demitri B. Shimkin et al., *The Extended Family in Black Society* (Chicago, 1978).

3. A. J. R. Russell-Wood, "The Black Family in the Americas," *Societas, A Review of Social History* 8 (1978), 1–38.

4. Stephen Gudeman, "An Anthropologist's View of The Black Family in Slavery and Freedom," *Social Science History* 3 (1979), 56–65.

INDEX